Sri Lanka

Jaffna &
the North
p270

The
West
Coast
p87

The Ancient
Cities
p202

The East
p243

Colombo
p56

The Hill
Country
p149

The South
p106

Anirban Mahapatra,
Ryan Ver Berkmoes, Bradley Mayhew, Iain Stewart

Contents

PLAN YOUR TRIP

ON THE ROAD

EGG HOPPER P36

POLONNARUWA P215

ISURUMUNIYA VIHARA
P234, ANURADHAPURA

Contents

Welcome to Sri Lanka

Endless beaches, timeless ruins, welcoming people, oodles of elephants, rolling surf, cheap prices, fun trains, famous tea and flavourful food make Sri Lanka irresistible.

The Undiscovered Country

You might say Sri Lanka has been hiding in plain sight. Countless scores of travellers have passed overhead on their way to someplace else, but years of uncertainty kept Sri Lanka off many itineraries.

Now, however, all that has changed. The country is moving forward quickly as more and more people discover its myriad charms. Lying between the more trodden parts of India and Southeast Asia, Sri Lanka's history, culture and natural beauty are undeniably alluring. It's the place you haven't been to yet, that you should.

So Much in So Little

Few places have as many Unesco World Heritage Sites (eight) packed into such a small area. Sri Lanka's 2000-plus years of culture can be discovered at ancient sites where legendary temples boast beautiful details even as they shelter in caves or perch on prominent peaks. More recent are evocative colonial fortresses, from Galle to Trincomalee.

Across the island, that thing that goes bump in the night might be an elephant heading to a favourite waterhole. Safari tours of Sri Lanka's pleasantly relaxed national parks encounter leopards, water buffaloes, all manner of birds and a passel of primates.

Rainforests & Beaches

When you're ready to escape the tropical climate of the coast and lowlands, head for the hills, with their temperate, achingly green charms. Verdant tea plantations and rainforested peaks beckon walkers, trekkers and those who just want to see them from a spectacular train ride. And then there are the beaches. Dazzlingly white and often untrodden, they ring the island so that no matter where you go, you'll be near a sandy gem. Should you beat the inevitable languor, you can surf and dive world-class sites without world-class crowds. And you're always just a short hop from something utterly new.

It's So Easy

Distances are short: see the sacred home of the world's oldest living human-planted tree in the morning (Anuradhapura) and stand awestruck by the sight of hundreds of elephants gathering in the afternoon (Minneriya). Discover a favourite beach, meditate in a 2000-year-old temple, exchange smiles while strolling a mellow village, marvel at birds and wildflowers, try to keep count of the little dishes that come with your rice and curry. Wander past colonial gems in Colombo, then hit some epic surf. Sri Lanka is spectacular, affordable and still often uncrowded. Now is the best time to discover it.

Why I Love Sri Lanka

By Ryan Ver Berkmoes, Writer

My fascination with Sri Lanka began when I read Paul Theroux's *The Great Railway Bazaar* as a child. His wonderment at the island's endless contradictions stayed with me. In 2004 I was in the west and south in the weeks after the tsunami. I was struck by the stories of the survivors. In the years since, I have been endlessly amazed by the ability of Sri Lankans to overcome disaster, war and other challenges. And I am slack-jawed at how one small island-nation can embody so much beauty and wonder. It seems so much bigger than it is.

For more about our writers, see p352

Above: Traditional fishing, Galle (p107)

Sri Lanka

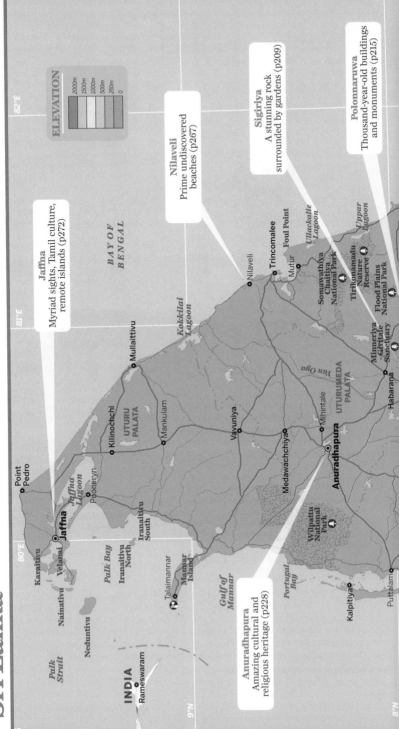

Jaffna
Myriad sights, Tamil culture, remote islands (p272)

Nilaveli
Prime undiscovered beaches (p267)

Sigiriya
A stunning rock surrounded by gardens (p209)

Polonnaruwa
Thousand-year-old buildings and monuments (p215)

Anuradhapura
Amazing cultural and religious heritage (p228)

ELEVATION
2000m
1500m
1000m
500m
250m
0

50 km
25 miles

INDIA
Rameswaram

Palk Strait
Palk Bay

Point Pedro
Karaitivu
Nainativu
Neduntivu
Velanai
Jaffna
Pooneryn
Jaffna Lagoon

BAY OF BENGAL

Mullaittivu

Kokkilai Lagoon

Nilaveli
Trincomalee
Foul Point
Mutur
Ullackalie Lagoon

Kilinochchi
UTURU PALATA
Mankulam

Talaimannar
Iranaitivu North
Iranaitivu South
Mannar Island

Gulf of Mannar

Vavuniya

Yan Oya

Somawathiya Chaitiya National Park
Trikonamadu Nature Reserve
Uppar Lagoon

Medawachchiya

UTURUMEDA PALATA

Minneriya-Giritale Sanctuary
Flood Plains National Park

Portugal Bay

Mihintale
Anuradhapura
Habarana

Wilpattu National Park

Kalpitiya

Puttalam

8°N
9°N
80°E
81°E
82°E

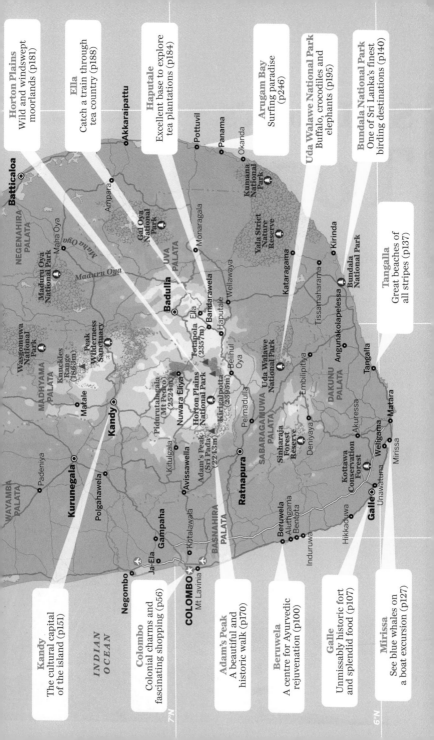

Kandy
The cultural capital of the island (p151)

Horton Plains
Wild and windswept moorlands (p181)

Ella
Catch a train through tea country (p188)

Haputale
Excellent base to explore tea plantations (p184)

Arugam Bay
Surfing paradise (p246)

Uda Walawe National Park
Buffalo, crocodiles and elephants (p195)

Bundala National Park
One of Sri Lanka's finest birding destinations (p140)

Tangalla
Great beaches of all stripes (p137)

Colombo
Colonial charms and fascinating shopping (p56)

Adam's Peak
A beautiful and historic walk (p170)

Beruwela
A centre for Ayurvedic rejuvenation (p100)

Galle
Unmissably historic fort and splendid food (p107)

Mirissa
See blue whales on a boat excursion (p127)

Akkaraipattu

Pottuvil

Panama

Okanda

Batticaloa

Ampara

NEGENAHIRA
PALATA

Maha Oya

Maha Oya

Maduru Oya

Maduru Oya National Park

Monaragala

Kumana National Park

UVA
PALATA

Badulla

Wellawaya

Bandarawela

Ella

Totapola (2357m)

Haputale

Belihul Oya

Katagarama

Yala Strict Nature Reserve

Kirinda

Wasgomuwa National Park

Knuckles Range (1863m)

Peak Wilderness Sanctuary

Matale

MADHYAMA
PALATA

Pidurutalagala (Mt Pedro) (2524m)

Nuwara Eliya

Horton Plains National Park

Kirigalpotta (2395m)

Pelmadulla

Uda Walawe National Park

Tissamaharama

Bundala National Park

Angunakolapelessa

WAYAMBA
PALATA

Padeniya

Kurunegala

Polgahawela

Kandy

Kitulgala

Avissawella

Adam's Peak (Sri Pada) (2243m)

Ratnapura

Embilipitiya

DAKUNU
PALATA

Tangalla

Matara

SABARAGAMUWA
PALATA

Deniyaya

Sinharaja Forest Reserve

Akuressa

Weligama

Gampaha

Kotalawala

BASNAHIRA
PALATA

Beruwela
Aluthgama
Bentota

Kottawa Conservation Forest

Galle

Unawatuna

Mirissa

Negombo

Ja-Ela

COLOMBO

Mt Lavinia

Indaruwa

Hikkaduwa

INDIAN OCEAN

7°N

6°N

Sri Lanka's
Top 20

Stunning Beaches

1 There are long, golden-specked ones, there are dainty ones with soft white sand, there are wind- and wave-battered ones, and ones without a footstep for miles. Some have a slowly, slowly vibe and some have a lively party vibe, but whichever you choose, the beaches of Sri Lanka really are every bit as gorgeous as you've heard. In a land where beaches are simply countless, consider the beaches of Tangalla (p137; pictured below), each with its own personality, and each beguiling in its own way, yet all easily visited in a day.

Travelling by Train

2 Sometimes there's no way to get a seat on the slow but oh-so-popular train to Ella (p188; pictured right), but with a prime standing-room-only spot looking out at a rolling carpet of tea, who cares? Outside, the colourful silk saris of Tamil tea pickers stand out in the sea of green; inside, you may get a shy welcome via a smile. At stations, vendors hustle treats, including some amazing corn and chilli fritters sold wrapped in somebody's old homework paper. Munching one of these while the scenery creaks past? Sublime.

Uda Walawe National Park

3 This huge chunk of savanna grassland centred on the Uda Walawe (p195) reservoir is the closest Sri Lanka gets to East Africa. There are herds of buffalo (although some of these are domesticated!), sambar deer, crocodiles, masses of birds, and elephants – and we don't just mean a few elephants. We mean hundreds of the big-nosed creatures. In fact, we'd go so far to say that for elephants, Uda Walawe is equal to, or even better than, many of the famous East African national parks.

Ancient Anuradhapura

4 At Anuradhapura (p228), big bits of Sri Lanka's cultural and religious heritage sprawl across 3 sq km. In the centre is one of the world's oldest trees, the Sri Maha Bodhi (more than two thousand years old). That it has been tended uninterrupted by record-keeping guardians for all those centuries is enough to send shivers down the spine. The surrounding fields of crumbling monasteries and enormous dagobas (stupas) attest to the city's role as the seat of power in Sri Lanka for a thousand years. Biking through this heady past is a thrilling experience.
Isurumuniya Vihara (p234)

Soaring Sigiriya

5 The rolling gardens at the base of Sigiriya (p209) would themselves be a highlight. Ponds and little artificial rivulets put the water in these water gardens and offer a serene idyll amid the sweltering countryside. But look up and catch your jaw as you ponder this 370m rock that erupts out of the landscape. Etched with art and surmounted by ruins, Sigiriya is an awesome mystery, one that the wonderful museum tries to dissect. The climb to the top is a wearying and worthy endeavour.

Bundala National Park

6 With all the crowds heading to nearby Yala National Park, its neighbour to the west, Bundala National Park (p140), often gets overlooked. But with the park's huge sheets of shimmering waters ringing with the sound of birdsong, skipping it is a big mistake. Bundala has a beauty that other parks can only dream of and is one of the finest birding destinations in the country. Oh, and in case herons and egrets aren't glam enough for you, the crocodiles and resident elephant herd will put a smile on your face.

Adam's Peak Pilgrims

7 For over a thousand years, pilgrims have trudged by candlelight up Adam's Peak (Sri Pada; p170) to stand in the footprints of the Buddha, breathe the air where Adam first set foot on earth and see the place where the butterflies go to die. Today tourists join the throngs of local pilgrims and, as you stand in the predawn light atop this perfect pinnacle of rock and watch the sun crawl above waves of mountains, the sense of magic remains as bewitching as it must have been for Adam himself.

Kandy Cultural Capital

8 Kandy (p151) is the cultural capital of the island and home to the Temple of the Sacred Tooth Relic (pictured bottom), said to contain a tooth of the Buddha himself. For the Sinhalese, this is the holiest spot on the island, but for tourists Kandy offers more than just religious satisfaction: there's a pleasing old quarter, a pretty central lake, a clutch of museums and, in the vicinity, some beautiful botanical gardens. In case you need further blessings from the gods, there's also a series of fascinating ancient temples.

Unmissable Galle Fort

9 Human and nature have joined forces in Galle Fort (p108) to produce an architectural work of art. The Dutch built the streets and buildings, the Sri Lankans added the colour and style, and then nature got busy covering it in a gentle layer of tropical vegetation, humidity and salty air. The result is an enchanting old town that is home to dozens of art galleries, quirky shops, and boutique cafes and guesthouses, plus some splendid hotels. For tourists, it's without doubt the number one urban attraction in the country.

Surfing at Arugam Bay

10 The heart of Sri Lanka's growing surf scene, the long right break at the southern end of Arugam Bay (p246) is considered Sri Lanka's best. From April to September you'll find surfers riding the waves; stragglers catch the random good days as late as November. Throughout the year you can revel in the surfer vibe: there are board-rental and ding-repair joints plus plenty of laid-back cheap hangouts offering a bed or a beer or both. And if you need solitude, there are nearby breaks up and down the coast

Feeling the Healing Ayurveda

11 If you start to feel the burden of the centuries while in Sri Lanka, you might appreciate an irony while you feel the tensions melt out of your body in an Ayurvedic sauna (p100): the design is more than 2500 years old. Ayurveda is an ancient practice and its devotees claim enormous benefits from its therapies and treatments. Herbs, spices, oils and more are used on and in the body to produce balance. Some people go on multiweek regimens in clinics; others enjoy a pampering afternoon at a luxury spa. The west coast, particularly around Beruwela, is rife with these treatments.

WWSOO1 / SHUTTERSTOCK ©

The East's Undiscovered Beaches

12 Truly magnificent beaches in Sri Lanka's east and north are luring travellers away from their more famous counterparts in the west and south. Horizon-reaching ribbons of white sand are just awaiting discovery – and your footprints. A prime place to start is in Nilaveli (p267; pictured above), just north of the nascent traveller hangout of Uppuveli. Perfect white sand shaded by palms stretches on and on. There are no cafes, guesthouses or people. Pick any dirt lane off the lonely coast road for your private patch of paradise.

Savouring Rice & Curry

13 Venture into a large Sri Lankan market and you'll see and smell the nation's rich diversity of foods and flavours. An average Sri Lankan cook spends hours each day tirelessly roasting and grinding spices while mincing, slicing and dicing all manner of foods. The seemingly humble rice and curry can consist of dozens of intricately prepared dishes, each redolent of a rich and, yes, at times fiery goodness. You can enjoy splendid rice and curries across Sri Lanka; Galle's Spoon's Cafe (p116) is wonderfully typical.

Horton Plains & World's End

14 The wild, windswept Horton Plains (p181), high, high up in Sri Lanka's Hill Country, are utterly unexpected in this country of tropical greens and blues, but they are far from unwelcome. You'll need to wrap up (a morning frost isn't uncommon) for the dawn hike across these bleak moorlands – it's one of the most enjoyable walks in the country. And then, suddenly, out of the mist comes the end of the world and a view over what seems like half of Sri Lanka.

Whale-Watching at Mirissa

15 People once visited the beaches of southern Sri Lanka to laze under palm trees and maybe go and peer at a few little fish on a diving excursion. Then somebody realised that the deep blue was home to more than just schools of workaday fish. It turns out that the waters off Sri Lanka are home to the planet's biggest creature, the blue whale (not to mention the nearly as huge sperm whale). Now, every morning in season, boats leave Mirissa (p131) in search of creatures like no other.

Visiting a Tea Plantation

16 It wasn't really all that long ago that Sri Lanka's Hill Country was largely a wild and ragged sweep of jungle-clad mountains, but then along came the British, who felt in need of a nice cup, so they chopped down all the jungle and turned the Hill Country into one giant, verdant tea estate. Sri Lankan tea is now famous across the world. Visiting a tea estate such as the Lipton-built Dambatenne Tea Factory (p184) near Haputale and seeing how the world's favourite cuppa is produced is absolutely fascinating.

17

18

THOMAS WYNNESS / SHUTTERSTOCK ©

Jaffna & the Islands

17 In Jaffna (p272), everything seems different, especially the language: the rapid-fire staccato of spoken Tamil is a real change from singsong Sinhala. So too is the cuisine: singularly spiced and, in season, complemented by legendary mangoes. The city has never looked better, with new hotels and energy. Sights include its vast colonial fort, leafy suburbs and ancient relics of a lost kingdom. Get a bike and catch a rickety ferry to the nearby islands like Neduntivu, where you can get lost in their end-of-the-earth appeal. Naga Pooshani Amman Kovil (p286), Nainativu

Colonial Legacy

18 Yes, the Brits were chased out at independence in 1948, but their legacy lives on in much more than an often impenetrable bureaucracy addicted to forms. The heart of Colombo, Fort (p58), is where you'll see the structures of the empire at its most magnificent. Along the capital's wide, tree-shaded streets, the National Museum building evokes the British Empire. You'll find colonial legacies of the Dutch and Portuguese as well, not just in Colombo's popular Dutch Hospital but in old fortresses that ring the nation's coasts. T-Lounge by Dilmah (p76)

Polonnaruwa's Stupendous Structures

19 Arrayed around a vast grassy quadrangle like the chess pieces of giants, Polonnaruwa's (p215) intricately carved buildings and monuments offer a visitor-friendly briefing on what was the centre of the kingdom some thousand years ago. Handy plaques are loaded with information, although you may find the buildings too extraordinary to switch your concentration to signage. Catch sight of the ruins at sunrise and sunset, when rosy rays of light bathe the complex in a romantic glow.

19

Shopping in Colombo

20 Part of the magic of Colombo is plunging into the shopping maelstrom of the city. The timeless markets of Pettah (p83) heave with goods and just general chaos. Shouting porters will knock you aside even as a laden cart bears down on your back. It's not for the faint-hearted, but it's a sensory overload that will leave you bewildered – and thrilled. And if you'd like something calmer and more stylish, the city has a growing collection of chic boutiques, stores and malls, and lovely quarters like Cinnamon Gardens. Federation of Self Employees Market (p60)

EFESENKO / SHUTTERSTOCK ©

20

Need to Know

For more information, see Survival Guide (p319)

Currency
Sri Lankan Rupee (Rs)

Languages
Sinhala, Tamil and English

Visas
Free transit visas are good for 48 hours. Thirty-day visitor visas cost US$25 to US$100, depending on your nationality. Apply in advance online (www.eta.gov.lk).

Money
ATMs available in cities and large towns. Credit cards accepted at most midrange and all top-end hotels.

Mobile Phones
Local SIM cards are cheap for unlocked phones.

Time
Sri Lanka Standard Time (GMT/UTC + 5½ hours)

When to Go

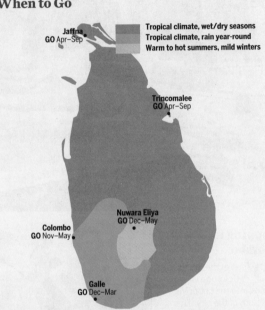

Tropical climate, wet/dry seasons
Tropical climate, rain year-round
Warm to hot summers, mild winters

Jaffna GO Apr–Sep
Trincomalee GO Apr–Sep
Nuwara Eliya GO Dec–May
Colombo GO Nov–May
Galle GO Dec–Mar

High Season (Dec–Mar)
➡ The Hill Country plus west- and south-coast beaches are busiest – and driest.

➡ With beds in demand, prices peak.

➡ The Maha monsoon season (October to January) keeps the East, North and ancient cities wet.

Shoulder (Apr & Sep–Nov)
➡ April and September offer the best odds for good weather countrywide.

➡ New Year's celebrations in mid-April cause transport to fill beyond capacity.

➡ A good time to wander without a set schedule.

Low Season (May–Aug)
➡ The Yala monsoon season (May to August) brings rain to the south and west coasts plus the Hill Country.

➡ The weather in the North and East is best.

➡ Prices nationwide are lowest.

Useful Websites

Lonely Planet (www.lonelyplanet.com/sri-lanka) Destination information, hotel bookings, traveller forum and more.

Ceylon Today (www.ceylontoday.lk) News, sports, entertainment and a handy ticker with exchange rates.

Yamu (www.yamu.lk) Excellent restaurant reviews, sights listings and more.

Hiru News (www.hirunews.lk) Excellent news aggregation site.

Meteo (www.meteo.gov.lk) Weather forecasts nationwide.

The Man in Seat 61 (https://seat61.com/SriLanka.htm) Encyclopaedic and inspiring information about Sri Lankan train travel.

Important Numbers

All regions have a three-digit area code followed by a six- or seven-digit number. Mobile numbers usually begin with ☎07 or ☎08 and have up to 12 digits.

Country code	☎94
International access code	☎00
Emergencies	☎118/119

Exchange Rates

Australia	A$1	Rs 123
Canada	C$1	Rs 126
Europe	€1	Rs 182
Japan	¥100	Rs 139
New Zealand	NZ$1	Rs 111
UK	UK£1	Rs 201
USA	US$1	Rs 152

For current exchange rates, see www.xe.com.

Daily Costs

Budget: Less than Rs 6000

➡ Simple guesthouse: Rs 2000–3500

➡ Local rice and curry: Rs 150–350

➡ Bus fares: under Rs 300 per day

Midrange: Rs 6000–20,000

➡ Double room in a good place: Rs 3500–9000

➡ Meals at hotel/restaurant: Rs 1000–3000

➡ Hire bikes, ride trains and use a car and driver some days: average per day Rs 3000

Top end: More than Rs 20,000

➡ Top-end hotel: Rs 9000 and up

➡ Meals at top-end places: from Rs 3000

➡ Daily use of car and driver: from Rs 9000

Opening Hours

Apart from tourist areas much is closed on Sunday.

Bars Usually close by midnight; last call is often a sobering 11pm.

Restaurants and cafes 7am to 9pm daily, later in areas popular with travellers

Shops 10am to 7pm Monday to Friday, 10am to 3pm Saturday

Shops and services catering to visitors 9am to 8pm

Arriving in Sri Lanka

Bandaranaike International Airport (Colombo) Sri Lanka's one main airport is 30km north of Colombo. From the airport, prepaid taxis cost about Rs 2600 to to Rs 3500 depending on destination; it's 30 minutes to one hour to Fort via the toll road. Pre-arranged rides with Colombo hotels are Rs 3000 to 5000. Air-con buses via the toll road to Central Bus Station cost Rs 150 and take about one hour.

Getting Around

Bus Sri Lanka's buses are the country's main mode of transport. They cover most towns, are cheap and are often crowded. Only a few routes have air-con buses. Private buses may offer a bit more comfort than government buses.

Car Many travellers use a hired car with a driver for all or part of their trip. This allows maximum flexibility and is the most efficient way to get around. Many drivers are very helpful and founts of local knowledge.

Train The improving railway network serves major towns and can be more comfortable than buses (excepting third-class carriages). Some routes such as Haputale to Ella and Colombo to Galle are renowned for their scenery.

For much more on **getting around**, see p327

First Time Sri Lanka

For more information, see Survival Guide (p319)

Checklist

➡ Make sure your passport is valid for at least six months past your arrival date.

➡ Check on the need for vaccinations.

➡ Arrange for appropriate travel insurance.

➡ Check the airline baggage restrictions.

➡ Inform your debit-/credit-card company.

➡ Arrange your visa online about one week before you depart.

What to Pack

➡ A good pair of earplugs.

➡ Effective mosquito repellent – hard to find in Sri Lanka (unlike mosquitoes).

➡ Sunscreen – another surprisingly hard-to-find item.

➡ Tampons – nearly impossible to find outside Colombo.

➡ Extra phone-charging cables – difficult to find in remote areas.

Top Tips for Your Trip

➡ Explore the beaches, especially in the north and east, where there are vast, deserted and beautiful swaths of sand. If you see a road heading towards the coast, take it and see what you find.

➡ Ride the trains: you'll enjoy the scenery, have comfort greater than buses and travel with a cross-section of locals.

➡ Hit the markets. Even if you don't want 100 green bananas, you'll see the country's bounty, meet people and get caught up in the frenzy.

➡ Eat with the locals. A busy 'hotel' (cafe) in a town centre or near a bus terminal will serve rice and curry that's properly spicy, something impossible to find at any place catering to tourists.

➡ Watch the calendar: *poya* (full moon) nights are when celebrations take place across the country.

What to Wear

Shorts and a T-shirt will work most of the time, but bathing suits and bikinis are never proper off tourist beaches. Bring a cover-up for shoulders and arms, and a long skirt, sarong or light pants for visiting temples. Sandals are always fine and are good for slipping off quickly when visiting temples. Something slightly dressy is required only for the very best restaurants in Colombo. For the elements, a lightweight waterproof jacket or poncho is useful in case of sudden downpours, and a warm layer if spending time high up in the temperate mountains.

Sleeping

Guesthouses Family run guesthouses are found everywhere; they can provide very good value and offer a great way to interact with locals.

Hostels Geared to backpackers, these are rare but numbers are growing in the main tourist centres.

Hotels Range from modest to grand and from back-road to beachfront.

Resorts Offering one-stop luxury, the best resorts are found on the west and south coasts and around national parks.

Ayurvedic spas Many offer accommodation-and-wellness packages.

Rented villas Offer grand accommodation; some even have a private beach.

Local Economics

Although Sri Lanka's economy is quickly expanding, people still work very hard to get by. Earnings compared to First World nations are low.

➡ Minimum wage on plantations: Rs 730 per day.

➡ Minimum wage for servers/hotel staff: Rs 10,000 per month.

➡ Commissioned military officer: US$7400 per year.

Bargaining

Unless you are shopping at a fixed-price shop, you must bargain. Generally, if someone quotes you a price, halve it. The seller will come down about halfway to your price, and the last price will be a little higher than half the original price. Try and keep a sense of perspective. Chances are you're arguing over less than US$1.

Tipping

Although a 10% service charge is added to food and accommodation bills, this usually goes straight to the owner rather than the worker.

Restaurants and bars 10% in cash to servers beyond the 'service charge'

Drivers 10%

Room cleaners Up to Rs 100 per day

Bag carriers/porters Rs 50 per bag

Shoe minders at temples Rs 30

Guides Varies greatly; agree to a fee *before* you set out

Temple of the Sacred Tooth Relic (p152)

Etiquette

Sri Lanka is an easy place to navigate if you remember a few key points.

Temple footwear Remove shoes and hats at temples. Socks are OK for walking scorching pavements.

Clothing Cover shoulders, arms and legs at temples as directed.

Buddha statues Never pose beside or in front of a statue (ie with your back to it), as this is considered disrespectful.

Buddha images Displaying body art or wearing clothing that includes an image of the Buddha can get you arrested and deported.

Photography Ask permission before photographing people. A few business-oriented folk like the stilt fishermen at Koggala will ask for payment.

Beach attire Nude and topless sunbathing are not allowed on beaches.

Modesty Overt displays of affection are frowned upon.

Avoid left hands These are considered unclean. Use both hands or just your right.

Language

Many Sri Lankans speak English, but your efforts to speak their language are always appreciated. In tourist areas, English will serve you well.

What's New

Huge New Projects, Colombo

Colombo Port City (p70) is a vast 269-hectare addition to the city taking shape off Fort and Galle Face Green. This enormous new neighbourhood will be home to financial companies, condos and much more. Meanwhile Cinnamon Life (p70), a vast and glitzy new mall and residential complex, is taking shape near Slave Island.

Restored Buildings, Colombo

Hot on the heels of other high-profile and successful renovations of colonial landmarks such as the Dutch Hospital, Arcade Independence Square is an 1800s mental hospital that's been turned into a stylish mall. (p83)

New Hotels, Colombo

Stylish hotels are opening for all budgets in the capital. A hot new midrange property is the high-rise Cinnamon Red (p73), which has a popular rooftop bar. Two high-profile luxury hotels set to open during 2017 are the Grand Hyatt Colombo (p70) and the Shangri-La Hotel (p70).

Colombo–Jaffna Trains

Repaired tracks once again link Colombo and Jaffna. It's a scenic ride you can enjoy on train rides lasting eight to 10 hours.

Jaffna's New Roads

As the capital of the north is revitalised, so to is the infrastructure. New and improved roads along with greatly decreased security precautions have opened up the islands (p285) and the Northeast Shore (p284).

Dutch Hospital, Galle Fort

This fine historic structure, which once hosted ailing colonial officers, has been restored to its former glory. Today it's home to some of Galle's best cafes and restaurants. (p109)

Unawatuna Beach Improvements

The east side of this glorious bay, until recently an eyesore of concrete sea defences, has re-emerged as a broad sandy beach after a regeneration program. (p118)

Ella's New Hotels

A roster of stylish new hotels and guesthouses have opened, and Ella now has the best accommodation selection in the Hill Country. (p193)

New Kalpitiya Resorts & Activities

There are now more than half a dozen kitesurfing camps on the peninsula. Alankuda has a handful of top-end resorts, including a couple of very stylish options. (p95)

Anuradhapura's New Budget Hotels

Dozens of small family-run budget guesthouses have opened in this Ancient City, making it one of Sri Lanka's best places for budget accommodation. (p234)

Pidurangala's Popularity

This rock has gone from a secret spot to a backpacker must-see, with dozens of people perched here at sunset enjoying the fantastic views over Sigiriya. (p213)

For more recommendations and reviews, see **lonelyplanet.com/ sri-lanka**

If You Like...

Beaches

If Sri Lanka looks outlined in white from space, it's due to the beaches that encircle the island. You can rarely travel any part of the coast for long without coming upon a simply stunning stretch of sand. More amazing is that many are almost empty.

Thalpe With its smattering of comfy guesthouses and quiet sands, this beach is a welcome respite from crowds. (p124)

Marakolliya Beach So what if the swimming isn't always safe? The beach itself is simply gorgeous. (p137)

Rekawa Beach Long and windswept, this beach attracts turtles and folks who love a lonely, dramatic landscape. (p137)

Arugam Bay Classic hangout for surfers and anyone who likes mellow, easy vibes. (p246)

Uppuveli & Nilaveli Beautiful beaches in an idyllic eastern corner; there's a small travellers' scene and untouched nature. (p23)

Northeast Shore Most of the sands this far north are totally isolated; for explorers and dreamers only. (p284)

Water Sports

Sri Lanka's diving scene is developing along with its surf scene. Excellent places for aquatic pleasures can be found right around the coast; most are still seldom visited. The west coast south of Colombo has been the centre of diving but other, better areas like the south and east are coming on strong. Surfing is also huge in the south and east.

Arugam Bay A beautiful crescent of sand where you can go from guesthouse to break in 10 minutes. (p246)

Bar Reef Little-exploited and near-pristine reefs where dolphins play in their hundreds. (p95)

Great Basses Reefs Tricky access and fickle conditions only add to the mystique of Sri Lanka's best dive site. (p144)

Pigeon Island National Park A shallow coral reef with tons of life where it's equally satisfying to snorkel or dive. (p268)

Weligama Sweet surf town down south, where you can learn to ride or just hang. (p126)

Batticaloa The HMS *Hermes* is for technical divers, but the rock dives here are for everyone. (p258)

Walking

Sure it's a bit hot during the day and it might rain, but there are oodles of places where you can stretch your legs and appreciate Sri Lanka's remarkable natural beauty, rich culture and ancient monuments.

Colombo The main streets may be choked but other roads in the capital are tree-lined and have a genteel charm. (p56)

Polonnaruwa The ancient monuments here are in a lush park-like setting that rewards explorers. (p215)

Adam's Peak Walk in the footsteps of the Buddha with hundreds of pilgrims. (p171)

Knuckles Range Rain-soaked and densely vegetated, the Knuckles Range offers exciting hiking. (p167)

Galle After the endlessly walkable Fort, continue to the tropical fantasy of Jungle Beach. (p107)

Jaffna This old town has colonial buildings, the nation's most intriguing fort and tree-lined streets. (p272)

Buddhist Temples

More than 2000 years of religious heritage can be found in the temples great and small that dot this island. Time your visit with a festival for an extraordinary experience.

Gangaramaya Temple Among many high-profile Colombo temples, this is the centre for the most extravagant Vesak celebrations. (p62)

Mulkirigala Rock Temples Hiding inside a series of caves is this beautiful and little-visited temple. (p140)

Temple of the Sacred Tooth Relic Containing a tooth of the Buddha, this is local Buddhism's heart and soul. (p152)

Sri Maha Bodhi The world's oldest documented living tree is the focus of this very sacred site in Anuradhapura. (p229)

Mihintale This temple of legends has more than 1800 steps to its mountaintop location. (p237)

Nagadipa Temple A simple temple on a little island in the far north where the Buddha, legend has it, once visited. (p286)

Wildlife

The island may be small, but the animals are big, especially the herds of Asian elephants that live inside and outside the national parks. Leopards and water buffaloes are just some of the other creatures you might spot.

Uda Walawe National Park If you've ever wanted to see a wild elephant, try your luck here. (p195)

Minneriya National Park The site of 'the Gathering', when over

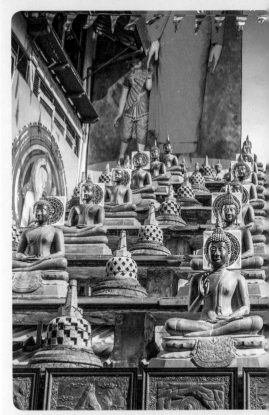

Top: Gangaramaya Temple (p62), Colombo

Bottom: Main Fish Market (p89), Negombo

400 pachyderms gather in an awesome spectacle. (p226)

Pottuvil Lagoon safaris can bring you tantalisingly close to elephants, monitor lizards and crocodiles. (p251)

Yala National Park Drawing huge crowds, a leopard safari here can reward, but beware at busy times. (p145)

Kumana National Park There are leopards, elephants and birds galore at this remote park, which is much less crowded than Yala. (p254)

Shopping

Given that it's such a lush country, it's no surprise that Sri Lanka grows many of its best goods. Tea is an obvious purchase; all manner of spices are another. In addition there are various handicrafts and a growing range of designer items.

Colombo Stylish designer boutiques, galleries and markets galore sell just about anything, with plenty of surprises on offer. (p82)

Negombo Charming and ramshackle, with a busy town centre and a beachfront lined with souvenir shops. (p89)

Galle A surfeit of classy galleries, independent designer boutiques and quirky bric-a-brac shops make Galle unmissable. (p117)

Hill Country At tea plantations and factories you can buy excellent teas – many hard to find elsewhere. (p149)

Ayurveda

Ayurveda is an ancient system of medicine and thera-

pies designed to heal and rejuvenate. It's widely used in Sri Lanka for a range of ailments and draws many visitors each year; some stay in clinics and spas for weeks.

Siddhalepa Ayurveda You can enjoy a full range of treatments in Colombo at places such as this authentic spa. (p68)

Sanctuary Spa Follow a hard day swimming in Unawatuna's surf by getting your inner balance restored. (p119)

Jetwing Ayurveda Pavilions In Negombo, Pavilions offers rooms that include spa treatments. (p92)

Barberyn Reef Ayurveda Resort A complete health resort in Beruwela, this place includes yoga and meditation. (p100)

Heritance Ayurveda Maha Gedara A west-coast retreat where the quality of the resort matches the quality of the treatments. (p100)

Heritage Sites

Unesco has recognised eight World Heritage Sites in Sri Lanka, an impressive number for a small island.

Galle Fort The Dutch fort forms a beautiful urban environment; stroll the walls at sunset. (p108)

Kandy The Royal City and temples are the heart of culture. (p151)

Sinharaja Forest Reserve One of the last remaining slabs of dense montane rainforest is a birdwatcher's dream. (p197)

Dambulla The cave temples and their extraordinary paintings are works of art. (p205)

Sigiriya The rock monastery which, yes, many people still think was a fort or temple. (p209)

Polonnaruwa A vast range of surviving structures populate this medieval capital. (p215)

Anuradhapura The sacred and the secular come together in a sprawling precinct spanning centuries of history. (p228)

Central Highlands Sri Pada Peak Wilderness, Horton Plains and Knuckles Range shelter outstanding biodiversity. (p149)

Colonial Architecture

The Dutch, the Portuguese and the British all literally left their marks on Sri Lanka. Their legacies are today's atmospheric sights.

Colombo's Fort The Dutch Hospital is one of many colonial beauties in Fort; many more treasures abound. (p58)

Colombo's Cinnamon Gardens The National Museum was once a British compound; elegant mansions shelter behind hedges. (p63)

Galle Fort Take a sunset walk along the fort walls and summon up a time long past. (p108)

Nuwara Eliya Stay in one of the grand old hotels and feel the Raj flicker back to life. (p173)

Jaffna See Portuguese-era churches, a grand old fort and elegant homes on tree-lined streets. (p272)

Batticaloa The compact neighbourhood of Puliyanthivu has colonial gems and a big fort. (p256)

Month by Month

January

At the peak of the tourist season when crowds are at their largest, many popular towns have special events such as the respected literary festival at Galle.

✯ Duruthu Perahera

Held on the *poya* (full moon) day at the Kelaniya Raja Maha Vihara in Colombo, and second in importance only to the huge Kandy *perahera* (procession), this festival celebrates the first of Buddha's three visits to Sri Lanka. (p68)

✯ Thai Pongal

Held in mid-January, this Hindu winter-harvest festival honours the sun god Surya. It is important to Tamils in Sri Lanka and South India. Look for the special sweet dish, *pongal*, which is made with rice, nuts and spices.

February

The tourist crowds continue strong, with wintering Europeans baking themselves silly on the beaches. This is a busy month for Sri Lankans, with an important national holiday.

✯ Independence Day

Sri Lanka gained independence on 4 February 1948 and this day is commemorated every year with festivals, parades, fireworks, sporting events and more across the nation. In Colombo, motorcades shuffle politicians from one event to the next.

✯ Navam Perahera

First celebrated in 1979, Navam Perahera is one of Sri Lanka's biggest and most flamboyant *peraheras*. Held on the February *poya*, it starts from the Gangaramaya Temple and travels around Viharamahadevi Park and Beira Lake in Colombo.

March

This is an important month for many of Sri Lanka's Buddhists. You'll see them observing Maha Sivarathri in the Ancient Cities areas and the portions of the west coast where they are in the majority.

✯ Maha Sivarathri

In late February or early March the Hindu festival of Maha Sivarathri commemorates the marriage of Shiva to Parvati with all-night vigils and more. It's the most important day for Shaivites, who comprise the majority of Sri Lanka's Hindus.

April

Although Christians comprise only 6% of Sri Lanka's population, secularised versions of Christian holidays are popular. Don't be surprised when you see an Easter bunny at the mall.

✯ Aurudu (New Year)

New Year's Eve (13 April) and New Year's Day (14 April) are nonreligious holidays. There is a period of a few hours between the old and new year called the 'neutral period' (*Nonagathe*); all activities are meant to cease. Over the days before and after, buses and trains are jammed as people go to their home villages.

Top: Poya (p28), Unawatuna
Bottom: Deepawali festival (p28), Colombo

May

The Yala monsoon blows in for five months, bringing huge rains from the Indian Ocean that drench the Hill Country and the beach towns in the southwest.

🎎 Vesak Poya

This two-day holiday commemorates the birth, enlightenment and death of the Buddha. Amid the festivities, the high point is the lighting of paper lanterns and displays of coloured lights outside every Buddhist home, shop and temple. Night-time Colombo is a riot of colours.

June

Sri Lanka's Buddhists barely have a chance to catch their breath after Vesak before another major religious event occurs – and they'll want to catch their breath...

🎎 Poson Poya

The Poson *poya* day celebrates the bringing of Buddhism to Sri Lanka by Mahinda. In Anuradhapura there are festivities in the famous temples, while in nearby Mihintale thousands of white-clad pilgrims ascend the lung-busting 1843 steps to the topmost temple.

July

Light-bulb vendors do a huge business as Buddhists gear up for Esala Perahera, which begins at the end of the month. Light displays are an integral part of the Kandy festivities.

Vel

This festival is held in Colombo and Jaffna. In Colombo the gilded chariot of Murugan (Skanda), the god of war, is ceremonially hauled from Pettah to Bambalapitiya. In Jaffna the Nallur Kandaswamy Kovil has a 25-day festival.

Kataragama

Another important Hindu festival is held at Kataragama, where devotees put themselves through a whole gamut of ritual masochism. It commemorates the triumph of the six-faced, 12-armed war god Skanda over demons here.

August

The Kandy Esala Perahera is important, but smaller versions are held across Sri Lanka. Many celebrations feature dancers and other performers such as stilt-walkers who practise all year.

Kandy Esala Perahera

The Kandy Esala Perahera, Sri Lanka's most spectacular and prominent festival, is the climax of 10 days and nights of celebrations during the month of Esala. This great procession honours the sacred tooth relic of Kandy and starts in late July.

Nallur Festival

Jaffna's Nallur Kandaswamy Kovil is the focus of an enormous and spectacular Hindu festival over 25 days in July and August, which climaxes on day 24 with parades of juggernaut floats and gruesome displays of self-mutilation by entranced devotees.

October

This is a month of meteorological mystery as it falls between the two great monsoon seasons. Rains and squalls can occur any place, any time. These are the final days of peak east-coast surfing.

Deepawali

The Hindu festival of lights takes place in late October or early November. Thousands of flickering oil lamps celebrate the triumph of good over evil and the return of Rama after his period of exile.

December

Sri Lanka's second annual monsoon season, the Maha, brings huge rains to the northeast part of the island.

POYA

Every *poya* (full moon) day is a holiday. *Poya* causes buses, trains and accommodation to fill up, especially if it falls on a Friday or Monday. No alcohol is supposed to be sold on *poya* days and many establishments close. Some hotels discreetly provide cold beer 'under the table'.

Note that the official full-moon day for *poya* does not always coincide with the same designated full-moon day in Western calendars. Because of the religious time used to calculate the exact moment of full moon, the *poya* day may be a day earlier or later than that shown on regular lunar calendars.

This is not the time to plan a Jaffna beach holiday.

Adam's Peak

The pilgrimage season, when pilgrims of all faiths (and the odd tourist) climb Adam's Peak near Ella, starts in December and lasts until mid-April. The trek begins shortly after midnight so that everyone can be in place for sunrise.

Unduvap Poya

This full-moon day commemorates Sangamitta, who in 288 BC brought a cutting from the sacred Bodhi Tree in India to Anuradhapura. The resulting tree, the Sri Maha Bodhi, is considered the oldest living, human-planted tree in the world. The ceremonies attract thousands in their finest.

Christmas

Outside of Sri Lanka's Christian communities – mostly around Colombo – this day has become a popular secularised holiday. Ersatz versions of Western Christmas traditions can be found everywhere, from bone-thin Santas in strange masks to garish artificial trees.

Itineraries

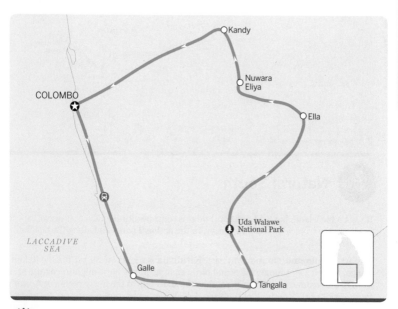

 Essential Sri Lanka

This compact trip covers a core selection of Sri Lanka's must-see sights.

Start in **Colombo**, exploring the markets and visiting the city's revitalised Fort district. Then take the train south along the coast to beguiling **Galle**, avoiding the often traffic-clogged road on the west coast and the ho-hum towns along it.

From Galle, go get some beach time. The **Tangalla** region has a growing selection of lovely beach places on its beautiful and uncrowded ribbon of sand. Head inland and venture up to **Uda Walawe National Park**, where you'll see dozens of elephants and many other animals. Take the winding road up into the heart of the Hill Country and put down roots for a few days in **Ella**, a cool town with a fun traveller vibe.

Take one of the world's most beautiful train rides to the stop for the British colonial heritage town of **Nuwara Eliya**, where you'll enter a time warp. Visit tea plantations and stop in iconic **Kandy** for temples and gardens. From here it's an easy jaunt back to Colombo or the airport.

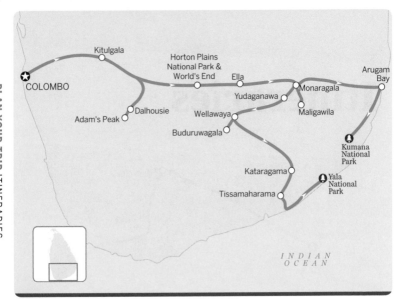

 Natural South

It's not a big island, but Sri Lanka still retains some beautiful wilderness areas, especially among the tropical peaks and valleys, in the national parks and along the beach-lined southern coast.

Start in **Colombo**. On your way east, **Kitulgala** is a gateway for rafting the Kelaniya Ganga, as well as for jungle hikes and birdwatching. Movie buffs might recognise scenes from *Bridge on the River Kwai* here. Take the short hop to the misty region of **Adam's Peak (Sri Pada)**. The climb of this sacred peak is an important pilgrimage for many. **Dalhousie** is the traditional starting point for the pre-dawn ascent. Spend a few days in the region tasting fragrant single-estate teas and bed down in luxurious ex-colonial tea planters' bungalows, or cosy guesthouses. Head east to **Horton Plains National Park** where you'll find **World's End**, a 9.5km looping walk to a stunning vantage point with stops at waterfalls. Now make the short drive to a Hill Country highlight: **Ella**. This village has more hiking, wonderful views and guesthouses renowned for having some of Sri Lanka's tastiest home-cooked food. Continue to **Monaragala**, a low-key gateway to the east and the jumping-off point for one of Sri Lanka's most atmospheric ancient Buddhist sites at **Yudaganawa**. Also nearby, **Maligawila** is home to an 11m-tall standing Buddha that's more than a thousand years old.

On the coast is the popular **Arugam Bay**, with its easygoing surfer vibe and excellent seafood. It's easy to spend an extra day or three here, swinging in a hammock at one of the beach guesthouses. Don't miss a boat trip exploring the nearby Pottuvil Lagoon. Explore the seldom-visited wilds of **Kumana National Park**, then veer back inland via Monaragala to **Wellawaya** and find time for a brief detour to Sri Lanka's tallest standing Buddha at **Buduruwagala**. Soak up the beauty of the tiny lakes and listen to the birds. Descend from Wellawaya to the coastal plains of **Kataragama**, the terminus of the Pada Yatra, a pilgrimage that begins at the other end of the island. Nearby **Tissamaharama** has a lovely lakeside setting, which is also a convenient entry point for the hugely popular safaris into **Yala National Park**, where you can spot elephants, leopards and most of Sri Lanka's other iconic critters.

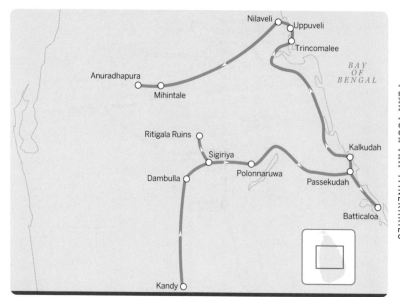

The Cultured Centre

This tour covers the uncrowded middle of Sri Lanka, which is at the heart of the country's rich culture. You'll see ancient temples and towns, along with some of the natural beauty that has inspired generations.

Start in **Kandy**, which has a lakeside setting with real natural beauty and was the capital of the last Sinhalese kingdom until the early 19th century. Head north to **Dambulla**, with its series of cave shrines painted with vivid Buddhist murals. From here it's a short jaunt to **Sigiriya**, a 200m-tall rock outcrop that was once a monastery and is truly one of the island's most amazing sights. A short drive northwest will bring you to the Ritigala Strict Nature Preserve. Deep inside this land is one of Sri Lanka's most mysterious sites: the **Ritigala Ruins**. Your inner Indiana Jones will enjoy exploring the remains of this once vast and ancient place.

Further east the former royal capital of **Polonnaruwa** offers an inspiring collection of Buddhist sculptures and monastery ruins dating back nearly a thousand years. Continue east to the coast and the beaches at **Passekudah** and **Kalkudah**. The former is a broad long ribbon of deserted and beautiful sand. The latter is part of a vast new resort development. Follow the coast south to **Batticaloa**, a historic port that has provided refuge to ships for years. It has a Dutch fort, while offshore is one of Sri Lanka's most fabled dive sites: the HMS *Hermes*, a British aircraft carrier sunk in WWII.

Going north you'll pass through nature preserves and deserted beaches until you reach the idyllic natural harbour of **Trincomalee**. It has a colourful history going back centuries as evidenced by its fort, which has Kandasamy temple right inside. Continue north to the beach town of **Uppuveli** with its cool travellers' scene and the beguiling and untrodden sands of **Nilaveli**. Now head due west into the heart of the country. Prepare for a steep climb up the hillside at **Mihintale** to appreciate the Buddhist history here that dates back to the 3rd century BC. A mere 13km further west brings you to **Anuradhapura**, one of the top sights in all of South Asia. Wander or bike around this sprawling landscape of temples, ruins and more.

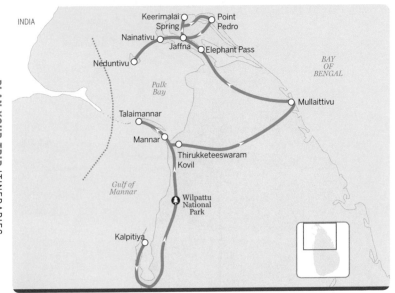

INDIA

Keerimalai Spring ○ ─── ○ Point Pedro

Nainativu ○ ─── Jaffna ○ Elephant Pass

Neduntivu ○

Palk Bay

BAY OF BENGAL

Talaimannar

Mannar ○ ─── ○ Thirukketeeswaram Kovil

Mullaittivu

Gulf of Mannar

Wilpattu National Park

Kalpitiya

Emerging North

Visitors are now discovering the beauty, beaches and culture of Sri Lanka's north, which was off-limits for many years. Roads are in excellent shape and train lines to Jaffna and other points are all open.

Start at **Kalpitiya**, the main town on the long finger of land that juts up into the Indian Ocean. The beaches here are OK, but the kitesurfing and dolphin-watching are spectacular. Hook your way around north to **Wilpattu National Park**. This treasure has leopards and many other large mammals. Next, explore another beautiful spit of Sri Lanka extending into the sea: **Mannar** is an island that looks to be thumbing a ride to the subcontinent. Amid African baobab trees, remote **Talaimannar** looks out at Adam's Bridge, a chain of reefs and islets, that almost forms a land bridge to India. Until service was halted by the war in the 1990s, this was where train ferries ran to India.

Hook around again to the Jaffna peninsula. On the mainland near the coast, just east of Mannar Town over the historic causeway, imposing **Thirukketeeswaram Kovil** is one of the *pancha ishwaram*, the five historical Sri Lankan Shiva temples established to protect the island from natural disaster. Now cruise on the newly improved roads right across the island to **Mullaittivu**, a town that was isolated during the war years. Legacies of that time abound, including the bizarrely compelling Sea Tiger Shipyard, where the LTTE tried to build submarines.

Head west on the smooth A35, then turn north on the A9 for **Elephant Pass**, with its stark beauty and bombastic war memorials. Continue on to **Jaffna**, where the rich Tamil culture offers temples on shady backstreets that await exploration. Cruise the colonial fort, bustling market area and good restaurants. Head north for **Keerimalai Spring**, a sacred site with legendary bathing pools. It's close to the Naguleswaram Shiva Kovil, which traces its past to the 6th century BC. Your next destination is east at **Point Pedro**, with its long swath of lonely white sand at Munai Beach. Jaffna has nearby islands well worth exploring for their sheer minimalist beauty, including **Nainativu**, a tiny speck of sand with Buddhist and Hindu temples, and **Neduntivu (Delft)**, a windswept place beyond the end of the road where wild ponies roam.

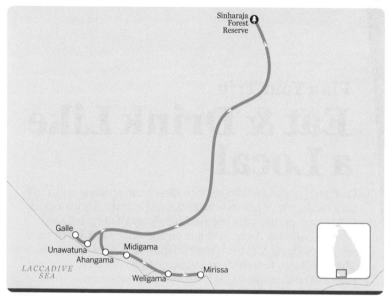

Quick Southern Jaunt

This fast trip will warm even the most frostbitten visitor escaping a frigid winter elsewhere in the world.

Begin your jaunt in **Galle**: founded by the Portuguese in the 16th century, it is one of Southeast Asia's best-preserved, fortified colonial cities. Walk the walls at sunset and enjoy the many cafes cropping up along streets lined with renovated and delightfully dilapidated old buildings. A vibrant foodie hotspot, Galle has some very stylish hotel bars for refined cocktail sipping.

Hit the beach at nearby **Unawatuna**, which has an alluring crescent of sand, cafes overlooking the surf and perfectly blue waters luring you in. The impressive Rumassala Peace Pagoda and pretty Jungle Beach are just a 15-minute walk west of Unawatuna.

Now find your inner Tarzan (many of the movies were shot in Sri Lanka) at the Unesco-recognised **Sinharaja Forest Reserve**, Sri Lanka's last major tropical rainforest. The only way to get about the reserve is by foot, and excellent park rangers or freelance guides can lead you along slippery trails, pointing out the wealth of stunning plant, bird and animal life.

Back on the south coast, Sri Lanka has a fast-breaking surf scene and you'll find lessons, board rentals and cheap surfer dives in **Ahangama** and **Midigama**.

Another short jaunt east brings you to **Weligama**, which has beach resorts and a lively fishing village with fascinating markets. It's also a hotspot for surfers (best for beginners).

Not far away is the sandy gem of the south, **Mirissa**, where cute guesthouses are hidden in the palms. Mirissa Harbour, across the peninsula from the west end of the beach, is always buzzing with boats, and the one very popular activity is a whale-watching boat trip. Spend the last bit of your trip soaking up the sun by the beach, which is an absolute dream.

Plan Your Trip

Eat & Drink Like a Local

Combining intricate flavours, incredibly fresh produce and a culinary heritage that blends indigenous and extraneous influences, Sri Lanka is perhaps the original Spice Island. Eating out here is a delight, whether it's tucking into an authentic roadside rice and curry or enjoying surf-fresh seafood from an oceanfront restaurant table. You'll also find Western and other Asian (Chinese, Thai and Japanese) dishes available in the most popular resorts.

The Year in Fruit

Sri Lanka's diverse topography means that the variety of fruit is staggering.

Year-round

Many fruits including bananas (over 20 varieties!), papayas and pineapples are available year-round.

Apr–Jun

The first mangoes appear in April in the north: the Karuthakolamban (or Jaffna) mango thrives in dry parts of the island and is prized for its golden flesh and juicy texture. Rambutans (a peculiar-looking red-skinned fruit with hairy skin), meanwhile, are at their best in June. They taste like lychees; you'll see them stacked in pyramids by the roadside.

Jul–Sep

It's peak season for durian, that huge spiky yellow love-it-or-hate-it fruit that smells so pungent that it's banned on the Singapore metro – you won't find this one on the breakfast buffet. Mangosteens, delicately flavoured purple-skinned fruit, are also harvested at this time. The fruit do not travel well, so it's best to sample these at source in the tropics.

Food Experiences

From the Sea

➡ **Elita Restaurant** (p116) For lighthouse views and seafood to die for.

➡ **Bu Ba** (p81) With candlelit tables right on Mt Lavinia beach.

➡ **Cool Spot** (p105) Family run and serves a mighty fine seafood platter.

➡ **Coconut Palm Beach Seafood Restaurant** (p135) Enjoy ocean-fresh seafood and fish by the waves.

Intense Flavours

➡ **Sanctuary at Tissawewa** (p236) Refined dining in the former residence of a British governor.

➡ **Nihonbashi Honten** (p77) Gourmet Japanese that's one of Colombo's best dining experiences.

➡ **Bedspace Kitchen** (p122) Deceptively casual garden restaurant where the cooking is highly accomplished and contemporary.

➡ **Fort Printers** (p116) A historic Galle setting for a modern, inventive East-meets-West menu.

➡ **Matey Hut** (p190) Shack in the hills where flavours are authentic to the max.

Dramatic Settings

➡ **Hill Club** (p180) Classic baronial-style dining room with British menu and adjacent billiards room.

➡ **Sharon Inn** (p160) Offers stupendous views of the Kandy hills and richly spiced local cuisine.

➡ **Church Street Social** (p116) Dine on the street-facing verandah or in the atmospheric colonial dining room.

Colonial Class

➡ **Governor's Restaurant** (p81), **Colombo** Classy hotel-restaurant that's perfect for Sunday lunch.

➡ **Margosa** (p277), **Jaffna** This 19th-century manor house makes a sublime setting for a memorable meal.

➡ **Empire Café** (p159), **Kandy** An old favourite in atmospheric colonial premises.

➡ **Royal Dutch Cafe** (p116), **Galle** Sip fine teas and coffees or enjoy a meal in this elegant colonnaded structure.

Cafe Cool

➡ **Old Railway Cafe** (p116), **Galle** Fine cafe well worth venturing outside the Fort's walls for.

➡ **Dutch Bank Cafe** (p264), **Trincomalee** Great snacks and meals in a converted colonial building that faces the harbour.

➡ **Dambulla Heritage Resthouse Restaurant** (p209), **Dambulla** Tour the caves, then recharge with a coffee here.

➡ **Queens Art Cafe** (p122), **Unawatuna** An inviting shady spot for a bite and a drink just off the beach.

➡ **Barefoot Garden Cafe** (p77), **Colombo** Stylish courtyard cafe in the Barefoot gallery.

Time for Tea

➡ **High Tea at the Grand** (p180), **Nuwara Eliya** For cucumber sandwiches, dainty cakes and a vast selection of different teas.

➡ **T-Lounge** (p76), **Colombo** An atmospheric setting for a cuppa in a landmark building.

➡ **Mlesna Tea Centre** (p187), **Bandarawela** Acclaimed tea shop in the heart of tea country.

Cheap Treats

➡ **Kotthu** A spicy stir-fried combo of chopped *rotti* bread, vegies and meat or egg. Try it at the Hotel De Pilawoos (p81), Colombo.

➡ **Paratha** A filling flatbread that's pan-fried on a hot plate. Those at Mangos (p278) in Jaffna are excellent.

➡ **Vadai** Generic term for disc- or doughnut-shaped deep-fried snacks, usually made from lentils.

➡ **Coconut rotti** Sold by street vendors, locals eat this toasted minibread with a chilli-salt topping.

➡ **Samosa** The ubiquitous snack, usually stuffed with spicy cooked vegies.

RICE & CURRY

The national dish, Sri Lankan rice and curry is a complex, intricately spiced array of individual vegetable (and often meat and fish) dishes, served with rice. Chutneys and *sambol* (a condiment made from ingredients pounded with chilli) add heat and additional flavour. Poppadoms are usually present too.

Virtually all Sri Lankan curries are based on coconut milk and a blend of spices: chilli, turmeric, cinnamon, cardamom, coriander, *rampe* (pandanus leaves), curry leaves, mustard and tamarind. Dried fish is also frequently used to season dishes.

As you're travelling around the country, you're likely to pull over at many a local restaurant for a rice and curry feed. Some of the best places are simple family owned roadside restaurants with a selection of around five to 10 individual dishes (mainly vegetarian but there's usually a meat or fish option too).

Many restaurants only serve rice and curry at lunchtime. Guesthouses will often prepare it for dinner but you'll need to order it early in the day and leave the cooks to work their magic.

Cooking Classes

Sri Lanka does not have an abundance of places offering cooking classes, but as interest grows the possibilities are expanding.

➡ **Matey Hut Cooking Classes** (p188), **Ella**

➡ **Mamas Galle Fort Cafe** (p116), **Galle**

➡ **Sonjas Health Food Restaurant** (p119), **Unawatuna**

➡ **Rawana Holiday Resort Cooking Classes** (p188), **Ella**

Sri Lankan Specialities

Rice is the staple of Sri Lankan cuisine and the national dish (rice and curry) and rice flour is also a basis for some unique foods. Many Sri Lankans are vegetarian, so meat-free eating is easy and vegetables are plentiful. Coconut is also added to most dishes. 'Devilled dishes' are any type of meat or fish cooked in a spicy, sweet-and-sour-style sauce with onion and peppers.

Rice

Hoppers Bowl-shaped pancakes (also called *appa* or *appam*) made from rice flour, coconut milk and palm toddy. If eggs are added it becomes an egg hopper. *Sambol* is often added for flavouring.

Dosas (*thosai*) Paper-thin pancakes made from rice batter and usually served stuffed with spiced vegetables.

Kola kanda A nutritious porridge of rice, coconut, green vegetables and herbs.

Rice and curry The national dish is a selection of spiced dishes made from vegetables, meat or fish.

Biryanis Fragrant basmati rice cooked with plenty of turmeric, garlic and cardamom, often with chunks of chicken or lamb.

Vegetable Dishes

Mallung Slightly like a tabbouleh, this salad combines chopped local greens (like kale), shredded coconut and onion.

Jackfruit curry The world's biggest fruit combines beautifully with rich curry sauces, as its flesh actually has quite a meaty texture.

Breads

Bakeries are common throughout the country, but can be disappointing.

Rotti Thick flatbreads cooked on a hot plate and served with sweet or savoury fillings.

Kotthu Chopped *rotti* fried with vegetables and/ or egg, cheese or meat on a hot plate. Try Hotel De Pilawoos (p81) in Colombo.

Uttapam A Tamil speciality, this thick pancake is prepared with onion, chillies, peppers and vegetables.

Seafood

Jaffna crab Recipes vary but in the north tamarind and coconut are key ingredients to bring out the flavour of this unique dish.

Ambulthiyal This fish curry is a southern speciality, made with *goraka*, a fruit that gives it a sour flavour.

Condiments

Pol sambol Shredded coconut, lime juice, red onions, chilli and spices.

Lunu miris Red onions, salt, chilli powder, lime juice and dried fish.

Desserts & Sweets

Wattalappam (*vattalappam* in Tamil) A coconut milk and egg pudding with jaggery and cardamom.

Pittu Steamed in bamboo, these cylindrical cakes are made from flour and coconut.

Curd Slightly sour cream that tastes like natural yoghurt; it's served drizzled with *kitul* treacle made from raw palm sugar.

Pani pol A small pancake made with a sweet topping of cinnamon and cardamom-infused jaggery.

Bolo fiado A layered cake said to have been first introduced by the Portuguese.

Ice Cream Widely available; indeed there are two specialist places in Galle.

Eating in Sri Lanka

When to Eat

Sri Lankans generally eat three meals a day. Interestingly the type of food consumed at each meal is quite distinct, so you usually won't find lunch foods (like rice and curry) available at dinner time.

Breakfast A typical local breakfast might take place around sunrise and consist of hoppers and some fruit. Milky tea is usually taken with breakfast; in the cities some favour coffee. In hotels and

Top: Dosa (paper-thin rice- and lentil-flour pancake)

Bottom: Sri Lankan breakfast

RHONDA GUTENBERG / GETTY IMAGES ©

guesthouses popular with tourists, Western-style breakfasts are almost always available.

Lunch Eaten between midday and 2.30pm. Rice and curry, the definitive Sri Lankan meal, is an essential experience that simply can't be missed – it can be quite a banquet or a simple pit stop depending on the place.

Dinner Usually eaten between 7pm and 9pm. If you really don't fancy a hot curry for dinner you'll find seafood and fish usually very lightly spiced, and fried rice is mild.

Where to Eat

Compared with most Asian countries, Sri Lanka is quite unusual in that most locals prefer to eat at home. Things are different in beach resorts and the capital, but in many towns there are actually very few restaurants, or even street-food stalls.

Accommodation You'll usually eat breakfast in your hotel. Evening meals are often available too, though guesthouses will ask you to order ahead, so they can purchase ingredients. Larger hotels usually offer buffet lunches and dinners with Western and local food.

'Hotels' When is a hotel not a hotel? When it's in Sri Lanka. Confusingly, restaurants here are also called 'hotels'. Usually these places are in towns and cities, pretty scruffy, and will consist of a store at the front selling snacks and drinks and tables at the rear for sit-down meals. Rice and curry is the lunchtime staple; for dinner *kotthu*, rice and noodle dishes are popular.

Restaurants In Colombo, beach resorts and tourist-geared towns (like Galle), you'll find excellent restaurants offering everything from Mexican to gourmet local cuisine.

Bakeries These sell what locals call 'short eats', essentially an array of meat-stuffed rolls, meat-and-vegetable patties (called cutlets), pastries and *vadai*. At some places, a plate of short eats is placed on your table and you're only charged for what you eat. Many bakeries (and some restaurants) also offer a 'lunch packet', which is basically some rice and a couple of small portions of curry.

Drinks

Sri Lanka's heat means that refreshing beverages are an important – if not vital – part of the day's consumption.

Tea & Coffee

Tea with spoonfuls of sugar and hot milk is the locally preferred way to drink the indigenous hot drink. If you don't have a sweet tooth, be very assertive about lowering the sugar dose.

Coffee, while not traditionally favoured, is now literally a hot commodity in Colombo and areas popular with tourists. Cafes with espresso machines are catching on, though are not that widespread as yet. Out in the sticks be prepared for instant, or something fresh-ish that tastes like instant.

Soft Drinks

Lime juice is excellent. Have it with soda water, but ask for the salt or sugar to be separate. If not, you could be in for a serious sugar hit. Indian restaurants and sweet shops are a good spot for a *lassi* (yoghurt drink). Ginger beer is an old-school, very British option, offering refreshment with a zing – look out for the Elephant or Lion brands. *Thambili* (king coconut) juice still in the husk can be found on sale at roadside stalls everywhere.

Beer

Locally brewed Lion Lager is a crisp and refreshing brew that is widely sold. Lion also sells a very good stout (also known as Sinha Stout) with coffee and chocolate flavours, though it's lethal at 8.8% alcohol. Three Coins and Anchor are less delicious local lagers. The licensed versions of international brands like Carlsberg and Heineken are also available.

Craft beer is available in Colombo, but very rare elsewhere.

Toddy & Arrack

Toddy is a drink made from the sap of palm trees. It has a sharp taste, a bit like cider. There are three types: toddy made from coconut palms, toddy from *kitul* palms and toddy from palmyra palms. Toddy shacks are found throughout the country, but are very much a male preserve. Arrack is a fermented and (somewhat) refined toddy. It can have a powerful kick and give you a belting hangover. The best mixer for arrack is the local ginger ale.

Sri Lankan coast

Plan Your Trip
Beaches & Activities

Sri Lanka is blessed with astonishing beaches, from ocean-washed surfing strongholds to sheltered sandy coves. Water-based activities include scuba diving and whale-watching, but if horizontal lounging is more your thing, you've come to the right place too.

PLAN YOUR TRIP BEACHES & ACTIVITIES

Best Beaches For...

Diving & Snorkelling

Pigeon Island off Nilaveli beach offers crystal waters, shallow reefs, colourful fish, and diving and snorkelling that's great for a beginner or the experienced.

Whale-Watching

Whales can be seen all along the Sri Lankan coast but Mirissa is the best base for seeing the blue whales that surge past Dondra Head.

Exploring

Jaffna's islands offer a stunning array of white-sand bays and remote coves, perfect for beach-hopping on a scooter or bicycle.

Indulgence

Bentota beach has an unrivalled collection of sublime boutique hotels. When you're done with pampering, the beach itself ain't bad.

Solitude

We almost want to keep this one to ourselves, but seeing as you asked nicely...Talalla beach is utterly empty and utterly divine – for the moment.

When to Go

Sri Lanka is pretty much a year-round beach destination. When it's raining in the East it's normally sunny in the West and vice versa.

➡ The main tourist season coincides with the northeast monsoon, which runs from December to March. At this time the beaches on the west and south coasts are bathed in sunshine and the tourist industry for this part of the country is in full swing. The east coast, by contrast, is often wet and many hotels are closed.

➡ Between May and September, when the stronger southwest monsoon hits the island and the southwest coast is drenched, head straight for the east coast, which sits in the rain shadow of the highlands and will be sunny and idyllic.

➡ Don't take the seasons as gospel: even during the height of the southwest monsoon it can often be sunny in the morning on the west-coast beaches before afternoon thunderstorms roll in.

➡ The north of the island is generally much drier so you could come here any time and get your beach towel out.

Beaches

For many people the beach *is* Sri Lanka. You'll encounter ravishing stretches of sand around much of this island nation's sparkling shoreline.

➡ The west coast is the most developed beach area and is where the majority of the package-tour resorts can be found, but don't let that put you off because some of the beaches here are up there with the best in the country.

➡ With its stunning beaches, good selection of accommodation and activities that range from diving to sunning to surfing, it's no surprise that the south coast of the island is the most popular area with beach-bound independent travellers. However, heavy development is bringing more package tourists.

➡ For years war and unrest had kept the east-coast beaches largely off the radar of all but the most adventurous, but with peace a coastline littered with absolutely corking beaches is now starting to open up. New hotels are springing up fast but the East is still much less developed than the West or South.

➡ Finally, there's the far north, where a beach to yourself isn't just a possibility but more of a given. However, tourist development up here remains minimal and locals aren't used to foreign beach worshippers.

Safe Swimming

Every year drownings occur off Sri Lanka's beaches. If you aren't an experienced swimmer or surfer, it's easy to underestimate the dangers – or be totally unaware of them. (Don't worry though, as not all of Sri Lanka's beaches are surf battered: Unawatuna, Passekudah and Uppuveli are some of the calmest, safest swimming beaches and are perfect for less confident swimmers and children.) There are few full-time lifesaving patrols, so there's usually no one to jump in and rescue you. A few common-sense rules should be observed:

➡ Don't swim out of your depth. If you are a poor swimmer, always stay in the shallows.

➡ Don't stay in the water when you feel tired.

➡ Never go swimming under the influence of alcohol or drugs.

➡ Supervise children at *all* times.

➡ Watch out for rips. Water brought onto the beach by waves is sucked back to sea and this current can be strong enough to drag you out with it. Rips in rough surf can sometimes be seen as calm patches in the disturbed water. It's best to check with someone reliable before venturing into the water.

➡ If you do get caught in a rip, swim *across* the current towards the breaking waves. The currents are usually less where the waves are actually breaking and the surf will push you shoreward. Never try and swim against the current. If it's too strong for you to swim across it, keep afloat and raise a hand so that someone on shore can see that you are in distress. A rip eventually weakens; the important thing is not to panic.

➡ Exercise caution when there is surf.

➡ Beware of coral; coming into contact with coral can be painful for the swimmer and fatal for the coral. Always check with someone reliable if you suspect the area you're about to swim in may have coral.

➡ Never dive head-first into the water. Hazards may be lurking under the surface or the water may not be as deep as it looks. It pays to be cautious.

Tangalla (p137)

Beach Culture

By and large Sri Lankans are an easygoing and accepting lot and on the south and west coasts they are also very used to foreign tourists and their skimpy beachwear. For much of the East and North, though, the situation is a little different: women in bathing suits, even modest one-piece numbers, can attract a lot of unwelcome attention. Even in the now very popular east-coast beach resorts such as Arugam Bay and the beaches north of Trincomalee the attention can be excessive (and there have been sexual assaults). On these beaches and especially in more remote locations, women will not want to travel alone and should consider wearing a T-shirt and shorts into the water.

Even in the more trodden beaches in the South and West it's worth remembering that the vast majority of Sri Lankans remain very conservative. Topless sunbathing is a no-no anywhere. Few local women would dare wear a bikini, so although nobody is likely to say anything to you about wearing one on a tourist beach you might risk offence, and possibly worse, if you were to leave the beach and venture off around the village or town in skimpy clothing.

Most resort hotels have pools where you can sunbathe freely without fear of offence or hassle.

Best Beaches

Talk about opening a can of worms, but in the interest of sun-lounger debates across Sri Lanka here's our pick of the nation's finest stretches of sand.

➡ **Talalla**

A near-perfect crescent of white sand, fringed by forest and almost completely untouched by development.

➡ **Hiriketiya**

This horseshoe-shaped mini-cove in the South has it all: surf breaks, sheltered swimming, azure water and a relaxed, utterly tropical vibe.

➡ **Tangalla**

Tranquil tropical coves and endless sweeps of white sand mean Tangalla has something for everyone.

➡ **Mirissa**

Idyllic south-coast beach with something of a party scene and the best whale-watching base.

White-water rafting on the Kelaniya Ganga, Kitulgala (p169)

➡ Uppuveli

Stunning Uppuveli is the beach of choice for many independent travellers on the east coast.

➡ Arugam Bay

One of the best surf spots in the country and the most developed east-coast beach resort.

➡ Bentota

A near-empty swath of golden sand backed by boutique hotels.

Surfing

Sri Lanka has consistent surf year-round, but the quality of waves is far lower than the nearby Maldives and Indonesia. You visit Sri Lanka more for the culture, climate and ease of travelling than for the chance to get barrelled.

On the east coast, surf's up from April to October. On the west and south coasts, the best surfing is from November to April, with the start and end of this season more consistent than January and February (when, bizarrely, most surfers choose to visit). On the flip side, however, the swells at this time can be less clean and easterly winds can badly affect some spots.

Sri Lanka is a superb place to learn how to surf or for intermediate surfers to get their first reef-break experiences. Many of the spots are very close to shore and surf access couldn't be easier, which makes Sri Lanka an ideal destination for a surfer with a nonsurfing partner. Boards can be hired (expect to pay Rs 1200 to 1500 per day) and lessons are available at most beach towns; courses start at around Rs 2500.

Best Surf Spots

➡ **Midigama** (p125) The best spot along the south coast, with a mellow left point, a nearby consistent beach break and a short and sharp right reef, which offers about the only frequently hollow wave in Sri Lanka.

➡ **Arugam Bay** (p13) Sri Lanka's best-known wave is at Arugam Bay on the east coast. Surf's up at this long right point from April to October.

➡ **Weligama** (p126) On the south coast, Weligama seems custom-made for learning to surf and a number of surf schools and camps have recently sprung up there.

→ **Hikkaduwa** (p102) The reefs here on the west coast are a long-time favourite, although more for the ease of living than for the quality of the waves.

White-Water Rafting, Kayaking & Boating

You don't have to be a beach babe to enjoy Sri Lankan water sports. High up in the hills, rivers tumble down mountains to produce some memorable rafting conditions.

Currently the best-known white-water rafting area is near Kitulgala, where you can set out on gentle river meanders (around US$30 per person) or, for experienced rafters, exciting descents of Class IV to V rapids. However, new dams under construction will likely curtail the white-water fun here in the next few years.

Action Lanka (p69) is the biggest player in Sri Lankan rafting and organises expeditions from its Colombo base; rates start at US$65.

Kayaking is possible at many spots along the coast, including the lagoons around Tangalla. Boat or catamaran trips for sightseeing, birdwatching and fishing are offered around Negombo, Bentota and from east-coast and south-coast beach resorts.

Windsurfing & Kitesurfing

Sri Lanka isn't renowned for its windsurfing or kitesurfing but that doesn't mean there's no action. Negombo has a well-run kitesurfing school (p90) that runs courses (three days for €359) and trips down the coast. Further north, the Kalpitiya area has gained a reputation as one of the best kitesurfing areas in South Asia and there are plenty of board-hire places and kitesurfing schools, such as Sri Lanka Kite (p96).

Further south, Bentota is an emerging windsurfing centre with two established operators: Sunshine Water Sports Center (p98) and Diyakawa Water Sports (p98). It's a good place for learners and lessons are possible; windsurfing courses cost around US$150.

Whale-Watching & Dolphin-Watching

Sri Lanka is a world-class whale-watching location. The big attraction is big indeed – blue whales, the largest of all creatures. Mirissa (p131) is the best place from which to organise a whale-watching trip. On the east coast, Uppuveli and Nilaveli offer quieter but less-reliable whale-watching. In the northwest the Kalpitiya area is another possible base; here large pods of dolphins are encountered, along with (less reliably) sperm whales and Bryde's whales.

In all these places local boat tours are available. One excellent nationwide tour operator is **Eco Team Sri Lanka** (Map p64; 📞 011-583 0833; www.srilankaecotourism.com; 20/63 Fairfield Gardens), which offers whale-watching (and dolphin-watching) tours on both the south and west coasts.

The season for whales (and dolphins) off the south coast and Kalpitiya is from December to April, while on the east coast it runs from May to October.

Diving & Snorkelling

There are plenty of opportunities to live like a fish in Sri Lanka. However, marine conditions are not ideal for diving as limited visibility and big waves make diving or snorkelling challenging.

Dive schools can be found all along the coast (except the far north). In Sri Lanka it's more about the fish than the reefs, but there are a few exceptions including some wrecks. Offshore waters include the full dose of tropical Indian Ocean fish species including such pretty little numbers as angel fish, butterfly fish, surgeon fish and scorpion fish. Higher up the scale come black- and white-tip reef sharks, though you'll be lucky to encounter these.

Along the west coast, the best time to dive and snorkel is generally from November to April. On the east coast, the seas are calmest from April to September. But at none of these times can underwater visibility be described as breathtaking.

Diving shops can be found in the major west-coast resorts. They hire and sell gear, including snorkelling equipment. PADI courses cost around US$325 to US$390

Top: Mirissa Beach (p130)

Bottom: Diving with whale sharks

BEST DIVE SPOTS

Great Basses reefs (p144) Several kilometres off the coast near Kirinda, these remote reefs are ranked by divers as about the best in the country. Eagle rays and white-tip reef sharks are the big fish to see here. But take note – conditions are tricky and the reefs are for expert divers only.

Bar Reef (p95) These offshore reefs in the northwest of the country offer pristine reef systems, masses of fish, and dolphins and whales to boot, but again it's experienced divers only.

Pigeon Island (p268) Accessible for beginners but still rewarding for experts, the beautiful, colour-splashed reefs off this pinprick of an island put a smile on everyone's face. Around 300 species of fish and other marine life have been recorded here. Also a great snorkelling spot.

Unawatuna (p118) It's all about wreck diving here – one boat was even sunk exclusively for the purpose of improving the diving. Several dive schools, lots of facilities and good for all levels of experience.

Batticaloa (p258) Calm waters for exploring the wreck of HMS *Hermes*, a WWII British naval ship.

Negombo (p90) Looking at the rather brown waters here you might not expect it to be a very good dive area, but that brown water hides reefs bustling with fish just offshore.

and are also available with the following respected dive schools:

➡ **Poseidon Diving Station** (p102), Hikkaduwa

➡ **Ocean Lanka Scuba** (p96), Kalpitiya

➡ **Unawatuna Diving Centre** (p119), Unawatuna

➡ **Weligama Bay Dive Center** (p127), Weligama

➡ **Sri Lanka Diving Tours** (p258), Batticaloa

➡ **Poseidon Diving Station** (p268), Nilaveli

➡ **Colombo Divers** (p90), Negombo

Safety Guidelines for Diving

Before embarking on a scuba-diving trip, carefully consider the following points to ensure a safe and enjoyable experience:

➡ Possess a current diving certification card from a recognised scuba-diving instructional agency.

➡ Be sure you are healthy and feel comfortable diving.

➡ Obtain reliable information about physical and environmental conditions at the dive site (eg from a reputable local dive operation).

➡ Dive only at sites within your realm of experience; if available, engage the services of a competent, professionally trained dive instructor or dive master.

Responsible Diving

Please consider the following tips when diving and help preserve the ecology and beauty of reefs:

➡ Never use anchors on the reef and take care not to ground boats on coral.

➡ Avoid touching or standing on living marine organisms or dragging equipment across the reef. Polyps can be damaged by even the gentlest contact. If you must hold on to the reef, only touch exposed rock or dead coral.

➡ Be conscious of your fins. Even without contact, the surge from fin strokes near the reef can damage delicate organisms. Take care not to kick up clouds of sand, which can smother organisms.

➡ Practise and maintain proper buoyancy control. Major damage can be done by divers descending too fast and colliding with the reef.

➡ Take great care in underwater caves. Spend as little time within them as possible as your air bubbles may be caught within the roof and thereby leave organisms high and dry. Take turns to inspect the interior of a small cave.

➡ Resist the temptation to collect or buy corals or shells or to loot marine archaeological sites.

➡ Ensure that you take home all your rubbish and any litter you may find as well. Plastics in particular are a serious threat to marine life.

➡ Do not feed fish and minimise your disturbance of marine animals.

Plan Your Trip
National Parks & Safaris

Sri Lanka is one of the finest wildlife-watching countries in Asia; many of its national parks are relatively accessible and the variety of habitats and the diversity of wildlife is exceptional. Even a visitor with only the most casual interest can't help but be overawed by the sight of great herds of elephants, enormous whales, elusive leopards, schools of dolphins, thousands of colourful birds and rainbow-coloured tropical fish.The Sri Lankan tourism industry hasn't been slow to cotton on to the country's wildlife-watching potential, and an impressive array of national parks, protected zones and safari options exist that allow anyone, from dedicated naturalist to interested lay person, to get out there with a pair of binoculars and make the most of the Sri Lankan wilderness.

Best Wildlife Experiences

West, South & East
The West is best for marine life, but Wilpattu National Park has large mammals and birders will like Muthurajawela Marsh. The south coast is home to several species of whales, dolphins and turtles, while Yala National Park is one of the best places in Asia to see leopards. In the East are quiet national parks and bird species that prefer drier climates.

The Hill Country
The hills have rainforests, moorlands and savanna parks with everything from elephants to endemic high-country birds.

The Ancient Cities
Numerous national parks filled with big-ticket mammals and great dry country birding. Even the region's ruined cities provide ideal habitat for many creatures.

Wildlife

For its size, Sri Lanka boasts an incredible diversity of animalia: 125 mammal species, 245 butterflies, 463 birds, 96 snakes and more than 320 species of tropical fish. Given the fragility of the environment in which they live, it should come as no surprise that quite a few are vulnerable.

Mammals

Sri Lanka's mammals include some of the most easily observable of the country's animal species, as well as some of the most invisible. Hard to spot are the solitary and mostly nocturnal leopard, Sri Lanka's top predator; the scavenging golden jackal; the shaggy sloth bear; the civet (a catlike hunter related to the weasel); the mongoose; and the shy, armour-plated Indian pangolin, with overlapping scales made from modified hair.

Very audible but not always visible are troops of tree-bound cackling primates,

BEST PLACES FOR ELEPHANTS

Uda Walawe National Park (p195) With around 500 elephants present year-round, this park offers the most reliable elephant-spotting in the country.

Minneriya National Park (p226) Each August hundreds of elephants home in on this park in an elephant spectacle known as 'the gathering'.

Kaudulla National Park (p227) Over 250 elephants call this park home.

Bundala National Park (p140) Consistent elephant sightings in a beautiful watery setting.

Yala National Park (p145) Lots of elephants but can be surprisingly hard to see.

like common langurs, also known as Hanuman or grey langurs; endemic purple-faced langurs; hairy bear monkeys; and toque macaques, notable for their distinctive thatch of middle-parted hair. The slow movements of the slender loris belie its ability to snatch its prey with a lightning-quick lunge.

More often crossed, albeit at different times of the day, are the majestic Asian elephant; the omnivorous and tusked wild boar of Sri Lanka; and cervine creatures like the big, maned sambar and smaller white-spotted Axis deer. The bushy-tailed, five-striped palm squirrel is commonly seen scurrying around gardens and town parks. These are often also the locations of the large trees in which Indian flying foxes (large fruit-eating bats) camp by the hundreds.

Mammals don't just hide out in the forests and savannas. The biggest of all mammals are to be found in the waters off Sri Lanka. Blue whales, sperm whales, fin whales and Bryde's whales swim along migration corridors off the coast here. The seas off Mirissa and around neighbouring Dondra Head are perhaps the best place in the world to see blue whales. Various dolphins are usually encountered on whale-watching trips, including megapods of spinner dolphins.

Birds

A tropical climate, long isolation from the Asian mainland and a diversity of habitats have helped endow Sri Lanka with an astonishing abundance of birdlife. Some 463 species have been recorded, 26 of which are unique to Sri Lanka; others are found only in Sri Lanka and adjacent South India. Of the 200 migrant species, most of which are in residence from August to April, the waders (sandpipers, plovers etc)

are the long-distance champions, making the journey from their breeding grounds in the Arctic tundra.

Birders may wish to contact the **Field Ornithology Group of Sri Lanka** (http://fogsl.cmb.ac.lk), the national affiliate of Birdlife International.

Tips for Birdwatchers

➡ Visit a variety of habitats – rainforest, urban parks and bodies of water in the dry zone – to see the full diversity of birdlife in Sri Lanka.

➡ February to March is the best time for birdwatching. You miss the monsoons, and the migrant birds are still visiting.

➡ Waterbirds are active for most of the day.

➡ Although morning is always the best time to go birdwatching, in the evening you will see noisy flocks of birds preparing to roost.

BEST PLACES FOR BIRDS

Sinharaja Forest Reserve (p197) A slab of rainforest with around 160 bird species.

Knuckles Range (p167) Little-known montane forests filled with hill-country and forest birds.

Bundala National Park (p140) This wetland park is the classic Sri Lankan birdwatching destination.

Kumana National Park (p254) Superb low-country birdwatching with around 150 species present.

Muthurajawela Marsh (p91) Excellent wetland birding close to Colombo.

Pottuvil Lagoon (p251) Numerous waders and waterbirds in this little-visited east-coast wetland.

➡ Consider taking a tour with a specialist if you're keen to see the endemic species and achieve a healthy birdwatching tally, particularly if time is short.

Planning Your Safari

Where to Go

Where to go depends entirely on what you want to see and what kind of safari you want to take. For example Yala National Park in the far southeast is the most popular overall park and is fantastic for leopards, but it's also very busy and can become something of a circus with minibuses chasing each other around in search of cats. If you want your leopard-spotting quieter (and less certain), try Wilpattu National Park.

National Parks & Reserves

More than 2000 years ago, enlightened royalty declared certain land areas off limits to any human activity. Almost every province in the ancient kingdom of Kandy had such *udawattakelle* (sanctuaries). All animals and plants in these reserves were left undisturbed.

Today's system of parks and reserves is mostly an amalgamation of traditionally protected areas, reserves established by the British, and newly designated areas set aside for things like elephant corridors. There are more than 100 of these areas under government guard, covering approximately 8% of the island. They are divided into three types: strict nature reserves (no visitors allowed), national parks (visits under fixed conditions) and nature reserves (human habitation permitted). Sri Lanka also has two marine sanctuaries – the Bar Reef (west of Kalpitiya peninsula) and Hikkaduwa National Park – as well as dozens of protected island and coastal zones.

Off the Beaten Track

A full 82% of Sri Lanka's land is controlled by the state in some form or another, and is therefore subject to a raft of legislation to combat destructive activity and protect sensitive areas like the scores of natural forests. There are 63 sanctuaries in the country, a long list of forest reserves and countless wetlands both with and without official titles.

Given the overcrowding at some of the better-known natural areas, new attention has been directed to other deserving national parks, such as Lunugamvehera (which serves as a link between Yala and Uda Walawe National Parks, allowing elephants to pass freely between the two) as an alternative to Yala, and Wasgomuwa instead of Gal Oya or Minneriya.

Sri Lanka is a signatory to the Ramsar Convention on Wetlands, which currently recognises six zones in the country. These include Bundala National Park and the 915-hectare Madu Ganga Estuary near Balapitiya, 80km south of Colombo on the A2, site of one of the last pristine mangrove forests in Sri Lanka. There's also the Anawilundawa Wetland Sanctuary, just west of the A3 about 100km north of Colombo, a cluster of ancient, human-made, freshwater reservoirs that are now a safe haven for awesome wetland biodiversity.

For further listings of out-of-the-way green escapes, contact the government conservation departments or consult **LOCALternative Sri Lanka** (www.localternative.com).

FIELD GUIDES & WILDLIFE BOOKS

There are plenty of good field guides out there. These are some of our favourites:

A Photographic Guide to Mammals of Sri Lanka (Gehan de Silva Wijeyeratne) This well-known Sri Lankan naturalist has also published extensively on the country's birds and butterflies, among other things.

A Selection of the Birds of Sri Lanka (John and Judy Banks) A slim, well-illustrated tome that's perfect for amateur birdwatchers.

A Field Guide to the Birds of Sri Lanka (John Harrison) A pricier hardback with colour illustrations; one of the best field guides available.

The Nature of Sri Lanka (L Nadaraja) With stunning photographs, this is a collection of essays about Sri Lanka by eminent writers and conservationists.

Top: Monkey, Kandy (p151)

Bottom: Elephants in Uda Walawe National Park (p195)

ANTON GVOZDIKOV / SHUTTERSTOCK ©

When to Go

Sri Lanka is a year-round wildlife-watching destination but generally the best times correspond with the main November-to-April tourist season. At this time of year all the big parks are open and the dry conditions mean that animals start to gather around water holes, making them easier to spot (this is especially so between February and early April). If you come in the May-to-October southwest monsoon season, head to the parks around the Ancient Cities and in the east of the island.

How to Book

For all the major national parks and other protected areas, organising a safari couldn't be easier. Groups of safari jeep drivers can normally be found in the nearest town or gathered outside the gates, and hotels can also organise safaris. It's normally just a case of turning up the evening before and discussing a price and your needs. Entry fees to all parks are paid directly at entrance gates.

At extremely busy parks such as Yala it pays to plan ahead. One good local operator based in nearby Tissamaharama is Ajith Safari Jeep Tours (p143).

MAJOR NATIONAL PARKS & RESERVES

PARK	AREA	FEATURES	BEST TIME TO VISIT
Bundala National Park	62.2 sq km	coastal lagoon, migratory birds, elephants	year-round
Gal Oya National Park	629.4 sq km	grasslands, evergreen forest, deer, Senanayake Samudra (tank), elephants, sloth bears, leopards, water buffaloes	Dec-Sep
Horton Plains National Park	31.6 sq km	Unesco World Heritage Site, montane forests, marshy grasslands, World's End precipice, sambars	Dec-Mar
Kaudulla National Park	66.6 sq km	Kaudulla Tank, evergreen forest, scrub jungle, grassy plains, elephants, leopards, sambars, fishing cats, sloth bears	Aug-Dec
Knuckles Range	175 sq km	Unesco World Heritage Site, traditional villages, hiking trails, caves, waterfalls, montane pygmy forest, evergreen forest, riverine forest, grasslands, scrub, paddy fields, over 30 mammal species	Dec-May
Kumana National Park	356.6 sq km	grasslands, jungle, lagoons, mangrove swamp, waterfowl	May-Sep
Lunugamvehera National Park	235 sq km	grasslands, reservoir, elephants	May-Sep
Minneriya National Park	88.9 sq km	Minneriya Tank, toque macaques, sambars, elephants, waterfowl	May-Sep
Sinharaja Forest Reserve	189 sq km	Unesco World Heritage Site, sambars, rainforest, leopards, purple-faced langurs, barking deer, 147 recorded bird species	Aug-Sep, Jan-Mar
Sri Pada Peak Wilderness Reserve	224 sq km	Unesco World Heritage Site, Adam's Peak, hiking trails	Dec-May
Uda Walawe National Park	308.2 sq km	grasslands, thorn scrub, elephants, spotted deer, water buffaloes, wild boar	year-round
Wasgomuwa National Park	393.2 sq km	evergreen forest, hilly ridges, grassy plains, elephants, leopards, sloth bears	Jun-Sep
Wilpattu National Park	1317 sq km	dry woodland, scrub, saltgrass, leopards, sloth bears, deer, crocodiles	Jan-Mar
Yala National Park	141 sq km	tropical thorn forest, lagoons, leopards, elephants, sloth bears, water buffaloes, lesser flamingos	Nov-Jul

Plan Your Trip

Travel with Children

Like a good rice and curry, Sri Lanka offers a dazzling array of choices. This is obviously not a first-world country, so the child who expects a packaged Disneyland experience won't be happy, but the love of Sri Lankans for children helps compensate for bumps along the way.

Sri Lanka for Kids

Sri Lankans have a special affinity for children, and visitors travelling with children will find the young ones are sure-fire icebreakers.

Sri Lanka is an easy-going place for children, even if it lacks kid-targeted sights such as amusement parks and similar attractions. The beaches, historical sites, national parks with elephants can all fascinate and entertain kids. However, the lack of special facilities means that kids will benefit from the same sense of adventure in exploring the country that serves adults well.

With preparation and mindfulness of a few things while in country, travel with children in Sri Lanka can be great fun.

Children's Highlights

There aren't many attractions dedicated solely to children in Sri Lanka, but there are a lot of sights they'll love.

➡ **Uda Walawe** (p195) One of the best national parks for wildlife-spotting safaris.

➡ **Elephant Transit Home** (p196) Not far from Uda Walawe, this is a well-regarded halfway house for injured and orphaned elephants.

Best Regions for Kids

The West

It's beaches all along this sandy coast. There are all manner of child-friendly resorts where you can relax and maybe build a castle or two. Overall, this is probably the most child-friendly area.

The South

More beaches, lots of water-based activities and in the east there are elephants.

The Hill Country

Many of the attractions here are more adult orientated, but the mild temperatures are a good respite from the heat elsewhere. Tea plantations and trains are an unbeatable day out.

The Ancient Cities

Ancient temples, forts, ruins, jungles and elephants. Hello, Indiana Jones!

The East

Outside of surfing high season (May to October), the surf on these beautiful beaches can be mild. Kids love the snorkelling at Pigeon Island National Park.

➡ **Minneriya** (p226) A national park renowned for its herds of elephants.

➡ **Pigeon Island National Park** (p268) Off beautiful Nilaveli beach, this island has great snorkeling that kids love.

➡ **Turtle hatcheries** (p99) On the west coast, these are popular.

➡ **Unawatuna** (p118) Fringing reefs mean the beach here is safe and shallow for little ones.

➡ **Polonnaruwa** (p215) Kids can run themselves silly at the vast and car-free ancient heritage sites such as this one, with its very cool ruins.

➡ **Three-wheelers** (p330) Buzzing, blowing and completely unlike a ride anyplace else, these ubiquitous transport options are good for a thrill.

➡ **Hill Country Train Rides** (p330) Kids will love hanging out the doors of chugging trains (and giving their parents heart attacks!).

Planning

Accommodation

➡ Sri Lankan hotels and guesthouses often have triple and family rooms, plus extra beds can be supplied on demand.

➡ Baby beds are in short supply.

➡ Don't expect to find 'kids clubs' or the like, which are common in first-world luxury resorts.

What to Pack

➡ Bring an extra mosquito net, as hotels rarely have spares if you get an extra bed.

➡ Bring sunscreen and children's mosquito repellent with you; you won't find it in Sri Lanka.

➡ Entertainment for long car rides, especially video downloads, as trying to download in Sri Lanka can take a long time.

➡ For very young children, either a backpack or some other form of carrier. Prams are tough going on uneven or nonexistent footpaths.

➡ Car seats are uncommon; if you want to use one, bring it from home.

➡ For all-round information and advice, check out Lonely Planet's *Travel with Children*.

Eating with Kids

➡ Sri Lankan hospitality means that people will go to any length to please young and finicky eaters, and most places offer at least a few Western-style dishes, though child-specific menus are rare.

➡ To ease children into Sri Lankan food, try a breakfast of *pittu*. The combination of coconut and rice will be kind to their palates. Also try hoppers (bowl-shaped pancakes), especially the string variety, or nice and mild *rotti* flatbreads with a filling.

➡ The profusion of fresh and exciting fruit varieties means that everybody will find something they like, even if it's never been tried before.

➡ Highchairs (in restaurants) are uncommon.

Other Tips

➡ Buy pharmaceutical supplies, imported baby food and disposable nappies/diapers at Cargills Food City and Keells supermarkets throughout the country.

➡ Nappie/diaper sizes run small in Sri Lanka.

➡ Breastfeeding in public is accepted, but parents will struggle to find dedicated baby-changing rooms. It's not a major problem, as it's acceptable for toddlers to be naked in public.

➡ Rabies and animal-borne parasites are present in Sri Lanka, so keep children away from stray animals, including cats, dogs and monkeys.

➡ Bring kid-friendly snacks for car and train trips in case vendor offerings don't suit young tastes.

Regions at a Glance

Colombo

Sunsets
Urban Life
Shopping

Amazing Colours

Built right up to the shores of the Indian Ocean, Colombo faces west into the setting sun. Many evenings begin with an explosion of magenta and purple on the horizon that you can share with others at a hotel bar or with the real people along the shore.

Pettah Market

The first time you almost get run down by a madman with a cart full of goods in the markets of Pettah, you may regret your decision to come. But soon you'll be in the chaotic thick of things dodging from stall to vendor with aplomb.

Glitzy Luxury

From artwork to tea, you can find unique and desirable goods and gifts in Colombo, especially along the leafy streets of Cinnamon Gardens and in flashy new shopping areas.

p56

The West Coast

Beaches
Activities
Lodging

Sand for All

From all-inclusive package-tour resorts to former hippy hangouts and little-visited sands, the beaches of the west coast span the entire spectrum and keep everyone happy.

Watery Pleasures

Ride the waves and dive the reefs of Hikkaduwa, birdwatch on the marshes, explore the back blocks, see the dolphins in the north, get pampered in a spa and take a boat safari around Bentota.

Top Resorts

The beaches around Bentota are home to some breathtaking boutique hotels that rank among the finest in the country. Cheerful Negombo also contains some memorable accommodation. Forget every care on an all-inclusive holiday.

p87

The South

Beaches
Activities
Wildlife

Stunning Strands

There are beaches here with a real traveller vibe and there are beaches with barely another person in sight, but the uniting factor is that they're almost all stunning.

Surfing

The area between Galle and Matara is arguably the finest slice of surf country in South Asia: Ahangama, Midigama and Weligama are known to surfers everywhere – or should be. Each has its own flavour and vibe.

Creature Features

Monkeys crash through the trees, whales splash through the seas, leopards slink through the night, birds flap through the skies, turtles emerge on the beach and animal lovers can't stop smiling.

p106

The Hill Country

Walking
Wildlife
Eating

Verdant Hikes

Hack through jungles, shiver over high plateaus, traipse to vertigo-inspiring viewpoints, tiptoe through tea plantations and walk in the footsteps of gods.

Elephants & More

No other part of Sri Lanka offers such varied wildlife habitats. There are steamy rainforests filled with noisy birds, grassland savannahs ruled by elephants, and highland forests covered in delicate lichens and moss.

Guesthouse Dining

Eating in Sri Lanka is rarely anything but a pleasure, but it's in the Hill Country where the preparation and consumption of food becomes an art form, and the best food comes from your guesthouse kitchen.

p149

The Ancient Cities

Monuments
Temples
Cycling

Ancient Treasures

The Polonnaruwa Quadrangle, the ancient quarter of Anuradhapura, the jaw-dropping sight of the rock monastery at Sigiriya: just some of the remarkable ruins ready for exploration.

Sri Maha Bodhi

Amid the leaf-shrouded ruins of Anuradhapura is Sri Maha Bodhi, a tree that has seen history and devotion for 2000 years. Nearby, a welter of temples and monuments will inspire your own devotion.

Biking the Temples

The ruins of the Ancient Cities are sited within much larger parks and reserves. You can pedal between the wonders along palm-shaded paths and never see a car. Guesthouses have bikes for hire.

p202

The East

Beaches
Activities
Wildlife

Lonely Sands

Most of the east coast's endless stretches of beach are untouched, but even those that are developed are sandy wonderlands, with just the right amounts of palm trees, white sands and low-key scenes.

Snoozing & Diving

The East generously provides activities to alternate with napping on beach hammocks. The ocean here isn't just calm and gorgeous, it also has the reefs and wrecks for great snorkelling and diving, and the right waves for surfing.

Kumana National Park

Tucked away in the far south, Kumana National Park doesn't have the size of its neighbour Yala. On the plus side it lacks Yala's tourist population, which means the leopards, elephants and birds here are all yours.

p243

Jaffna & the North

Discovery
History
Seashores

Off the Beaten Path

All but shut down to travel for years, the North is now one of the best places in Sri Lanka for directionless travel. Roads have never been better, making it easy to discover surprises like the abandoned port at the end of Mannar Island.

Ancient Sites

Hindu gods and goddesses painted in exquisite riots of colour animate towering and legendary temple gateways all over the North.

Islands & Coasts

Seemingly endless coastlines curl around the Jaffna region's mainland. There's even more to discover amid the turquoise waters that surround lonely coast roads and causeways. Take boat rides to isolated islands with sublime beauty.

p270

On the Road

Colombo

⏏ 011 / POP 760,000

Best Places to Eat

➡ Nihonbashi Honten (p77)
➡ Nana's (p76)
➡ Good Market (p77)
➡ Bu Ba (p80)

Best Places to Sleep

➡ Cinnamon Red (p73)
➡ Cinnamon Grand Hotel (p73)
➡ Havelock Place Bungalow (p74)
➡ Colombo City Hostel (p71)
➡ YWCA (p71)

Why Go?

Although it's unlikely it will reclaim its 19th-century moniker 'the garden city of the East', Colombo has nevertheless emerged as a must-see stop in Sri Lanka. No longer just the sprawling city you have to endure on your way to the beaches, it has become a worthy destination in its own right and makes an excellent start – or finish – to your Sri Lankan adventures.

The legacies of colonial Colombo's garden roots are still very much intact along its often-shady boulevards. Fort is a compelling place thanks to ongoing restoration of its landmark colonial architecture, while Pettah brims with markets and rampant commerce. Even traffic-clogged Galle Rd is getting spiffier with glossy new hotel complexes.

Colombo's cosmopolitan side supports ever-more stylish eateries, galleries and shops. Surprises abound: with a little exploration you'll find great local food, characterful shops and tiny, convivial cafes. Meanwhile, a building boom like no other is transforming the city's skyline.

When to Go
Colombo

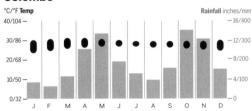

| **Jan–Mar** The driest season, with night-time cool breezes. More tourists, so book hotels in advance. | **May** The important religious celebration of Vesak sees the city come alive in colours, lights and festivities. | **Dec** Although Christians are a minority, Christmas is popular and festive decorations abound. |

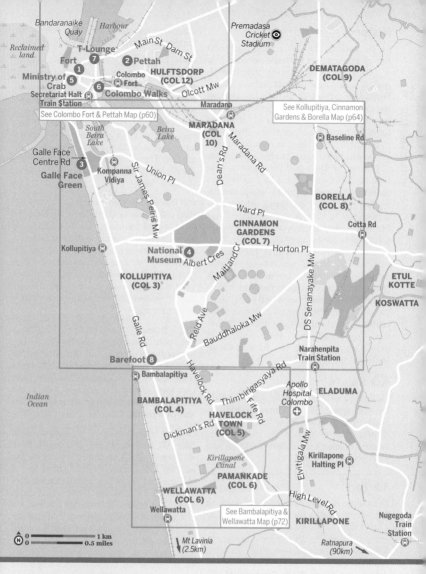

Colombo Highlights

1 Fort (p58) Revelling in the restoration of this compelling historic quarter.

2 Pettah (p59) Plunging into the timeless commercial madness of the shops, stalls and markets.

3 Galle Face Green (p59) Catching a sunset amid families and courting couples on Colombo's front lawn.

4 National Museum (p63) Soaking up Sri Lanka's history and discovering its treasures in the remarkable first five rooms.

5 Ministry of Crab (p76) Getting splattered with goodness at this hugely popular restaurant.

6 Walking tour (p68) Exploring this fascinating old city on foot.

7 Tea (p76) Enjoying the best of Sri Lanka's national beverage in a stylish cafe such as T-Lounge.

8 Shopping (p82) Prowling through landmark stores such as Barefoot, where you can revel in the beauty and creativity of local merchandise.

History

As far back as the 5th century, Colombo served as a sea port for trade between Asia and the West. During the 8th century Arab traders settled near the port and in 1505 the Portuguese arrived. By the mid-17th century the Dutch had taken over, growing cinnamon in the area now known as Cinnamon Gardens, but it wasn't until the British arrived that the town became a city. In 1815 Colombo was proclaimed the capital of Ceylon.

During the 1870s the breakwaters were built and Fort was created by flooding surrounding wetlands. Colombo was peacefully handed over when Sri Lanka achieved independence in 1948. A new parliament was built in Sri Jayawardenepura-Kotte, an outer suburb of Colombo, in 1982.

Bomb attacks in Fort over the years of war caused Colombo's major businesses and institutions to disperse across the city. With peace, Colombo is changing fast, with a great deal of development north and south along the coast, a building boom of high rises in the centre, and relentless – and mostly charmless – sprawl eastward. Huge amounts of money are pouring into the city from China, India and the Middle East.

⊙ Sights

Lacking signature must-see sights, Colombo's real appeal lies in its many neighbourhoods, which span many eras from the earliest colonial days to the city's present nascent boom. Start in Fort or Pettah and work your way south.

⊙ Fort

During the European era Fort was indeed a fort, surrounded by the sea on two sides and a moat on the landward sides. Today it's literally at the centre of Colombo's resurgence, with grand old colonial-era buildings being restored amid a mix of modern structures, such as the **World Trade Center** (Map p60; Bank of Ceylon Mawatha).

Security remains in evidence in this area, as the fenced-off **President's House** (Map p60) and various government ministries are here. You may have to detour around a bit, but it's a compact area and can be appreciated on a short stroll, starting at the Old Galle Buck Lighthouse.

The busy harbour on the north side of Fort is mostly walled off, but you can enjoy sweeping views from the tiny terrace of the otherwise humdrum top-floor cafe of the once-grand Grand Oriental Hotel (p71).

★ **Dutch Hospital**　　　HISTORIC BUILDING
(Map p60; Bank of Ceylon Mawatha, Col 1) Centrepiece of the vibrant Fort, this colonial-era complex dates back to the early 1600s. Lavishly restored, it is home to shops, cafes and restaurants run by some of Colombo's best operators. Enjoy a pause for a cold drink amid the incredibly thick columns of its arcades. There's an annex in a 19th-century British building on the backside that faces Chatham St.

Old Galle Buck Lighthouse　　　LIGHTHOUSE
(Map p60; Marine Dr, Col 1) Climb up onto the large central terrace of this 1954 lighthouse for views of the ocean, and the rapidly expanding commercial port and mega offshore developments such as Colombo Port City (p70). Ceremonial cannons point over what was open water just a couple of years ago. A modest cafe across the street offers refreshments.

Clock Tower　　　LANDMARK
(Map p60; Janadhipathi Mawatha, Col 1) The restored clock tower at the junction of Chatham St and Janadhipathi Mawatha (once Queen St) was originally a lighthouse that was built in 1857. It's now right at the heart of officialdom and you can expect a few watchful guards.

Central Point　　　HISTORIC BUILDING
(Map p60; Chatham St, Col 1; ⊙ museum 8.30am-4pm Mon-Fri) FREE Chatham St is seeing the ongoing renovations of old buildings, one of the grandest being the old colonnaded 1914 Central Bank building known as Central Point. The beautifully restored interior is a riot of Greco-Roman detailing and features the tallest chandelier in Asia. There's a small museum off the lobby about local money that's worth the time simply for the display on why bartering a cow for fish was a bad idea, thus leading to the invention of currency.

Lloyd's Buildings　　　HISTORIC BUILDING
(Map p60; Sir Baron Jayathilaka Mawatha, Col 1) Sir Baron Jayathilaka Mawatha has the grandly restored Lloyd's Buildings. Several other imposing colonial piles on the street are also in various stages of renovation, such as the neighbouring Whiteaways with its arched wooden windows. The regal air of when this was the fiscal heart of Ceylon is definitely returning.

Cargills Main Store HISTORIC BUILDING
(Map p60; York St, Col 1) Local retail giant Cargills once had its main store on York St. The now mostly empty ornate 1906 red building still shows its faded elegance in its long arcades with old store signage such as the one noting 'toilet requisites'. Ground-floor colonnades like those here were once a feature across colonial Colombo, allowing people to get around sheltered from monsoon deluges. There's a tiny modern Cargills convenience store inside with tables where you can pause for a cool drink.

St Peter's Church CHURCH
(Map p60; Church St, Col 1; ⊘ 7am-5pm Tue-Sun) Reached along the arcade on the north side of the Grand Oriental Hotel, this converted Dutch governor's banquet hall was first used as a church in 1821. Inside it has an original iron roof framing and myriad plaques attesting to its work with seamen through the years.

◉ Pettah

Immediately inland from Fort, the bustling bazaar of Pettah is one of the oldest districts in Colombo and one of the most interesting places to spend a few hours. It is the most ethnically mixed place in the country. Large religious buildings represent a plethora of faiths, while more earthly pursuits can be found in market stalls and shops selling seemingly everything.

The crowds in Pettah can become overwhelming during the morning and late-afternoon rush hours, but the streets are still thronged during most daylight hours. Vendors hurrying with carts piled high with impossible loads, zooming three-wheelers, cars trying to fit down narrow lanes and people rushing here and there can make for an exhausting experience. Your best bet is to find a shady doorway out of traffic and just observe the timeless manic swirl around you. **Wolfendhal Lane** is a typical side-street refuge: wander past its textile stores and exchange gentle 'hellos' with the locals.

Various streets in Pettah each have their specialities (p83).

★**Dutch Period Museum** MUSEUM
(Map p60; ☑ 011-244 8466; 95 Prince St, Col 11; adult/child Rs 500/300; ⊘ 9am-5pm Tue-Sat) This unique museum was originally the 17th-century residence of the Dutch governor and has since been used as a Catholic seminary, a military hospital, a police station and a post office. The mansion contains a lovely garden courtyard and has a nice faded feel since a 1977 restoration. Exhibits include Dutch colonial furniture and other artefacts.

It's here in 1638 that King Rajasinghe II of the Kingdom of Kandy signed the treaty that opened up Ceylon to the Dutch.

★**Old City Hall** HISTORIC BUILDING
(Map p60; Main St, Col 11; ⊘ 8am-5pm Mon-Sat) **FREE** Dating to 1865, this municipal building

COLOMBO SIGHTS

COLOMBO IN...

One Day
Start at the bustling markets of Pettah, taking time for small Hindu temples and the **Dutch Period Museum**. Head west to Fort (p58) and pause to appreciate the restoration of colonial gems such as the **Old Dutch Hospital** (p58). Rub elbows with busy locals over a spicy crab curry and rice at **Mayura Hotel** (Map p60; 46 Sri Kathiresan St, Col 11; mains Rs 200-500; ⊘ noon-10pm).

In the afternoon visit the eclectic Buddhist **Gangaramaya Temple** (p62) and wander down to **Viharamahadevi Park** (p67). Later, as the sun sets, take a stroll along the ocean front with Sri Lankan families at **Galle Face Green** (Map p64) and enjoy a snack from a vendor.

Two Days
Have a classic local breakfast of string hoppers while enjoying a view of the Indian Ocean at **Curry Pot** (Map p64; ☑ 011-237 0119; www.currypotlk.com; 314/1/A Marine Dr, Col 3; mains Rs 150-400; ⊘ 6.30am-4.30pm; 🛜) before tackling the excellent **National Museum** (p63). Afterwards go shopping at the many excellent stores and boutiques, such as **Paradise Road** (p83), in leafy **Cinnamon Gardens** and **Kollupitiya**. For dinner, head down to Mt Lavinia and dig into seafood by the seashore at **Bu Ba** (p80).

Colombo Fort & Pettah

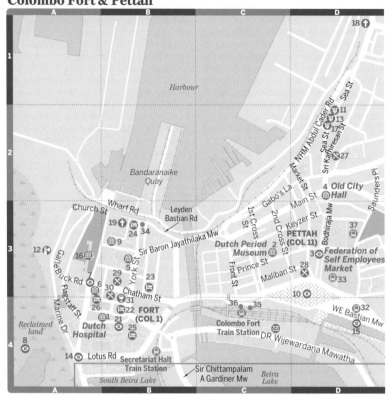

from the British era is mostly empty today, save for some old trucks and municipal equipment on display in the ground-floor galleries. But let the attendants lead you up the vintage mahogany stairs (tip them Rs 100) and you'll discover something of a waxworks in the old council chambers. There, covered in dust, are replicas of the town's first councillors in 1906.

Wolvendaal Church CHURCH
(Christian Reformed Church; Map p60; Wolvendaal Lane, Col 11; ⊙9am-4pm) The 1749 Wolvendaal Church is the most important Dutch building in Sri Lanka. When the church was built, this area was a wilderness beyond the city walls. The Europeans mistook the packs of roaming jackals for wolves and the area became known as Wolf's Dale, or Wolvendaal in Dutch. The church is in the form of a Greek cross, with walls 1.5m thick, but the real treasure is its Dutch furniture. Overdue repairs began in 2017.

★**Federation of
Self Employees Market** MARKET
(Map p60; off Olcott Mawatha, Col 11; ⊙7am-4pm) The concentrated and manic commerce of Pettah is concentrated even further in its markets. Stretching along 5th Cross St, this don't-miss market is a hive of household goods interspersed with artful displays of fruit and veg, such as towering pyramids of limes. Garish toys add colour.

Manning Market MARKET
(Map p60; Olcott Mawatha, Col 11; ⊙6am-2pm) Just east of Fort train station, Manning Market is ripe with everything grown in Sri Lanka. It's the city's wholesale fruit and veg centre and is a monkey's dream of bananas.

Pettah Floating Market PLAZA
(Map p60; WE Bastian Mawatha, Col 11; ⊙8am-midnight) A perfect example of how quickly Colombo is changing: what was an industrial

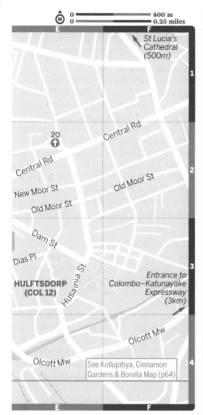

N 0 —— 400 m
0 —— 0.25 miles

St Lucia's Cathedral (500m)

Central Rd

Central Rd

New Moor St

Old Moor St

Old Moor St

Dam St

Dias Pl

HULFTSDORP (COL 12)

Husainia St

Entrance to Colombo–Katunayake Expressway (3km)

Olcott Mw

Olcott Mw

See Kollupitiya, Cinnamon Gardens & Borella Map (p64)

Colombo Fort & Pettah

canal has been reborn as a waterfront district with simple cafes, food vendors, shops, and chairs under umbrellas for relaxing. Local couples stroll the wooden boardwalks, holding hands and pausing for simple pleasures.

Pettah Hindu Temples   TEMPLES
Known as *kovils,* Hindu temples are numerous in Colombo, with a particularly high concentration in Pettah. On Sea St, the goldsmiths' street, you'll find three temples in a row: **Sri Muthu Vinayagar Swamy Kovil** (Map p60; Sea St, Col 11), **Old Kathiresan Kovil** (Map p60; Sea St, Col 11; ⊙6am-6pm), and **New Kathiresan Kovil** (Map p60; Sea St, Col 11; ⊙6am-6pm), which was built in 1830 and is one of Colombo's largest.

The temples are dedicated to the war god Murugan (Skanda), and are the starting point for the annual Hindu Vel festival held in July/August, when the huge *vel* (trident)

chariot is dragged to various *kovils* on Galle Rd in Bambalapitiya (Col 4). Note the many garland and flower sellers nearby.

⊙ Galle Face Green

Colombo's front porch is immediately south of Fort. So popular that it's more brown (dirt) then green (grass), this is where Colombo comes to unwind. Galle Face Green is now under threat as looming new high-rise hotels, apartments and offices cut off dawn light to the east, and the vast Colombo Port City (p70) cuts off some of the open ocean on the west.

At the south end of the green is the luxe Galle Face Hotel (p73). Sunsets here are enjoyed by one and all.

Pelican Perches   LANDMARK
(Map p60; Galle Face Green, Col 1) Huge pelicans perch on light poles and otherwise lounge about at this roundabout. Watch where you walk.

⊙ Slave Island & Union Place

After Pettah, Colombo's oldest neighbourhoods are found here. Slave Island was once mostly surrounded by water and it's where the Dutch kept slaves during colonial times. Largely a backwater during the war, its proximity to Fort and Galle Face Green make it the centre of vast new developments, including the enormous Cinnamon Life (p70). While multilevel malls, posh condos and the Lotus Tower rise up, you can still find streets of timeless character, but don't delay.

Already in the shadow of new buildings, Union Place is on the cusp of transformation. But until bulldozers arrive, its narrow lanes pulse with life little changed in centuries. Start at the row of **colonial storefronts** (Map p64; Union Pl, Col 2) on Union Pl (which aren't looking particularly healthy, what with the trees growing out their facades) and then plunge into the neighbourhood by walking south on **Church St** and prowling random alleys to the west. Tiny shopfronts sell goods of uncertain provenance and each alley holds a surprise. Wind your way south until you reach Nawam Mawatha and South Beira Lake.

⊙ South Beira Lake & Around

South Beira Lake is the pretty centrepiece of the city. Pelicans vie for space on the water with rental **swan boats** (Map p64; Sir James Peiris Mawatha, Col 2; rental per 30min Rs 150; ⊙9am-5pm), which courting couples looking for a little privacy lethargically paddle

about. Stroll the waterside walk with local families, while their children race over the cable-stayed bridge to the playground and immaculate gardens on the small island.

Seema Malakaya
Meditation Centre   RELIGIOUS SITE
(Map p64; South Beira Lake, Col 2; Rs 300; ⊙6am-6pm) One of Colombo's most photographed sights is on an island on the east side of the South Beira Lake. This small but captivating meditation centre was designed by Geoffrey Bawa in 1985 and is run by Gangaramaya Temple. The pavilions – one filled with Thai bronze Buddhas, another centred on a bodhi tree and four Brahmanist images – are especially striking when illuminated at night. New additions appear less sympathetic to the poetic original.

Gangaramaya Temple   BUDDHIST TEMPLE
(Map p64; ☑ 011-232 7084; www.gangaramaya.com; Sri Jinaratana Rd, Col 2; museum donation Rs 100; ⊙5.30am-10pm) Run by one of Sri Lanka's more politically adept monks, Galboda Gnanissara Thera, this bustling temple complex has a library, a **museum** and an extraordinarily eclectic array of bejewelled and gilded gifts presented by devotees and well-wishers over the years (plus one lonely and chained temple elephant named Ganga). Gangaramaya is the focus of the Navam Perahera on the February *poya* (full moon) day each year. This is the centre for the most extravagant Vesak celebrations in Colombo.

⊙ Kollupitiya

This long commercial strip along traffic-choked Galle Rd is jammed with myriad shops, businesses and hotels both modest and grand (many older properties are being torn down for glossy replacements). It makes for a good stroll as surprises abound. Several places popular for snacks are along here as well. Improvements to Marine Dr are harbingers for seaside development.

Geoffrey Bawa House   MUSEUM
(Number 11; Map p64; ☑ 011-433 7335; www.geoffreybawa.com; 11 33rd Lane, Col 3; cash-only admission Rs 1000; ⊙tours 10am, noon, 2pm & 3.30pm Mon-Sat, 10am Sun) At the end of this quiet little street is the house where the renowned architect Bawa lived from 1960 to 1970. The house combines his usual love for traditional local forms with the stark white architectural palette he favoured. You can tour the

small gardens as well as the interior with its custom furnishings. If you say, 'Gee I'd like to live here', you can also arrange to stay in one part of the house (p73). Book tours in advance.

St Andrew's Church CHURCH
(Map p64; 73 Galle Rd, Col 3) As compact as a fresh haggis, this 1834 granite church is an island of calm back from Galle Rd. Inside the cool interior, the walls are lined with fulsome memorials to the long-forgotten colonial Scots who built the church. A minor restoration is tidying up the whitewashed interior.

University of Colombo UNIVERSITY
(University of Ceylon; Map p64; 011-258 1835; www.cmb.ac.lk; Cumaratunga Munidasa Mawatha, Col 3) The 50-acre University of Colombo campus, which originally opened as the Ceylon Medical School in 1870, is surrounded by long tree-lined avenues lined with colonial-era mansions. Of note is Cumaratunga Munidasa Mawatha along the southwest side of the sporting green. Ponder the gracious lives of the people who built the Italianate baroque **Saifee Villa** (Map p64; Cumaratunga Munidasa Mawatha) in 1910 and the nearby turreted **College House** (Map p64; Cumaratunga Munidasa Mawatha, Col 3) in 1912. The school has over 11,000 students.

◉ Cinnamon Gardens

About 5km south of Fort and inland from Kollupitiya, Cinnamon Gardens is Colombo's most gentrified area. A century ago it was covered in cinnamon plantations. Today it contains elegant tree-lined streets with posh mansions, embassies, stylish cafes and shops, sports grounds and a cluster of museums and galleries.

Colombo's vivid white, domed 1928 **Old Town Hall** (White House; Map p64; FR Senanayaka Mawatha, Col 7) overlooks the area's heart, Viharamahadevi Park. To the south is the striking Nelum Pokuna Mahinda Rajapaksa Theatre (p82), which opened in 2011.

★ National Museum MUSEUM
(Map p64; 011-269 4767; www.museum.gov.lk; Albert Cres, Col 7; adult/child Rs 600/300; ⊙9am-6pm, last entrance 5pm) A large 9th-century stone Buddha greets you with an enigmatic smile as you enter Sri Lanka's premier cultural institution, which gets better (in small increments) each year. In galleries dating back as far as 1877, you'll encounter all manner of art, carvings and statuary from Sri

COLOMBO'S MAIN NEIGHBOURHOODS

Colombo is split into 15 postal-code areas, which are often used to identify the specific districts. Pettah, for example, is also referred to as Colombo 11 (or just Col 11) and so on. Note that street numbers start again each time you move into a new district. Thus there will be a '100 Galle Rd' in several different neighbourhoods. These are the main areas of interest.

DISTRICT	SUBURB
Col 1	**Fort** The restored and bustling centre of the city; historic and chic
Col 2	**Slave Island** Not an island at all (though it really was used for keeping slaves in the Dutch colonial era); some of Colombo's oldest – and most threatened – historic areas are here, including Union Pl; also the site of huge new developments
Col 3	**Kollupitiya** The dense commercial heart of the city, with myriad shops, hotels and businesses along Galle Rd
Col 4	**Bambalapitiya** An extension of Col 3
Col 5	**Havelock Town** Gentrifying southern extension of Col 4
Col 6	**Wellawatta** More commercial sprawl south along Galle Rd; inland, **Pamankada** is a newly stylish enclave
Col 7	**Cinnamon Gardens** Colombo's swankiest district has the National Museum, Viharamahadevi Park, old colonial mansions and trendy shops and cafes
Col 8	**Borella** The quieter eastern extension of Cinnamon Gardens
Col 11	**Pettah** Old quarter just east of Fort, with thriving markets
Col 13	**Kotahena** Alongside the port north of Pettah; home to old neighbourhoods and important religious buildings

Kollupitiya, Cinnamon Gardens & Borella

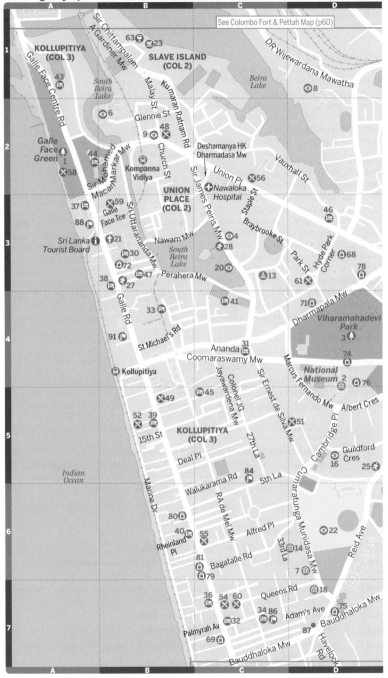

See Colombo Fort & Pettah Map (p60)

KOLLUPITIYA
(COL 3)

SLAVE ISLAND
(COL 2)

Beira Lake

DR Wijewardana Mawatha

South Beira Lake

Galle Face Green

Galle Face Centre Rd

Sir Mohamed Macan Markar Mw

Kompanna Vidiya

Church St

Glennie St

Malay St

Kumaran Ratham Rd

Sir Chittampalam A Gardiner Mw

UNION PLACE
(COL 2)

Deshamanya HK Dharmadasa Mw

Union Pl

Nawaloka Hospital

Sir James Peiris Mw

Staples St

Braybrooke St

Vauxhall St

Sri Lanka Tourist Board

Nawam Mw

South Beira Lake

Perahera Mw

Sri Uttarananda Mw

Park St

Hyde Park Corner

Galle Face Tce

Galle Rd

St Michael's Rd

Kollupitiya

Ananda Coomaraswamy Mw

Colonel JG Jayawardena Mw

27th La

Sir Ernest de Silva Mw

Marcus Fernando Mw

Dharmapala Mw

Viharamahadevi Park

National Museum

Albert Cres

Cambridge Pl

Guildford Cres

15th St

KOLLUPITIYA
(COL 3)

Deal Pl

Walukarama Rd

RA de Mel Mw

5th La

Cumaratunga Munidasa Mw

Marine Dr

Indian Ocean

Rheinland Pl

Bagatalle Rd

Alfred Pl

33rd La

Queens Rd

Reid Ave

Adam's Ave

Bauddhaloka Mw

Havelock Rd

Palmyrah Av

Bauddhaloka Mw

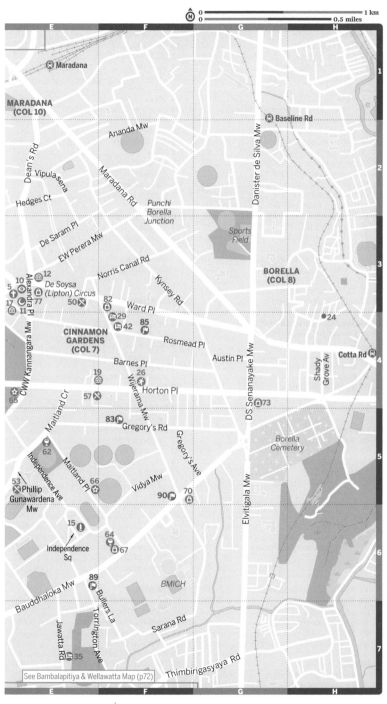

0 _____ 1 km
0 _____ 0.5 miles

Ⓝ N

Ⓡ Maradana

MARADANA
(COL 10)

Ⓡ Baseline Rd

Ananda Mw

Dean's Rd

Vipulasena

Hedges Ct

Maradana Rd

Punchi
Borella
Junction

Danister de Silva Mw

Sports
Field

De Saram Pl

EW Perera Mw

Norris Canal Rd

Kynsey Rd

BORELLA
(COL 8)

12
10
5
De Soysa
(Lipton) Circus
50 ✕
17
11
77
82
Ward Pl
29
42
85

24

Ⓡ Cotta Rd

CWW Kannangara Mw

CINNAMON
GARDENS
(COL 7)

Rosmead Pl

Austin Pl

Shady
Grove Av

19
65
26
57 ✕
Barnes Pl
Horton Pl

Wijerama Mw

DS Senanayake Mw

73

83
Gregory's Rd

Maitland Cr

62

Gregory's Ave

Borella
Cemetery

Independence Ave

53 ✕
Phillip
Gunawardena
Mw

Maitland Pl

66
Vidya Mw

90
70

Elvitigala Mw

15
Independence
Sq

64
67

89
Bauddhaloka Mw

Bullers La

BMICH

Jawatta Rd

Torrington Ave

Sarana Rd

35

Thimbirigasyaya Rd

See Bambalapitiya & Wellawatta Map (p72)

Kollupitiya, Cinnamon Gardens & Borella

Lanka's ancient past, as well as swords, guns and other paraphernalia from the colonial period. There are 19th-century reproductions of English paintings of Sri Lanka and a collection of antique demon masks.

★ **Viharamahadevi Park**   PARK
(Map p64; Col 7) Colombo's biggest park was originally called Victoria Park, but was renamed in the 1950s after the mother of King Dutugemunu. It's notable for its superb flowering trees, which bloom in March, April and early May. Elephants used for ceremonies sometimes spend the night in the park, chomping on palm branches. It has been given a major sprucing up and now boasts comfy benches (often occupied with caressing couples), walkways, landscaping and playgrounds. You'll even still see the odd snake charmer.

De Soysa (Lipton) Circus   LANDMARK
(Map p64; Col 7) One corner of this bustling roundabout is occupied by the popular Odel (p83) department store. Opposite is the **Cinnamon Gardens Baptist Church** (Map p64; De Soysa (Lipton) Circus, Col 7), which dates to 1877. Located just south of the church is the **Dewata-Gaha Mosque** (Map p64; Alexandra Pl, Col 7), a rambling structure dating to 1802 that bustles with people following the Friday afternoon prayers. Meanwhile, the ragtag confection of red and white bricks that was once the **Eye Hospital** (Map p64; De Soysa (Lipton) Circus, Col 7) now houses the Coroner's Court while awaiting its own rescue from fate.

Saskia Fernando Gallery   GALLERY
(Map p64; ☑ 011-742 9010; www.saskiafernandogallery.com; 41 Horton Pl, Col 7; ⊗ 10am-6pm) Some of the best contemporary Sri Lankan artists are displayed in this whitewashed compound. Look for the huge elephant sculpture, created from old mechanical parts. The namesake owner is the daughter of local design maven Shanth Fernando of Paradise Road fame.

Lionel Wendt Centre   ARTS CENTRE
(Map p64; ☑ 011-269 5794; http://lionelwendt.org; 18 Guildford Cres, Col 7; ⊗ 9am-1pm & 2-5pm Mon-Fri, 10am-noon & 2-5pm Sat & Sun) Has a constantly changing line-up of cultural events, with regular art exhibitions as well as performances and theatre. It's worth turning up just to see what's on.

Independence Memorial Hall   MONUMENT
(Map p64; Independence Sq, Col 7) Really a large memorial building to Sri Lanka's 1948 independence from Britain, this huge stone edifice is loosely based on Kandy's Audience Hall. It's now at the centre of buzz due to the glitzy new Arcade Independence Square (p83) shopping mall just south.

◉ Southern Colombo

South of Kollupitiya and Cinnamon Gardens is more of the same, only less so. The commercial strip of Galle Rd continues south through Bambalapitiya and Wellawatta. Inland, Havelock Town is a more relaxed version of Cinnamon Gardens. It has several midrange hotels. The one area here with buzz is **Pamankada**, which has some interesting shops and cafes along Stratford Ave.

Traditional Puppet Art Museum   MUSEUM
(☑ 011-271 4241; www.puppet.lk; Anagarika Dharmapala Mawatha, Col 5; Rs 500; ⊗ 9am-5pm) Puppet shows were long a part of traditional entertainment in Sri Lankan villages. Performing troupes would stage shows with intricate plots that lasted for hours. This engaging museum keeps the traditional puppet arts alive. Dozens and dozens of colourful puppets – some quite huge – are displayed. Many are surprisingly animated even when still.

◉ Mt Lavinia

Long Colombo's beach retreat, Mt Lavinia makes for a good respite from the city's cacophony and fumes. The **beach** is not bad, although some rivers just north empty dodgy water into the ocean after rains and the undertow can be prohibitive. If you're heading to the famous beaches south there's no need to stop here. Otherwise Mt Lavinia's many beachside cafes are lovely places to laze away the hours until sunset. It's only 15 minutes by train from Fort, a ride that's a treat in itself.

◉ Kotahena

Immediately northeast of Pettah, Kotahena is closely linked to Colombo's port, which forms the west boundary. It's not as rampant with commerce as Pettah, but also boasts many old buildings and streets. You could easily visit the Kotahena sights with the services of a taxi or three-wheeler.

St Anthony's Church CHURCH
(Map p60; www.kochchikade.churchlk.com; St Anthony's Mawatha, Col 13; ☺6am-6pm) One of the city's most interesting shrines is St Anthony's Church. Outside it looks like a typical Portuguese Catholic church, but inside the atmosphere is distinctly subcontinental. There are heaving queues of devotees offering *puja* (offerings or prayers) to a dozen ornate statues; a likeness of St Anthony said to be endowed with miraculous qualities is the centre of devotions from people of many faiths.

St Lucia's Cathedral CHURCH
(☑011-243 2080; St Lucia's St, Col 13; ☺5.30am-noon & 2-7pm) This enormous 1881 cathedral lies in the Catholic heart of the Kotahena district. The biggest church in Sri Lanka has an exterior inspired by St Peter's in Rome. It can hold up to 5000 worshippers in its rather plain interior.

☉ North & Northwest of Colombo

The busy old commercial road linking Colombo with Negombo and the north is often traffic-choked and is lined with an untidy mishmash of strip malls aimed at Sri Lanka's burgeoning middle class. It's much the same for the first few kilometres of the road to Kandy, although lush green landscapes soon provide relief.

Kelaniya Raja Maha Vihara BUDDHIST TEMPLE
(☑011-291 1505; www.kelaniyatemple.org; Biyagama Rd, Kelaniya) It's believed Buddha visited the site of this temple on his third visit to Sri Lanka. Suitably grand and labyrinthine, it has a dramatic past. The original temple was destroyed by Indian invaders, restored, and then destroyed again by the Portuguese in the 16th century. The Dutch restored it again in the 18th century in order to curry favour locally.

Activities

★ Spa Ceylon SPA
(Map p64; ☑011-233 7111; www.spaceylon.com; 103 Galle Rd; massage per hour from Rs 3000; ☺9am-9pm) This is the most lavish branch of this chain of luxury spas. It offers both Ayurvedic treatments and regular spa services in chic surrounds and has numerous luxe therapies.

Kemara SPA
(Map p64; ☑011-269 6498; www.kemaralife.com; 14 Phillip Gunawardena Mawatha, Col 7; therapies from Rs 2500; ☺10am-8pm) Holistic health treatments and luxurious beauty and health products, many based on fruits and herbs. A long list of therapies and spa treatments is available.

Siddhalepa Ayurveda SPA
(Map p64; ☑011-269 8161; www.siddhalepa.com; 33 Wijerama Mawatha, Col 7; therapies from Rs 2000; ☺7.30am-8pm) This full-service Ayurvedic spa offers all manner of treatments and therapies. It also has a small spa outlet at Bandaranaike International Airport (in the departure concourse) that usefully treats jet lag.

Kanduboda Siyane Meditation Center MEDITATION
(☑011-240 2306; www.insight-meditation.org; Delgoda-Pugoda Rd, Kanduboda, Delgoda; by donation) This is a major centre for meditation instruction in the style of the late Mahasi Sayadaw. Accommodation and meals are offered free of charge, though donations are expected. Most participants stay for an initial three-week training period, after which they can meditate on their own for as long as they like. The centre is located 25km east of Colombo in Delgoda; Pugoda bus 224 passes by and can be caught from the Central Bus Station.

Edge ADVENTURE SPORTS
(Borderlands; Map p72; ☑011-441 0110; www.discoverborderlands.com; 15 Stratford Ave, Col 6; activities from US$40; ☺8.30am-5pm Mon-Fri) This well-organised adventure-tour company offers a range of activities including abseiling, hiking, river canoeing, sea kayaking and much more. Standards are high and safety is paramount. At the high-style shop with an industrial vibe, you can also buy all manner of gear for your own adventures.

Tours

★ Colombo Walks WALKING
(☑077 560 0333; www.colombowalks.com; tours adult/child from Rs 4000/1000; ☺6.45am, 11am, 4pm) Colombo expert Harold Sandrasagara leads daily walking tours of the historic precincts of Fort and Pettah that last 2½ to three hours. He provides insights into these fascinating areas that you could never discover on your own. Tours (which include a stop for a snack) leave from the Dutch Hospital; book in advance.

★ Colombo by Jeep DRIVING
(☑077 733 0900; www.colombobyjeep.com; 3½hr tour for 1-4 people US$100) Feel like an occupying force as you tour Colombo in a restored

WWII jeep. Your tour guide is Nishantha Abeysekara, who is even more interesting than his vehicles. Expect a highly entertaining romp around just about everything worth seeing in Colombo.

★ Colombo City
Hostel Walking Tour   WALKING

(Map p64; ☑ 077 485 2650; 177 RA de Mel Mawatha, Col 3; tours Rs 3000; ⊙10.30am) This hostel runs daily walking tours that are also open to nonguests. The five-hour itineraries include top sights as well as transport over some longer distances. Water and snacks are also included.

★ Action Lanka   OUTDOORS

(☑ 011-450 3448; www.actionlanka.com; 366/3 Rendapola Horagahakanda Lane, Talangama, Koswatta) Arranges outdoor activities including white-water rafting, kayaking, diving, mountain biking and walks. Experienced guides hold international Swift Water Rescue certificates and all have first aid training.

Srilanka Bicycle Trips   CYCLING

(☑ 011-622 3378; www.srilankabicycletrips.com; tours from Rs 10,500) This company organises guided cycling trips from one to 14 days around Sri Lanka. There are thematic

tours or you can let the company organise the logistics and you guide yourself. It also offers a day trip south from Colombo to a tea plantation where you can ride amid the rolling green hills.

Colombo City Tour   BUS

(☑ 011-281 4700, 077 759 9963; www.colombocity tours.com; tour adult/child from US$25/12) Tour Colombo's sprawl from high above the traffic in an open-top double-decker bus. The narration is in English and snacks and water are included. There are three routes and tours depart daily, including a weekend night-time tour. Book and check schedules in advance.

 Festivals & Events

Special events, such as street rally races and open-air concerts by the ocean, are blossoming in Colombo.

★ Vesak Poya   RELIGIOUS

(⊙May) The birth, enlightenment and death of Buddha is celebrated across Colombo (and Sri Lanka), but the festivities around Gangaramaya Temple and South Beira Lake are mind-blowing. Huge eruptions of coloured light displays vie with hundreds of smaller displays made by competing groups.

COLOMBO FESTIVALS & EVENTS

GEOFFREY BAWA'S ARCHITECTURE

The most famous of Sri Lanka's architects, Geoffrey Bawa (1919–2003) fused ancient and modern influences in his work.

Using courtyards and pathways, Bawa developed pleasing connections between the interior and exterior of his structures. These connections frequently included contemplative spaces, as well as framed areas that enabled glimpses of spaces yet to be entered.

His designs were based within the environment. And he was not averse to the environment claiming his structures – at times he encouraged jungle growth along walls and roofs.

While Bawa created aesthetic beauty, he was also concerned with the functional aspects of architecture, opening and exposing structures to air and light while ensuring shelter and protection from harsh climatic elements. His approach was important not only for its originality but also for its influence on architecture in Sri Lanka and abroad.

Bawa's work outside Colombo includes the landmark **Heritance Kandalama Hotel** (p208) near Dambulla. In Colombo, don't miss the following:

Gallery Cafe (p77) The historic building used to be Bawa's office and is now used as an exhibition space for art and photography.

Seema Malakaya Meditation Centre (p62) A gem-like space on an island on South Beira Lake.

Geoffrey Bawa House (p62) The house where Bawa once lived is now a museum.

Parliament of Sri Lanka (www.parliament.lk; Parliament Approach Rd, Kotte) Bawa's grand masterpiece is located on a lake island in Kotte, 11km southeast of Fort. Visits require a complex series of approvals as outlined on the website.

COLOMBO TRANSFORMED

Every month seems to bring another colossal building project to Colombo. Collectively, they are forever altering the city's skyline and even its shape. New projects include the following:

Colombo Port City (Map p60; www.colomboportcity.lk) The huge dredges you see working offshore of Fort and Galle Face Green are building the initial stages of this enormous 269-hectare addition to the city. At an untold cost of billions to the Chinese investors, this glossy new neighbourhood is envisaged to be a home of commercial high rises, glossy condos, canals, recreation areas and much more. It's already blocking views of the Indian Ocean and could well make Fort a landlocked precinct. The investors cite the famous artificial Palm Islands of Dubai as their inspiration.

Cinnamon Life (Map p64; www.cinnamonlife.com; off Glennie St, Col 2) Sri Lanka's Cinnamon Group is behind this vast mixed-use development that will overwhelm the west side of Slave Island. Its eye-catching modern design will house a huge new luxury hotel, condos, a 30-storey office building and a vast five-storey indoor mall.

Colombo Lotus Tower (Map p64; DR Wijewardana Mawatha, Col 2) Casting a shadow over Slave Island, the 350m Lotus Tower is set to open by sometime in 2018. With a bulbous top meant to resemble the namesake blossom, this soaring erection (24m taller than the Eiffel Tower) will have telecommunications equipment and an array of tourist attractions, including an observation deck at the top and a restaurant at the base. Like most other recent megaprojects in Sri Lanka, it is being financed by China.

Altair (Map p64; www.altair.lk; 121A Sir James Peiris Mawatha, Col 2) Another of Colombo's new instant landmarks, the 240m-tall Altair is a stunning edifice that takes its name from its soaring A-shape. Balconies texturise the otherwise smooth exterior.

Dansala stands, where food and treats are given away, are everywhere.

Vel   RELIGIOUS
(☉ Jul or Aug) During the Vel, the gilded chariot of Murugan (Skanda), the Hindu war god, is ceremonially hauled from the Kathiresan *kovil* (temple) to a *kovil* at Bambalapitiya.

Navam Perahera   RELIGIOUS
(☉ Feb) Held on the February *poya* and led by 50 elephants; it starts from Gangaramaya Temple (p62) and is held around Viharamahadevi Park and South Beira Lake.

Duruthu Perahera   RELIGIOUS
(☉ Jan) Held at the Kelaniya Raja Maha Vihara (p68) on the January *poya* (full moon).

Colombo Jazz Festival   MUSIC
(www.colombojazzfestival.com; day pass Rs 5000; ☉ mid-Feb) Colombo's nascent jazz festival is well-funded and attracting big names. It's held at the Galle Face Hotel (p73).

🛏 Sleeping

Like much else in the capital, the accommodation scene in Colombo is improving quickly. New top-end hotels such as the **Grand Hyatt** (Map p64; www.grand.hyatt.com; Galle Rd, Col 3) and **Shangri-La Hotel** (Map p64; www.shangri-la.com; 1 Galle Face Centre Rd, Col 2) are being built and older ones refurbished. There's a fast-growing selection of high-quality budget and midrange places.

Amid this new hostelry energy, some older properties continue to limp along on past glories. Fort and Galle Rd have shabby hotels that are little changed in decades.

🛏 Fort & Pettah

Fort is home to international-style high-rise hotels and several new budget hotels aimed at travellers. This is also where you can find historic hotels with rates that make their shortcomings palatable.

Colombo YMCA   GUESTHOUSE $
(Map p60; ☎ 011-232 5252; ymcacbo@sltnet.lk; 39 Bristol St, Col 1; dm Rs 1500, s/d from Rs 2050/2600, r with air-con Rs 5720; ❄ 🛜) This old Y is a bit shabby, but if you're on a very tight budget this could be it. It offers male-only dorms and a few very basic single and double rooms that are open to both men and women: some share bathrooms and some have fans. A few

rooms have private bathrooms and air-con. Wi-fi is lobby-only.

City Rest Fort HOTEL $$
(Map p60; ☑ 011-233 9340; http://cityrestfort colombo.bookings.lk; 46 Hospital St, Col 1; dm/r from US$27/60; ❈ 🛜) This very professionally managed hotel and hostel has an ideal location just east of the Dutch Hospital. In its renovated four-storey building there are private rooms, as well as 73 hostel beds in 17 rooms. There are male, mixed and female rooms. The hotel has a modern cappuccino colour scheme.

Grand Oriental Hotel HOTEL $$$
(Map p60; ☑ 011-232 0392, 011-232 0391; www. grandoriental.com; 2 York St, Col 1; r US$60-120; ❈ 🛜) Opposite the harbour, this was Colombo's finest hotel a century ago, a place to see and be seen. Although it's no longer the case, there's a certain frumpy charm here and the veteran staff are very helpful and obliging. Rooms have a tired, generic look; request one facing the quiet inside. Stay here before someone guts it and does a full luxury renovation.

There are superb harbour views from the 4th-floor restaurant and terrace; go for a drink, skip the food.

Hilton Colombo Hotel HOTEL $$$
(Map p60; ☑ 011-249 2492; www.hilton.com; 2 Sir Chittampalam A Gardiner Mawatha, Col 2; r from US$150; ❈ @ 🛜 ⊕) This large international business-class hotel buzzes with activity around the clock. It has 382 rooms in regular- and executive-floor flavours, six restaurants, a pub, a 24-hour business centre, a fully equipped sports and fitness club, and an attractive garden and pool area.

Steuart BOUTIQUE HOTEL $$$
(Map p60; ☑ 011-557 5575; www.citrusleisure.com; 45 Hospital Lane; r US$90-130; ❈ 🛜) The Steuart is set in a renovated colonial-era building with parts dating back to 1835. The 50 rooms have a fairly simple purple-and-white decor with old Scottish heraldry on the walls (reflecting the origins of the building's original owners). Rooms include fridges; premium rooms with extra amenities cost only slightly more; the quality of views varies greatly.

🛏 Kollupitiya

Colombo's best large hotels (with several new ones under construction) are in this central area, near the ocean and noisy Galle Rd. On back roads to the east you'll find numerous interesting choices.

★Colombo City Hostel HOSTEL $
(Map p64; ☑ 077 485 2650; www.colombocityhostel. com; 177 RA de Mel Mawatha, Col 3; dm with fan/ air-con Rs 1500/1800, r with fan/air-con US$25/30; ⊙ reception 7am-9pm; ❈ 🛜) Colombo's best hostel has a rooftop lounge/kitchen/chill space with great views over the city, including nearby Temple Trees, home of the PM. There are 33 beds in dorms on three floors. It's down some quiet lanes yet close to the action; look for signs. The hostel also runs excellent walking tours (p69) that are open to nonguests.

Clock Inn HOTEL $
(Map p64; ☑ 011-250 0588; www.clockinn.lk; 457 Galle Rd, Col 3; dm/s/d from US$10/40/45; ❈ 🛜) Great value and style in a central location are the appeal of this clean and well-run hotel. The four- and six-bed dorm rooms have a dash of style, while the regular rooms have queen-size beds with cable TV and private bathrooms.

★YWCA GUESTHOUSE $$
(Map p64; ☑ 011-232 4181; www.ywcacolombo.com; 393 Union Pl, Col 2; r with cold water & fan/hot water & air-con Rs 4700/6750; ❈ 🛜) Of the several Ys offering budget accommodation, this is easily the best. Enjoy modest colonial splendour in this leafy compound in a frenetic and popular part of Colombo. The nine rooms are basic, but you can lounge on comfy rattan chairs on the shady porch in an island of calm. The breakfast room is an oasis of serenity.

Drift B&B B&B $$
(Map p64; ☑ 011-250 5536; www.facebook.com/ driftbnb; 646 Galle Rd, Col 3; dm/r from US$15/45; ❈ @ 🛜) In a courtyard building just behind the noise of Galle Rd, this flashpacker special has 10 roomy, comfy rooms, and four- and six-person dorms. The common spaces have artwork and a clean-lined vibe. Although the stairs are a hike, there's a mechanical luggage hoist. Breakfast is optional.

YWCA National Headquarters GUESTHOUSE $$
(Map p64; ☑ 011-232 3498; natywca@sltnet.lk; 7 Rotunda Gardens, Col 3; r per person with fan/air-con Rs 2500/3000; ❈ @) This place has three tidy, very basic rooms that surround a leafy courtyard in a five-star part of Colombo. It's a secure refuge for female travellers; men can stay if they're with a female companion.

Bambalapitiya & Wellawatta

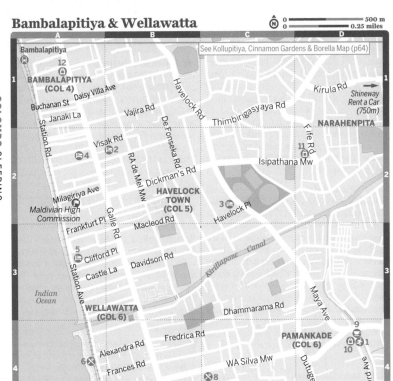

Bambalapitiya & Wellawatta

Whitehouse Residences   GUESTHOUSE **$$**
(Map p64; ☎ 077 413 2832; whitehousecolombo@
gmail.com; 265/2 RA de Mel Mawatha, Col 3; r from
US$45-80; ⌘ ⓦ) Self-sufficient travellers will
appreciate the large rooms and limited staff
interface at this multistorey guesthouse,
down a small lane. It's all spick and span.
Some rooms have bright views and balco-
nies, especially the top-floor suite.

Ivy Lane   GUESTHOUSE **$$**
(Map p64; ☎ 011-257 5733; www.ivylane.lk; 538
Galle Rd, Col 3; s/d from US$50/55; ⌘ ⓦ) A real
urban retreat, the 15 rooms here have a light
colour scheme *and* are flooded with light.
Many have balconies. It's down a quiet lane
away from Colombo's bustle.

★**Cinnamon Red** HOTEL $$$
(Map p64; ☑ 011-214 5145; www.cinnamonhotels.com; 59 Ananda Coomaraswamy Mawatha, Col 3; r from US$90; ❄@🛜🏊) Hugely popular from the day it opened, this 26-floor hotel from the ubiquitous Cinnamon Group is its debut of a new concept in 'lean luxury'. The 242 rooms are good sized with tables that allow for work; many have sweeping views.

★**Lake Lodge** GUESTHOUSE $$$
(Map p64; ☑ 011-242 4246; www.taruhotels.com; 20 Alvis Tce, Col 3; r US$90-120; ❄🛜) This hotel gets everything just right. The 13 rooms are well equipped and stylish in a minimalist way. Long concrete counters are good for work and the rooftop terraces have views of South Beira Lake. Service is excellent and the hotel is well managed. You can easily walk to much of what's interesting in Colombo.

★**Cinnamon Grand Hotel** HOTEL $$$
(Map p64; ☑ 011-243 7437; www.cinnamonhotels.com; 77 Galle Rd, Col 3; r US$150-250; ❄@🛜🏊) Colombo's best large hotel has a central location well back from Galle Rd. It buzzes with energy as there always seems to be an elite wedding on or some high-profile politician strolling the huge, airy lobby. The 501 rooms are large; ask for a high floor to enjoy views. Service is excellent.

There's a fitness centre, a big outdoor swimming pool and numerous top-notch restaurants.

★**Colombo Courtyard** BOUTIQUE HOTEL $$$
(Map p64; ☑ 011-464 5333; www.colombocourtyard.com; 32 Alfred House Ave, Col 3; r US$80-150; ❄🛜🏊) All the comforts you could ask for (decent work areas, rain showers, welcome fruit basket and more) are appealingly packaged at this new small hotel. Some rooms look onto the pool area. The entire property feels more like a posh urban retreat than mere hotel. Need some action? The rooftop terrace bar, Cloud Cafe (p82), is a popular hang out.

Hotel Renuka &
Renuka City Hotel HOTEL $$$
(Map p64; ☑ 011-257 3598; www.renukahotel.com; 328 Galle Rd, Col 3; r US$65-120; ❄🛜🏊) The well-run Renuka is bifurcated into two different buildings. Its 99 rooms are well maintained and have safes, fridges and 24-hour room service. It's well maintained; the decor is unadorned modern. Be sure to get a room not facing Galle Rd. The staff are good, as is the basement Palmyrah restaurant, known for its Jaffna dishes.

Taj Samudra HOTEL $$$
(Map p64; ☑ 011-244 6622; www.tajhotels.com; 25 Galle Face Centre Rd, Col 3; r US$155-250; ❄@🛜🏊) Part of the well-regarded Indian chain, this vast edifice has elegant public areas and a lovely 11-acre garden, as well as myriad restaurants and bars, including a 24-hour cafe. The 270 rooms have a plush, red motif. Opt for one facing west for sunset views. Better yet, get a room with a balcony.

Galle Face Hotel HERITAGE HOTEL $$$
(Map p64; ☑ 011-254 1010; www.gallefacehotel.com; 2 Galle Rd, Col 3; r US$130-250; ❄@🛜🏊) The grande dame of Colombo faces Galle Face Green to the north and the sea to the west. The sweeping staircases recall the hotel's opening in 1864. Comprehensive renovations have restored the former grandeur and created refined, modern luxury. Service has had an upgrade, as have the prices.

Number 11 INN $$$
(Map p64; ☑ 011-433 7335; www.geoffreybawa.com; 11 33rd Lane; rates for 1-4 people US$200-305) Geoffrey Bawa fans can stay in his Colombo home. Within his artful estate, which is a popular place for tours (p62), a suite of two bedrooms is rented out. Only one guest party may rent at any one time. The apartment includes a sitting room, breakfast, and access to a 3rd-floor loggia and a top-floor open-air deck.

ℹ️ **SWIMMING**

Skip the polluted waters off Galle Face Green; the only place you might consider an ocean dip is at Mt Lavinia.

Rather, if you are staying somewhere without a pool – or just want a change of scenery – consider paying to swim at a hotel with a pool. Many properties will allow you to use the facilities for a fee of Rs 1000 to 2000. Two good choices are the pool at the **Cinnammon Lakeside Hotel** (Map p64; ☑ 011-249 1000; 115 Sir Chittampalam A Gardiner Mawatha, Col 2; nonguests adult/child Rs 1500/750) and the magnificently positioned pool at the **Mount Lavinia Hotel** (Map p75; ☑ 011-271 5227; 100 Hotel Rd, Mt Lavinia; non-guests Rs 1000).

🛏 Cinnamon Gardens

The tree-lined streets here offer at least the illusion of genteel charm.

Black Cat Bed & Breakfast   B&B $
(Map p64; ☑ 011-267 5111; www.blackcatcolombo. com; 11 Wijerama Mawatha; r from US$55; ✳🛜) One of Colombo's best cafes also rents out five rooms (four with king beds, one with twin beds). Just like the great coffees downstairs, the decor is rich in browns and creams. There's a shared lounge and breezy balcony.

Paradise Road
Tintagel Colombo   BOUTIQUE HOTEL $$$
(Map p64; ☑ 011-460 2060; www.tintagelcolombo. com; 65 Rosmead Pl, Col 7; r incl breakfast US$150-250; ✳@🛜🏊) Set inside an old mansion with a notorious past (when it was a home for local politicians), this stylish hotel dazzles with its dark, minimalist design, elegant contours and idiosyncratic artworks. Part of the Paradise Road design empire, each of the 10 rooms is unique and some include a private splash pool. All have private outside access.

🛏 Bambalapitiya, Havelock Town & Wellawatta

South of the centre, you'll realise some savings in both money and, at least on the side streets, noise. There are new options appearing close to the ocean.

Hotel Sunshine   HOTEL $$
(Map p72; ☑ 011-401 7676; www.hotelsunshine.lk; 5A Shrubbery Gardens, Col 4; r with fan/air-con from Rs 2500/4000; ✳🛜) This small budget hotel is tall and narrow and hemmed in by even taller neighbours. It has 24 clean but plain rooms at reasonable rates (cheaper ones are fan-only) and is just a half-block from the sea (a few rooms have partial views). The staff are professional and the address will appeal to Monty Python fans everywhere.

★ Havelock Place Bungalow   GUESTHOUSE $$$
(Map p72; ☑ 011-258 5191; www.havelockbunga low.com; 6-8 Havelock Pl, Col 5; r from Rs 7800; ✳@🛜🏊) This appealing guesthouse has seven rooms in two sizes spread across two colonial houses. Modern luxury is matched with antiques that feel authentic to the period, as well as wooden floors. It's on a quiet lane and has lush gardens and a small lap pool. The outdoor cafe is a good place to while away the hours.

Colombo Hotel
Ceilão Villas   BOUTIQUE HOTEL $$$
(Map p64; ☑ 011-723 5232; www.ceilaovillas.com; 47/1 Jawatta Rd, Col 5; r US$60-120; ✳🛜🏊) Close to Cinnamon Gardens and other hotspots but isolated from the street mayhem, this relaxed estate has six lovely rooms in an elegant and restful modern mansion. Trees and gardens help you forget the chaotic city nearby. Besides the large garden pool, there's a rooftop plunge pool. It's great value and books out weeks in advance.

Casa Colombo   BOUTIQUE HOTEL $$$
(Map p72; ☑ 011-452 0130; www.casacolombo.com; 231 Galle Rd, Col 4; r US$140-300; ✳🛜🏊) This vast 200-year-old mansion shelters behind a row of storefronts on Galle Rd. Protected from the noise, it's an urban refuge with huge old trees and an infamous pink-hued swimming pool. Designed by Lalin Jinasena, the 12 large suites are all decorated in colonial colours that mix modern and minimalist with the odd Moorish touch. Concierge service is lavish.

Ozo Colombo   HOTEL $$$
(Map p72; ☑ 011-255 5570; www.ozohotels.com; 36-38 Clifford Pl, Col 4; r from US$110; ✳@🛜🏊) High-rise casual comfort on Colombo's waterfront; this striking blue hotel has 158 rooms spread over 14 floors across from Wellawatta's beach (and train station). There are comforts and conveniences such as big work desks and modern tech gadgets aplenty, while the rooftop has a perfect cafe for sundowners.

🛏 Mt Lavinia

If you want a quieter alternative to Colombo, but don't want to go as far as beach towns such as Negombo, Mt Lavinia is a 30-minute drive from Fort and has a modest beachy charm. There are simple guesthouses aimed at local weekend travellers along the aptly named Hotel Rd as well as De Saram and College Rds. Inspect a couple before deciding. The Mt Lavinia train station is central to a number of properties.

Cottage Gardens Bungalows   HOTEL $$
(Map p75; ☑ 077 794 7804; www.cottagegardenbun galows.com; 42-48 College Ave, Mount Lavinia; r from US$35; ✳🛜) A little bit of Bali in Mount Lavinia, this walled compound hosts several bungalows that have wide terraces that look onto gardens. It's very clean and the rooms have large beds. The beach is a two-minute walk.

Blue Seas Guest House   GUESTHOUSE **$$**
(Map p75; 📞011-271 6298; 9/6 De Saram Rd, Mt Lavinia; r Rs 2500-4600; ✳🛜) This well-managed house has 15 clean and spacious rooms, some with balconies. There's a large sitting room and a garden. Budget rooms are fan-only. Guests enjoy a warm welcome, even by local standards. It's down a short lane; the beach is a two-minute walk.

Tropic Inn   GUESTHOUSE **$$**
(Map p75; 📞011-273 8653; www.tropicinn.com; 30 College Ave; dm/s/d from US$10/34/38; ✳@🛜) This four-storey hotel features 16 tidy rooms. There's an internal courtyard and many of the rooms have a small balcony. The engaging staff are helpful.

Mount Lavinia Hotel   HOTEL **$$$**
(Map p75; 📞011-271 1711; www.mountlaviniahotel.com; 100 Hotel Rd, Mt Lavinia; r US$100-150; ✳🛜🏊) Part of this grand seafront hotel dates to 1806, when it was the residence of the British governor. The appropriately named 'governor's wing' has colonial decor and smallish rooms; the remainder is modern and rooms have balconies. The beautifully positioned pool and terrace have sweeping ocean views. The beach is just north of the hotel. The Sunday lunch is hugely popular.

 Eating

Colombo boasts a good and growing selection of restaurants. Besides great Sri Lankan food, you'll find food from across the region and further afield. There are upscale and stylish cafes aimed at the well heeled, but perhaps even more interesting are the many high-quality places aimed at Colombo's burgeoning middle class.

The websites www.yamu.lk and www.tasty.lk are good resources for the fast-changing Colombo dining scene.

✖ Fort & Pettah

Hordes of office workers, traders, commuters and residents support excellent snack stands and restaurants, most aimed at the masses. In the Fort's high-profile Dutch Hospital you'll find an array of chic restaurants and outdoor cafes.

Pagoda Tea Room   BAKERY **$**
(Map p60; 📞011-232 5252; 105 Chatham St, Col 1; mains Rs 200-500; ⏱9am-8pm) Hungry like the wolf? Duran Duran filmed its classic 1980s video for that very song in this venerable establishment opened in 1884 (sadly, there are

Mt Lavinia

⊕ Activities, Courses & Tours
1 Mount Lavinia Hotel A3

⊟ Sleeping
2 Blue Seas Guest House.......................B1
3 Cottage Gardens Bungalows B2
4 Mount Lavinia Hotel A3
5 Tropic Inn..B2

⊗ Eating
6 Bu Ba A3
  Governor's Restaurant................(see 4)
7 La Voile Blanche...................................A2

⊕ Drinking & Nightlife
8 Shore By O..A2

no monkeys or snake charmers at Pagoda these days). Although rice and curry is on the menu, the main focus is inexpensive pastries.

New Palm Leaf Hotel   SRI LANKAN **$**
(Map p60; 📞077 654 7611; 237 Olcott Mawatha, Col 11; meals Rs 200-330; ⏱6am-10pm) Like elsewhere in Sri Lanka, 'hotel' here means 'simple eating place'. Across the very busy road from Fort station and close to Pettah's market madness, pause here for a tea and cake or one of many excellent curries that

are properly fiery. English is spoken and everything is also offered for takeaway.

★T-Lounge by Dilmah   CAFE $$

(Map p60; ☑011-244 7168; www.dilmaht-lounge. com; Dutch Sq, 18 Chatham St, Col 1; mains Rs 500-900; ☺8am-10.30pm; ☎) A product of Sri Lanka's best tea producer, Dilmah, this gem of a cafe is in an annexe to the hugely successful Old Dutch Hospital. The interior complements the restored colonial exterior. The walls are lined with books about Sri Lanka and tea, while the menu has a range of tasty snacks such as crepes, sandwiches and desserts, plus cocktails.

Heladiv Tea Club   CAFE $$

(Map p60; ☑011-575 3377; www.heladivteaclub. com; Old Dutch Hospital, Col 1; mains Rs 500-1200; ☺9am-midnight; ☎) Tapas standards, spicy local nibbles, burgers, salads and much more are served at this casual cafe that's one of the best places to take a break in Fort. Choose from a huge range of fine teas (the peach iced tea is plummy) or settle back on the terrace with a cocktail.

★ Ministry of Crab   SEAFOOD $$$

(Map p60; ☑011-234 2722; www.ministryofcrab. com; Old Dutch Hospital, Col 1; mains Rs 2000-8000; ☺6-11pm Mon-Fri, noon-11pm Sat & Sun) Crabs are a major income earner for Sri Lanka's fishing industry, but most are exported. This high-profile restaurant rectifies this loss by celebrating the crustaceans in variations ranging from Singaporean chilli crab to locally spiced crab curry. The garlic pepper preparation is sublime. Two owners are former captains of the Sri Lanka cricket team plus there's famous chef Dharshan Munidasa.

Easily one of Colombo's top restaurants, a couple can easily drop Rs 15,000 on a truly superb meal with drinks (an average-sized crab for one costs Rs 6600). Be sure to book ahead.

✖ Kollupitiya, Slave Island & Union Place

Old favourites can be found along Galle Rd. Head east for restaurants and cafes along quieter and often tree-lined streets.

★Nana's   STREET FOOD $

(Map p64; Galle Face Green, Col 3; ☺5-10pm) One of the best food vendors on Galle Face Green, Nana's is a legend for its excellent grilled meats and rice dishes. Choose a battered plastic stool and slightly leaning table and enjoy a fresh meal by the glow of sunset or under the stars. Note that there are numerous copycats with 'Nana's' in the name.

The original – and the best – is directly across from the main entrance to the Taj Samudra hotel.

Burger's King   BURGERS $

(Map p64; ☑011-230 4504; www.burgerskingsl. com; cnr Malay St & Union Pl, Col 2; mains Rs 200-250; ☺8am-11pm) Don't for one second confuse this Sale Island institution with the worldwide chain with the copycat name. The smiling dudes behind the big windows here dish up 15 kinds of very tasty burgers (beef, chicken, shrimp and veggie), plus kebabs and, yes, fries.

Green Cabin   SRI LANKAN $

(Map p64; ☑011-258 8811; 453 Galle Rd, Col 3; meals Rs 200-450; ☺7.30am-11.30pm) This local institution is famous for baked goods and an inexpensive array of rice and curry variations, all served in a leafy dining area. The lunchtime vegetarian buffet (Rs 300) is excellent value – the mango curry, if it's on, is very good.

Carnival   ICE CREAM $

(Map p64; ☑011-257 6265; 263 Galle Rd, Col 3; cones Rs 100; ☺10am-11pm) Unchanged in decades, you don't visit Carnival for the ice cream (which is more icy than creamy), but rather for the timeless ice-cream-parlour surrounds. Still, where else can you get a banana split for Rs 200?

Keells   SUPERMARKET $

(Map p64; 199 Union Pl, Col 2; ☺8am-10.30pm) This Western-style supermarket chain is popular for its large selection of imported goods. This location has a big range of ready-made meals; a second branch can be found in Crescat Boulevard (Map p64; 89 Galle Rd, Col 3; ☺8am-10.30pm).

Park Street Mews   CAFE $$

(Map p64; ☑011-230 0133; www.parkstreetmews restaurantcolombo.com; 50/1 Park St, Col 2; mains Rs 500-2200; ☺10am-11pm; ☎) The namesake cafe of the smart little lane of stylish shops and eateries has a suitably hip vibe with an industrial motif and pillows on the concrete floor for lounging – along with tables, chairs and more traditional soft seating. The menu mixes burgers, salads and Asian fare. Party folk will bless the restorative 'morning after' juice.

★**Nihonbashi Honten**   JAPANESE **$$$**
(Map p64; ☎ 011-232 3847; www.nihonbashi.lk; 11 Galle Face Tce; mains from Rs 1200; ⏱ noon-2.30pm & 6-10.30pm) Gird the expense account for an adventure at Colombo's best Japanese restaurant. The sushi, *donburi* and Kobe beef are as good as you can find anywhere in Asia. The interior is jewel-like, the service superb. This is where you go when you want an exquisite evening out. Don't miss the Yakitori Garden, where you can savour sake and cocktails surrounded by bamboo.

Barefoot Garden Cafe   CAFE **$$$**
(Map p64; ☎ 011-258 9305; www.barefootceylon. com; 704 Galle Rd, Col 3; mains Rs 750-1200; ⏱ 10am-7pm; 🔊) Located in the courtyard of the splendid Barefoot gallery, this casual but stylish cafe serves sandwiches, salads and daily specials that usually include Sri Lankan and Asian dishes. The wine list is good, and it also has fresh juices and tasty desserts. On Sunday there's popular live jazz in the afternoon.

Paradise Road Gallery Cafe   ASIAN **$$$**
(Map p64; ☎ 011-258 2162; www.paradiseroad. lk; 2 Alfred House Rd, Col 3; mains Rs 500-1500; ⏱ 10am-midnight; 🔊) The trim colonial bungalow that houses Shanth Fernando's Gallery Cafe used to be the office of Sri Lanka's most famous architect, Geoffrey Bawa. The open-air dining area looks over an intimate courtyard and reflecting pool. The Sri Lankan–inspired dishes focus on fresh ingredients and bold, clean flavours. Desserts focus on chocolate.

Curries made with black pork and prawns are popular. There's a huge range of luscious cakes you can snack on through the day. A small shop sells signature Paradise Road designer items.

✖ **Cinnamon Gardens**

Stylish little cafes and more ambitious restaurants can be found along the genteel streets of Colombo's classiest district.

★**Good Market**   MARKET **$**
(Map p64; ☎ 077 020 8642; www.goodmarket.lk; Colombo Racecourse, Phillip Gunawardena Mawatha, Col 7; ⏱ 10am-6pm Sat) 🍃 This organic and artisan food market is held in the northeast parking lot of the Colombo Racecourse and attracts a range of high-quality vendors. Breads, prepared foods, organic fruit and veg, smoothies, snacks and much more are on offer. There is live entertainment and

some appealing handicrafts for sale. Look for the treasure-filled booth of Deen the Bookman.

Milk & Honey Cafe   VEGETARIAN **$$**
(Map p64; ☎ 011-523 4347; 44 Horton Pl, Col 7; meals Rs 300-800; ⏱ 9am-6pm Mon-Sat) Eating vegetarian never tasted so good; in a simple house shared with a kids bookshop, this groovy little cafe has an ever-changing menu of fresh fare, such as slow-roasted veggies with pesto and a scrumptious mushroom and cream cheese focaccia. Enjoy a fresh juice while perched on an old wooden milk carton.

Commons   BISTRO **$$**
(Map p64; ☎ 011-269 4435; 39A Sir Ernest de Silva Mawatha, Col 7; mains Rs 400-1000; ⏱ 8.30am-midnight Sun-Thu, to 2am Fri & Sat; 🔊) This cafe has a strong following among Colombo's hipster set (plus among staff from the Russian embassy across the road). Customers lounge in soft seats around low tables and enjoy popular breakfasts, *rotti,* excellent burgers, pastas, desserts and more. The garden at the back is a shady urban retreat. Good kids menu.

Boulevard   FOOD HALL **$$**
(Map p64; ☎ 011-462 5800; Odel, 5 Alexandra Pl, Col 7; meals Rs 200-750; ⏱ 10am-8pm) Fronting the entrance to the popular and chic Odel department store is this silver-hued swath of food stalls in a sleek outdoor food court. Outlets of well-known local vendors serve up sandwiches, Indian fare, health food, pizza, various snacks, gelato and even cocktails. A recent reconstruction added fountains.

Coco Veranda Cafe   CAFE **$$**
(Map p64; ☎ 011-763 5635; www.cocoveranda. com; 32 Ward Pl, Col 7; mains Rs 500-1000; ⏱ 7am-11.30pm; 🔊) In a small building with

ATTILA JANDI / SHUTTERSTOCK ©

1. National Museum (p63), Colombo 2. Dutch Fort (p290), Mannar Town 3. Galle Fort (p108) 4. Pillar box, Galle (p107)

PAUL KENNEDY / GETTY IMAGES ©

Historic Sri Lanka

Sri Lanka has more than 500 years of colonial heritage. The earliest imported architecture was the fortifications built by the Portuguese, but most are now in ruins or were subsequently rebuilt during the Dutch era (which lasted almost two centuries). Alongside Portuguese and Dutch buildings, there is also a tangible British legacy, stretching across every corner of the nation.

Portuguese

Reminders of 16th- and 17th-century Portuguese influence are dotted around the entire coastline. Tiny islands like Velanai and prominent settlements like Jaffna, Galle and Trincomalee all have the remains of once-important Portuguese defences. Many, such as Mannar fort (p290), are crumbling or ruined, while Colombo's once-substantial Portuguese enclave (home to many churches and convents) was destroyed by the Dutch in 1655–56.

Dutch

The most impressive testament to Dutch rule is Galle's remarkable Unesco-listed Fort (p108), a walled city replete with grand mansions and administrative buildings, an elegant old hospital and towering ramparts. Colombo also has important reminders of Dutch rule, including the Wolvendaal church (p60) and 17th-century Governor's Mansion (p59), now the Dutch Period Museum. Elsewhere, there are fine Dutch-period structures in Matara and Dutch-built canals on the west and east coasts.

British

British-era buildings are everywhere in Sri Lanka, from the monumental tea-processing factories and graceful plantation bungalows of the Hill Country to the neoclassical National Museum (p63) in Colombo and landmark lighthouses like Dondra Head (p134). For a taste of 'Little England', head to Nuwara Eliya, home to grand old stone-clad hotels like the Hill Club (p177) and Victorian-style formal gardens. Functional, emblematic reminders of London's rule endure in the quintessentially British red postboxes and scarlet phone booths that dot roadsides around the country.

designer-clothing shops, this cool little cafe has an extraordinarily long menu of teas, coffee drinks, frappés and fresh juices. There are sandwiches and pastas, as well as very alluring desserts, including a 'Death by Chocolate' option. Breakfasts are Western, fresh and tasty.

Paradise Road Cafe   CAFE $$
(Map p64; ☑ 011-268 6043; www.paradiseroad.lk; 213 Dharmapala Mawatha, Col 7; mains Rs 350-700; ☺10am-7pm) Part of the designer empire, this smart cafe serves coffee drinks, milkshakes, luscious cakes and a plethora of teas in its 2nd-floor location above the popular shop. Mains include sandwiches and pasta. Get upscale picnic fare from the deli to enjoy in Viharamahadevi Park.

✖ Wellawatta

Local favourites dominate the options of this southern quarter, which has Galle Rd as its spine. Look for a dose of hip over on Stratford Ave in Pamankada.

★Bombay Sweet Mahal   SWEETS $
(Map p72; ☑ 011-258 3561; 161 Galle Rd, Col 6; sweets from Rs 50; ☺9am-8pm) Galle Rd boasts many vendors of Indian sweets, but this tiny open-fronted shop is the best. An array of treats sits colourfully in the display cases. We especially like the thick and chewy nut musket. Buy by weight to go or grab a cool juice at a table at the back. The engaging staff will explain the many offerings.

DON'T MISS

SUNSETS

The Indian Ocean can yield up sunsets so rich in vivid colours that your eyes and brain can't quite cope. Many people opt for the outdoor bars in the cloistered surrounds of the Galle Face Hotel, but you can have a much more authentic experience joining Colombo's great and many on Galle Face Green (p62). Nature's beauty is a moment best shared with others and you can enjoy a local snack from the many vendors. The beachside cafes of Mt Lavinia are also good sunset venues. Note that the day's weather is no indication of sunset quality: a dreary grey day can suddenly erupt in crimson and purple at dusk.

Yaal Restaurant   SRI LANKAN $$
(☑ 011-566 1212; Marine Dr, Col 6; mains Rs 400-1000; ☺7am-10pm) The unique spicy cuisine of Jaffna's Tamils features at this simple yet very well-managed restaurant across from the seashore. The speciality is the truly unique *odiyal kool,* a famous Jaffna dish consisting of vegetables and seafood combined in a creamy porridge. Also popular is the crab curry.

Curry Leaves   INDIAN $$
(Map p72; ☑ 011-566 3322; 68 WA Silva Mawatha, Col 6; mains Rs 400-900; ☺11am-3pm & 5-11pm) South Indian is served in well-mannered surrounds at this very popular restaurant. Besides good versions of the standards it has a good selection of crab at popular prices. Thirsty? The same owners run the adjoining Sri Siam sports bar, where you can quaff lager cheap.

Beach Wadiya   SEAFOOD $$$
(Map p72; ☑ 011-258 8568; www.beachwadiya.com; 2 Station Ave, Col 6; mains Rs 600-1600; ☺10am-11pm) Renowned for its seafood, Beach Wadiya has attracted a popular following for decades. The location is a tropical dream; cross the train tracks at the seashore and enter a walled enclave lit by romantic little lights. Waiters describe what's fresh – there's always crab, prawns and lobster – then enjoy something cold while your dish is cooked. Book a few days ahead.

✖ Mt Lavinia

The beachfront here is lined with cafes offering up drinks (cold Lions at sunset are Rs 250 to Rs 400), simple meals and seafood. Cross the tracks at any of many points and see what you find.

La Voile Blanche   CAFE $$
(Map p75; ☑ 011-456 1111; www.lvb.lk/beach; 26/11 De Saram Rd; mains Rs 600-1000; ☺11am-midnight) Amid the often rather shabby Mt Lavinia beachfront cafes, this very popular vision in white stands out. Under seven iconic palm trees, a range of comfy chairs and loungers beckon. The drinks list is long and the menu offers up sandwiches, pasta and seafood. Look for the cafe across the tracks behind the Mount Breeze Hotel.

★Bu Ba   SEAFOOD $$$
(Map p75; ☑ 011-273 2190; www.bubabeach.com; Mt Lavinia beach; mains Rs 800-3200; ☺8am-midnight) With candlelit tables right on the

HOTEL DE PILAWOOS

Just known as **Pilawoos** (Map p64; ☑ 077 741 7417; www.pilawoos.lk; 417 Galle Rd; meals Rs 200-400; ⊗24hr), this open-fronted purveyor of short eats is renowned for what may be the best *kotthu* in town. Starchy, savoury and very addictive, this purely Sri Lankan dish starts with *rottis* (preferably day-old), which are then rather dramatically sliced up along with vegetables, meats, cheese or some such combination thereof. The results are cooked on a very hot iron sheet and served steaming.

Possibly invented here, although no one is sure, cheese *kotthu* are rapidly becoming the most popular version. Expect anyone and everyone to drop by to grab one, often with a fresh juice. In the wee hours, many customers are clearly looking for absorbent fare, of which *kotthu* is ideally suited; in the morning, you'll see bleary-eyed patrons looking for the restorative magic for which *kotthu* is so good.

Note that this is the true and original Pilawoos. As is often the case in Sri Lanka, the restaurant's success has inspired dozens of competitors to adopt some version of the name; ersatz Pilawoos abound.

sandy beach, this seafood pub is a hidden treat. In the heat of the day you can retreat under the grove of palm trees; at night let the sky open overhead and the starlight rain down. To find it, walk about 50m south alongside the tracks from Mt Lavinia train station.

Governor's Restaurant
BUFFET $$$

(Map p75; ☑ 011-271 1711; www.mountlaviniahotel.com; Mount Lavinia Hotel, 100 Hotel Rd, Mt Lavinia; buffet from Rs 1900; ⊗6.30-10.30am, 12.30-3pm & 7-10.30pm) The main restaurant at the Mount Lavinia Hotel has buffets three times a day, with themes that change daily. The special Sunday lunch, however, is the local legend: there's live jazz and blues, and patrons get to use the hotel's beautiful pool. It's catnip for expat families. Book a table with an ocean view.

Drinking & Nightlife

Finding a spot for sunset drinks is an essential Colombo experience (try Galle Face Green or Mt Lavinia); otherwise, many of the best cafes are good for a drink. Note that last call comes early: technically 11pm, although many places keep pouring much later.

The local club scene is small, but starting to develop wings.

★Cloud Red
LOUNGE

(Map p64; ☑ 011-214 5175; www.cinnamonhotels.com; Cinnamon Red, 59 Ananda Coomaraswamy Mawatha, Col 3; ⊗5pm-midnight) The rooftop bar high atop the popular Cinnamon Red hotel has the kinds of views you'd expect from the 26th floor, but for once the drinks at this kind of aerie match the sights, as do the snacks and small meals. It gets crowded;

beware of poseurs blabbing about their $4200 watch.

41 Sugar
LOUNGE

(Map p64; ☑ 011-268 2122; www.sugar.lk; 41 Maitland Crescent, Col 7; ⊗6pm-midnight) Rise above it all at this stylish (low-rise) rooftop cocktail lounge. Long tables outside have views of the ever-changing Colombo skyline, while inside there's lots of low leather sofas for slouching and looking cool. There's a long list of frilly drinks, plus tapas bites to chase away the munchies.

Kopi Kade
COFFEE

(Map p72; ☑ 077 055 2233; www.facebook.com/thekopikade; 15/3 Stratford Ave, Col 6; ⊗noon-8pm Wed & Thu, to 9pm Fri-Sun) Fairtrade organic coffee, with many beans roasted locally, is reason enough to stop by this little coffee bar on the Stratford strip. Vintage carvings frame the doors, adding an artful air of class.

Re.Pub.Lk
LOUNGE

(Map p60; ☑ 011-744 6654; www.facebook.com/therepublk; 57 Hospital St, Col 1; ⊗5-11pm Sun-Thu, to 2.30am Fri & Sat) Once a colonial bar dating back to 1924, the facade may be the same, but the inside has been completely reborn as a stylish, modern lounge. The cocktail list is long and creative, and various tapas options are on hand to keep hunger at bay. Service is great.

Shore By O
BAR

(Map p75; ☑ 011-438 9428; www.facebook.com/TheShoreByO; College Ave, Mount Lavinia; ⊗5-11pm Mon & Tue, 11am-11pm Wed-Sun) Feel the sand between your toes at this upscale beach club. Tables and loungers are set over two

CASINOS
···

Gaming is legal in Colombo, but only for holders of foreign passports. Most of the clientele is from the region and the casinos – despite adopting names familiar to Vegas high rollers – are very modest affairs with no connection to their famous namesakes, although some big-ticket operators have been vying to change this.

levels, the better to accommodate the sunset rush. There's a kiddie pool and a pizza oven cooking up decent pies.

Asylum   LOUNGE
(Map p64; ☑ 011-406 1761; www.asylum.lk; Arcade Independence Sq, 30 Bauddhaloka Mawatha, Col 7; ☺ 11am-late) No subtlety here; Asylum takes its name from the original use of its now upscale mall surrounds. The bar is dark and posh. Expect excellent cocktails made by talented bartenders and upscale bites to go with the drinks.

Cloud Cafe   COCKTAIL BAR
(Map p64; ☑ 011-464 5333; www.colombocourt yard.com; Colombo Courtyard, 32 Alfred House Ave, Col 3; ☺ 5pm-midnight Sun-Thu, to 1am Fri & Sat) The rooftop bar atop the three-storey Colombo Courtyard hotel is popular most nights for its breezy, sweeping views. Cute little chairs cradle your rump while you enjoy fine cocktails and upscale bar snacks. There's live music on Friday night and classic movies on other nights.

7° North   COCKTAIL BAR
(Map p64; ☑ 011-249 1000; Cinnamon Lakeside Hotel, 115 Sir Chittampalam A Gardiner Mawatha, Col 2; ☺ 5pm-1am) The one compelling reason to visit this otherwise forgettable hotel is the posh sprawling bar that overlooks Beira Lake from a large deck. Catch the skullers out rowing at sunset and enjoy high-end cocktails under the stars.

Silk   CLUB
(Map p64; ☑ 071 482 4398; www.sugarcolombo. com/club-silk; 41 Maitland Cres, Col 7; ☺ 9pm-2am Wed & Thu, to 4am Fri & Sat) Close to other nightspots, including 41 Sugar, this club is among the city's most popular. The vibe is mainstream, with music from salsa to house.

B52   CLUB
(Map p60; ☑ 011-232 0320; www.facebook.com/ B52NightclubCMB; Grand Oriental Hotel, 2 York St,

Col 1; ☺ 9pm-4am Thu-Sun) Somewhat cramped, this club draws a mixed crowd of locals, sailors and lost visitors who take to the dance floor to thump the night away till nearly dawn.

☆ Entertainment

Colombo's after-dark entertainment has not expanded as quickly as the skyline. There are very few places for music; the club scene is nascent at best. Sri Lankans do love cricket, so if you can get into a match, it will be memorable.

Sri Lanka Cricket   CRICKET
(Map p64; ☑ 011-267 9568; www.srilankacricket.lk; 35 Maitland Pl, Col 7; ☺ ticket office 8.30am-5.30pm) The top sport in Sri Lanka is, without a doubt, cricket. You can buy tickets for major games from Sri Lanka Cricket, at the office near the oval. Major matches are played at Premadasa Cricket Stadium, northeast of the centre.

**Nelum Pokuna
Mahinda Rajapaksa Theatre**   THEATRE
(Map p64; ☑ 011-266 9019; www.lotuspond.lk; Ananda Coomaraswamy Mawatha, Col 7) This glossy venue is located in a high-profile spot south of Viharamahadevi Park. Its stunning design is based on the Nelum Pokuna, the 12th-century lotus pond in Polonnaruwa. Look for important productions here.

Lionel Wendt Art Centre   CULTURAL CENTRE
(Map p64; ☑ 011-269 5794; www.lionelwendt.org; 18 Guildford Cres, Col 7; ☺ gallery & office 9am-7pm Mon-Fri, 10am-noon & 2-7pm Sat & Sun) Among other cultural happenings, this gallery hosts live theatre and other events at night.

🛍 Shopping

Colombo's markets, with their vast selection of everyday goods, are much more compelling as places to visit than venues for finding gifts and goods to take home. Otherwise, Colombo has many stores making that extra bag essential, and glossy new malls are expected to open in the next few years as megaprojects progress. High-quality tea is sold everywhere.

★ Barefoot   CRAFTS, BOOKS
(Map p64; ☑ 011-258 9305; www.barefootceylon. com; 704 Galle Rd, Col 3; ☺ 10am-7pm Mon-Sat, 11am-5pm Sun) Designer Barbara Sansoni's beautifully laid out shop, located in an old villa, is justly popular for its bright handloomed textiles, which are fashioned into bedspreads, cushions, serviettes and other

household items (or sold by the metre). You'll also find textile-covered notebooks, lampshades and albums, and a large selection of stylish, simple (but not cheap) clothing. There's also a lovely courtyard cafe (p77).

Within the much-lauded designer shop is an excellent book department. This is where you'll find a carefully selected range of locally published books, the full range of Michael Ondaatje's works and much more.

⭐ **Plâté** HOMEWARES
(Map p64; ☎ 011-250 3366; www.platelimited.com; 580 Galle Rd; ☼ 10am-7pm) An engrossing treasure of a store selling antiques, old photos, art, books and more in a genteel, wood-panelled setting. Also has a busy photo studio.

Arcade Independence Square MALL
(Map p64; ☎ 078 556 1315; www.arcadeindependencesquare.com; 30 Bauddhaloka Mawatha, Col 7; ☼ 7am-11pm) Another massive restoration of a colonial landmark. In this case, the sprawling colonial 'hospital for the insane' has been reborn as an upscale mall after spending the last few decades in bureaucratic decrepitude. It has dozens of upscale international chains, a good food court and some high-concept eateries. Between expenditures, rest up in the gardens. The new name derives from Independence Memorial Hall (p67), which is just north.

Selyn HOMEWARES
(Map p72; ☎ 011-259 5151; www.selyn.lk; 102 Fife Rd, Col 5; ☼ 10am-7pm Mon-Sat, to 6pm Sun) Fairtrade goods made on local handlooms are the main items for sale here; the inventory spans all forms of housewares and is colorful and stylish. The big shop works exclusively with Sri Lankan producers.

Odel DEPARTMENT STORE
(Map p64; ☎ 011-462 5800; www.odel.lk; 5 Alexandra Pl, Col 7; ☼ 10am-7pm) A high-profile department store that combines international and local brands in one glitzy labyrinth. From fashions to homewares to cosmetics and gift items, Odel's selection is tops. It's always crowded with both visitors and the local elite. Many pause for a break at the stylish Boulevard (p77) food court out front.

Dilmah Tea Shop TEA
(Map p64; www.dilmahtea.com; Odel, 5 Alexandra Pl, Col 7; ☼ 9am-7pm) Sri Lanka's top tea brand has its own posh shops, including this outlet in glitzy Odel. A second branch is located in

Crescat Boulevard (Map p64; Crescat Boulevard, 89 Galle Rd, Col 3; ☼ 9am-7pm).

Vijitha Yapa Bookshop BOOKS
(Map p72; ☎ 011-259 6960; www.vijithayapa.com; Unity Plaza, Galle Rd, Col 4; ☼ 9.30am-6pm Mon-Fri, to 7pm Sat, 10am-6pm Sun) Stocks a comprehensive collection of foreign and local novels, magazines and pictorial tomes on Sri Lanka. There's a second branch in **Crescat Boulevard** (Map p64; ☎ 011-551 0100; Crescat Boulevard, 89 Galle Rd, Col 3).

Paradise Road HOMEWARES
(Map p64; ☎ 011-268 6043; www.paradiseroad.lk; 213 Dharmapala Mawatha, Col 7; ☼ 10am-7pm) In addition to a variety of colonial and Sri Lankan collectables, you'll find a vast selection of original homewares and designer items in this crammed-to-the-rafters boutique from famous designer Shanth Fernando. Small gifty items can also be found in the shop adjoining the Paradise Road Gallery Cafe (p77).

House of Fashions CLOTHING
(Map p64; ☎ 011-215 4555; www.houseoffashions.lk; 101 DS Senanayake Mawatha, Col 7; ☼ 10am-5pm Mon, to 8pm Tue-Sun) Colombo's legendary multistorey surplus outlet for the nation's garment industry is actually a tad upscale. It has unbeatable textile and clothing prices, but now it's cultivating its own style, too.

Tropic of Linen CLOTHING
(Map p64; ☎ 011-267 2972; www.tropicoflinen.com; 1 Wijerama Mawatha; ☼ 10am-7pm) There's

---

PETTAH'S SHOPPING STREETS

Pettah's market stalls and shops sell seemingly everything. When plunging into the age-old district's commercial madness, it's handy to note that many thoroughfares have their own shopping specialities:

1st Cross St at Bankshall St plastic flowers

2nd Cross St at Bankshall St lace & ribbons

2nd Cross St jewellery

3rd Cross St fake flowers, decorative garlands on sale at the southern end

4th Cross St hardware, potatoes and garlic being traded in huge bags

Gabo's Lane at 5th Cross St Ayurvedic medicines

plenty of goods here made from the name-sake material, as well as cool cotton. Refit your wardrobe with a new bright and comfy tropical look.

Cotton Collection CLOTHING
(Map p64; ☑ 011-230 7005; www.cotton-collection. com; 143 Dharmapala Mawatha, Col 7; ⊙ 10am-7pm) Two floors of casual, high-quality clothes for both sexes are on offer in this big store in a compound off the busy road.

PR CLOTHING
(Map p64; ☑ 011-269 9921; www.pr.lk; 41 Horton Pl, Col 7; ⊙ 10am-6pm) The fashion branch of the Paradise Road design conglomerate is run by Annika Fernando and is housed with her sister Saskia Fernando's eponymous gallery. All the clothing is from Sri Lankan and Indian designers.

Kala Pola Art Market MARKET
(Map p64; Ananda Coomaraswamy Mawatha, Col 7; ⊙ 8am-noon) Every Sunday morning the broad avenue Ananda Coomaraswamy Mawatha south of Viharamahadevi Park comes alive with colour as local artists display their works at the Kala Pola Art Market. This weekly explosion of colour is an outgrowth of the original market, a huge annual event still held the third Sunday of January when up to 500 artists display their work.

Sri Lanka Cashew Corporation FOOD
(Map p64; ☑ 011-257 5119; 518 Galle Rd, Col 3; ⊙ 8.30am-6pm Mon-Sat) Cashews were brought by the Portuguese to Sri Lanka from Brazil in the 16th century. They've clearly found the climate agreeable as the nuts are now a major export item. This small shop is packed full of fulsome cashews of a size and quality that are usually hard to find, especially in that dodgy bag of mixed nuts.

Arpico FOOD & DRINKS
(Map p64; ☑ 011-473 4725; 62 Hyde Park Corner, Col 2; ⊙ 9am-10pm) A huge store good for replacing almost anything you left at home. Imported foods (get your Marmite here), cosmetics, sunscreen, a pharmacy, travel gadgets such as plug adapters and much, much more. It has a good, casual cafe where you can rest up and hone your shopping list.

Sri Lanka Tea Board Shop TEA
(Map p64; ☑ 011-258 7814; 574 Galle Rd, Col 3; ⊙ 9am-7pm Mon-Sat) One-stop tea shopping: this large but unflashy shop has many of the smaller brands of Ceylon tea that can be hard to find. It also has most of the top brands, such as Mackwoods, and all sorts of tea-related merchandise.

Gandhara HOMEWARES
(Map p72; ☑ 011-259 6329; www.gandharacrafts. com; 28 Stratford Ave, Col 6; ⊙ 10am-7pm) This stylish designer shop on the trendy stretch of Stratford Ave sells everything from candles to coffee tables. Gift items pegged to the season are displayed in profusion and there is a good selection of books on Sri Lankan art.

Laksala ARTS & CRAFTS
(Map p64; ☑ 011-258 0579; 215 Bauddhaloka Mawatha, Col 7; ⊙ 9am-9pm) Part of a large government-run chain of arts-and-crafts shops popular with groups, Laksala offers cheap carved elephants, well-crafted handicrafts and handmade jewelry and clothing. There's another outlet in the **National Museum** (Map p64; ☑ 011-269 8263; National Museum, Nelum Pokuna Rd, Col 7; ⊙ 9am-9pm), which also has a good cafe.

Buddhist Book Centre BOOKS
(Map p64; ☑ 011-268 9786; 380 Bauddhaloka Mawatha, Col 7; ⊙ 10am-6pm) Filled with books on Buddhism; about a third of the stock is in English.

ⓘ Information

DANGERS & ANNOYANCES
Colombo is a very safe city by international standards. Violence towards foreigners is uncommon, although you should take the usual safeguards.

➠ Solo women should be careful when taking taxis and three-wheelers at night; if, as sometimes happens, your taxi turns up with two men inside, call another.

➠ Colombo has its share of touts and con artists. You may be approached by someone who, after striking up a conversation, asks for a donation for a school for the blind or some such cause – these artists are invariably con artists. Street offers for guides and 'special' tours should also be shunned.

EMERGENCY

Ambulance & Fire	☑ 110, ☑ 011-242 2222
Medi-Calls Private Ambulance	☑ 011-255 6605
Police	☑ 119, ☑ 011-243 3333
Tourist Police	☑ 1912, ☑ 011-242 1052

INTERNET ACCESS
Many cafes and most hotels in Colombo offer wi-fi. Mobile service is LTE.

MEDIA

The daily English-language newspapers, the *Daily Mirror,* the *Daily News* and the *Island* all have local news and entertainment listings.

Good websites include:

Ceylon Today (www.ceylontoday.lk) News, sports and entertainment.

Daily Mirror (www.dailymirror.lk) Best of the newspaper websites.

Yamu (www.yamu.lk) Good source for events, dining out, sights and more.

MEDICAL SERVICES

Avoid government hospitals, such as Colombo General. **Nawaloka Hospital** (Map p64; ☑ 011-557 7111; www.nawaloka.com; 23 Deshamanya HK Dharmadasa Mawatha, Col 2) is a private hospital that has a good reputation and English-speaking doctors.

MONEY

There are banks and ATMs everywhere in the city. Exchange services can be found in the arrivals hall at Bandaranaike International Airport, in Fort and along Galle Rd.

POST

Sri Lanka Post (Map p60; ☑ 011-232 6203; DR Wijewardana Mawatha, Col 1; ⊙7am-6pm) Has branches around the city.

TOURIST INFORMATION

Sri Lanka Tourist Board (SLTB; Map p64; ☑ 011-243 7059; www.srilanka.travel; 80 Galle Rd, Col 3; ⊙7am-9pm) The country's national tourism office has maps and lavish brochures and can answer questions.

❶ Getting There & Away

AIR

Although **Bandaranaike International Airport** (CMB; ☑ 011-226 4444; www.airport.lk; Katunayake) is at Katunayake, 30km north of the city, it is called Colombo (CMB) in airline schedules. Arriving by air – especially late at night – it is easiest to spend your first night near the airport, in Negombo, or in the city. You can then easily move on by road, rail, bus or private car to other parts of the country.

LONG-DISTANCE BUSES FROM COLOMBO

DESTINATION	DEPARTURE STATION	PRICE (RS)	DURATION (HR)
Anuradhapura	Saunders Pl	350-500	6
Galle	Bastian Mawatha	150-550	1½-3¼
Hikkaduwa	Bastian Mawatha	130-245	3
Jaffna	Saunders Pl	700-1300	8-10
Kandy	Bastian Mawatha	155-240	3-4
Kataragama	Bastian Mawatha	260-860	6-8½
Kurunegala	Saunders Pl	120-240	3½
Matara	Bastian Mawatha	200-510	2½-5
Negombo	Saunders Pl	60-120	1-2
Nuwara Eliya	Bastian Mawatha	240-480	6
Polonnaruwa	Saunders Pl	265	6
Tangalla	Bastian Mawatha	160-860	3-6
Trincomalee	Saunders Pl	450	7

LONG-DISTANCE TRAINS FROM COLOMBO

DESTINATION	PRICE (RS)	DURATION (HR)	FREQUENCY
Anuradhapura	280-900	5	5
Batticaloa	480-1250	9	2
Galle	100-180	2¼-3½	7-9
Jaffna	320-1100	6-8	4
Kandy	180-500	2½-3	9-11
Trincomalee	305-1250	8	2

BUS

Colombo's bus stations are chaotic, but have frequent buses going in all directions. The city has three main bus terminals, all just east of Fort train station on the south edge of Pettah. Long-distance buses leave from **Bastian Mawatha** (Map p60; Olcott Mawatha) and **Saunders Pl** (Map p60; Saunders Pl). **Central Bus Station** (Map p60; Olcott Mawatha) has suburban buses.

There are fast buses that leave from the southern suburbs for Galle via the Southern Expressway.

TRAIN

The landmark main train station, **Colombo Fort** (Olcott Mawatha), is very central. Trains in transit often stop only for two or three minutes. **JF Tours & Travels** (Map p60; ☑ 011-244 0048; www.jftours.com; Colombo Fort Train Station; ☺ 9am-5pm) has an office at the front of Fort station; the helpful staff know everything about transport in and out of Colombo. Or you could try the information desk in the station. There is **left-luggage storage** (Map p60; Colombo Fort Train Station; per bag per day Rs 100; ☺ 5.30am-9.30pm) at the extreme left end as you face the station.

❶ Getting Around

Like most big cities, Colombo can grind to a halt due to traffic congestion on weekdays. However the city is also spread out, so however you choose to get about, plan on it taking some time. (One hint: if you want to see a lot of Colombo fast, do so on a Saturday or Sunday when congestion is less of an issue.) Buses are bewildering and often jammed. However various taxi services can be quite cheap.

TO/FROM THE AIRPORT

Completion of the Colombo–Katunayake Expressway has greatly reduced travel time between Bandaranaike International Airport and the city. From its start 4km northeast of Fort at Kelani Bridge, you can reach the airport in 30 minutes. Unfortunately the city streets remain as congested as ever during the day so add plenty of time for navigating Colombo itself. Avoid the old Colombo–Negombo Rd as it can take up to two hours.

Bus Fast airport buses using the expressway depart from Central Bus Station around the clock, take about 45 minutes and cost Rs 150. At the airport you'll find buses in the parking lot at the far left end of the terminal as you exit the arrivals hall.

Car You can arrange an airport car with most Colombo-area hotels for Rs 3000 to 5000. Hotels as far as Galle and beyond also often arrange airport transport. Drivers will meet you in the arrivals area of the airport.

Taxi You can book a car into Colombo (or elsewhere in Sri Lanka) at the desks in the arrivals hall or you can use the hassle-free taxi service outside. Rides cost Rs 2600 to 3500 depending on where you are going in Colombo. Be sure to specify you want to use the expressway and pay the Rs 300 toll.

BUS

The best way to find out which bus to take is just to ask people at the nearest stop. Buses going down Galle Rd from Fort or Pettah include the 100. Fares vary from Rs 10 to 50, depending on distance. Service is frequent; there is usually an English-language destination sign on the front of the bus.

TAXI

Most taxis are metered, but often the driver won't use the meter – agree on the fare before setting off. A taxi from Fort train station to Galle Face Hotel (a little over 2km) should cost about Rs 300; Mt Lavinia should cost around Rs 1400.

Dispatched cabs are popular and good value. Taxis take from five to 20 minutes to arrive. Reliable companies include:
Ace Cabs (☑ 011-281 8818; www.acecabs.lk)
Kangaroo Cabs (☑ 011-258 8588; www.2588588.com) Offers service in small cars that dart through traffic.
In addition, Uber is active in Colombo and is reliable and cheap. A local version of ride-sharing, PickMe, also offers app-based dispatching.

THREE-WHEELER

Also known as tuk-tuks and tri-shaws, these are ubiquitous. Although you're likely to get wet if it rains and the cramped back seats have limited views out, a ride in a three-wheeler is part of the Colombo experience. Drivers dart fearlessly between huge buses, an experience that's exhilarating for some and frightening for others.

Many three-wheelers now have meters and are the cheapest means of getting around. Some drivers, however, will try to not use the meter or won't have one. Avoid meter-free three-wheelers or agree to a firm price before setting out. From Fort, expect to pay Rs 300 to get to Cinnamon Gardens, Rs 600 to Bambalapitiya and Rs 1000 to Mt Lavinia. Avoid drivers who are parked as they'll charge more; hail one passing by instead.

TRAIN

You can use the train to get to the suburbs dotted along Galle Rd – Kollupitiya, Bambalapitiya, Wellawatta, Dehiwala and Mt Lavinia; as a bonus, the line follows the seashore. Timetables are clearly marked at the stations, though service is frequent. If you board the train at Fort train station, double-check that it stops at all stations or you may end up in Galle. Train fares are about the same as bus fares.

The West Coast

Best Places to Eat

➜ Lords (p93)

➜ Home Grown Rice & Curry (p105)

➜ Petit Restaurant (p93)

➜ Spaghetti & Co (p105)

Best Places to Sleep

➜ Ging Oya Lodge (p94)

➜ Shangri-Lanka Villa (p98)

➜ Saman Villas (p100)

➜ Camellia Dwellings (p103)

Why Go?

You don't have to be on Sri Lanka's west coast for long to realise that the coastline has something of a multiple personality. North of the capital is Negombo, a cheerful beach town crowned with church spires that is, thanks to its proximity to the airport, a staple of almost every visitor's Sri Lankan journey. Head further north, though, and you enter a wild and little-visited region that seems to consist of nothing but coconut plantations and lagoons, sparkling in the sun and filled with dolphins.

South of Colombo's chaos is a world that oscillates between the dancing devils of traditional Sri Lankan culture in Ambalangoda, the chic boutique hotels and uncluttered golden sands of Bentota and the slightly scrappy but ever-popular backpacker party town of Hikkaduwa.

Whichever part of the west coast you choose, a beach stay here makes for the perfect beginning or end to your Sri Lankan adventure.

When to Go
Negombo

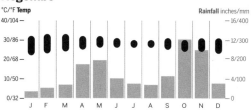

Jan Schools of dolphins party daily in Dutch Bay; backpackers party nightly in Hikkaduwa.

Mar–Apr Sri Lanka's Christians stage Easter passion plays in Negombo and Talawila.

Nov If you prefer your beaches (mostly) tourist free, November is the month to come.

West Coast Highlights

1 Kalpitiya
(p95) Scanning the horizon for schools of playful dolphins or learning to kitesurf in protected lagoon waters.

2 Negombo
(p89) Finding your feet and strolling the beach after a long flight in this oh-so-easy resort town.

3 Bentota
(p98) Feeling the stress levels drop as you are pampered under palm trees in one of the area's boutique hotels.

4 Muthurajawela
(p91) Ticking off egrets and herons during a waterborne birdwatching safari through this salt marsh.

5 Wilpattu National Park
(p96) Scouring the undergrowth for leopards and spotted deer from the back of a safari jeep.

6 Brief Garden
(p97) Enjoying the artful horticulture of Bevis Barwa's former home near Bentota.

7 Hikkaduwa
(p101) Raising a toast to the sunset after a hard day's diving and surfing in this lively backpacker hangout.

NORTH OF COLOMBO

Leaving Colombo most eyes look south, but for those with time on their hands and a sense of curiosity, or for those on the slow road towards Anuradhapura, the northbound A3 heads out of Colombo, skirts some charming old Dutch canals, slides past some sandy beaches and gets utterly lost among a matted tangle of coconut groves and wildlife-filled woodlands. It all adds up to a wonderful sense of discovery.

For the moment, aside from workaday Negombo, which sits close to Bandaranaike International Airport, much of this area remains fairly unexplored by tourists, except for a hardcore band of kitesurfers who flock to Kalpitiya. Change is happening fastest on the sleepy Kalpitiya peninsula, where new resorts are blossoming and an ambitious project is under way to transform the northern tip of the peninsula into the kind of high-end, exclusive beach tourism that dominates the neighbouring Maldives.

Negombo

📞 031 / POP 141,000

Negombo is a modest beach town located just 10km from Bandaranaike International Airport. With a stash of decent hotels and restaurants to suit all pockets, a friendly local community, an interesting old quarter and a reasonable (though somewhat polluted) beach, Negombo is a much easier place to find your Sri Lankan feet than Colombo.

The Dutch captured the town from the Portuguese in 1640, lost it, and then captured it again in 1644. The British then took it from them in 1796 without a struggle. Negombo was one of the most important sources of cinnamon during the Dutch era, and there are still reminders of the European days.

The busy centre of Negombo town lies to the west of the bus and train stations. Most places to stay, however, line the main road that heads north from the town centre, with the beachside hotel strip starting about 2km north of town.

👁 Sights

Negombo is dotted with churches – so many locals converted to Catholicism that the town is sometimes known as 'Little Rome'.

Negombo Beach   BEACH
(Map p92) Even though it could never compete in a beauty contest against many Sri Lankan beaches, Negombo's beach, which stretches north from the town right along the hotel strip before fading into a palm-tree distance, is pleasant enough and makes for a good sunset stroll. The water does have a distinct brown colour thanks to estuary run-off and pollution, but it's no longer bad enough to stop people swimming.

Foreign tourists can normally access the beach in front of most big hotels even if you're not staying (act rich and confident), but for a more colourful (and noisier) scene join the locals at what is known as **Negombo Beach Park** (Map p92).

Main Fish Market   MARKET
(Map p90) Each day, fishers take their *oruvas* (outrigger canoes) and go out in search of the fish for which Negombo is famous. They're a fine sight as they sweep home into the lagoon after a fishing trip. Fish auctions on the beach and sales at the fish market near the fort are a slippery and smelly affair, but one that's well worth forgoing some pool time for.

The catch is not all from the open sea: Negombo is at the northern end of a lagoon that is renowned for its lobsters, crabs and prawns. Across the lagoon bridge there's a second **fish market** (Map p90). If you can stagger out of bed at 6am, it's a good place to watch much bigger fishing boats return with their catches.

Hamilton Canal   CANAL
(Map p90) The Dutch showed their love of canals here like nowhere else in Sri Lanka. Canals extend from Negombo all the way south to Colombo and north to Puttalam, a total distance of over 120km. You can hire a bicycle in Negombo from various hotels and ride the canal-side paths of the Hamilton Canal, enjoying picturesque views and small villages along the way.

Dutch Fort   RUINS
(Map p90) Close to the seafront near the lagoon mouth are the ruins of the old Dutch fort, which has a fine gateway inscribed with the date 1678. Also here is a green, called the **Esplanade**, where cricket matches are a big attraction. As the fort grounds are now occupied by the town's prison, the only way you'll get a peek inside is by committing a serious crime. You'd need to be very interested in old Dutch architecture to go to such lengths.

Angurukaramulla Temple   BUDDHIST TEMPLE
(Temple Rd) East of the town centre the Angurukaramulla Temple, with its 6m-long reclining Buddha, is worth seeing; take a three-wheeler for around Rs 200.

Negombo (Town)

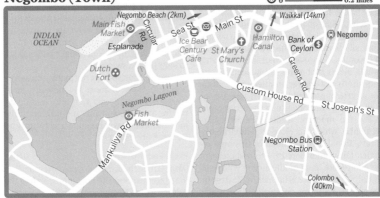

St Mary's Church
CHURCH

(Map p90; Main St) The fading pink chamber of St Mary's Church, in the town centre, has some thunderous religious ceiling paintings covering the nave.

🏃 Activities & Courses

If this is your first stop in Sri Lanka, hotels can fix you up with guides and drivers for trips elsewhere in the country.

Colombo Divers
DIVING

(Map p92; ☑077 736 7776; www.colombodivers. com; Porutota Rd, Ethukala) The waters around Negombo offer much better diving than many people imagine and this well-regarded agency can take you to meet the fish at over forty different reef sites. A two-tank dive costs US$75. Novices can opt for a Discover Scuba day (US$100) or full PADI open water course (US$450). Contact Sherick Fernando.

Serendib Watersports Paradise
DIVING

(Map p92; ☑077 738 5505; Pearl Guesthouse, 13 Porutota Rd) The Pearl guesthouse can put you in touch with this long-established and reputable dive outfit. It charges €380 for the PADI Open Water dive course.

Kite Centre Negombo
KITESURFING

(Map p92; ☑031-492 7744; Pearl Guesthouse, 13 Porutota Rd) Want to skim like a flying fish over the surface of the ocean? Kitesurfing courses using decent equipment and run by experienced surfers are available here through the Pearl guesthouse. A three-day course costs €359; one short hour with a teacher is €49. Equipment rental is possible for experienced surfers.

★Ceylon Adventure Tours
ADVENTURE SPORTS

(☑077 717 3007; www.ceylonadventuretours.com; 189/10A, Lewis Place, Negombo) Expertly guided motorbike and car tours, plus camping and trekking trips. It also rents bikes and tuk-tuks for DIY touring.

Lucky Tours
BIRDWATCHING

(Map p92; ☑077 357 8487; lucky-tour55@hot mail.com; 146 Lewis Pl) Specialist birdwatching tours in the Negombo region, including half-day tours (per one/two people Rs 5000/7000, including transport) to the Muthurajawela Marsh (p91).

🛏 Sleeping

There are masses of places to stay in all price bands, including many new homestays. Many people spend their first or last Sri Lankan night in Negombo, so it pays to book ahead at the more popular places. Generally, the closer the accommodation is to town, the rougher around the edges it is.

Jeero's Guest House
GUESTHOUSE $

(Map p92; ☑031-223 4210, 077 616 1619; 239 Lewis Pl; r Rs 3000-4000) With latticework window frames, comfortably worn-in furniture and breezy balconies, this is a well-priced and friendly option with just four rooms set above a pleasing family house just back from the beach. Ask for a sea-view room when booking.

Villa Rodrigo
GUESTHOUSE $$

(Map p92; ☑077 590 6277; www.villa-rodrigo-lk. book.direct; 38/3 Peter Mendis Rd, Cemetery 2nd Lane, Kudapaduwa; d/ste US$28/40; ❄🛜) The three air-con rooms above this family house are modern and spotless, even if prices are at the top end of good value. It's a five-minute walk from the beach in a quiet residential backstreet. The owner's son, Christian, runs a tight ship and can arrange for his father, a fisherman, to take guests out fishing in the lagoon.

There are a few cheaper fan-only rooms (d US$15) with shared bathroom on the ground floor, often marketed online as 'Rodrigo Lite'.

Angel Inn GUESTHOUSE $$
(Map p92; 031-223 6187; www.angelinnlk.com; 189/17 Lewis Pl; r 5000; ✳🛜) This is one of the best-run cheap guesthouses in Negombo. Rooms might not have sea views, but the beach is only 20m away and in every other way it's excellent value, with simple but flawlessly spick-and-span rooms set around a small garden courtyard.

Blue Water Boutique Hotel HOTEL $$
(Map p92; 031-223 7233; info@bluewaterboutiquehotels.com; 281/1 Lewis Place; s/d incl breakfast US$80/89; ✳🛜) This modern and fresh hotel has spacious split-level rooms that are all about sleek minimalism. The hotel doesn't have much natural light, but there's good rooftop seating and guests can use the pool of the neighbouring Paradise Beach Hotel. Breakfast is served on the sun-blasted roof terrace.

Holiday Fashion Inn GUESTHOUSE $$
(Map p92; 031-223 7550; www.holidayfashioninn.bookings.lk; 109 Cemetery Rd; r incl breakfast US$50, ste US$90; ✳🛜) There's an inviting family vibe to this smart guesthouse a short stroll back from the main strip. Rooms are spacious and immaculate and have little kitchenettes (minus a cooker).

Ice Bear Guest House GUESTHOUSE $$
(Map p92; 071 423 7755; www.icebearhotel.com; 95 Lewis Pl; s €26-39, d €48-81; ✳🛜) A gorgeous traditional villa with lots of colour and flair (or 'Swissness', as the sign says – to which you could also add 'and a little eccentricity'). This 'budget boutique' hotel has hammocks, sun loungers and a variety of rooms, the priciest of which offer sea views. The rooms have flower-sprinkled beds and homey touches. There's also a breezy cafe with tasty treats such as homemade muesli, with classical music often wafting through the palms. Book the five-course captain's dinner in advance (Rs 1800).

Pearl GUESTHOUSE $$
(Map p92; 031-492 7744; www.pearl-negombo.com; 13 Porutota Rd; s/d incl breakfast €39/52; ✳🛜) This small German-run beachfront pad might be discreet, but it packs all mod cons, along with plenty of sun loungers and a good restaurant. The six immaculate rooms are brightened by cheeky modern art; corner rooms have a sea view. If you're into watersports, it's a good bet as it's the home base of well-regarded diving and kitesurfing outfits.

Hotel Silver Sands HOTEL $$
(Map p92; 031-222 2880; www.silversandsnegombo.com; 229 Lewis Pl; r with fan Rs 2500-3800, with air-con Rs 4900; ✳🛜) An excellent, budget beachfront option with Arabian-style arched portals and neatly tiled rooms that have a balcony/terrace and odd tent-like mosquito nets. Wi-fi is in the lobby only.

THE WEST COAST NEGOMBO

WORTH A TRIP

MUTHURAJAWELA MARSH

Evocatively translated as 'Supreme Field of Pearls', **Muthurajawela Marsh** is a little-known gem of a wetland at the southern end of Negombo's lagoon. A trip here offers sightings of some 75 bird species, including purple herons, cormorants and kingfishers, as well as crocodiles, monkeys and even some very rarely seen otters.

The area had been a rich rice-growing basin before the Portuguese constructed a canal that flooded the fields with sea water. Over the centuries, Mother Nature turned Muthurajawela into Sri Lanka's biggest saline wetland.

The **Muthurajawela Visitor Centre** (011-403 0150; www.muthurajawelavisitorcentre.org; boat trip per person Rs 1200; ⏰7am-6pm) is at the southern end of the road along Pamunugama (the narrow belt of land between the gulf and the lagoon that stretches much of the way from the northern suburbs of Colombo to Negombo), next to the Hamilton Canal. It has some moth-eaten displays and a 25-minute video on the wetland's fauna. Much more interestingly, particularly for birders, it also runs 90-minute boat trips through the wetlands. Call and reserve a boat ride in advance as it gets busy at weekends and on holidays. A percentage of the profits goes toward local conservation initiatives.

THE WEST COAST NEGOMBO

Negombo (Beach Area)

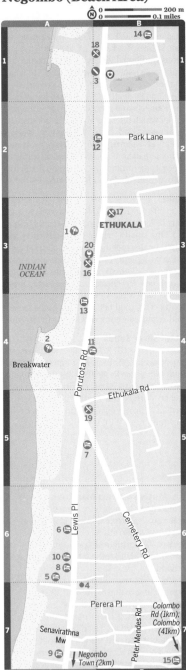

Negombo (Beach Area)

Jetwing Beach　　　　　　　　RESORT $$$
(Map p92; ☑031-227 3500; www.jetwinghotels.
com; Porutota Rd; s/d incl breakfast US$270/290;
❄@🛜🏊) With its imposing entrance and
high ceilings, this place feels like a temple –
a temple to minimalist luxury, that is. The
rooms are luxurious, with sea-view balco-
nies, and glass-walled bathrooms that boast
walk-in showers and circular two-person
bathtubs. There's also an impressive pool
complex that's lit up at night by flaming
torches. It's as magical as you could hope for.

There's even an in-house naturalist who
will happily answer all of your birds-and-
bees questions. Online discounts bring a
double room down to US$180.

**Jetwing
Ayurveda Pavilions**　　AYURVEDA RESORT $$$
(Map p92; ☑031-227 6719; www.jetwinghotels.
com; Porutota Rd, Ethukala; s/d incl breakfast
US$65/80, villa US$105-160; ❄@🛜🏊) The spacious private villas here are excellent value,
with minimalist yet luxurious furnishings. The
bathrooms are the real highlight and soaking
in one of the steamy, flower-petal-covered

outdoor baths with someone special on a rainy afternoon is every bit as romantic as you'd expect.

Most people are here on a package that includes Ayurvedic treatments and food, but you can also book individual treatments (in your villa) from US$35.

Villa Araliya   BOUTIQUE HOTEL $$$
(Map p92; ☑ 071 272 8504, 031-227 7650; www.villaaraliya-negombo.com; 154/10 Porutota Rd; r with fan US$60, with air-con US$80-120; ✳ ⚙ ☲) This stand-out choice has a variety of modern rooms – most featuring exposed red-brick walls and dark wooden furniture – but the uniting factor is that they're all supremely comfortable, with four-poster beds, high ceilings and bathrooms that you'll be happy to splash about in. The crystal-clean swimming pool will likely entice you in for a few pre-breakfast laps. Rates include breakfast.

The hotel is family-friendly (it has children's toys, cots and high chairs) and is on a quiet side street that's a five-minute walk from the beach. Small groups can opt for the spacious three-bedroom villa across the road.

✖ Eating

There are lots of very ho-hum restaurants and cafes stringing the main road along the beach, with more exciting options in between.

Petit Restaurant   SRI LANKAN, SEAFOOD $$
(Map p92; ☑ 077 628 7682; 100/7 Porutota Rd; mains Rs 750; ⊙11am-10pm) Potted plants and flowers surround the entrance of this suitably small, family-run restaurant. The menu serves up most of the Sri Lankan classics, but is especially strong on seafood; there are some more unusual dishes on offer such as the 'prawn fiesta' (essentially prawns dusted in coconut shavings).

It's very popular, so reservations are a good idea; be warned that the wait for your meal can be a long one.

Dolce Vita   ITALIAN $$
(Map p92; ☑ 031-227 4968; 27 Porutota Rd; mains Rs 700-1100; ⊙9am-10pm Tue-Sun) This casual Italian-owned beachside cafe and restaurant is the kind of place where people end up frittering away half a day sitting in the breezy shade drinking real espresso and tucking into pizza, caprese salad and house-made gelato (as well as local seafood).

★**Lords Restaurant**   FUSION $$$
(Map p92; ☑ 077 285 3190; www.lordsrestaurant.net; 80B Porutota Rd, Ethukala; dishes Rs 900-1500;

⊙1.30-11.30pm) By far Negombo's most creative eating experience, with dishes that are a hybrid of Western and Eastern flavours. Martin, the British owner, is a rare thing among expat restaurant owners in that he actually works on the floor and in the kitchen, making sure that everything is just spot on. It's the one place in town worth a splurge; credit cards are accepted.

The Thai and Sri Lankan curries are recommended, especially the prawn, coconut and arak curry, and it's also a great place for cocktails (try the mango and passionfruit mojito), with afternoon and evening happy hours. The lunch special (Rs 950 for two courses) is a deal. There's lots going on here – multiple dining spaces, live music, shisha pipes – so check out the website.

Tusker Restaurant   SEAFOOD $$$
(Map p92; ☑ 031-222 6999; 83 Ethukala Rd; mains Rs 1000-2500; ⊙11am-2pm & 6-10.30pm) The airy, elephant-lined Tusker is one of the smarter places to eat in town. Although its menu is wide-ranging in its geo-culinary diversity, its real strong point is seafood. Expect a warm welcome from the expat owners, if they are around.

⚓ Drinking & Nightlife

Most people drink in their hotel bar, but an increasing number of bars and cafes are popping up, especially in the northern part of the strip.

Ice Bear Century Cafe   CAFE
(Map p90; ☑ 031-223 8097; 25 Main St; ⊙9am-6pm) In a lovingly restored peach-pink colonial-era townhouse, this calm retreat in the heart of Negombo offers a touch of refined class, all manner of Sri Lankan brews (coffee Rs 270), mountains of homemade cakes and lunch specials, such as fisherman's soup or a hearty Swabian stew (mains Rs 540 to Rs 840).

Rodeo Pub   PUB
(Map p92; ☑ 031-227 4713; 35 Porutota Rd; ⊙10am-1am) Graffiti-sprayed bar busy with expats and tourists. There's live music on Tuesday nights, DJs the rest of the time, and a long list of cocktails with sexy names. It also does a range of classic Western and Sri Lankan dishes (Rs 600 to Rs 1000).

ℹ Information

There are a couple of ATMs along the main tourist strip, with most bank branches in the town proper.
Bank of Ceylon (Map p90; Broadway; ⊙8.30am-3pm Mon-Fri, to 1pm Sat & Sun) Changes cash in the centre of town.

HSBC (Colombo Rd; ⊙9am-3pm Mon-Fri) One of several banks in a row that changes foreign currency and has a 24-hour ATM accepting foreign cards.

Post Office (Map p90; Main St; ⊙7am-8pm Mon-Sat) In the centre of town.

Tourist Police (Map p92; ☑031-227 5555; Porutota Rd, Ethukala; ⊙24hr) At the northern end of the hotel strip; helpful in an emergency.

🛈 Getting There & Away

Government, private and intercity express buses run between **Negombo bus station** (Map p90) and Saunders Pl, Colombo (regular/air-con Rs 57/100, two hours, every 20 minutes). A faster air-con bus goes via the new highway (Rs 120, one hour) until 8pm. Long queues form at the bus station on weekend evenings, when day trippers return to the capital.

There are nine trains a day to Colombo (2nd/3rd class Rs 70/40, two hours), but they're slower and less frequent than the buses.

For Kandy, buses run four times a day until 3.30pm (Rs 150); the journey takes around three hours.

Bus 240 for Bandaranaike International Airport (Rs 24, 40 minutes), leaves from the bus station in town every 15 minutes between about 6am and 7pm. A three-wheeler costs about Rs 500 from Negombo town or Rs 900 from Lewis Pl. A taxi costs double this.

From the airport, find a taxi at an office just outside the terminal or catch a three-wheeler on the main road just outside the airport. Hotels can also arrange transport. The journey takes about 20 to 30 minutes.

🛈 Getting Around

To get from the bus station to Lewis Pl or Porutota Rd, you can catch a Kochchikade-bound bus or splash out Rs 300 on a three-wheeler.

Waikkal

☑031

The area around Waikkal and the neighbouring suburb of Kammala just off the A3 about 10km north of Negombo is a much quieter alternative to the bars and tourist shops of Negombo. A huge plus for this area is that the nearby beaches are long, golden and generally fairly untarnished in comparison to Negombo.

While there are several self-contained package-tour hotels in the area, there are also several excellent places more suited to independent travellers that offer a far more intimate, nature-based experience. Restaurants are limited to local rice-and-curry places on the main A3, 3km inland from the beach. Most people eat in their hotels.

🛏 Sleeping & Eating

★ Ging Oya Lodge   LODGE $$

(☑031-227 7822; www.gingoya.com; Kammala North; s/d incl breakfast €50/57; ❋@🛜⛱) The Belgium artist-owners of this place were inspired by the safari lodges of Africa and they've done a sterling job of replicating the rustic-chic luxury. There are seven spacious cottages with filigree window carvings, beautiful four-posters and semi-open-plan bathrooms, plus a wonderful pool, birds and butterflies everywhere, and total and utter peace. It's the kind of place you only tell your best friends about.

Set three-course dinners (€11) prepared by the owner Leo are served to classical music in the open-sided dining room. The beach is a shady 1km walk or cycle away (bikes available) or you can paddle a kayak (free) down to the sea. To get here independently take a Chilaw bus to Kammala or a train from Negombo or Colombo to Bolawatta; either way it's then a 3km three-wheeler ride (Rs 200). The hotel organises airport drops for Rs 2000.

Ranweli Holiday Village   RESORT $$$

(☑031-227 7359; www.ranweli.com; Waikkal; s/d with full board from US$225/250; ❋@🛜⛱) On the coast near Waikkal, the Ranweli Holiday Village has a fine beachside location if you don't mind the tour-group vibe, with 90 rooms and buffet-style meals. The ecofriendly management operates birdwatching tours by boat and has won dozens of environmental awards. The gentle punt over the canal separating it from the mainland sets a particularly romantic mood. Online rates are often discounted to US$135.

🛈 Getting There & Away

Frequent buses between Negombo and Chilaw can drop you in Waikkal, from where it's a short three-wheeler ride to the resorts or beach. Many people reach Waikkal by taxi or with a car and driver.

Negombo to Kalpitiya

Although the A3 stays close to the coast, there are few ocean views from the road between Negombo and Kalpitiya. Rather, you'll pass through an endless series of coconut plantations, which have their own rhythmic beauty.

Roughly halfway, the fishing town of **Chilaw** has a strong Roman Catholic flavour, with elaborate statues of saints and cardinals in the centre. About 7km south of Chilaw, pop into the roadside **Murugan (Kataragama) Temple** (A3 Hwy; ⊙ dawn-dusk), a Hindu shrine with building-sized statues of Vishnu and Hanuman. **Munneswaram**, 5km to the east of Chilaw, has another place of Hindu pilgrimage. The central of the three shrines is dedicated to Shiva.

The tiny village of **Udappuwa**, 12 kilometres north of Chilaw, has a hectic morning fish market and an important Hindu temple with a large *gopuram* (gateway tower). In August festival devotees here and at Munneswaram test their strength by walking on red-hot coals. Buses are frequent along the A3, though you may have to change in Chilaw.

Kalpitiya Peninsula

Dolphins and kitesurfing are what brings people to the relatively undeveloped Kalpitiya peninsula. Schools of dolphins hundreds strong can often be seen playing in the offshore waters; boat safaris offer close-up views of these aquatic mammals. Meanwhile, for those who want to act like a dolphin dancing through the waves, Kalpitiya, with its near-constant strong winds, is widely considered to have the best kitesurfing conditions in South Asia.

As well as all the water-sports activities, most hotels can also organise Wilpattu National Park safaris, but it's a fairly long drive and you'll miss dawn, which is the best time for seeing animals.

◉ Sights & Activities

At **Talawila**, halfway up the peninsula, there's a Catholic shrine to St Anne. The church features satinwood pillars and is pleasantly situated on the seafront. Thousands of pilgrims come here in March and July, when major festivals honouring St Anne are held. The festivals include huge processions, healing services and a fair. The two main beaches are Kalpitiya Beach and Alankuda Beach, a short way to the south.

Dolphin- & Whale-Watching

Boat safaris to watch schools of hundreds of spinner dolphins run most mornings between November and March, when dolphins (and even whales) are seen around 80% of the time. Sperm whales and Bryde's whales are frequently seen between December and mid-April.

Every hotel can organise a safari, but try and suss out how knowledgeable your

CHANGING KALPI

Changes are afoot in the   sula. The government, lo   the island's tourist indu   in a project to turn the   la and its string of offsh   one of Sri Lanka's prime   destinations. The blueprints call for huge resorts, a domestic airport, golf courses, high-speed boat safaris and much more.

Environmentalists are concerned about the impact these projects will have on the populations of dolphins, sperm whales and dugongs that use the waters around Dutch Bay, while many locals are angered by the banning of fishing in certain areas and corruption in the development process itself (the minister of economic development has admitted that land deeds have been forged in some places). So far there is minimal sign of development, but things will likely change soon.

captain is about dolphins beforehand. Prices start from US$40 per person, which includes a US$9 wildlife conservation fee.

Kitesurfing

Kalpitiya lagoon and beach is fast gaining a reputation for having South Asia's best kitesurfing conditions, and there are several excellent residential kitesurfing camps, which also rent out equipment.

A nine-hour (two or three days) course should get you surfing solo and costs around US$300 in a group of three, or $380 with private tuition, including gear hire. The best places work with two-way radios to speed up learning. Training takes place on the protected lagoon from bases on Kalpitiya Beach. Sri Lanka Kite (p96) is located right on the lagoon; other camps such as Kitesurfing Lanka (p96) have a 20-minute drive to the site.

The monsoon months of May to October are the prime months for wind, though seas can be rough. At other times conditions are generally best in the afternoon.

Snorkelling & Scuba Diving

There are some spectacular offshore reefs here with plenty of big fish. The prime dive site is Bar Reef, which sits several kilometres off the northwest tip of the peninsula and is said to be one of the finest dive sites in Sri Lanka. Most hotels can organise snorkelling

...rips, with dives costing from US$85.

...uda Beach
BEACH

...nkuda is the peninsula's busiest and best beach for non-kitesurfing beach bums. If you squint your eyes and blot out the string of giant wind turbines stretched right out along the length of the beach, the massive coal-fired power plant at the far end and its long and ugly jetty, then Alankuda is a lovely stretch of sand.

Kalpitiya Beach
BEACH

Kalpitiya Beach at the northern end of the peninsula consists of a long spit of sand most easily reached by boat across the Kalpitiya lagoon. It's a lovely stretch of sand, but there are few facilities here and it can get very windy – too windy to really enjoy lying about on a towel.

Kalpitiya Discover Diving
DIVING

(☑ 077 003 0033; www.kalpitiyadiving.lk) This dive school is the closest to the resorts on Alankuda Beach. A two-tank dive costs US$85 and it also runs snorkelling trips to Bar Reef.

Ocean Lanka Scuba
DIVING

(☑ 071 0822 231; www.oceanlankainfo.com; Kudawa) This dive school is the closest to the kitesurfing schools around Kalpitiya Beach.

🛏 Sleeping & Eating

There's been a surge of hotel construction in the past two years, most of it centred around top-end options. There are two main areas to stay: Alankuda Beach, with its mixture of midrange and top-end accommodation, and Kalpitiya Beach, home to several kitesurfing camps.

Several of the Alankuda resorts sit right under a line of huge wind turbines. They may not be very attractive, but they don't make much noise.

Omeesha Beach Hotel
CABANAS $$

(☑ 072 787 8782; www.omeeshabeach-kalpitiya.com; Alankuda Beach; s/d with fan Rs 3000/4500, with air-con Rs 5000/7000; ❄🛜) This friendly, family-run and good-value place looks out onto a fine section of beach. The rooms are a little ramshackle (wooden budget cabanas are the best value, with open-air bathrooms), but there's a good beachside restaurant and loungers for guests. Rates include breakfast.

Sri Lanka Kite
RESORT $$

(☑ 077 252 8567; www.srilankakite.com; Sethawadiya; s/d with shared bathroom US$50/90, cottage from US$80/110; 🛜) Down a maze of confusing tracks from Kalpitiya town, this place is aimed squarely at kitesurfers. Rooms vary from basic tents and dorms (US$40 per person) to comfortable cottages and luxurious villas (s/d US$155/180). Big pluses are the warm staff, sociable restaurant area and the lagoon-front location with a free boat shuttle to the beach. Rates are full board.

To get here take the turn-off 1.5km south of Kalpitiya town towards the Muslim village of Sethawadiya.

Kitesurfing Lanka
RESORT $$

(☑ 072 190 7894; www.kitesurfinglanka.com; Kandakuliya; tent per person €35, s €60-75, d €100-115; 🛜) This French-run kitesurfing camp has a good range of accommodation aimed at surfers, from simple tents to comfortable en suite villas. There's a sociable bar and restaurant area and the beach is just a short walk away. Rates include full board.

To get here turn off the Kalpitiya road at Kandakuliya (36/37km post) and drive 3km west.

Rosaanne Beach Resort
RESORT $$$

(☑ 077 182 5455; www.rosaannebeach.lk; Alankuda Beach; s/d incl breakfast US$70/90; ❄🛜🏊) Probably the best bet around Alankuda Beach, this stylish and friendly place has nine whitewashed, thatched cottages huddled under the palms, 100m from the beach. The vibe is Robinson Crusoe but with all mod-cons.

ℹ Getting There & Away

Two very-early-morning direct buses run between Negombo and Kalpitiya (Rs 180, four hours), but it's generally easier to change in Puttalam or at the Palavi junction (15km post), from where buses run to Kalpitiya (Rs 75) every 15 minutes.

For the accommodation at Alankuda Beach get off at Norochcholai and take a three-wheeler (Rs 150) for the remaining 3km. Buses between Alankuda and Kalpitiya cost Rs 50.

Buses from Puttalam run frequently to Negombo (normal/air-con Rs 85/250) and Colombo (normal/air-con Rs 160/320), with through buses passing by outside the bus station to Anuradhapura.

Wilpattu National Park

Wilpattu means 'natural lakes' in Sinhala and '10 lakes' in Tamil and lakes are exactly what you'll find at **Wilpattu National Park** (☑ 025-385 5691; www.dwc.gov.lk/library/Np_wilpattu.html; adult/child US$15/8, service charge per group US$8, jeep entry Rs 250, plus overall tax

12%; ⊙6am-6.30pm; last entry 4.30pm). Visitor numbers remain low, even in high season, which gives it a genuine sense of wilderness.

At 1317 sq km, Wilpattu is Sri Lanka's largest national park. Hidden in the dense, dry woodland, you'll (hopefully) find an array of wildlife that includes leopards (this is the second-best park after Yala for leopards, with 16 leopards per 100 sq km), sloth bears, spotted deer, wild pigs and crocodiles. Birders in particular will love Wilpattu with its abundance of dry forest, water and even coastal birds.

Be sure to note, however, that the dense forest and general skittishness of the animals means that actually sighting wildlife is less of a sure thing than in the country's more-visited parks. This is a place for the more dedicated safari-goer.

The national park is visited via jeep safari. The easiest option is to organise a safari through your accommodation, as this will also include transport to the national park, but you can hire six-seater 4WDs for safaris from beside the park entrance gate and ticket office. Prices run from Rs 4500 to 5500 for a half-day tour.

🛏 Sleeping & Eating

Teal Cottage HOTEL **$$**
(☑077 784 4998; www.wilpattutealcottage.com; Wilpattu Junction, Pahala Maragahawewa; d Rs 3500-4500; ❋🔊) This reliable family-run hotel is an appealing base for visiting Wilpattu, especially as it has its own safari jeeps. Choose from the quiet and immaculate seven back rooms with lake views of Timbire Wewa or the slightly cheaper rooms nearer the road. It is on the main road, 600m east of the turn to Wilpattu.

Mahoora Safari Camp LODGE **$$$**
(☑Colombo 011-583 0833; www.mahoora.lk; s US$720-920, d US$880-1040, all incl full board; 🔊) 🏃 This is safari the old-fashioned, decadent way. Mahoora offers a luxury tented camp on the edge of Wilpattu Park. Whatever safari tent type you opt for you can expect a bush-chic luxury stay and quality safari jeeps and guides. Full board includes all activities for one night and two days.

It's essential to book in advance – not only do they not accept walk-ins, but the camp itself may not even be set up.

❶ Getting There & Away

The turn-off to the park on the Puttalam–Anuradhapura Rd (A12) is 45km northeast of Puttalam and 26km southwest of Anuradhapura. From here it's a further 7km to the park entrance

at the barely discernible village of Hunuvilagama (Rs 500 by three-wheeler).

Frequent buses pass through the park turn-off en route to Anuradhapura, Puttalam and Colombo, though you are not guaranteed a seat.

SOUTH OF COLOMBO

Escaping the frenetic and sticky capital for the road south is a giant sigh of relief. Out go the congested streets and dark clouds of exhaust fumes and in come the sultry beaches of the Sri Lankan dream.

Most independent travellers make a beeline for surf-focused Hikkaduwa, with its wide range of accommodation, but the Bentota area offers quieter and even more stunning, beaches with a sprinkling of boutique hideaways amid the luxury resorts. Hire a scooter for a day and you'll quickly find your own stretch of private deserted sand.

Bentota, Aluthgama & Induruwa

🗺 034

Protected from noisy Galle Rd by the sluggish sweep of the Bentota Ganga, the ribbon of golden sand that makes up Bentota Beach is a glorious holiday sun-and-fun playground. There's a good mix of uberluxe resorts and smaller boutique places catering to independent travellers. There are more such places bordering Aluthgama, a small town on the mouth of an inlet and straddling the main road between Beruwela and Bentota. The town of Aluthgama has a raucous fish market, local shops and the main train station in the area. Induruwa doesn't really have a centre – it's spread out along the coast.

◉ Sights

Brief Garden GARDENS
(☑034-227 4462; Rs 1000; ⊙8am-5pm) You'll find the Brief Garden 10 kilometres inland from Bentota. A barely controlled riot of a garden out of *The Jungle Book*, the grounds are a lovely place to get lost in. The house, which used to be the home of Bevis Bawa, brother of renowned architect Geoffrey Bawa, has an eclectic range of artwork on display – from homoerotic sculpture to a wonderful mural of Sri Lankan life in the style of Marc Chagall.

Past visitors include Vivien Leigh and Laurence Olivier who stayed here in 1953 during the filming of *Elephant Walk*.

To get here, follow Mathugama Rd north-east inland from Aluthgama and branch northwest to the village of Dharga Town. From here you will periodically see yellow signs saying 'Brief', but as everyone knows this place, it's easy enough to ask directions. There's no public transport; a three-wheeler will cost around Rs 1000 return.

Galapata Raja Temple   BUDDHIST TEMPLE
(☉ dawn-dusk) FREE About 3km inland from Bentota, on the south bank of the Bentota Ganga, this unexpected 12th-century temple has some lovely murals and a 2500-year-old dagoba that is said to hold the canine tooth of Buddha's main disciple, Kasyapa. To reach it, cross the bridge south of Aluthgama and take the Elpitiya Rd to your left for 1.5km, keeping straight when the main road swings right and continuing for a further 1km.

 Activities

The protected lagoon and river mouth of the Bentota Ganga make this an excellent area for water sports. Windsurfing, waterskiing, jet-skiing, deep-sea fishing and everything else watery are offered by local operators. Independent operators **Sunshine Water Sports Center** (☏ 034-428 9379; www.srilanka watersports.com; River Ave, Aluthgama; ☉ 9am-dusk) and **Diyakawa Water Sports** (☏ 077 916 5330; www.srilankawatersports.lk; 10 River Ave, Aluthgama; ☉ 8am-5.30pm) are both right on the riverfront in Aluthgama. Besides renting out a wide range of equipment, they also offer tuition, including windsurfing (from Rs 14,000) and waterskiing (Rs 5600). There are also snorkelling tours, canoeing and scuba-diving courses.

Boat journeys along the Bentota Ganga are a peaceful, popular and bird-filled way to pass a late afternoon. **Tours** (per group Rs 2500-5000) travel through the intricate coves and islands on the lower stretches of the river, which is home to more than a hundred bird species. Most trips last for three hours. Sunshine Water Sports and Diyakawa Water Sports both organise trips, otherwise all hotels can point you to operators.

Sleeping & Eating

In among the resort bubbles are a number of charming boutique hotels and guesthouses, as well as one or two rare budget offerings.

Almost all the hotels and guesthouses double as restaurants; seafood is generally at the top of the list of offerings.

If you want to escape the confines of your hotel, there are a number of busy, tasty and cheap places in Aluthgama town.

Bentota

The fine beach of Bentota has a good mix of uberluxe resorts and smaller boutique places, some inland, catering to upmarket independent travellers.

Dedduwa Boat House   GUESTHOUSE $$
(☏ 077 027 6169, Colombo 011-452 9901; www. jetwinghotels.com; Dedduwa Junction; s/d incl breakfast Rs 3000/4000, house boat US$250; ✳️ 🛜) Head inland a couple of kilometres and you'll find this hidden villa in a lush, green lakeside setting of utter tranquillity. The five good-value rooms are carefully tended and you could spend hours just watching the birdlife on neighbouring Dedduwa Lake. The floating houseboat is sheer luxury.

Hotel Susantha Garden   GUESTHOUSE $$
(☏ 034-227 5324; www.hotelsusanthagarden.com; Bentota; s/d with fan from Rs 4850/5450, with air-con from Rs 6500/6850; ✳️ @ 🛜) Shady gardens, traveller-savvy staff, easy access to the northern part of Bentota Beach and an array of colourful rooms make this a very popular place to drop your backpack for a few days. You can enter the gates right from the platform of Bentota (not Aluthgama) train station. Deluxe rooms are quietest and the best value.

⭐ **Shangri-Lanka Villa**   BOUTIQUE HOTEL $$$
(☏ 034-227 1181; www.shangrilankavilla.com; 23 De Alwis Rd, Bentota; s/d incl breakfast US$110/125; ✳️ 🛜 🏊) The peaceful, rural setting of this intimate and beautiful British–Sri Lankan guesthouse, a kilometre inland from the main road and beach, means at night you'll fall asleep to the sound of cicadas singing to the moon rather than honking buses. The rooms are enormous, with bright splashes of colour, and there's tasteful art on the walls.

The food and the service are as good as the accommodation, and the centrepiece of the garden is an immaculate pool. Brits will enjoy the beans on toast and bacon and sausages for breakfast.

Club Villa   BOUTIQUE HOTEL $$$
(☏ 034-227 5312; www.club-villa.com; 138/15 Galle Rd, Bentota; s/d incl breakfast from US$180/220; ✳️ @ 🛜 🏊) Ever wondered what happened to the hippies who bummed across Asia in the 1960s and '70s? Well, while some dropped out of life completely, others went home and

became investment bankers who now spend their dollars reminiscing in hotels like this Bawa-designed masterpiece. From the antique furniture to the blissed-out Buddha and Shiva statues, everything about this place reeks of ethnic chic.

Even the giant catfish that haunt the numerous ponds seem to cruise about in a stoned state of permanent indolence.

Amal Villa   BOUTIQUE HOTEL **$$$**
(☎ 077 603 7541; www.amal-villa.com; 135 Galle Rd, Bentota; s/d with half board Rs 15,000/17,000; ✦ ⸙ ⸙) This beautifully maintained hotel is split into a beachside building and a landside villa. The smaller inland building is our

favourite, with a gorgeous infinity pool (the huge luxury rooms with private balcony are worth the extra Rs 3000), but the beachside building, which doesn't have a pool, is more sheltered from road noise. Pamper yourself with a steam bath in the good Ayurvedic spa.

Wunderbar
Hotel and Restaurant   SEAFOOD **$$**
(☎ 034-227 5908; Galle Rd, Bentota; mains Rs 650-1200; ⊙ 8am-11pm) The Wunderbar Hotel and Restaurant has an enjoyable 1st-floor cabana-style restaurant open to nonguests and sea breezes, and a decent selection of seafood and Western dishes.

HATCHING TURTLES

Five species of sea turtles lay eggs along the west and south coasts of Sri Lanka. The green turtle is the most common, followed by the olive ridley and the hawksbill. The leatherback and loggerhead are both huge, reaching 2m or more in length. During what should be long lives (if they don't end up in a net or soup pot), female turtles make numerous visits to the south coast to lay eggs in the sand of the same beach where they themselves were born. A few weeks later, hundreds of baby turtles make a perilous journey back to the water.

Most of the tiny turtles are quickly gobbled up by birds, fish, people and other critters. And many never hatch at all, since human egg-poachers work overtime to satisfy the demand for turtle omelettes. However, the turtle hatcheries on the coast around Bentota and Kosgoda claim to increase the odds for the turtles by paying locals for the eggs at a rate slightly above that which they would fetch on the market. The eggs are then incubated by the hatchery. After a short stay in a tank the babies are released under the cover of darkness (in the wild, the babies also emerge at night).

The reality of the situation is that the turtle hatcheries might be doing more damage than good. When a baby turtle hatches it retains a part of the yolk from the egg, which acts as a vital energy source when the turtles first swim out to sea. By keeping the babies for even a very short time in a tank, they do not gain the benefit of this first food source. In addition, mature female turtles like to return to the beach where they hatched in order to lay their own eggs: if they have been born in captivity, they will not have obtained a 'magnetic imprint' of their beach of birth and thus they are thought to be unable to return to shore to lay their eggs. For a truly sustainable turtle conservation effort, it's better that the eggs are simply left on the beach where they were laid and given protection there. For more on this see www.srilankaecotourism.com/turtle_hatchery_threat.htm.

Although the conservation benefits of the hatcheries are limited, there's no denying that the turtles are awfully cute and make for an entertaining visit. Visits rarely last more than about 20 minutes. Expect to see babies, as well as adults who have been injured by nets or in other calamities. Many environmental groups recommend you do not visit the more commercial hatcheries around Bentota area.

Kosgoda Sea Turtle Conservation Project (☎ 091-226 4567; www.kosgodaseaturtle.org; 13A Galle Rd, Mahapalana; Rs 1000; ⊙ 8.30am-5.30pm) On the beachside of Galle Rd, just north of Kosgoda, this volunteer-run operation has been here for 18 years. It's a very simple affair.

Kosgoda Turtle Hatchery (Victor Hasselblad Sea Turtle Sanctuary; ☎ 077-326 2553; Rs 500; ⊙ 7am-6pm) Turn down a small track on the A2 at the Km72/73 post to find this operation, located in a quiet spot right on a pristine beach. Look for the 50-year-old turtle and the blind albino turtle, both of which have miraculously survived both humans (nets) and nature (tsunami). Arrive at 6pm and you can help release the three-day-old hatchlings into the ocean (Rs 1500).

AYURVEDA IN PARADISE

The area around Beruwela, a short way north of Bentota, has a number of regarded Ayurveda resorts, including several of the centres that we have recommended here. **Jetwing Ayurveda Pavilions** (p92), in Negombo, is a good option north of Colombo, while **Aditya Resort** (p104) is just south of Hikkaduwa.

Saman Villas (☑ 034-227 5435; www.samanvilla.com; Aturuwella; d from US$625; ❀ @ 🛜 🌊) We would love to tell you just how incredible this place is, but the simple truth is that there are no words to describe the sheer opulence of this hotel complex. How opulent? Well, some of the rooms have private swimming pools – inside the bathroom!

Temple Tree Resort & Spa (☑ 034-227 0700; www.templetreeresortandspa.com; 660 Galle Rd, Induruwa; s/d incl breakfast from US$120/140; ❀ 🛜 🌊) Picture a minimalist loft apartment transported to a tropical beach and you get the Temple Tree Resort. The polished-concrete and stone rooms with electric-white walls are opulent, and deluxe rooms have a whirlpool bathtub that you can soak in while staring at the ocean. All rooms have balconies overlooking the two pools and superb beach.

Heritance Ayurveda Maha Gedara (☑ 034-555 5000; www.heritancehotels.com; Beruwela; s/d with full board from US$205/320; ❀ 🛜 🌊) You only have to visit a few Ayurveda hotels to realise that the quality of the accommodation often plays second fiddle to the treatments. Not here. At the Heritance, not only are the treatments first rate with very experienced doctors, but the Bawa-designed hotel itself is a wonderful luxury retreat tucked among the frangipani trees. Rates include treatments and yoga.

Barberyn Reef Ayurveda Resort (☑ 034-227 6036; www.barberynresorts.com; Beruwela; s/d with full board from €85/150, plus compulsory Ayurveda treatments per person per day €80; ❀ 🛜 🌊) One of the best-regarded Ayurveda resorts in Sri Lanka, with the full compliment of treatments and excellent doctors. Most people stay for a minimum of a week. It also offers yoga, meditation, free local excursions and Ayurveda cooking demonstrations. The cheaper rooms are fan only. The resort is 4km north of central Aluthgama.

🛏 Aluthgama

The town of Aluthgama has a few small guesthouses that line the lagoon; great if you want to be close to the transport and commercial options of a town environment.

Hotel Hemadan　　　　GUESTHOUSE **$$**
(☑ 034-227 5320; www.hotelhemadan.com; 25 River Ave, Aluthgama; s/d from Rs 6040/6900; ❀ 🛜) A cosy Danish-owned guesthouse that has 10 clean rooms in an ageing river-front building. There's prime river-viewing opportunities from the villa-style restaurant, dock and beer garden, all of which enjoy riverside breezes. The rooms themselves are simple; smaller ones come with a balcony, and only deluxe rooms have air-con. It's a good choice if you want to be closer to town and transportation. There are free boat shuttles across the river to the ocean-side beach and a baby cot for those travelling with little ones.

High Rich River View Resort　GUESTHOUSE **$$**
(☑ 034-227 4050; www.highrichresort.com; 97 Riverside Rd, Aluthgama; r/ste Rs 6600/8500; ❀ 🛜)

This riverside hotel's six slightly musty rooms contain wooden beds, dressing tables and hot-water showers, but it's the pleasant deck and riverfront restaurant that make it worthwhile.

🛏 Induruwa

Induruwa lies at the quieter southern end of Bentota Beach. There are a couple of luxury resorts here, mixed with one or two budget options, which are good if you want a quiet beach break. There's little in the way of restaurants or shops here.

Long Beach　　　　　　HOTEL **$**
(☑ 034-227 5773; www.longbeachcottageinduruwa. com; 550 Galle Rd, Induruwa; tw Rs 2750; 🛜) The five fan-cooled rooms here might be basic, but if you want paradise on the cheap, this family-run place is your best choice. There is a shady coconut grove of a garden and – with a feature that matches all the big-boy hotels – a gorgeous beach so close that you can lie in bed and listen to the waves.

❶ Information

Commercial Bank (339 Galle Rd, Aluthgama; ⊘9am-3pm Mon-Fri) Just north of the river; has an ATM.

Post office (Elpitiya Rd; ⊘9am-5pm Mon-Sat) East of Bentota.

Tourist office (☑ 091-393 2157; Galle Rd, Bentota; ⊘8.30am-4.30pm Mon-Fri) Outside the Bentota Beach Hotel.

❶ Getting There & Away

Beruwela and Bentota are both on the main Colombo–Matara railway line, but Aluthgama, the town sandwiched between them, is the station to go to as many trains don't make stops at these smaller stations. Aluthgama has five or six express trains daily to Colombo (2nd/3rd class Rs 110/55, 1½ to two hours) and a similar number to Hikkaduwa (2nd/3rd class Rs 70/35, one hour). The 3.40pm express to Colombo fort connects with a service to Kandy (2nd class Rs 260). The ticket office is on the unusual middle-platform station.

Aluthgama is also the best place to pick up a bus, although there is no trouble getting *off* any bus anywhere along the Galle Rd (if for example you are headed to Induruwa). There is frequent service to Colombo (regular/air-con Rs 85/150, three hours) and Hikkaduwa (regular/air-con Rs 57/120, one hour) until 5pm.

The easiest way to get between the hotels of Aluthgama, Bentota and Induruwa is by three-wheeler, though you can jump on and off any bus travelling the main Galle Rd that links the three locations.

Hikkaduwa & Around

☑ 091

Hikkaduwa has been a firm fixture on the Sri Lankan tourist map since the 1970s, and this long exposure to tourism has left it a little worse for wear. A kilometre-long strip of guesthouses, shops and restaurants lines the beach, which is quite badly eroded in its northern stretch. The busy Colombo–Galle Rd, with its crazy high-speed bus drivers, runs right through the middle of Hikkaduwa, which can make stepping outside of your guesthouse as deadly as a game of Russian roulette!

But it's not all bad. There are plenty of charming places to stay, a string of mellow beach bars and restaurants, good diving and surf schools and plenty of interesting excursions accessible by three-wheeler or rental scooter. For years there has been talk about a possible bypass road around Hikkaduwa, which if it were to materialise would do wonders for this paradise lost.

◉ Sights

Hikkaduwa National Park   NATIONAL PARK

(adult/child Rs 30/15) Hikkaduwa's marine park stretches along the northern end of the beach and is an easy way to get a glimpse of some of Sri Lanka's undersea life. Snorkelling gear can be rented from places around the park **ticket office** (⊘7am-6pm) for around Rs 600 for two hours.

Hikkaduwa Lake   LAKE

Hikkaduwa Lake, with its monitor lizards and numerous birds, makes for a pleasant excursion away from the beach. Boat tours can sometimes be organised on the lake; ask around. The lakeside hotel Kalla Bongo (p104) offers kayak hire if you are having lunch there. To get there head along Baddegama Rd for 2km, then turn north.

Seenigama Vihara   BUDDHIST TEMPLE

(⊘dawn-dusk) About 2km north of Hikkaduwa is the Seenigama Vihara, perched on its own island. It's one of only two temples in the country where victims of theft can seek retribution. People who have been robbed visit the temple and buy a specially prepared oil made with chilli and pepper. With the oil they light a lamp in their homes and recite a mantra. Sooner or later the thief will be identified when they're struck down with misfortune.

Boats shuttle visitors out to the island in calm weather.

Gangarama Maha Vihara   BUDDHIST TEMPLE

(off Baddegama Rd; ⊘dawn-dusk) This interesting Buddhist temple has lots of popular educational paintings that are the work of one man over nearly a decade. The monks are happy to show you around.

Activities

For many people, a visit to Hikkaduwa begins and ends on the beach. The widest bit of sand extends south from the Hotel Moon Beam to the southern suburb of Narigama. Most of the sun loungers here belong to hotels, but you can normally use them if you order a drink or lunch. There are lovely beach walks to the south.

To take a break from the beach scene, rent a bicycle or scooter to explore any of the minor roads heading inland. They lead to a calmer, completely different, rural world.

Diving

The diving season runs from November to April. Novices can opt for a day-long Discover Scuba taster (US$50 to US$85) or a longer

THE WEST COAST HIKKADUWA & AROUND

Hikkaduwa & Around

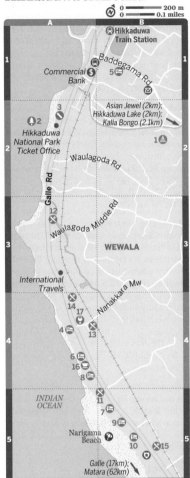

Hikkaduwa & Around

several places rent snorkelling gear (around Rs 600 for two hours). Stay alert in the water so that you don't get mowed down by the many glass-bottomed boats. You may be asked to buy a ticket for the offshore Hikkaduwa National Park from the ticket office (p101).

Surfing
The conditions for surfing are at their best from November to April. The Wewala and Narigama areas of the beach have a handful of tame reef breaks as well as a beach break, all of which are perfect for beginner-to intermediate-level surfers. These waves, combined with the relatively energetic nightlife, have made Hikkaduwa the most popular surf spot in Sri Lanka.

Most guesthouses and several dedicated surf shops rent out surfboards for around Rs 400 per hour, and there are several places offering surf lessons, but pick carefully because the 'teachers' at some of the better-known surf schools are more interested in looking cool than teaching.

PADI open water dive course (from US$375). The best local dives are to the wrecks of the *Conch,* a well-preserved 19th-century steam-powered tanker, and *The Earl of Shaftesbury,* an 1892 four-masted sail boat.

There are half-a-dozen dive schools, including **Poseidon Diving Station** (☏091-227 7294; www.divingsrilanka.com; 304 Galle Rd; ⊗8am-6pm), which also has a restaurant and accommodation for divers. A two-tank dive costs US$75.

Snorkelling
Horseshoe-shaped Hikkaduwa Beach at the northern end of the strip has a section of coral reef just offshore in around 3m of water;

⊟ Sleeping
Virtually all of Hikkaduwa's accommodation is strung out along Galle Rd. Most plots of land along the strip are quite narrow, which

means that guesthouses will only have a few pricey rooms with views of the water. In contrast, rooms closest to the road get a lot of noise, so be sure to get a room well away from the traffic. Many places are jammed right up against each other.

Dewasiri Beach Restaurant & Hotel HOTEL **$**
(☑ 091-227 5555; 472 Galle Rd; r with fan Rs 2500-4000, with air-con Rs 4500; 🛜) Ideal for surfers on a budget, this slightly ramshackle place overlooks Main Reef and has a variety of simple but clean (cold-water) rooms, the priciest of which let you drift off to sleep with the sound of the surf in your ears. It's the friendly family and their culinary skills that really make it stand out from the budget pack.

★Camellia Dwellings GUESTHOUSE **$$**
(☑ 071 227 7999; www.camelliadwellings.com; Baddegama Rd; d US$30; 🌀🛜) The five rooms in this colonial-style villa are spacious and well tended, making it excellent value. Major pluses are the friendly owner and staff and the proximity to the train and bus stations, but other highlights include the antique Morris Minor in the driveway and breakfast alfresco in the garden. If full, the owner can often book you for the same price in the nearby Arcadia Resort, an equally good villa with the added attraction of a pool.

Neela's GUESTHOUSE **$$**
(☑ 091-438 3166; www.neelasbeachinn.com; 634 Galle Rd; r with fan/air-con from US$30/70; 🌀🛜) This welcoming and well-run choice has something for everybody. Even the cheapest rooms are spotlessly clean and come with pleasing decor, while the more expensive top-floor suites (US$115) are very luxurious. Breakfast in the beachside restaurant is included with most rooms. If you fancy a drink, pop next door to the sociable Drunken Monkey Bar.

Blue Ocean Villa HOTEL **$$**
(☑ 091-227 7566; blueoceanvilla420@gmail.com; 420 Galle Rd; r with fan/air-con Rs 4000/7000; 🌀🛜) This slice of a guesthouse has well-furnished upper-floor air-conditioned rooms overlooking the beach, and cheaper but darker side rooms that have more of a budget feel.

Hotel Moon Beam HOTEL **$$**
(☑ 091-505 6800; hotelmoonbeam@hotmail.com; 548/1 Galle Rd; r with fan Rs 5500, with air-con Rs 6000-7500; 🌀🛜) A smart midrange option with 28 spick-and-span rooms that are enlivened by pictures and wooden decorations. Piping-hot water gushes forth from the showers and the best back rooms have balconies with partial surf views. Rates include breakfast in the pleasant restaurant. Subtract Rs 1000 for single occupancy.

Drifters Hotel HOTEL **$$**
(☑ 091-2275 692, 077 706 7091; www.driftershotel.com; 602 Galle Rd; d with fan/air-con US$35/60; 🌀🛜🏊) The small but well-kept pool at this beachside property alone makes it worth the money, but add in large and nicely presented rooms and a decent patch of beach out front and you have a solid bet, even if the public areas are a bit cramped. The seafront triples (US$70) are the best choice. The same management also have an inferior (but not bad)

THE WEST COAST HIKKADUWA & AROUND

REMEMBERING THE TSUNAMI

Two museums 3.5km north of Hikkaduwa tell the story, through photographs and newspaper features, of that dreadful day in 2004 when the Indian Ocean tsunami struck Hikkaduwa and Sri Lanka. The **Tsunami Education Centre and Museum** (☑ 077 731 6664; Galle Rd, Telwatta; by donation; ⊙ 8am-6pm) focuses on tsunami education for locals, but also has some dramatic and harrowing photos, including some of dead bodies. Just to the north is the ramshackle **Tsunami Photo Museum** (☑ 091-390 0884; Galle Rd, Telwatta; by donation; ⊙ 8am-6.30pm), with more powerful images that render most visitors silent.

Just south of the museums in Peraliya is a small **memorial** (Galle Rd, Peraliya) to the roughly 35,000 people who lost their lives to the tsunami just in Sri Lanka and the hundreds of thousands of others whose lives were changed profoundly. It was also assumed here that the tsunami washed away a packed commuter train with the loss of over 1200 lives – the world's worst ever train disaster and just one story from that terrible day.

A few hundred yards further south is the **Tsunami Honganji Vihara** (Galle Rd) **FREE**, where a statue of a standing Buddha faces the waves with his hands in the *abhaya mudra* (Buddha pose conveying fearlessness and protection). The statue is a replica of Afghanistan's Bamiyan Buddha, which was destroyed by the Taliban in 2001.

AMBALANGODA'S DEVIL MASKS

Ambalangoda is a sweaty, workaday town, which is completely overshadowed by nearby Hikkaduwa as a tourist destination. The main reason for visiting is to dig under the surface of the Sri Lankan souvenir scene and discover the magical meanings behind the ubiquitous 'devil' masks. Genuine devil dances, which drive out spirits causing illness, still occur irregularly in the hinterland villages. Ambalangoda is 13km north of Hikkaduwa on the main transport route between Colombo and Hikkaduwa; buses and trains are frequent.

Southern Antiques & Reproductions (☑ 091-225 8640; 32 Galle Rd, Urawatte) Anyone with a penchant for interior design will enjoy visiting this Aladdin's Cave of treasures. Most of the pieces are too big to transport (lots of wooden pillars and reclaimed wood), but it's fun to browse and dig through the inner rooms stuffed full of more portable treasures, including antique masks.

Ariyapala Mask Museum (☑ 091-225 8373; www.masksariyapalasl.com; 426 Main St; ⏱ 8.30am-5.30pm) This museum, with its dioramas and explanations in English, gives an interesting insight into Sri Lankan masks and the meanings behind them. It also sells the booklet *The Ambalangoda Mask Museum,* a useful publication if you want to delve into the mysterious world of *kolam* dance, legend and exorcism, and the psychology behind the masks.

Ariyapala Traditional Masks (☑ 091-225 4899; 432 Galle Rd; ⏱ 8.30am-5.30pm) Ariyapala Traditional Masks is a small ground-floor museum starring a life-sized statue of the last king and queen of Kandy. It also has a shop selling quality pieces. It's across the road from the Ariyapala Mask Museum.

hotel on the landward side of the road – don't get them mixed up.

Hotel Ritas　　　　　　　GUESTHOUSE $$
(☑ 091-227 7496; www.hotelritas.com; Galle Rd; r with fan/air-con incl breakfast US$40/50; ❄ 🛜) Keeping passing travellers content for years, lovely Ritas has simple but tidy ground-floor budget rooms, while midrange cruisers will like the fancier ocean-facing rooms, the best of which come with a private balcony (US$75). The good restaurant backs onto a nice section of beach equipped with loungers.

★ **Aditya Resort**　　　　　　RESORT $$$
(☑ 091-226 7708; www.aditya-resort.com; 719/1 Galle Rd, Devenigoda; r incl breakfast from US$465, ste US$995; ❄ 🛜) This sublime place is crammed with Buddhist statues, tropical flowers and masses of high-quality antiques. The huge rooms have carved wooden headboards and the semi-open-air bathrooms boast your own private koi pond and a plunge-pool bath that doubles as a jacuzzi.

The hotel overlooks an empty stretch of beach, but most of its small number of lucky guests just relax by the pool and indulge in spa and Ayurveda treatments. Light sleepers can select the firmness of their pillow from a designated menu. It's 6km south of Hikkaduwa.

★ **Kalla Bongo**　　　　　　BOUTIQUE HOTEL $$$
(☑ 091-438 3234; www.kallabongo.com; Lane 3, Field View, Baddegama Rd; s/d incl breakfast from Rs 13,500/14,500; ❄ 🛜) A serene Buddha greets new arrivals at this beautiful lakeside Dutch-run hideaway; the sense of calm continues throughout the property. Standard rooms overlook the pool, while the five deluxe rooms (Rs 2000 more) have wonderful lake views. Canoes are free for a sunset paddle.

Asian Jewel　　　　　　BOUTIQUE HOTEL $$$
(☑ 091-493 1388; www.asian-jewel.com; Lane 3, Field View, Baddegama Rd; r incl breakfast from US$115; ❄ 🛜) This small boutique hotel close to Hikkaduwa lake has lush, glitzy rooms, a beautiful pool and excellent food, though it's not actually on the lake. What really makes a stay here special are the staff – within seconds of arriving they'll have memorised your name and be bending over backwards to help.

The British-influenced menu stretches to English breakfasts and fish and chips. It's 3km inland, just off Baddegama Rd.

🍴 Eating & Drinking

Most of Hikkaduwa's places to eat are connected to hotels and guesthouses; few are all that memorable. Down on the sandy shores of Narigama, you can table-hop from one spot to the next throughout the night. Many places are good just for a drink and a few stay open past 11pm.

No 1 Roti Restaurant SRI LANKAN $
(☑ 091-491 1540; 373 Galle Rd; snacks Rs 150-280; ⊘ 10am-9.30pm) Away from the beach restaurant scene, this local roadside joint sells over 60 kinds of *rotti* (folded crepe-like pancake), ranging from garlic chicken to banana and honey. Two make a decent meal. There are also fresh shakes and lassis.

★**Home Grown**
Rice & Curry Restaurant SRI LANKAN $$
(☑ 072 440 7858; 140/A Wewala; curry Rs 500-750; ⊘ 8am-10pm) Half-buried under palm trees and flowering plants, this is a sweet little garden-terrace restaurant on a quiet (at least compared to the main road) side street. The family who run it are as lovely as the setting, and dish up fresh, tasty homemade curries, toasted sandwiches and pricier seafood (Rs 1200) at reasonable rates. No beer. There are only around half-a-dozen tables and it's very popular, so get there early or book ahead.

Bookworm SRI LANKAN $$
(☑ 077 622 5039; Galle Rd; veg/fish curries Rs 700/950; ⊘ 6.30-8.30pm) For some of the best home-cooked curries in town order dinner in this family-run place a couple of hours in advance. Dinner is upstairs; downstairs the family lends books (Rs 300) and rents out motorbikes (Rs 800 to 1000).

Spaghetti & Co ITALIAN $$$
(☑ 077 669 8114; 587/2 Galle Rd; meals Rs 800-1000; ⊘ 6-11pm) The lush gardens that surround this colonial-style villa go some way to hiding busy Galle Rd, which helps enhance the enjoyment of the ultra-thin-crust pizzas and creamy pastas this spot serves.

Cool Spot SEAFOOD $$$
(☑ 077 233 4900; 327 Galle Rd; mains Rs 600-2300; ⊘ 11am-11pm) This family-run place has been serving up fresh seafood from a vintage roadside house at the northern end of the strip since 1972. There's a cool veranda where you can peruse the blackboard menu that details the morning catch, from lobster salad or chilli crabs to snapper in Thai curry.

Sam's Bar BAR
(Roger's Garage; ☑ 077-725 2550; www.hikkaduwasamsbar.com; 403 Galle Rd; ⊘ 10am-midnight) A laid-back and spacious bar with pool tables (Rs 250 for 30 minutes) that broadcasts major sports events and serves good value food (mains Rs 400 to 700). It's about as far

removed from a typical Sri Lankan bar as you can get.

Coffee Shop CAFE
(536 Galle Rd; ⊘ 9am-7pm; ☎) Real Italian coffee (Rs 320), including hangover-busting espresso, and excellent cakes give a post-surf boost at this fashionable cafe.

ℹ️ Information

Commercial Bank (Galle Rd; ⊘ 9am-3pm) One of several banks on the main strip that changes cash and has ATMs.

Main post office (Baddegama Rd; ⊘ 9am-5pm Mon-Sat) A five-minute walk inland from the bus station.

Tourist police station (☑ 091-227 5554; Galle Rd; ⊘ 24hr) At the southeastern end of the tourist strip; not all the police here speak English – which rather defeats the purpose of the place!

ℹ️ Getting There & Away

BUS

There are frequent buses from Colombo (normal/air-con Rs 127/245, three hours). Buses also operate frequently to Galle (Rs 40 to 50, 30 minutes). Buses to Galle or beyond will drop you south of the bus station along the guesthouse strip. When leaving Hikkaduwa, your chances of getting a seat are best if you start at the **bus station** (Galle Rd).

CAR

There are two roads connecting Hikkaduwa with Galle and Colombo. The old Colombo–Galle Rd runs right through the middle of Hikkaduwa. Travelling along this road to central Colombo takes at least three hours and you should allow four or five hours to get to the airport (at quiet times you can do it faster than this). If driving yourself or taking a taxi to Colombo it's worth taking the Southern Expressway, a toll road that runs 15 minutes inland from the coast.

TRAIN

Service on the coast line is fairly frequent, but it's hard to get a seat when starting in Hikkaduwa; avoid the slow trains that stop everywhere. Check at the station for express departure times. Destinations include Colombo (2nd/3rd class Rs 160/85, two to three hours), Galle (2nd/3rd class Rs 40/20, 30 minutes) and beyond to Matara.

ℹ️ Getting Around

A three-wheeler from the train or bus stations to Wewala or Narigama costs about Rs 150. A motorbike gives you wonderful freedom to explore the deserted beaches, temples and sights around Hikkaduwa. **International Travels** (Galle Rd) is a reliable place to rent mopeds (Rs 800) and trail bikes (Rs 1700).

The South

Best Places to Eat

➡ Bedspace Kitchen (p122)
➡ Fort Printers (p116)
➡ Jinas Vegetarian and Vegan Restaurant (p121)
➡ Church St Social (p116)
➡ Mango Shade (p139)

Best Places to Sleep

➡ Blue Turtle (p141)
➡ Fort Bazaar (p114)
➡ Mirissa Hills (p131)
➡ Chill (p138)
➡ Lonely Beach Resort (p138)
➡ Pilgrim's Hostel (p112)

Why Go?

Prepare your senses for overload, for the South is Sri Lanka at its most sultry and enticing: a glorious shoreline of dazzling white curves of sand set against emerald forested hills. Yes, you'll find the region a delight to explore, with each bend in the coastal highway revealing yet another idyllic cove to investigate. Galle, an utterly captivating walled city replete with historic interest, is undoubtedly the South's cultural highlight, but there's also astonishing Buddhist-inspired art in lonely caves and the sacred precinct of Kataragama, an important pilgrimage town.

No matter what you're after you'll find it here. Surfers return year after year to pursue the perfect break. There's the chance to see blue whales surging through offshore swells and turtles crawling onto moonlit beaches. Meanwhile, in the national parks, leopards move like spirits in the night and elephants trumpet across the forest to acclaim the first light of day.

When to Go
Galle

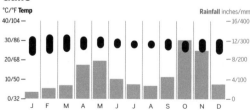

Dec–Apr Whales roll through the sea, the beaches buzz and everything is open.

Jul–Aug Pilgrims perform acts of self-mortification at the unforgettable Kataragama festival.

Nov The monsoon rains die out, beach resorts wake up and crowds are yet to arrive.

Galle

🎵 091 / POP 103,600

Galle is a jewel. A Unesco World Heritage Site, this historic city is a delight to explore on foot, an endlessly exotic old trading port blessed with imposing Dutch-colonial buildings, ancient mosques and churches, grand mansions and museums. Wandering its rambling lanes you'll pass stylish cafes, quirky boutiques and impeccably restored hotels owned by local and foreign artists, writers, photographers and designers.

Built by the Dutch, beginning in 1663, Galle's core is the Fort, a walled enclave surrounded on three sides by the ocean. A key part of the Fort's appeal is that it isn't just a pretty place. Sure, tourism now dominates the local economy, but this unique city remains a working community: there are administrative offices and courts, export companies, schools and colleges.

Most travellers are utterly seduced by Galle's ambience, and it's undoubtedly southern Sri Lanka's one unmissable sight.

History

Some historians believe Galle may have been the city of Tarshish – where King Solomon obtained gems and spices – though many more argue that a port in Spain seems a more likely candidate. Either way, Galle only became prominent with the arrival of the Europeans. In 1505 a Portuguese fleet bound for the Maldives was blown off course and took shelter in the harbour. Apparently, on hearing a cock (*galo* in Portuguese) crowing, they gave the town its name. Another slightly less dubious story is that the name is derived from the Sinhala word *gala* (rock).

THE SOUTH GALLE

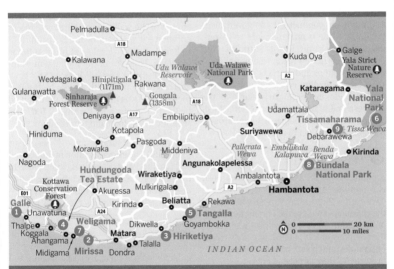

The South Highlights

1 **Galle** (p107) Strolling the lanes of this uniquely atmospheric Unesco World Heritage Site.

2 **Blue whale tours** (p131) Achieving the dream of a lifetime: seeing the world's largest living creatures on a boat tour out of Mirissa.

3 **Hiriketiya** (p135) Discovering that most perfect of beaches.

4 **Handunugoda Tea Estate** (p124) Learning about the gourmet tea trade at this famous white-tea plantation.

5 **Tangalla** (p137) Enjoying long walks along empty oceanic beaches.

6 **Yala National Park** (p145) Spotting a leopard or camera-snapping a croc in this famous reserve.

7 **Weligama** (p126) Learning to surf in a backpacker-friendly town.

8 **Bundala National Park** (p140) Scanning these wetlands for flamingos, ibis and eagles.

9 **Tissamaharama** (p141) Watching the mist rise off Tissa Wewa in the pink glow of sunset.

In 1589, during one of their periodic squabbles with the kingdom of Kandy, the Portuguese built a small fort, which they named Santa Cruz. Later they extended it with a series of bastions and walls, but the Dutch, who took Galle in 1640, destroyed most traces of the Portuguese presence.

After the construction of the Fort in the 17th century, Galle was the main port for Sri Lanka for more than 200 years and was an important stop for boats and ships travelling between Europe and Asia. However, by the time Galle passed into British hands in 1796, commercial interest was turning to Colombo. The construction of breakwaters in Colombo's harbour in the late 19th century sealed Galle's status as a secondary harbour, though it still handles some shipping and yachts.

⊙ Sights

The Fort area is home to about 400 historic houses, churches, mosques, temples and many old commercial and government buildings. Galle is an experience to savour, taste and touch; revel in its surprises. And don't neglect the new town, where you'll find interesting shops and markets.

A large Muslim community lives and works inside the Fort, particularly at the southern end of the walled town. Some businesses close for a couple of hours around noon on Friday for prayer time.

⊙ The Fort Walls

Ambling along the Fort's ramparts at dusk is a quintessential Galle experience. As the daytime heat fades away, you can walk almost the complete circuit of the Fort along the top of the wall in an easy hour or so. You'll be in the company of lots of residents, shyly courting couples, and plenty of kids diving into the protected waters or playing cricket.

Note that you can tell which parts of the walls were built by the Portuguese and which by the Dutch: the latter designed much wider walls to allow for cannons to be mounted. If you examine the walls closely you can make out chunks of coral mixed in with the stone and mortar.

★ Flag Rock   HISTORIC SITE
(Rampart St) Flag Rock, at the southernmost end of the Fort, was once a Portuguese bastion. Today it is easily the most popular place to catch a sunset. During daylight hours you may see daredevil locals leaping into the water from the rocks. Numerous vendors sell good street food such as fresh papaya with chilli powder from carts.

During the Dutch period, approaching ships were signalled from the bastion atop Flag Rock, warning them of dangerous rocks – hence its name. Musket shots were fired from Pigeon Island, close to the rock, to further alert ships to the danger. Later, the Dutch built a lighthouse here; since removed, the nearby street name survives.

★ Old Gate   HISTORIC SITE
A beautifully carved British coat of arms tops the entrance to the Old Gate on the outer side. Inside, the letters VOC, standing for Verenigde Oostindische Compagnie (Dutch East India Company), are inscribed in the stone with the date 1669, flanked by two lions and topped by a cockerel. A section of the fortifications here also served as a spice warehouse.

Main Gate   HISTORIC SITE
(Lighthouse St) The Main Gate in the northern stretch of the wall is a comparatively recent addition – it was built by the British in 1873 to handle the heavier flow of traffic into the old town. This part of the wall, the most intensely fortified because it faced the land, was originally built with a moat by the Portuguese, and was then substantially enlarged by the Dutch who split the wall in 1667 into separate Star, Moon and Sun Bastions.

Point Utrecht Bastion   HISTORIC SITE
(Hospital St) The eastern section of Galle's wall ends at the Point Utrecht Bastion, close to the powder magazine, which bears a Dutch inscription from 1782. Today this is the location of Galle's lighthouse (Hospital St).

Lighthouse Beach   BEACH
(off Hospital St) A slim swathe of sand right on the east side of the Fort. However it's not that great for a dip as there are rocks offshore and the beach is often littered.

⊙ Inside the Fort

Most of the older buildings within the Fort date from the Dutch era. Many of the streets still bear their Dutch names, or are direct translations. The Dutch also built an intricate sewer system that was flushed out daily by the tide. With true efficiency, they then bred musk rats in the sewers, which were exported for their musk oil.

Visitors to Galle 20 years ago will be surprised by what they find today: crumbling streets resurfaced with tidy paving stones and myriad historic building renovations both completed and ongoing. And just when it all seems a bit chi chi, a screaming monkey will go leaping overhead.

★**Dutch Reformed Church**   CHURCH
(Groote Kerk, Great Church; cnr Church & Middle Sts; ☉9am-5pm) Originally built in 1640, the present building dates from 1752. Its floor is paved with gravestones from Dutch cemeteries, while other impressive features include the organ and an imposing pulpit made from calamander wood and topped by a grand hexagonal canopy. You may encounter the friendly caretaker who will likely point out the (slightly bizarre) carved wooden memorial dedicated to a former Commander of Galle, Abraham Samlant – the tiny cotton shirt is said to be the one he was baptised in.

Marine Archeological Museum   MUSEUM
(Church St; adult/child Rs 710/355; ☉8am-5pm) This spacious maritime museum occupies a colossal old spice warehouse built by the Dutch and dating back to the late 17th century. The structure was originally part of the main gateway to the Fort and it still forms part of its ramparts. An introductory video presentation sets the scene and there are interactive displays that illuminate the city's maritime past, including the many shipwrecks in Galle's surrounding waters. It covers two levels that snake through the city walls.

National Maritime Museum   MUSEUM
(Queens St; adult/child Rs300/150; ☉9am-4.30pm Tue-Sat) Nestled in the old walls, this small museum is worth a quick look for its skeleton of a Bryde's whale and a very useful model that explains how tsunamis occur. There are also some dusty displays demonstrating old fishing techniques and examples of local boats.

Dutch Hospital   HISTORIC BUILDING
(Hospital St) Now fully restored and home to myriad upmarket boutiques and restaurants, this vast, colonnaded colonial landmark dates from the 18th century. Its size was necessary as both the voyage to Ceylon and life in the tropics proved very unhealthy to the Dutch, who died in droves from various diseases and the tropical heat. There are fabulous bay views from its upper balcony.

Historical Mansion   HISTORIC BUILDING
(31-39 Leyn Baan St; ☉9am-6pm) **FREE** More of an antique store than a museum, this Fort townhouse (which dates back to the Dutch days) contains the private collection of a longtime local family. Many exhibits have price tags; look for oodles of colonial artefacts, including collections of antique typewriters, VOC china and jewellery. Also look out for craftspeople busy polishing gems and weaving lace; a guide will show you around.

Amangalla   HISTORIC BUILDING
(10 Church St) The Amangalla was built in 1684 to house the Dutch governor and officers. Later, as the New Oriental Hotel, it was the lodging of choice for 1st-class P&O passengers travelling to and from Europe in the 19th century. During much of the 20th century, it was in a decades-long slow decline and was run by the legendary Nesta Brohier, a grand lady who was actually born in room 25.

National Museum   MUSEUM
(☏091-223 2051; Church St; adult/child Rs 300/150; ☉9am-5pm Tue-Sat) This museum is housed in what's thought to be the oldest Dutch building in Galle, dating back to 1686. Displays are somewhat dusty and dated but include information on the lace-making process, traditional masks and religious items, including a relic casket.

◉ New Town

Although the Fort rightfully gets most of the attention, Galle's new town is also worth a stroll. Shops and markets are hives of activity throughout the day. Havelock Pl near the railway station has interesting businesses that can't afford the ever-ascending rents inside the Fort.

Dutch Market   MARKET
(Main St; ☉7am-6pm) Look for the Dutch Market with its displays of fruits and vegetables under a 300-year-old columned roof. It's located on busy Main St, close to other food and spice merchants.

**Galle International
Cricket Stadium**   STADIUM
(Main St) Once a racecourse for wagering British colonials, Galle's cricket ground was established over 100 years ago. Since 1998 it has been used for international matches; in 2010 it was the site of the legendary last appearance of Sri Lanka's great bowler, Muttiah Muralitharan. There's a great perspective of the ground from the Sun Bastion to the south.

🏃 Activities & Tours

Spa Sandeshaya   SPA
(☏071 740 8494; www.spasandeshaya.com; 44 Lighthouse St; ☉10am-7pm) A professionally

THE SOUTH GALLE

Galle

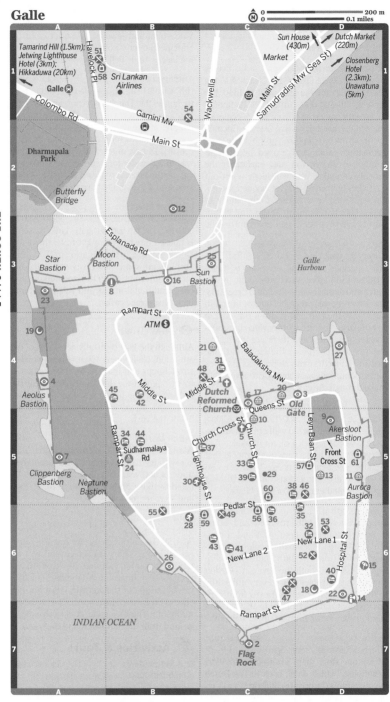

N 0 _____ 200 m
0 _____ 0.1 miles

Tamarind Hill (1.5km);
Jetwing Lighthouse
Hotel (3km);
Hikkaduwa (20km)

Sun House
(430m)

Dutch Market
(220m)

Closenberg
Hotel
(2.3km);
Unawatuna
(5km)

Sri Lankan
Airlines

Galle

Colombo Rd

Gamini Mw

Market

Main St

Samudradisi Mw (Sea St)

Wackwella

Main St

Dharmapala
Park

Butterfly
Bridge

Esplanade Rd

Star
Bastion

Moon
Bastion

Sun
Bastion

Galle
Harbour

Rampart St

ATM

Baladaksha Mw

Aeolus
Bastion

Middle St

Dutch
Reformed
Church

Queens St

Old
Gate

Akersloot
Bastion

Rampart St

Sudharmalaya
Rd

Church Cross St

Church St

Leyn Baan St

Front
Cross St

Aurora
Bastion

Clippenberg
Bastion

Neptune
Bastion

Lighthouse St

Pedlar St

New Lane 1

Hospital St

New Lane 2

INDIAN OCEAN

Rampart St

Flag
Rock

Dutch Market
(220m)

Galle

run spa with excellent massage therapists in an an impressive art-deco building. A foot massage and scrub is Rs 3500, while back massages start at Rs 4000.

Galle Fort Spa　　　　　　　　　　SPA
(☏ 077 725 2502; www.gallefortspa.com; 63 Pedlar St; massage per hour from Rs 5500; ⊙10am-6.30pm Mon-Sat) A top-end spa where you can enjoy a range of therapies (try a serenity massage) and services (including excellent manicures and pedicures), all with fine-quality products, potions and lotions.

★**Galle Fort Walks**　　　　　　WALKING
(☏ 077 683 8659; julietcoombe@yahoo.com.au; Serendipity Arts Cafe, 60 Leyn Baan St; tours from US$25) Author and photographer Juliet

Coombe leads excellent walking tours of the Fort. These include a Mystical Fort Tour, which delves into local legends and myths; a Meet the Artists tour, taking in an optional mask-making course (24 hours' notice required); and even evening walk exploring the city's black magic traditions and legends. Great culinary tours (including street food) are also offered.

Galle Fort Tours　　　　　　　　TOURS
(Church St; tours from Rs 3000; ⊙9am-5pm) Several of Galle's tuk-tuk drivers offer tours around Galle, though the Fort is best explored on foot. They wait around the Galle Fort Hotel or Old Gate. These guys are real characters.

✨ Festivals & Events

Galle Literary Festival   CULTURAL
(www.galleliteraryfestival.com; ☺ Jan) One of Sri Lanka's most important cultural events, this annual festival brings together renowned Asian and Western writers for workshops, talks and literary lunches and dinners.

🛏 Sleeping

The Fort has a fast-expanding selection of places to stay, including some outstanding heritage hotels, though few really good budget places. Definitely book ahead in high season as demand keeps spiralling ever upward. The surrounding region also has several options, including resort-style hotels with pools.

THE SOUTH GALLE

🛏 Fort

★ Pilgrim's Hostel   HOSTEL $
(☎ 077 698 0257; pilgrimsgalle@yahoo.com; 6 Sudharmalaya Rd; dm US$13; 🛜) Virtually opposite the Sudharmalaya Buddhist temple, this excellent new hostel has two good-quality mixed dorms; each bed is equipped with a private reading light, fan, mossie net and electric socket. A complimentary breakfast is included and there's a dining area for socialising and tea sipping or beer quaffing.

Pedlar's Inn Hostel   GUESTHOUSE $
(☎ 091-222 7443; www.pedlarsinn.com; 62 Lighthouse St; dm US$12-17, r US$50-60; ❄🛜) A bright, inviting guesthouse that features very good hostel rooms. Each has three or four beds, is fan-cooled and boasts reading lights and lockers. Two private rooms have air-con. You can rent bikes and serve yourself from the breakfast bar; there's no curfew.

Mrs ND Wijenayake's Guest House   GUESTHOUSE $
(Beach Haven; ☎ 091-223 4663; www.beachhaven-galle.com; 65 Lighthouse St; r Rs 2500-6000; ❄🛜) The wonderful Mrs Wijenayake and her family have been hosting grateful backpackers since 1968 and their hospitality shows in this comfy guesthouse. The rooms range from the clean and simple with shared bathrooms to fancier air-con rooms; all beds have mossie nets. Lonely Planet cofounder Tony Wheeler had an extended stay here in 1977.

Light House View Inn   GUESTHOUSE $
(☎ 091-223 2056; www.lighthouseviewinn.com; 44 Hospital St; r basic Rs 2500, r with fan/air-con Rs 3500/7000; ❄🛜) A popular budget inn that enjoys a superb position opposite Galle's

---

🏃 Town Walk
The Historic Fort

START CLOCK TOWER
FINISH CLOCK TOWER
LENGTH 2.75KM; THREE TO FOUR HOURS

This walk will take you past many of Galle's highlights as you traverse over four centuries of history. One of the Fort's great charms is that detours and aimless wanderings are rewarded, so don't hesitate to stray from the following route.

Start at the **①Clock Tower**, which, unlike so many worldwide, actually displays the correct time thanks to the fine engineering of the 1882 British mechanism inside. Stop to look out across the cricket stadium to the New Town, with its ceaseless bustle. Walk down along the inside of the wall and pause at the British-built **②Main Gate** (p108). Avoid the careening three-wheelers and cross Lighthouse St, following the walls to the **③Sun Bastion**, with its fine views of the harbour.

Head back down off the wall and proceed up Church St to the heart of old Dutch Galle. Admire the deep porches of the **④Amangalla** (p109) hotel, then cross Middle St to the cool confines of the **⑤Dutch Reformed Church** (p109). Across from the church is a 1901 **⑥bell tower**, which rings for tsunami warnings. Continue south on Church St to **⑦All Saints Anglican Church** at the corner of Church Cross St. Constructed 1868–71, its solid rock structure would look right at home in an English village. Leave some money in the donation box, as relentless repairs are necessary to preserve the building. Just further south is the impressive facade of the 17th-century **⑧Fort Bazaar** (p114) hotel.

Retrace your steps and turn east on Queens St. Admire the 1683 **⑨Dutch Governor's House**. A slab over the doorway bears the date 1683 and Galle's ubiquitous cockerel symbol. Walk down the gentle hill and stop to admire both sides of the **⑩Old Gate** (p108). Now make your way back up the walls to the Fort's northeast corner and the **⑪Zwart Bastion**, thought to be Portuguese built. It

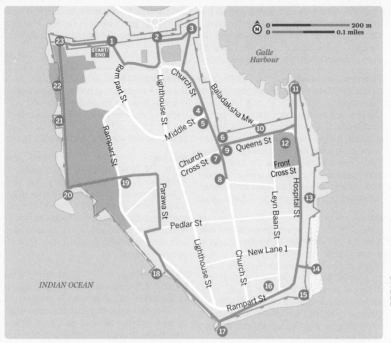

is the oldest of the Fort bastions, with some portions dating to 1580.

Make your way down to the vast leafy expanse of **12 Court Sq**. As the name implies, various courts and related offices ring the sides. On weekdays you'll see people in the shade of the huge banyan trees nervously awaiting their turn in court. Follow Hospital St south and you'll encounter the lavishly restored **13 Dutch Hospital** (p109), which once was filled with victims of the plague, but now boasts a slew of smart cafes. You might even consider a dip at **14 Lighthouse Beach** (p108).

At the southeast corner of the Fort you can't miss the British-built **15 lighthouse** (p108). Just west along Rampart St is the shining white and imposing **16 Meeran Mosque**, the centre of Galle's vibrant Muslim community. Continue west to the fun and frolic at **17 Flag Rock** (p108), a good place to see so many of the submerged rocks that have claimed dozens of ships through the centuries. Walk the walls northwest to **18 Triton Bastion**, a great place to be at sunset.

Now come down off the wall to the cafe-lined Pedlar St and make a quick turn north on Parawa St. These two narrow blocks have

some of the most typical of the old Dutch colonial houses, complete with characteristic thick columns and shaded porches. Curve west and at the corner of Rampart St you'll find **19 Sudharmalaya Temple** with its compact dagoba and large reclining Buddha. If you have the good fortune to be here on a full-moon day, you can expect to see all sorts of ceremonies, many featuring coloured lights and candles after dark.

Head back up onto the wall at **20 Clippenberg Bastion**. In the usually gentle surf surging around the rocks and sand below you may well see sea turtles feeding at dusk. Head north along the walls and enjoy the vast grassy expanse that until very recently was part of Galle's modern-day army base. Today you're more likely to see a cow chewing its cud than a recruit standing at attention.

North of **21 Aeolus Bastion**, look for the small **22 tomb** of the Muslim saint Dathini Ziryam outside the wall. At the northwest corner of the Fort, pause at the **23 Star Bastion**, which has ample evidence of the area's dark past; the fortifications were used at various times by the Dutch as a prison and slave quarters. Now complete your circuit at the Clock Tower.

landmark lighthouse. Accommodation is less inspiring than the view, but adequate: book a balcony room for *those* vistas; note that the cheapest options share a bathroom. Expect an early alarm call from the mosque next door.

Seagreen Guest House
GUESTHOUSE **$$**

(☑ 091-224 2754; www.seagreen-guesthouse.com; 19B Rampart St; s/d US$45/52; ❄ ☏) A simple elegance defines this fine guesthouse. Its five whitewashed, air-conditioned rooms feature colourful Indian textiles and a splash of artwork, while some have excellent ocean views. The bathrooms are some of the best in this price range and the rooftop terrace has sublime sunset views over the ramparts and the salt-spraying Indian Ocean. Breakfast is extra.

Frangipani Motel
GUESTHOUSE **$$**

(☑ 091-222 2324; www.frangipanigallefort.com; 32 Pedlar St; r US$45-65; ❄ ☏) Frangipani is a comfortable family-run guesthouse with rooms in two buildings that straddle Pedlar St. Choose from five different price tariffs; the most expensive have two double beds; all have air-con and an en suite bathroom. Decor is somewhat garish and a tad kitsch, but rooms are well-maintained and there's a lovely front garden for socialising.

Fort Dew Guesthouse
GUESTHOUSE **$$**

(☑ 091-222 4365; www.fortdew.com; 31 Rampart St; r from Rs 5500; ❄ ☏) Set close to the ancient city walls on the quieter side of the Fort, this small guesthouse has a simple yet tasteful theme of white walls and dark wood.

GALLE READS

The following books are on sale at shops within the Fort:

➡ *Galle: As Quiet As Asleep* by Norah Roberts. Galle's long-time librarian offers an interesting and very readable take on local history.

➡ *Around the Fort in 80 Lives* by Juliet Coombe and Daisy Perry. Profiles residents of the Fort who recount stories both amazing and illuminating.

➡ *Drawn to Galle Fort* by Juliet Coombe. This exhaustive guide includes themed walks of the Fort and details of the new town and the sights beyond.

➡ *Galle Fort* by Mark Thompson and Karl Steinberg. A compact and detailed illustrated tour of the Unesco sites.

---

and rooms enjoy shared balconies overlooking the ramparts towards the sea. There's a rooftop terrace cafe and bar.

New Old Dutch House
HOTEL **$$**

(☑ 091-223 2987; www.newolddutchhouse.lk; 21 Middle St; r US$44-55; ❄ ☏) This place (with the timeless name) has beautifully presented, spacious rooms with creaky, polished wooden floors and lovely soft beds; all have satellite TV, fridge and air-con. Breakfast can be enjoyed under the courtyard's papaya trees.

Fort Inn
GUESTHOUSE **$$**

(☑ 091-224 8094; rasikafortinn@yahoo.com; 31 Pedlar St; r Rs 3500-5000; ❄ @ ☏) The ever-beaming owner of this guesthouse offers decent, basic rooms and a perfect people-watching balcony. Economy rooms are somewhat cramped, but you can enjoy amenities such as a fridge and air-con in the more expensive options.

★ Fort Printers
BOUTIQUE HOTEL **$$$**

(☑ 091-224 7977; www.thefortprinters.com; 39 Pedlar St; r US$185-190; ❄ @ ☏ ❋) In the heart of the Fort, this imposing 1825 structure once housed printing presses, and later school classrooms. Today it's divided into two sections: rooms in the older part have enormous wooden beams and are supremely spacious, while the other wing houses more contemporary rooms with sleek, modern decor. The in-house restaurant (p116) is one of the best in Galle.

★ Antic Guesthouse
BOUTIQUE HOTEL **$$$**

(☑ 077 901 9324; www.antic.lk; 3 New Lane 1; r US$60-75; ❄ ☏) This historic property has been sympathetically converted into an inviting guesthouse by the friendly, artistic hosts who have a keen eye for design. Rooms have stylish lighting, painted floorboards and seaside appeal, as well as mod cons including air-con, flat-screen TVs and hairdryers. A delicious breakfast is included.

★ Fort Bazaar
HERITAGE HOTEL **$$$**

(☑ 077 363 8381; www.teardrop-hotels.com/fort-bazaar; 26 Church St; r/ste from US$175/295; ❄ @ ☏) An outstanding nine-year renovation has transformed this 17th-century townhouse into one of Galle's most evocative hotels, with 18 gorgeous, commodious rooms and suites, each with espresso machines and wonderful bathrooms, and finished in natural tones. It's also home to the excellent Church Street Social restaurant and bar, and boasts a small library and a spa. A pool is planned, too.

Amangalla BOUTIQUE HOTEL **$$$**
(☑ 091-223 3388; www.amanresorts.com; 10 Church St; r from US$500; ✳@🖥🖂) One of the Fort's most famous buildings, this Aman hotel boasts lashings of colonial opulence. Its reception rooms (all polished teak floors and period furnishings) are quite something: witness spiffily dressed staff waltzing around bearing gifts (cocktails) to guests. There are several categories of rooms – all luxurious and immaculately presented, and with four-poster beds – though the least expensive are small-ish. In its previous incarnation as the New Oriental Hotel, the building housed generations of travellers. You can recall those days – and the Dutch family who ran the place – in the beautiful library, which, like the gorgeous pool, offers a reason to leave your room.

Galle Fort Hotel BOUTIQUE HOTEL **$$$**
(☑ 091-223 2870; www.galleforthotel.com; 28 Church St; r/ste from US$310/375; ✳@🖥🖂) Following a Unesco-commended renovation, this former 17th-century Dutch merchant's house is now a breathtaking boutique hotel. The rooms are all different: some have two levels and others stretch across entire floors. Linens are exquisite and you won't find any distractions such as TVs – rather, you can enjoy the courtyard pool and serenity.

Fortaleza BOUTIQUE HOTEL **$$$**
(☑ 091-223 3415; www.fortaleza.lk; 9 Church Cross St; r US$125-165; ✳🖥) This former spice warehouse has been transformed into a fabulous small hotel. Each room exudes relaxed luxury, with furnishings that have a colonial feel, without the pomp, and spacious bathrooms. Opt for the Library Room, which has a huge round window that bathes the interior in light.

🛏 Around Galle

Maggie Garden Hostel HOSTEL **$**
(☑ 091-223 2836; www.facebook.com/maggiehostel; 492 Dangedera Mawatha; dm US$10, r US$30-45; @🖥) This new hostel is 3km inland from the Fort, but it's an easy ride by bus or three-wheeler, or there are bicycles for hire. The detached building is highly attractive, there's a lovely garden to enjoy, and a kitchen for guest use. Rates are good considering the quality of the fan-cooled dorms (mixed and female) and private rooms.

Tamarind Hill BOUTIQUE HOTEL **$$$**
(☑ 091-222 6568; www.asialeisure.lk; 288 Galle Rd; r/ste from US$160/270; ✳🖥🖂) This 19th-century former British admiral's mansion is

now a terrific boutique hotel with 10 luxurious rooms, fine service and a jungle-fringed pool. Rooms are set in long colonnaded wings and are furnished with antiques, oil paintings and oriental rugs. Guests get the run of a high-ceilinged guest lounge, dining room and bar. It's 2km west of the new town.

Sun House BOUTIQUE HOTEL **$$$**
(☑ 091-438 0275; www.thesunhouse.com; 18 Upper Dickson Rd; r/ste from US$160/240; ✳🖥🖂) This gracious old villa, built in the 1860s by a Scottish spice merchant, is located on the shady hill above the new town. The eight rooms vary in size, although even the smallest is a crisply decorated gem. There's a good collection of books to browse in the lounge, a lovely garden to enjoy and fine dining in the restaurant.

Jetwing Lighthouse Hotel RESORT **$$$**
(☑ 091-222 3744; www.jetwinghotels.com/jetwing lighthouse; Galle Rd; r from US$220; ✳@🖥🖂) Parts of this large resort hotel, located 3km up the coast from the Fort, were designed by legendary Sri Lankan architect Geoffrey Bawa, though other sections are more mundane. Rooms and restaurants won't disappoint, but this Jetwing's trump card is its magnificent ocean-side location, private beach and two gorgeous pools (one 40m).

Closenberg Hotel HISTORIC HOTEL **$$$**
(☑ 091-222 4313; www.closenberghotel.com; 11 Closenberg Rd; r US$90-130; ✳@🖥🖂) Built as a 19th-century P&O captain's residence in the heyday of British mercantile supremacy, this rambling hotel sits on a promontory with views over Galle harbour and the Fort (which is five minutes west by three-wheeler). The rooms are comfortable and atmospheric, though some of the fixtures and fittings could use an upgrade. There's a lovely infinity pool.

🍴 Eating

Be sure to find a table before 9pm as the town gets sleepy fast. Also, many places do not serve any alcohol.

🍴 Fort

You can't beat dining inside the Fort for atmosphere. Note, however, that few places are air-conditioned, so dinner is usually a better option for a relaxed, romantic meal, rather than sweaty lunch.

Dairy King DESSERTS **$**
(☑ 091-222 5583; 69A Church St; treats from Rs 250; ⏰11am-10pm) The King family have been

whipping up Galle's best ice cream for many years from their window-front outlet. The crunchy cashew and passionfruit flavours are simply divine, and satisfyingly rich cakes are also sold.

★ Spoon's Cafe
SRI LANKAN $$

(☑ 077 938 3340; 100 Pedlar St; meals from Rs 450; ⊙ 11am-9pm) For authentic Galle-style rice and curry, this minuscule place (there are only four tables) can't be beat. Chef Shamil Roshan Careem hails from one of the Fort's oldest families and he prepares traditional family recipes. Save room for dessert; try his superb 'Silk Route Toffee'.

★ Royal Dutch Cafe
CAFE $$

(☑ 077 177 4949; 72 Leyn Baan St; meals Rs 550-850; ⊙ 8am-7pm; 🕏) The sign says 'Relax Zone' and this is a fine place to sit back and enjoy the company of cafe owner Fazal Badurdeen, who has a million stories to tell. He also seems to have almost that many teas and coffees, from cinnamon to cardamom to ginger. There's a small menu of curries and good banana pancakes for breakfast.

There are just four tables, or enjoy Galle street life from the colonnaded terrace.

Mamas Galle Fort Cafe
SRI LANKAN $$

(☑ 091-223 5214; 67 Church St; mains Rs 450-750; ⊙ 11am-9pm) Malini Perera and her daughters have been cooking for curry-hunting travellers for decades, and their much-loved and dead-simple rice and curries still hit the spot, though prices have invariably risen. Breakfast, either Western or Eastern (with hoppers) is filling, fresh and delicious, too. Good cooking classes (US$30) include a trip to the new town market.

Serendipity Arts Cafe
INTERNATIONAL $$

(☑ 091-224 6815; 65 Leyn Baan St; meals Rs 500-900; ⊙ 8am-9pm; 🕏) This boho cafe has a fusion menu that includes Western sandwiches and Eastern curries, fresh juices and shakes, bacon-and-egg hoppers and filter coffee. It's a very casual place, with a pretty patio and lots of artwork to enjoy.

Heritage Cafe
INTERNATIONAL $$

(☑ 091-224 6668; 53 Lighthouse St; meals Rs 500-950; ⊙ 8am-10pm; 🕏) The menu here covers all bases with filling sandwiches, pasta, steaks and, yes, even local curries. Choose between eating on the sunny terrace, under the lazy interior fans or out in the courtyard garden. Or just cool off with a fresh juice, shake or iced coffee on one of Galle's typically sultry days.

Cafe Punto
SRI LANKAN $$

(42 Pedlar St; meals Rs 500-800; ⊙ 11am-9pm) The praise for this rice-and-curry joint is far wider than its narrow dining room. It also serves tasty Chinese-style fried rice and noodle dishes and decent fish and chips. Lassis, juices and fresh coconuts are well-priced, too.

★ Fort Printers
INTERNATIONAL $$$

(☑ 091-224 7977; www.thefortprinters.com; 39 Pedlar St; meals Rs1000-1800; 🕏) The ideal venue for a memorable meal, this hotel restaurant offers a concise menu featuring fresh seafood and organic local produce. It's especially good for Mediterranean-inspired dishes (such as slow-roasted leg of goat), while traditional Sri Lankan rice and curry is also excellent. Dine in the frangipani-shaded courtyard at the rear or in the imposing dining room.

★ Church Street Social
INTERNATIONAL $$$

(☑ 077 007 2597; www.teardrop-hotels.com; Fort Bazaar Hotel, 26 Church St; meals Rs1200-3500; ⊙ 7am-10pm; 🕏) A classy retreat from Galle's steamy streets, this refined air-conditioned hotel restaurant is the perfect setting for a great meal, with the formality of its colonial dining rooms offset with hip lighting to eclectic effect. The menu is varied: sandwiches, wraps and burgers, starters including fine tuna sashimi, and mains such as Moroccan lamb tagine or pork tenderloin.

Elita Restaurant
SEAFOOD $$$

(☑ 077 242 3442; www.facebook.com/elita.restaurant; 34 Middle St; meals Rs 650-2000; ⊙ 8am-11pm) Thirteen years of work as a chef in Belgium gave Krishantha Suranjith myriad skills in preparing seafood. His restaurant has great views out to the lighthouse and harbour and is a fine place to sample the local salt water bounty. Opt for a table out front or upstairs in the cute dining room.

🍴 New Town

South Ceylon Bakery
SRI LANKAN $

(☑ 091-223 4500; 6 Gamini Mawatha; snacks Rs 100-300; ⊙ 8.30am-9pm) Opposite the bus station, this highly popular lunch spot, with its impossible-to-resist sweet and savoury short eats and tasty curries, is an authentic place to eat in the new town.

★ Old Railway Cafe
CAFE $$

(☑ 077 626 3400; www.theoldrailwaycafe.wordpress.com; 42 Havelock Pl; mains Rs 600-900; ⊙ 10am-6pm Mon-Sat; 🕏) Right across the small canal from the namesake station, this fashionable upstairs cafe has artfully mismatched furnishings and a boho vibe. You'll find an enticing menu of creative soups, salads and mains, with dishes such as pesto-crusted chicken patties with coleslaw, as well as espresso coffee and good juices. After you've eaten, browse the clothes, jewellery and bags in the store downstairs.

Drinking & Nightlife

Galle is not known for its nightlife, but you can find a few spots for a relaxing beverage.

Amangalla COCKTAIL BAR
(☑ 091-223 3388; www.aman.com/resorts/amangalla; 10 Church St; ☺ 11am-11pm; 🛜) Live the dream and sip an exquisite mixed drink (mocktails Rs 800, cocktails start at Rs 1200) or a glass of fine wine at Galle's landmark hotel. The setting, either on the classy front veranda or in the stately Zaal lounge, is simply stunning.

Shopping

Galle's history makes it a natural spot for antique shopping. You'll also find a growing number of designer-owned shops and up-market boutiques. Many stores in the new town close on Sunday.

★ **Withered Leaves** TEA
(☑ 077 225 0621; www.witheredleaves.com; Dutch Hospital, Hospital Rd) Specialist tea store with an amazing range of top-quality green teas, white teas, Ceylon garden teas, blended teas and single-estate teas. There's no hard sell and staff are highly informed.

★ **Stick No Bills** ART
(☑ 091-224 2504; www.sticknobillsonline.com; 35 Church St; ☺ 8am-8pm) Super-stylish reproduction posters (Rs 3000) and postcards (Rs 350) covering Sri Lanka through the decades. Many of the beautiful vintage airline images for Ceylon sell a tropical paradise of fantasy. The classic film posters are also superb.

★ **Shoba Display Gallery** ARTS & CRAFTS
(☑ 091-222 4351; www.shobafashion.org; 67A Pedlar St; ☺ 7.30am-10pm) 🖉 Beautiful lacework made right here. The shop teaches local women dyeing crafts and ensures them a fair price for their work. Even if you're not buying, pop in to witness the process of making lace, or sign up to a lace-making (Rs 2000) or papermaking (Rs 1800) class. There's a small cafe, too.

Old Railway CLOTHING
(☑ 077 626 3400; www.theoldrailwaycafe.wordpress. com; 42 Havelock St; ☺ 10am-6pm Mon-Sat) An eclectic, interesting store where most of the clothing, jewellery, bags, toys and gifts are designed in-house, made from locally sourced materials, and created right on the premises. Check out the upstairs cafe, too.

Barefoot ARTS & CRAFTS
(☑ 091-222 6299; www.barefootceylon.com; 41 Pedlar St; ☺ 9am-8pm Mon-Sat, 10am-6pm Sun) Chic boutique selling colourful local clothing, jewellery, linen and rugs, crafts and gifts. The book section has an excellent selection of Sri Lanka–related titles.

Olanda Antiques ANTIQUES
(☑ 091-223 4398; www.olandafurniture.com; 30 Leyn Baan St; ☺ 9am-6pm) A vast Aladdin's cave of antique furniture and perfect reproduction pieces are among the treasures you'll find in this Dutch colonial house. There's also an attached cafe. Look out for the vintage cars (a 1936 Austin and a 1945 Morris Minor) parked outside.

ℹ Information

Galle has a few scammers and small-time hustlers – a firm 'I have no interest in anything you have to offer' should do the trick. Dark corners of the ramparts are best avoided at night.

There is no shortage of banks and ATMs, both in the Fort and the new town.

ATM (Lighthouse St) In the Fort.

Main post office (Main St; ☺ 8am-5pm Mon-Fri, to 1pm Sat) Near the market.

Post office (Church St; ☺ 8am-4.30pm Mon-Thu & Sat, 8-11.45am Fri) A small branch office in the Fort.

SriLankan Airlines (☑ 091-224 6942; 3rd fl, 16 Gamini Mawatha) You can book flights here; it also offers a full range of travel services.

ℹ Getting There & Away

BUS

There are plenty of local buses linking the towns along the coastal road, though very few air-con services. Buses leave from the **bus station** (Main St) in the new town and operate roughly every 10 to 20 minutes between 4.30am and 8pm on all routes. Destinations include the following:

Colombo (via coastal road) Rs 143, 3¼ hours
Hikkaduwa Rs 36, 30 minutes
Matara Rs 65, 1¼ hours
Weligama Rs 28, 40 minutes

EX001 air-conditioned buses using the Southern Expressway from Colombo to Galle (Rs 400 to 550, 1½ hours, every 20 minutes) use a terminal in the southern Colombo suburb of Maharagama; there are also buses from Kadawatha. Buses that take the expressway save at least two hours compared with the coastal road. Note that it can take up to 2½ hours from Galle to Bandaranaike International Airport, but this will shorten as additional sections of expressway are opened.

CAR
Galle is an exit on the Southern Expressway, a toll road.

TRAIN
The railway route along the coast from Colombo Fort to Galle is easily the most scenic and atmospheric way to journey between the two cities. The website www.seat61.com is far more user-friendly for checking services and prices than the official Sri Lanka Railways one. There are at least six express trains a day on the Colombo–Matara line, which all stop at Galle. There's also one daily 5.10am service from Kandy to Galle (2nd/3rd class Rs 320/175, 6½ hours), returning from Galle at 2.45pm. Note the southern railway line is being extended as far east as Kataragama; work is expected to be completed by 2018.

Destinations include the following:

Colombo Fort 2nd/3rd class Rs 180/100, 2¼ to 3½ hours, seven to nine daily

Hikkaduwa 2nd/3rd class Rs 40/20, 30 minutes, six to nine daily

Matara 2nd/3rd class Rs 80/40, one to 1½ hours, five to seven daily

Unawatuna & Around
☑ 091 / POP 4800

With palm-lined beaches, turquoise waters and a good selection of guesthouses and restaurants, Unawatuna is very popular with travellers. The resort's location is superb, with the historic city of Galle just 6km away and a wooded headland to the west dotted with tiny coves.

Years of insensitive development, however, have resulted in an unappealing sprawl of concrete hotels and restaurants packed together right on the shore, blocking views of the bay in many spots.

Erosion caused by the construction of ill-advised breakwaters have also hit Unawatuna hard, causing massive loss of sand to its fabled beaches. By 2012 the resort was in a poor state. But recent initiatives have certainly improved things, as the authorities have pumped sand from deep water offshore to widen the beach, which is now looking in better shape than it has for years.

Atmosphere-wise, Unawatuna is lively without being rowdy: think sunset drinks rather than all-night raves.

◉ Sights & Activities

Unawatuna doesn't have a lot in the way of surf breaks thanks to a fringing reef, though there is a gentle break right at the western end of the bay that a few locals ride. The main beach is fine for frolicking and body-surfing. You can easily rent gear to **snorkel** the reefs a short distance from the west end of the beach.

There are several interesting **wreck dives** around Unawatuna, as well as reef and cave diving. Wrecks include the *Lord Nelson,* a cargo ship that sank in 2000; it has a 15m-long cabin to explore. The remains of a 100-year-old British steamer, the 33m *Rangoon,* are a 30-minute boat ride south of Unawatuna.

Yatagala Raja
Maha Viharaya   BUDDHIST TEMPLE
(donation Rs 100) Just 4km inland from Unawatuna, the Yatagala Raja Maha Viharaya is a quiet rock temple with a 9m reclining Buddha. The mural-covered walls are painted in the typical style of the Kandyan period. Monks have been living here for at least 1500 years. You'll seldom find crowds here, which only adds to the appeal. As you ascend the long flights of stairs, there are good views over the rice fields.

Buddhist Temple   BUDDHIST TEMPLE
This small Buddhist temple at the west end of the beach has amazing bay views and also a vigilant monk ready to chase away anyone who is hoping to feign some piety in return for a shady rest.

★ **Sri Yoga Shala**   YOGA
(☑ 076 569 1672, 077 300 2802; www.sriyogashala.com; Durage Watta, Metaramba; 90min class Rs 1900; ☏) This incredible rural retreat, 3km inland from Unawatuna is one of Sri Lanka's very best, with amazing facilities including a yoga studio with jungle views and a gorgeous saltwater pool; a garden cafe is also planned. There are three daily yoga sessions (in vinyasa, Iyengar, hatha, slow-flow and yin styles); workshops, teacher training and treatments are also available. Various accommodation packages with local hotels are possible; consult the website for details. Sri Yoga Shala is Rs 400 in a three-wheeler from Unawatuna.

Yoga with Asiri   YOGA
(☑ 077 176 4662; www.yogawithasiri.net; 6 Wella Dewala Rd; classes from Rs 1200; ⊙ classes 9.30am daily, also 6pm Dec-Apr) Asiri is a popular instructor who wins plaudits for his teaching style and general enthusiasm. Treatments and massages (Rs 3000 per hour) are also available.

Sanctuary Spa SPA

(☑ 077 307 8583; www.sanctuaryspaunawatuna.com; 136 Wella Dewala Rd; 1hr full body massage Rs 3200; ☉ 9am-6pm) If a holiday means doing nothing more strenuous than being utterly pampered, the Sanctuary Spa should be music to your knotted muscles. Reflexology, aromatherapy and a good variety of massages are offered.

Unawatuna Diving Centre DIVING

(☑ 091-224 4693; www.unawatunadiving.com; off Galle-Matara Rd; 2-tank boat dives €60, PADI courses from €215) The only dive shop with a decompression unit. It offers refresher programs (€40), discovery dives and rents out underwater cameras.

Sea Horse Scuba Diving Centre DIVING

(☑ 091-228 3733; www.seahorsedivinglanka.com; off Galle-Matara Rd; snorkel gear hire per day Rs 1000, shore dive €25) A well-regarded PADI outfit that offers a range of snorkelling and dive tours, including trips to the wreck of the *Rangoon,* as well as night dives.

Sonjas Health Food Restaurant COOKING

(☑ 077 961 5310, 091-224 5815; Wella Dewala Rd; half-day course Rs 3000) These enjoyable cookery courses involve you preparing five different curry dishes and will have you mixing your own curry powder in no time. The course is led by the lovely Karuna and a trip to Galle market is included in the price. Book ahead.

🛏 Sleeping

Unawatuna is home to a good number of small budget and midrange guesthouses. Most beachside hotels are unattractive and several are built atop landfill. There are also budget places right on busy Galle-Matara

Rd: avoid them unless you enjoy being serenaded by honking buses and trucks.

Dutch Hostel HOSTEL $

(☑ 077 144 5732; www.facebook.com/TheDutch Hostel; Maharamba Rd; dm/r Rs 1200/2400; 🛜) A sociable hostel run by helpful crew with four mixed dorms, all with shared bathrooms, and a double room with an en suite. There's a nice roof terrace, a large lounge area and a guest kitchen. Breakfast is included. It is well inland from the beach, however, and the restrictions are a tad ageist – no over 40s.

★ **Villa Malena** GUESTHOUSE $$

(☑ 077 112 7156; www.facebook.com/villamalena unawatuna; 61C Bulathwatta; s/d US$26/28) On a quiet road off the main Galle-Matara highway, this fine modern guesthouse has immaculately clean and inviting rooms with high-quality furnishings and four-poster beds. It's exceptional value for money, though you are 2km from the beach (Rs 400 in a three-wheeler). There are bikes for hire.

Saadhana Bird House GUESTHOUSE $$

(☑ 091-222 4953; www.birdhouseun.wordpress.com; Yaddehimulla Rd; r US$45-65; 🗙 🛜) A charming – and yes, a bird-loving – family run this guesthouse. It's simple, clean and close to the beach, with both old rooms and better modern rooms. The road is quiet. There's good birding from the rooftop terrace and there's plenty of feathered-friend spotting info on offer. Tasty local fare is also available.

Weliwatta House GUESTHOUSE $$

(☑ 091-222 6642; www.weliwattahouseunawatuna. com; Yaddehimulla Rd; r with fan US$27-39, with air-con US$49; 🗙 🛜) Offering character and

THE SOUTH UNAWATUNA & AROUND

SHORT WALKS

There are numerous good walks in and around Unawatuna. For views to the other side of the promontory with Galle Fort far in the distance, head up the hill behind Yaddehimulla Rd.

Another pleasant option is to walk north around the rocky outcrop at the west end of the beach to **Rumassala**, known for its protected medicinal herbs. Legend has it that Hanuman, the monkey god, dropped herbs carried from the Himalayas here.

You can also wander up to the **Rumassala Peace Pagoda** FREE on top of the hill. This impressive pagoda was built by Japanese Buddhist monks of the Mahayana sect in 2005, as part of their scheme to build peace temples in conflict zones (the Sri Lankan war was raging at the time). It's a (steep) 20-minute hike from the west end of Unawatuna beach.

Isolated **Jungle Beach** on the north side of the peninsula is also a popular destination, and if you don't feel up for the 2km walk over the hill through dense canopy to this bay, you can access it by scooter or three-wheeler via the Galle-Matara Rd. One of those 'secret' spots that everyone seems to knows about, there are a couple of slim-line sandy coves here, some snorkelling offshore (though the reef is degraded) and a cafe (the venue for excellent DJ-driven parties on Wednesdays in high season).

Unawatuna

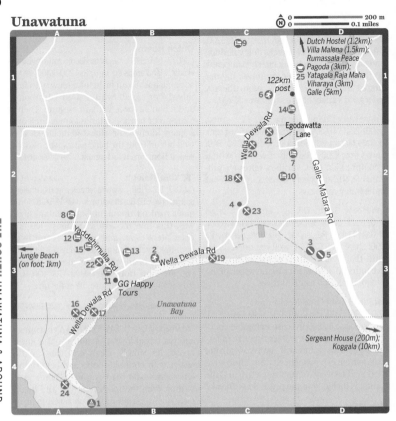

charm, this attractive buttercup-yellow villa was built in 1900 and has a lush garden to enjoy (where you may spot monkeys, monitor lizards and woodpeckers). There

are a couple of spacious and tidy rooms with hot-water bathrooms in the main building and newer and more comfortable rooms behind.

Srimali's Residence   GUESTHOUSE **$$**
(📞 077 337 7826; nalakakk@gmail.com; 206 Galle-Matara Rd; r US$28; ✳️ 🛜) Located down a tiny lane on the beach side of the Matara highway, Srimali's has a convenient location and offers fine value. Rooms are bright and airy, with four-poster beds, mosquito nets, balconies and hot-water private bathrooms. The family owners are helpful, rent bikes and scooters, and can help with onward transport.

Bedspace Guesthouse   HOTEL **$$**
(📞 091-225 0156; www.bedspaceuna.com; Egodawatta Lane; r US$50-72; ✳️ 🛜) A superb guesthouse run by two expat mates (one from the UK, one from New Zealand), located down a quiet lane set back from the beach. Rooms are spacious and well presented, all with air-con and iPod docks, and some with colossal beds. It's perfect for foodies, as the owners are top chefs: breakfast is a magnificent spread, while dinner is a memorable occasion.

Palm Grove   GUESTHOUSE **$$**
(📞 091-225 0104; www.palmgrovesrilanka.com; off Wella Dewala Rd; r US$50-65; ✳️ 🛜) This little English-run gem of a guesthouse has five spacious rooms, all with air-con and ceiling fans, that are very comfortable and have nice private outdoor porches. Upstairs is a roof terrace filled with hammocks. Breakfast is extra, but worth the $US4 charged.

Nooit Gedacht   HISTORIC HOTEL **$$**
(📞 091-222 3449; www.nooitgedachtheritage.com; Galle-Matara Rd; r US$45-80; ✳️ @ 🛜 🏊) At the heart of this compound is an atmospheric 1735 Dutch colonial mansion, which is slightly tumbledown but perfectly enchanting. Rooms are divided between an old wing and a newish two-storey block. Mountain bikes are available for rent, Ayurvedic treatments can be arranged, and there are two pools in the lush, beautiful garden.

Primrose Guest House   GUESTHOUSE **$$**
(📞 077 607 4428, 091-222 4679; www.primrose.wz.cz; Yaddehimulla Rd; r with fan/ air-con from US$35/45; ✳️ 🛜) This bright three-storey guesthouse is close to the beach and has pleasant communal balconies for chilling. The tidy and spacious rooms are well maintained, though the decor is mismatched and perhaps a tad kitsch.

Sergeant House   BOUTIQUE HOTEL **$$$**
(📞 077-356 5433; www.sergeanthouse.com; 381 Galle-Matara Road; r US$145-280, bungalow US$600;

✳️ 🛜 🏊) Set well back from the busy road, these very comfortable units (rooms, suites and a three-bedroom bungalow) all have a homely ambience thanks to rugs, carvings, art and the American owner's decorative taste. There's a supremely fecund tropical garden, with a 20m pool, plus a games room (with dartboard), a small gym and a spa.

Secret Garden   GUESTHOUSE **$$$**
(📞 091-224 1857; www.secretgardenunawatuna.com; off Wella Dewala Rd; r/ste from US$100/130; ✳️ 🛜) This renovated 140-year-old house has a range of rooms that are colour coordinated with the flowers in the lovely garden. Choose from rooms, suites and good-value bungalows. There are twice-daily yoga sessions during the main holiday season and Ayurvedic treatments are also available.

Dream House   GUESTHOUSE **$$$**
(📞 091-438 1541; www.dreamhouse-srilanka.com; off Yaddehimulla Rd; d/tr US$65/75; ✳️ 🛜) This Italian-owned house has four intimate rooms that have been decorated in a Rome-meets-the-tropics fusion. It's got a large terrace that's great for relaxing while you count the monkeys leaping overhead; there's a good in-house Italian restaurant, too. There are substantial discounts during low season.

🍴 Eating

Most hotels and guesthouses offer meals, and the beach is lined with places that are good for fresh seafood. For self-catering, there are simple grocery stores on the inland portion of Wella Dewala Rd.

Roti Shop   SRI LANKAN **$**
(Wella Dewala Rd; snacks from Rs 80; ⏲ 10am-10pm) A very simple place with a couple of street-side tables. Offers tasty *rottis,* including dozens of sweet and savoury breads jammed full of cheeses, fruits and more, that make for a tasty snack.

★ Jinas Vegetarian and Vegan Restaurant   VEGETARIAN **$$**
(📞 091-222 6878; Wella Dewala Rd; meals Rs 500-800; ⏲ 11am-9pm) This mighty fine place offers a wide array of Indian food (thalis and masala dosas) as well as great falafel, wholesome soups and Mexican-style dishes such as *huevos rancheros* (eggs in a spicy tomato sauce). Cold-pressed juices are superb, too. As it's always busy and everything is freshly prepared, you may have to wait a while – enjoy the garden setting.

HIGH TIDE HIGHJINKS

After the 2004 tsunami, laws were passed forbidding construction within 100m of the high-tide line on any beach in Sri Lanka. Unfortunately, a quick drive along many coastal areas will show that these laws have been widely ignored. This is especially apparent on the south coast, where the tsunami's destruction was so complete that most structures date from the last decade or so.

Powerful ocean currents and tides have always made this coastline sensitive to erosion, something the Coast Conservation Department tried to tackle by constructing breakwaters along the coast. Critics say this is being done without adequate scientific research. At Unawatuna the situation was compounded by illegal construction far too close to the shore, resulting in a double environmental whammy.

Regional authorities have attempted to redress the balance by demolishing several such structures in 2011 and placing giant concrete blocks and boulders as improvised sea defences. The shoreline, however, remained a mess. Then in March 2015 authorities hired a ship to suck sand from the sea bottom offshore and to pump it onto Unawatuna's eastern section of beach, resurrecting a broad sandy bay (though some pedants complained the new sand was too coarse). The much-maligned breakwater was also reduced in height.

It remains to be seen whether these measures will be enough to safeguard Unawatuna Beach. Many locals believe that erosion will cease only when the breakwater is completely removed.

Mati Gedara
SRI LANKAN $$

(☑077 790 6723; Egodawatta Lane; meals Rs 350-500; ⊙8am-9.30pm; ⊛) For inexpensive, authentic rice and curry, this appealingly rustic place is well worth seeking out. *Mati gedara* refers to the large earthenware pots the food is served in; a full veggie buffet is just Rs 350; meat and fish dishes are also available. The rich curd and honey is a treat for dessert.

Le Cafe Francais Bakery & Boutique
CAFE $$

(☑077 740 1014; 55/1 Wella Dewala Rd; meals Rs 500-800; ⊙10am-6pm; ⊛) A lovely, civilised little French-owned cafe where you can savour wonderful croissants, cakes and sandwiches, while sipping a latte or cup of tea from a china pot. Staff bake a selection of fine artisan breads and rustle up a mean breakfast, too.

Sunrise Seafood Restaurant
SEAFOOD $$

(off Wella Dewala; mains Rs 650-1200; ⊙11am-9pm) This simple beachfront place gets our vote as the best location in Unawatuna, tucked away near the temple on the west side of the resort, away from the crowds. The menu reflects whatever has been culled from the fishing boats resting on the sand. Order your shrimp with plenty of garlic.

Koko's on the Beach
BURGERS $$

(Wella Dewala Rd; meals Rs 600-1100; ⊙9am-11pm) The beach bar for those who literally can't wait to get home for a tasty burger and fries or authentic fish and chips. Chicken kebabs and fish tacos are other good choices. Gary, the owner, runs a tight ship and the bay views are epic.

Queens Art Cafe
CAFE $$

(☑077 555 1633; Yaddehimulla Rd; mains Rs 450-1000; ⊙8am-9pm; ⊛) A popular traveller cafe with fine espresso coffee and good snacks and meals (curries, fish dishes and breakfasts) in a street-facing, open-sided dining room. There are numerous vegetarian options, too, and books to buy and borrow.

Hot Rock
SRI LANKAN $$

(☑091-224 2685; Wella Dewala Rd; meals Rs 500-1000; ⊙9am-10pm) At this family-run beachside restaurant you can enjoy good local fare plus seafood and cheap beer with your feet in the sand and your eyes on the ocean-filled horizon. The menu trumpets many pork dishes (which are not normally common on local menus).

★Bedspace Kitchen
INTERNATIONAL $$$

(☑091-225 0156; www.bedspaceuna.com; Egodawatta Lane; mains Rs 900-1600; ⊙noon-3.30pm & 6-10pm; ⊛) One of the most progressive, enjoyable restaurants in the country, Bedspace Kitchen has it all right. Around 95% of their ingredients are sourced in Sri Lanka, most are organic and local, and the menu is concise and unpretentious. Stand-out dishes include black pork curry, the sublime sea platter, and the coconut lemon-grass soup;

lunch is more casual. Book ahead as it's wildly, deservedly popular.

Bedspace has an open kitchen and tables dotted around a shady garden.

Bedspace Beach SRI LANKAN **$$$**
(☑ 091-225 0156; www.bedspaceuna.com; 147 Wella Delaya Rd; meals Rs 600-1600; ☺ 8am-10pm; 🛜) This new place offers a mod take on Sri Lankan cooking, with perfect hoppers available all day (including fusion-versions of this dish – try the eggs Benedict hoppers with smoked salmon), a huge selection of authentic curries (including gluten-free and vegan choices) and a dozen or so sambals and relishes. There's great coffee and half of the attractive premises is air-conditioned.

 Drinking & Nightlife

Kat's Coffee CAFE
(☑ 076 856 8495; www.katscoffee.com; 235 Galle-Matara Rd; ☺ 9am-6pm Wed-Mon; 🛜) For the best cafe in Unawatuna, head to Kat's. The German owner only uses premium arabica beans and though prices aren't cheap (a flat white is Rs 480) the coffee is divine, as are the homemade cakes. It's on the badass-busy main highway, but there's ample parking for scooters outside.

ℹ **Information**

GG Happy Tours (☑ 091-225 0376; www.gghappytours.com; Yaddehimulla Rd; ☺ 9am-10pm) Internet access (Rs 250 per hour) and a good place to arrange tour and car-hire services.

ℹ **Getting There & Away**

Coming by bus from Galle (Rs 18, 10 minutes) you can get off at the beach access lane (Wella Dewala Rd) at the 122km post, or get off at the next stop, where the ocean meets the main road. A three-wheeler to or from Galle costs about Rs 500.

Thalpe & Koggala

☑ 091

Beyond Unawatuna, the road runs close to the coast through Thalpe, Dalawella and Koggala, and on to Ahangama and beyond. This is posh country, with beautiful albeit narrow beaches and a long stretch of walled estates and hotels.

Along this part of the coast you will see **stilt fishermen** perching precariously like storks above the waves at high tide. Each

fisherman has a pole firmly embedded in the sea bottom, close to the shore, on which they perch and cast their lines. Stilt positions are passed down from father to son and are highly coveted. You'll be amazed at how fast they can get off those stilts and run up to you for payment if you even vaguely wave a camera in their direction.

👁 **Sights**

★ **Martin Wickramasinghe Folk Art Museum** MUSEUM
(www.martinwickramasinghe.info; off Galle-Matara Rd, Koggala; Rs 200; ☺ 9am-5pm) This interesting museum includes the house where respected Sinhalese author Martin Wickramasinghe (1890–1976) was born (the traditional southern structure dates back 200 years and has some Dutch architectural influences). Exhibits are well displayed, with information in English, with a good section on dance (including costumes and instruments), puppets, *kolam* (masked dance-drama) masks (including one of a very sunburnt British officer), carriages and Buddhist artefacts. Look for the turn near the 131km post, across from the Fortress Hotel.

Koggala Lake LAKE
(☺ boat trips 8am-4.30pm) Next to the road, Koggala Lake is alive with birdlife and dotted with islands, one of which features a Buddhist temple that attracts many visitors on *poya* (full moon) days, another that contains an interesting cinnamon plantation and also an (overpriced and touristy) herb-garden island.

Kataluwa Purwarama Temple BUDDHIST SITE
(☺ 24hr) Rarely crowded, this feels like the temple time forgot. Dating from the 13th century, it has some recently restored murals, including some large ones depicting foreigners in flowing robes. A friendly monk will open the building and explain the murals. Some of the Jataka tales (stories from the Buddha's previous lives) painted here are 200 years old. Turn inland and drive for 1.2km right at the 134km post; there are some signposts to help you navigate the way.

🛏 **Sleeping & Eating**

This stretch of shoreline is dotted with villas and upmarket hotels. There are very few independent restaurants, but virtually all of the large hotels have a fine choice of dining options.

🛏 Thalpe

Thalpe is popular with those looking for a more sedate alternative to nearby Unawatuna. The beach is largely hidden from the road by a solid line of villas, houses and hotels, each with thick walls and massive gates.

★ Frangipani Tree   BOUTIQUE HOTEL $$$
(☑ 091-228 3711; www.thefrangipanitree.com; 182 Galle-Matara Rd, Thalpe; ste from US$250; ❈ 🛜 🏊) Cement, of all things, is the basis for this starkly modern vision of contemporary architecture on the coast. There are nine suites in three houses: all are named after turtle species and have soaring ceilings, private verandahs and ocean views. There's a lovely infinity pool and palm-fringed beach.

Why House   BOUTIQUE HOTEL $$$
(☑ 091-222 7599; www.whyhousesrilanka.com; off Galle-Matara Rd, Thalpe; r from US$250; ❈ 🛜 🏊) This feels more like a private estate than a small hotel, with its expansive grounds and rooms in a colonial house (or cottages). Personal service is emphasised, children are catered to, and all manner of meals can be prepared. However it is a kilometre inland from the shore – look for the turn off from the main road at the 124km post.

Wijaya   INTERNATIONAL $$$
(☑ 091-228 3610; www.wijayabeach.com; Galle-Matara Rd, Thalpe; mains Rs 900-2300; ⊙ 9am-11pm; 🛜) This boutique hotel's restaurant is one of southern Sri Lanka's most renowned places to dine out, famed for its pizza cooked in wood-burning ovens. Bar staff whip up mean cocktails and the seafood specials also win rave reviews. No reservations by phone; use the website to book a table.

🛏 Koggala

Koggala is home to a long, wide, but wave-lashed stretch of beach. The road runs quite close to the shore, but most of the time it remains just out of sight, hidden by the high walls of estates.

Fortress   HOTEL $$$
(☑ 091-438 9400; www.thefortress.lk; Galle-Matara Rd, Koggala; r from US$280; ❈ 🛜 🏊) From the outside this vast place, with its high walls, looks exactly like a prison and a formidable one at that. But inside you'll find it's all wide open in the one direction it should be: the sea. There's a stunning infinity pool, 53 chic urban-style rooms with whirlpool baths and rain showers, and great dining.

Era Beach Hotel   BOUTIQUE HOTEL $$$
(☑ 091-228 2302; www.jetwinghotels.com; 834 Galle-Matara Rd, Thalpe; r US$200; ❈ 🛜 🏊) This is a small boutique hotel, where wood and stone combine to create a Zen-like sense of happiness (the ocean-side setting, coconut-tree-studded lawn and gorgeous pool help out with this, too). However, some of the spacious rooms, with four-posters and polished wood floors, catch a little road noise, and the shore here is rocky – there are fine sands a short walk away.

Mumbo Jumbo   INTERNATIONAL, SRI LANKAN $$$
(☑ 091-228 2497; Galle-Matara Rd, Koggala Beach, Habaraduwa; meals Rs 950-1700; ⊙ 7.30am-10pm; 🛜) A fine new beachfront place run by a young team who know their way around a menu. It's perhaps a tad pricey, but the seafood is excellent: try the crab with black pepper sauce or mahi-mahi with cashews. There are free sun loungers for customers.

DON'T MISS

HANDUNUGODA TEA ESTATE

An exquisite tea plantation in the hills above Koggala, **Handunugoda Tea Estate** (☑ 077 329 0999; www.hermanteas.com; off Kathaluwa Rd; ⊙ 8am-5pm; 🛜) offers (free) highly informative tours of the estate. You'll sample and learn how they produce over 25 varieties of tea here, including the fabled Virgin White tea, a delicate brew made from the tiniest and newest leaves. Where the average large plantation worker will pick 23kg of black tea in a day, the workers here manage but 150 grams of virgin white leaves. It's 6km inland from the coastal highway; signposted from the 131km post.

Handunugoda is owned by Herman Gunaratne, one of the legends of the island's tea industry. Be sure to pick up a copy of Gunaratne's autobiography, *The Suicide Club: A Virgin Tea Planter's Journey*, which is a remarkably entertaining and insightful read about his life, tea and Sri Lanka, from the waning days of the British Raj to today.

ℹ️ Getting There & Away

Buses between Galle and Matara pass through Thalpe and Koggala every 10 to 15 minutes during daylight hours.

Cinnamon Air (Map p60; ☎ 011-247 5475; www.cinnamonair.com) runs a daily scheduled flight between Colombo's Bandaranaike International Airport and the airstrip at Koggala (one-way US$206).

Tuk-tuks are locally available for short journeys, and car rentals (with driver) are convenient for excursions.

Ahangama & Midigama

 041

The Ahangama and Midigama area are home to the most consistent, and possibly the best, surf in Sri Lanka. Development is ongoing in parts, but for now it remains a relatively low-key region with a mix of surfer-friendly accommodation and the odd villa. The shoreline consists of slim sandy bays and rocky outcrops, though the highway often runs very close to the shore.

🏃 Activities & Courses

The first surf spot heading east is the consistent beach break at **Kabalana Beach**, which normally has something to ride even when waves are tiny elsewhere.

In **Midigama** itself, a pint-sized village built beside a curve of sand, there are a couple of reef breaks. Lazy Left is the aptly named wave that bends around the rocks and into the sandy bay – it's perfect for that first reef experience. A few hundred metres further down is Ram's Right, a hollow, shallow and unpredictable beast. It's not suitable for beginners. Plantations is a reef break that's usually a right, with some lefts depending on the swell.

Note that just below sea level there are loads of rocks, coral and other hazards. Plantation Surf Inn (p126) offers ding repairs, surf lessons and board rental.

Lion Yoga   YOGA
(☎ 041-225 0990; www.lions-rest.com; Lion's Rest Hotel, Midigama Beach; per class US$12) This small hotel has twice-daily yoga sessions from visiting instructors during the main tourist season. Weekly/fortnightly deals are available.

★ **Subodinee Surf School**   SURFING
(☎ 077 765 9933; www.subodinee.com; off Galle–Matara Rd, Midigama; 2hr course €30, 3 courses

€75) Yannick Poirier, a Frenchman, is something of a local legend and runs one of the better surf schools in the area, in conjunction with the Subodinee Guesthouse. He also has the best range of boards for hire (from €6 per half-day).

🛏️ Sleeping & Eating

Accommodation sprawls along the coast from Ahangama to Midigama.

Most people eat in their hotel or guesthouse on this stretch of coast as restaurants are slim on the ground.

🛏️ Ahangama

Many surfers stay in Ahangama and ride the waves in Midigama. Stilt fishermen offshore add colour, while the short commercial strip has services and ATMs. Some of the guesthouses are quite isolated.

Wadiya on the Beach   GUESTHOUSE $$
(☎ 070 390 4357, 041-228 2863; wadiyahotel@gmail.com; Galle–Matara Rd, Ahangama; r US$50; ❄️🛜) Overlooking a lagoon-like cove beach, right on top of the waves, this excellent little place has six immaculately presented and spacious rooms (and two more planned) each with good mattresses and furniture, hot-water private bathrooms and access to a shared balcony or terrace. It's run by a friendly Russian, and there's good swimming directly offshore as the bay is nicely sheltered.

Haus Sunil   GUESTHOUSE $$
(☎ 041-228 3988; sunil.walgamage@yahoo.com; Galle–Matara Rd, Ahangama; r Rs 3500-4000; 🛜) An isolated guesthouse with two basic rooms; the upper room has the kind of oceanic views (including a small island) you can ponder for days. The modest building is well off the road and there is a tiny beach, too. Food is available. It's just east of the 137km post.

🛏️ Midigama

This tiny town has a few basic services and a few worthwhile cheap guesthouses.

Subodinee Guesthouse   GUESTHOUSE $
(☎ 077 765 9933; www.subodinee.com; off Galle–Matara Rd, Midigama; r/cabanas from Rs 1800/5500; ❄️@🛜) Long-time owners Jai and his wife Sumana offer 19 very different rooms, from hot concrete cubes with shared bathrooms to pleasing individual cabanas and rooms in

a modern building over the road. Surfers are catered to. Turn inland off the main road at the 139km post and go just past the clock tower and the train station.

Plantation Surf Inn   GUESTHOUSE $
(☑ 077 643 8912; www.plantationsurfinn.com; off Galle–Matara Rd, Midigama; ☺ s/d from US$16/23; 🗟) This attractive family-run surf inn has a pretty garden and five fan-cooled rooms, two with en suite bathrooms and one which can sleep up to four people. The food here is excellent as the owner worked as a chef for years in Colombo. It's set just back from the highway and beach, on the inland side.

Ram's Guesthouse   GUESTHOUSE $
(☑ 041-225 2639; ramssurfingbeach@gmail.com; Galle–Matara Rd, Midigama; r from Rs 2200; @🗟) It's now a tad run down and the road noise is invasive, but the 15 rooms at this surfers camp are certainly cheap. It's located just west of the 140km post, right in front of the best wave on the island: Lazy Right. Note that locals are not allowed to stay here as guests.

🛏 Midigama Beach

At the 140km post, look for a tiny road heading 100m towards the water from the main road. At the end you'll discover a splendid oasis of calm. There's a long beach and the several places to stay are all real finds. This area is also called Gurubebila.

Villa Tissa   HISTORIC HOTEL $$
(☑ 041-225 3434; www.villatissa.lk; Midigama Beach; r US$45-90; ❇🗟⊠) Set in pleasant beachfront gardens, the huge, well-appointed rooms here line a colonnaded terrace and recall bygone days; many do not have air-con. There's a large swimming pool, a narrow patch of beach out front and a cute little cafe.

★ **Villa Naomi Beach**   HISTORIC HOTEL $$$
(☑ 041-225 4711; www.villanaomibeach.com; Midigama Beach; r Rs 10,000; ❇🗟) In a gorgeous shore-front location, with ocean views through a strip of coconut trees, this beautiful colonial villa has whitewashed rooms with antique furnishings and plush bathrooms. The terrace with rattan rockers is perfect for a sundowner. Rates vary widely according to the season.

Lion's Rest   GUESTHOUSE $$$
(☑ 041-225 0990; www.lions-rest.com; 5A Kadabeddagama, Midigama Beach; s US$50-90, d US$60-100;

❇🗟⊠) Directly opposite the Coconuts break, this attractive hotel draws surfers and yogis for its daily classes. Its has eight pleasant, modern rooms set in a two-storey complex surrounding a pool; upper-floor units have ocean views across the green, while the decor is all whitewashed plaster and dark wood. There's a small seafood restaurant.

❶ Getting There & Away

Buses run every 15 minutes along the busy coastal road connecting Ahangama and Midigama with Galle (Rs 35) and Matara (Rs 38). Many Colombo–Galle–Matara trains stop at Ahangama. Only a few local trains stop at Midigama.

Weligama

☑ 041 / POP 14,200

Weligama (meaning 'Sandy Village') is an interesting blend of lively fishing town and beach resort. The sprawling main settlement and coastal road is somewhat scruffy and not that easy on the eye, but you'll find the sandy beach is attractive once you're away from the main section; there's a couple of cove beaches west of the centre. At the east end of the beach, there's an enormous new concrete Marriott hotel, which towers over the surrounding buildings and looks completely out of place.

Weligama's benign beach break is ideal for novice surfers and many independent travellers learn to ride their first waves here. There's a strip of surf shacks on the main beachfront, across the road from the Hang Ten hostel, where instructors rent boards (from Rs 1200 per day) and offer lessons (from Rs 2500). After fun in the ocean you can marvel at (and feast on) the denizens of the deep, who end their days being hacked up and sold from roadside fish stalls.

◉ Sights & Activities

Bandrawatta Beach   BEACH
This lovely natural cove beach is well away from the main highway, has sheltered swimming and also a surf break further offshore. Look out for stilt fishermen in the sea just below the Cape Weligama hotel. It's 3km southwest of Weligama.

Taprobane   ISLAND
(www.taprobaneisland.com; island rental per day US$1995; 🗟) Just offshore – you can walk out to it at low tide – is this tiny island. It looks like an ideal artist's or writer's retreat, which

indeed it once was: novelist Paul Bowles wrote *The Spider's House* here in the 1950s. The island was developed in the 1920s by the French Count de Mauny Talvande who perched his mansion on the tiny rock. You can stay or dine on the island with advance planning; five staff are allocated to cater for your stay.

Weligama Bay Dive Center　　　　DIVING
(☑ 041-225 0799; www.scubadivingweligama.com; 126 Kapparathota Rd; boat dives from US$35, snorkel gear rental per day US$15) Snorkelling and diving around Weligama is quite good. This operation, just off the highway at the western end of the beach, runs PADI courses as well as night dives and wreck dives. It also organises whale- and dolphin-watching trips and snorkelling excursions.

🛏 Sleeping & Eating

Hang Ten　　　　　　　　　　HOSTEL $
(☑ 071 415 6135; www.hangtimehostel.com; 540 Weligama Rd; dm/r from Rs 1500/3500; ✹ 🎧) Take a dated concrete hotel on the seafront, pimp it up with backpacker-geared appeal (yoga deck, rooftop bar-resto, surfboard racks) and end up with the Hang Ten hostel. The private rooms are on the ground level and have private verandahs, while dorms have attached hot-water bathrooms, mosquito nets, reading lights and individual fans and lockers. Excursions are offered, including booze cruises and safaris.

Samaru Beach House　　　　HOTEL $$
(☑ 041-225 1417; www.samarubeachhouseweligama.com; 544 New Matara Rd; r US$40-80; ✹ 🎧) Located close to the middle of the bay, this small traveller-savvy place is on the beach and has light and airy rooms (some fanonly). The better rooms have a verandah. Bikes and surfboards can be rented and the genial owner can organise local tours and activities.

★ Cape Weligama　　　　RESORT $$$
(☑ 041-225 3000; www.resplendentceylon.com; Abimanagama Rd; r from US$485; ✹ 🎧 ☒) Perched on a promontory above the Indian Ocean, this astonishing hotel has stunning vistas and a sublime 60m crescent-shaped infinity pool (should you get bored of your own private pool that many of the villas are equipped with, or indeed the huge kid-friendly 'cove pool'). There's a spa, a dive school and several restaurants, including a cliff-edge steakhouse.

Eraeliya Villas & Gardens　　VILLA $$$
(☑ 041-225 0461; www.eraeliya.com; 299 Walliwala; villas from US$265; ✹ 🎧 ☒) Located in Weligama's most attractive and peaceful location, this villa complex enjoys a delightful oceanfront situation and its air-conditioned villas (sleeping two to eight) are very spacious and are kitted out with mod cons including flatscreen TVs and kitchenettes. There's a spa, a lovely pool and a restaurant.

AVM Cream House　　INTERNATIONAL $
(3 Samaraweera Pl; meals Rs 200-350; ⊙ 9am-9pm) A bustling little place serving filling meals including noodle and fried-rice dishes as well as tasty snacks (the shawarmas are superb). There's good ice cream and fresh fruit juices; a delicious melon lassi is Rs 240. It's opposite the bus station in the town centre and has a menu in English.

🍷 Drinking & Nightlife

Tiki Clifftop　　　　　　　BAR
(☑ 071 200 1483; www.facebook.com/tikiweligama; 1 Awariyawaththa; ⊙ 10am-late; 🎧) Tucked away in a remote cliff-side spot 3km southwest of the centre, this cool bar-resto is well worth a tuk-tuk ride. The ocean views are mesmerising and DJs pump up the dance floor with house and party vibes, and reggae on Wednesdays.

❶ Getting There & Away

There are buses every 15 minutes to both Galle (Rs 50, one hour) and Matara (Rs 32, 30 minutes).

Weligama is on the Colombo–Matara train line. Destinations include Colombo (2nd/3rd class Rs 220/120, 2½ to four hours), Galle (2nd/3rd class Rs 60/30, 40 minutes to one hour) and Matara (2nd/3rd class Rs 30/15, 20 to 30 minutes). Four to six trains stop daily at Weligama.

Mirissa
☑ 041

Crack open a coconut, slip into a hammock and rock gently in the breeze, allowing the hours, days and even weeks to slip calmly by. Welcome to Mirissa, a stunning crescent beach. Modest guesthouses abound and there's a string of simple restaurants at the back of the sand.

Paradise is compromised slightly by an erosion problem on the east side of Mirissa, which is partly due to a government-built breakwater and partly due to sand-encroaching construction.

PAUL PRESCOTT / SHUTTERSTOCK ©

1. Unawatuna (p118)
The re-emergence of this broad sandy beach has seen travellers flock to its perfectly blue waters.

2. Galle Fort (p107)
Galle's vibrantly coloured fort is an architectural work of art.

3. Bundala National Park (p140)
Sri Lanka's classic birdwatching destination, this wetland park rings with the sound of birdsong.

4. Mirissa (p127)
Mirissa Harbour is always buzzing with boats.

3

In recent years Mirissa has developed a reputation as a party destination for young travellers, and in high season DJs spin pumping tunes till late several nights a week. If you're looking for solitude and zen-like calm, this may not be the beach for you.

◉ Sights & Activities

★ Mirissa Beach   BEACH
A vision of tropical bliss, Mirissa Beach boasts powdery pale sand, while its azure water is framed by an arc of coconut palms. The west side is the nicest and has the broadest expanse of sand; as the bay curves gently around to the east it meets up with the roar of the Galle–Matara Rd. Close to the centre of Mirissa bay is a much-photographed sandbar that connects to a tiny island that you can walk to at low tide.

Secret Root Spa   SPA
(☑ 077 329 4332; www.secretrootspa.com; off Galle-Matara Rd; massage per hour Rs 2700; ☎) Just inland from the east end of the beach is this family-run sanctuary of calm. It's an Ayurvedic centre with male and female therapists who are experts in relieving tension. Try a herbal steam bath after your massage.

Cinnamon Plantation Tour   TOURS
(☑ 041-225 0980; www.mirissahills.com; Mirissa Hills Hotel, Henwalle Rd, off Galle-Matara Rd; 45min tour & meal Rs 2000; ⊙ 9am-4.30pm) Tours of this magnificent 24-hectare hilltop estate are an excellent introduction to the cultivation and harvesting of cinnamon, the queen of spices. You get to examine the bushes, which can be up to 40 years old, and see how a skilled worker removes the bark by hand using a specialist brass instrument. The tour includes a meal on the hotel's wonderful terrace, and you're then free to tour the hotel's remarkable contemporary art gallery. It's essential to book ahead.

🛏 Sleeping

You'll find a thicket of good-value guesthouses and modest beach hotels at the west end of Mirissa, on and off tiny Gunasiri Mahimi Mawatha. Inland, there are some excellent family-run places along tiny lanes a short walk from the beach. Beware of road noise at the east end of the beach and loud and late music near the beach cafes.

Sunrise Dream   GUESTHOUSE $
(☑ 077 783 4436; ranudituktuk@gmail.com; 432 Yatipila Rd; r with fan/air-con Rs 2000/3000; ❄ ☎)

A fine little guesthouse with just three very clean and spacious rooms located in a separate block to the side of a garden compound. All have a front verandah, ceiling fan and two beds. It's about 500m inland from the beach and the friendly owner also offers tours of the region.

Calidan   HOMESTAY $
(☑ 077 754 7802; calidan.mirissa@gmail.com; Sunanda Rd; r with fan/air-con from Rs 2800/3600; ❄ ☎) This welcoming two-storey homestay features simple, attractive rooms painted in cheery colours, and big smiles from the owners. It's a five-minute walk back from the west end of the beach.

Amarasinghe Guest House   GUESTHOUSE $
(☑ 071 689 9787; www.amarasingheguesthouse. com; off Galle-Matara Rd; r with fan/air-con Rs 2500/3500; @ ☎) Adrift in a web of rural lanes a five-minute walk inland from the highway, this family-owned place has a selection of agreeable rooms and cottages scattered around a garden compound. The owners grow all their own vegetables and spices, and the food is authentic and cheap – try one of their cooking courses (Rs 2500).

★ Rose Blossom   HOMESTAY $$
(☑ 077 713 3096; mirissa.roseblossom@gmail. com; off Galle-Matara Rd; r with fan/air-con from Rs 4500/6500; ❄ ☎) This cute little place has smallish but well-decorated rooms and wonderfully charming owners, who take real care of their guests, love chatting and prepare excellent breakfasts. It's a leafy five-minute walk inland from the eastern end of the beach.

Poppies   GUESTHOUSE $$
(☑ 077 794 0328; www.poppiesmirissa.com; off Galle-Matara Rd; s/d with fan US$30/40, with air-con US$50/60; ❄ ☎) Offering good value, the pristine rooms here are set around a pretty, shady courtyard; each has a nice outside sitting area and hammock. It's just inland from the eastern end of the beach, though expect some traffic noise from the highway.

Palm Villa   GUESTHOUSE $$
(☑ 041-225 0022; www.palmvillamirissa.com; Galle-Matara Rd; r with fan/air-con from €50/65; ❄ ☎) Each of the eight lovely rooms in this colonial-style manor is uniquely decorated in a bright and modern fashion and represents good value. The more expensive are set right on the beach – perhaps a little *too* close to the shore for some – expect some noise and lots

of passing people traffic. There's a two-night minimum, and a fine restaurant.

★ Mirissa Hills   BOUTIQUE HOTEL $$$

(☑ 041-225 0980; www.mirissahills.com; Henwalle Rd, off Galle-Matara Rd; r US$90-300; ❄️🛜🍽️) One of southern Sri Lanka's most remarkable places to stay, this working cinnamon farm has a selection of fine accommodation, including a renovated estate house and a spectacular hilltop retreat. Meals are excellent, with dramatic coastal views from the dining terrace, while the contemporary art gallery contains many important sculptures. The entrance is 1.1km inland from the highway's 148km post.

Spice House   HOTEL $$$

(☑ 077 351 0147; www.thespicehousemirissa.com; Galle-Matara Rd; r US$85-100; ❄️🛜🍽️) Set back from the road, a short walk from Mirissa's east shoreline, this attractive hotel has nine

---

BLUE WHALE TOURS

Only in recent years have marine biologists realised that blue whales – the world's largest living mammal – are remarkably similar to many holidaying humans: they like Sri Lanka's coast. In fact, the waters off Mirissa and Dondra Head to the east often host some of the world's largest number of blue whales. (On the east coast, Trincomalee is another excellent place for whale spotting.)

The stats for blue whales are as extraordinary as their size: 30m long and weighing up to 200 tonnes (which makes them heavier than any known dinosaur by a significant amount). They are thought to live for more than 80 years, but this is not well understood as research has been scant, primarily because there were so few blue whales left – an estimated 5000 (just 1% of the population from 200 years before) – after whaling finally ended in the 1970s. Since then numbers have recovered slightly and there are now an estimated 10,000 to 25,000 spread around the world's oceans.

Mirissa-based boat tours to spot blue whales are a major draw for visitors and there are many competing operators. Besides the blues, it's common to spot their (slightly) smaller cousins: fin whales (the world's second largest at up to 27m), sperm whales, Bryde's whales and various dolphins. Megapods of spinner dolphins, numbering over 500, are regularly encountered. A few points to consider:

➡ Although blue whales have been spotted throughout the year, December and April seem to be the peak months.

➡ Avoid May to July as monsoon season makes the waters very rough.

➡ Most tours depart around 6.30am and generally last from two to five hours, depending on how long it takes to find whales. This can make for a long day if seas are rough.

➡ Established tour boats have at least two levels for viewing, plus proper toilet facilities.

➡ Look for tours that respect international conventions about approaching whales. Ask about this before you book.

➡ Avoid rogue operators or chartered fishing boats as many of these are known to harass whales, for example by boxing one animal between two boats.

➡ Ask about food and drink availability, and find out if there are binoculars for passengers to use.

Recommended operators include the following:

Raja and the Whales (☑ 071 333 1811; www.rajaandthewhales.com; Mirissa Harbour; adult/child Rs 6000/3000) Uses a two-level trimaran for trips and follows international guidelines for approaching whales.

Paradise Beach Club (☑ 041-225 1206; www.paradisebeachmirissa.com; Gunasiri Mahimi Mawatha; tours US$50) This small beach resort runs its own tours on a good, custom-built boat.

Blue Water Cruise (☑ 077 497 8306; Galle-Matara Rd; adult/child Rs 7000/3500) A professional, responsible outfit with well-maintained boats.

well-appointed and inviting rooms, and three more in a separate villa at the rear. It's owned by a welcoming British–Sri Lankan couple and you'll find plenty of chill-out areas for relaxing, and a lovely garden and pool to enjoy.

Eating & Drinking

Numerous places set up tables and chairs right up to the tide day and night. Wander and compare which one has the freshest seafood. All are good for a beer; some also serve espresso coffee.

★**No1 Dewmini Roti Shop**   SRI LANKAN $$
(☑ 071 516 2604; www.dewminirotishop.wordpress. com; off Udupila Rd; meals Rs 200-550; ⊗8am-9pm; 🐾) The original and still the best local *rotti* shop. It also makes *kotthu* (*rotti* chopped up and mixed with vegies) and delicious, more substantial rice-and-curry-style dishes. The ever-smiling chef and owner also offers **cooking classes** (Rs 2000 for six curries). It's 350m north of the coastal highway.

Papa Mango   INTERNATIONAL $$
(☑ 041-454 5341, 077 772 6546; www.facebook. com/papamangomirissasl; off Galle-Matara Rd; meals Rs 650-1200; ⊗8am-10pm or later; 🐾) This restaurant has a prime beachfront location on the east side of Mirissa with tables dotted around a large garden shaded by palms. The menu takes in seafood, local curries and Western dishes and it regularly hosts parties with live bands and DJs.

Zephyr Restaurant & Bar   BAR
(☑ 077 750 2222; www.facebook.com/zephyrmirissa; off Galle-Matara Rd; ⊗9am-4pm & 6-11pm; 🐾) One of the coolest beach hang-outs, Zephyr offers a cosmopolitan ambience thanks to well-selected lounge tunes. Later on, expect live music or a DJ, dancing in the sand and a party vibe. It also has a full menu, though portions are small and you can expect to wait a while.

ⓘ Getting There & Away

Very regular buses, running about every 15 minutes, connect Mirissa with Galle (Rs 55, one hour) and Matara (Rs 30, 25 minutes). If you're heading to Colombo by bus, head to Matara or Galle and take an express service from there.

The bus fare to/from Weligama is Rs 15 (10 minutes); a three-wheeler costs Rs 400.

Drivers charge Rs 10,000 for a one-way ride to Colombo airport; the journey time is around 2½ hours.

Matara

 ☑ 041 / POP 72,600

Matara is a busy, booming and sprawling commercial town that owes almost nothing to tourism – which can make it a fascinating window on modern Sri Lankan life. Matara's main attractions are its ramparts, Dutch architecture, a well-preserved fort and its street life.

⊙ Sights

You can spend half a day wandering Matara. The long strip of beach along Sea Beach Rd is somewhat tatty and commercial and can be missed.

★**Star Fort**   FORT
(Main St; ⊗8.30am-4.30pm Wed-Mon) **FREE** This fort was built by the Dutch to compensate for deficiencies in the neighbouring rampart, but it's so small it could only have protected a handful of bureaucrats. Look out for the construction date (1765) embossed over the main gate, along with VOC insignia and the coat of arms of the governor of the day. Inside there's a small **museum** with modest displays about the history of Matara, and you can view former soldiers' sleeping quarters and prisoners' cells.

Old Dutch Trade Centre   HISTORIC BUILDING
(Nupe Market; Anagarika Dharmapala Mawatha) **FREE** On the western side of town, this magnificent T-shaped building (once the town's market) will fascinate architectural buffs: it has an imposing, steeply pitched roof, three conical towers and a grand gabled entrance. It's open-sided and supported by colossal wooden beams and columns.

Matara Fort   AREA
This historic, though run-down district, was once the heart of Dutch, and later British, Matara. There are no real sights, but it's an intriguing area architecturally, and a quick wander will reveal many fine old colonial mansions in various states of disrepair. The river bank at the west corner is serene; see if you can spot one of the rumoured crocodiles.

Polhena Beach   BEACH
(Polhena Rd) The best beach in the area is a small sandy cove that's sheltered by a reef offshore. There's good snorkelling in the bay, and though visibility is not that great, turtles are very regularly spotted here. It's popular with locals at weekends who rent goofy inflatable toys and frolic in the surf, but it's usually quiet on weekdays.

Matara

🛏 Sleeping & Eating

Sunil Rest Guest
House & Restaurant   GUESTHOUSE $
(📞041-222 1983; sunilrestpolhena@yahoo.com;
16/3A Second Cross Rd; r from Rs 2500; 🛜) Run
by Sunil and Ureka, a charming local couple, this fine guesthouse is about 150m from
the beach. Rooms in the main building are
simple and clean, or there are other options
managed by the family close by. Ureka is an
excellent cook, too. As they don't pay commission, many three-wheeler drivers will tell
you it's closed – it's not.

Galle Oriental
Bakery Restaurant   SRI LANKAN $
(41 Anagarika Dharmapala Mawatha; meals Rs 130-
280; ⏲8am-8pm) The best central option is
a creaky but historic place with lots of little
dining rooms, a wooden interior and warped
display cases bulging with baked and savoury treats. The soups and curries are good
and prices are cheap.

⭐ Dutchman's Street   SRI LANKAN $$
(📞041-223 6555; www.thedutchmansstreet.com;
Court Rd; meals Rs 500-1300; ⏲9am-10pm; 🛜) A
cool new cafe-restaurant serving well-priced
international dishes (saucy fried chicken
wings, battered fried prawns) in the colonial

enclave of Matara Fort. It occasionally hosts
DJs and live music events and has a lovely
sea-facing garden.

ℹ Information

All the main roads in the centre have banks and
ATMs.
Police station (📞041-222 2222; Main St;
⏲24hr) Centrally located near the market.
Post office (New Tangalla Rd; ⏲8am-5pm
Mon-Sat) Near the bus station.

ℹ Getting There & Away

BUS

Matara's **bus station** (New Tangalla Rd;
⏲24hr) is a vast multilevel place; look for tiny
destination signs over the queuing pens. As
Matara is a regional transport hub, services are
frequent in all directions; most buses are not air-
conditioned. For Kandy, travel via Colombo.

TRAIN

Matara's **train station** (Railway Station Rd)
is the present terminus of the coastal railway,
although work is progressing on an extension
as far as Kataragama, which is scheduled to be
completed by 2018. Destinations include the
following:
Bentota 2nd/3rd class Rs 140/70, two hours,
five to six daily

LONG-DISTANCE BUSES FROM MATARA

DESTINATION	PRICE (RS)	DURATION (HR)	FREQUENCY
Colombo (via coastal road)	regular/semi-luxe 191/410	5	every 15min
Colombo (via expressway)	air-con luxury 510	2½	hourly 4am-7pm
Ella	270	5	5 daily
Galle	50	1	every 15min
Kataragama	215	4	hourly
Ratnapura	225	4½	6.20am, 7am, 12.40pm
Tangalla	58	1	every 15min

Colombo 2nd/3rd class Rs 230/130, 2¾ to four hours, five to six daily

Galle 2nd/3rd class Rs 80/40, one to 1½ hours, six to eight daily

Kandy (via Colombo) 2nd/3rd class Rs 360/195, seven hours, daily

Dondra

The small town of Dondra was one of the island's primary places of worship until its grand Tenavaram temple was destroyed by the Portuguese back in the 16th century. Today it's famous as marking the southernmost point in Sri Lanka. There are short eats available around the Tenavaram temple. Nearby Matara has a good choice of restaurants.

The landmark **Dondra Head Lighthouse** (Lighthouse Rd) provides an exclamation mark to the southernmost point of Sri Lanka. Visitors are not currently permitted to enter the lighthouse compound or climb up the structure's interior, but if the rules change you'll find the coastal views from the top remarkable. The fine ocean-side setting is still inspiring. It's 1.2km south of the centre.

The **Tenavaram Kovil** compound is now the the largest temple in town after the original vast complex of Tenavaram Dondra was destroyed in 1587. Sadly, a couple of (chained) elephants can usually be found here.

Buses from Matara (every 15 minutes) will drop you in the centre of Dondra. From here you can catch a three-wheeler or walk to the lighthouse.

Talalla

📞 041

Strongly contesting the award for Sri Lanka's most beautiful beach, Talalla is an utterly sublime curve of sand that's been only very lightly touched by tourism. Indeed as you walk the idyllic kilometre-long shoreline, virtually the only artificial features you'll encounter are small fishing boats. Nature feels very close here at the idyllic western end of the beach, where patches of tropical forest are home to swinging monkeys and snoozing iguanas.

The eastern side of Talalla is less attractive as the highway runs much closer to the shore.

🛏 Sleeping & Eating

There are several simple guesthouses back off the beach, a villa or two and a fine hotel.

There are just a couple of places for snacks and drinks; most accommodation has a restaurant.

⭐**Talalla Sunshine Beach**   GUESTHOUSE **$$**
(📞 077 514 1533; www.talalla-sunshine-beach.com; r with fan/air-con from Rs 3800/4700; ❄🐾) The incredibly hospitable owners really make this budget-friendly place, located just behind the beach. All four rooms have partial sea views, mosquito nets, optional air-con, and private bathrooms with hot water. Food here is a real highlight: Nisansala's rice and curries and hopper breakfasts are very special indeed; she also offers cooking lessons.

Paradise Beach House   GUESTHOUSE **$$**
(📞 077 270 8092; off Matara-Tangalla Rd; r Rs 4500; 🐾) Offering clean tiled rooms with fresh linen, mosquito nets and cold-water en suites, this is a good choice located just 200m from the beach. The owners speak very limited English, but are friendly enough.

Secret Bay Hotel   GUESTHOUSE **$$**
(📞 041-438 1089; www.secretbayhotel.jimdo. com; off Matara-Tangalla Rd; r from US$55; ❄🐾) About 250m from the beach, this guesthouse has rooms split between humble bungalows (best) and a rather looming three-storey main building. Decor is simple but accented with vivid blues. The top-floor restaurant has sweeping views.

★ **Talalla Retreat**   RESORT $$$
(☎ 041-225 9171; www.talallaretreat.com; off Matara-Tangalla Rd; r US$50-110; ❄ 🛜 🌊) One of the island's foremost retreats, many guests at this healthy sanctuary are on yoga, wellness or surf-instruction packages. The location is inspirational, set back from the shore with views of the ocean from the wonderful restaurant. Some accommodation, however, is poorly designed: many rooms are open-sided (windowless) so expect visits from raiding monkeys and squirrels, and some noise issues.

ℹ Getting There & Away

All buses travelling between Matara and Tangalla (running about every 15 minutes) pass by the access road, located at the 171km post, to Talalla.

There's no public transport to the beach itself, though a tuk-tuk from the highway is Rs 250.

Dikwella
🗺 041

Little more than a wide spot in the road with a few shops useful to locals, Dikwella – 22km east of Matara – is close to a couple of interesting sights. The area's low-key stretch of coast features some beautiful beaches in perfect little coves off the main road.

◉ Sights

Ho-o-maniya Blowhole   LANDMARK
(Rs 250; ⊙ dawn-dusk) The Ho-o-maniya blowhole is sometimes spectacular and other times a fizzle. During the southwest monsoon (June is the best time), high seas can force water 23m up through a natural chimney in the rocks and then up to 18m in the air. At other times the blowhole will leave you limp. From the parking area, it's a 300m up-and-down walk past numerous vendors and, sadly, lots of rubbish.

Wewurukannala Vihara   BUDDHIST SITE
(Wewurukannala Rd; Rs 200; ⊙ dawn-dusk) A 50m-high seated Buddha figure – the largest in Sri Lanka – is a highlight of this somewhat gaudy temple, which is often thronged with worshippers. Before reaching the Buddha you pass through a hall of horrors full of life-sized models of demons and sinners. The punishments depicted include being dunked in boiling cauldrons, sawn in half and disembowelled. The temple is 1.5km inland from Dikwella, towards Beliatta.

🍴 Sleeping & Eating

There are a few hotels and guesthouses on the beach here. This region is largely limited to local places on the highway serving rice and curry and short eats.

★ **Dickwella Beach Hotel**   HOTEL $$
(☎ 041-225 5522; www.dickwellabeach.lk; 112 Mahawela Rd; r with fan/air-con from US$28/36; ❄ 🛜) This family-run place has two blocks, a modern structure with a prime beachfront location where the rooms have dreamy sea views, and budget rooms by the road. The lovely ocean-side dining zone is just perfect for sipping a fresh coconut and gazing at the waves. Look for the turn-off from the main road about 1km east of Dikwella.

**Coconut Palm Beach
Seafood Restaurant**   SEAFOOD $$
(☎ 071 803 1141; Tangalla Rd; meals from Rs 650; 🛜) A fine place to taste the fruits of the sea, with delicious crab, prawn, squid and fish dishes served up right by the ocean. Located on a pretty little sandy cove 1km west of central Dikwella, though it is close to the coastal highway.

ℹ Getting There & Away

Dikwella is connected to Matara (Rs 20, 30 minutes) and Tangalla (Rs 36, 40 minutes) by very regular buses from 5.30am to 7pm.

Hiriketiya
🗺 041

Fringed by tropical forest and lapped by surging surf, this tiny horseshoe-shaped cove is fast becoming one of Sri Lanka's coolest beaches. For now it's still somewhat off the radar and draws an in-the-know crowd of independent travellers and ex-pats. Hiriketiya's appeal is easy to understand: it's tucked well away from the highway traffic that curses many southern Sri Lankan beaches and there are no looming concrete hotels, only a handful of low-key guesthouses. For now.

Surfing is a huge draw. Novices and the less-experienced will love the waves close to the central shoreline, while there are bigger breaks on the eastern edge of the bay. You'll find boards for rent racked up right on the beach and most guesthouses can organise lessons. Swimming is usually good close to shore and on the western edge of the bay.

🛏 Sleeping & Eating

Everything is located close the beach. The jungle is still quite dense, so expect to encounter some wildlife, including monkeys and lizards. Most guesthouses also offer meals. Expect a wait in high season.

Dot's Bay House GUESTHOUSE $$
(📞 077 793 5593; www.dotsceylon.com; ⊙ r US$50; ❄ 🛜) Five small artistically decorated rooms in a guesthouse known for its good vibes and chilled atmosphere; you'll pay extra for air-con. The rooms are a tad pricey, but such is Hiriketiya's draw they're often fully booked. It's a good place to meet others and socialise and there's a great cafe.

Salt House GUESTHOUSE $$$
(📞 041-225 6819; www.salthousesrilanka.net; Hiriketiya Rd; r US$85; ❄ 🛜) A stylish, up-market guesthouse with six rooms (some open-sided, so expect some noise, others enclosed and air-conditioned) and there's a spacious chill-out space on the top deck. Next door there's a lovely garden with a superb forest-facing yoga studio and a fine healthy-eating restaurant. It's 100m inland from the shore.

Beach House Hiriketiya GUESTHOUSE $$$
(📞 076 617 6969; www.beachhousehiriketiya.com; r US$80; ❄ 🛜) There's a row of simple beach-chic rooms here at the back of the restaurant, all thoughtfully designed in creams and whites; the beds have deep, comfortable mattresses and all boast outdoor en suite bathrooms. Book well ahead as it's very popular.

Dot's Surf Cafe CAFE $$
(meals Rs 500-800; ⊙ 8am-6pm; 🛜) Tucked away just back from the shore by a little lagoon, this lovely cafe has a cool vibe and serves up meaty burgers, crisp waffles, fine juices and espresso coffees.

ⓘ Getting There & Away

Hiriketiya is only a kilometre or so from Dikwella. Very regular buses buzz between Matara (Rs 20, 30 minutes) and Tangalla (Rs 36, 40 minutes) from 5.30am until 7pm; all pass through Dikwella.
  A tuk-tuk from Dikwella is Rs 250.

Goyambokka
📞 047
There's nothing much to tiny Goyambokka, which consists of some pretty sandy coves and a selection of coastal hotels. Look out for the turn-off, Goyambokka Rd, just west of the 194km post.

🛏 Sleeping & Eating

Most hotels here are somewhat dated and quite pricey for what you get.
  It's mainly about hotel restaurants on this stretch, though there are a few shacky beach cafes. Head into Tangalla for more choice.

★ Goyambokka Guest House GUESTHOUSE $$
(📞 047-224 0838; www.goyambokkaguesthouse. com; Goyambokka Rd; r Rs 4000-5000, villa Rs 8000-10,000; ❄ 🛜 🏊) This excellent property has recently expanded and now has a good choice of accommodation, from fan-cooled rooms to sleek units in two-storey villas and other options for families. All are dotted around a tropical garden with dancing palm trees, and are a short walk from the beach.

Green Garden Cabanas HOTEL $$
(📞 077 624 7628; www.greengardencabanas.com; Mahawela Rd; r with fan/air-con from US$28/40; ❄ 🛜 🏊) Set back from the beach, this hotel has a range of accommodation, including well-kept stone and wooden cabanas with tidy bathrooms. Rooms in the main building have private terraces with views out to the fruit-filled gardens; there's a decent restaurant, too. The turn is at the 196km post.

★ Amanwella LUXURY HOTEL $$$
(📞 047-224 1333; www.amanresorts.com; off Mata-ra-Tangalla Rd; ste from US$655; ❄ @ 🛜 🏊) A true temple of luxury living, Amanwella's suites all have private plunge pools, preloaded iPods and gloriously tasteful and modish design touches. Indeed the mood is so sybaritic you may need to be bribed to leave. All units have ocean views, but suites 110, 111 and 112 are nearest the beach. The entrance is just east of the 193km post. The infinity pool is one of Sri Lanka's best, measuring 50m.

Think Club SEAFOOD, SRI LANKAN $$
(📞 077 364 1739; off Goyambokka Rd; meals Rs 600-1000) Quirky but brilliant shack on the beach run by a father-and-son team; you climb a rickety ladder to an ocean-facing deck for your meal. The seafood is surf-fresh and delicious and there are cold beers. The owners also rent out a very basic hut here if you don't want to stumble home.

ⓘ Getting There & Away

Any bus (they pass every 10 minutes) travelling between Matara and Tangalla will drop you at the Goyambokka turn-off. A three-wheeler from Tangalla bus station costs Rs 400.

Tangalla & Around

☑ 047 / POP 11,200

Tangalla is the gateway to the wide-open spaces and wide-open beaches of southeast Sri Lanka. It's the last town of any size before Hambantota and has some old-world charm. But you're really here to find your perfect beach, and there are several nearby.

◉ Sights & Activities

Tangalla's harbour is an interesting place for a minor exploration. There's evidence of the Dutch all around here. Follow Harbour Rd around the point and into the military area (which is usually wide open); there are great vistas from the **viewpoint** along the grassy verge.

Turtle Watch Rekawa   TOURS
(☑ 076 685 7380; www.turtlewatchrekawa.org; Rekawa Beach; adult/child Rs 1000/500; ⊙ 8.30pm-midnight.) Five species of turtles struggle ashore to lay their eggs on Rekawa Beach. Groups are led to nest sites to witness these beautiful creatures. Unfortunately, as groups are sometimes huge (up to 100 people; weekends are busiest), some nights the commotion can be deeply disturbing for the turtles. Until management of the project improves, it's difficult to recommend these tours wholeheartedly.

⌂ Sleeping

There are several areas in and around Tangalla in which to stay. The beach places close to town are convenient, but tend to be packed together. As you go east, many hotels are more secluded and lie at the end of rough tracks off the Hambantota Rd.

⌂ Tangalla

The town beaches south of the centre are pretty, but sadly the busy main road runs very close to the edge of the sand, meaning lots of fascinated bus passengers watching you lounge about in a bikini.

Moonstone Villas   HOTEL **$$$**
(☑ 047-224 0320; www.moonstonevillas.com; 336 Matara Rd; s/d from US$72/90; ❋ 🔊 ☎) Offers modern and pleasantly decorated rooms in leafy, lush grounds, though rates are a tad

steep given the location: the beach is down and across the busy main road.

⌂ Medaketiya Beach

The long sandy beach here, which extends northeast away from the town, is lined with both good and bad budget guesthouses and cafes. The sand is golden, but dumping waves can make swimming dangerous. At the northeast end, the busy road turns inland and it becomes quieter. Unfortunately, new breakwaters here are messing up the flow of the ocean and causing erosion.

Starfish Beach Cafe   GUESTHOUSE **$**
(☑ 047-224 1005; starfishtangalle@gmail.com; Vijaya Rd; r Rs 2000-4500; ☎) Run by a bunch of energetic and music-loving young guys, this guesthouse has large, airy, tidy rooms and is popular with backpackers. This is a good place to get a *rotti* from the seaside stand.

Villa Araliya   GUESTHOUSE **$$**
(☑ 047-224 2163; www.villa-araliya.net; Vijaya Rd; r €40-50, villa €180; ☎) A German-run beachside place set in luxuriant gardens with bungalows decorated with vintage furniture, including lovely carved wardrobes. The compound has a charm that's lacking nearby, while the villa has three bedrooms and is perfect for friends sharing or a family.

Frangipani Beach Villas   GUESTHOUSE **$$**
(☑ 071 533 7052; www.frangipanibeachvilla.com; Jayawardana Rd; r US$35-75; ❋ 🔊 ☎) Located close to town, this guesthouse is a designers' nightmare – the garish, clashing decor, dodgy murals and dated furnishings could not be more mismatched. But aesthetics aside, the owners are warm and friendly, and there's a very pleasant beachside cafe. Note the pool is located about 300m along the shore.

⌂ Marakolliya Beach

Virtually a continuation of Medaketiya Beach, but much further out of town, the beach here is utterly breathtaking. Unfurling along the coast is a seemingly endless tract of soft sand backed by palms, tropical flowers and mangrove lagoons. However, note that the dramatic surf that pounds the beach here has undertows, and it's frequently too dangerous to swim.

There are two access roads: Madilla Rd is at times a rough continuation of Vijaya Rd in Tangalla, while another partially paved track extends from the main Hambantota Rd at the 200km post. At night, turtles lumber ashore to lay eggs; by day, a lone traveller scours the sands for seashells. Plenty of guesthouses and hotels offer lagoon tours, birdwatching and kayak rental.

Panorama Rock Cafe BUNGALOW $
(☑047-224 0458, 077 762 0092; www.facebook.com/Panorama-Rock-Cafe; Madilla Rd, Medaketiya Beach; r Rs 2200-5000; 🛜) This older property has rooms in cement bungalow-style units. The site is nicely shaded with mature plants, while the open-front cafe has a good water's-edge view along the narrow beach. You can arrange mangrove outings here.

★**Chill** GUESTHOUSE $$
(☑077 671 0711; www.chillenjoycabanas.com; off Hambantota Rd, Marakolliya Beach; s/d US$30/40; ❋🛜) This beautiful new place is owned by a Hungarian–Sri Lankan couple who've worked in hospitality for years and run a tight ship. Their two huge detached bungalows are the best value in the area, immaculately furnished and boasting generous verandahs with hammocks. It's about 400m from the beach, close to the lagoon and has a good restaurant, and bikes for hire.

★**Lonely Beach Resort** BUNGALOW $$
(☑071 816 4804; www.lonelybeachresort.com; off Hambantota Rd, Marakolliya Beach; r US$30-40; 🛜) While the planet is not lonely, this corner of the beach near the lagoon certainly is – indeed it's perfect for those in search of a tranquil beachside base. Rooms are neat and tidy; those at the rear are cheaper. The cafe has lovely sea views and you can ponder the scene from a hammock strung between palm trees.

★**Ganesh Garden** BUNGALOW $$
(☑047-224 2529; www.ganeshgarden.com; Madilla Rd, Marakolliya Beach; r US$40-75; ❋🛜) A very well-run place with an array of different cabanas. There are mud-walled abodes next to the lagoon at the rear, while others near the beach are timber-and-thatch, and some are straight concrete – all are comfortable and well designed. It's on a fine stretch of beach, has a good cafe-restaurant, and there are kayaks available to explore the lagoon.

Cinnabar Resort BUNGALOW $$
(☑077 965 2190; www.cinnabarresort.wordpress.com; Madilla Rd, Marakolliya Beach; r US$20-50; 🛜) Everything you need to know about Cinnabar is that one of its rooms is a treehouse. If you're bored it wouldn't be much effort to find

driftwood on the beach to build another – this really is a rustic experience. Cinnabar has a social ambience and its atmospheric beach cafe is the perfect spot for a sundowner or meal.

Serein Beach BOUTIQUE HOTEL $$
(☑047-224 0005; www.sereinbeach.com; Madilla Rd, Marakolliya Beach; r US$45-90; ❋🛜) This smart three-storey hotel has nine very attractive rooms featuring stylish modern furniture; book one on the upper floor for full-frontal sea views. Solar energy is used to heat water, staff are professional and there's a wonderful rooftop deck. The location is sun-drenched and the beach out front is blissful.

Mangrove Chalets BUNGALOW $$
(☑077 790 6018; www.beachcabana.lk; off Hambantota Rd, Marakolliya Beach; r from €45; 🛜) These large bungalows (some sleep up to four) have spacious verandahs facing the sea or lagoon. It's a good spot for families, as the mangrove waters are calm for swimming. You can access the site by a very Hollywood-feeling creaky bamboo bridge.

Sandy's GUESTHOUSE $$
(☑077 622 5009; www.sandycabana.com; off Hambantota Rd, Marakolliya Beach; r from US$40; 🛜🏊) Classic Robinson Crusoe–style beach hang-out with palm-thatch open-air cabanas (some have bedrooms open to the stars and sea breezes). Conditions can be basic (and you may have to inspect a couple to find a clean unit). The dinner buffet (Rs 1500) is pricey, but quite a spread.

🛏 Rekawa Beach

Around 10km east of Tangalla, this is another corker of a beach. Like Marakolliya, but even less developed, it's an endless stretch of wind- and wave-battered sand that isn't safe for swimming. It's also famous for nesting turtles, of no fewer than five different species. An access road wanders off the Hambantota Road at the 203km post.

Buckingham Place RESORT $$$
(☑047-348 9447; www.buckingham-place.com; Rekawa Beach; r from US$210; ❋🛜🏊) This gated compound holds a very secluded luxe resort set back from the beach on a slim sandbar. Rooms boast a contemporary look, with polished concrete floors, elegant furniture and gorgeous semi-open bathrooms. It's close to the turtle-viewing area and there's excellent birdlife on the neighbouring lagoon – be sure to take out a kayak.

Tangalla & Around

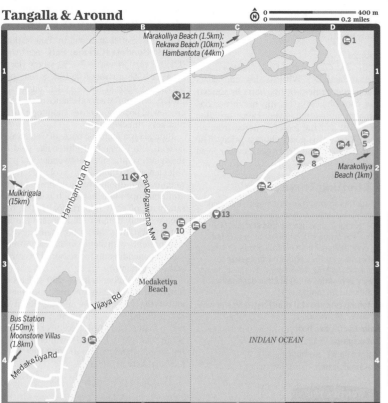

THE SOUTH TANGALLA & AROUND

⚹ Eating & Drinking

Just about all the places to stay serve meals. Many have cafes with dreamy ocean views, and seafood is always a good choice.

★**Mango Shade**   SRI LANKAN **$$**
(☎077 720 1859; Pangngawana Mawatha 141, Medaketiya Beach; meals Rs 350-750; ☺8am-9.45pm; 🛜) Down a lane, 300m inland from the beach, this is the place for home cooking, Sri Lankan style, with richly spiced sauces, fresh seafood and very moderate prices for the area (rice and curry with fish is Rs 350). It's run by a kindly couple and you sit (as the name indicates) under mango trees and coconut palms.

Saliya Restaurant   SEAFOOD **$$**
(☎047-224 2726; Hambantota Rd; meals Rs 250-500; ☺7am-10pm; 🛜) Sitting on wobbly stilts 1.5km east of the town centre near the 198km post, this eccentric wooden shack is

Tangalla & Around

worth considering for the mangrove views; the food is fine, but it's the setting that is really great.

Lounge BAR
(📞 077 342 4723; Madilla Rd, Medaketiya Beach; ⊙ 10am-2am; 🛜) With tables and seats made from crates, swing chairs by the bar and cool playlists, this hip beach bar has its own individual style. There are fine cocktails, and the food (prepared from an open kitchen) is good, though pricey. The chatty sports-mad Sri Lankan owner lived in London for years.

ℹ Getting There & Away

Tangalla is an important bus stop on the main coastal road; you can flag buses anywhere on the coastal road or use the **bus station** (Main Rd) in the centre of town; most buses are not air-conditioned. There are four luxury air-con buses daily via the Southern Expressway to Colombo (Rs 860, three hours). Frequent buses (every 15 minutes or so) to other destinations include the following:

Colombo (via coastal road) regular/semi-luxe RS 160/324, six hours

Galle Rs 107, two hours

Kataragama Rs 121, 2½ hours

Matara Rs 58, one hour

Tissamaharama Rs 101, two hours

Bundala National Park

Much less visited than nearby Yala National Park, **Bundala National Park** (adult/child US$10/5, plus per vehicle Rs 250, service charge per group US$8, plus overall tax 15%; ⊙ 6am-6pm, last entrance 4.30pm) is an excellent choice for birders, and you've a good chance of spotting crocs, wild boar, mongooses, monitor lizards, monkeys and elephants.

Bundala is a fantastic maze of waterways, lagoons and dunes that glitter like gold in the dying evening sun. This wonderland provides a home to thousands of colourful birds ranging from diminutive little bee-eaters to grotesque open-billed stalks. It is a wetland sanctuary of such importance that it has been recognised under the Ramsar Convention on Wetlands. Many big mammals are also present, with between 15 and 60 elephants depending on the season (December is the best month).

The park shelters almost 200 species of birds within its 62-sq-km area, with many journeying from Siberia and the Rann of Kutch in India to winter here, arriving between August and April (December to March is the peak time). It's also a winter home to the greater flamingo; up to 2000 have been recorded here at one time.

WORTH A TRIP

MULKIRIGALA

Dangling off a rocky crag 16km northwest of Tangalla and nestled away among a green forest of coconut trees are the peaceful **Mulkirigala Rock Temples** (Mulkirigala Rd; Rs 500; ⊙ dawn-dusk). Clamber up the 500 or so steps and you'll encounter a series of seven cleft-like caves on five different terraced levels. Housed in the caves are a number of large reclining Buddha statues interspersed with smaller sitting and standing figures.

Vying with these for your attention are some fantastical wall paintings depicting sinners pleasuring themselves with forbidden fruit on Earth and then paying for it with an afterlife of eternal torture – apparently it was worth it! Further on up, and perched on top of the rock some 206m from the base, is a small dagoba with fine views over the surrounding country.

Temples, in some form or another, have been located here for over 2000 years, but the current incarnations, and their paintings, date from the 18th century. Nearby is a Buddhist school for young monks.

Pali manuscripts found in the monastic library here by a British official in 1826 were used for the first translation of the Mahavamsa (Great Chronicle), which unlocked Sri Lanka's early history to the Europeans. For more detail on the site and a series of photographs, see www.srilankaview.com/mulkirigala_temple.htm.

Mulkirigala can be reached by bus from Tangalla via either Beliatta or Wiraketiya. (Depending on the departures, it might be quicker to go via Wiraketiya than to wait for the Beliatta bus.) A three-wheeler from Tangalla costs about Rs 1800 for a return trip.

Bundala also has civets, giant squirrels and lots of crocodiles. Between October and January, four of Sri Lanka's five species of marine turtles (olive ridley, green, leatherback and loggerhead) lay their eggs on the coast.

Bundala stretches nearly 20km along a coastal strip between Kirinda and Hambantota. The entrance is west of the 251km post. There's a visitor centre at the main gate that has views over the marshes; check out the skeleton of a fearsomely huge crocodile. Bundala is open year-round, allowing wildlife junkies to get a wet-season fix.

There's no accommodation in the park itself and most people stay in Tissamaharama. There are a couple of hotels on the highway close to the entrance, but you'll still need to hire jeeps to access the park. There are no eating options in the park; bring your own supplies.

Bundala is 18km from Tissamaharama or 10km from Hambantota. There's no public transport inside the park. Most people organise tours (p143) of Bundala (or hire jeeps) from Tissamaharama; exact rates of safari packages depend on numbers, guides and the vehicle.

Tissamaharama

☑ 047 / POP 11,300

In Tissamaharama (usually shortened to Tissa), eyes are automatically drawn upwards and outwards. Upwards to the tip of its huge, snowy-white dagoba and outwards, beyond the town's confines, to nearby wildlife reserves crawling with creatures large and small. With its pretty lakeside location, Tissa is an ideal mellow base for the nearby Yala and Bundala National Parks.

⊙ Sights

★ Tissa Dagoba   BUDDHIST STUPA
(off Rubberwatte Rd) FREE This large much-restored dagoba looming between Tissa town centre and the *wewa* is believed to have been originally built around 200 BC by Kavantissa, a king of Ruhunu, located in present-day Tissamaharama. The white stupa has a circumference of 165m and stands 55.8m high. It is thought to have held a sacred tooth relic and forehead bone relic. It's attractively lit up at night.

★ Tissa Wewa   LAKE
The centrepiece of the town and its surrounds is the lovely Tissa Wewa (Tissa Tank), a huge

artificial lake. In the evening, check out the flocks of egrets that descend onto the trees around the lake to roost. The road along the southern edge has a wide **Lakeside Walkway** for strolling. Don't be tempted to swim here as crocodiles are sometimes spotted.

★ Yatala Wehera   BUDDHIST STUPA
(Tissamaharama Rd) Lotus ponds surround this site, which has a wealth of elephant details in the carvings (note the footpads). It was built 2300 years ago by King Mahanaga in thanks both for the birth of his son, Yatala Tissa, and for his safe escape from an assassination attempt in Anuradhapura. It's an easy walk from town.

Museum   MUSEUM
(Tissamaharama Rd; ⊙8am-5pm) FREE This small museum, next to Yatala Wehera, contains an extraordinary range of treasures including an ornate, ancient bidet, which – as well as an elaborate filtration system that limited water pollution – had murals of ugly faces carved into it in order to stop the user thinking about sex! Note that hours vary as the caretaker is not always around.

Wirawila Wewa   LAKE
West of Tissa, the Hambantota–Wellawaya Rd runs over this large lake (via a causeway). It's home to resident waders and visited by migrating birds.

🛏 Sleeping

Prices are lower here than on the coast and there are pleasant hotels and guesthouses scattered all about Tissa. Lakeside ones have obvious appeal; just about every place has a restaurant. Note that for Yala tours, hotels along the park access roads and near the beach in Kirinda are also good options.

🛏 Tissa Wewa & Town Centre

Hotel Tissa   GUESTHOUSE $
(☑071 711 5744; www.hoteltissa.com; Main Rd; r US$15-25, cottage US$35; 🅰@🛜) Just 100m from the bus station, the functional, decent-value rooms here are divided between the main building and quieter block out back. All have air-con, while more deluxe units have fridges and hot water.

★ Blue Turtle   BOUTIQUE HOTEL $$
(☑077 548 6836; www.blueturtlehotel.com; 119/2 Tissamaharama Rd; r US$34-54; 🅰@🛜🏊) Offering exceptional value, this hotel sits in a large, tranquil compound with accommodation

Tissamaharama

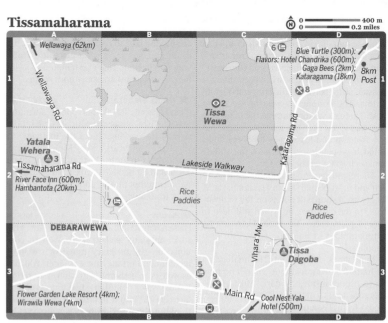

Tissamaharama

facing a stunning 20m pool and elegant lobby-restaurant. Rooms are in attractive two-storey cottages, all with balconies or verandahs, and are beautifully presented with contemporary furnishings. The restaurant offers fine Sri Lankan and Western food. There's a bar, too.

★ My Village
GUESTHOUSE $$
(☑ 077 350 0090; www.myvillagelk.com; 69 Court Rd; r US$30-60; ❄☎) A very stylish three-bedroom guesthouse, My Village is actually the modernist dream creation of a local designer. There's a stylish open-plan cafe and communal area for socialising. The shady grounds are peaceful and have hammocks. Guests can use bicycles for free. Do check out the totally spotless open kitchen where your complimentary breakfast is prepared.

Cool Nest Yala Hotel
(☑ 047-322 1303; www.thecoolnestyala.com; 137/a Halambagaswala Rd, off Rubberwatte Rd; s/d from Rs 3250/3650; ❄☎) Scoring high marks for value, cleanliness and comfort, this place has two attractive white villas; you can either rent a room (all have en suite bathrooms) or families could book an entire property. Staff can help book transport and tours; it's just 500m from the bus station.

Traveller's Home
GUESTHOUSE $$
(☑ 077 601 0208, 047-223 7958; www.travellershomeyala.com; Main Rd; r US$20-40, 3-bed unit US$100; ❄@☎) This traveller-aware guesthouse is just off Main Rd and has a variety of bright, refurbished rooms all with a balcony or patio and private hot-water bathrooms. Cheaper fan-cooled options and a three-bed bungalow are also available. There are free bicycles for guests and a good restaurant.

Gaga Bees
BUNGALOW $$

(☑ 071 620 5343; www.gagabeesyala.com; off Sandagirigama Rd; r Rs 5000-6000; ❋ ⎙ ⛱) This compound of nine rustic bungalows is in a serene setting surrounded by rice fields. All have been built from natural materials – mud bricks, palm thatch and local wood – and have two beds, air-con and verandahs. There's a small on-site cafe and pool. It's 1.7km east of the main road after a turn at the Hotel Chandrika.

Hotel Chandrika
HOTEL $$$

(☑ 047-223 7143; www.chandrikahotel.com; Kataragama Rd; r US$85-120; ❋ ⎙ ⛱) This large hotel enjoys beautifully landscaped grounds and is very popular with tour groups. Its 40 comfortable rooms are set around a palm-lined courtyard and good pool; those in the newer wing are more stylish. Staff are attentive and the restaurant does a tasty curry.

🛏 Deberawewa

West of Tissa, there are some good choices amid lush rivers and wide lakes.

River Face Inn
GUESTHOUSE $$

(☑ 077 389 0229; www.yalariverfaceinn.com; off Hambantota Rd; r US$30-80, tree houses from US$80; ❋ ⎙) Family-run riverside guesthouse blessed with a huge covered terrace where an array of tables with chairs, comfy loungers and hammocks await the weary big-game-spotter. Choose from fan-cooled or air-con rooms, or book a tree house for something really different. There is tasty food available at night. It's 3km west of Tissa.

Flower Garden Lake Resort
HOTEL $$

(☑ 047-223 9980; www.flowergardenlakeresort.com; off Wewa Rd; r US$54-88; ❋ ⎙ ⛱) In a quiet and remote location about 3km west of central Tissa, this small hotel has a grand lakeside setting on Wirawila Wewa. There's nothing other than the song of birds to interrupt the silence. Rooms have satellite TVs and there is a small pool. The cafe is good, and wine and beer are served.

✖ Eating

★ Royal Restaurant
SRI LANKAN $$

(☑ 071 085 1361; Main Rd; meals Rs 300-700; ☻ 8am-10pm) A good bet for cheap and tasty curries or Chinese-ish-style dishes (try the seafood fried rice). Always busy with lots of local families and a sprinkling of travellers. Although in the centre, it is off the road, so the open-sided dining rooms are quiet.

JEEP TOURS

Tissamaharama is the most popular starting point for jeep tours (p146) to Yala National Park and Bundala National Park. Drivers can be arranged at your accommodation or directly with the operators at the **Independent Jeep Association** (off Tissamaharama Rd) car park by the lake, or at the park entrances. Tour rates to the national parks vary a lot depending on the jeep, but start at about Rs 4000/8000 per half-day/full-day. Fine-tune your bargaining skills before you arrive. **Ajith Safari Jeep Tours** (☑ 077 790 5532, 047-223 7557; www.yalawild.com; 414 Debarawewa) is a well-established private safari operator specialising in trips to Yala, Uda Walawe and Bundala National Parks. Guides are well-trained and modern 4WDs are in good shape.

Flavors
SRI LANKAN, INTERNATIONAL $$

(☑ 077 760 4190; www.facebook.com/flavors.tissamaharama; Kataragama Rd; meals Rs 500-900; ☻ 1-10pm; ⎙) Flavors' owner/chef has honed his cooking skills overseas and prepares good Italian and Chinese food, as well as excellent local devilled dishes and curries. It's a small roadside place with nice wooden seating.

New Cabanas Restaurant
SRI LANKAN $$

(Kataragama Rd; mains Rs 600-1200; ☻ 11am-10pm; ⎙) A simple, open-sided restaurant popular for rice and curry. There are regular fresh seafood specials that are right off the grill, as well as lunch buffets.

ℹ Getting There & Away

Tissa's centrally located **bus station** (off Main St) has very regular services along the coast. There are very few buses up to the Hill Country, but very regular services from the Wirawila junction (Rs 16, 15 minutes) west of town, most via Wellawaya (Rs 82). For Arugam Bay change at Wellawaya. There are no buses to Yala National Park. There are four luxury air-con buses daily via the Southern Expressway to Colombo (Rs 860, 5½ hours). Other major bus destinations from Tissa (departing every 15 to 30 minutes) include:

Colombo (via coastal road) regular/semi-luxe, Rs 222/448, eight hours

Kataragama Rs 37, 30 minutes

Kirinda Rs 28, 20 minutes

Tangalla Rs 101, two hours

Three-wheelers around town will cost Rs 150 to Rs 250.

Kirinda

♪ 047

Oceanside Kirinda, 12km south of Tissa, is a place on the edge. On one side its sandy streets and ramshackle buildings give way to a series of magnificently bleak and empty beaches (heavy undertows make swimming here treacherous) that are perfect for long evening walks. In the other direction, tangled woodlands and sweeps of parched grasslands merge into the national parks.

The village itself centres on a Buddhist shrine dramatically perched atop huge round rocks right at the shore.

◉ Sights & Activities

Visible offshore are the wave-smashed **Great Basses reefs** with their lonely lighthouse.

The diving out on these reefs is ranked as about the best in the country, but it's not for inexperienced divers – conditions are often rough. The best time is only between mid-March and mid-April.

Kirinda Temple   BUDDHIST SHRINE

Kirinda centres on this imposing hilltop Buddhist shrine, which includes a stupa and huge standing Buddha. It's dedicated to Queen Viharamahadevi, who lived in the 2nd century BC and is at the heart of a local legend: when raging waters threatened Ceylon, King Kelanitissa ordered his youngest daughter, then a princess, into a boat as a sacrifice. The waters were calmed and the princess miraculously survived. Some 2000 years later, the temple was a place of refuge during the 2004 tsunami.

HAMBANTOTA

Once Hambantota was a dusty little workaday fishing port where nothing much ever happened. But during the presidency of Mahinda Rajapaksa (who hails from here) this deeply provincial town was well and truly put on the map as the location for a roster of vast presidentially-directed construction projects. Now Rajapaksa has been removed from power things have cooled down, though many ill-advised, bombastic reminders of his rule remain.

The bumpy two-lane coast road gives way to huge freeway interchanges as you enter Hambantota. The new roads are peppered with buildings including a landmark hospital, conference centre and an industrial park. These huge projects, dubbed white elephants by the Sri Lankan press, garnered much controversy, even in a country where Rajapaksa's whims were seldom questioned.

Mahinda Rajapaksa International Cricket Stadium This was built for the 2011 World Cup, has a capacity of 35,000 and boasts floodlights and smart media facilities. However as it's 32km from Hambantota in a rural area, its stands have rarely been filled and it's rapidly deteriorating. Farmers dry beans on the stadium access road and animals graze on its grass.

Mattala Rajapaksa International Airport Named after the Rajapaksa family, this vast facility 28km north of Hambantota cost well over US$200 million and opened in 2013. Today it's a gleaming facility that lacks one thing: passengers. Since its opening, flights have been very few and wild animals have to be chased from its 3.5km runway (which is big enough for Airbus A380s). Many airlines refuse to fly here because the neighbouring wetlands and lakes are home to hundreds of thousands of birds, causing several collisions. Today it's served by just two scheduled flights.

Magampura Mahinda Rajapaksa Port Also named after the president's family, this huge port near the centre of town has cost an estimated US$1.3 billion (so far). It was meant to relieve Colombo's container port facility, although the low-capacity roads have hampered access and the port has had to be dredged to allow ships to dock. Faced with alarming running costs, the Sri Lankan government sold 80% of its holding in the port to a Chinese firm in November 2016.

It was largely China that funded the spending spree of the Rajapaksa years, and now China again which is tasked with making the facilities function financially. One proposal is to create a Free Trade area in the Hambantota region, where imported Bangladeshi workers will make Chinese-branded cars in a tax-free zone.

🛏 Sleeping & Eating

⭐ **Suduweli**

Beauties of Nature   GUESTHOUSE $$
(📞 072 263 1059; www.beauties-of-nature.net; Yala Junction; r US$25-50; ⊚) Accommodation at this rural idyll consists of basic but clean rooms in the main house and a handful of comfortable, vaguely alpine-style cottages in the gardens. There's a small lake on the grounds; wildlife abounds, including iguanas and peacocks. The owners are a welcoming Swiss–Sri Lankan couple.

Kirinda Beach Resort   HOTEL $$$
(📞 077 020 0897; www.yalawildlifebeachresortsrilanka.com; r from $70; ❄🌐🏊) Right next to a wild, oceanic, boulder-strewn beach, this quirky compound is perfect for long days exploring the coast and for those that enjoy nature. Gaze upon the pounding surf from the uniquely elevated swimming pool, then enjoy a meal in the large, airy cafe before retiring to a rustic wood chalet or earthy mud hut. It's 1km southwest of the Kirinda temple.

Elephant Reach   RESORT $$$
(📞 077 106 5092; www.elephantreach.com; Yala Junction; r/chalet from US$88/104; ❄🌐🏊) Rooms and chalets at this pleasant lodge have an attractive, natural feel thanks to the stone floors, hemp curtains, coir rugs, and walls decorated with wildlife photography and art. Outside, the large pool curls like a water snake around the gardens.

❶ Getting There & Away

There is a bus from Tissa to Kirinda every half-hour or so (Rs 28, 20 minutes); a three-wheeler is Rs 500.

Yala National Park

Sri Lanka's most famous national park, Yala (www.yalasrilanka.lk; adult/child Rs 3690/1040, jeep & tracker Rs 250, service charge per group US$8, plus overall tax 15%; ⊘ 5.30am-6pm mid-Oct–Aug) forms a total area of 1268 sq km of scrub, light forest, grassy plains and brackish lagoons. It's very rich in wildlife and you're virtually certain to encounter elephants, crocodiles, buffaloes and monkeys. Plan your trip carefully, however – such is Yala's appeal that the main tracks and viewing spots can be crowded.

Yala National Park is divided into five blocks, with the most visited being Block I (141 sq km). Also known as Yala West, this zone was originally a reserve for hunters, but was given over to conservation in 1938. It's the closest to Tissa. The entrance fees are payable at the main office, which is near the west entrance. The only practical way to visit the park is on a tour or safari.

With over 20 leopards thought to be present in Block I alone, Yala is considered one of the world's best parks for spotting these big cats. *Panthera pardus kotiya,* the subspecies you may well see, is unique to Sri Lanka. The best time to spot leopards is February to June or July, when the water levels in the park are low.

The park's estimated 300 elephants can be more elusive, although some regularly appear in the most visited areas. Other animals of note include the shaggy-coated sloth bear and fox-like jackals. Sambars, spotted deer, boars, buffaloes, mongooses and monkeys are also here, along with startlingly large crocodiles.

Over 200 species of birds have been recorded at Yala, many of which are visitors escaping the northern winter, such as white-winged black terns, curlews and pintails. Locals include jungle fowl, hornbills, orioles and peacocks by the bucketload.

Despite the large quantity of wildlife, the light forest can make spotting animals quite hard; however, small grassy clearings and lots of waterholes offer good opportunities. The end of the dry season (March to April) is the best time to visit, as during and shortly after the rains the animals disperse over a wide area.

As well as herds of wildlife, Yala contains the remains of a once-thriving human community. A monastic settlement, **Situlpahuwa**, appears to have housed 12,000 inhabitants. Now restored, it's an important pilgrimage site. A 1st-century BC *vihara* (Buddhist complex), **Magul Maha Vihara**, and a 2nd-century BC *chetiya* (Buddhist shrine), **Akasa Chetiya**, point to a well-established community, believed to have been part of the ancient Ruhunu kingdom.

Yala is a very popular park: there were over 400,000 visitors in 2016, a number which has quadrupled since 2009. At times jeeps can mimic a pack of jackals in their pursuit of wildlife. It's a good idea to discuss with your driver and/or guide where you can go to get away from the human herd. Be sure, however, to make time for the park's **visitor centre** (⊘ 6am-6pm) at the western

THE SOUTH YALA NATIONAL PARK

entrance. It has excellent displays about Yala and a good bookshop.

🛏 Sleeping & Eating

The national park manages four simple lodges inside the park. These are mainly geared to Sri Lankan groups of 10 or more, but you can book online in advance via the Yala National Park website (www.yalasrilanka.lk). You can also sleep inside the park on an organised camping trip; these are best set up in Tissa.

Several top-end resorts are located off the 12km road that runs into the park from Yala Junction. There are no restaurants inside Yala. Visitors are permitted to bring picnics and snacks to eat at designated spots.

Jetwing Yala   RESORT $$$
(☎047-471 0710; www.jetwinghotels.com; r from US$170; ❋ @ 🛜 🏊) Only 4km from the park entrance, this posh resort is set amid the dunes near the beach. Its modish rooms boast stunning views from their balconies, or book a luxury tented villa for a more intimate experience. Staff can arrange sunset picnics on the beach and there's a 50m pool and spa, too.

Cinnamon Wild Yala   LODGE $$$
(☎047-223 9449; www.cinnamonhotels.com; r from US$120; ❋ 🛜 🏊) 🍴 This lodge offers bush-chic accommodation in individual luxe bungalows. The hotel runs on solar power, some of the waste water is recycled and there's a tree-planting scheme. At night elephants often wander through the grounds. There are two bars and a fine restaurant.

❶ Getting There & Away

There's no public transport to the park. The drive to Yala takes about one hour due to road conditions whether you take the 22km route via Yala Junction from Tissa, or a somewhat shorter road past some remote and pretty lakes.

NATIONAL PARK TOUR ESSENTIALS

Most people visit Yala and Bundala National Parks on jeep tours from Tissamaharama (p143). Half-day tours start with a Tissa hotel pick-up at around 4.30am followed by a one-hour drive to the park for a dawn start. You are usually back by noon. Dusk tours run about 3pm to 7pm. Full day tours run 4.30am to 5pm and include stops at beaches and other sights.

Standards between the jeeps vary greatly, although almost all are open-sided, with a high roof for shade. Broadly, the operators and their jeeps fall into three groups:

Normal Often very old vehicles, these often have inward-facing seats along the sides which is very bad for animal spotting. Rates average Rs 4500 per half-day.

Luxury Usually three rows of two forward-facing seats that are stepped up towards the back so you can see over the heads of those in front of you. The seats may be worn or in a few cases broken. Rates average Rs 5500 per half-day.

Super Luxury The newest jeeps are usually Land Rovers or Toyotas and have two or three rows of comfortable seats. Rates start from Rs 6000 per half-day.

The differences between luxury and super luxury can be minor; the most important consideration is that the jeep is in good shape (newer models have better suspension) and that its seats are comfortable. Avoid any jeep with middle seats. Shop around as prices are negotiable. Other considerations:

➡ Are the services of a guide included? This is not always necessary as many of the drivers are very good at animal-spotting. You will also usually be offered a tracker; these guys work for tips (for a half-day tour, tip the driver and any guide at least Rs 500 per person).

➡ Does your prospective driver seem in a rush? One common complaint is about drivers who zip across the countryside reducing the tour to a gut-wrenching blur.

➡ Does the driver provide binoculars? Ask also about water and snacks.

➡ Hoping for tips, drivers aim to please, perhaps too much so. The merest hint of a large animal can spark a convoy of jeeps. You can do your part to keep things calm by asking your driver to refrain from madcap chases. The resulting quiet is more conducive for spotting anyway.

Kataragama

♪ 047 / POP 12,600

This most holy of towns is a compelling mix of pomp and procession, piety and religious extravagance. Along with Adam's Peak (Sri Pada), Kataragama is the most important pilgrimage site in Sri Lanka; a holy place for Buddhists, Muslims, Hindus and Veddah people.

It is one of those wonderful destinations where the most outlandish of legends becomes solid fact and magic floats in clouds of incense. Many believe that King Dutugemunu built a shrine to Kataragama Deviyo (the resident god) here in the 2nd century BC, but the site is thought to have been significant for even longer.

In July and August, the Kataragama Festival draws thousands of pilgrims. Apart from festival time, the town is busiest at weekends and on *poya* (full moon) days. It's easily visited from Tissa.

◉ Sights

The sacred precinct is set on the other side of Menik Ganga, a chocolate-coloured river in which pilgrims wash before continuing towards the shrines. The site's wide promenades are lined with grey monkeys always on the lookout for a handout – or a dropped personal item. Watch your stuff!

★ Maha Devale   HINDU SHRINE

This is Kataragama's most important shrine. It contains the lance of the six-faced, 12-armed Hindu war god, Murugan (Skanda), who is seen as identical to the Kataragama Deviyo. Followers make offerings at daily *puja* at 4.30am, 10.30am and 6.30pm (no 4.30am offering on Saturday). Outside this shrine are two large boulders, against which pilgrims smash burning coconuts while muttering a prayer.

Kirivehara   BUDDHIST STUPA

An impressive 29m white dagoba in the north of the sacred compound. It's thought to have been built during the reign of King Mahasena (AD 276–303) who also constructed the Jetavanarama Dagoba in Anuradhapura and many large tanks.

Ul-Khizr Mosque   MOSQUE

The second holy site you see as you pass through the holy compound. This beautiful mosque features intricate coloured tile work and wooden lintels, and the tombs of two

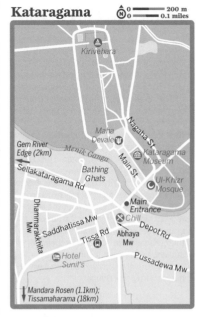

Kataragama

holy men (who originated from Central Asia and India).

Kataragama Museum   MUSEUM

(Rs 650; ☉ 8.30am-4.30pm Wed-Mon) This archaeological museum inside the complex has a collection of Hindu and Buddhist religious items, as well as huge fibreglass replicas of statues from around Sri Lanka. The labelling, however, is woeful.

✻ Festivals & Events

★ Kataragama Festival   RELIGIOUS

(www.kataragama.org; ☉ late Jul-early Aug) This predominantly Hindu festival draws thousands of devotees who make the pilgrimage (the Long Walk to Kataragama) over a two-week period.

⊨ Sleeping & Eating

Kataragama's accommodations are limited. Book well ahead during the festival, or find a bed in neighbouring Tissa and visit as a day-trip. You'll find simple snack stands along Tissa Rd and at the parking lots.

Hotel Sunil's   GUESTHOUSE $

(♪ 047-567 7172; www.hotelsunilskataragama.com; 61 Tissa Rd; r with fan/air-con Rs 2500/3000; ❄ 🛜) This cheery little guesthouse is right on the

THE LONG WALK TO KATARAGAMA

Forty-five days before the annual Kataragama Festival starts on the Esala *poya* (full moon) in July, a group of Kataragama devotees start walking the length of Sri Lanka for the Pada Yatra pilgrimage. Seeking spiritual development, the pilgrims believe they are walking in the steps of the god Kataragama (also known as Murugan) and the Veddahs, who made the first group pilgrimage on this route.

The route follows the east coast from the Jaffna Peninsula, via Trincomalee and Batticaloa to Okanda, then through Yala National Park to Kataragama. It's an arduous trip, and the pilgrims rely on the hospitality of the communities and temples they pass for their food and lodging. Although often interrupted during the war years, the walk is again hugely popular.

Pilgrims arrive in Kataragama just before the festival's feverish activity. Elephants parade, drummers drum. Vows are made and favours sought by devotees, who demonstrate their sincerity by performing extraordinary acts of penance and self-mortification on one particular night: some swing from hooks that pierce their skin, others roll half-naked over the hot sands near the temple. A few perform the act of walking on beds of red-hot cinders – treading the flowers, as it's called. The fire-walkers fast, meditate and pray, bathe in Menik Ganga (Menik River) and then worship at Maha Devale before facing their ordeal. Then, fortified by their faith, they step out onto the glowing path while the audience cries out encouragement.

The festival officially ends with a water-cutting ceremony (said to bring rain for the harvest) in Menik Ganga.

main drag of the quiet strip that passes for Kataragama's centre. The 10 rooms are brightly painted and all have air-con, private hot-water bathrooms and cable TV.

Gem River Edge HOMESTAY **$$**
(☑ 047-223 6325; www.gemriveredge.com; off Sella Rd; r from US$52; ☏) A riverside ecolodge that offers a special, rural location 2km northwest of the centre. Take one of the bikes and explore the countryside, have a dip in the river, and watch the butterflies and birds. There's superb home-cooked pure veg food, too, but be aware rooms are a little dark, only two are en suite and there's no hot water.

Mandara Rosen HOTEL **$$$**
(☑ 047-223 6030; www.mandararesorts.com; Tissa Rd; r from US$110; ❋☏☰) The smartest address in the area is the Rosen, which is surrounded by woodlands 2km south of the centre. The rooms are good, but the hotel's most unusual asset is the pool, which has an underwater music system (though its odd shape is not great for laps). There's also

a spa and fitness centre, and a good, shady cafe open to all.

Chill SRI LANKAN **$$**
(40 Abhaya Mawatha; meals Rs 250-650; ⊙ 7am-11pm) The best eatery in town, this busy little place serves up good local and Chinese dishes at very fair rates. Doubles as a store, so you can stock up on snacks here, too.

❶ Getting There & Away

There are frequent buses to Tissamaharama and Colombo. The **bus station** (Tissa Rd) is centrally placed and has connections including the following:

Colombo (via coastal road) regular/semi-luxe Rs 252/476, 8½ hours, every 30 minutes
Colombo (via expressway) luxury air-con Rs 860, six hours, four daily
Tissamaharama regular Rs 37, 30 minutes, every 20 minutes

The coastal train line was being extended to Kataragama at the time of research and was scheduled for completion in 2018.

The Hill Country

Best Places to Eat

➡ Matey Hut (p190)

➡ Sharon Inn (p160)

➡ High Tea at the Grand (p180)

➡ Hill Club (p180)

Best Places to Sleep

➡ Rainforest (p200)

➡ Chamodya Homestay (p193)

➡ Baramba House (p167)

➡ Tea Trails (p172)

➡ Waterfall Homestay (p193)

➡ Clock Inn Kandy (p157)

Why Go?

Sri Lanka's Hill Country is the island at its most scenic, a mist-wrapped land of emerald peaks and stupendous views, of hillsides carpeted with tea plantations and graced by astonishing waterfalls. This is a place where you can wear a fleece in the daytime and cuddle up beside a log fire in the evening. Where you can enjoy a memorable meal in the eternal city of Kandy or at a roadside shack in lovely Ella. A region where you can walk to the end of the world, stand in the footsteps of the Buddha and be surrounded by a hundred wild elephants. Ride a train utterly bewitched by the vistas. Paddle a raft down a raging river. Enjoy the drumbeat of traditional dance and then savour the silence on a lonely mountaintop.

When to Go
Nuwara Eliya

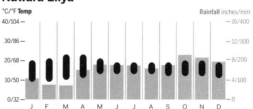

Jan Perfect for clear days, crisp nights and the pilgrimage up Adam's Peak.

Apr The Sinhalese New Year means horse racing and a hectic social calendar in Nuwara Eliya.

Jul–Aug Rain showers do little to deter the crowds who gather for the Esala Perahera festival.

The Hill Country Highlights

1 Horton Plains (p181)
Hiking across a high plateau to the viewpoint of World's End.

2 Nuwara Eliya (p173)
Taking high tea in an atmospheric colonial-era hotel.

3 Adam's Peak (p171)
Joining devout pilgrims and ascending the sacred mountain by flickering torchlight.

4 Hills Railways (p191)
Travelling on a scenic rail journey from Haputale to Ella.

5 Sinharaja Forest Reserve (p197) Discovering your inner birdwatcher in this impressive rainforest reserve.

6 Ella (p188) Savouring the vistas in this small town with big views.

7 Knuckles Range (p167)
Trekking through montane forests, well off the beaten path.

8 Uda Walawe National Park (p195) Counting elephants in this wildlife-rich reserve.

9 Kandy (p151) Explpre the Sri Lankan centre of Buddhism and the country's main arts base.

Colombo to Kandy

The uphill journey from Colombo to Kandy passes through the lush foothills of Sri Lanka's central mountains. Dotted along the route are several attractions worth visiting.

The first place of interest is the **Henerathgoda Botanic Gardens** (Gampaha Botanical Garden; ☑ 033-222 2316; Gampaha; ⊗ 8.30am-5pm), about 30km northwest of Colombo, where the first rubber trees in Asia were planted (in 1876, after being brought here from Brazil). These lush, tropical gardens cover 17 hectares and are home to over 400 plant species, including towering palms and a good orchid collection.

About 50km from Kandy is **Cadjugama**, famous for its cashew nuts. At the 48km post is **Radawaduwa**, notable for woven cane items.

Kegalle, 77km from Colombo, is surrounded by several spice farms and is the nearest town to the Pinnewala Elephant Orphanage.

Initially created to protect abandoned or orphaned elephants, the **Pinnewala Elephant Orphanage** (☑ 035-226 6116; http://nationalzoo.gov.lk/elephantorphanage; adult/child Rs 2500/1250; ⊗ 8.30am-5.30pm) is one of Sri Lanka's most popular attractions. It's a highly commercialised experience, with hefty entrance fees for foreigners (25 times the local price) and mahouts demanding extortionate tips for photos. Sure, you get up close to elephants and see them bathing, but the orphanage's conservation value is questionable and organisations including Born Free (www.bornfree.org.uk) have published negative critiques of the centre. Overall, national parks are the best places to see Sri Lankan elephants.

Two kilometres from Pinnewala on the Karandupona–Kandy road is the **Millennium Elephant Foundation** (☑ 035-226 3377; http://millenniumelephantfoundation.com; adult/child Rs 1000/500; ⊗ 8.30am-4pm; ☎), which houses elephants rescued from aggressive mahouts and elephants retired from working in temples. Be aware that though elephants are well-cared for here, they are chained for quite long periods and elephant rides are offered. Volunteers are welcome at the foundation.

Nearby is **Utuwankandu**, a rocky hill from where the 19th-century Robin Hood-style highwayman Saradiel preyed on travellers until the British executed him.

At **Kadugannawa**, just after the road and railway make their most scenic climbs – with views southwest to the large Bible Rock – is a tall pillar erected in memory of Captain Dawson, the English engineer who built the Colombo–Kandy road in 1826.

ℹ Getting There & Away

The A1 Hwy is always busy, particularly on weekends. Traffic congestion should ease once the EO4 expressway is completed (perhaps by 2019).

Cadjugama, Kegalle and Kadugannawa are on the A1, easily accessible by bus between Colombo and Kandy. Catch a train to Kadugannawa and the Henerathgoda Botanic Gardens at Gampaha.

The Pinnewala Elephant Orphanage is a few kilometres north of the A1 Colombo–Kandy road, accessible by three-wheeler from Karandunpona on the A1 Hwy or from Rambukkana station.

Kandy

☑ 081 / POP 112,000 / ELEV 500M

Some days Kandy's skies seem perpetually bruised, with stubborn mist clinging to the hills surrounding the city's beautiful centrepiece lake. Delicate hill-country breezes impel the mist to gently part, revealing colourful houses amid Kandy's improbable forested halo. In the centre of town, three-wheelers careen around slippery corners, raising a soft spray that threatens the silk saris worn by local women. Here's a city that looks good even when it's raining.

And when the drizzle subsides, cobalt-blue skies reveal a city of imposing colonial-era and Kandyan architecture, none more impressive than the Temple of the Sacred Tooth Relic, one of Buddhism's most sacred shrines.

History and culture are on tap. Yes, the city is renowned for the great Kandy Esala Perahera festival (held annually in July/August), but its vibrant cultural life and attractions more than justify a visit at any time of year.

History

Kandy served as the capital of the last Sinhalese kingdom, which fell to the British in 1815 after defying the Portuguese and Dutch for three centuries. It took the British another 16 tough years to finally build a road linking Kandy with Colombo. The locals still proudly see themselves as a little different – and perhaps a tad superior – to Sri Lankans from the island's lower reaches. Indeed, some grumble that when the new expressway from Kandy is completed (perhaps by 2019 or 2020), the cultured character of the city will inevitably be diluted.

THE HILL COUNTRY COLOMBO TO KANDY

⊙ Sights

★ Temple of the Sacred Tooth Relic

BUDDHIST TEMPLE

(Sri Dalada Maligawa; www.sridaladamaligawa.lk; off Dalada Vidiya; adult/child Rs 1500/free; ⊘ temple 5.30am-8pm, puja 5.30-6.45am, 9.30-11am & 6.30-8pm) The golden-roofed Temple of the Sacred Tooth houses Sri Lanka's most important Buddhist relic – a tooth of the Buddha. During *puja* (offerings or prayers), the heavily guarded room housing the tooth is open to devotees and tourists. However, you don't actually see the tooth. It's kept in a gold casket shaped like a dagoba (stupa), which contains a series of six dagoba caskets of diminishing size.

As well as the revered main temple, the complex includes a series of smaller temples, shrines and museums.

Freelance guides will offer their services around the entire temple complex for around Rs 600, and free audio guides are available at the ticket office. An elevator facilitates access for travellers with disabilities.

The complex can get crowded as it receives many worshippers and tourists, and backpackers, Chinese tour groups and Thai monks all jostle for space. Wear clothes that cover your legs and your shoulders, and remove your shoes.

➡ Alut Maligawa

BUDDHIST TEMPLE

(entrance included in temple ticket; ⊘ 5.30am-8pm) The three-storey Alut Maligawa is a large shrine hall displaying dozens of sitting Buddhas donated by devotees from Thailand. Its design resembles a Thai Buddhist temple, reflecting the fact that Thai monks reestablished Sri Lanka's ordination lineage during the reign of King Kirti Sri Rajasinha.

Set on the upper two floors, the **Sri Dalada Museum** (⊘ 7.30am-6pm) displays a stunning array of gifts donated by several presidents and Buddhist leaders from across the world to the Temple of the Sacred Tooth Relic. Letters and diary entries from the British era reveal the colonisers' surprisingly respectful attitude to the tooth relic. More recent photographs reveal the significant damage caused to the temple complex by a truck bomb detonated by the LTTE in 1998.

➡ Audience Hall

NOTABLE BUILDING

(entrance included in temple ticket; ⊘ 5.30am-8pm) To the north of the Temple of the Sacred Tooth Relic, but still within the compound, is the 19th-century Audience Hall, an open-air pavilion with stone columns carved to look like wooden pillars. Adjacent in the **Rajah Tusker Hall** (entrance included in temple ticket; ⊘ 5.30am-8pm) are the stuffed remains of Rajah, a Maligawa tusker who died in 1988.

➡ World Buddhism Museum

MUSEUM

(Rs 500; ⊘ 8am-7pm) Housed inside the former High Court buildings, the World Buddhism Museum contains lots of photographs, models and displays illustrating Buddhism around the world. Note that a large number of the statues and other exhibits are actually reproductions. The museum is within the Temple of the Sacred Tooth Relic complex and can only be accessed via the temple.

Kandy Lake

LAKE

Dominating the town is Kandy Lake. A leisurely stroll around it, with a few stops on the lakeside seats, is a pleasant way to spend a few hours, although diesel-spurting buses careening around the southern edge of the lake can mar the peace somewhat. The nicest part to walk along is the area around the Temple of the Sacred Tooth Relic. Due to some past cases of harassment, single women should not walk here alone after dark.

National Museum

MUSEUM

(☑ 081-222 3867; www.museum.gov.lk; adult/child Rs 600/300, camera/video camera Rs 250/1500; ⊘ 9am-5pm Tue-Sat) This museum once housed Kandyan royal concubines and now features royal regalia and reminders of pre-European Sinhalese life. One of the most impressive exhibits is Rajasinha II's golden crown, but for visitors the museum is let down by poor lighting, labelling and general layout. The tall-pillared audience hall hosted the convention of Kandyan chiefs that ceded the kingdom to Britain in 1815.

One of the displays is a copy of the 1815 agreement that handed over the Kandyan provinces to British rule. This document announces a major reason for the event: '...the cruelties and oppressions of the Malabar ruler'.

Sri Wickrama Rajasinha was declared 'by the habitual violation of the chief and most sacred duties of a sovereign', to be 'fallen and deposed from office of king' and 'dominion of the Kandyan provinces' was 'vested in... the British Empire'.

The museum, along with four *devales* (complexes for worshipping deities) and two monasteries – but not the Temple of the

Sacred Tooth Relic itself – make up one of Sri Lanka's cultural triangle sites.

Kandy Garrison Cemetery CEMETERY
(⊙8am-6pm) FREE This well-maintained cemetery contains 163 graves from colonial times. Perhaps the most striking aspect of a visit here is learning just how young most people were when they died – if you made it to 40 you were of a very ripe old age. Some of the deaths were due to sunstroke, elephants or 'jungle fevers'. You'll probably be shown around by the highly informed caretaker, who once guided the UK's Prince Charles here, and who seems to have a tale for every tomb.

St Paul's Church CHURCH
(Deva Veediya) Construction of this impressive red-brick colonial-era church began in 1843 and was completed five years later. Built in neo-Gothic style, it originally served as a garrison church for British troops based nearby.

Udawattakelle Sanctuary FOREST
(adult/child Rs 650/375; ⊙6am-6pm) This forest on the north side of Kandy Lake has soaring hardwood trees and giant bamboo, good birding and loads of cheeky monkeys.

Birdwatchers can arrange guides (Rs 500) at the ticket office. There are two main paths you can follow, and smaller tracks too.

Be careful if you're visiting alone. Muggers are rare, but not unknown; solo women should take extra care. Enter by turning right after the post office on DS Senanayake Vidiya. Last tickets issued at 4.30pm.

Devales
There are four Kandyan *devales* to the gods who are followers of Buddha and protect Sri Lanka.

Natha Devale BUDDHIST TEMPLE
(⊙24hr) The 14th-century Natha Devale is the oldest of Kandy's *devales*. It perches on a stone terrace with a fine *vahalkada* (solid panel of sculpture) gateway. Bodhi trees and dagobas stand in the *devale* grounds.

Vishnu Devale BUDDHIST TEMPLE
(⊙24hr) The Vishnu Devale is reached by carved steps and features a drumming hall. The great Hindu god Vishnu is the guardian of Sri Lanka, demonstrating the intermingling of Hinduism and Buddhism.

HISTORY OF THE TOOTH

The sacred tooth of the Buddha is said to have been snatched from the flames of the Buddha's funeral pyre in 483 BC and smuggled into Sri Lanka during the 4th century AD, hidden in the hair of a princess. At first it was taken to Anuradhapura, then it moved through the country on the waves of Sri Lankan history before ending up at Kandy. In 1283 it was carried back to India by an invading army, but it was retrieved by King Parakramabahu III.

The tooth gradually grew in importance as a symbol of sovereignty, and it was believed that whoever had custody of the tooth relic had the right to rule the island. In the 16th century the Portuguese apparently seized the tooth, took it away and burnt it with devout Catholic fervour in Goa. Not so, say the Sinhalese. The Portuguese had actually stolen a replica tooth while the real incisor remained safe. There are still rumours that the real tooth is hidden somewhere secure, and that the tooth kept in Kandy's Temple of the Sacred Tooth Relic is only a replica.

The temple was constructed mainly under Kandyan kings from 1687 to 1707 and from 1747 to 1782, and the entire temple complex was part of the Kandyan royal palace. The imposing pinky-white structure is surrounded by a moat. The octagonal tower in the moat was built by Sri Wickrama Rajasinha and used to house an important collection of *ola* (talipot-palm leaf) manuscripts. This section of the temple was heavily damaged in a 1998 bomb blast.

The main tooth shrine – a two-storey rectangular building known as the Vahahitina Maligawa – occupies the centre of a paved courtyard. The eye-catching gilded roof over the relic chamber was paid for by Japanese donors. The 1998 bomb exposed part of the front wall to reveal at least three layers of 18th- to 20th-century paintings depicting the *perahera* (procession) and various Jataka tales (stories of the Buddha's previous lives).

Sri Lankan Buddhists believe they must complete at least one pilgrimage to the temple in their lifetime, as worshipping here improves one's karmic lot immeasurably.

Kandy

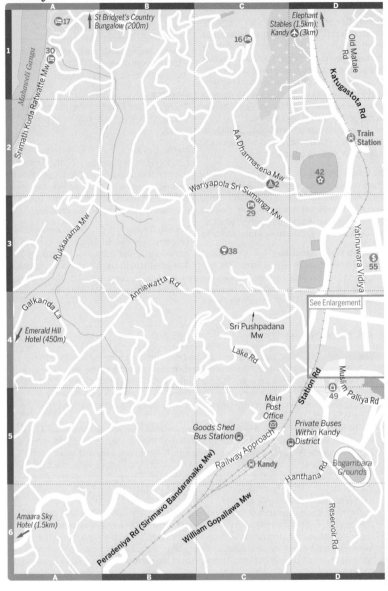

THE HILL COUNTRY KANDY

Pattini Devale BUDDHIST TEMPLE
(Temple St; ⊙ 24hr) The very popular, simple-looking Pattini Devale temple is dedicated to the goddess of chastity. It's frequented by pregnant women and those seeking a cure from disease.

Kataragama Devale HINDU TEMPLE
(Kotugodelle Vidiya; ⊙ 24hr) The brightly painted tower gateway of the Kataragama Devale demands attention amid the bustle on Kotugodelle Vidiya. Murugan, the god of war, has six heads and 12 hands wielding weapons.

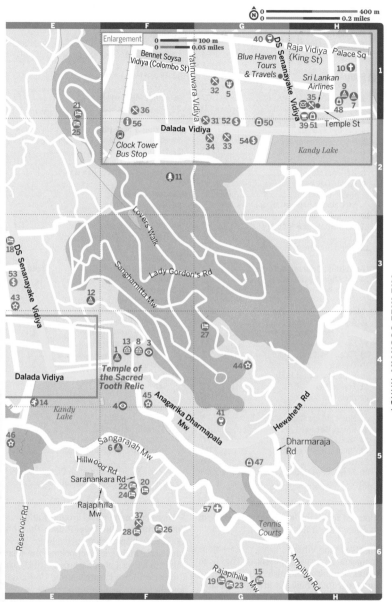

THE HILL COUNTRY KANDY

Viharas

The principal *viharas* (Buddhist complexes) in Kandy have considerable importance – the high priests of the two best known, Malwatte and Asgiriya, are the most important in Sri Lanka. These *viharas* are the headquarters of two of the main *nikayas* (orders of monks).

Malwatte Maha Vihara   BUDDHIST SITE
(Sanagaraja Mawatha) One of the principal *viharas* in Kandy, the Malwatte Maha Vihara

Kandy

is located across the lake from the Temple of the Sacred Tooth Relic (p152).

Asgiriya Maha Vihara   BUDDHIST SITE
(Wariyapola Sri Sumanga Mawatha) The head monks here also administer the Temple of the Sacred Tooth Relic. Inside, there's a large reclining Buddha. It's located 1km northwest of the town centre.

 Activities

Visitors can learn or practise meditation and study Buddhism at several places in the Kandy area. Ask at the Buddhist Publication Society (p161) for details about courses.

There are many walks around Kandy, including through the **Royal Palace Park** (Rs 100; ⊙8.30am-5pm), constructed by Sri Wickrama Rajasinha and overlooking the lake. The Peradeniya Botanic Gardens (p165) are also perfect for a leisurely stroll. Up on Rajapihilla Mawatha there are lovely views over the lake, the town and the surrounding hills. For longer walks, there are paths branching out from Rajapihilla Mawatha.

Sri Lanka Trekking   HIKING
(☑071 499 7666, 075 799 7667; www.srilanka trekking.com; Expeditor Guest House, 41 Sarankara Rd) These professionals can arrange trekking around Kandy, and camping and

trekking (and birdwatching) expeditions to the rugged Knuckles Range. They also offer safaris to Wasgamuwa National Park (and many other reserves), plus mountain-biking and rafting trips. For a standard overnight trek in the Knuckles expect to pay €75. The per-person price decreases with group size. They have an office in the Expeditor Guest House.

Joy Motorboat Service
BOATING

(20min Rs 2000; ⏰ 9am-6pm) Put on an eye patch and set sail like a pirate into the great blue...lake. Little puttering boats can be hired from this place on the jetty at the western end of the lake.

🛏 Sleeping

Kandy has many good guesthouses, and the more comfortable hotels often occupy spectacular hilltop or riverside locations.

In the city centre, the highest concentration of accommodation is along or just off Anagarika Dharmapala Mawatha and Saranankara Rd (buses 654, 655 and 698 will get you there, or just ask for 'Sanghamitta Mawatha' at the clock tower bus stop). Most places have in-house restaurants.

⭐ Clock Inn Kandy
HOSTEL $

(☎ 081-223 5311; www.clockinnkandy.lk; 11 Hill St; dm/d from US$13/45; ❄ 🌐) A lot of know-how has gone into this very well-set-up hostel, with its inviting air-con dorms (all with lockers, comfy bunks and reading lights) and lovely private doubles with en suites. They also offer some totally wacky rooftop capsule-style tube-beds (not for the claustrophobic!). There are ample lounging zones for socialising and it's located close to the train station.

Hotel Mango Garden
GUESTHOUSE $

(☎ 081-223 5135; www.mangogarden.lk; 32/A Saranankara Rd; r Rs 3000-4000; ❄ 🌐) Manager Malik and his French wife run a tight ship here. Rooms are plain but spacious with good bedding, though the bathrooms are more prosaic. There's a lovely terrace restaurant for drinks and excellent meals (open to all). Call them for free pick-up from the bus or train station.

Expeditor Guest House
GUESTHOUSE $

(☎ 081-490 1628, 081-223 8316; www.expeditor kandy.com; 41 Saranankara Rd; r Rs 2500-5500; ❄ 🌐) Lots of potted plants, balconies with views, a warm welcome, spotless rooms (some have shared bathrooms) and the opportunity to mix with the hospitable proprietors give Expeditor a cosy bed-and-breakfast feel. Speak to the owners about treks in the Knuckles mountains and other regions.

McLeod Inn
GUESTHOUSE $

(☎ 081-222 2832; www.mcleodinnkandy.com; 65A Rajapihilla Mawatha; r Rs 3200-4200; ❄ 🌐) A fine family-run guesthouse with lovely lake views from some of its 10 comfortable, clean and well-presented rooms. You'll enjoy the dining area and its valley views for that essential end-of-the-day combination: a good book and a cold drink.

Freedom Lodge
HOMESTAY $$

(☎ 081-222 3506; www.freedom-lodge-kandy-sri-lanka.en.ww.lk; 30 Saranankara Rd; r incl breakfast from Rs 5000; 🌐) This popular, well-established guesthouse is owned by a friendly family, one of whom worked in hospitality for years, and is surrounded by towering palm trees. The rooms are attractive and have modern en suites with hot water. Those on the upper floor have the best views. Home-cooked meals can be requested; you eat communally, so can mix with other guests.

Day's Inn
GUESTHOUSE $$

(☎ 081-224 1124; www.daysinn-kandy.com; 66A Rajapihilla Mawatha; d/tr/apt US$49/56/96; ❄ 🌐 🏊) Staying at this intimate six-room guesthouse

---

KANDY FOR CHILDREN

Kandy isn't as obviously child-friendly as Sri Lanka's beaches and national parks, but there are a few sights and activities that'll keep little ones – and therefore you as well – happy and sane. Renting a boat from **Joy Motorboat Service** for a putter about the lake and then hiring a tuk-tuk to buzz around the city streets is sure to delight. Children can burn off energy in the Udawattakelle Sanctuary (p153) and Peradeniya Botanic Gardens (p165), and, with their elaborate costumes and fire eaters, Kandy's various **dance shows** will surely meet with approval. The Temple of the Sacred Tooth Relic (p152) has enough exotica to capture the imagination of most children and there's also a surprisingly good children's **play park** (Sanagaraja Rd; ⏰ 7am-6pm Tue-Sun) at the eastern end of the lake.

HELGA'S FOLLY

'If expecting a regular hotel experience best look elsewhere' says the marketing blurb, and that's 100% accurate, for **Helga's Folly** (☏ 081-223 4571; www.helgasfolly.com; off Rajapihilla Mawatha; r US$100-130, nonguest admission US$3; ✳ 🛜 🏊) could have been dreamt up as a joint project between Gaudí and Dalí. This hotel/art gallery/surrealist dream has to be the most extraordinary hotel in Sri Lanka. Indeed, the Stereophonics famously wrote the song 'Madame Helga' about the owner.

It's run and designed by the outlandish Helga da Silva, who grew up in a world of 1950s Hollywood celebrities, artists, writers, politicians and general intrigue, and she has to be one of the only hotel owners who prefers her property not to be full! As extraordinary as it all is, once you've peeled through all the decorations you'll see that the place is actually looking pretty tatty. Rather than staying in this self-styled 'antihotel' we recommend just popping past for a poke about and a drink – for many people it's actually one of the most interesting sights in Kandy. Writers and artists get half-price rates (six nights minimum).

is a pleasure. It's bursting with pictures, colour and decorations and has a warm, homely feel. Rooms are all en suite and good food is available. Note that the pool is a short walk away, where the family apartment is located.

St Bridget's Country Bungalow HOMESTAY $$
(☏ 081-221 5806; www.stbridgets-kandy.com; 125 Sri Sumangala Mawatha, Asgiriya; r from Rs 2800; @ 🛜) Hemmed in by jungly forest filled with birds, this traditional homestay has eight simply furnished rooms, a very warm welcome and fine home-cooked breakfasts and dinners. It's a 20-minute uphill walk from town, or Rs 250ish in a three-wheeler.

Kandy Cottage GUESTHOUSE $$
(☏ 081-220 4742; www.kandycottage.com; 160 Lady Gordon's Dr, Sri Dalada Thapowana Mawatha; s Rs 2000-3200, d Rs 3600-4800; 🛜) Run by Thomas and Mani, a very welcoming couple, this slightly bohemian place is a great escape from the city, a Sri Lankan cottage tucked away in a forested valley on the fringes of the Udawattakelle Sanctuary. There are three rooms (or you can rent the entire cottage) with chunky wooden furniture and polished concrete floors, though no air-con.

It's about 2km north of the centre.

Anna Shanthi Villa GUESTHOUSE $$
(☏ 081-222 3315; annashanthivilla@gmail.com; 203 Rajapihilla Tce; s/d incl breakfast US$52/58; ✳ 🛜) Tucked away up a quiet lane, not far from the lake, this well-run guesthouse has seven rooms with good-quality furnishings and a lot more style than many similarly priced places. The standard of service is excellent, with staff going out of their way to help.

Sharon Inn HOTEL $$
(☏ 081-220 1400; 59 Saranankara Rd; r incl breakfast Rs 6500-8500; ✳ @ 🛜) This small hilltop place is one of Kandy's longest-established hotels and it has excellent views and scrupulously clean rooms decorated with Sri Lankan arts and crafts. Staff are genuinely welcoming and fully switched on to travel information and tours. Don't miss the dinner buffet (p160) here, which is one of the best dining experiences in Kandy.

Nature Walk Resort GUESTHOUSE $$
(☏ 077 771 7482; www.naturewalkhr.net; 9 Sanghamitta Mawatha; r incl breakfast US$22-55; ✳ 🛜) Terracotta tiles and French doors lead to balconies with, from some rooms, excellent forest views. The rooms are spacious and airy, and you can look forward to troops of monkeys in the morning and squadrons of bats at dusk.

Blue Haven Guesthouse GUESTHOUSE $$
(☏ 081-222 9617; bluehavtravels@gmail.com; 30/2 Poorna Lane, Asgiriya; incl breakfast dm Rs 1500, r from Rs 3500; ✳ 🛜 🏊) The rooms here are quite ordinary, but the pool is a big plus and there are fantastic views out over the Knuckles Range. The proprietor, Mr Linton, is an entertaining host who can arrange car hire and tours of the country. It's north of the centre; a three-wheeler ride into town costs Rs 300.

Forest Glen GUESTHOUSE $$
(☏ 081-222 2239; www.forestglenkandy.com; 150/6 Lady Gordon's Dr, Sri Dalada Thapowana Mawatha; s/d/tr Rs 3500/5500/7000; 🛜) This wonderfully secluded, though slightly faded, family guesthouse is on the edge of Udawattakelle Sanctuary and has fine forest views from its

terrace. Indra is a welcoming host and prepares tasty local and Western food. It's 1.5km north of central Kandy.

★ **Clove Villa**   BOUTIQUE HOTEL **$$$**
(☑ 081-221 2999; www.clovevilla.com; 48 P B A, Weerakoon; r US$170-205; ❄ 🖥 ☒) A superb converted villa with seven gorgeous rooms, all with plush, tasteful furnishings and a dash of art, and kitted out with all the mod cons you could want. There's fine in-house dining, a billiards table and a library. It's 5km north of the centre, located on a bend in the river.

★ **Villa Rosa**   BOUTIQUE HOTEL **$$$**
(☑ 081-221 5556; www.villarosa-kandy.com; Asgiriya; s US$95-160, d US$140-235; ❄ 🖥) Dotted with antiques, and with stunning views over a secluded arc of the Mahaweli Ganga, Villa Rosa is an inspiring place to stay. Spacious wooden-floored rooms in cool, neutral tones share the limelight with relaxing lounges and a lovely reading room. A separate pavilion houses yoga and meditation centres. Two-night minimum stay required.

It's very popular, so book well ahead.

Elephant Stables   BOUTIQUE HOTEL **$$$**
(☑ 081-743 3201; www.elephantstables.com; 46 Nittawela Rd; r incl breakfast from US$174; ❄ 🖥 ☒) This stunning villa was once the home of Sir Cudah Ratwatte, the first elected mayor of Kandy. Today, it's been lovingly converted into a beautiful hotel, with excellent service, earthy tones, polished concrete and gnarled wood. Two rooms have balconies overlooking an inviting pool and the not-so-distant mountains. There's a fab bar, and a reading room well stocked with Sri Lanka–related titles. True to its name, elephants used to be stabled here.

Cinnamon Citadel   RESORT **$$$**
(☑ 081-223 4365; www.cinnamonhotels.com; 124 Srimath Kuda Ratwatte Mawatha; r incl breakfast from US$98; ❄ 🖥 ☒) This well-designed hotel boasts a stunning location, its large pool located right by the riverbank. Designer-chic rooms in chocolate tones and grey slate are fine value given the facilities, which include a spa, gym, cafe and lounge bar. It's 5km west of Kandy; a taxi costs around Rs 600 one way.

🍴 Eating

Kandy, like many other Sir Lankan towns, does not have much of a dining scene. Most travellers eat in their hotel or at one of a handful of restaurants in the centre. Some fancier places to eat have recently opened, and Kandy now has a good selection of cafes serving Western-style snacks, cakes and treats.

★ **Empire Café**   INTERNATIONAL **$$**
(☑ 081-223 9870; www.empirecafekandy.com; 21 Temple St; meals Rs 365-780; ⊗ 8.30am-8.30pm; 🖥) This flamboyantly styled, very inviting restaurant, in historical colonial-era premises,

KANDY ESALA PERAHERA

This *perahera* (procession) is held in Kandy to honour the sacred tooth enshrined in the Temple of the Sacred Tooth Relic (p152). It runs for 10 days in the month of Esala (July/August), ending on the Nikini *poya* (full moon).

The first six nights are relatively low-key. On the seventh night, proceedings escalate as the route lengthens and the procession becomes more splendid (and accommodation prices increase accordingly). The procession is led by thousands of Kandyan dancers and drummers beating drums, cracking whips and waving colourful banners. Then come long processions of up to 50 elephants. The Maligawa tusker is decorated from trunk to toe. On the last two nights of the *perahera* it carries a huge canopy sheltering the empty casket of the sacred relic cask. A trail of pristine white linen is laid before the elephant.

The Kandy Esala Perahera has been performed annually for many centuries and is described by Robert Knox in his 1681 book *An Historical Relation of Ceylon*. There is also a smaller procession on the *poya* day in June, and special *peraheras* may be put on for important occasions.

The ceremony is certainly one of South Asia's most spectacular. But before you go ahead and book tickets, you may want to consider the elephants' welfare. Sri Lankan campaigners point out that the cacophonous *perahera* noise can deeply affect the mammals, which have very sensitive hearing, and that the constant prodding by mahouts and their *ankus* (hooks) is painful. Chains and buckles are used to control elephants and constrain their mobility. Their long journey to Kandy is made either on the back of a truck (in the scorching sun) or on foot, treading on sizzling tarmac.

has a selection of vibrantly painted (pink and turquoise) dining rooms that make for a great place to take a break from a sightseeing session. Tuck into tasty breakfasts, rice and curries, pastas, wraps, salads, juices and milkshakes.

Kandy Muslim Hotel SRI LANKAN **$$**
(Dalada Vidiya; meals Rs 150-510; ⊙6.30am-9pm) No, it's not a hotel, but this bustling eatery offers Kandy's best samosas, authentically spiced curries and heaving plates of frisbee-sized, but gossamer-light, flat breads. However, what people really come for are the *kotthu* (*rotti* chopped and fried with meat and vegetables), which come in a variety of styles, flavours and prices (chicken starts at Rs 220).

Cafe Divine Street INTERNATIONAL **$$**
(☑077 699 2799; www.facebook.com/cafedivine street; 139 Colombo St; meals from Rs 300; ⊙10am-9pm Wed-Sun) Run by an industrious local, this tiny, inexpensive cafe offers great burgers, kebabs, subs and fried rice dishes; all are well seasoned and attractively presented. There are more tables upstairs, with good street views.

Cafe Walk CAFE **$$**
(Dalada Vidiya; meals Rs 350-900; ⊙9am-6pm; 🖎) This open-sided cafe is where many of Kandy's bright young things like to hang out, with tables facing busy Dalada Vidiya. It's great for breakfast (with good almond pancakes) as well as sandwiches, paninis and salads. All your favourite espresso coffee options are also available.

Devon Restaurant INTERNATIONAL **$$**
(11 Dalada Vidiya; meals Rs 175-725; ⊙7.30am-8pm) This large and busy restaurant and bakery has a long menu of Sri Lankan and Chinese staples, a biryani or two and a few lacklustre Western offerings. Rice and curry (from Rs 175) is a winner and includes four side dishes. The main dining hall is a smart canteen-like affair.

Bake House SRI LANKAN **$$**
(☑081-223 4868; www.bakehousekandy.com; 36 Dalada Vidiya; meals from Rs 220; ⊙7.30am-8pm) Old-timer Bake House now has a smart (air-conditioned) dining room as well as the ground-floor cafe. On the dependable, but not wildly exciting, menu you'll find baked goodies, curries, sandwiches and Chinese and Indian dishes. Pop in just after 3pm, when the second bake of the day comes out and the short eats are still warm.

★**Sharon Inn** SRI LANKAN **$$$**
(☑081-220 1400; 59 Saranankara Rd; meals Rs 500-1300; ⊙7-9pm; 🖎) The nightly buffet dinner (Rs 1100) at this hotel (p158), served at 7.30pm sharp in the starlit rooftop restaurant, is a tasty short cut to falling in love with Sri Lankan cuisine. It's a true feast of veggie curry – jackfruit, banana leaf, aubergine and others are all lovingly prepared. Get here for sunset and the views are remarkable. The Sharon Inn is 2km south of Kandy city centre.

Drinking & Nightlife

In this sacred city, the legislation for pubs, bars and clubs is very strict (indeed, many establishments are not permitted liquor licences). Nevertheless, there are a few places for an end-of-day gin and tonic.

★**Royal Bar & Hotel** BAR
(☑081-222 4449; http://royalbarandhotelkandy. com; 44 Raja Vidiya/King St; ⊙7am-11pm; 🖎) The best place in Kandy for a drink, the Royal has benefited from a stunning, sympathetic recent renovation. With a couple of atmospheric bars, a lovely central courtyard and a wonderful upper balcony-terrace, this landmark colonial building offers many choices for a leisurely G&T, malt whisky or cool draught beer. Drink prices are steep; happy 'hour' runs from 5.30pm to 7.30pm. There's also a restaurant menu (mains Rs 1200 to 1500) for Asian dishes and Western classics.

★**Slightly Chilled Lounge Bar** BAR
(www.slightly-chilled.com; 29A Anagarika Dharma-pala Mawatha; ⊙11am-11pm; 🖎) With views out over the lake, pool tables, Premier League football, decent Chinese food and a 5pm to 6pm happy hour, this place is always busy. There's local wine by the glass (Rs 125), arrack drinks, cocktails and imported bottled lagers.

Blackout CLUB
(www.swissresidence.lk/blackout.html; Swiss Residence Hotel, 23 Bahirawakanda; admission incl 1 drink Rs 1000-1500; ⊙9pm-4am Fri & Sat; 🖎) The best nightlife option in Kandy, with credible local and visiting DJs playing progressive and deep house, minimal and techno. Draws a wealthy clubbing crowd who love to dress up. Friday night is the big night.

Natural Coffee CAFE
(☑081-220 5734; http://naturalcoffee.lk; 5 Temple St; ⊙8.30am-7pm; 🖎) A homely cafe with wood-trimmed decor that's perfect for a freshly ground, organic caffeine pick-me-up

DANCERS & DRUMMERS

With elaborate costumes, gyrating dance moves and show-stopping, fire-breathing stunts, a Kandyan dance performance is one of the defining experiences of a stay in Kandy. Calling it a traditional Kandyan dance performance is something of a misnomer as the shows are very much aimed at audience entertainment and contain dance routines and costumes from across the country, including the famous 'devil' dances of the west coast (which are very hard to see in their home region). There are three main venues. All have nightly performances that last an hour (arrive there 30 minutes in advance to get a better seat). None of the venues have air-con, and all can get hot.

Kandy Lake Club (077 367 0763; www.facebook.com/kandylakeclub; 7 Sanghamitta Mawatha; Rs 1000; ⊙ show starts 5pm) Located 300m up Sanghamitta Mawatha, this place has arguably the best costumes of any of the venues staging traditional Sri Lankan dance shows. Performances often conclude with a 'fire walking' (stepping on burning coals) finale. Arrive early for good seats.

Kandyan Art Association & Cultural Centre (www.facebook.com/KandyanArt Association; 72 Sangarajah Mawatha; Rs 500; ⊙ show starts 5pm) This is the busiest dance-show venue and in high season it can be overwhelmingly crammed with tour groups. However, the auditorium makes it easier to take photographs here than at other venues. It's on the northern lake shore. Be sure to arrive well ahead of time to secure seats.

Mahanuwara YMBA (081-223 3444; 5 Rajapihilla Mawatha; Rs 500; ⊙ show starts 5.30pm) Southwest of the lake, the YMBA guesthouse is a low-key venue for Sri Lankan dance; the performances here are entertaining and the crowds somewhat thinner.

You can also hear Kandyan drummers every day at the Temple of the Sacred Tooth Relic (p152) and the other temples surrounding it – their drumming signals the start and finish of the daily *puja* (offering or prayers).

However, it's a tad pricey, with filter coffee costing Rs 400 and a cappuccino Rs 500.

☆ Entertainment

The modest, attractive **Asgiriya Stadium** (off B70 Hwy), 2km north of the centre, hosts college, national and international cricket matches. Tickets are sold on the day, or you can book ahead via the **Sri Lanka Cricket office** (081-223 8533).

Rugby is played between May and September at the Nittawella rugby grounds.

Alliance Française CULTURAL CENTRE
(081-222 4432; www.afkandy.lk; 642 Peradeniya Rd; ⊙ 9am-5pm Tue & Thu-Sun) The Alliance hosts film nights (free on the first Friday of the month), and has books and periodicals. Good coffee is available. Nonmembers can browse the library.

British Council CULTURAL CENTRE
(081-222 2410; www.britishcouncil.lk; 88/3 Kotugodelle Vidiya; ⊙ 9am-5.30pm Tue-Sat, to 3pm Sun) British newspapers, CDs, videos and DVDs, and occasional film nights, exhibitions and plays. Nonmembers may read newspapers on presentation of a passport.

🔒 Shopping

Central Kandy has shops selling antique jewellery and silver belts, and you can buy crafts in the colourful **main market** (Station Rd; ⊙ 8am-7pm).

Selyn FASHION & ACCESSORIES
(081-223 7735; www.selyn.lk; 7/1/1 Temple St; ⊙ 8.30am-6pm) 🌿 Fair-trade textiles, clothing (including saris, sarongs and shirts) and jewellery made of recycled fabric, paper and other materials.

Odel Luv SL CLOTHES
(www.odel.lk/luvsl; shop no L3-3, 5 Dalada Vidiya; ⊙ 10am-7pm) Wacky T-shirts, tacky tourist goods, kitsch flip-flops and some good souvenirs: this shop under the arcades of the Queens Hotel has the lot.

Buddhist Publication Society BOOKS
(081-223 7283; www.bps.lk; 54 Victoria Rd; ⊙ 9am-4.30pm Mon-Fri, to 12.30pm Sat) The Buddhist Publication Society, on the lakeside 400m northeast of the Temple of the Sacred Tooth Relic, is a nonprofit charity that distributes the Buddha's teachings. There's a fine selection of books for sale and

a comprehensive library. This is a good place to ask about meditation courses.

Jayamali Batiks Studio
CLOTHING

(www.jayamalibatiks.com; 196 Main Market) Fine batik clothing and homeware (bedspreads and wall hangings) in modern, artistic styles created by designer Upali Jayakody. It's on the upper floor of the main market.

Rangala House Gallery
ART

(http://rangalahouse.com/gallery; 2nd fl, 7/1/1 Temple St; ⊙10am-5.30pm) The works of local and Colombo-based artists are displayed and sold here. It also sells a range of organic jams made in the hills surrounding Kandy.

Kandyan Art Association & Cultural Centre
ARTS & CRAFTS

(Sangarajah Mawatha; ⊙9am-5pm) Worth browsing for good-quality local lacquerware, brassware and other craft items. There are some craftspeople working on the spot. Prices are slightly inflated.

Cultural Triangle Office
BOOKS

(⊙8am-4.15pm) Has a selection of books on the Ancient Cities for sale. *Kandy*, by Dr Anuradha Seneviratna, is an informative guide to the city's heritage. Also available is *The Cultural Triangle*, published by Unesco and the Central Cultural Fund, which provides background information on the ancient sites.

ℹ Information

DANGERS & ANNOYANCES

The back alleys of the town centre are worth avoiding after dark as they are the natural habitat of drunks and shady characters.

Solo women travellers are sometimes hassled around the lakeside at dusk and after dark. Get a three-wheeler back to your guesthouse to keep safe.

INTERNET ACCESS

Virtually every hotel and guesthouse, and many cafes, have wi-fi access.

MEDICAL SERVICES

Lakeside Adventist Hospital (☑081-222 3466; http://lakesideadventisthospital. blogspot.co.uk; 40 Sangaraja Mawatha) Has English-speaking staff.

MONEY

The following banks all have ATMs and exchange facilities:

Bank of Ceylon (Dalada Vidiya; ⊙9.30am-4.30pm Mon-Fri, to noon Sat)

Commercial Bank (Kotugodelle Vidiya; ⊙9am-5pm Mon-Fri, 9.30am-1pm Sat)

Hatton National Bank (Dalada Vidiya; ⊙9am-5pm Mon-Fri, to noon Sat)

HSBC (Kotugodelle Vidiya; ⊙9am-5.30pm Mon-Fri, 9.30am-1pm Sat)

POST

The **main post office** (⊙7am-7pm Mon-Sat, 8am-5pm Sun) is opposite the train station. A more central post office is at the intersection of Kande Vidiya and DS Senanayake Vidiya.

TOURIST INFORMATION

Cultural Triangle Office (☑081-222 2661; 16 Deva Vidiya; ⊙8am-4pm Mon-Fri) Information on the cultural triangle sites (including Anuradhapura, Polonnaruwa and Dambulla) as well as Kandy's attractions. It's located in a colonial building near the Temple of the Sacred Tooth Relic. Note that there are no longer any cultural triangle tickets for sale.

Kandy Tourist Information Center (☑081-312 2143; Dalada Vidiya; ⊙8.30am-7pm) The main tourist office is right by the clock tower bus stop. Staff have a few leaflets to dispense and can help with train and dance performance schedules.

BUSES FROM KANDY

DESTINATION	BUS STATION	FARE (RS) LUXURY	FARE (RS) NORMAL	DURATION (HR)	FREQUENCY
Anuradhapura	Goods Shed	372	206	3½	every 30min
Badulla	Goods Shed	215	160	3	every 45min
Colombo	Station Rd	240	155	3-4	every 15min
Negombo	Station Rd	248	162	3-4	hourly
Nuwara Eliya	Goods Shed	250	180	3½	every 30min
Polonnaruwa	Goods Shed	272	180	3½	every 30min
Ratnapura	Goods Shed	–	173	3½	hourly
Trincomalee	Goods Shed	–	232	5	4 daily

ⓘ Getting There & Away

AIR

Cinnamon Air (Map p60; ☎ 011-247 5475; www.cinnamonair.com) Runs scheduled flights once or twice daily to and from Colombo and a daily direct flight (US$199 one-way) to Weer-awila airport (for southern Sri Lanka, including Yala National Park).

SriLankan Airlines (☎ 081-223 2495; 17 Temple St; ☺ 8am-6pm Mon-Fri, to 1pm Sat) Ticket reservations can be made here.

BUS

Kandy has one main bus station (the manic Goods Shed) and a series of bus stops near the clock tower. The Goods Shed bus station has long-distance buses, while regular local buses, such as those to Peradeniya (Rs 20), Ampitiya (Rs 18), Matale (Rs 48) and Kegalle (Rs 65), leave from near the clock tower. However, some private intercity express buses – to Negombo and Colombo, for example – leave from Station Rd between the clock tower and the train station. If you're not sure where to go, ask someone to point you the right way.

For Sigiriya, you must change in Polonnaruwa and for Dalhousie you normally have to go to Hatton and change there. Heading to Ella, you'll have to change in Badulla.

TAXI

Cars can generally be hired, with a driver and petrol, for approximately Rs 6000 per day. Many long-distance taxi drivers hang around the Temple of the Sacred Tooth Relic, or ask at your guesthouse or hotel.

Some guesthouses advertise day trips to all three cultural triangle destinations (Sigiriya, Anuradhapura and Polonnaruwa), but this is an exhausting itinerary for both driver and passengers, and one that encourages manic driving. An overnight stay in Anuradhapura, Sigiriya or Polonnaruwa is a saner and safer option.

Blue Haven Tours & Travels (☎ 077 737 2066; www.bluehaventours.com; 25 DS Senanayake Vidiya) One recommended car hire company, charging around US$50 per day.

Nishantha Maldeniya (☎ 077 084 9137; nishantha.maldeniya71@gmail.com) Offers fair rates for local and long-distance trips.

TRAIN

Kandy is a major railway station, and trains to and from here are very popular with visitors. Posh privately run ExpoRail and Rajadhani Express air-conditioned carriages are attached to several trains to and from Kandy. Seats are also very popular in the 1st-class observation saloon on the Badulla-bound train. This train originates in Colombo and after Kandy stops in Hatton (near Adam's Peak), Nanu Oya (for Nuwara Eliya), Haputale, Ella and a number of other Hill Country stations. Observation-class tickets cost a set Rs 1000 for anywhere between Kandy and Nanu Oya and Rs 1250 for any of the stations east of there. Note that delays are common on the line to Hatton.

If you are unable to reserve a seat at the ticket window, enquire with the stationmaster, who can sometimes release further seating for tourists.

Trains run to the following (prices are for unreserved tickets):

Badulla (2nd/3rd class Rs 270/145; 7-8hr; 5 daily)

Colombo (2nd/3rd class Rs 190/105; 2½-3½hr; 7-9 daily)

Ella (2nd/3rd class Rs 240/130; 6-7hr; 5 daily)

Haputale (2nd/3rd class Rs 210/115; 5-6hr; 5 daily)

Hatton (2nd/3rd class Rs 110/65; 2½-3hr; 5 daily)

Nanu Oya (for Nuwara Eliya; 2nd/3rd class Rs 160/90; 3½-4hr; 5 daily)

ⓘ Getting Around

BUS

Buses to outlying parts of Kandy and nearby towns such as Peradeniya, Ampitiya, Matale and Kegalle leave from near the clock tower.

TAXI

With metered air-con taxis, **Radio Cabs** (☎ 081-223 3322) provides a comfortable alternative to three-wheelers. You may have to wait some time for your cab, especially if it's raining and demand is heavy. With taxis (vans) that are not metered, settle on a price before you start your journey.

THREE-WHEELER

Expect to pay around Rs 300 for a three-wheeler from the train station to the southeast end of the lake.

Around Kandy

There are a few things worth seeing around Kandy that can be done as a half-day trip (best undertaken by tuk-tuk or taxi). The Three Temples Loop (including the Lanka-tilake, Gadaladeniya and Embekka temples) is a worthwhile excursion. You might then choose to hit the botanic gardens for the afternoon to make it a full day out.

◉ Sights

★ **Peradeniya Botanic Gardens** GARDENS (www.botanicgardens.gov.lk; adult/child Rs 1500/750; ☺ 7.30am-5pm) These stunning gardens

Around Kandy

See Kandy Map (p154)

Around Kandy

were once reserved exclusively for Kandyan royalty. Today, even commoners are allowed in to enjoy the most impressive and largest (60 hectares) botanic gardens in Sri Lanka.

Highlights include a fine collection of orchids, a stately avenue of royal palms, the extraordinary, aptly named cannonball fruit tree and 40m-high Burma bamboo. Another big hit is the giant Javan fig tree on the great lawn, with its colossal central trunk and umbrella-like canopy of branches. Peradeniya is 6km from central Kandy.

You'll share the gardens with thousands of wing-flapping fruit bats, hundreds of monkeys and dozens of canoodling courting couples.

Inside the grounds are an overpriced cafeteria (mains Rs 550 to Rs 1000), serving Western and Sri Lankan food, and a small cafe by the exit gate. A better option is to stock up on picnic items.

Bus 644 (Rs 16) from Kandy's clock tower bus stop goes to the gardens. A three-wheeler from Kandy is about Rs 400 one way. Many taxi drivers incorporate a visit to the gardens with the Kandy Three Temple Loop.

★Lankatilake Temple
BUDDHIST, HINDU TEMPLE

(Rs 300; ◷8am-6pm) This impressive 14th-century temple, mounted on a rocky bluff, is the most imposing in the region. It's divided into two halves – one half Buddhist and one half Hindu – and features a seated Buddha image, Kandy-period paintings, rock-face inscriptions and stone elephant figures. A caretaker or monk will unlock the shrine if it's not already open. A *perahera* (procession) takes place in August.

The setting is as memorable as the temple. It's located 15km southwest of Kandy.

From Kandy, you can go directly to the Lankatilake Temple on bus 644 heading towards Pilimatalawa. Get off at Dawulagala Rd, from where it's around a 750m walk to the temple. You can also reach Lankatilake from the neighbouring temple of Embekka Devale via a 3km stroll beside rice paddies.

Embekka Devale
HINDU TEMPLE

(Rs 300; ◷8am-6pm) Dedicated to the worship of the Hindu deity Mahasen, this beautiful temple, with its finely carved wooden pillars depicting swans, eagles, wrestling men and dancing women, was constructed in the 14th century. The best carvings are in the so-called drummers' hall.

To get here by public transport, catch the frequent bus 643 (to Vatadeniya via Embekka) from near the Kandy clock tower for Rs 38. The village of Embekka is about 7km beyond the Peradeniya Botanic Gardens (about 45 minutes from Kandy). From the village, it's a pleasant rural stroll of about 1km to the temple.

Gadaladeniya Temple
BUDDHIST, HINDU TEMPLE

(Rs 300; ◷8am-6pm) This Buddhist temple with a Hindu annex dates from the 14th century, and the main shrine room contains a stunningly beautiful, gilded seated Buddha. Built on a rocky outcrop and covered with small pools, the temple is reached by a series of steps cut into the rock.

You may encounter it protected by scaffolding and a tin roof to prevent further rain-induced erosion. It's 13km southwest of central Kandy.

From Kandy, bus 644 (Rs 28), among others, will take you to the temple. The turn-off from the A1 Hwy is close to the 105km post, from where it's 1km to Gadaladeniya.

Ceylon Tea Museum   MUSEUM

(📞081-380 3204; www.ceylonteamuseum.com; Hantane; adult/child Rs 800/400; ☺8.30am-3.45pm Tue-Sat, to 3pm Sun) This museum occupies the 1925-vintage Hantane Tea Factory, 4km south of Kandy on the Hantane road. Abandoned for more than a decade, it was recently refurbished and has good exhibits on tea pioneers James Taylor and Thomas Lipton, and lots of vintage tea-processing paraphernalia. A quick tour (all guides are knowledgable, but you feel some just go through the motions) is included and there's a free cuppa afterwards in the top-floor tearoom.

Degal Doruwa
Raja Maha Vihara   BUDDHIST TEMPLE

(Lewella; by donation; ☺8am-6pm) Hidden away in Kandy's leafy outskirts is the little-visited, but fascinating, Degal Doruwa Raja Maha Vihara cave temple, constructed (with the help of some obliging boulders) in the 18th century. The interior of the cave is painted head to toe in slightly faded, but captivating murals. These fine Kandyan-era paintings depict scenes from the Jataka stories (tales from the previous lives of the Buddha).

In among these are some out-of-place paintings depicting men with guns. These are likely to have been inspired by the first firearms to have arrived in Sri Lanka. Alongside the paintings is a large reclining Buddha. Visitors are likely to be shown around by one of the five resident monks.

Kandy War Cemetery   CEMETERY

(www.cwgc.org; Deveni Rajasinghe; by donation; ☺10am-noon & 1-6pm) This small and beautifully melancholic cemetery is maintained by the Commonwealth War Graves Commission. It is the final resting place for those who died defending Sri Lanka during WWII.

🏃 Activities

There are several well-regarded meditation centres close to Kandy.

Nilambe Buddhist
Meditation Centre   MEDITATION

(📞077 780 4555; www.nilambe.net; donation requested) Offers daily classes (mainly silent and sitting meditation) spread over a minimum of three- to five-day stays. Basic accommodation is available. Days start with a 4.45am wake-up gong and end with group chanting and meditation around 9pm. Reservations should be made through the website at least two weeks in advance.

The centre is 24km south of Kandy. It can be reached by bus 633 (catch a Delthota bus via Galaha and get off at Office Junction). From Office Junction, you can walk a steep 3km through tea plantations or take a three-wheeler for Rs 250 to the centre. A three-wheeler/taxi from Kandy costs about Rs 1200 one way.

Amaya Hills   AYURVEDA

(📞081-447 4022; www.amayaresorts.com; Heerassagala; facials from Rs 4000, oil massages & steam baths Rs 8000) The nicest Ayurveda centre in the Kandy area with professional staff and wonderful massages and treatments – try a Udvarthana body scrub. Try to make a day of it: have lunch and spend a few hours around the stunning pool. Amaya Hills is high in the hills on a winding road. A three-wheeler here from Kandy costs around Rs 600.

Dhamma Kuta
Vipassana Meditation Centre   MEDITATION

(📞081-238 5774; www.kuta.dhamma.org; Mowbray, Hindagala; donation requested) This centre offers courses from one to 10 days following the SN Goenka system of meditation. Booking ahead is mandatory. There's dorm accommodation with separate male and female quarters. Take a Mahakanda-bound bus from the clock tower bus stop in Kandy and get off at the last stop. It's a steep 2km walk.

🛏️ Sleeping & Eating

As Kandy becomes increasingly congested, the verdant rolling hills around town gain in appeal as a base. There's a growing number of hotels and guesthouses in this highly scenic region. Restaurants are limited, but most hotels and guesthouses offer meals.

Nisha Tourist Home   HOMESTAY $$

(📞077 084 9137; nishantha.maldeniya71@gmail.com; 47/9A Riverside, Galaha Rd, Peradeniya; r US$25; ✱ 🛜) Run by an intelligent, kind host family, the rooms in this family home are kept clean and have hot-water en suites. The location is very quiet, though quite isolated, so make use of the bikes for rent. Pick-ups can be arranged from Peradeniya Junction station (3.5km away), cooking lessons are offered and Nisha is an excellent driver/guide.

Emerald Hill Hotel   HOTEL $$

(📞081-465 1651; www.emeraldhill.lk; 70/18 Riverdale Rd, Aniwatte; r from US$45; ✱ 🛜 ☀) This hotel enjoys some of the most spectacular views in the entire Kandy area from its ridgetop perch, with astonishing vistas across the

Mahaweli river valley from the balconies of its modern rooms. However, there's nothing else around, so you'll need to hire tuk-tuks or have your own wheels.

Chaya Hills HOTEL **$$**
(077 350 6962; www.chayahillskandy.com; 1 Chaya Hills; dm/d US$18/40;) Around 6km southwest of Kandy, this good-value hotel has a selection of very well-presented rooms (including air-con dorms with four beds) and very spacious doubles with cable TV. Book one on the upper floor for sweeping valley views.

★ **Baramba House** BOUTIQUE HOTEL **$$$**
(081-220 0173; www.barambalanka.com; 22 Upul Mawatha, Primrose Hill; r incl breakfast US$85-95;) The Swiss–Sri Lankan owners of this idyllic little three-room guesthouse have created a small slice of bliss here. There are cool, high-ceilinged rooms with fans swishing lazily away above giant four-poster beds, and a crystal-clear pool. Terraces with views over jungle-clad hills and beautiful home-cooked meals only add to Baramba's appeal.

No children under 12 years are allowed. It's 5km from central Kandy.

★ **Kandy House** BOUTIQUE HOTEL **$$$**
(Amunugama Walauwa; 081-492 1394; www.the kandyhouse.com; Amunugama Walauwa, Gunnepana; r incl breakfast from US$325;) Thanks to masses of exotic tropical flora, the air you breathe at this divine hotel, once home to a Kandyan chief, literally tastes perfumed. Now fully restored, its nine rooms are furnished with colonial antiques, and service is courtesy of a butler who is assigned on arrival. An infinity pool segues to emerald-green rice paddies and eating here is a real highlight.

Note that no children under 12 years are allowed.

Amaara Sky Hotel BOUTIQUE HOTEL **$$$**
(081-223 9888; www.amaarasky.com; 72/22 AB Damunupola Mawatha; r incl breakfast from US$140;) Boutique hotel in a suburban location atop the hills of Kandy. The rooms enjoy wonderful views from their balconies and are some of the largest in town, while the restaurant serves up delicious local and international food.

Kandy Samadhicentre BOUTIQUE HOTEL **$$$**
(077 771 0013; www.thekandysamadhicentre. com; Kukul Oya Rd, Kandy; s/d from US$95/120;) A bohemian Ayurvedic and yoga centre

23km from Kandy with mud huts, rooms and pavilions dotted around a forested hillside, each furnished with Asian textiles and four-poster beds. Various packages that include treatments and yoga sessions are offered; however, rates are pricey. Food is both organic and vegetarian (dinner US$15), and no alcohol is served.

🛍 Shopping

Waruna Antiques ANTIQUES
(081-447 0925; www.warunaantique.com; 761 Peradeniya Rd; 9am-6pm) About 2km southwest of the centre, this warren of an antique shop is a fine place to root around for old masks, jewellery, coins, textiles, maps and art. Prices are fair.

ℹ Getting There & Away

Many people rent a three-wheeler for the day to get around this area; expect to pay around Rs 3000 from central Kandy. A car will be around Rs 6000; try Nishantha Maldeniya (p163).

Buses operate along the main highways. If you're combining public transport with walking, you'll need to ask the way occasionally, and note: there's a fair amount of walking involved.

Knuckles Range

Sri Lanka's central mountains have recently been included as one of Unesco's World Heritage Sites, and the craggy, biodiverse Knuckles Range forms a key part of that recognition. This massif is home to pockets of rare montane and cloud forest, and offers fine hiking and birdwatching possibilities. The name 'Knuckles' derives from the mountains' profile, which looks like a closed fist. This rugged highland region remains relatively unknown to foreign visitors and is one of the best areas in the Hill Country to get off the beaten tourist path.

If you are coming here in order to hike then you'll need to be well prepared. A knowledgable guide is virtually essential.

Hotels in the Knuckles Range can organise guided hiking trips. In Kandy, contact Sri Lanka Trekking (p156). A guide for the high peaks is compulsory, and some serious wet-weather gear and leech protection are essential. For anything more ambitious than a couple of hours' stroll around the foothills, you will need to be totally self-sufficient, with camping equipment and food.

The foothills of the Knuckles are covered in small villages and there are no restrictions

VISITING THE VEDDAHS

Sri Lanka was inhabited long before the Sinhalese or Tamils arrived on the scene. These original inhabitants, known as the Veddahs (or hunters), are thought to have first arrived on the island some 18,000 years ago and until fairly recently they have lived alongside their fellow Sri Lankans without too many issues. Today, though, as with aboriginal communities across South Asia, the remaining Veddah communities are under intense pressure and only a few hundred traditional Veddah remain.

The last Veddah stronghold is in the countryside around the village of **Dambana**, which is east of the small town of **Mahiyangana**. If you want to meet the Veddah, once in Dambana you need to find a translator-guide and then get to the pretty hamlet of **Kotabakina**, the most frequently visited Veddah village. Once here, you will (for a fairly substantial sum) most likely be entertained with dancing, singing and a 'hunting' display by the Veddah people.

Perhaps not surprisingly, the whole experience can feel rather staged, but it should also be borne in mind that the money tourism pumps into the villages, and the tourists' desire to see traditional tribal 'culture', might actually be enough to stop the last of the Veddah from being swallowed up by mainstream Sri Lankan culture.

The best base for a visit to this area is Mahiyangana, a sprawling and sparsely settled town. The only highlight in the town itself is the **Mahiyangana dagoba** where, according to legend, the Buddha preached on his first visit to Sri Lanka. Leaving Kandy, there are two routes towards the town. The spectacular A26 north road goes past the Victoria Reservoir to Madugoda, before twisting downhill through 18 hairpin bends to the Mahaweli lowlands and the dry-zone plains. Going up you worry about overheating and going down it's all about the brakes. Drivers prefer the road along the southern shores of the Victoria and Randenigala Reservoirs, which is much faster and in better condition.

There are a few lodging options in Mahiyangana, none of which are very accustomed to foreign guests, and there are buses to Kandy, Badulla and Polonnaruwa, among other destinations.

on walking here. The high massif, though, is a protected zone and entrance is Rs 650. Tickets cannot be purchased at the gate itself, but will normally be obtained by your guide from a forestry department office.

🛏 Sleeping & Eating

There are some excellent mountain lodges and boutique hotels in this highland area. You'll find several places around the village of Elkaduwa, which is a good base for the Knuckles Range. Virtually all hotels and guesthouses provide meals; otherwise, eating options are very limited.

Green View HOTEL **$$**
(📞 077 781 1881; bluehavtravels@gmail.com; Karagahinna, Elkaduwa; s/d incl breakfast from Rs 2800/3600; 🛜🍽) A well-managed lodge, this cheery hillside place has spectacular views of a forested mountain valley. Rooms are clean, plain but showing their age a little. Staff will happily lead you on easy, low-level strolls or much tougher hikes around the edge of the Knuckles Range. Book ahead and they'll pick you up from Kandy.

★**Rangala House** BOUTIQUE HOTEL **$$$**
(📞 081-240 0294; www.rangalahouse.com; 92B Bobebila Rd, Makuldeniya, Teldeniya; s/d half-board US$171/235, studios from US$288; 🛜🍽) Located at around 1000m, this gorgeous former tea planter's bungalow enjoys a temperate, sometimes coolish climate on a steep forested hillside surrounded by spice trees. It has three double rooms and a studio for families. You'll love the large living and dining room (with fireplace) and views down to the distant bright lights of Kandy.

Rangala organises very good hiking tours in the Knuckles Range.

Madulkelle Tea & Ecolodge BOUTIQUE HOTEL **$$$**
(📞 081-380 1052; www.madulkelle.com; Madulkelle Village; d from US$268; 🛜🍽) 🌿 Definitely glamping not camping, this upmarket lodge's luxe tents are scattered around a verdant hillside, and are all equipped with commodious beds, fully equipped bathrooms and wooden writing desks. Stroll around the Madulkelle estate, then relax in the infinity pool, gazing over mountain creases and the deep greens of the surrounding tea plantations.

The main building, containing the grand dining room, is filled with polished antiques and leather armchairs set beside a roaring log fire. Note, the access road is very rough and a high-clearance car is usually necessary.

Amaya Hunas Falls Hotel HOTEL $$$
(☎081-494 0320; www.amayaresorts.com; Elkaduwa; r/ste incl breakfast from US$145/252; ❇ @ 🛜 ⛲) On the edge of a tea plantation and spice garden, this hotel has elegant rooms and a bucolic location. The building itself is an elongated, somewhat ungainly concrete construction, but the surrounding landscape is stunning. There are several memorable settings for a special meal, including a lakeside terrace, and there's a pub-style bar for drinks.

❶ Getting There & Away

Hiking trips to the Knuckles from Kandy usually include return transport. Otherwise, a tuk-tuk/taxi from Kandy to Elkaduwa should cost Rs 900/1800. Alternatively, take a bus to Wattegama (from near the clock tower in Kandy), and then catch another to Elkaduwa.

Kitulgala
☑036

West of the road from Kandy to Nuwara Eliya, Kitulgala is a popular adventure-sports centre located amid thickly forested hills. Most visitors are the young and energetic of Colombo, but foreign visitors are also starting to discover the region's white-water rafting, jungle trekking, birdwatching and cave exploration.

The town's other main claim to fame is that David Lean filmed his 1957 Oscar-winning epic *Bridge on the River Kwai* here on the banks of the Kelaniya Ganga, though there's little physical evidence left to see.

A few kilometres from Kitulgala is a large **cave system** where the 28,500-year-old remains of early humans were discovered. Many hotels in the area can arrange a guide to the caves.

◉ Sights

Only the concrete foundations of the 'Bridge on the River Kwai' remain. To reach the site, follow the signs from the main road, about 1km from Plantation Hotel in the direction of Adam's Peak. Wannabe guides will attempt to show you the way, but are not necessary. Apparently, the actual railway carriages used in the movie now lie at the bottom of the river, after being sunk in an explosive

conclusion. You'll have to bring your own scuba gear if you want to look.

Classic Car Museum MUSEUM
(Plantation Hotel, 250 Kalukohuthanna; ⊙8am-6pm) **FREE** It's more of a hotel garage than a museum, but this fine collection of classic cars is well worth a peek. Just buy a drink at the hotel and someone will open it up for you. Models, most from the 1960s, include several Rolls-Royces, Jaguars and an original Mini Cooper. One of the Rolls is said to have shepherded the Queen of England around the country on an official trip.

🏃 Activities

Birdwatching
The area is famous for birdwatching – 23 of Sri Lanka's 27 endemic bird species inhabit the surrounding forest. Rafter's Retreat (p170) has the best ornithological guides. A half-day of birdwatching is around Rs 2800.

White-Water Rafting
At the time of research, the Kelaniya Ganga, the river that runs through Kitulgala, offered the best white-water rafting in Sri Lanka. However, the construction of two new dams upstream (scheduled to be finished by perhaps 2019) will disrupt the river and impact on future rafting trips. Contact Rafter's Retreat (p170) or Borderlands (p170) for the latest situation.

For now, the typical rafting excursion takes in seven Class 2-3 rapids in 7km for US$30 per person, including transport and lunch. You'll be on the water for around two hours. Experienced rafters can opt for more difficult Class 4-5 rapids by special arrangement. Some operators also combine river canyoning with a rafting trip.

Almost every hotel can organise rafting trips with over a dozen local operators. All offer pretty similar packages, but not all have insurance – ask to see their papers first. **Xclusive Adventures** (☎072 456 9615; www.xclusive-adventures.com; Gingathhena Rd) has a good reputation, running white-water rafting (from US$20), canyoning, mountain-biking and trekking excursions.

Trekking
The sheer hills surrounding Kitulgala are covered in rainforest and the area makes for some decent, but quite strenuous, jungle hikes. You will need a guide, good footwear, waterproofs and leech repellent. Most hotels can arrange a guide and suggest a suitable

THE HILL COUNTRY KITULGALA

route; Channa Perera at Rafter's Retreat is the most experienced 'jungle man' in the area and is knowledgable about the local flora and fauna. A half-day trek costs around US$20.

🛏 Sleeping & Eating

There's an expanding range of accommodation in Kitulgala, but prices are high (perhaps because of its popularity with visitors from Colombo).

Breetas Garden HOTEL **$$**
(☑ 051-224 2020; www.breetasgarden.com; Kitulgala-Ginigaththena Rd; r US$60; 🛜 🗷) This converted tea plantation residence is now a tasteful guesthouse and restaurant, with eight spacious, well-presented rooms, many with private balconies. There are stunning mountain views, and you can gaze over an ocean-like expanse of forest from the lovely little pool. It's 7km east of Kitulgala on the road to Hatton, with good walking nearby.

★ Royal River Resort BOUTIQUE HOTEL **$$$**
(☑ 011-273 2755; www.plantationgrouphotels.com; Eduru Ella; s/d incl half-board Rs 11,500/13,900; 🗷 🛜 🗷) In a remote rainforest location, 6km north of Kitulgala via a rough road, this hotel is fantastically secluded. It has four timber cottages built around, on to and into a series of boulders and waterfalls. The rooms are pleasantly decorated in colonial shades. There's a good restaurant and a sublime river-fed pool.

Rafter's Retreat HUT **$$$**
(☑ 031-228 7598; www.raftersretreat.com; s/d incl half-board US$75/90; 🛜) This old colonial-era bungalow serves as the hub for a rafting and birdwatching outfit that sprawls along the riverbank. The 10 quirky riverside cottages are basic and fan-cooled. You just pull up a blind to see the gushing river.

The breezy riverside restaurant is a great place for a few beers, and jovial owner Channa can organise all manner of tours and activities.

Borderlands CAMPGROUND **$$$**
(☑ 077 789 9836, Colombo 011-441 0110; www.discoverborderlands.com; riverside, off Kalukohuthanna; per person incl half-board US$66; 🛜) Borderlands is a riverside activities camp offering kayaking, rafting, biking, hiking and more, and it's run by a fun-loving, young and international crowd. Accommodation is basic but quite pricey, in either screened open-sided cabanas or large tents with beds. There's a separate bathroom block and a cool terrace/dining area. Be warned that school groups can swamp the place from time to time.

Packages including full board and two activities cost US$125 per person.

ℹ Getting There & Away

It's easy to stop at Kitulgala even if you are travelling by bus. Coming from Colombo, catch the bus to Hatton and get off at Kitulgala (Rs 186). When you're over Kitulgala, flag a bus on to Hatton from the main road (Rs 72). For Nuwara Eliya and Kandy, change in Hatton.

Adam's Peak (Sri Pada)
☑ 051 / ELEV 2243M

Located in a beautiful area of the southern Hill Country, this lofty peak has sparked the imagination for centuries and been a focus for pilgrimage for more than 1000 years.

It's variously known as Adam's Peak (the place where Adam first set foot on earth after being cast out of heaven), Sri Pada (Sacred Footprint, left by the Buddha as he headed towards paradise), or perhaps most poetically as Samanalakande (Butterfly Mountain; where butterflies go to die). Legends attribute the huge 'footprint' crowning the peak to St Thomas, the early apostle of India, or even Lord Shiva.

The pilgrimage season begins on *poya* day in December and runs until the **Vesak festival** in May. In season, pilgrims and tourists alike make the climb up the countless steps to the top. At other times, the summit's temple can be unused, and is often obscured by clouds.

🏃 Activities

The moderately tough, steep hike up to the sacred summit of Adam's Peak is a challenge undertaken by many Sri Lankans and travellers from Dalhousie.

During the pilgrimage season (December to May), the route is illuminated by a sparkling ribbon of lights that is visible from miles around and from afar looks like a trail of stars leading into the heavens. Out of season, you will need a torch.

Definitely wear hiking boots if you have them, or good-quality sports shoes at a push. Bring warm clothes and pack plenty of water. If you're in Dalhousie in the pilgrimage season, you'll find stalls at the market selling warm jackets and headgear (although on busy nights the crush of humanity can be so intense that you'll be kept warm simply by the close proximity of so many other people). Otherwise, try the market at Nuwara Eliya or stores in Ella for outdoor gear.

The Climb

You can start the 7km climb from Dalhousie soon after dark – bring a good sleeping bag to keep you warm overnight at the top – or you can wait until about 2am to start. The climb is up steps most of the way (about 5200 of them), and on a quiet day you'll reach the top in 2½ to four hours. A 2.30am start should easily get you there before dawn, which is around 6.30am. Start on a *poya* day or a weekend, though, and the throng of pilgrims will add hours and hours to your climb.

From the car park, the slope is gradual for the first half-hour, passing under an entrance arch and then by the Japan–Sri Lanka Friendship Dagoba. The pathway gets steeper until it becomes a continuous flight of stairs. There are teahouses all the way to the top; in season, they open through the night. A few are open out of season. The authorities have banned litter, alcohol, tobacco, meat and recorded music, so the atmosphere remains reverential.

Many pilgrims prefer to make the longer, more tiring – but equally well-marked and lit – seven-hour climb from Ratnapura via the Carney Estate because of the greater merit thus gained.

Between June and November, when the pathway isn't illuminated and there aren't many people around, travellers are urged to do the hike at least in pairs. Expect to pay around Rs 1000 for a guide.

The Summit

The summit can be cold, so it's not worth getting there too long before dawn and then sitting around shivering.

As dawn illuminates the holy mountain, the diffuse morning light uncovers the Hill Country rising in the east and the land sloping to the coast to the west. Colombo, 65km away, is easily visible on a clear day.

Adam's Peak saves its most breathtaking moment for just after dawn. The sun casts a perfect shadow of the peak on to the misty clouds down towards the coast. As the sun rises higher, this eerie triangular shadow races back towards the peak, eventually disappearing into its base.

Some pilgrims wait for the priests to make a morning offering before they descend, but

the sun and heat rise quickly, so it pays not to linger.

The Descent

Many people find the hardest part is coming down. The endless steps can shake the strongest knees, and if your shoes don't fit well, you can add in crushed toes and blisters. Walking poles or even just a sturdy stick will make the descent much less jarring on your legs. Take a hat, as the morning sun intensifies quickly. Remember to stretch your legs when you finish, and booking a massage is highly recommended too.

🛏 Sleeping & Eating

Dalhousie is the best place to start the climb, but accommodation standards are pretty average overall and not great value for money.

Most guesthouses are on your left as you reach Dalhousie.

Dalhousie has simple restaurants, and stores selling snacks. Most guesthouses and hotels offer meals.

🛏 Dalhousie

Ayos Hill Hotel GUESTHOUSE $

(☑076 925 5998; Sri Pada Rd; r Rs 2500-3800; ⓐ) Operated by friendly locals, this lakeside place's rooms are well kept and have bright bedspreads and en suites. The restaurant/tea centre serves a fine brew and tasty food at fair rates. Bikes are available for guests and there's a free shuttle service to the starting point of Adam's Peak, which is about 4km away.

White House HUT $

(☑077 791 2009; www.adamspeakwhitehouse. com; r incl half-board Rs 3200-4800; ⓐ) This place has helpful staff and a pretty riverside location next to a swimming hole with lots of hammocks and easy chairs. Accommodation, ranging from basic to fairly smart rooms, could be better maintained, but all have en suites (with hot water) and are fine for a night or two. Guided walks through tea estates can be organised.

★ Slightly Chilled GUESTHOUSE $$

(☑052-205 5502, 071 909 8710; www.slightly chilled.tv; r incl half-board US$45-70; @ⓐ) Dalhousie's best option is Slightly Chilled in name and very chilled in nature. You'll find spacious, comfortable and colourful rooms with polished wooden floors, many with great views of Sri Pada, and there's an airy restaurant. Mountain bikes can be hired and there's lots of information on other trails in the area.

Punsisi Rest HOTEL **$$**
(☏ 051-492 0313; www.facebook.com/punsisirest adamspeak; r incl breakfast from Rs 4200; ☏) An ever-expanding collection of ageing concrete rooms with hot showers – you do have to climb up about a million steps to reach some of them. There's a restaurant here for Chinese and local food. Punsisi offers free pick-ups from Hatton train station if you book ahead. Wi-fi is spotty.

🛏 Around Adam's Peak

After ascending Adam's Peak, most people take their strained leg muscles straight off for a well-deserved rest, and what better place to do so than in one of the delightful tea-estate bungalows that can be found dotted about the beautiful countryside near Adam's Peak.

★ Tea Trails HISTORIC HOTEL **$$$**
(☏ Colombo 011-774 5700; www.resplendent ceylon.com/teatrails; Dikoya; s/d full board from US$453/582; ❄ ☏ ⛱) Tea Trails comprises a collection of five stunning colonial-style residences built for British tea plantation managers. Completely refurbished, the bungalows each has four to six large bedrooms, spacious dining and living areas, and verandas and gardens with views over rolling tea estates. 'Summerville' is very special indeed as it's located on a spit of land that juts into the Castlereigh Reservoir.

Rates are all-inclusive, even laundry. Western and Sri Lankan meals are prepared by a resident chef, along with complimentary drinks (yes, that means alcohol, and single-estate teas). There are self-guided walks through the region's tea-carpeted hills. All bungalows are well stocked with fine books to browse. And after a gourmet dinner, sipping a single malt whisky around your bungalow's log fire is one of Sri Lanka's unique experiences.

The Farm Resorts HISTORIC HOTEL **$$$**
(☏ 051-222 3607; www.thefarmresorts.com; Norton Rd, Dikoya; cottages US$66-132; ☏) These beautifully presented cottages, with attractive furnishings and a stylish touch, are in a lovely spot under eucalyptus trees on the edge of the Castlereigh Reservoir. Resident staff prepare meals in a lovely dining room and can arrange a boatman for tours on the lake.

ℹ Getting There & Away

A taxi from Hatton to Dalhousie costs Rs 2600 and a three-wheeler is Rs 1800. On busy pilgrimage nights, the roads to Dalhousie can get clogged with traffic in the early evenings and it can take hours to cover the final kilometres into town, so try to set off for Dalhousie as early as you can in the day.

BUS

Buses run to Dalhousie from Kandy (from the Goods Shed bus station), Nuwara Eliya and Colombo in the pilgrimage season. Otherwise, you need first to get to Hatton or to Maskeliya, about 20km along the Hatton–Dalhousie road.

Throughout the year, there are services to Hatton from Colombo (Rs 252), Kandy (Rs 116) or Nuwara Eliya (Rs 88). There are also limited direct buses from Nuwara Eliya and Colombo to Maskeliya.

There are buses from Hatton to Dalhousie via Maskeliya every 30 minutes in the pilgrimage season (Rs 80, two hours). Otherwise, you have to take a bus from Hatton to Maskeliya (Rs 42, last departure about 6pm) and then another to Dalhousie (Rs 38, last departure about 7pm).

Out-of-pilgrimage-season buses may drop you off in Dalhousie's main square, but during the season buses stop wherever they can find a space.

THE HILL COUNTRY ADAM'S PEAK (SRI PADA)

PILGRIMAGE ON A POYA DAY

Thinking of climbing Adam's Peak on a *poya* (full moon) day or weekend? Go for it! It'll likely turn out to be one of the most memorable things you do in Sri Lanka. But take note: the last time we climbed the mountain on such a night we got within 800m of the summit and then stood in a queue for nearly three hours. We advanced forward by around only 100m before giving up (as did most other tourists there who were not so spiritually enlightened). We've heard of some travellers taking more than nine hours to reach the summit on a *poya* day. This doesn't mean you should avoid climbing on such days; there's a real carnival-like atmosphere on the mountain, the tea shops are packed and there's plenty of colour and noise – some Hindu pilgrims even dress up as Shiva himself! Just don't expect to have a silent moment of reflection as the sun rises above the mountains.

TRAIN

Hatton is the nearest station to Dalhousie. There are five daily trains between Colombo and Nanu Oya, all via Kandy and Hatton. From Kandy, trains cost Rs 163/98 (2nd/3rd class) and take 2½ to three hours. However, note delays are common on this line, particularly on pilgrimage season weekends.

From Nanu Oya, it costs Rs 60/30 (2nd/3rd class) and the journey time is between 1½ and two hours. Advance reservations in either of these classes is Rs 600 and an observation-class seat in either direction is Rs 1000.

Kandy to Nuwara Eliya

The road from Kandy to Nuwara Eliya climbs nearly 1400m as it winds through jade-green tea plantations and reservoirs. The 92km of asphalt allow for plenty of stops at waterfalls and tea outlets.

Kothmale Reservoir (also known as Puna Oya Reservoir) can be seen on the way. It's part of the Mahaweli Development Project and blamed by some locals for climatic quirks in recent years. **Ramboda Falls** (108m), about 1.5km from the road, is a spectacular double waterfall.

Nearing Nuwara Eliya, the road gains elevation abruptly, passing several tea estates, then roadside stalls overflow with all sorts of veggies and flowers.

◉ Sights

Blue Field Tea Estate   FACTORY
(www.bluefieldteagardens.com; ⊘ 8am-4pm Mon-Sat) **FREE** This large tea estate is 20km north of Nuwara Eliya. Short tours are offered and there's a decent restaurant here too. Blue Field Tea Estate has no processing on Sunday.

Glenloch Tea Estate   FACTORY
(⊋ 052-225 9646; A5 Hwy, Katukithula; ⊘ 8am-4.45pm) **FREE** Around 27km north of Nuwara Eliya, tours of this factory are fairly informative, explaining cultivation, types of tea and the drying and packing processes. There's some fine old machinery from the UK still in use. Unlike in many tea factories, photography is allowed here.

**Mackwoods Labookellie
Tea Factory**   FACTORY
(www.mackwoods.com; A5 Hwy; ⊘ 8am-5.15pm) **FREE** On the A5, 11km northwest of Nuwara Eliya, the Labookellie Tea Factory is a convenient factory to visit as it's right on the roadside. Its tours are very brief, but do include a free cup of tea. Be warned that many

hundreds of visitors stop here in high season and the place can be rammed. There's a cafe and also well-priced quality teas to buy.

🛏 Sleeping & Eating

There are a few hotels along the route, but far more choice in both Kandy or Nuwara Eliya. The highway is dotted with the odd roadside restaurant, and some tea plantations have cafes.

Ecolanka   LODGE **$$$**
(⊋ 051-223 3133; www.ecolanka.com; Maussawa Estate, Pundaluoya; s/d from €42/60, cottages €90; 🕾) In a remote location 28km north of Nuwara Eliya, this rustic lodge is just the place to get all off-grid and don your walking boots – you'll find several good trails nearby. Some rooms have shared bathrooms, or book the deluxe cottage for more comfort. There are gorgeous views of central Lanka's rolling hills, and fine nutritious food is prepared.

ⓘ Getting There & Away

Buses (regular/express Rs 250/180, 3½ hours) connect Kandy and Nuwara Eliya every 45 minutes or so.

Nuwara Eliya

⊋ 052 / POP 26,120 / ELEV 1889M

Often referred to as 'Little England', this genteel highland community does have a rose-tinted, vaguely British-country-village feel to it, with its colonial-era bungalows, Tudor-style hotels, well-tended hedgerows and pretty gardens. Indeed, Nuwara Eliya was once was *the* favoured cool-climate escape for the hard-working and hard-drinking English and Scottish pioneers of Sri Lanka's tea industry.

A recent construction boom has blighted the scene to a degree, and the dusty and bustling centre is a thoroughly Sri Lankan urban tangle, but Nuwara Eliya still makes a fine base for a few days' relaxation. The verdant surrounding countryside of tea plantations, carefully tended vegetable plots and craggy hills is highly scenic. Treat yourself to a night in one of Nuwara Eliya's colonial hotels, play a round of golf or a few frames of billiards, and soak up the town's unique bygone heritage.

A rainy-day, misty-mountain atmosphere blankets the town from November to February so don't come expecting tropical climes. But during April's spring release, the town is crowded with domestic holidaymakers enjoying horse racing and sports-car hill climbs, and celebrating the Sri Lankan New Year. The cost of accommodation escalates wildly, and Nuwara Eliya becomes a busy, busy party town.

History

Originally an uninhabited system of forests and meadows in the shadow of Pidurutalagala (aka Mt Pedro; 2524m), Nuwara Eliya became a singularly British creation, having been 'discovered' by colonial officer John Davy in 1819 and chosen as the site for a sanatorium a decade later.

Later the district became known as a spot where 'English' vegetables and fruits, such as lettuce and strawberries, could be successfully grown for consumption by the colonists. Coffee was one of the first crops grown here, but after the island's coffee plantations failed due to disease, the colonists switched to tea. The first tea leaves harvested in Sri Lanka were planted at Loolecondera Estate, in the mountains between Nuwara Eliya and Kandy. As tea experiments proved successful, the town quickly found itself becoming the Hill Country's 'tea capital', a title which endures.

As elsewhere in the Hill Country, most of the labourers on the tea plantations were Tamils, brought from southern India by the British. Although the descendants of these 'Plantation Tamils' (as they are called to distinguish them from Tamils in northern Sri Lanka) have usually stayed out of the ethnic strife that has rocked Jaffna and the North, there have been occasional outbreaks of tension between the local Sinhalese and Tamils. The town was partially ransacked during the 1983 riots.

At nearby Hakgala, there is a significant Muslim population, but internecine strife is not a problem.

◉ Sights

Victoria Park PARK
(Rs 300; ⊙ 7am-6pm) This is one of the country's most attractive, and best-maintained, town parks. A stroll around its paths, past manicured lawns, is a pleasure. The park comes alive with flowers around March to May, and August and September. It's also home to quite a number of hill-country bird species, including the Kashmir flycatcher, Indian pitta and grey tit.

Galway's Land National Park NATIONAL PARK
(Hawaeliya; US$10 plus tax 15%; ⊙ 6am-5pm) One of Sri Lanka's newest (2006) and smallest (29 sq hectares) national parks, Galway's Land

is a dense patch of montane forest a couple of kilometres east of town. It is renowned for its birdlife, including 10 Sri Lankan endemics, as well as buffalo, wild boar, barking deer and other mammals. There's very little on-site information, but guides are available (by donation) from the park office and a 2km-long walking trail also leaves from here.

◉ Around Nuwara Eliya

Hakgala Gardens GARDENS
(adult/child Rs 1500/750; ⊙ 7.30am-5.30pm) These attractive gardens, 10km southeast of Nuwara Eliya, are a peaceful retreat. Highlights include a fine rose garden, a Japanese garden, an orchid collection, cedars and giant cypresses. However, the entrance fee is very steep for foreigners. Planting season is between January and late March and at these times the gardens don't really look their best. To get here, take a Welimada-bound bus (Rs 22, 20 minutes).

Seetha Amman Temple HINDU TEMPLE
(A5 Hwy, Sita Eliya) FREE This colourful Hindu temple, 7km southeast of Nuwara Eliya, is said to mark the spot where Sita was held captive by the demon king Rawana, and where she prayed daily for Rama to come and rescue her. On the rock face across the stream are circular depressions said to be the footprints of Rawana's elephant.

Lovers Leap VIEWPOINT
From the Pedro Tea Estate (p176), take a very enjoyable 5km (round-trip) walk to Lovers Leap, an impressive waterfall. From the tea factory, cross the main road and follow the signs to the tea manager's bungalow along the dirt road. At the first crossroads go left and at the three-way junction take the middle path until, after about 15 minutes, you hit a dirt parking area. A foot-only track heads left through the tea gardens towards the forest and a rock face. Follow this trail and, just beyond the small Shiva shrine, you'll see the spluttering waterfalls.

🏃 Activities

The Grand Hotel (p177), St Andrew's Hotel (p177), Hill Club (p177) and Hotel Glendower (p177) all have snooker rooms. The Hill Club also has four clay tennis courts.

Nuwara Eliya Golf Club GOLF
(☑ 052-223 2835; www.nuwaraeliyagolfclub.com; green fees Rs 5900-7200, club & shoe hire Rs 2500; ⊙ 6am-6pm) It didn't take the tea planters long to lay out land for drives and putts in

Nuwara Eliya

0 —— 100 m
0 —— 0.05 miles

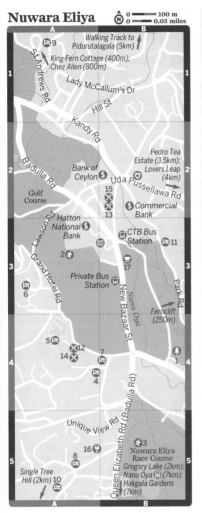

Nuwara Eliya

& 6.30-9pm) includes classic bland English cuisine, such as lamb chops with mint sauce, and an increasing number of Asian dishes.

Royal Turf Club HORSE RIDING
(📞 077 030 9090; www.royalturfclub.com; Race Course; tickets from Rs 100) The Royal Turf Club hosts horse racing at the 1875-vintage Nuwara Eliya Race Course. The most important event every year is the Governor's Cup race, held over the April Sinhala and Tamil New Year season.

Cycling

There are steep dirt trails radiating into the hills from the outskirts of town. Ask at the Single Tree Hotel about mountain-bike rental (p176). A relatively challenging, but undeniably spectacular, day trip is through the verdant blanket of tea plantations to the Labookellie Tea Factory (p173). There are a few hills to climb, but the reward of swooping downhill makes it worthwhile.

Hiking

Sri Lanka's highest mountain, **Pidurutalagala** (2524m), also known as Mt Pedro, rises

their holiday town, and the golf club was founded in 1889. Nuwara Eliya Golf Club is beautifully kept and has a retinue of languid sleeping dogs guarding more than a few of the greens. Watch out for thieving crows, which pinch golf balls!

Temporary members pay Rs 500 per day. As with most golf clubs, a certain standard of dress applies (shirts and trousers or shorts of a 'respectable' length). The club has a convivial wood-lined bar and a billiard room. Dinner in the **dining room** (📞 052-222 2835; www.nuwara -eliya-golf-club-nuwara-eliya-sri-lanka.en.ww.lk; Nuwara Eliya Golf Club; meals from Rs 850; ⊙ noon-3pm

THE HILL COUNTRY NUWARA ELIYA

WORTH A TRIP

PEDRO TEA ESTATE

To see where your morning cuppa originates, head to the **Pedro Tea Estate** (Rs 200; ⊘8-11am & 2-4pm), about 3.5km east of Nuwara Eliya on the way to Kandapola. You can take a 20-minute guided tour of the factory, originally built in 1885 and still packed with 19th-century engineering. However, due to the type of tea produced here (a very light tea), processing only takes place at night when it's colder, so you're unlikely to see much action.

Overlooking the plantations is a pleasant teahouse. Photography inside the factory is forbidden.

A three-wheeler from Nuwara Eliya should cost Rs 450 return, including waiting time. Alternatively, you could hop on a Ragalla-bound bus (Rs 15) from the main bus station in Nuwara Eliya.

behind the town. On top stands the island's main TV transmitter; however, the summit is out of bounds to foreigners. You can walk about 4km up, as far as a concrete water tank; beyond is a high-security zone. Follow the path from Keena Rd, along a ravine through eucalyptus forest (the town's source of firewood) and into the rare cloud forest.

An alternative walk is up **Single Tree Hill** (2100m), which is a three-hour return hike. Walk south on Queen Elizabeth Rd, go up Haddon Hill Rd as far as the communications tower and then take the left-hand path. Guesthouses can supply you with a rudimentary map.

For longer hikes, ask at the Single Tree Hotel. Most guided walks in the surrounding hills cost between Rs 3000 and 5000. Staff can also arrange longer camping trips.

Tours

Most hotels in town can arrange day trips by motorbike taxi, car or 4WD to Horton Plains National Park (p181). The standard price for up to five passengers is Rs 4000 or so (excluding park fees). One of the better 4WD tours is organised by Single Tree Hotel. It's about an hour's drive to the park gates.

Single Tree can also arrange trips to the Pedro Tea Estate and Lovers Leap (p174) for Rs 1500. For the ultimate waterfall experience, join its waterfall day trip (per van

Rs 3500 to 9000), which takes in between six and 18 different cascades and two tea plantations.

Sleeping

Staying in a colonial-style hotel, revelling in the heritage ambience, is one of Sri Lanka's unique experiences. That said, don't expect great value for money and note that around Sri Lankan New Year (April), room rates rocket in price. You'll need blankets at almost any time of year. Some hotels light log fires on chilly nights – you won't find a toastier way to keep warm. There aren't many backpacker-oriented guesthouses.

Chez Allen   GUESTHOUSE $$
(☑052-222 2581; 45/B St Andrew's Rd; ⊘r from Rs 4500; 🛜) Resembling an alpine chalet, this fine hillside guesthouse has outstanding views from its balconies and homely rooms. Food is available, tasty and freshly cooked. It's located 3km north of town, around Rs 300 in a three-wheeler.

Trevene   HISTORIC HOTEL $$
(☑052-222 2767, 072 230 4220; www.hotel trevenenuwaraeliya.com; 17 Park Rd; r incl breakfast Rs 4000-8000; 🛜) A very pleasant colonial villa set in flowering gardens and filled with little hideaways where you can curl up with a book on a wet afternoon. Rooms are a mixed bag and it definitely pays to check out a few first: some have high ceilings, wood panelling and fireplaces, others just feel dated. Call for free pick-up from the town centre.

Single Tree Hotel   GUESTHOUSE $$
(☑052-222 3009; singletreehtl@sltnet.lk; 178 Haddon Hill Rd; s/d/tr US$30/35/40; 🛜) This popular travellers' guesthouse is spread over two neighbouring buildings, with a sociable vibe and helpful staff. Rooms, some with lots of wood trim, are a shade pricey and pretty functional, but the bed linen is fresh and the place is clean. The switched-on owners offer lots of good tours of the region, and rent bikes (per half-day/day Rs 1000/1500) and scooters.

Ceybank Rest   HISTORIC HOTEL $$
(☑052-222 3855; www.ceybank-rest-nuwaraeliya -sri-lanka.en.wiw.lk; 119 Badulla Rd; s/d incl breakfast Rs 8600/9800; 🛜) This historic residence was once a British governor's mansion and has stunning gardens. Its plus points include a lovely lounge area and a fine old bar. Rooms, though spacious, are somewhat neglected, with tired carpets and cheap curtains.

King Fern Cottage GUESTHOUSE $$
(☑ 077 358 6284; www.kingferncottage.com; 203/1A St Andrews Rd; r Rs 3200-6500; @🖭) A quirky place to stay, King Fern is a minimalist's nightmare with its clashing colours, garish bedspreads, huge handmade beds and logwood tables. However, for those of an artistic persuasion, somehow it all works. The setting is good, in a timber pavilion beside a bubbling stream. Call for free pick-up from Nanu Oya station.

★ **Ferncliff** BOUTIQUE HOTEL $$$
(☑ 072 231 9443; www.ferncliff.lk; 7/10 Wedderburn Rd; r incl breakfast US$182; 🖭) Set in spacious lawned grounds, this colonial-era bungalow is straight out of a period drama – even the sprucely turned-out staff hovering in the background play their parts perfectly. There are just four spacious rooms, each with modish en suites, and you'll love the guests' lounge complete with log fire. Dining here is excellent, with delicious, filling meals.

Grand Hotel HERITAGE HOTEL $$$
(☑ 052-222 2881; www.tangerinehotels.com; Grand Hotel Rd; r/ste incl breakfast from US$222/277; ✱@🖭) This huge mock-Tudor edifice has immaculate lawns, a reading lounge and an impressive partly open dining terrace. Rooms are comfortable and well-equipped, but do lack the character of other heritage hotels in Nuwara Eliya – that's because much of the hotel is actually an extension. Facilities are good, including a gym and wood-panelled snooker room.

Hill Club HERITAGE HOTEL $$$
(☑ 052-222 2653; www.hillclubsrilanka.lk; 29 Grand Hotel Rd; r incl breakfast US$160-180; @🖭) Judged in pure value-for-money terms, the somewhat tired rooms at this quintessentially colonial hotel don't really cut it. However, a stay at the Hill Club is still many travellers' most memorable Sri Lanka experience. Chance your arm in the billiards room, stroll the sweeping lawns, admire the stone-clad exterior, sip a G&T in the bar and soak up the unique ambience.

St Andrew's Hotel HERITAGE HOTEL $$$
(☑ 052-222 3031; www.jetwinghotels.com; 10 St Andrews Rd; r incl breakfast US$139-198; 🖭) North of town on a beautifully groomed rise overlooking the golf course, this striking colonial residence was once a planters' club. Today, it's a luxurious, carefully renovated heritage hotel, well managed by the Jetwing group. Highlights include a graffiti-stained cocktail bar, a library filled with dusty books and a roaring log fire, a billiards room and a decent restaurant.

Teabush Hotel HISTORIC HOTEL $$$
(☑ 052-222 2345; www.teabush-hotel.com; 29 Haddon Hill Rd; s/d incl breakfast from US$95/125; 🖭) This 140-year-old tea planter's bungalow certainly has bags of character with its antique furniture and colonial ambience. However, the heritage charm of the shared, public areas is tempered by more prosaic rooms. Restaurant views are superb.

Hotel Glendower HISTORIC HOTEL $$$
(☑ 052-222 2501; www.hotelglendower.com; 5 Grand Hotel Rd; r/ste incl breakfast US$90/110; 🖭) This rambling colonial building has bundles of ye-olde-worlde English charm to it (or a South Asian version of it, anyway), thanks to its terrific bar, lounge, billiard rooms and garden (complete with croquet set). However, rooms need upgrading, with carpets patched up and somewhat bygone facilities. Still, it's not a bad choice for those who love nostalgia.

🛏 Around Nuwara Eliya

Stashed away among the tea estates around Nuwara Eliya are some fabulous places to stay. Ideally, you'll have your own transport if staying at one of these.

★ **Highest Village Bungalow** GUESTHOUSE $
(☑ 052-205 1938, 077 617 1208; highestvillagebungalow@yahoo.com; 222 School Rd, Shanthipura; r Rs 3000; 🖭) Run by a very hospitable family, this charming little guesthouse is located up in the hills, 4km northwest of town, in a mountain village said to be the highest in Sri Lanka. There are fine views, good local walks, excellent food and clean rooms. Call for free pick-up from the town centre.

★ **Heritance Tea Factory** BOUTIQUE HOTEL $$$
(☑ 052-555 5000; www.heritancehotels.com; Kandapola; r incl breakfast from US$188; ✱🖭) High in mist-wrapped hills 13km northeast of Nuwara Eliya, this unique place has been built into and around a century-old tea factory. Blurring the line between museum and luxury hotel, much of the factory machinery is still in situ and has been incorporated into the design. Rooms are stately and plush and have heating. Service is first rate.

There are two different restaurants (one inside an old steam-train carriage) serving some of the best meals in the hills. Note: there's a pretty strict dress code for dinner.

178

THOMAS WYNESS / SHUTTERSTOCK ©

SAIKO3P / SHUTTERSTOCK ©

orton Plains National Park (p181)
ational park is a hotbed of wildlife, including
rely seen black-lipped green lizard.

lla (p188)
kilometres out of Ella, the Nine Arch Bridge
hotogenic crossing.

da Walawe National Park (p195)
reds of elephants roam this national park,
f the best places in the country for elephant-
ng.

dam's Peak (p170)
ilgrims on their trek to the top of this
cle of rock to see the predawn light.

ANTON GVOZDIKOV / SHUTTERSTOCK ©

Langdale HOMESTAY **$$$**

(☎ 052-492 4959; www.amayaresorts.com; Radetta, Nanu Oya; s/d incl breakfast US$170/180; 🖥 🛏) For the ultimate luxury 'homestay', try this offering from the Amaya chain. It's a converted old colonial building set, of course, in a tea estate, around 11km west of Nuwara Eliya on the road to Hatton. It all feels like a very posh homestay and the service is first rate. You'll love the grass tennis court and croquet lawn.

Eating

Dining options are surprisingly limited. You'll find cheap options in the town centre, but for dinner you'll probably want to eat at your guesthouse or at one of the ritzier hotel eateries.

De Silva Food Centre SRI LANKAN **$**

(90 New Bazaar St; mains Rs 200-660; ⊙ 8am-9pm) This inexpensive eatery located along a busy main street serves Sri Lankan and Chinese-style fried rice dishes. A few vegetarian *rotti* make a good lunchtime snack while rice and curry (lunch only) starts at Rs 250.

Milano Restaurant SRI LANKAN **$**

(94 New Bazaar St; meals Rs 180-500; ⊙ 7.30am-10pm) This restaurant's premises are decidedly dated, but service is friendly and there's a reliable menu of Sri Lankan, Chinese and Western dishes, including good sizzlers. It also sells very cheap snacks such as mushroom buns (Rs 30 each) from a counter on the ground floor.

Coffee Bar CAFE **$$**

(http://tangerinehotels.com; Grand Hotel Rd; snacks from Rs 200; ⊙ 7am-7pm; 🖥) This small modern cafe on the driveway to the Grand Hotel is perfect for cakes and espresso coffee. However, their short eats (samosas and pastries) can be a bit dry and disappointing.

LOCAL KNOWLEDGE

STRAWBERRY TIME

Around 11km west out of Nuwara Eliya, on the road to Hatton, is the village of Radella. Here you'll find the **Somerset Farm** (☎ 052-567 5550; Somerset Radella; snacks from Rs 250; ⊙ 7.30am-5.30pm) shop and cafe where those in the know buy fresh-from-the-farm strawberries, as well as jam and tea. There are some outdoor tables at which to enjoy them.

King Prawn Restaurant CHINESE **$$**

(Hotel Glendower, 5 Grand Hotel Rd; mains Rs 500-900; ⊙ noon-2pm & 6-10pm; 🖥) Chinese is the overriding culinary influence here, delivered in a dining room transplanted from 1930s England. There's a good array of seafood on offer. While the food isn't that memorable, it does make a nice change from rice and curry. Watch out for the additional taxes when you settle up.

★ **Hill Club** INTERNATIONAL **$$$**

(☎ 052-222 2653; 29 Grand Hotel Rd; set menu US$25; ⊙ 7-10.30pm) Dinner at the Hill Club is an event in itself. The menu focuses on traditional English dishes such as roast beef with all the trimmings and rich puddings – in cuisine terms it's far from sophisticated, but will be familiar (for homesick Brits at least). The whole thing is carried off with faded colonial panache. All diners must wear formal attire.

★ **Grand Indian** INDIAN **$$$**

(http://grandhotel.tangerinehotels.com; Grand Hotel Rd; mains Rs 600-1300; ⊙ noon-3pm & 6.30-10pm; 🖥) Far and away the town's favourite restaurant, so much so that in the evenings you often have to wait for a table. The food here is the rich, delicious fare of northern India; try the *palek paneer* (puréed spinach with fresh cheese) or the tandoori chicken.

★ **High Tea at the Grand** CAFE **$$$**

(☎ 052-222 2881; www.tangerinehotels.com; Grand Hotel, Grand Hotel Rd; high tea Rs 1250; ⊙ 3.30-6pm) High tea is served either outside on the lawn or in the open-sided tea lounge. At 3.30pm sharp, waiters in white livery unveil a bulging buffet of perfectly groomed triangular sandwiches and dainty cakes which get washed down with a vast selection of different teas.

Indian Summer INDIAN **$$$**

(☎ 052-222 4511; www.indiansummerlk.com; Badulla Rd; meals from Rs 750; ⊙ 10am-10pm; 🖥) The sign says 'fusion cuisine' but this smart restaurant with lake views is best for authentic North Indian curries. Prices are quite high, but service is efficient, flavours authentic and the attractive premises are comfortable. No alcohol is served.

Drinking & Nightlife

Several colonial hotels have fine bars that are perfect for an evening G&T, including the Hill Club (p177) and Glendower (p177). For the best tea experience in town, don't miss afternoon High Tea at the Grand.

Victoria Restaurant
CAFE
(off New Bazaar St, Victoria Park; ⊗7am-7pm) A relaxing place for an afternoon tea, or one of the many different coffees, after a stroll through Victoria Park. It also does simple meals (Rs 300), all served with a prime park view (and quite a lot of road noise).

Lakeview Pub
BAR
(Alpine Hotel, 4 Haddon Hill Rd; ⊗4pm-late; 🛜) With wood-panelled walls and friendly bar staff, this bar is a popular spot. There's also billiards, darts and a terrace with (distant) lake views.

❶ Information

Each of the following banks has an ATM and exchange facilities:

Bank of Ceylon (Lawson Rd; ⊗8.30am-6pm Mon-Fri, 9am-1.30pm Sun)

Commercial Bank (Park Rd; ⊗9am-3pm Mon-Fri)

Hatton National Bank (Badulla Rd; ⊗8am-3pm Mon-Fri)

Police (Jayathilaka Mawatha) Centrally located.

Post Office (Badulla Rd; ⊗8am-4.30pm Sun-Fri) Located in the town centre.

❶ Getting There & Away

AIR
Cinnamon Air (Map p60; 📞011-247 5475; www.cinnamonair.com) Runs twice-weekly scheduled flights (US$153, 30 minutes) to and from Colombo.

BUS
The government **CTB bus station** (off New Bazaar St) is by the main roundabout in the town centre. The **private bus station** (New Bazaar St) is just up the road. There are buses to/from the following destinations:

Colombo (normal Rs 240, intercity express Rs 480; 6hr; every 45min)

Ella (Rs 150; 3hr; 4 daily)

Haputale (Rs 116; 2hr; 3 daily)

Hatton (Rs 102; 2hr; 7 daily)

Kandy (normal Rs 180, intercity express Rs 250; 3½hr; every 30min)

Matara (Rs 360; 7-8hr; 2 morning departures)

Welimada (Rs 56; 1hr; every 30min)

TRAIN
Nuwara Eliya is served by the Nanu Oya train station, 9km along the road towards Hatton and Colombo. Most Nuwara Eliya accommodation will pick you up – often for free – if you have already booked. A taxi from the station is around Rs 800 and a three-wheeler is Rs 450.

A 1st-class observation carriage seat is Rs 1000 no matter where you get on or off. The limited number of seats in this class are in high demand, so try to book ahead. Not all trains have a 1st-class carriage. A 2nd-class reserved seat is Rs 600 to anywhere between Kandy and Badulla.

Badulla (2nd/3rd class Rs 140/80; 3¼-5hr; 5 daily)

Bandarawela (2nd/3rd class Rs 90/50; 2-3hr; 5 daily)

Colombo (2nd/3rd class Rs 450/270; 6-7½hr; 4 daily)

Ella (2nd/3rd class Rs 110/60; 2½-3hr; 5 daily)

Haputale (2nd/3rd class Rs 80/40; 1½hr; 5 daily)

Hatton (2nd/3rd class Rs 60/30; 1½hr; 6 daily)

Kandy (2nd/3rd class Rs 160/90; 4-5hr; 4 daily)

Horton Plains National Park & World's End

Horton Plains is an eerie, starkly beautiful highland plateau popular with walkers that includes the fabled viewpoint of World's End. If you're travelling from the Central Highlands down to the coast, the road through the national park is an utterly spectacular route to follow.

◉ Sights

★ Horton Plains National Park
NATIONAL PARK
(adult/child US$15/8, jeep/car Rs 250/125, service charge per group US$8, plus overall tax 15%; ⊗6am-6pm) Horton Plains has excellent hikes and is located in the shadows of Sri Lanka's second- and third-highest mountains, Kirigalpotta (2395m) and Totapola (2357m). The 'plains' form an undulating plateau over 2000m high, covered with wild grasslands and interspersed with patches of thick forest, rocky outcrops, filigree waterfalls and misty lakes. The surprising diversity of the landscape is matched by the wide variety of wildlife (p182), although many of the larger animals are very elusive. Birdwatchers will be well rewarded.

★ World's End
VIEWPOINT
The Horton Plains plateau comes to a sudden end at World's End, a stunning escarpment that plunges 880m. The walk here is 4km, but the trail then loops back to Baker's Falls (2km) and continues back to the entrance (another 3.5km). The 9.5km round trip takes a leisurely three hours. Unless you

VISITING HORTON PLAINS NATIONAL PARK

This stunning national park is one of the few in Sri Lanka where visitors can walk on their own (on designated trails). Although the main focus of the park is on World's End, don't underestimate the joy of the walk across the grassland plains. Longer and more challenging walks up Mt Kirigalpotta and Mt Totapola are also possible.

Almost every guesthouse in Nuwara Eliya and Haputale operates trips to Horton Plains and World's End; expect to pay Rs 4000 or 4500 respectively. Park fees are not included, and must be paid at the National Park Office near Farr Inn. The last tickets are sold at 4pm.

Wildlife

As an important watershed and catchment for several year-round rivers and streams, the Horton Plains hosts a wide range of wildlife. There are a few leopards, sambar deer and wild boars about, but you'd be very lucky to see a boar or leopard. The shaggy bear monkey (aka purple-faced langur) is sometimes seen in the forest on the Ohiya road, and occasionally in the woods around World's End (listen for a wheezy grunt). You may also find the endemic toque macaque.

Birdwatching

The area is popular with birdwatchers. Endemic species include the yellow-eared bulbul, the fan-tailed warbler, the ashy-headed babbler, the Ceylon hill white-eye, the Ceylon blackbird, the Ceylon white-eyed arrenga, the dusky-blue flycatcher and the Ceylon blue magpie. Birds of prey include the mountain hawk-eagle.

Flora

A tufty grass called *Chrysopogon* covers the grasslands, while marshy areas are home to copious bog moss (sphagnum). The umbrella-shaped, white-blossomed keena *(Calophyllum)* stand as the main canopy over montane forest areas. The stunted trees and shrubs are draped in lichen and mosses. Another notable species is *Rhododendron zeylanicum*, which has blood-red blossoms. The poignant purple-leafed *Strobilanthes* blossoms once after five years, and then dies.

get there early, the view from World's End is often obscured by mist, particularly during the rainy season from April to September.

All you can expect to see from World's End after around 9am is a swirling white wall. The early morning (between 6am and 10am) is the best time to visit, before the clouds roll in. That's when you'll spy toy-town, tea-plantation villages in the valley below, and an unencumbered view south towards the coast.

Try to avoid doing this walk on Sundays and public holidays, when it can get crowded.

Guides at the national park office expect about Rs 800. There's no set fee for volunteer guides, but expect to donate a similar amount. Some guides are well informed about the area's flora and fauna, and solo women travellers may want to consider hiring one for safety. Two guides who are genuinely enthusiastic about the park and unusually knowledgable on the area's fauna and flora are **Mr Nimal Herath** (☑ 077 618 9842; hrthnimal@gmail.com) and **Mr Kaneel Rajanayeka** (☑ 077 215 9583;

nuwaraeliyatrekkingclub@hotmail.com) – just Raja to friends. Both normally work as guide/jeep drivers through the Single Tree Hotel (p176) in Nuwara Eliya, but are available on a freelance basis as well.

Wear strong and comfortable walking shoes, a hat and sunglasses. Bring sunscreen, food and water. Ask your guesthouse to prepare a breakfast package for you, and reward yourself with an alfresco brekkie once you reach World's End. The weather can change very quickly on the plains – one minute it can be sunny and clear, the next chilly and misty. Bring a few extra layers of warm clothing (it's very cold up here at 6am).

It is forbidden to leave the paths, which can be slippy and tough to negotiate in places. There are no safety rails around World's End and there have been a couple of accidents where people have fallen to their deaths. If you have young children with you keep a very firm grip on them as you approach the cliff edge.

Farr Inn   LANDMARK

A local landmark, Farr Inn was a hunting lodge for high-ranking British colonial officials, but now incorporates a basic but expensive cafe and a visitor centre with displays on the flora, fauna and geology of the park. A small souvenir stand nearby has books about Horton for sale.

It can be reached by road from Ohiya or Nuwara Eliya and is situated next to the car park from which almost all visitors start the walk to World's End.

🛏 Sleeping & Eating

The vast majority of visitors base themselves in Nuwara Eliya; Haputale is another possible base.

There are a few accommodation options around Ohiya, 10km east of the park, including a good mountain lodge. But if you base yourself here you'll need to organise transport to get to Horton Plains.

The **Department of Wildlife Conservation** (☑011-288 8585; www.dwc.gov.lk; 382 New Kandy Rd, Malambe) manages two bungalows, Giniheriya Lodge and Mahaeliya Lodge, inside Horton Plains National Park. The bungalows have 10 beds each, and the charge for foreigners is US$30 per day plus US$2 per group for linen hire and a US$30 per group service charge. Bring rations and kerosene. The lodges open up only when people are staying, and you must book ahead.

There are also two camp sites (signposted near the start of the World's End track). These can also be booked through the Department of Wildlife Conservation. There's a cafe at Farr Inn beside the national park office. Otherwise bring your own picnic.

★ **Hill Safari Eco Lodge**   LODGE **$$**

(☑071 277 2451; www.hill-safari-eco-lodge-ohiya -sri-lanka.en.ww.lk; Lower Bray Estate, 5km south of Ohiya; r US$25-50) Located in a tea plantation, this fine mountain lodge enjoys outstanding views – on very clear days you can even see the Dondra Lighthouse on the South coast. There are five rooms, all with hot-water private bathrooms, and those in the new wing have amazing vistas. The lodge serves filling local food and is an ideal base for trekkers; there are walking maps available.

There's no wi-fi or phone signal. Hill Safari is 5km from Ohiya train station, via a rough access road that tuk-tuks just about cope with (but which drivers without high clearance may not want to tackle). It's at an altitude of around 2000m, so pack some warm clothes.

ℹ Information

National Park Office (⊘6am-6pm) This is where you buy entrance tickets. Last tickets are sold at 4pm. It's near Farr Inn.

ℹ Getting There & Away

Note that even if you want to just drive through the park you have to pay the hefty national park entrance fees.

Nuwara Eliya Most people come from Nuwara Eliya, a trip that takes about an hour one way (around Rs 4000 return by van). If taking a tour from Nuwara Eliya, you can ask to be dropped afterwards at Pattipola train station to catch the afternoon train to Haputale and Ella.

Ohiya The village of Ohiya is 10km east of Horton Plains and has a train station served by five daily trains to Haputale and Nanu Oya. From here you can hire a tuk-tuk (around Rs 1800, including waiting time) to the park's Farr Inn. The road rises in twists and turns through forest before emerging on the open plains. Keep your eyes peeled for monkeys.

Haputale You can also get to Farr Inn from Haputale. It takes about 1½ hours by road (Rs 4500 return).

Belihul Oya

Belihul Oya is a pretty hillside region worth passing through on your way to or from the Hill Country. There are numerous waterfalls in the area, including the dramatic Bambarakanda Falls, and good hiking.

Bambarakanda Falls   WATERFALL

(Kalupahana; Rs 150; ⊘8am-5.30pm) At 240m, the remote Bambarakanda Falls are the highest in Sri Lanka. March and April are the best months for viewing the falls, but any visit after heavy rainfall should be worthwhile. At other times, the water may be reduced to a disappointing trickle. The waterfalls are located off the A4 Hwy, between Belihul Oya and Haputale.

The turn-off to the falls is Kalupahana Junction. From here, it's 6km along a rough track, which many cars won't be able to manage. Waiting three-wheelers charge up a barely there track. For a return ride with an hour's wait, it's Rs 1000.

Bambarakanda
Holiday Resort   GUESTHOUSE **$**

(☑057-357 5699; www.bambarakanda.com; r incl full board Rs 2500-4000) A few hundred metres before the Bambarakanda Falls is this rustic guesthouse. There are three mudbrick cottages and a couple of rooms; all are pretty basic but in fair shape, and the setting, with waterfall views, is certainly spectacular. Ideally, you'll have your own transport to get here; note the access road is in very poor shape.

Belihul Oya Rest House   HISTORIC HOTEL **$$**
(☏ 045-228 0156; www.chcresthouses.com/belihul oya; Ratnapura-Haputale Rd; s/d incl breakfast from US$58/68; 🛜) This rest house is pleasantly situated next to the fast-flowing Belihul Oya river. Its six rooms are pretty tired in terms of decor, but the hotel has a faint colonial vibe and the garden setting is enjoyable. Watch out for monkeys and don't leave windows open. Good local and Western meals (from Rs 600) are served on the lovely river-facing terrace.

ℹ️ Getting There & Away

Belihul Oya is on the A4 Hwy. Buses run approximately hourly to both Haputale (Rs 52, one hour) and Ratnapura (Rs 121, two hours).

Haputale

☏ 057 / POP 5500 / ELEV 1580M

Perched at the southern edge of the Hill Country, the largely Tamil town of Haputale clings to a long, narrow mountain ridge with the land falling away steeply on both sides. On a clear day you can view the south coast from this ridge, and at night the Hambantota lighthouse pulses in the distance. On a not-so-clear day, great swaths of mist cling magnetically to the hillsides. Either way, it's a spectacular part of the country.

The scruffy town centre is a dusty ribbon of traffic, three-wheelers and small-scale commerce. But take a short walk and you'll be rewarded with extraordinary views. The railway hugs one side of the ridge in a minor victory for 19th-century engineering. Haputale is a useful base for trips to Horton Plains; guesthouses arrange vans for Rs 4500 per person.

History

Haputale today mainly reflects the influence of Sinhalese and Tamil cultures, but the legacy of the British tea planters also lives on. Tea estates blanket the hillsides, punctuated by graceful planters' bungalows, all enveloped in a damp and heavy climate that must have made the British settlers feel right at home. The pretty Anglican church (St Andrew's) on the Bandarawela road has a graveyard filled with poignant memories of earlier times.

◉ Sights & Activities

★ **Dambatenne Tea Factory**   FACTORY
(Rs 250; ⊙ 8am-6pm) This popular tea factory was built in 1890 by Sir Thomas Lipton, one of the most famous figures in tea history. The tour through the works is an education on the processes involved in the fermentation, rolling, drying, cutting, sieving and grading of tea. It's probably the most comprehensive tea-factory tour around, and afterwards you can sip a cuppa. On Sundays no processing takes place, so there's little to see. Dambatenne is 9km northeast of Haputale. Buses (Rs 28, 20 minutes) from Haputale pass the factory every 30 minutes. A three-wheeler one-way/ return costs Rs 600/1000 from Haputale.

★ **Adisham Monastery**   MONASTERY
(☏ 057-226 8030; www.adisham.org; adult/child Rs 150/50; ⊙ 9am-4.30pm Sat & Sun, poya days & school holidays) This beautiful Benedictine monastery once belonged to tea planter Sir Thomas Lester Villiers. To recreate his

---

SIR THOMAS LIPTON – ONE VERY CANNY SCOTSMAN

His name lives on in the hot-beverage aisle of your local supermarket, but Sir Thomas Lipton was a major success in business even before he became the biggest player in the global tea industry.

From 1870 to 1888 he grew his parents' single grocery shop in Glasgow to a nationwide chain of 300 stores. Recognising the potential of tea, he cannily bypassed the traditional wholesale markets of London, and went straight to the source by purchasing his own tea plantations in Sri Lanka. His network of 300 stores provided him with guaranteed distribution to sell tea at lower prices to an untapped working-class market. It also inspired the winning advertising slogan, 'Direct from the tea gardens to the tea pot'.

Lipton's planet-spanning ambition wasn't only limited to trade. In 1909 he donated the Thomas Lipton Trophy for an international football competition 21 years before the first World Cup, and he was tireless in his (unsuccessful) attempts to win yachting's America's Cup. His well-publicised interest in the two sports ensured his brand became a household name on both sides of the Atlantic.

Haputale

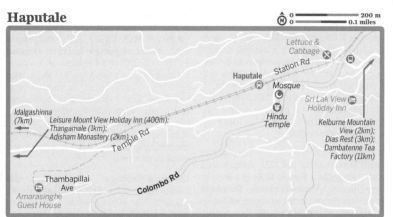

English lifestyle, he developed some English country-cottage gardens, which are still enchanting visitors today. Inside, visitors are allowed to see the living room and library, which is filled from floor to ceiling with dusty tomes. If you like the monastery so much you want to stay, well, you can, as there's a small guesthouse (p186). No photography is permitted inside the building.

Lipton's Seat   VIEWPOINT
(person/vehicle Rs 50/100; ⊙24hr) The Lipton's Seat lookout is one of Sri Lanka's most impressive viewpoints (unless it's misty and cloudy of course, which is why early morning is the best time to visit). The Scottish tea baron Sir Thomas Lipton used to survey his burgeoning empire from here, and today it's said you can see across emerald hills and tea estates to no fewer than seven different provinces.

To hike to the lookout, take the signed narrow paved road from the Dambatenne Tea Factory and climb about 8km through lush tea plantations. It's also possible to drive up – tuk-tuks charge around Rs 2500 return from Haputale. Look forward to the company of Tamil tea pickers going off to work as you walk uphill. Enterprising locals sell drinks and snacks at the top.

Thangamale   NATURE RESERVE
This woodland west of town is called a bird sanctuary, but it's more of a highland forest with a pleasant ridge-top walking trail. You can access the reserve from the Adisham Monastery (p184), from where a path leads west through the reserve to Idalgashinna, 4.3km away.

Hiking
For spectacular views – weather permitting – take the train to **Idalgashinna**, 8km west of Haputale. Walk back beside the train tracks, enjoying a spectacular view with the terrain falling away on both sides.

Some visitors hike along the train lines from Haputale to **Pattipola** (14km, an all-day hike), the highest train station in Sri Lanka. From Pattipola you can continue via foot or tuk-tuk to Ohiya train station, and from there to the Horton Plains.

Mr Amarasinghe, the genial owner of Amarasinghe Guest House (p186), is planning to open up a new hiking route to the hilltop above town.

🛏 Sleeping & Eating

Possibly due to increasing traffic congestion, Haputale's popularity with tourists has diminished in recent years. Nevertheless, there's a good stock of budget accommodation, and it's fine value compared with nearby, busier tourist towns.

There are a number of OK places for short eats, dosas (paper-thin pancakes), *rotti,* and rice and curry in the town centre.

Leisure Mount
View Holiday Inn   GUESTHOUSE $
(☑057-226 8327; www.leisuremountview.com; 163/3 Temple Rd; r Rs 1500-4500; ☎) A fine place to stay with four cheap, basic rooms in the family house and a smart, new two-storey block with modern, spacious 'deluxe' rooms, all with breathtaking views. Dining on the rooftop terrace is a pleasure, with dramatic vistas and good local food.

Amarasinghe Guest House   HOMESTAY $

(☑ 057-226 8175; agh777@sltnet.lk; Thambapillai Ave; r Rs 2500-3500; ☎) This orderly, well-run family guesthouse in a tranquil location (with no views) has been in business for decades. There are five new rooms with a contemporary finish plus three older units, all well-presented and clean. The kindly owner, Mr Amarasinghe, will pick you up from the train station or bus stand for no charge and good meals are available.

Dias Rest   GUESTHOUSE $

(White Monkey; ☑ 057-568 1027; diarest@yahoo.com; Thotulagala; r from Rs 1800; ☎) Run by very friendly, welcoming people (the owner is an experienced guide and can advise on local treks), this place has simply astonishing views. Yes, rooms are fairly basic (and a tad chilly), but they are kept tidy and the Sri Lankan food (rice and curry and breakfasts) is excellent and very affordable. It's 3km east of the town centre.

Sri Lak View Holiday Inn   HOTEL $

(☑ 057-226 8125; www.srilakviewholidayinn.com; Sherwood Rd; s/d incl breakfast from Rs 1500/1700; @☎) Offering fine value, this inn has spotless rooms split across two buildings. Views stretch a few hundred kilometres from the decent restaurant and some rooms. It's popular with backpackers for its central location, cheap rates and travel info.

Adisham Monastery Guesthouse   HERITAGE HOTEL $$

(☑ 057-226 8030; www.adisham.org; r incl full board per adult/child Rs 3000/1500) For a unique experience, check into this monastery (p184), which has only recently permitted outside guests. There are nine clean neat rooms with private hot-water bathrooms and fresh bedlinen. Meals provided are generous in portion and delicious in taste. No alcohol or tobacco are permitted. Guests are asked to maintain silence as much as possible and to book at least three weeks ahead.

★Kelburne Mountain View   BOUTIQUE HOTEL $$$

(☑ 057-226 8029, 011-257 3382; www.kelburnemountainview.com; Kelburne Tea Estate; bungalows Rs 19,600-22,000; ☎) Kelburne is a simply sublime spot to relax for a few days, with homely accommodation in immaculately renovated former tea-planters' bungalows and dapper white-suited staff attending to your needs. What really makes the property stand out, though, are the beautiful flower gardens, the surrounding tea estates and stupendous views.

Lettuce & Cabbage   INTERNATIONAL $$

(Station Rd; meals from Rs 300; ⊙ 11am-9pm; ☎) Above a row of shops, this fancy-looking cafe has modern white seating, big views and a good menu featuring Western grub like bacon and avocado salad as well as local dishes like *kotthu*. It's run by the owner of the Amarasinghe Guest House, and reliable independent travel info is available.

❶ Getting There & Away

BUS

Buses depart from stops close to the main junction on the east side of the town centre. There are regular services to Badulla (Rs 76, two hours), Bandarawela (Rs 28, 30 minutes), Welimada (Rs 55, 1½ hours) and Wellawaya (Rs 93, 2½ hours). Three daily buses run to Nuwara Eliya (Rs 116, 2½ hours). For Ella, change in Bandarawela. To get to Tangalla or Embilipitiya, change in Wellawaya.

TRAIN

Haputale is on the Colombo–Badulla line, so you can travel by train directly to and from Kandy or Nanu Oya (for Nuwara Eliya). A 1st-class observation ticket is Rs 1000 for anywhere between Badulla and Nanu Oya and Rs 1250 from Nanu Oya to Kandy. A 2nd-class reservation is Rs 600.

TAXI

Guesthouses can arrange shared minibus 'taxis' to take you to Horton Plains (Rs 4500 return trip

TRAINS FROM HAPUTALE

DESTINATION	PRICE (2ND/3RD CLASS)	DURATION	FREQUENCY (DAILY)
Bandarawela	Rs 20/15	30min	5
Colombo	Rs 330/180	8½-9hr	4
Ella	Rs 50/25	1hr	5
Kandy (incl Peradeniya Junction)	Rs 210/115	5½hr	5
Nanu Oya	Rs 80/40	1½-2hr	5
Ohiya	Rs 30/20	30-45min	5

including waiting time), Ella (Rs 2200) and Uda Walawe National Park (Rs 7000).

Bandarawela

☎ 057 / POP 7970 / ELEV 1230M

Bandarawela is a busy market town with an agreeable climate that makes a possible base for exploring the surrounding area. However, it's somewhat cursed by heavy traffic as buses, trucks and three-wheelers joust for space. Each Sunday morning the town has a lively market, but, otherwise, Bandarawela has little to attract tourists.

⦿ Sights

Dowa Temple BUDDHIST TEMPLE
(Map p192; Badulla Rd; Rs 100) The highlight of the charming Dowa Temple, 6km east of Bandarawela, is a 4m-high standing Buddha cut into the rock face. The walls of the adjacent cave shrine, carved from solid rock, are covered with excellent Sri Lankan–style Buddhist murals. It's said that King Valagamba (Vattajamini Ahhya) took refuge here in the 1st century BC during his 14-year exile from Anuradhapura. Legend also has it that a secret underground tunnel stretches from this temple all the way to Kandy. The temple, which is on the road to Badulla, is easy to miss if you're coming by bus, so ask the bus conductor to tell you when to alight. A three-wheeler or taxi from Bandarawela should cost Rs 750 return.

Church of the Ascension CHURCH
(Bandarawela-Welimada Rd) On the northwest side of town, this attractive stone church dates back to 1908, and was later extended in 1936 and 1938. Its tower was added in 1952.

🛏 Sleeping & Eating

Very few travellers stay in Bandarawela, and options are very limited. You'll find snack bars for short eats around the clock tower and central roundabout.

Bandarawela Hotel HISTORIC HOTEL $$$
(☎ 057-222 2501; www.aitkenspencehotels.com; 14 Welimada Rd; s/d incl breakfast US$90/106; 🛜) Around 90 years ago, they wisely stopped updating the furniture at this venerable tea planters' club. Now, in the 21st century, this hotel is a jolly fine show. So don your pith helmet, walk shorts and long socks, settle into one of the easy chairs, and enjoy the classy bar. Rooms are small, but have original features and en suites with bath-tubs.

Bandarawela

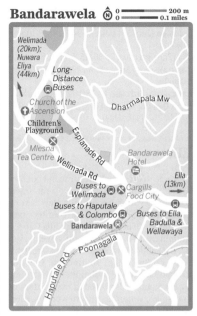

Mlesna Tea Centre CAFE $
(www.mlesnateas.com; Welimada Rd; tea Rs 80-120; ⊙8am-8pm Mon-Sat, to 6pm Sun) This superb tea store has high-quality leaves from across the hills and lots of china and teapots for sale. Its tearoom is perfect for a refined brew and slice of cake.

Cargills Food City SUPERMARKET $
(7 Welimada Rd; ⊙8am-10pm) Open long hours and perfect for stocking up on food supplies.

ⓘ Getting There & Away

BUS
Confusingly, buses leave from several stops dotted around town. Regular services run to the following destinations:
Badulla Rs 66, 1¼ hours
Ella Rs 36, 30 minutes
Haputale Rs 35, 30 minutes
Nuwara Eliya Rs 83, 2¼ hours
Welimada Rs 56, one hour

TRAIN
Bandarawela is on the Colombo–Badulla railway line. First-class observation tickets through the hills cost Rs 1000 for anywhere between Nanu Oya and Badulla. From Nanu Oya to Kandy is Rs 1250. A reserved 2nd-class ticket is Rs 600.

Badulla (2nd/3rd class Rs 60/30; 1½hr; 5 daily)

Colombo (2nd/3rd class Rs 340/185; 8-10hr; 4 daily)

Ella (2nd/3rd class Rs 30/15; 30min; 5 daily)

Haputale (2nd/3rd class Rs 20/15; 20-30min; 5 daily)

Kandy(2nd/3rd class Rs 230/125; 6hr; 5 daily)

Nanu Oya (for Nuwara Eliya; 2nd/3rd class Rs 90/50; 2-2½hr; 5 daily)

Ella

📱 057 / POP 4820 / ELEV 1041M

Welcome to everyone's favourite hill-country village, and the place to ease off the travel accelerator with a few leisurely days resting in your choice of some of the country's best guesthouses. The views through Ella Gap are stunning, and on a clear night you can even spy the subtle glow of the Great Basses lighthouse on Sri Lanka's south coast. Don't be too laid-back though; definitely make time for easygoing walks through tea plantations to temples, waterfalls and viewpoints. After building up a hiking-inspired appetite, look forward to Sri Lanka's best home-cooked food and a reviving cuppa.

In recent years, Ella's popularity has soared and the town's attractiveness has been somewhat compromised by some multistorey concrete eyesores.

🏃 Activities & Courses

Most people are in town to hike, or just chill, but when it's time to rest your boots, you'll find cooking classes too.

Hiking

Ella is a great place for walking. Most accommodation can give you a hand-drawn map of local paths. Kick off with a stroll to what is locally dubbed **Little Adam's Peak**. Go down Passara Rd until you get to the Ella Flower Garden Resort, just past the 1km post. Follow the track past guesthouses The Chillout and The One; Little Adam's Peak is the biggest hill on your right and is clearly signposted. Take the second path that turns off to your right and follow it to the top of the hill. Part of this path passes through a tea estate. The approximately 4.5km round trip takes about 45 minutes each way. The final 20 minutes or so is uphill, but otherwise it's an easy walk. Get an early start from your guesthouse – around 7am – and you'll meet Tamil families heading off to work in the tea plantations along the way. From atop Little Adam's Peak,

waterfalls and a couple of tea factories shimmer from out of the mist that's often welded persistently to the surrounding hills.

Walking to **Ella Rock** (Map p192) is more demanding and a guide is a very good idea (it's easy to miss the turn-off from the railway track and get lost in the forest that covers the upper slopes). Most guesthouses can organise a guide for Rs 1800 per group. It's a three- to four-hour round trip and the views from the top are extraordinary. If you do decide to attempt it yourself, go in a group. Follow the train tracks in the direction of Bandarawela for 45 minutes. Just after the black bridge there's a small shrine on the left. Turn left a metre or so after this and down a short embankment. Cross a concrete bridge over the Rawana Falls and then go right up the dirt track immediately after the bridge. Now start climbing uphill. From here on it's easy to get lost, especially on misty or cloudy days. Watch for the occasional faded blue way-marker. There's often someone selling overpriced tea and other drinks at the summit.

For an easier walk (2.5km from town) without a guide, follow the route to Ella Rock, but only go as far as the small **Rawana Falls**.

Cooking Classes

Matey Hut Cooking Classes   COOKING
(Map p189; Main St; Rs 1500) These cooking classes have become so popular that chef-owner Madu now offers them twice daily. You'll learn the ropes and prepare up to eight different veggie dishes.

Rawana Holiday Resort Cooking Classes   COOKING
(Map p189; 📱 057-222 8794; http://rawanaholiday. com; Rawana Holiday Resort; half-day classes Rs 2000) Here you'll cook up to 10 different dishes, including sweet-and-sour eggplant, spicy potato curry and Rawana's signature garlic curry, made with whole cloves of the 'stinking rose'.

🛏 Sleeping

Ella has a very high standard of accommodation and some fine new guesthouses have recently opened, though there are few real cheapies. During the peak Christmas/New Year period, prices can double.

Expect some attention on the train from touts telling tall tales about the hotel of your choice being closed down or rat-infested and the like. These guys are just fishing for a

Ella

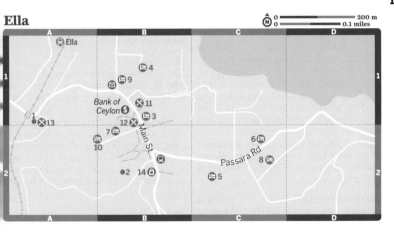

commission and hope you'll go with them to a place that pays one.

Freedom Guest Inn HOMESTAY $
(Map p189; 📞 071 689 7778; freedomguestinn@ gmail.com; 132/1 Passara Rd; r incl breakfast Rs 4000; 🛜) A traditional homestay where you're assured of a warm welcome from the helpful owner, who can provide a hiking map and advise about public and private transport options. Rooms are neat and clean and there's a pretty covered terrace to eat breakfast on.

Sita's Heaven GUESTHOUSE $
(Map p189; 📞 057-205 0020; www.sitasheavenella. com; off Passara Rd; r Rs 2700-4000; 🛜) Down a quiet forested lane five minutes' walk from central Ella, Sita's Heaven offers the best of both worlds, with privacy and great views. The owners are switched on to travellers' needs and it's the kind of place where visitors end up staying longer than they planned.

Sun Top Inn GUESTHOUSE $
(Map p189; 📞 057-222 8673; suntopinn@yahoo. com; r incl breakfast from Rs 3000; 🛜) A sunset-orange guesthouse with welcoming owners who prepare some of the best breakfasts in town and also offer cooking lessons. Rooms are small and well-kept, and bikes are available for cycling adventures (Rs 1500 per day).

Little Folly CHALET $
(Map p189; 📞 057-222 8817; www.facebook.com/ LittleFollyInElla; Passara Rd; cottages incl breakfast Rs 3000-4000; 📶🛜) Quaint Little Red Riding Hood wooden cottages squirrelled away in a forest that, if not the home of a big bad

wolf, is probably home to a monkey or two. The cottages are airy, bright and clean and everything is made of logs and bamboo. There's a great roadside **tea and cake shop** (cakes Rs 150; ⏰8am-8pm; 🛜), too.

Eeshani Guest Inn HOMESTAY $
(Map p189; 📞 057-222 8703; eeshaniguestinn@ yahoo.com; r Rs 2200-4500; 🛜) This five-room homestay is run by an endearing old couple who'll bustle you in and sit you down for a nice cuppa and a chat. The house is filled with sepia photos of their family and there's

a pretty flower-filled garden and great local food available.

Dream Café Guest House HOTEL **$$**
(Map p189; ☑ 057-222 8950; www.dreamcafe-ella.com; Main Rd; r from Rs 5500; ☎) Located above the restaurant (p190) of the same name, this hotel's accommodation is immaculate and ideal for families. Many of the offerings are mini-apartments with two bedrooms and balconies, while all have fine-quality furnishings and polished wooden floors. It's located on the busy high street, but as rooms face the rear (not the road), traffic noise is not too bothersome.

Okreech Cottages COTTAGE **$$**
(Map p189; ☑ 077 238 1638, 077 779 4007; www.ellaokreechcottages.com; r from US$35; ☎) There's an artistic touch evident in this place, which has a collection of attractive, slightly quirky two-storey cottages scattered around a hillside garden. All are quite plain inside but attractive, with great balconies and modern hot-water private bathrooms.

Zion View GUESTHOUSE **$$$**
(Map p189; ☑ 072 785 5713; www.ella-guesthouse-srilanka.com; r incl breakfast US$60-110, apt from US$180; ☎) A wonderful guesthouse where the rooms have enormous glass-panel windows and terraces strewn with hammocks and chairs. Eating breakfast on the sunny terrace with views down through the Ella Gap is what Sri Lankan dreams are made of. The owners go out of their way to help; call for free pick-up from the train station or bus stop.

✕ Eating

There's a wide choice of cafes and restaurants on Ella's main drag. However, you'll find some of the best food in the simplest guesthouses, and these are great for home-cooked authenticity; just be sure to order in advance. Some places offer rice- and curry-making classes too.

Curd (made with buffalo milk) and treacle (syrup from the *kitul* palm; sometimes misnamed 'honey') is a much-touted local speciality.

Curd Shop INTERNATIONAL **$**
(Map p189; Main St; meals Rs 200-380; ☎7am-9pm) Tiny hole-in-the-wall spot near the bus stand that's good for a cheap breakfast before or after an early-morning stroll to Little Adam's Peak. It's a classic backpacker-style place and, as the name suggests, is *the* spot

to try curd and honey or *kotthu*. It's also handy for picking up sandwiches if you're going walking.

★ Matey Hut CAFE **$$**
(Map p189; www.facebook.com/janikath; Main St; meals Rs 300-600; ☎noon-8pm) A neo-rustic log cabin that looks suspiciously like a backwoods hipster hang-out but is actually just a simple, very cheap roadside joint run by a jovial, talented chef. You can't go wrong with a rice and curry (which might take in mango, pumpkin and okra dishes and a dash of coconut sambal). It's tiny, so be prepared to wait for a table. They also offer excellent cooking classes here.

★ Cafe Chill INTERNATIONAL **$$**
(Map p189; www.facebook.com/cafechillnescoffeeshop; Main St; meals Rs 500-800; ☎10am-10pm; ☎) Run by an engaging local team, this huge, stylish roadside cafe-bar-restaurant goes from strength to strength. Its latest addition is an upper deck scattered with cushions and tables that's graced with a sculpted, wave-inspired wooden roof. Background music is modern and carefully selected. Oh, and the food is excellent too, with flavoursome local and Western dishes and espresso coffee.

Try the *lamprais* (meat and veggies cooked slowly in a banana leaf) or one of their 10 different curries.

Dream Café INTERNATIONAL **$$**
(Map p189; www.dreamcafe-ella.com; Main St; meals Rs 560-1250; ☎8am-9.30pm; ☎) This cosmopolitan cafe-restaurant has good espresso coffee, well-executed Western dishes including breakfasts (Rs 490), roasted veggie wraps, paninis and pizzas, and fine sizzling pepper steaks (Rs 1250). There are also smoothies and salads for the healthy traveller.

🛍 Shopping

Main St is lined with stores selling travel essentials, clothing and souvenirs.

T-Sips TEA
(Map p189; ☑ 077 788 3434; Wellawaya Rd; ☎9am-7.30pm) 🌿 This fair-trade tea shop (selling leaves rather than cups of tea) helps local tea-estate children. It donates 5% of all money made to community projects. It sells an array of local teas and infusions.

ℹ Information

Almost every guesthouse and most bigger restaurants have wi-fi.

Bank of Ceylon (Map p189; Main St; ⊘ 8.30am-5pm Mon-Fri, to 1pm Sat) Has an ATM.

Post Office (Map p189; Police Station Rd; ⊘ 8am-4.30pm Mon-Sat)

❶ Getting There & Away

BUS
Buses leave from Main Street (Map p189), from stops just south of the Passara Rd turn-off. Schedules change fairly often, so ask for an update at the Curd Shop (p190). No buses originate in Ella and many are full (standing room only) by the time they pass through.

➡ Regular buses go to Badulla (Rs 48, 45 minutes), Bandarawela (Rs 36, 30 minutes) and Wellawaya (Rs 67, one hour).

➡ For Kandy, you must change in Badulla.

➡ There are five direct buses to Matara (Rs 270, five hours), the last at 2.30pm; or you can always catch a bus to Wellawaya and change there for a service to the south coast or for Monaragala (for Arugam Bay).

➡ A bus heads to Galle every morning at 8am (Rs 340, seven hours).

TRAIN
Ella is an hour or so from Haputale and Badulla on the Colombo–Badulla line. The stretch from Haputale (through Bandarawela) is particularly lovely scenery. Roughly 10km north of Ella, at Demodara, the line performs a complete loop around a hillside and tunnels under itself at a level 30m lower. A few kilometres out of Ella, the train passes over **Nine Arch Bridge**, a picturesque crossing and iconic landmark.

Ella's pretty train station is so quaint it has won the 'Best Kept Station' award. It's like Thomas the Tank Engine come to life. Station manager, Mr Ashendria Disanayake, deserves mention for winning the 'Most Helpful Station Manager' award.

Fares and timetables are well posted. Observation class is Rs 1000 for anywhere between Nanu Oya and Badulla and Rs 1250 to Kandy and Colombo. A 2nd-class advance reservation is Rs 600 to any of the following destinations. There are five daily trains to each of these destinations, and four daily to Colombo.

Destination	Price (2nd/3rd Class)	Duration
Badulla	Rs 40/20	1hr
Bandarawela	Rs 30/15	35min
Colombo	Rs 350/190	9hr
Haputale	Rs 50/25	1-1½hr
Kandy	Rs 240/130	6-10hr
Nanu Oya (for Nuwara Eliya)	Rs 110/60	2½-3hr
Ohiya	Rs 70/40	2hr

TAXI
Private minibus taxis gather on the roadside close to the Dream Café and charge the following rates:

Colombo (Rs 16,000)
Galle (Rs 14,000)
Horton Plains (Rs 8500)
Mirissa (Rs 12,000)
Nuwara Eliya (Rs 7500)
Tangalla (Rs 10,000)
Tissamaharama (Rs 6500)

Around Ella

There are a number of interesting sights in the vicinity of Ella. Some can be reached by public transport or, for more convenience, on a half-day tour by tuk-tuk or taxi.

◉ Sights

★ Uva Halpewaththa
Tea Factory   FACTORY
(Map p192; www.halpetea.com; adult/child Rs 300/150; ⊘ tours 8am-4pm) The Uva Halpewaththa Tea Factory, 5km north of Ella, runs some of the better tea plantation tours in Sri Lanka. After you've enriched yourself with knowledge, treat your taste buds by trying samples of the estate's different teas. There's also a small shop selling leaves and tea-related paraphernalia. Tours take place throughout the day, but the frequency of tours varies slightly depending on the kind of tea being processed. To be safe, visit in the morning.

To get here, catch a bus towards Bandarawela, get off at Kumbawela junction, and flag a bus going towards Badulla. Get off just after the 27km post, near the **Halpe Temple** (Map p192). From here you have a very steep 2km walk to the factory. A three-wheeler from Ella will charge Rs 1000 return.

Rakkhiththakanda
Len Viharaya Cave Temple   BUDDHIST TEMPLE
(off Wellawaya Rd) The rock face around this remote and little-visited cave temple, which is signed off the road to Wellawaya, is covered in faded Kandyan-era paintings including one of the British Royal coat of arms. Inside, the paintings are in far better condition and completely cover all the walls. There's also a reclining Buddha. It's 21km south of Ella.

Rawana Ella Falls   WATERFALL
(Map p192; Wellawaya Rd) The 19m-high Rawana Ella Falls are about 6km down Ella Gap

Around Ella

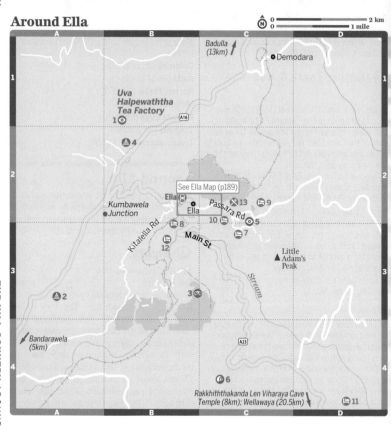

Around Ella

⊚ Top Sights
1 Uva Halpewaththa Tea Factory	B1

⊚ Sights
2 Dowa Temple	A3
3 Ella Rock	B3
4 Halpe Temple	B2
5 Newburgh Green Tea Factory	C2
6 Rawana Ella Falls	C4

🛏 Sleeping
7 98 Acres Resort	C3
8 Chamodya Homestay	B3
9 Chill Ville	C2
10 Ella Flower Garden Resort	C2
11 Planters Bungalow	D4
The Chillout	(see 7)
The One	(see 7)
12 Waterfall Homestay	B3

⊗ Eating
13 Adam's Breeze	C2

towards Wellawaya. During rainy months, the water comes leaping down the mountainside in what is claimed to be the 'wildest-looking' fall in Sri Lanka, but during the dry season it may not flow at all. There are vendors selling food and trinkets. Catch any bus heading towards Wellawaya.

Newburgh Green Tea Factory　　FACTORY
(Map p192; Newburgh Tea Estate, Passara Rd; adult/child Rs 500/free; ⊙8am-6pm Mon-Sat) The tours at this green-tea factory are pretty rushed and the guide may or may not be informative – some are more intent on flogging leaves. Newburgh is owned by Finlays, one of the world's larger tea producers. It's a half-hour walk from town.

🛏 Sleeping & Eating

★**Chamodya Homestay**　　HOMESTAY **$**
(Map p192; ☑ 077 743 7795; r incl breakfast Rs 4500; 🛜) One of the best homestays in the

Ella region, Chamodya is run by a lovely couple who take very good care of their guests. Guests get to enjoy a glorious outlook over a forested valley and the five rooms are very well-presented and attractive, all with hot-water bathrooms. Do eat here. It's 2km west of the centre, via a track; a three-wheeler costs Rs 250.

★ **The One** GUESTHOUSE $$
(Map p192; ☑ 077 533 0532; dammikaediri@gmail.com; Passara Rd; ⊙ r US$45-50; 🛜) Owned by a talented musician and master carpenter, these beautifully finished rooms boast gorgeous handmade fixtures and fittings (shelves, clothes rails) and fuse contemporary design with a traditional touch. Each has a flat-screen TV with satellite channels and a generous balcony. Two units were complete at the time of research; a total of six are planned.

★ **Waterfall Homestay** GUESTHOUSE $$
(Map p192; ☑ 057-567 6933; www.waterfalls-guesthouse-ella.com; s/d incl breakfast from Rs 5000/6000; 🛜) A delightfully secluded homestay run by an Australian couple with a flair for art and design. The building melds into the hillside and offers views over the Rawana Falls. Expect some original art or a statue in each individually decorated room. Memorable meals are served on the terrace. It's 1.5km from town.

Closes from 10 to 19 April, and the first three days of every other month.

The Chillout GUESTHOUSE $$
(Map p192; ☑ 077 404 9777; dhanushka4048@gmail.com; off Passara Rd; r incl breakfast US$40; 🛜) Run by a welcoming family and located right by the start of the trail to Little Adam's Peak, these three well-appointed rooms with fans and minibar enjoy sweeping views and share a large balcony.

★ **Chill Ville** COTTAGE $$$
(Map p192; ☑ 077 180 4020; www.chillvillehotel.com; 8 Mile Post, Passara Rd; cottages US$80; ✳🛜🏊) Totally renovated, this once supremely tacky hotel now has seven perfectly designed, sleek, modern bungalows, each with stupendous valley views from their generous balconies. It's a delightfully isolated 8km from Ella, and run by the efficient Cafe Chill (p190) team. Chill Ville opened in 2017, and the owners plan to renovate the on-site restaurant and open a yoga *shala*.

A three-wheeler from Ella is about Rs 400.

Planters Bungalow HISTORIC HOTEL $$$
(Map p192; ☑ 077 127 7286, 057-492 5902; www.plantersbungalow.com; 10 Mile Post, Wellawaya Rd; d/ste incl breakfast US$85/130; 🛜🏊) Ten clicks south of Ella, this converted tea-planters' bungalow is fringed by blossoming, beautiful gardens carefully cultivated by the owners (one of whom worked in art publishing in England). Its rooms have been impeccably renovated and are filled with religious imagery, fine antiques and works of art. For families there's a suite that can accommodate up to six people.

Ella Flower Garden Resort GUESTHOUSE $$$
(Map p192; ☑ 057-205 0480; www.ellaresort.com; Passara Rd; r US$55-80; 🛜) Right beside the trail to Little Adam's Peak, this hotel is a horticultural paradise with blooming flower gardens. There are three classes of accommodation, all well maintained – book a chalet for more space. However, there's a lot of ongoing construction around the hotel that even the caged birds can't drown out.

98 Acres Resort RESORT $$$
(Map p192; ☑ 057-205 0050; www.resort98acres.com; Uva Greenland Tea Estate; r/ste incl breakfast from US$180/300; 🛜🏊) Set in tea gardens 2km east of town, the elegant stilted cottages here have fabulous views towards Little Adam's Peak. Rooms are of the earthy, rustic-luxury type and the tea-bush-hemmed swimming pool is a huge bonus. There's also an in-house spa and Ayurveda centre. However, the price tag is very hefty and dining options could be improved.

Adam's Breeze INTERNATIONAL $$
(Map p192; Passara Rd; meals from Rs 500; ⊙ 7am-9pm; 🛜) A casual family-run thatched place close to the turn-off for Little Adam's Peak, with delicious *kotthu*, noodle dishes, curries and Western food. Prices are moderate and service is warm.

ⓘ Getting There & Away

From Ella, you can hop on buses heading to towns including Wellawaya, Bandarawela and Badulla to access the sights in this region. However, hiring a tuk-tuk is more convenient; expect to pay around Rs 2200 for a half-day trip.

Wellawaya
☑ 055 / POP 4230

Wellawaya is a small crossroads town and, apart from the considerable allure of the nearby Buduruwagala carvings, there's not much of interest in the area. It's surrounded by dry plains that were once home to the ancient Sinhalese kingdom of Ruhunu.

Roads run north through the spectacular Ella Gap to the Hill Country, south to Tissamaharama and the coast, east to the coast and west to Colombo.

◉ Sights

★ **Buduruwagala** MONUMENT
(Rs 300; ⊘6.30am-6pm) The beautiful, 1000-year-old, rock-cut Buddha figures of Buduruwagala are the region's biggest attraction. The gigantic standing Buddha (at 15m, it is the tallest on the island) here still bears traces of its original stuccoed robe, and a long streak of orange suggests it was once brightly painted. It's surrounded by smaller carved figures. This remote site is located 9km south of Wellawaya, accessed by a scenic side road.

➡ **The Central Figures**
The central of the three figures to the Buddha's right is thought to be the Mahayana Buddhist figure Avalokitesvara (the bodhisattva of compassion). To the left of this white-painted figure is a female figure thought to be his consort, Tara. Local legend says the third figure represents Prince Sudhana.

➡ **The Other Figures**
Of the three figures on the Buddha's left-hand side, the crowned figure at the centre of the group is thought to be Maitreya, the future Buddha. To his left stands Vajrapani, who holds a vajra (an hourglass-shaped thunderbolt symbol) – an unusual example of the Tantric side of Buddhism in Sri Lanka. The figure to the right may be either Vishnu or Sahampath Brahma. Several of the figures hold up their right hands with two fingers bent down to the palm – a beckoning gesture.

The name Buduruwagala is derived from the words for Buddha (Budu), images (*ruva*)

ⓘ TRANSPORT HUB: BADULLA

Badulla marks the southeast extremity of the Hill Country and is a transport gateway to the east coast. It is one of Sri Lanka's oldest towns, occupied briefly by the Portuguese, who torched it upon leaving. For the British, it was an important social centre, but beyond the pretty gardens and clock tower, any vestiges of a past – including a racecourse and cricket club – are lost in Badulla's typical Sri Lankan bustle. The railway through the Hill Country from Colombo terminates here.

Very few tourists stay overnight in Badulla and in recent years the town's cheaper guesthouses have developed a reputation for being hire-by-the-hour kinds of places. Pricier places tend to be used as wedding-reception venues and can be noisy. **Hotel Onix** (☎055-222 2090, 055-222 2426; 69 Bandaranayake Mawatha; d incl breakfast with/without air-con Rs 4800/3600; ❀🛜❄) is about the best Badulla has to offer.

Most Sri Lankans visiting Badulla stop at either **Muthiyagana Vihara** (off Passara Rd) or **Kataragama Devale** (Lower King St).

Bus
There are two daily luxury air-conditioned night buses (Rs 910, six hours) to Colombo leaving at 11pm and 11.30pm. The bus station (King St) is centrally located. Frequent regular buses run to the following destinations:

Colombo Rs 330 to 490, six to seven hours

Ella Rs 48, 45 minutes

Kandy Rs 160 to 215, three hours

Monaragala Rs 118, two hours

Nuwara Eliya Rs 120, two hours

Train
Observation class is Rs 1000 to anywhere between Badulla and Nanu Oya and Rs 1250 for anywhere beyond Nanu Oya. Reserved 2nd-class tickets are Rs 600.

Five daily trains head to Colombo (2nd/3rd class Rs 370/205) via Kandy (2nd/3rd class Rs 270/145).

and stone *(gala)*. The figures are thought to date from around the 10th century and belong to the Mahayana Buddhist school, which enjoyed a brief heyday in Sri Lanka during this time.

An ancient stupa has recently been uncovered halfway along the road from the junction to the carvings.

➡ **Practical Tips**

You may be joined by a guide, who will expect a tip. A three-wheeler from Wellawaya costs about Rs 700 return. Some people walk (or cycle) from the junction of the main road, which is very pleasant but can also be very hot. The 4km track crosses a series of delicate lakes. Keep an eye out for local birdlife, including many egrets and herons.

🛏 Sleeping & Eating

Little Rose GUESTHOUSE $
(☎055-567 8360; www.littlerosewellawaya.com; 101 Tissa Rd; incl breakfast s with/without air-con Rs 3000/2000, d with/without air-con Rs 4000/2500; ❄🛜) Just 500m from the bus station, this is a good budget option if you're staying overnight to wait for onward transport. This country home is in a quiet rural setting, surrounded by rice paddies and run by a welcoming family. Its 17 rooms are well-kept, and have mossie nets, fans (or air-con) and private bathrooms. Good, inexpensive meals are available.

⭐ **Jetwing Kaduruketha** HOTEL $$$
(☎055-471 0710; www.jetwinghotels.com; r US$112; ❄🛜🏊) In a rural location 2km north of Wellawaya, this fine new hotel has well-appointed, smart and modern rooms that overlook rice fields and across towards the bulk of the central highlands. The only thing that might disturb the peace here are songbirds and peacocks. There are free bikes for guests. During quiet times, rates can be slashed by 50%.

Living Heritage Koslanda BOUTIQUE HOTEL $$$
(☎077 935 5785; www.koslanda.com; Koslanda; r incl breakfast US$295-395; 🛜🏊) 🌿 Set within 32 hectares of grounds, which include tangled forest and even a waterfall, the planters-style bungalows here are cool, calm and impeccably decorated. They were constructed by local craftspeople using traditional techniques, but, fear not, gorgeous open-air bathrooms and private jacuzzis have also been incorporated and there's a glorious infinity pool. However, rates are steep indeed.

DIYALUMA FALLS

The 171m-high **Diyaluma Falls** is Sri Lanka's third-highest waterfall. Cascading down an escarpment of the Koslanda Plateau, the falls leap over a cliff face and plunge (in one clear drop) to a pool below. It's more impressive in the rainy season. Diyaluma Falls is 13km west of Wellawaya; any bus heading to Haputale passes by.

A path to the upper part of the falls leaves from close to KM 207.5 on the A4 Hwy. It's a steep 45-minute hike to the top.

ℹ Getting There & Away

Wellawaya is a common staging post between the Hill Country and the south and east coasts. You can usually find a connection here until mid-afternoon. For Tissamaharama, change at Pannegamanuwa Junction (Rs 92). Buses leave when full.

Badulla (Rs 96; 1½hr; every 30min)
Ella (Rs 67; 1hr; every 30-40min)
Embilipitiya (Rs 141; 2½hr; 5 daily)
Monaragala (Rs 74; 1hr; every 20min)
Tangalla (Rs 172; 3½hr; every 30min)

Uda Walawe National Park

Framed by soaring highlands on its northern boundary, the **Uda Walawe National Park** (adult/child US$15/8, service charge per group US$8, vehicle charge per group Rs 250, plus overall tax VAT 15%; ⏲6am-6pm) is one of the world's best places to see wild elephants. Largely comprised of grasslands and bush forest, it's also one of the best national parks in Sri Lanka for game spotting, with herds of elephant, wild buffalo, sambar and spotted deer, and giant squirrel.

Elephants are Uda Walawe's key attraction, with around 600 in the park in herds of up to 50. There's an elephant-proof fence around the perimeter of the park, (supposedly) preventing elephants from getting out and cattle from getting in. The best time to observe elephant herds is from 6.30am to 10am and again from 4pm to 6.30pm.

The park, which centres on the 308.2-sq-km Uda Walawe Reservoir, is lightly vegetated, but it has a stark beauty and the lack of dense vegetation makes game-watching easy.

The entrance to the park is 12km from the Ratnapura–Hambantota road turn-off and 21km from Embilipitiya. Visitors buy tickets in a building a further 2km on. Most people take a tour organised by their guesthouse or hotel, but a trip with one of the 4WDs waiting outside the gate should be around Rs 3800 for a half-day for up to eight people with driver. Last tickets are usually sold at 5pm. A park guide is included in the cost of admission and these guys, who all seem to have hawk-like wildlife-spotting eyes, are normally very knowledgable about the park and its animals. A tip is expected.

Besides elephants, sambar deer and wild buffalo (although most buffalo you'll see in the park are domesticated), there are also mongooses, jackals, water monitor lizards, lots of crocodiles, sloth bears and the occasional leopard. There are 30 varieties of snakes and a wealth of birdlife – 210 species at last count; northern migrants join the residents between November and April.

◉ Sights

★ **Elephant Transit Home**   ZOO
(CP de Silva Rd; adult/child Rs 500/250; ⊙ feedings 9am, noon, 3pm & 6pm) Supported by the Born Free Foundation (www.bornfree.org.uk), this complex is a halfway house for orphaned elephants. After rehabilitation, the elephants are released back into the wild, many into the Uda Walawe National Park. Although you can't get up close and personal with the elephants, seeing them at feeding time (from a viewing platform) is still a lot of fun. It's on the main lakeside road, about 5km west of the Uda Walawe National Park entrance. Elephants here are not normally chained at night (unlike at other elephant 'orphanages') in Sri Lanka. Over 100 elephants have been rehabilitated at the Elephant Transit Home and subsequently released into the wild. Around 40 or so juvenile pachyderms are usually here at any one time. Most tour operators include a visit to the Elephant Transit Home in their trips. There are also decent information displays where you can learn all about elephants and their ancestors. Try to avoid weekends and holidays, when dozens of people are packed together on the viewing platform.

🛏 Sleeping & Eating

There's a wide choice of places to stay on the fringes of the park. Rates are high, though – expect to pay more than you would on the coast or up in the highlands. All the hotels around the park have restaurants.

★ **Silent Bungalow**   GUESTHOUSE $
(☑ 071 271 8941; off Dakunu Ala Rd, Uda Walawe; r incl breakfast Rs 1500-3000; 🗑) A welcoming place offering good budget accommodation in simple, quite spacious fan-cooled rooms with cold-water private bathrooms. Breakfasts, indeed all meals, are excellent. Sudath, the owner, organises very good safaris from here at fair rates and you've a good chance to share costs with others as it's a popular base for independent travellers. Book ahead. It's behind the army camp in Uda Walawe town.

Superson Family Guest   GUESTHOUSE $
(☑ 047-347 5172; 90B CDE Pl, Uda Walawe; s/d Rs 1200/2000, d with air-con Rs 3200; ❄🗑) Run by Percy and Mali, a charming local couple, this budget guesthouse has clean rooms, a nice garden and good home-cooked food. The owners will help out with transport advice

---

UDA WALAWE UNDER THREAT

Wildlife in Uda Walawe is under threat for several reasons, including illegal settlement and the associated grazing of cattle. Another problem is poaching and the use of 'Hakka Patas', small explosive devices that are concealed in food and left on the banks of the Uda Walawe Reservoir, where wild boar graze. Though the explosives target wild boar, several elephants have been severely injured in recent years.

All along the main road fringing the park, shops sell fruit to passing motorists who then attempt to hand feed the wild elephants that gather along the edge of the park fence. Be aware that feeding the elephants encourages dependence and erodes their fear of humans. This frequently leads to human–elephant conflict (each year around 50 people in Sri Lanka are killed by elephants and over 100 elephants are killed by farmers).

Fences around the park also cause the elephants stress, preventing movement to waterholes and good grazing. Indeed, there's evidence that Uda Walawe's park-confined elephants are struggling to feed themselves adequately. Elephants prefer feeding on grass, but as forests inside Uda Walawe regenerate, so its grasslands diminish.

and setting up safaris; many backpackers stay here. Prices are pretty flexible.

Athgira River Camping CAMPGROUND $$
(☑ 047-223 3296; www.nilukasafari.com; Mudunmankada Rd; s/d half-board US$70/85; 🛜) This safari camp has comfortable canvas tents strung along the river bank with attached (cold-water) bathrooms and proper beds (with mossie nets). It's a social place and the friendly staff organise frequent riverside barbecue nights. There are bikes for hire too.

If arriving by public transport, hop off the bus at the Elephant Transit Home and go to the Athgira Restaurant opposite; they'll provide onward transport.

Elephant Safari Hotel LODGE $$$
(☑ 047-567 8833; www.elephantsafarihotel.lk; 60 Aloka Mawatha; s/d half-board US$139-232; ❄@≋) This lodge has huge cottages, built from mudbrick and thatch, which are spacious and quite stylish, with open-air showers. However, the pool is often out of action and overall maintenance should be better for the rates asked. It's down a maze of bumpy rural lanes but well-signed; the turn-off is a couple of kilometres west of the park gate.

Grand Uda Walawe RESORT $$$
(☑ 047-223 2000; www.grandudawalawe.com; 912 Thanamalwila Rd; s/d half-board US$155/195; ❄🛜≋) This large, resort-like place centres on an impressive pool complex; it's every tour group's favourite place to stay. Although it doesn't blend seamlessly into the environment, it's slickly run and offers luxury and comfort for those who need it. Facilities include a gym and snooker room.

ℹ Getting There & Away

Tours of the park are offered from Ella, Ratnapura, Tissa and many south-coast resorts.

Buses from Embilipitiya (Rs 46, every 45 minutes) pass the park entrance, where jeeps for safaris can be hired.

Most of the cheaper accommodation is in or close to the small town of Uda Walawe. More upmarket places can be found strung along the road between the park entrance and Uda Walawe village. Bus drivers will usually drop you off outside your hotel of choice, though note many places are located down dusty side tracks.

BUSES FROM EMBILIPITIYA

Embilipitiya is sometimes used as a base for tours to Uda Walawe National Park, as it's only 23km south of the park's ticket office. However, with the increasing range of accommodation around the park itself, there's much less reason to stay in this otherwise busy, dusty agricultural town.

Buses leave from the central bus station (A18 Hwy, Embilipitiya) frequently for the following destinations:

Matara (Rs 142; 2½hr; every 20min)
Ratnapura (Rs 166; 3hr; every 30min)
Tangalla (Rs 88; 2hr; every 30min)
Uda Walawe (Rs 46; 45min; every 30min)

Sinharaja Forest Reserve

The largest lowland rainforest in Sri Lanka, Sinharaja Forest Reserve (adult/child Rs 644/325, compulsory guide per person from Rs 1000, video camera Rs 560; ⊙6.30am-6pm, ticket office to 4.30pm) is an abundant, biodiverse habitat, bordered by rivers and rich in wildlife, including rare mammals and many endemic birds. Unlike most Sri Lankan national parks, access to the forest is only on foot, accompanied by a ranger or guide. Most visitors base themselves in the nearby settlements of Deniyaya or Kudawa, where entrance tickets are sold at the main Forest Department offices.

Because the forest is so dense, wildlife-spotting is not as easy here as it is in many other Sri Lankan reserves and parks. A good guide certainly helps. On most days, the jungle is shrouded by copious rain clouds, which replenish its deep soils and balance water resources for much of southwestern Sri Lanka. Recognising its importance to the island's ecosystem, Unesco declared the Sinharaja Forest Reserve a World Heritage Site in 1989.

There are 22 villages around the forest, and locals are permitted to enter the area (on motorbikes) to tap palms to make jaggery (a hard brown sweet) and treacle, and to collect dead wood and leaves for fuel and construction. Medicinal plants are collected during specific seasons. Rattan collection is of more concern, as the demand for cane is high. Sinharaja attracts illegal gem miners, too, and abandoned open pits pose a danger to humans and animals, and cause erosion. There is also some poaching of wild animals.

History

In 1840 the forest became British crown land, and from that time some efforts were made towards its preservation. However, in 1971 loggers moved in and began selective logging. The logged native hardwoods were replaced with mahogany (which does not occur naturally here), logging roads and

THE HILL COUNTRY SINHARAJA FOREST RESERVE

trails snaked into the forest and a woodchip mill was built. Following intense lobbying by conservationists, the government called a halt to all logging in 1977. Machinery was dismantled and removed, the roads gradually grew over and Sinharaja was saved. Much of the rest of Sri Lanka's rainforest stands on mountain ridges within a 20km radius of the forest.

Sights

Aside from the forest reserve, the region fringing Sinharaja has some interesting temples and several waterfalls worth investigating.

Getabaruwa Raja
Maha Viharaya   BUDDHIST SITE
This superb early-17th-century rock temple is just west of Kotapola, 11km south of Deniyaya. There's a steep access road then steps up to the site, which has a seated gilded Buddha and a small stupa.

Kolawenigama Temple   BUDDHIST TEMPLE
The Kolawenigama Temple, 6km southwest of Deniyaya, is of modest proportions,

but has a unique structure that resembles Kandy's Temple of the Sacred Tooth Relic. It was built by King Buwanekabahu VII in recognition of the protection given to the tooth relic by the villagers. The shrine has Kandyan-style frescoes.

Kiruwananaganga Falls   WATERFALL
The impressive Kiruwananaganga Falls, some of the largest in Sri Lanka (60m high in stages and up to 60m wide during the height of the rainy season), are 5km east of Kotapola on the road towards Urubokka. There are other falls in the area too.

Activities

The only access to the Sinharaja forest is via a guided walk, either using freelance guides (based at the park entrances) or as part of a tour. Tours are possible not only from Deniyaya and Kudawa, but are also offered as day trips by operators in several south-coast resorts including Unawatuna and Galle.

Exact guiding rates depend on how many are in your group, but you can expect to pay around US$25 for a half-day guided walk.

SINHARAJA ATTRACTIONS

Wildlife
The largest carnivore here is the leopard. Its presence can usually be gauged only by droppings and tracks, and it's seldom seen. Even rarer are rusty spotted cats and fishing cats. Sambar, barking deer and wild boar can be found on the forest floor. Groups of 10 to 14 purple-faced langurs are fairly common. There are three kinds of squirrels: the flame-striped jungle squirrel, the dusky-striped jungle squirrel and the western giant squirrel. Porcupines and pangolins waddle around the forest floor, mostly unseen. Civets and mongooses are nocturnal, though you may glimpse the occasional mongoose darting through the foliage during the day. Six species of bat have been recorded here.

Birdlife
There is a wealth of birdlife: 160 species have been recorded, with 19 of Sri Lanka's 20 endemic species seen here. The forest is renowned for its mixed 'bird wave'. This is when several different species of bird move in a feeding flock together. It's commonly seen in many parts of the world, but in Sinharaja it's worth noting for the length of time a flock can be viewed and the number of species (up to a dozen). It sometimes even contains mammals (such as ground squirrels).

Reptiles
Sinharaja has 45 species of reptile, 21 of them endemic. Venomous snakes include the green pit viper (which inhabits trees), the hump-nosed viper and the krait, which lives on the forest floor. One of the most frequently found amphibians is the wrinkled frog, whose croaking is often heard at night.

Plant Life
Sinharaja has a wild profusion of flora. The canopy trees reach heights of up to 45m, with the next layer down topping 30m. Nearly all the subcanopy trees found here are rare or endangered. More than 65% of the 217 types of trees and woody climbers endemic to Sri Lanka's rainforest are found in Sinharaja.

As it can rain in the reserve at any time of year, waterproofs are advisable, and leech gear is essential.

🛏 Sleeping & Eating

There are several possible bases from which to explore the reserve, including Kudawa on the north side and Deniyaya on the south side. All guesthouses and hotels provide meals.

🛏 Kudawa & Around

This village is the settlement of choice for many visitors with their own transport. The forest is a little less disturbed on this side of the park. The Forest Department at Kudawa also has some bungalows with fairly basic accommodation. Contact the **Forest Department HQ** (📞 011-286 6633; forest@slt.lk; 82 Rajamalwatte Rd, Battaramulla) in Colombo for information.

Rock View Motel   HOTEL **$$**
(📞 045-567 7990; www.rockviewmotel.com; Rakwana Rd, Weddagala; d/tr incl breakfast Rs 5250/7000; ❄🛜) Rock View offers functional and airy rooms with balconies that have views over rolling hills of forest and tea bushes. It's 2km east of Weddagala and about the best-value deal in these parts. However, expect noise at weekends when it often hosts wedding parties.

Blue Magpie Lodge   GUESTHOUSE **$$$**
(📞 077 320 6203; www.bluemagpie.lk; Kudawa; s/d incl breakfast US$80/95; ❄) In a peaceful location just a short walk from the park entrance, this lodge has 12 rustic cabanas, which are a little tired and dark, and six smarter modern rooms. It's expensive, even considering the remote location, but it has good forest and birding guides available.

Boulder Garden   BOUTIQUE HOTEL **$$$**
(📞 045-225 5812; www.bouldergarden.com; Sinharaja Rd, Koswatta; s/d US$188/272; ❄) For something very different, check out this brilliantly designed ecoresort. There are 10 rustic rooms – two of them in actual caves – built among boulders and streams, and the amazing restaurant is located underneath a huge overhanging rock. It's 15km northwest of the Kudawa entrance to the Sinharaja Forest Reserve.

🛏 Deniyaya

If you don't have your own wheels, the small town of Deniyaya is a convenient base.

ℹ LOOK OUT FOR LEECHES

Sinharaja has leeches in abundance. In colonial times the British, Dutch and Portuguese armies rated leeches as their worst enemy when they tried to conquer the hinterland (which was then much more forested), and one British writer claimed leeches caused more casualties than all the other animals put together. These days you needn't suffer as much because all guides carry antileech preparations.

Accommodation also tends to be better value here.

Deniyaya Rest House   HOTEL **$**
(📞 041-227 3600; r Rs 3000; 🛜) Like most former government rest houses in Sri Lanka, this place has the best location in town, with great views over the countryside. The large, spartan rooms are ageing but serviceable, and there's a bar-restaurant where you can tally up your leech bites over a stiff drink. It's just off the main road in the town of Deniyaya.

**★ Sinharaja Rain
Forest View Villas**   HUT **$$**
(📞 071 801 0700; http://rainforestviewvillas.com; s/d/tr US$25/35/45; 🛜) These well-constructed wooden forest cabins are delightful, each with a double bed, stylish attached bathroom (with hot water) and verandah. There are views over the Sinharaja Forest Reserve, friendly, helpful hosts (speak to them about tours) and tasty grub. It's fine value for the area. It's 6km north of Deniyaya via some rough tracks.

Sinharaja Rest   GUESTHOUSE **$$**
(📞 041-227 3368; www.sinharajarest.com; Temple Rd, Deniyaya; r incl breakfast US$24-40; 🛜) Brothers Palitha and Bandula Rathnayaka are both certified forest guides, so staying here makes it easy to maximise your time. The rooms at their home are fairly basic, but there's good home cooking and a lovely private garden. Day trips to the Sinharaja Forest Reserve cost Rs 4000 per person and include transport, guiding and lunch (but exclude park entrance fees). Trips are also open to nonguests, and overnight stays in forest bungalows are possible (with advance notice). The same family also has smart chalets that sleep four (US$100 to $120 including breakfast) a short way up the road.

Rainforest Lodge HOTEL **$$**
(📞 041-492 0444; www.rainforestlodge-srilanka.de; off Temple Rd, Deniyaya; incl breakfast s €25-55, d €44-68; 🛜) In an isolated spot within a tea plantation, 2km west of Deniyaya, the Rainforest Lodge has spacious, plain but decent-value rooms with en suites. The views include a green trifecta of rainforest, rice paddies and tea gardens, and good food is served.

Forest trips cost Rs 4500 for one person or Rs 7000 for two, including food, transport and guiding fees.

★ **Rainforest** BOUTIQUE HOTEL **$$$**
(📞 Colombo 011-558 8714; www.rainforest-ecolodge.org; s/d incl breakfast US$180/215; 🛜) 🌿 On the edge of the Sinharaja reserve (very rare purple-faced langurs are regularly seen) this is one of the remotest hotels in Sri Lanka. Highly original rooms with stupendous views have been created out of metal shipping containers. The staff are trained from the local community, water comes from nearby springs and there's also an impressive recycling scheme. It's 17½ rather tortuous kilometres north of Deniyaya.

❶ Getting There & Away

There are several park access points, but the most relevant to travellers are those via Kudawa in the northwest and via Mederapitiya (reached from Deniyaya) in the southeast. The Mederapitiya entrance is the easiest to reach by public transport.

BUS

From Ratnapura to Deniyaya there are four daily buses (Rs 218, five hours) from 6.30am until 2.30pm. There are also three daily buses to and from Galle (Rs 164, three hours).

Heading to Kudawa can be complicated and slow going. From Ratnapura, regular buses go to Kalawana (Rs 68, 1½ hours) and from there to Weddagala (4km before Kudawa; Rs 32, 20 minutes), and then, finally, you hop on one to Kudawa (Rs 18, 15 minutes).

CAR

The road through Hayes Tea Estate, north of Deniyaya en route to Madampe and Balangoda (for Belihul Oya, Haputale or Ratnapura), is very scenic. Trying to loop from the north to the south entrances of the park is also a fine drive, but slow and painful as the roads are rough.

Ratnapura

📞 045 / POP 55,640

A bustling, congested city, Ratnapura hosts few travellers but is a famous trading centre for the area's wealth of gemstones. As you explore the town, you're sure to encounter some hustle from pushy salespeople eager to flog you a gemstone (or a piece of polished glass). Another reason to visit Ratnapura is that it's the take-off point for one of the oldest routes up Adam's Peak (p170). Climatically, expect humidity and regular downpours.

⊙ Sights

Maha Saman Devale BUDDHIST TEMPLE
This Buddhist temple, 4km northwest of the city, is an architectural treasure well worth visiting. Perched on a small hill, it has a handsome series of broad courtyards and multiroofed, whitewashed pavilions in the Kandyan style. Originally built in the 13th century, the temple was destroyed by the Portuguese and then rebuilt during Dutch times. The main sanctuary is dedicated to Saman, while side shrines honour the Buddha and Pattini. A three-wheeler from Ratnapura is about Rs 250.

The major festival is a *perahera* on Esala *poya* (July/August).

Gemmological Museum MUSEUM
(📞 045-223 0320; 6 Ehelepola Mawatha; ⊙ 9am-5pm Tue-Sat) **FREE** Established by a local gemmologist, this impressive private collection of precious stones (plus quartz, fossils and artefacts) is a good place to learn about gem mining in Sri Lanka. Yes, there are gemstones for sale, but staff are not pushy, and there's a little cafe too. It's 2.5km southwest of the centre, off the A4 Hwy.

🛏 Sleeping & Eating

Hotel Gem Land GUESTHOUSE **$**
(📞 076 696 6533; www.rohangems.com/hotelgemland; 12 Mudduwa Rd; r with fan/air-con US$17/29; ❄🛜) Away from the bustle of the city centre, this guesthouse has functional rooms with solid wooden beds and furniture; some rooms have balconies. Eating options are good (you'll never dine alone as there's a resident hornbill!) and there's a pool table. Staff seem to enjoy working here and helping out guests with travel arrangements and gem tours.

Ratna Gem Halt GUESTHOUSE **$**
(📞 045-222 3745; www.ratnapura-online.com; 153/5 Outer Circular Rd; r with fan/air-con from Rs 1250/3000; ❄🛜) This family-run, eight-room guesthouse north of town has warm hospitality, good Sri Lankan food and fine views of emerald-green rice paddies. The

CITY OF GEMS

Sri Lanka has been associated with precious stones since antiquity (its ancient names of Serendip and Ratna Dweepa both have gem connections); Marco Polo reported gem mining here during his travels in 1292. Nowhere in the nation is more associated with precious stones than Ratnapura; indeed, the name is derived from the Sanskrit for 'city of gems'. Rivers gushing down from the central highlands come laden with rocks and rubble bearing gems, particularly sapphires and rubies.

The British royals have long prized Sri Lankan sapphires. Queen Elizabeth's Crown Jewels are studded with them, and Prince Charles gave Lady Diana Spencer a large sapphire engagement ring. When Prince William married Kate Middleton, the same Ceylon sapphire was used to create his bride's ring. The virtually flawless 563-carat 'Star of India' currently exhibited in New York's Museum of Natural History is actually a sapphire from Sri Lanka.

cheapest rooms have no hot water and no views. It's run by a gem dealer who also runs **gemmology courses** (per day Rs 4000). Trips to the gem mines and markets, parks and waterfalls are also possible.

Shopping

Ratnapura Gem Bureau, Museum & Laboratory   JEWELLERY
(☑ 045-222 2469; Pothgulvihara Mawatha; ⊙ 9am-4pm) This reputable place to purchase gems adopts a relatively low-pressure approach to sales. There's a good display of local minerals and precious stones, as well as information on mining and polishing. A return three-wheeler trip from the centre of

town should cost about Rs 400, including waiting time.

ⓘ Getting There & Away

Ratnapura has good road links to Colombo, but no train connections anywhere.

The bus station is centrally located. For west-coast resorts like Hikkaduwa you should travel via Kalutara and get a connection there.

Services include the following:
Colombo (Rs 175; 3hr; every 15min)
Deniyaya (Rs 228; 5hr; 4 daily)
Haputale (Rs 167; 3hr; every 30min)
Kalutara (Rs 182; 3hr; hourly)
Kandy (Rs 203; 4hr; hourly)
Matara (Rs 278; 6-7hr; 3 daily)

THE HILL COUNTRY RATNAPURA

The Ancient Cities

Best Places to Eat

➡ Sanctuary at Tissawewa (p236)

➡ Hotel Shalini (p236)

➡ Traditional Foods Sales Centre (p208)

Best Places to Sleep

➡ Rice Villa Retreat (p225)

➡ Sigiri Lion Lodge (p212)

➡ Jim's Farm Villas (p204)

➡ Ulagalla (p235)

➡ Sanctuary at Tissawewa (p236)

Why Go?

Crumbling temples, lost cities and sacred Buddhist sites are the reason to head up country to the cultural heartland of Sri Lanka. It was here on the central plains that ancient Sinhalese dynasties set up their first capitals and supported massive artistic and architectural endeavours. Eventually these kingdoms fell, slowly to be reclaimed by the forest and jungles.

For more than a century archaeologists have been slowly stripping the many layers of history from this overgrown landscape. The rock fortress at Sigiriya, the monumental dagobas (stupas) of Anuradhapura and the refined carvings of Polonnaruwa are but a few of the sites now ranking as national treasures. Home to four Unesco World Heritage Sites, this 'Cultural Triangle' is a heaven for amateur archaeologists and historians.

Besides the amazing ruins, save time for the national parks, which teem with elephants and outstanding birdlife, and try to visit at least one off-the-beaten-track temple site.

When to Go
Dambulla

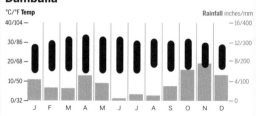

Jun A great festival, the Poson Poya, is held at Mihintale on the full-moon night.

May–Sep Elephants gather in the central and easily visited Minneriya National Park.

Nov Ceremonies in Anuradhapura for Unduvap Poya, marking the sacred bodhi tree's arrival.

Ancient Cities Highlights

1 Abhayagiri Dagoba
(p231) Feeling utterly humbled by the epic scale of the former capital of Anuradhapura.

2 Sigiriya (p209) Scaling the great rock for epic views, outstanding murals and intriguing ruins.

3 Polonnaruwa (p215) Admiring the exquisite carved

temples and Buddhas at the fascinating ruins of this former Sinhalese stronghold.

4 Minneriya (p226) Spotting elephants, crocodiles and birdlife on the lake shores and in the jungles.

5 Dambulla Cave Temples (p205) Peering at some of

Sri Lanka's most stunning Buddhist murals and images.

6 Ridi Vihara (p241) Getting off the beaten track at this little-visited site.

7 Mihintale (p237) Climbing monumental stairways to the stupas and viewpoints where Buddhism first took root in Sri Lanka.

Matale

☑ 066 / POP 46,000

This midsize regional city at the heart of the island lies in a broad, fertile valley at an elevation of 300m. Matale is a featureless urban sprawl with a congested one-way system, so you're unlikely to want to linger long. However, the road north of town is lined with dozens of visitor-friendly spice plantations where vanilla, rubber, cinchona, jackfruit, cocoa and cardamom thrive. The area is also famous for *kohila* (a type of watercress) and small, mild chillies. The historical Buddhist site of Aluvihara just north of the town is also worth a visit.

◉ Sights

Aluvihara   BUDDHIST MONASTERY
(Rs 250; ⊙ 7am-6pm) Set in the foothills 3km north of Matale, surrounded by giant boulders, this monastery is a low-key, but intriguing, site. There's a charming series of Buddhist caves, religious paintings, and a stupa or two. It's easily accessible just off the main highway.

Legend has it that a giant used three of the rocks as a base for his cooking pot, and the name Aluvihara (Ash Monastery) refers to the ashes from the cooking fire.

**Sri Muthumariamman
Thevasthanam**   HINDU TEMPLE
(exterior/interior Rs 100/250; ⊙ 7am-noon & 4.30-7.30pm) Just north of the bus stand for Kandy (at the north end of town) is this interesting South Indian–style Hindu temple. A couple of garages to the side house five enormous, colourful ceremonial chariots pulled along by people during the annual Theru festival in February/March.

🛏 Sleeping & Eating

There's no compelling reason to stay in Matale (Kandy is just an hour away), but there are a couple of decent options.

Sesatha Hotel   GUESTHOUSE $$
(☑ 066-205 7080; h.sesatha@gmail.com; 40 Kohombiliwela Rd; d Rs 4500-5500; ❄ 🛜) An elegant, modern place with rice-field views from the balconies of the five rooms, Sesatha has delightful gardens, dotted with palm trees and overlooked by restaurant tables. The catch (and it's potentially a big one) is that it's also a popular wedding venue, so time your visit wrong and you'll end up

centre stage in a no-holds-barred Bollywood-style extravaganza. Sesatha is 1.5km south of town, about 200m off the main road, and easily missed.

★ **Jim's Farm Villas**   LODGE $$$
(☑ 077 782 8395; www.jimsfarmvillas.com; s/d/tr US$130/160/195; ❄ 🛜 🏊) 🍃 In the misty, verdant hills north of Matale, at an elevation of 450m, this working organic farm (harvesting coconuts, mangoes, bananas and papaya) is owned by an Englishman and run on an environmentally sustainable basis. The 14 rooms (divided between three villas) are beautiful, with attractive wooden furniture, Egyptian-cotton bed linen, a spa and generous balconies or verandahs.

The cooking is exceptional and meals (US$10 to US$20) are eaten communally. It's 20km north of Matale, 3km off the main road west of Madawala Ulpotha.

A&C Restaurant   SRI LANKAN $$$
(☑ 072 367 4501; 3/5 Sir Richard Aluvihara Mawatha; mains Rs 900; ⊙ 11am-3pm) For a step up in class from your standard-issue rice and curry, this unlikely location offers delicious Sri Lankan meals that are varied and flavourful.

ⓘ Getting There & Away

Buses 593 and 636 run from Kandy to Matale (normal/minibus Rs 50/80, 1½ hours) every 10 minutes. Buses to Dambulla or Anuradhapura will drop you at Aluvihara (Rs 10) or the spice gardens.

There are five trains daily on the pretty spur line between Matale and Kandy (3rd class Rs 25, 1½ hours). On Saturdays and Mondays there is a direct train to Colombo (3rd/2nd class Rs 125/220, 4½ hours) departing at 6.40am. The station is on the eastern edge of the town centre.

Nalanda Gedige

The venerable **Nalanda Gedige** (⊙ 7am-5pm) FREE enjoys a wonderfully peaceful location next to a *wewa* (artificial lake) with prolific local birdlife, and is a worthwhile stop between Dambulla and Kandy, if you have your own transport. This South Indian–style temple consists of an entrance hall connected to a taller *shikara* (holy image sanctuary), with a courtyard for circumambulations. There is no sign of Hindu gods, however, and the temple is said to have been used by Buddhists. It's one of the earliest stone buildings in Sri Lanka.

SPICE GARDENS

The A9 Hwy between Matale and Dambulla is famous for its spice gardens, with over 30 dotted along the road. All offer free tours of their gardens with an English-speaking guide who can explain the merits and health properties of herbs, spices and plants including cocoa, vanilla, cinnamon, cloves, coriander, coffee, nutmeg, pepper, cardamom, aloe vera, *iriweriya* (tulsi) and the henna plant.

Most visitors enjoy the tours and find them educational, but at some point you will be guided towards the gift shop, where some of the prices asked for products can be eye-watering; be prepared for a medium to hard sell and accept it as the price of your free tour.

Euphoria Spice & Herbal (☑ 077 270 9107; www.euphoriaspice.com; Madawala Ulpotha; ☺ 8.30am-4pm) Offers very detailed tours of its spice garden and has a shop selling all kinds of creams, potions and lotions that are said to help everything from sleeplessness to low sex drive. Staff are welcoming, there's a restaurant, and cooking demonstrations are also performed. Located 15km north of Matale on the road to Dambulla.

Heritage Spice & Herbs Garden (☑ 066-205 5150; 130 Center Land, Madawala Ulpotha; ☺ 8am-5pm) With an attractive, shady garden, this spice specialist runs informative tours and has a cafe for snacks and drinks. Around 15km north of Matale.

The temple's richly decorated stone-block walls, reassembled from ruins in 1975, are thought to have been fashioned during the 8th to 11th centuries. The plinth bears some Tantric carvings with sexual poses – the only such sculptures in Sri Lanka – but before you get excited, the carvings are weather-beaten and it's difficult to see much in the way of action.

Nalanda Gedige is about 25km north of Matale and 20km before Dambulla, 1km east of the main road; look out for the sign near the Km 49 post. Anuradhapura buses from Kandy or Matale will drop you at the turn-off.

Dambulla

☑ 066 / POP 72,500

Dambulla's famed rock cave temple is an iconic Sri Lankan image – you'll be familiar with its spectacular Buddha-filled interior long before you arrive in town. Despite its slightly commercial air, this remains an important holy place and should not be missed.

The town of Dambulla is of no interest, cursed by heavy traffic heading for one of Sri Lanka's biggest wholesale markets. A night here is tolerable, but consider visiting the site as a day trip from the more relaxing environs of Kandy or Sigiriya.

⊙ Sights & Activities

In recent years, two rival monastic groups have been fighting over legal control of the Dambulla caves, with the result that the **ticket office** (☺ 7am-5pm) has moved from the Golden Temple to an inconvenient and poorly signed location 1km west of the main highway, on the south side of the hillside leading up to the temples. The easiest thing to do is take a three-wheeler here to buy your ticket, climb 20 minutes to the cave temples on the side path from here and then descend down the main stairway to the Golden Temple on the main road.

★ **Cave Temples**   BUDDHIST TEMPLE
(adult/child US$10/5; ☺ 7am-6pm) The beautiful Royal Rock Temple complex sits about 160m above the road in the southern part of Dambulla. Five separate caves contain about 150 absolutely stunning Buddha statues and paintings, some of Sri Lanka's most important and evocative religious art. Buddha images were first created here over 2000 years ago, and over the centuries subsequent kings added to and embellished the cave art. From the caves there are superb views over the surrounding countryside; Sigiriya is clearly visible some 20km distant.

Dambulla is thought to have been a place of worship since the 1st century BC, when King Valagamba (also known as Vattagamani Abhaya), driven out of Anuradhapura, took refuge here. When he regained his throne, he had the interior of the caves carved into magnificent rock temples. Further paintings were made by later kings, including King Nissanka Malla, who had the caves' interiors gilded, earning the place the name Ran Giri (Golden Rock).

This process of retouching original and creating new artwork continued into the 20th century. Remarkably, the overall impact is breathtakingly coherent.

➡ Cave I (Devaraja Viharaya)

The first cave, the Temple of the King of the Gods, has a 15m-long reclining Buddha. Ananda, the Buddha's loyal disciple, and other seated Buddhas are depicted nearby. A statue of Vishnu is held in a small shrine within the cave, but it's usually closed.

➡ Cave II (Maharaja Viharaya)

The Temple of the Great King is arguably the most spectacular of the caves. It measures 52m from east to west and 23m from the entrance to the back wall; the highest point of the ceiling is 7m. This cave is named after the two statues of kings it contains. There is a painted wooden statue of Valagamba on the left as you enter, and another statue further inside of Nissanka Malla.

The cave's main Buddha statue, which appears to have once been covered in gold leaf, is situated under a *makara torana* (archway decorated with dragons), with the right hand raised in *abhaya mudra* (pose conveying protection). Hindu deities are also represented. The vessel inside the cave collects water that constantly drips from the ceiling of the temple – even during droughts – which is used for sacred rituals.

➡ Cave III (Maha Alut Viharaya)

This cave, the New Great Temple, was said to have been converted from a storeroom in the

18th century by King Kirti Sri Rajasinghe of Kandy, one of the last Kandyan monarchs. It is also filled with Buddha statues, including a beautiful reclining Buddha, and is separated from Cave II by only a masonry wall.

➡ Cave IV (Pachima Viharaya)

The relatively small Western Cave is not the most westerly cave – that position belongs to Cave V. The central Buddha figure is seated under a *makara torana*, with its hands in *dhyana mudra* (a meditative pose in which the hands are cupped). The small dagoba in the centre was broken into by thieves who believed that it contained jewellery belonging to Queen Somawathie.

➡ Cave V (Devana Alut Viharaya)

This newer cave was once used as a storehouse, but it's now called the Second New Temple. It features a reclining Buddha; Hindu deities, including Kataragama (Murugan) and Vishnu, are also present.

Museum of Wall Paintings MUSEUM
(adult/child Rs 300/150; ⏱ 8am-4pm) The English-language displays here are a good primer on Sri Lankan wall art – from cave paintings to 18th-century frescoes – but the poor reproductions fail to inspire the enthusiasm the subject deserves. The building is 500m south of the main caves' parking area.

Dambulla Produce Market MARKET
(Matale Rd; ⏱ noon-3am) Even if you're not looking to buy a truckload of bananas, this huge wholesale market south of the centre offers a fascinating look at the vast range of produce grown in Sri Lanka. What you see being carted about with manic energy (be careful and stay out of everybody's way) will be sold in Colombo tomorrow.

Golden Temple BUDDHIST TEMPLE
(www.goldentemple.lk; ⏱ dawn-dusk) **FREE** At the foot of the cave temples hill stands this modern temple, a kitschy structure and Buddhist museum completed in 2000 using Japanese donations. On top of the cube-shaped building sits a golden Buddha image in the *dhammachakka mudra* (wheel-turning pose) and a huge neon sign.

Lanka Ballooning BALLOONING
(☎ 077 472 7700; www.srilankaballooning.com; adult/child US$210/160; ⏱ Nov-Apr) This reliable company runs hour-long dawn balloon flights over the Kandalama lake area. You'll see Sigiriya in the distance and, if you're lucky, you might just see elephants from the

---

ℹ **CULTURAL TRIANGLE TICKETS**

Tickets are needed to visit the major Cultural Triangle sites as well as a few of the minor ones. Most are run by the Central Cultural Fund (CCF), which has a good website (www.ccf.gov.lk).

Admission tickets to the main sites are steep, and are charged per day:

Anuradhapura US$25

Aukana US$6.60

Dambulla US$10

Mihintale US$3.30

Polonnaruwa US$25

Sigiriya US$30

Dambulla

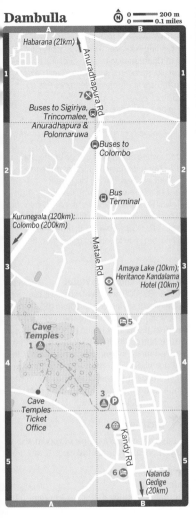

N
0 ——— 200 m
0 ——— 0.1 miles

Dambulla

Heritage Resthouse   HERITAGE HOTEL $$
(☏066-228 4799; www.chcresthouses.com; Kandy Rd; s/d/tr US$38/45/54; ⊛🖥) This former government rest house has been given the full Heritage treatment, and the four rooms now boast very classy interiors – the dark-wood furniture and elegant fabrics give more than a nod to colonial times. There's a great cafe-restaurant, too. But, and this is a considerable but, it's right next to the dreaded highway and traffic noise is omnipresent.

Sundaras   RESORT $$$
(☏072 708 6000; www.sundaras.com; 189 Kandy Rd; r incl breakfast US$75-85; ⊛🖥🌊) This smart midrange resort is within a short stroll of the caves and museum. The grounds aren't exactly spacious, but staff (some Swedish) are attentive and the well-equipped rooms all have a balcony overlooking the pool and its swim-up bar.

Lake Lodge   BOUTIQUE HOTEL $$$
(☏066-205 2500; www.lakelodgekandalama.com; 16 Division, Wewa Rd, Kandalama; s/d incl breakfast from US$190/230; ⊛🖥) The 12-roomed Lake Lodge lacks the scale of the big Kandalama resorts, but makes up for it with personalised service. Rooms are fresh and modern, with the upper-storey deluxe rooms boasting fine sunset views over the forest canopy. The hotel is French-run, so the coffee and food are good, with romantic candlelit dinners by the pool a highlight.

air. Children must be at least seven years of age; 13-year-olds and up pay full fare.

🛏 Sleeping

Trucks on Hwy A9, which cuts through the heart of Dambulla, thunder through town night and day, so bear this in mind when choosing a room.

Guesthouses tend to be near the cave temples, while the best top-end resorts are way out in the lush countryside by the Kandalama lake; for these you'll need your own transport or a three-wheeler.

THE ANCIENT CITIES DAMBULLA

AUKANA BUDDHA

According to legend, the magnificent 12m-high standing **Aukana Buddha** (adult/child Rs 1000/500; ⊘24hr) was sculpted during the reign of Dhatusena in the 5th century, though some sources date it to the 12th or 13th century. Aukana means 'sun-eating', and dawn – when the first of the sun's rays light up the huge statue's finely carved features – is the best time to see it.

Note that although the statue is still narrowly joined at the back to the rock face it is cut from, the lotus plinth on which it stands is a separate piece. The Buddha's pose, *ashiva mudra,* signifies blessings, while the burst of fire above his head represents the power of total enlightenment.

Don't miss the lily-filled rock-cut pond behind the white stupa at the edge of the site.

You'll need long trousers or a sarong to visit the statue; the ticket office is at the top of the first set of steep steps. A couple of vendors sell drinks near the parking area.

The statue is 800m from the village of Aukana. Buses between Dambulla and Anuradhapura stop at the junction town of Kekirawa (Rs 30, 30 minutes, every 30 minutes), from where there are local buses every 30 minutes for the 19km to Aukana (Rs 40, No 548). A three-wheeler from Kekirawa to Aukana is Rs 900 with waiting time.

Aukana is on the Colombo to Trincomalee rail line, but only four daily trains stop here: the station is 1km from the statue.

Kalundewa Retreat HOTEL $$$
(☎077 520 5475; www.kalundewaretreat.com; Kalundewa Rd; r US$270-655; ✳@🛱🏊) The attention to detail at Kalundewa Retreat is impressive, with six suites that feature polished-concrete floors, modern art and stylish wooden furniture that blend seamlessly into the nearby paddy fields and ponds, surrounded only by birdsong and undisturbed natural environment. It's a wonderfully exclusive experience.

Amaya Lake RESORT $$$
(☎066-446 1500; www.amayaresorts.com; r US$180-290; ✳@🛱🏊) The Amaya Lake complex has 100 stylish villas set in magnificent landscaped grounds on the north shore of Kandalama lake. The scale of the place will suit those looking for the full resort-hotel experience, as the facilities are superb (including tennis courts, a gorgeous pool and a spa) and there is evening entertainment and buffet banquets. It's 9km northeast of Dambulla.

Arika Boutique Villa BOUTIQUE HOTEL $$$
(☎066-493 5045; www.arikavillas.com; 40th Mile Post, Puwakattawala Rd; r incl breakfast US$220; ✳🛱🏊) A small, hip hotel with spacious, stylish rooms, four of which have balconies overlooking the stream. The upper-floor rooms with high ceilings are best. It's overpriced unless you get an online deal (as low as US$80). It's 9km south of Dambulla, just off the Kandy Rd.

Heritance Kandalama Hotel RESORT $$$
(☎066-555 5000; www.heritancehotels.com; Kandalama Wewa; s/d incl breakfast from US$335/395; ✳@🛱🏊) Designed by renowned architect Geoffrey Bawa, this is one of Sri Lanka's signature hotels. With 124 rooms, the hulking edifice emerges from the forest like a lost city, its walls and roofs covered in vines. Light floods into the beautifully appointed rooms and there's an infinity pool overlooking the Kandalama Wewa.

🍴 Eating

Dambulla town has a couple of good places to eat just north of the central clock tower area.

★ Traditional Foods
Sales Centre SRI LANKAN $
(A6 Hwy; snacks Rs 20-100; ⊘7am-7pm) This government-run stand exists to preserve local traditional foods, but for travellers it's an excellent chance to do some culinary exploration. Try a portion of *pittu* (steamed rice flour patty with savoury sauce) followed by a *narang kewum* (fried coconut and honey ball), washed down with a belimal flower tea, all for sale for pennies.

Mango Mango INTERNATIONAL $$
(Anuradhapura Rd; mains Rs 400-900; ⊘cafe 7am-10pm, meals 11am-3pm & 6-10pm) A smart, modern cafe-restaurant that serves good coffee and cake, as well as Western meals as diverse as breakfast pancakes, bangers and mash, and Chinese potstickers. It's a good place to

take a break. The dinner set meals are good value at Rs 300 to 490.

Dambulla Heritage Resthouse Restaurant INTERNATIONAL $$

(Kandy Rd; mains Rs 300-800; ⊙7am-10pm; 🛜)
This classy cafe-restaurant, all monochrome photographs and period furniture, is atmospheric for a drink or meals such as pot-roasted chicken and lake fish. There's a good wine selection and pleasant terrace seating.

❶ Getting There & Away

Dambulla is 72km north of Kandy on the road to Anuradhapura. The junction with the Colombo–Trincomalee road (A6) forms the centre of town.

The closest train station is in Habarana, 23km north. Local buses run frequently from the bus terminal to Kurunegala, Matale and Sigiriya (Rs 30, 45 minutes, every 45 minutes).

For other places you'll have to jump on a through bus and hope there's a seat. Buses to Kandy stop just outside the bus terminal. Buses to Anuradhapura (Rs 88, two hours), Habarana and Sigiriya stop just north of the clock tower, while buses to Colombo stop southwest of the clock tower.

Colombo Rs 150, five hours, every 30 minutes

Kandy Rs 100, two hours, every 30 minutes

Polonnaruwa Rs 78, 1¾ hours, every 45 minutes

Three-wheelers cost Rs 100 to 150 around town.

Sigiriya

📋 066 / POP 1800

Rising dramatically from the central plains, the enigmatic rocky outcrop of Sigiriya is perhaps Sri Lanka's single most dramatic sight. Near-vertical walls soar to a flat-topped summit that contains the ruins of an ancient civilisation, thought to be once the epicentre of the short-lived kingdom of Kassapa, and there are spellbinding vistas across mist-wrapped forests in the early morning. Sigiriya refuses to reveal its secrets easily, and you'll have to climb a series of vertiginous staircases attached to sheer walls to reach the top. On the way you'll pass a series of quite remarkable frescoes and a pair of colossal lion's paws carved into the bedrock. The surrounding landscape – lily-pad-covered moats, water gardens and cave shrines – only add to Sigiriya's rock-star appeal.

History

Peppered with natural cave shelters and rock overhangs – supplemented over the centuries by numerous hand-hewn additions and modifications – Sigiriya may have been inhabited in prehistoric times.

The established historical theory is that the rock formation served royal and military functions during the reign of King Kasyapa (r 477–495), who built a garden and palace on the summit. According to this theory, King Kasyapa sought out an unassailable new residence after overthrowing and murdering his own father, King Dhatusena of Anuradhapura. After 16 years on the throne Kasyapa eventually took his own life on the battlefield, following the return of his vengeful half-brother.

After the 14th century the complex was abandoned. British archaeologist HCP Bell rediscovered the ruins in 1898, which were further excavated by British explorer John Still in 1907.

Unesco declared Sigiriya a World Heritage Site in 1982.

◉ Sights

One of Sri Lanka's most famous monuments, **Sigiriya** (www.ccf.gov.lk/sigiriya.htm; adult/child US$30/15; ⊙tickets 7am-5.30pm) is an archaeological site, not a sacred site, so shorts are fine and a sarong is not necessary. Expect a visit to take half a day.

To avoid the fiercest heat and the thickest crowds, get as early a start as possible. A good strategy is to head straight for the rock itself so that you're climbing Sigiriya in the relative cool of the early morning. Then later in the morning you can amble around the gardens and tour the museum. The narrow staircases in particular get clogged with visitors after about 9.30am. The ascent involves steep climbs, so if you're not fit it may be tough. There's no shade on the exposed summit, so bring a hat and water.

Wasps build their nests on the rock face and can be a nuisance in July and August so take care if you are sensitive to stings.

Royal Gardens GARDENS

The base of the Sigiriya rock is a beautifully landscaped area dotted with formal water features, terraced gardens and natural boulders that were once home to numerous Buddhist shrines. It's a beautiful place to explore away from the crowds.

From the main entrance you pass a series of symmetrical **water gardens**, which extend to the foot of the rock and include bathing pools, little islands with pavilions

THE ANCIENT CITIES SIGIRIYA

Sigiriya

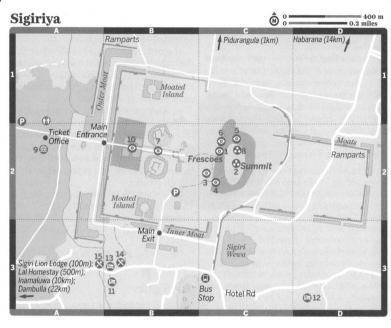

N 0 — 400 m
0 — 0.2 miles

that were used as dry-season palaces, and landscaped borders.

A series of steps continues up through terraced gardens to the western face of the rock, and then ascends it steeply.

The charming **boulder gardens**, closer to the rock itself and best seen on the descent from the rock, feature boulders that once formed the bases of monastery buildings. The step-like depressions in the sides of the boulders were the foundations of brick walls and timber columns. The cistern and audience-hall rocks are impressive, and the entire area is fun to explore.

★ **Frescoes**   HISTORIC SITE

Halfway up the Sigiriya rock an open-air spiral stairway leads to a long, sheltered gallery in the sheer rock face. The paintings of the buxom, wasp-waisted women are popularly believed to represent either *apsaras* (celestial nymphs) or King Kasyapa's concubines. Protected from the sun in the sheltered gallery, the frescoes remain in remarkably good condition, their colours still glowing.

Modern theory suggests the female forms represent aspects of Tara – a bodhisattva and one of the most important figures in Tantric Buddhism. They are similar in style to the rock paintings at Ajanta in India, but have a specific character in their classical realist style. No one knows the exact dates of the impressive frescoes, though it's unlikely they date as far back as the 5th century (when King Kasyapa reigned).

The paintings are at their best in the late-afternoon light. Photos are not allowed.

Mirror Wall   HISTORIC SITE

Beyond the Sigiriya frescoes, the path clings to the sheer side of the rock and is protected on the outside by a 3m-high wall. This wall (not the actual rock face) was coated with a smooth glaze upon which visitors felt impelled to note their impressions of the women in the gallery above – or so says local legend. The graffiti was inscribed between the 6th and 14th centuries.

You'll have to look hard beyond the modern mess to see the ancient messages. One typical graffito reads, 'The ladies who wear golden chains on their breasts beckon me. As I have seen the resplendent ladies, heaven appears to me as not good.' Another reads, 'A deer-eyed young woman of the mountainside arouses anger in my mind. In her hand she had taken a string of pearls and in her looks she has assumed rivalry with us.'

The graffiti is of great interest to scholars because they show the development of the Sinhala language and script, and because they demonstrate an age-old appreciation of art and beauty. Signs warn modern visitors not to add their own inscriptions.

Lion's Paws   HISTORIC SITE

At the northern end of the rock, a narrow pathway emerges on to the large platform from which the site derives its name – Sigiriya (from *sinha-giri*) means 'Lion Rock'. HCP Bell, the British archaeologist responsible for an enormous amount of archaeology in Sri Lanka, found the two enormous lion paws when excavating here in 1898.

At one time a gigantic brick lion sat at this end of the rock, and the final ascent to the top commenced with a stairway that led between the lion's paws and into its mouth. The lion symbolism serves as a reminder to devotees ascending the rock that Buddha was Sakya-Sinha (Lion of the Sakya Clan) and that the truths he spoke of were as powerful as the sound of a lion's roar.

The 5th-century lion has since disappeared, apart from the first steps and the paws. Reaching the top means clambering up across a series of metal stairs, but you can still see the original grooves and steps cut into the rock.

★ Summit   RUINS

The spectacular terraced summit of the rock covers 1.6 hectares. This is thought to be the site chosen by King Kasyapa for his fortified capital after he had assassinated his father. Today only the low foundations of structures exist, and the remains are visually unimpressive. Still, it's hard not to be captivated by the astonishing views from this lofty perch, which extend for kilometres across an emerald ocean of forest canopy.

A smooth stone slab (the so-called king's throne, possibly a meditation spot) sits 30m away from the ruins of a dagoba. The 27m-by-21m tank, hewn out of the rock, looks for all the world like a modern swimming pool, although it was doubtless used for water storage.

Cobra Hood Cave   CAVE

This rocky projection down in the Boulder Garden earned its name because the overhang resembles a fully opened cobra's hood. The plastered interior of the cave was once embellished with floral and animal paintings; a couple of faint traces remain. Generally, you pass by this cave after descending the rock on your way to the south gate and the car park.

Below the drip ledge is an inscription from the 2nd century BC that indicates it belonged to Chief Naguli, who donated it to a monk.

Sigiriya Museum   MUSEUM

(☉8.30am-5.30pm) This decent museum has a fine diorama of the site, providing an excellent overview and explaining Sigiriya's cultural importance beyond the obvious natural beauty. The theory that Sigiriya was a

---

PALACE OR MONASTERY?

Though the established view is that Sigiriya's summit was the site of Kasyapa's palace, some (including Dr Raja de Silva, Sri Lanka's former archaeological commissioner) are not convinced. In particular the absence of stone bases, post holes, visible foundations for cross walls or window sashes, and a lack of lavatory facilities has caused doubt and provoked heated academic debate as to the purpose of the structures. For de Silva, this site was a vast Buddhist monastery, embracing both Theravada and Mahayana practices, and existing for many centuries before and after Kasyapa's rule. The summit was a sanctuary for meditation, containing *kutis* (cells) for monks and paved paths for Buddhist perambulation.

Buddhist monastery is given here, although the established position that it was a palace or fortress prevails. Trade routes are explained, showing Sigiriya's connections with the Gulf, China, India and the Roman Empire.

🛏 Sleeping

New hotels and homestays are opening all the time around Sigiriya. It's easy to understand the appeal: the village is a mellow little place, off the main highway, and a far more preferable base than Dambulla town.

See Dambulla (p207) for rural hotels between Dambulla and Sigiriya that can also serve as a base for visiting the rock.

★ Sigiri Lion Lodge   GUESTHOUSE $
(☑ 071 479 3131; www.sigirilionlodge.com; 186 Main Rd; r Rs 2200-4000; ❄🛜) An outstanding place to stay, thanks to the genuine welcome and attention paid to guests by Ajith and Ramya, the owners. Rooms are divided between the quiet old building and a modern three-storey block that has large wood-clad rooms on the top floor. All are immaculately clean and spacious and have tables outside where you can linger over breakfast.

It's up a little lane about 500m west of the village. If you need air-conditioning, there's an extra charge of Rs 1000.

Lal Homestay   GUESTHOUSE $
(☑ 066-228 6510, 077 704 5386; lalhomestay@gmail.com; 209 Ehelagala; r Rs 1500-2000) For that living-with-a-family experience, Lal's is perfect. Your host family could not be more welcoming or friendly, offering home-cooked meals (try the delicious jackfruit curry) and useful travel info. The five fan-cooled rooms, each with verandah and hot-water bathroom, are kept clean and tidy. The two back rooms have less road noise.

River Retreat Homestay   GUESTHOUSE $
(☑ 077 242 9784; river.retreat@yahoo.com; r Rs 2000-4000; ❄🛜) This bungalow set back off the road has three spacious, quiet rooms next to a creek, with air-con and solar-heated hot water. It was just starting up at the time of writing, but promises to be good. Access it through the owner's sister's place, the **Flower Inn** (☑ 066-567 2197; s/d from Rs 1800/2500, with air-con Rs 3000/3500; ❄🛜), which has plainer and cheaper rooms.

Nilmini Lodge   GUESTHOUSE $
(☑ 066-567 0469; nilminilodge@gmail.com; r with/without air-con from Rs 3000/1500; ❄🛜) An old-school guesthouse owned by a family who

have been hosting travellers for years and can provide lots of useful tips about the region. Rooms are basic with cold water only (the cheapest share bathrooms), but are adequate and there are pleasant garden sitting areas. It's right in the village centre.

Fresco Lion Villa   GUESTHOUSE $$
(☑ 077 630 2070, 071 780 7634; www.frescolionvilla.com; Sigiriya Rd; r Rs 4000-5000; ❄🛜) This well-run place 9km outside Sigiriya (12km from Dambulla) has five stylish rooms in a leafy, rural compound south of the Kimbissa junction. Rooms vary from two air-con rooms in a duplex with balconies to a split-level family room without air-con. The Sri Lankan meals are excellent and Roy is a fabulous host.

Hideout Sigiriya   LODGE $$$
(☑ 077 771 6088; www.sigiriyahideout.com; Palatawa Rd, Kimbissa; r incl breakfast US$60-80, treehouse $85-110; ❄🛜🏊) The aptly named Hideout is indeed a real escape, tucked away at the end of a dirt road surrounded by paddy fields and with viewing platforms for spotting eagles and peacocks. Rooms are spacious, but perhaps a little prosaic for the prices asked (only some rooms have air-con). Still, the pool is a delight, the peaceful setting is pulse-lowering and the welcome is warm.

Fresco Water Villa   HOTEL $$$
(☑ 066-228 6161; www.frescowatervilla.com; Kimbissa; s/d US$125/130; ❄🛜🏊) Groups like the villa-style rooms, fine balconies and stylish design at this well-tended place. The 25m pool is heaven after a hard day tackling the rock, but you'll be lucky to nab one of the six loungers (for 72 rooms!). The in-house restaurant is unnecessarily pricey. It's 5km west of Sigiriya. Online rates drop as low as US$70.

Elephant Corridor   LUXURY HOTEL $$$
(☑ 066-228 6951; www.elephantcorridor.com; Kimbissa; r from US$220; ❄@🛜🏊) Set in over 80 hectares of unfenced grasslands, this high-end hotel is a terrific place to spot wildlife. Iguanas, monitor lizards and mongooses are all regularly encountered, and wild elephants wander through the area. The villas are spectacular and incredibly spacious, all with private indoor plunge pools, and there's a good spa and pool set in a forest clearing.

Jetwing Vil Uyana   LUXURY HOTEL $$$
(☑ 066-228 6000; www.jetwinghotels.com; Kimbissa; r from US$340; ❄@🛜🏊) For natural-world

EXPLORING AROUND SIGIRIYA

With a bike or scooter you can explore several spots around Sigiriya.

One place not to miss is **Pidurangala** (Rs 500; ⊙5am-6.30pm) rock, the temples of which actually predate Sigiriya. This prominent rock about 1km north of the Sigiriya site offers amazing views of Sigiriya from its wide summit. It's a 20-minute hike up to the top, past several small temples, a 12.5m reclining Buddha and a final tricky scramble over boulders. Most people come at sunset (bring a torch for the trip down), but a sunrise visit is equally beautiful and much less crowded. A return three-wheeler costs around Rs 700, including waiting time. If you explore the dirt roads north then west of here you'll find several water tanks that offer lovely reflected views of both rocks.

Another good longer bike or scooter ride follows backroads for 25km to Dambulla via the **Kandalama Wewa** reservoir.

En route you can stop at the **Dakinigiriya Vihara** (Kaludiya Pokuna) FREE, 2.5km off the main road down a dirt track past the Paradise Resort. Trails take you past a stupa, the standing monolithic stones of a prayer hall, several rock inscriptions and caves, a small tank and many fabulous trees. It'll likely be only you and the monkeys here.

immersion – crocodiles in the pond, monitor lizards in the grass and occasional visiting elephants – the Jetwing is a great choice. The huge, individual chalets (book a 'water' or 'forest' dwelling for the best views) have a rustic look outside, but inside they are equipped with all mod cons (including Bose sound systems).

Hotel Sigiriya HOTEL **$$$**
(☑ 066-493 0500; www.serendibleisure.com; Hotel Rd; s/d incl breakfast US$140/155; ❉@☎❄) There are truly remarkable views of the rock from the pool area at this hotel. The 40-year-old breeze block exteriors are dated, but the rooms have been renovated with polished concrete and modern bathrooms. Lots of tour groups stay here and it's also popular with twitchers, lured by its resident naturalist who leads much-lauded birdwatching trips (US$15 to US$25).

✖ Eating

There is a line of traveller-geared cafe-restaurants in Sigiriya village, and most guesthouses located outside of town offer meals. For a spellbinding blow-out consider dining at Jetwing Vil Uyana (p212).

Rasta Rant SRI LANKAN **$$**
(☑ 077 794 2095; mains Rs 350-500; ⊙11am-11pm) A young backpacker crowd frequent this chilled creek-side hang-out. It's as much a drinking place as a restaurant, but the food is good value, from breakfasts to fruit *rottis*, Bob Marley is on musical rotation, and there are plenty of hammocks and riverside loungers made out of shipping pallets.

The owner also runs 2½-hour kayak trips on a nearby *wewa* (tank) for Rs 1800 per person.

Chooti SRI LANKAN **$$**
(mains Rs 300-400; ⊙7am-10pm; ☎) Cooking up a *rotti* storm, this likeable restaurant serves up delicious, freshly cooked sweet and savoury *rotti* bread and excellent juices in the new upper-storey cabana-style restaurant. Sip a fresh coconut or slurp a fruit shake and you're sated. It's in the centre of the village.

❶ Getting There & Away

Sigiriya is about 10km east of the Inamaluwa junction on the main road between Dambulla and Habarana. Buses to Dambulla run every 30 minutes from 6.30am to 6pm (Rs 40, 45 minutes) from a small stop southeast of the site exit. A three-wheeler between Dambulla and Sigiriya is around Rs 800.

To get to Polonnaruwa either take the Dambulla bus to the Inamaluwa junction to catch a northbound bus there or, shorter, take a three-wheeler north to the junction with the Habanara–Pononnaruwa Rd and catch a bus from there.

Cinnamon Air (Map p60; ☑ 011-247 5475; www.cinnamonair.com) operates daily flights to/from Colombo (US$229) from the airport 5km west of town, but prices are steep.

Guesthouses can organise day trips with a private car to Anuradhapura or Polunnaruwa for around Rs 8000 return, or a one-way drop at Colombo airport for Rs 9000.

Sigiriya and its surrounds are ideally explored by bike (Rs 300 per day) or scooter (Rs 1500); most guesthouses can organise rentals.

THE ANCIENT CITIES SIGIRIYA

Habarana

📞 066 / POP 8700

This small town isn't a destination in itself, but it serves as a good base for Sigiriya and safaris to Minneriya and Kaudulla National Parks.

🛏️ Sleeping & Eating

In the last few years many new upmarket places have opened around Habarana. The town itself also has some good hotels, though budget places are limited.

Mutu Village   GUESTHOUSE $$

(📞 077 269 4579; www.mutuvillage.com; Kashyapagama; r incl breakfast US$40-80; ❄️🛜) This rural guesthouse is run by a very accommodating couple: Mutu is a superb cook and Ajith takes good care of guests. The environment is great, with a lovely garden to enjoy, away from the hubbub and traffic in town. There's a slightly ramshackle Ayurvedic spa. It's a 10-minute drive south then east of the main junction, down a side road.

Heritage Habarana   HOTEL $$

(📞 066-227 0003; www.chcresthouses.com; s/d incl breakfast US$42/50; ❄️🛜) Formerly the Rest House, this attractive historic structure has been very sensitively updated and offers high comfort levels and an excellent location right by the central crossroads. Its four rooms boast original (turquoise) window shutters and are fronted by a long, shaded verandah. Major renovations are planned, so things might change.

Cinnamon Lodge   LUXURY HOTEL $$$

(📞 066-227 0012; www.cinnamonhotels.com; r US$250-280; ❄️@🛜💧) A classy and professionally run hotel, Cinnamon blends Portuguese colonial design with traditional Sri Lankan stone architecture that takes its inspiration from the Ritigala ruins. A nature trail leads through 11 hectares of lush lakeshore landscaping to a tree-house platform for viewing birds (155 species), deer and monkeys. Rooms are tastefully presented with tropical decor and are very comfortable.

The elegant main restaurant area overlooks the lovely pool and is renowned for its buffet (with an entire room devoted solely to desserts) and there's even a dedicated bath sommelier(!). The hotel is just south of the main Habarana junction.

Galkadawala   LODGE $$$

(📞 077 373 2855; www.galkadawala.com; s/d incl breakfast from US$75/85; ❄️@🛜) Harmoniously built in a forest setting from recycled materials, this serene ecolodge is perfect for wildlife enthusiasts, with nature (outstanding birdlife and the odd elephant) very much on your doorstep – which is the local tank. Maulie, your amiable and well-informed host, is very knowledgeable about the area and Galkadawala's vegetarian (only) food is a real highlight.

Other Corner   LODGE $$$

(📞 077 374 9904, 076 624 6511; www.tocsrilanka.com; s/d incl breakfast US$110/130; ❄️@🛜💧) Cross the rope bridge into this ecolodge and you quickly feel a million miles from anywhere, even though it's just 1.5km from the centre. The nine gorgeous mudbrick and wood-thatched cabanas are set in extensive, shady grounds, and food is prepared freshly to order in the romantic restaurant. The excellent resident naturalist leads birdwatching walks and can arrange night safaris.

Aliya   RESORT $$$

(📞 066-204 0400; www.theme-resorts.com/aliya resort; s/d incl breakfast from US$185/220; ❄️@🛜💧) This bombastic temple of bling has raised the bar of luxury very high indeed. The fortress-like entrance, lovely open-sided restaurant and village-like collection of stylish chalets is designed to impress rather than charm, but the 30m infinity pool (with Sigiriya rock views at the end of each lap!) is breathtaking.

Heritage Avanhala   CAFE $$

(www.ceylonhotelscorporation.com; Heritage Habarana; mains Rs 550-800; ⏰7am-10pm; 🛜) The Heritage's cafe-restaurant is right on the main crossroads in town, so is perfect for people-watching. There's a classy, turn-back-the-years ambience and a wide choice of food: local-style curries, Western breakfasts (Rs 490), sandwiches, grilled meats and 'devilled' dishes. Those with a sweet tooth must check out the cake cabinet (try a piece of *rulang,* made from sesame and grain).

ℹ️ Getting There & Away

Transport links are excellent: Habarana has the nearest train station to both Dambulla and Sigiriya and sits on a busy crossroads.

BUS

Buses stop at the crossroads outside the Heritage Habarana hotel. Frequent services:

Anuradhapura Rs 90, 2½ hours, every 30 minutes

Dambulla regular/air-con Rs 25/40, 30 minutes, every 30 minutes

Polonnaruwa Rs 40, one hour, every 30 minutes

TRAIN
TRAIN
The train station is 2km north of town on the Trincomalee road. The infrequent train services include the following:

Batticaloa 2nd/3rd class Rs 210/115, 3½ hours, one day

Colombo 1st/2nd/3rd class Rs 620/300/160, five hours, two daily

Polonnaruwa 3rd class Rs 50, one to two hours, two daily

The station at Palugaswewa, 6km west, is served by more and faster trains.

Polonnaruwa

📞 027 / POP 15,800

Kings ruled the central plains of Sri Lanka from Polonnaruwa 800 years ago, when it was a thriving commercial and religious centre. The glories of that age can be found in the archaeological treasures that still give a pretty good idea of how the city looked in its heyday. You'll find the archaeological park a delight to explore, with hundreds of ancient structures – tombs and temples, statues and stupas – in a compact core. The Quadrangle alone is worth the trip.

That Polonnaruwa is close to elephant-packed national parks only adds to its popularity. And with good accommodation and plenty of bikes for hire, the town itself makes a pleasant base for a day or two, fringed by a huge, beautiful tank with a relaxed ambience.

Nearby Kaduruwela, 4km east of Polonnaruwa, has the lion's share of banks, shops and other facilities.

History

The South Indian Chola dynasty made its capital at Polonnaruwa after conquering Anuradhapura in the late 10th century, as Polonnaruwa was a strategically better place to guard against any rebellion from the Ruhunu Sinhalese kingdom in the southeast. It also, apparently, had fewer mosquitoes! When the Sinhalese King Vijayabahu I (r 1055–1110) drove the Cholas off the island in 1070, he kept Polonnaruwa as his capital.

Under King Parakramabahu I (r 1153–86), Polonnaruwa reached its zenith. The king erected huge buildings, planned beautiful parks and, as a crowning achievement, created a 25-sq-km tank, which was so large that it was named the Parakrama Samudra (Sea of Parakrama). The present lake incorporates three older tanks, so it may not be the actual tank he created.

Parakramabahu I was followed by Nissanka Malla (r 1187–96), who virtually bankrupted the kingdom through his attempts to match his predecessors' achievements. By the early 13th century, Polonnaruwa was beginning to prove as susceptible to Indian invasion as Anuradhapura had been, and eventually it, too, was abandoned and the centre of Sinhalese power shifted to the western side of the island. In 1982, Unesco added the ancient city of Polonnaruwa to its World Heritage list.

◉ Sights

Most visitors will find a day enough time to explore the **ruins** (📞 027-222 4850; www.ccf. gov.lk/polonnaruwa.htm; adult/child US$25/12.50; ⏱ 7.30am-6pm), which can be conveniently divided into five groups: the Royal Palace Group; the Quadrangle; the Northern Group (spread over a wide area); the small Island Park Group near the Archaeological Museum on the banks of the Tissa Wewa tank; and the small Southern Group, towards the New Town. There are also a few other scattered ruins. The main structures all have useful information plaques.

The main entrance to the central archaeological site is from Habarana Rd, about 500m north of the museum. Tickets are not usually needed to visit the Island Park or Southern Groups. A bike is an ideal way to explore the area. There's plenty of shade around the monuments and vendors sell drinks (including chilled king coconuts) and snacks.

Although tickets technically allow you only one entrance, you can ask a ticket collector to sign and date your ticket so you can return after lunch.

Archaeological Museum   MUSEUM
(⏱ 7.30am-5pm) This excellent museum has rooms dedicated to the citadel, the outer city, the monastery area (check out the model of the monks' hospital and medical instruments) and Hindu monuments. The latter room contains a wonderful selection of bronzes, including some outstanding Shiva statues. One depicts Shiva, ringed by an *aureole* (celestial arch), performing a cosmic dance while trampling on a dwarf. Photos are not allowed.

◉ Royal Palace Group

This group of buildings dates from the 12th-century reign of Parakramabahu I. The walled enclosure is the logical place to start

Polonnaruwa

0   400 m
0   0.2 miles

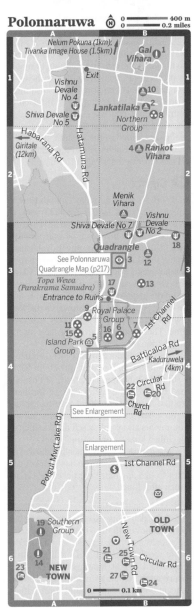

seven storeys. Today its crumbling remains look like giant cavity-ravaged molars.

The 3m-thick walls have holes to receive the floor beams for two higher floors; however, if there were another four levels, these must have been made of wood. The roof in this main hall, which had 50 rooms in all, was supported by 30 columns.

Audience Hall   RUINS
Parakramabahu I's Audience Hall is notable for the frieze of elephants, each of which is in a different pose. There are fine lions at the top of the steps.

Bathing Pool   RUINS
Just outside the southeast corner of the palace grounds, the Bathing Pool (Kumara Pokuna) has a central lotus island and two of its

a tour of Polonnaruwa, before continuing north to see the other principal monuments.

Royal Palace   RUINS
The Royal Palace constructed by Parakramabahu I was a magnificent structure measuring 31m by 13m, and is said to have had

THE ANCIENT CITIES POLONNARUWA

crocodile-mouth spouts remaining. The foundations to the right were a changing room.

◉ Quadrangle

Only a short stroll north of the Royal Palace ruins, the area known as the Quadrangle is literally that – a compact group of fascinating ruins in a raised-up area bounded by a wall. It's the most concentrated collection of buildings you'll find in the Ancient Cities – an archaeologist's playpen. Over time, the Atadage, the Vatadage and the Hatadage all likely housed the Buddha tooth relic, each one built by a successive king to show his personal devotion.

As well as the major ruins here, also look for the **recumbent image house, chapter house, Bodhisattva shrine** and **bodhi tree shrine**.

Vatadage   BUDDHIST TEMPLE
In the southeast of the Quadrangle, the Vatadage (circular relic house) is typical of its kind. Its outermost terrace is 18m in diameter, and the second terrace has four entrances flanked by particularly fine guardstones. The moonstone at the northern entrance is reckoned to be the finest in Polonnaruwa. Four separate entrances lead to the central dagoba with its four Buddhas. The flower-patterned stone screen is thought to be a later addition, probably by Nissanka Malla.

Thuparama Gedige   BUDDHIST TEMPLE
At the southern end of the Quadrangle, the Thuparama Gedige is the smallest *gedige* (hollow Buddhist temple with thick walls) in Polonnaruwa, but is also one of the best: it's the only one with its roof intact, supported by corbel arch-style supports. The inner chamber is delightfully cool and contains four beautifully executed standing Bodhisattva statues. The building's exterior shows a marked Hindu influence and is thought to date from the reign of Parakramabahu I.

Hatadage   MONUMENT
Erected by Nissanka Malla, the Hatadage monument is said to have been built in 60 *(hata)* hours. It's in poor condition today, but was originally a two-storey building (and may have once housed the Buddha tooth relic). Stand at the entrance and admire the symmetry of the pillars receding into the distance.

Latha-Mandapaya   RUINS
The busy Nissanka Malla was responsible for the Latha-Mandapaya. This unique structure

consists of a latticed stone fence – a curious imitation of a wooden fence with posts and railings – surrounding a very small dagoba. The dagoba is encircled by curved stone pillars shaped like lotus stalks, topped by unopened buds. It is said that Nissanka Malla sat within this enclosure to listen to chanted Buddhist texts.

Gal Pota   MONUMENT
The Gal Pota (Stone Book) is a colossal stone representation of an *ola* book. It is nearly 9m long by 1.5m wide, and 40cm to 66cm thick. The inscription on it – the longest such stone inscription in Sri Lanka – indicates that it was a Nissanka Malla publication. Much of it extols his virtues as a king, but it also includes the footnote that the slab, weighing 25 tonnes, was dragged from Mihintale, an astonishing 100km away.

Satmahal Prasada   MONUMENT
In the northeast corner of the Quadrangle stands the unusual ziggurat-style Satmahal Prasada, which consists of six diminishing storeys (there used to be seven), shaped like a stepped pyramid. Check out the figurines set in niches within its crumbling walls.

Atadage   MONUMENT
A shrine for the tooth relic, the Atadage is the only surviving structure in Polonnaruwa dating from the reign of Vijayabahu I.

Velaikkara Slab Inscription   MONUMENT
This 12th-century memorial slab records the oath taken by the Velaikkara royal guards to protect the Buddha tooth relic after an earlier rebellion was quashed.

Polonnaruwa Quadrangle

◉ Around the Quadrangle

Dotted around the fringes of the Quadrangle are a number of structures, including Shiva *devales* (Hindu temples), relics from the South Indian invasion of the 10th century.

Shiva Devale No 1   HINDU TEMPLE

Just south of the Quadrangle, the 13th-century Hindu temple Shiva Devale No 1 displays the Indian influence that returned after Polonnaruwa's Sinhalese florescence. It is notable for the superb quality of its stonework, which fits together with unusual precision. The domed brick roof has collapsed, but when this building was being excavated a number of excellent bronzes, now in the Archaeological Museum, were found.

Shiva Devale No 2   HINDU TEMPLE

Shiva Devale No 2 is the oldest structure in Polonnaruwa and dates from the brief Chola period, when the Indian invaders established the city. Unlike so many buildings in the Ancient Cities, it was built entirely of stone, so the structure today is much as it was when built. Look for the statue of Shiva's mount, Nandi the bull.

Pabula Vihara   BUDDHIST TEMPLE

Also known as the Parakramabahu Vihara, Pabula Vihara is a typical dagoba from the period of Parakramabahu I. This brick stupa is the third-largest dagoba in Polonnaruwa, and is set in a woodland clearing.

◉ Northern Group

These ruins, all north of the city wall, start about 1.5km north of the Quadrangle. They include the impressive **Alahana Pirivena group** (consisting of the Rankot Vihara, Lankatilaka, Kiri Vihara, Buddha Seema Prasada and the other structures around them). The name of the group means 'crematory college' – it stood in the royal cremation grounds established by Parakramabahu I.

Further north is Gal Vihara, probably the most famous group of Buddha images in Sri Lanka. A bike makes exploration of the Northern Group a lot easier.

★ Rankot Vihara   BUDDHIST TEMPLE

The 54m Rankot Vihara dagoba, the largest in Polonnaruwa and the fourth largest on the island, has been ascribed to the reign of King Nissanka Malla. Like the other major dagobas in Anuradhapura and Polonnaruwa, the dome consists of earth fill covered by a brick mantle and plaster. The construction clearly imitates the Anuradhapura style. Surgical instruments found in a nearby ruined 12th-century hospital are surprisingly similar to those used today; see examples in the Archaeological Museum.

Buddha Seema Prasada   RUINS

Set on a natural ridge, this was the monastery's convocation hall, where monks met fortnightly. This building features a fine *mandapaya* (raised platform with decorative pillars).

★ Lankatilaka   BUDDHIST TEMPLE

One of the most evocative structures in Polonnaruwa, the Lankatilaka temple was built by Parakramabahu I and later restored by Vijayabahu IV. This massive *gedige* has 17m-high walls, although the roof has collapsed. The cathedral-like aisle leads to a huge standing (headless) Buddha. Offerings of incense, and the structure's columns and arches, add to the distinctly devotional atmosphere.

Kiri Vihara   BUDDHIST TEMPLE

Construction of the dagoba Kiri Vihara is credited to Subhadra, King Parakramabahu I's queen. Originally known as the Rupavati Chetiya, the present name means 'milk white' because when the overgrown jungle was cleared away after 700 years of neglect, the original lime plaster was found to be in perfect condition. It is still the best-preserved unrestored dagoba at Polonnaruwa.

★ Gal Vihara   MONUMENT

This is a group of beautiful Buddha images that probably marks the high point of Sinhalese rock carving. They are part of Parakramabahu I's northern monastery. The Gal Vihara consists of four separate images, all cut from one long slab of granite. At one time, each was enshrined within a separate enclosure.

The **standing Buddha** is 7m tall and is said to be the finest of the series. The unusual crossed position of the arms and sorrowful facial expression led to the theory that it was an image of the Buddha's disciple Ananda, grieving for his master's departure for nirvana, since the reclining image is next to it. The fact that it had its own separate enclosure, along with the discovery of other images with the same arm position, has discredited this theory and it is now accepted that all the images are of the Buddha.

Continued on p223

STEFANO EMBER / SHUTTERSTOCK ©

Ancient Cities

Forming one of Asia's most impressive collections of Buddhist art and architecture, this utterly captivating region contains no fewer than four Unesco World Heritage Sites. The monumental dagobas (stupas), ruined palaces, elegant frescoes and outstanding sculptures and carvings comprise Sri Lanka's greatest monuments. Touring the Ancient Cities region is a delight; it's largely a rural area, and the main sites are surrounded by scenic dry-zone countryside and fringed by national parks.

Contents

➡ Anuradhapura
➡ Polonnaruwa
➡ Sigiriya
➡ Dambulla

Above Detail of the Vatadage (p217), Polonnaruwa

Ancient Cities

Anuradhapura

Prepare yourself: Anuradhapura (p228) represents early civilisation on a giant scale. The three colossal stupas that define this stupendous site are some of the largest monuments ever constructed in the ancient world, exceeded only by the pyramids at Giza, Egypt.

Founded in the 4th century BC, Anuradhapura was the epicentre of the island's Buddhist civilisation for around 1300 years, a city of magnificent monasteries and palaces sustained by an ingenious irrigation system and huge tanks (reservoirs). For Sri Lankans, it's an important pilgrimage site, home to the Sri Maha Bodhi (sacred Bodhi tree).

This incredible legacy of civil and religious structures is spread over a wide area, with four main zones. Highlights include the wooded Abhayagiri Monastery complex (which once housed 5000 monks), the Citadel and its ruined royal palace, and the Jetavanarama stupa.

Polonnaruwa

Famous for its elaborate carvings, sculpture and temples, Polonnaruwa (p215) was the island's capital from the 11th to the 13th century, a short but glorious period which allowed a flourishing of Buddhist arts and architecture.

The city's Quadrangle formed a sacred precinct and contained many of Polonnaruwa's most impressive structures, including the Vatadage and its famous moonstone. The Lankatilaka temple has a huge headless Buddha, and don't miss the artistry at Gal Vihara, which arguably represents the zenith of Sinhalese rock carving.

1. Vatadage (p217), Polonnaruwa
2. Dambulla Cave Temples (p205)
3. Abhayagiri Dagoba (p231), Anuradhapura

Sigiriya

The astonishing site of Sigiriya (p209) briefly flourished in the 5th century AD under King Kassapa, who constructed a near-inaccessible rocky mountaintop as a location for his royal palace. Clambering up the rock face to the summit, you'll pass the sculpted paws of a giant carved lion, Mirror Wall (which contains a tangle of ancient graffiti) and some superb

SRI LANKA'S ANCIENT CITIES

Anuradhapura (p228) A vast ancient Buddhist complex and a profoundly spiritual site.

Polonnaruwa (p215) Famous for its intricate carved monuments, temples and Buddhas.

Sigiriya (p209) A real rock star, topped by a palace and graced by outstanding murals.

Dambulla (p205) Remarkable cave temples containing Buddhist murals and statues.

Ridi Vihara (p241) Remote, but has some stunning Buddhist art.

Mihintale (p237) Birthplace of Buddhism in Sri Lanka.

Aluvihara (p204) Fine collection of cave art close to Matale.

Ritigala (p227) Huge ancient monastic complex.

Lion's Paws (p211). S

frescoes. Beneath the rock there's much more to explore: Boulder Gardens, Water Gardens and an impressive site museum.

Dambulla

Halfway up a hilltop, the magnificent Buddhist statues and murals in the cave complex of Dambulla (p205) were first fashioned in the 1st century BC, although the site was further embellished by royal patrons, including the kings of Kandy. The artistry is incredible and the condition of the paintings and sculpture remarkable. From the summit you can enjoy sweeping views across to the great rock temple of Sigiriya.

Continued from p218

The **reclining Buddha** depicted entering *parinirvana* (nirvana-after-death) is 14m long. Notice the subtle depression in the pillow under the head and the lotus symbols on the pillow end and on the soles of Buddha's feet. The other two images are both of the seated Buddha. The carvings make superb use of the natural marbling in the rock. The one in the small rock cavity is smaller and of inferior quality.

Nelum Pokuna   POND
A track to the left from the northern stretch of road leads to unusual Nelum Pokuna (Lotus Pond), nearly 8m in diameter, which has five concentric, descending rings of eight petals each. The pool was probably used by monks.

Tivanka Image House   BUDDHIST TEMPLE
Polonnaruwa's northern road ends at Tivanka Image House. Tivanka means 'thrice bent', and refers to the fact that the Buddha image within is in a three-curve position normally reserved for female statues. The building is notable for its fine frescoes depicting Buddha in his past lives – the only Polonnaruwa murals to have survived (photos not allowed). Some of these date from a later attempt by Parakramabahu III to restore Polonnaruwa, but others are much older.

⊙ **Southern Group**

The small Southern Group is close to several top-end hotels. By bicycle, it's a pleasant ride on Potgul Mawatha (Lake Rd) alongside the shores of the Topa Wewa (Parakrama Samudra) tank. It's particularly lovely at sunset. You'll likely find more cows (and their friends, the cattle egret) than you will people.

Potgul Vihara   MONUMENT
Also known as the library dagoba, the Potgul Vihara in the far south of Polonnaruwa is an unusual structure. A thick-walled, hollow, dagoba-like building, it is thought to have been used to store sacred books. It's effectively a circular *gedige*, and four smaller solid dagobas arranged around this central dome to form the popular Sinhalese quincunx arrangement of five objects in the shape of a rectangle (one at each corner and one in the middle).

Statue   STATUE
Standing nearly 4m high, this statue displays an unusually lifelike human representation, in contrast to the normally idealised or stylised Buddha figures. Exactly whom it represents is a subject of some debate. One theory is that it's the Indian Vedic teacher Agastya, holding a book. Alternatively, it could be that the bearded, stately figure is Parakramabahu I clasping the 'yoke of kingship'. Others say that the king is simply holding a piece of papaya.

⊙ **Island Park Group**

Concentrated just north of the Archaeological Museum are the ruins of **Nissanka Malla's Palace**, which have almost been reclaimed by the earth. On the way there, you'll pass the **Royal Baths**, still fed via a sluice from the main tank. Entry to this group of ruins is free.

King's Council Chamber   RUINS
This pillared hall is where the King Nissanka Malla's council would have met. Inscribed into each of the 48 columns in the chamber is the name of the minister whose seat was once beside it, while the royal throne, in the shape of a stone lion, dominates the head of the hall. Just offshore is a tiny island on which are the ruins of a small summer house used by the king.

🛏 **Sleeping**

Most hotels in town have a rural vibe, especially those just south of the central crossroads. Nearby Giritale is a good alternative accommodation base.

Sunset Tourist Home   GUESTHOUSE $
(☏027-222 7294; info@sunsettouristhome.com; r with/without air-con Rs 3000/2000; ❄ 🗢) This rural villa has high ceilings, pleasant balcony sitting areas and a quiet location amid the rice paddies, making it a peaceful choice. It's a bit far from the ruins but bike rental is available, as are meals. The next-door and connected Palm Garden offers similarly good accommodation.

Thisara Guest House   GUESTHOUSE $
(☏027-222 2654, 077 170 5636; www.thisaraguest house.com; New Town Rd; r with/without air-con Rs 3000/2000; ❄ 🗢) About 100m off the main road south of the Old Town, this place has clean, spacious rooms with terrace eating in two blocks; those at the rear with rice-paddy views are the ones to book. The two new rooms above the restaurant will be the best when finished.

Leesha Tourist Home
GUESTHOUSE $

(☏072 334 0591; leeshatourist@hotmail.com; 105/A New Town Rd; r with/without air-con Rs 2800/2000; ❄️🛜) Good vibes are guaranteed at this fine guesthouse thanks to the efforts of genial owner Upali and his family. Rooms are well-priced and sparkling clean, all with mosquito nets and sprung mattresses (though those abutting the main road suffer some traffic noise). It's a sociable place with tables for playing Parcheesi or sampling the delicious home cooking, with cookery classes possible.

Devi Tourist Home
HOMESTAY $

(☏027-222 3181; www.facebook.com/devitourist home; Church Rd; r Rs 2000-4500; ❄️@🛜) Down a quiet, leafy suburban lane, this well-run, inviting and orderly homestay owned by a Malay-Muslim couple is a good choice, with five rooms (the cheapest are fan-only) arranged around a pretty garden. Meals are filling (don't miss string hoppers for breakfast), bicycles are available (Rs 300 per day) and there's a three-wheeler for pick-ups.

Jayaru Guest House
GUESTHOUSE $

(☏027-222 2633, 071 563 6678; jayaruguest@gmail.com; Circular Rd; s/d Rs 1200/1500; 🛜) If you're looking for a really inexpensive room, this simple guesthouse is located in a quiet area and has a pleasant sitting area for chilling. Rooms are basic, with fans and cold-water bathrooms, but there are also a couple of air-con rooms (single/double Rs 3000/3500). Musicians might find themselves jamming with the owners, one of whom is a music teacher.

Manel Guest House
GUESTHOUSE $

(☏027-222 2481; www.manelguesthouse.com; New Town Rd; s/d incl breakfast Rs 2000/2500, new block Rs 4000/4500; ❄️@) There are two blocks at this friendly place. The old block rooms have a fan, but can be hot, while the new block has much more modern, spacious air-con rooms with balconies overlooking the rice paddies (upper-floor rooms are best). Both blocks share the pleasant restaurant. Ask the manager to play you a traditional local tune on his flute.

Hotel Ancient Village
HOTEL $$

(☏072 212 3063; www.hotelancientvillage.com; Sri Sudarshana Rd, Thopawewa; s/d incl breakfast US$28/35; ❄️🛜) At the end of a side road and surrounded on three sides by rice paddies, this modern 10-room hotel is close to the centre but feels relaxingly rural. The rooms are fresh and tiled, with balconies and there's a peaceful thatched cabana-style restaurant.

Tishan Holiday Resort
GUESTHOUSE $

(☏027-222 4072; www.facebook.com/TishanHoliday Resort; Habarana Rd, Bendiwewa; r incl breakfast Rs 3500-5500; ❄️🛜🏊) A good-value place (especially considering there's a pool with loungers) that straddles budget and midrange. It's 4.5km west of the centre of town, but they rent bicycles and scooters, and there's a good restaurant. There are also some budget ground-floor non-air-con rooms (singles/doubles Rs 2250/2750).

Lake Hotel
HOTEL $$$

(☏027-222 2411; www.thelakehotel.lk; Potgul Mawatha; s/d incl breakfast US$95/110; ❄️@🛜🏊) Right by the lake shore, this elegant two-storey hotel offers sublime views of the tank from its beautifully presented rooms, restaurant and pool area. The atmosphere is relaxing, with classical music in the lobby, monochrome photographs and attentive service. Upper-floor rooms have the best views.

Eating

There's little reason to venture far from your hotel or guesthouse for a meal as there are few standout selections locally.

Ariya Rest House
SRI LANKAN $$

(☏077 358 8060; www.ariyaresthouse.com; Bendiwewa; buffet Rs 500-750; ⏱11.30am-5pm) This large and well-run restaurant is set up for the tourist groups, but it's a convenient place to take a break between sightseeing. The lunch buffet is available all afternoon and the food is good, with tasty manioc, banana flower and wild mango curries. It's 4km from the centre, but easily reached by bicycle or three-wheeler.

Jaga Food
SRI LANKAN $$$

(☏077 665 2048; 22 Junction, Jayanthipura; buffet Rs 950; ⏱11.30am-4pm & 6.30-9pm) This family-run garden restaurant is halfway between Polonnaruwa (6km) and Giritale (7km), so you need transport, but it's worth the detour. The 10 or so curries on offer are cooked on traditional firewood stoves and guests are welcome to poke around the kitchen and even get a free cookery lesson (come at 5.30pm).

ℹ Information

Post office (Batticaloa Rd; ⏱8am-5pm Mon-Fri) In the centre of the Old Town.

Seylan Bank (Habarana Rd; ⊘9am-4pm Mon-Fri) Changes foreign currency and has a 24-hour ATM.

Tourist police (⌨027-222 3099; Batticaloa Rd) In the Old Town at the main traffic circle.

ⓘ Getting There & Away

BUS

Polonnaruwa's main bus station is in Kaduruwela, 4km east of Old Town on Batticaloa Rd. Buses to and from the west pass through Old Town, but to make sure you get a seat, start at Kaduruwela.

Buses run every 30 minutes or so until about 4pm on main routes, which include the following:

Anuradhapura Rs 145, three hours

Colombo Rs 265, six hours

Dambulla Rs 77, 1½ hours; take a Kandy, Kurunegala or Colombo bus

Kandy Rs 75, three hours

TRAIN

Polonnaruwa is on the Colombo–Batticaloa railway line and is about 30km southeast of Gal Oya, where the line splits from the Colombo–Trincomalee line. The train station is in Kaduruwela.

Trains include the following:

Batticaloa 2nd/3rd class Rs 150/85, 2½ hours, five daily

Colombo 1st/2nd/3rd class Rs 700/340/185, six to seven hours, two daily, including one sleeper (Rs 1250/630/480) leaving at 10.25pm

ⓘ Getting Around

Frequent buses (Rs 20) link Old Town and Kaduruwela. Three-wheeler drivers ask for Rs 250. Bicycles are great for getting around Polon-

naruwa's monuments, which are surrounded by shady woodland. Most guesthouses rent bikes for Rs 200 to 350 per day, and a few can find you a scooter for Rs 1500.

Giritale

⌨027 / POP 8200

Northwest of Polonnaruwa on the Habarana road, Giritale is a sleepy, spread-out settlement alongside the impressive 7th-century Giritale Wewa. It's essentially a rural community, with a few places to stay (all 7km to 15km from Polonnaruwa). It makes a good base for visiting Polonnaruwa and Minneriya National Park, and also the outlying ruins of the Mandalagiri Vihara.

🛏 Sleeping & Eating

There are a couple of simple local restaurants along the Giritale–Polonnaruwa Rd, but almost everyone eats dinner in their hotel.

Lak Nilla   HOMESTAY $
(⌨077 911 5265; www.laknilla.com; s/d Rs 2500/3000; ❋🛜) A simple, but hospitable, homestay with five clean rooms in a friendly local's house in a rural setting off the highway. A sumptuous dinner costs Rs 650, and bikes can be hired and safaris arranged. It's 2km east of Giritale junction then 700m up a side road; phone ahead for free pick-up.

★**Rice Villa Retreat**   GUESTHOUSE $$
(⌨077 630 2070; www.ricevillaretreat.com; 21st Mile Post, Polonnaruwa Rd, Jayanthipura; s/d Rs

THE ANCIENT CITIES GIRITALE

WORTH A TRIP

MANDALAGIRI VIHARA

This *vatadage* (circular relic house) is virtually identical to the one at Polonnaruwa, but while Polonnaruwa's is ringed by many other structures, **Mandalagiri Vihara** (Medirigiriya; ⊘dawn-dusk) stands alone atop a low hill. A granite flight of steps leads up to the *vatadage*, which has concentric circles of 16, 20 and 32 pillars around the dagoba and is noted for its fine stone screens. Four large Buddhas face the four cardinal directions. The site is uncrowded and accessed via a pretty country-road drive.

An earlier structure may have been built here around the 2nd century, but the one that stands today was constructed in the 7th century by Aggabodhi IV. There was once a hospital next to the *vatadage*, and you can still see one temple with three standing Buddhas.

At 3.5km past Medirigiriya, itself about 30km north of Polonnaruwa, Mandalagiri Vihara is best visited as a half-day trip from Giritale. There are no places to stay or eat nearby. A return three-wheeler costs around Rs 1500 from Polonnaruwa or Giritale. By scooter, make your way to Hingurakgoda, then 14km to Medirigiriya, then take the left branch at the clock-tower roundabout.

There was no-one selling tickets at the time of research, but this could change.

5500/6500; ❋@☎) A memorable place to stay, this beautifully located guesthouse enjoys an idyllic position overlooking an expanse of rice paddies, replete with the sounds of peacocks and bullfrogs. The five bungalows are well appointed, with modern bathrooms, terrace seating and contemporary design touches. Best of all, the hospitality from the family owners is warm and genuine.

Take off Rs 1000 if you don't need air-conditioning. The excellent meals are served in the wooden restaurant on stilts and free cooking classes are offered for guests. Reserve in advance and arrange free pick-up from the Giritale bus stop, 4km to the west. The owners are expert at arranging local transport to Polonnaruwa and beyond.

White House Bungalow BOUTIQUE HOTEL $$
(☏077 630 2070; www.whitehousebungalow.com; s/d incl breakfast Rs 4500/5500; ❋☎) This fresh, crisp white villa was new in 2017. The modern rooms come with colourful bedspreads and antique bed frames and there's a good rooftop restaurant. It's run by the same folks as the Rice Villa Retreat. Take off Rs 1000 if you don't need air-con.

Deer Park RESORT $$$
(☏027-777 7777; www.deerparksrilanka.com; r from US$180; ❋@☎≋) A large resort-style property made up of 85 rooms in dozens of cottages. The pool, bar area and restaurant are all excellent. Some rooms have outdoor showers, and the priciest rooms have a private deck with views of Giritale Wewa. Nature tours can be arranged; borrow some binoculars and you might spot elephants on the far side of the tank. It's south of Giritale junction.

Giritale Hotel HOTEL $$$
(☏027-224 6311; www.giritalehotel.com; r US$90-110; ❋@☎≋) Rooms at this slightly old-fashioned hotel are spacious and pleasant, but the real draw is the unmatched sunset view from the bar terrace – come for a drink if you have your own transport. It's behind the Deer Park hotel, 1.5km south of the Giritale junction.

❶ Getting There & Away

Frequent buses on the road between Polonnaruwa and Habarana (and other towns to the west) stop in Giritale village. None of the places to stay are especially near the stop, so arrange for pick-up.

Minneriya & Kaudulla National Parks

With their proximity to Polonnaruwa and Habarana, the Minneriya and Kaudulla National Parks offer an excellent chance of seeing elephants and other animals without the crowds of Yala National Park. On some days, you won't need to enter the parks to view elephants as they freely roam the countryside. You might even see elephants at dusk from beside the main Habarana–Giritale Rd. Be sure to keep a safe distance.

Before visiting, first speak to locals (guesthouse staff, tour companies or guides) as they'll know which of these two parks has the greatest concentration of elephants at any one time. Kaudulla is the less visited of the two parks.

Both parks are well served by tours: during busy times you'll find guides in jeeps waiting at the park gates. Typically, however, you'll arrange a trip with your guesthouse or hotel. With guide fees – and the many park fees – two people can expect to pay around US$90 for a four-hour safari.

Groups normally tip their driver (and guide if you have one) around 10%.

There are no places to stay in the national parks, so almost everyone visits from Habarana, Giritale or Polonnaruwa. There are no restaurants near the parks. Make an early start and take a packed breakfast.

Minneriya National Park NATIONAL PARK
(☏027-327 9243; adult/child US$15/8, service charge US$8, charge per vehicle Rs 250, plus 15% tax; ⊙6am-6.30pm) This national park is one of the best places in the country to see wild elephants, which are often present in huge numbers. Dominated by the ancient Minneriya Wewa, the park has plenty of scrub forest and wetlands in its 88.9 sq km to also provide shelter for toque macaques, sambar deer, buffalo, crocodiles and leopards (the latter are very rarely seen, however).

The dry season, from April to October, is reckoned to be the best time to visit (as by then water in the tank has dried up, exposing grasses and shoots to grazing animals). Elephants which can number 200 or more, come to feed and bathe during what is known as 'the Gathering'; and flocks of birds, such as little cormorants, painted storks, herons and large pelicans all fish in the shallow waters. However, it's also possible to see large numbers of elephants here at other times of year, too; we saw over 100 in February when we visited.

The park entrance is on the Habarana–Polonnaruwa Rd. A visitor centre near the entrance sells tickets and has a few exhibits about the park's natural history. The initial 40-minute drive (along a poor dirt road) into the heart of the park is through dense forest, where wildlife sightings are rare. But then the landscape opens up dramatically, and the views across the tank are superb. Early mornings are generally best for birds and late afternoon for elephants.

Kaudulla National Park
NATIONAL PARK

(☑ 027-327 9735; adult/child US$10/5, service charge US$8, charge per vehicle Rs 250, plus overall tax 15%; ☺6am-6pm) Like Minneriya, Kaudulla offers a good chance of getting up close and personal with elephants. In October, there are up to 250 elephants in the park, including herds of juvenile males. There are also leopards, fishing cats, sambar deer, endangered rusty spotted cats and sloth bears. The best time to visit is from January to March and, less reliably, May to June.

This park stands on the fringe of the ancient Kaudulla Wewa, 6km off the Habarana–Trincomalee Rd at Gal Oya junction. It is part of a 66.6-sq-km elephant corridor between Somawathiya National Park and Minneriya National Park.

❶ Getting There & Away

Everyone visits the parks as part of a jeep safari. It's possible to arrange your jeep at the park gates, but most people take the jeep from where they are overnighting. Figure on Rs 3000 to 4500 for the jeep costs alone.

Ritigala

Deep inside the Ritigala Strict Nature Reserve are the sprawling, jungle-covered **ruins** (adult/child US$2/1; ☺8am-4pm) of this extensive forest monastery.

Ritigala was probably a place of refuge (as long ago as the 4th century BC) and also has mythological status. It's claimed to be the spot from which Hanuman (the monkey god) leapt to India to tell Rama that he had discovered where Sita was being held by the king of Lanka.

Monks found Ritigala's caves ideal for an ascetic existence, and more than 70 have been discovered. Royals proved generous patrons, especially King Sena I, who in the 9th century made an endowment of a monastery to the *pamsukulika* (rag robes) monks.

Ritigala was abandoned following the Chola invasions in the 10th and 11th centuries, after which it lay deserted and largely forgotten until it was rediscovered and excavated by British surveyors in the late 19th century.

◉ Sights

The ruins of Ritigala forest monastery complex consist of two main groups, with dozens of smaller buildings and residences hidden among the boulders. Budget a couple of hours for a visit.

DON'T MISS

THE GATHERING

One of Asia's great wildlife spectacles occurs at Minneriya National Park in August and September. Known as 'the Gathering', 200 or more elephants gather for several weeks in one concentrated spot. Long thought to be driven by thirst during the dry season, only recently has it been learned that the natural factors behind the Gathering are much more complex.

The elephants surround the Minneriya Wewa, the huge reservoir first built in the 3rd century AD. It was assumed that they were there for the water, as it remains wet even when smaller waterholes dry up. However, biologists have discovered that the water's retreat from the land is what really lures the elephants. As the reservoir shrinks, it leaves behind vast swaths of muddy earth that are soon covered in rich, tender grass. It's a tasty feast for the elephants and they come in droves.

Unfortunately, recent actions by the water authority (which manages irrigation for local farmers) have threatened the Gathering in recent years. When the reservoir is full, new grasses won't emerge. The result can be a lot of elephants standing around looking for their food. Other pressing issues include illegal encroachment inside the park and the poaching of wildlife.

RITIGALA PEAK

Proving a lush backdrop to the ruins is the 766m Ritigala peak, a striking feature that looms above the dry central flatlands. Climbing it is a tempting three-hour endeavour, but for this you need permission from Colombo, which is hard to get.

Paths lead from the ticket office past an Archaeology Department bungalow to the huge *banda pokuna* (artificial pond), which still fills with water during the rainy season. From here, you cross the inlet over a stone bridge and follow the ceremonial staircase past the first of three round junctions.

The first main ruin is a large reception building. A path to the right leads to the *janthagara* (monastery bathhouse), with a central sunken bath surrounded by a roofed colonnade. You can still see the grinding stones used to prepare the baths.

Further up the flagstone staircase is the main roundabout, with two paths to the left. The first leads back past half-hidden ruins to a monolithic bridge and raised library. There are several other buildings here to explore.

Further up the main staircase you finally get to Building No 16, a *padhanaghara* (double-platformed building) set in a moat-like depression, used for meditation, teaching and ceremony. Look for the ornate latrine stone in the right corner.

There's nowhere to stay at Ritigala, so most people visit en route between Anuradhapura and Sigiriya.

There's nowhere to eat at Ritigala, so bring snacks and water.

❶ Getting There & Away

The turn-off for Ritigala is 15km northwest of Habarana on the road to Anuradhapura. It's then 5.5km on a good paved road followed by a dirt track for 2km. It may be impassable after heavy rains.

You might find a three-wheeler (Rs 1000 return) waiting at the junction on the main road; otherwise, you need your own transport.

Anuradhapura

🎧 025 / POP 64,000

The ruins of Anuradhapura are one of South Asia's most evocative sights. The sprawling complex contains a rich collection of archaeological and architectural wonders enormous dagobas, ancient pools and crumbling temples, built during Anuradhapura's thousand years of rule over Sri Lanka. Today, several of the sites remain in use as holy places and temples; frequent ceremonies give Anuradhapura a vibrancy that's a sharp contrast to the museum-like ambience at Polonnaruwa.

Current-day Anuradhapura is a pleasant albeit sprawling city; a small town that feels more like a large village. There's loads of good budget accommodation, easy bike hire and a relaxed pace, making it a good place to spend an extra day.

History

Anuradhapura became Sri Lanka's first capital in 380 BC under King Pandukabhaya, but it was under Devanampiya Tissa (r 307–267 BC) – during whose reign Buddhism reached Sri Lanka – that it first rose to great importance. Soon Anuradhapura became a great and glittering Buddhist complex, the importance of which was reinforced when the relic of Buddha's tooth was enshrined in the city in the 4th century AD.

In 204 BC the city was captured for the first time by the South Indian Chola dynasty – a fate that was to befall it repeatedly for more than 1000 years. It was almost a half-century until the Sinhalese hero Dutugemunu led an army from a refuge in the far south to recapture Anuradhapura. The 'Dutu' part of his name, incidentally, means 'undutiful' because his father, fearing for his son's safety, forbade him to attempt to recapture Anuradhapura. Dutugemunu disobeyed him, and later sent his father a woman's ornament to indicate what he thought of his courage.

Dutugemunu (r 161–137 BC) set in motion a vast building program that included some of the most impressive monuments in Anuradhapura today. Other important kings who followed him included Valagamba (r 103 BC and 89–76 BC), who lost his throne in another Indian invasion but later regained it, and Mahasena (r AD 276–303), the last 'great' king of Anuradhapura, who was the builder of the colossal Jetavanarama Dagoba. He also held the record for water-tank construction, building 16 of them in all, plus a major canal.

Anuradhapura was to survive until the early 11th century before finally being replaced as capital by Polonnaruwa. The

Anuradhapura site was sacked by the Cholas in 1017 and never retained its earlier heights, though a handful of monks continued to live here for another 200 years.

◉ Sights

You'll need a couple of days to properly explore the Unesco-recognised **Anuradhapura World Heritage Site** (www.ccf.gov.lk/anuradhapura. htm; adult/child US$25/12.50; ⊘24hr). You can buy the Anuradhapura ticket at the **Jetavanarama Museum** (⊘7.30am-6.30pm), the **Archaeological Museum** (⊘7.30am-6.30pm), at a **ticket office** (⊘7.30am-6.30pm) just east of the Citadel and sometimes at a ticket booth near the Abhayagiri site.

The scale of the ruins is huge. You can appreciate individual areas on foot, but a bicycle is an ideal way to get around the car-free trails and red-earthed walkways that link the main sites.

Anuradhapura has four main zones. The Mahavihara was the spiritual centre of Anuradhapura, home to Sri Maha Bodhi – the sacred bodhi tree. Nearby are the Citadel, a compact collection of structures about 1000 years old, and Jetavanarama, with a huge dagoba and important museum. Further north is the Abhayagiri Monastery, arguably the most evocative part of the entire site, with several temples and dagobas dating back more than 2000 years, spread over a large, forested area.

The Anuradhapura ticket is pricey and valid for only one day. To avoid having to buy more than one, you'll need to be strategic. Tickets are most closely inspected in the Abhayagiri and Jetavanarama collections of sites and museums. You could squeeze your touring of these important sites into one day and then use a second day for sites with their own entrance fees such as Sri Maha Bodhi and Isurumuniya Vihara.

◉ Mahavihara

This is the heart of ancient Anuradhapura and the focus of religious observances, which draw masses of people dressed in their finest. Relics here date from the 3rd century BC to the 11th century AD.

★ Sri Maha Bodhi   BUDDHIST SITE
(Rs 200; ⊘6am-noon & 2-9pm) The sacred bodhi tree is central to Anuradhapura in both a spiritual and physical sense. It was grown from a cutting brought from Bodhgaya in India and is said to be the oldest historically authenticated tree in the world, tended by an uninterrupted succession of guardians for over 2000 years. Today thousands of devotees come to make offerings, particularly on *poya* (full moon) days and weekends. Sunset is a magical time to visit.

The faithful believe it was Princess Sangamitta, daughter of the Indian Emperor Ashoka and sister of Mahinda (who introduced Buddhism to Sri Lanka), who brought the cutting from India. These days there is not one but many bodhi trees here; the oldest and holiest stands on the top platform. Railing and other structures around the trees are festooned with prayer flags.

In 1985, during the civil war, Tamil Tigers opened fire in the enclosure, killing several worshippers as part of a larger offensive that took the lives of almost 150 civilians.

April and December are particularly busy months as pilgrims converge on the site for *snana puja* (offerings or prayers).

★ Ruvanvelisaya Dagoba   BUDDHIST STUPA
This magnificent white dagoba is guarded by a wall with a frieze of 344 elephants standing shoulder to shoulder. Apart from a few beside the western entrance, most are modern replacements of the originals from 140 BC. Today, after incurring much damage from invading Indian forces, it rises 55m, considerably less than its original height; nor is its form the same as the earlier 'bubble' shape.

During the dagoba's consecration, a portion of Buddha's ashes were allegedly enshrined here, in a grand ceremony attended by monks from Rajagriha, Vaishali, Patna, Kashmir and Afghanistan. At the time, it was the biggest stupa in the world, with a 7m-deep foundation made of limestone broken with hammers and then crushed by elephants.

Ruvanvelisaya was commissioned by King Dutugemunu, but he didn't live to see its completion. However, as he lay on his deathbed, a false bamboo-and-cloth finish was placed around the dagoba so that Dutugemunu's final sight could be of his 'completed' masterpiece. A limestone statue in a small pavilion south of the great dagoba is popularly thought to be of Dutugemunu.

The land around the dagoba is dotted with the remains of ponds and pools, and collections of columns and pillars, all picturesquely leaning in different directions. Slightly southeast of the dagoba, en route to

THE ANCIENT CITIES ANURADHAPURA

Anuradhapura

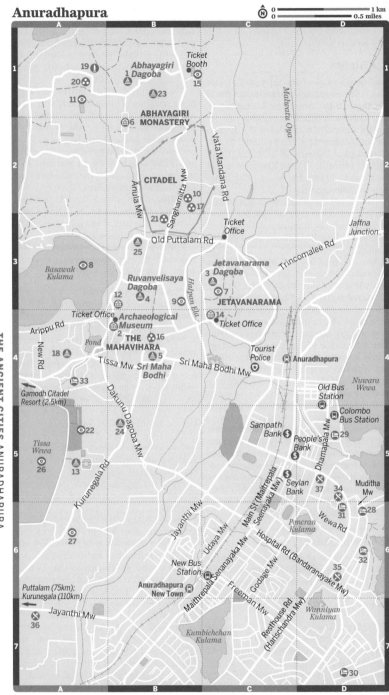

N

0 — 1 km
0 — 0.5 miles

Abhayagiri Dagoba 1

Ticket Booth 15

19
20
11
23

ABHAYAGIRI MONASTERY 6

Mahaveli Oya

CITADEL

Anula Mw

Sanghamitta Mw

Vata Mandana Rd

10
17
21

25

Old Puttalam Rd

Ticket Office

Jaffna Junction

Trincomalee Rd

Ruvanvelisaya Dagoba 4

Jetavanarama Dagoba 3

7

Basawak Kulama 8

12
9

JETAVANARAMA

Halpan Ela

Archaeological Museum 2

Ticket Office

16

14

Ticket Office

Arippu Rd

THE MAHAVIHARA

Tourist Police

Anuradhapura

Pond

New Rd

18

5

Sri Maha Bodhi

Tissa Mw

Sri Maha Bodhi Mw

Nuwara Wewa

Old Bus Station

33

Gamodh Citadel Resort (2.5km)

Dakunu Dagoba Mw

24

22

Colombo Bus Station 29

Dhamapala Mw

Sampath Bank

Tissa Wewa

26
13

People's Bank

Kurunegala Rd

Muditha Mw

Seylan Bank

37
34

Wewa Rd

31
28

27

Jayanthi Mw

Pomeran Kulama

32

Udaya Mw

Main St (Maithrepala Seenayaka Mw)

Maithrepala Senanayaka Mw

New Bus Station

Anuradhapura New Town

Godage Mw

Hospital Rd (Bandaranayake Mw)

35

Puttalam (75km); Kurunegala (110km)

36

Jayanthi Mw

Freeman Mw

Resthouse Rd (Hanschandra Mw)

Wanniyan Kulama

Kumbichchan Kulama

30

Anuradhapura

the Sri Maha Bodhi Temple, you can see one of Anuradhapura's many monks' refectories.

Lowamahapaya　　　　　　　RUINS
(Brazen Palace) So called because it once had a bronze-tiled roof, the ruins of the 'Brazen Palace' stand close to the bodhi tree. The remains of 1600 columns are all that is left of this huge pavilion, said to have had nine storeys and accommodation for 1000 monks and attendants.

It was originally built by King Dutugemunu more than 2000 years ago, but through the ages was rebuilt many times, each time a little less grandiosely.

Thuparama Dagoba　　　　　BUDDHIST STUPA
In a beautiful woodland setting north of the Ruvanvelisaya Dagoba, the Thuparama Dagoba is the oldest dagoba in Sri Lanka – indeed, probably the oldest visible dagoba in the world. It was constructed by King Devanampiya Tissa in the 3rd century BC and is said to enshrine the right collarbone of the Buddha. Its 'heap-of-paddy-rice' shape was restored in 1862 to a more conventional bell shape and to a height of 19m.

Abhayagiri Monastery

For the sheer delight of exploring an ancient city, much of it still enveloped in tropical forest, the 2000-year-old Abhayagiri Monastery area can't be beat. Head off the main trails and your only companions will be strutting egrets and the occasional dog-sized monitor lizard.

A map at the entrance shows how the forest surrounding the main dagoba was home to four main *mula* (colleges or faculties), each with its own residences, refectories, meditation centres and bodhi-tree shrines. An estimated 5000 monks lived here at its peak.

★ Abhayagiri Dagoba　　BUDDHIST TEMPLE
Dating back to the 1st century BC, this colossal dagoba was the ceremonial focus of the 5000-strong Abhayagiri Monastery. Originally over 100m high, it was one of the greatest structures in the ancient world, its scale only matched by the pyramids of Giza (and nearby Jetavanarama). Today, after several reconstructions, Abhayagiri Dagoba soars 75m above the forest floor. Visually, it's stunning, and your first glimpse of this brick monument through a gap in the surrounding forest is breathtaking.

The name means 'Hill of Protection' or 'Fearless Hill'. The Saddarma Rathnawaliya scripture records that a statue of a golden bull containing relics of the Buddha was buried in the core of the stupa.

Abhayagiri Dagoba has some interesting bas-reliefs, including one near the western stairway of an elephant pulling up a tree. A large slab with a Buddha footprint can be seen on the northern side, and the eastern and western steps have unusual moonstones made from concentric stone slabs (the word 'moonstone' relates to the shape of the stone, not the type of stone itself).

As you walk around the northern side of the stupa, look for the octagonal *yupa* (spire) and shaft that originally topped the dagoba before the current square top was added.

Moonstone   MONUMENT
Sitting northwest of the Abhayagiri Dagoba, this ruined 9th-century residential complex for monks is notable for having the finest carved moonstone in Sri Lanka; see how many species of animals you can find in its elaborate carvings. This is a peaceful wooded area full of butterflies, and makes a good place to stop and cool off during a tour of the ruins (there are drink and snack stands close by). Look for the fine steps held up by jovial *gana* (dwarfs).

Ratnaprasada   RUINS
Most of the 8th-century Ratnaprasada or 'Jewel Palace' lies in ruins today, though it was originally seven storeys high with a graceful, tiered roof. The entrance is marked by a beautifully carved *muragala* (guardstone), which depicts the Cobra King holding a vase of abundance and a flowering branch, with a dwarf attendant at his feet and his head framed by a cobra hood.

Abhayagiri Museum   MUSEUM
(⏱10am-5pm) This museum, south of the Abhayagiri Dagoba, is arguably the most interesting in Anuradhapura and contains a collection of squatting plates, jewellery, pottery and religious sculpture from the site. There's a lot of information about the many monuments of Anuradhapura, and a small bookshop.

Samadhi Buddha   BUDDHIST STATUE
This 4th-century statue, seated in the samadhi (meditation) pose, is regarded as one of the finest Buddha statues in Sri Lanka. When constructed, it was likely one of four statues placed at the cardinal directions.

Kuttam Pokuna   POND
(Twin Ponds) These swimming-pool-like ponds were likely used by monks from nearby Kaparamula residence hall. Water entered the larger pond through the mouth of a *makara* (a mythical hybrid beast featuring the body of a fish, the mouth of a crocodile and the trunk of an elephant) and then flowed to the smaller pond through an underground pipe. Note the five-headed cobra figure close to the *makara* and the nearby water-filter system, both at the northwestern end of the ponds.

Eth Pokuna   POND
(Elephant Pond) Surrounded by forest, this huge body of water is thought to have acted as an ancient water storage tank for the Abhayagiri monastery rather than as a pool for pachyderms. Such is the scale of the tank – 159m long, 53m wide and 10m deep – that six Olympic-sized swimming pools could comfortably fit inside it.

◉ Citadel
Despite dating from a later period than most of the Buddhist constructions, time has not been kind to the Citadel. Its once-great walls have almost entirely been reabsorbed by the earth, offering a fine Buddhist lesson in the nature of impermanence.

Royal Palace   RUINS
FREE Built in 1070 (some 12 centuries after Anuradhapura's heyday), this palace was an attempt by King Vijayabahu I to link his reign with the glories of the ancient Sinhalese capital. Little remains today except two fine, but surprisingly modest, guardstones.

THE WORLD'S MOST ORNATE TOILETS

In the 8th century, a new order of *tapovana* (ascetic) monks settled in the western fringes of Anuradhapura. Living among the lowest castes and dressed in scraps of clothing taken from the surrounding graveyards, they renounced the luxury of the main monastery and lived, it is said, on nothing more than rice.

To show their contempt for the effete, luxury-loving monks, the monks of the western monasteries carved beautiful stone squat-style toilets, with their brother monks' monasteries represented on the bottom. Their urinals illustrated the god of wealth showering handfuls of coins down the hole.

Ironically, these squatting plates remain some of the most beautifully ornate objects left in Anuradhapura; you can see fine examples at the Archaeological Museum, Abhayagiri Museum and the **Padhanagara** site, as well as in Ridi Vihara (p241).

Mahapali Refectory   RUINS
The Mahapali refectory, or alms hall, is notable mainly for its immense trough (nearly 3m long and 2m wide) that the lay followers filled with rice for the monks.

Dalada Maligawa   RUINS
In the Royal Palace area you can also find the Dalada Maligawa. The central relic chamber of this ruined temple may have been the first Temple of the Tooth in the 4th century AD. Other sources claim the tooth resided in the Abhayagiri Dagoba.

🔘 Jetavanarama

The huge Jetavanarama Dagoba dominates the eastern part of Anuradhapura.

⭐ Jetavanarama Dagoba   BUDDHIST STUPA
The Jetavanarama Dagoba's massive dome rises above the entire eastern part of Anuradhapura. Built in the 3rd century by King Mahasena, it may have originally topped 120m, but today is about 70m – similar to the Abhayagiri. When it was built it was almost certainly the third-tallest monument in the world, the first two being Egyptian pyramids.

Its vast, bulbous form is unplastered and said to consist of more than 90 million bricks. A British guidebook from the early 1900s calculated that this was enough bricks to make a 3m-high wall stretching from London to Edinburgh.

Around it stand the ruins of a monastery that housed 3000 monks. One building has door jambs over 8m high still standing, with another 3m still buried underground. This area was once part of an ancient pleasure park called Nandana Uyana, said to be the site of the first sermons on Buddhism preached by Mahinda in the 3rd century BC.

Jetavanarama Museum   MUSEUM
(⏰ 8am-5.30pm) A 1937 British colonial building provides a suitably regal venue for some of the treasures found at Jetavanarama. The objects displayed here range from the sublime (finely carved ivory finials) to the ridiculous (ancient toilet pipes). Highlights include the elaborately carved urinal in Room 1 and the tiny 8mm-long gold decoration featuring eight exquisite flowers in Room 2.

Buddhist Railing   HISTORIC SITE
A little south of the Jetavanarama Dagoba, on the other side of the road, there is a stone railing built in imitation of a log wall. It

---

ⓘ TEMPLE ETIQUETTE
....
Because so many of Anuradhapura's major sites are still considered sacred, it is important to be prepared to remove your shoes and hat, wear a sarong if you are wearing shorts or otherwise don modest dress as required. It's a good idea to bring a pair of socks for the hot and rocky ground.

Sri Lankan pilgrims wear white, which is considered a holy colour, a mode you might choose to copy out of respect (and also as it reflects strong sunlight).

---

encloses a site 42m by 34m, but the building within has long disappeared.

🔘 Museum Quarter

Anuradhapura's main Archaeological Museum covers most of the local sites. Two other museums, the Abhayagiri Museum (p232) and Jetavanarama Museum, are closely tied to their namesake sites.

⭐ Archaeological Museum   MUSEUM
(⏰ 8am-5pm, closed public holidays) **FREE** The old British colonial administration building has recently been renovated and has an interesting collection of artwork, carvings and everyday items from Anuradhapura and other historic sites around Sri Lanka. Exhibits include a restored relic chamber, found during the excavation of the Kantaka Chetiya dagoba at nearby Mihintale, and a large-scale model of Thuparama Dagoba's *vatadage* as it might have been if a wooden roof had existed.

Folk Museum   MUSEUM
(adult/child Rs 300/150; ⏰ 9am-4.30pm Tue-Sat, closed public holidays) A short distance north of the Archaeological Museum is this dusty museum with mildly interesting exhibits of country life in Sri Lanka's North Central Province.

🔘 Other Sites

South and west of the main historic and sacred areas are several important and enigmatic sites.

Mirisavatiya Dagoba   BUDDHIST STUPA
FREE This huge dagoba was the first built by King Dutugemunu after he recaptured the city in the 2nd century BC. The story goes

> ### TANKS
>
> Anuradhapura has three great artificial water tanks, commissioned by the city's kings to provide water for irrigation and to raise tax revenue for the Buddhist community.
>
> **Nuwara Wewa**, on the east side of the city, is the largest, covering about 12 sq km. It was built around 20 BC and is well away from most of the old city. The northwestern corner offers spectacular sunset views of the old city.
>
> The 160-hectare **Tissa Wewa** is the southern tank in the old city and is encircled by a dirt road. It's easily accessed from the behind the Isurumuniya Vihara or Royal Pleasure Gardens.
>
> The oldest tank, probably dating from around the 4th century BC, is the 120-hectare **Basawak Kulama** to the north.
>
> All are good for quiet bike rides and walks along the shorelines.

that Dutugemunu went to bathe in the tank, leaving his ornate sceptre implanted in the bank. When he emerged he found his sceptre, which contained a relic of the Buddha, impossible to pull out. Taking this as an auspicious sign, he had the dagoba built.

Royal Pleasure Gardens GARDENS
(Ranmasu Uyana) FREE Known as the Park of the Goldfish, these extensive 2000-year-old royal pleasure gardens cover 14 hectares and contain two ponds skilfully designed to fit around the huge boulders in the park. Look out for the fine elephant carvings.

Isurumuniya Vihara BUDDHIST MONUMENT
(Rs 200; ☉7am-8pm) This charming rock temple, dating from the reign of Devanampiya Tissa (r 307–267 BC), is set around a lovely lotus pond, the corner of which is carved with images of elephants playfully splashing water. The central temple has some particularly fine mural paintings. Climb around the back to the rock summit to see the bell-shaped stupa and a pair of Buddha footprints etched into the rock.

Vessagiriya HISTORIC SITE
FREE South of the Isurumuniya Vihara are the faint remains of the Vessagiriya cave monastery, a series of evocative, gravity-defying boulder overhangs etched with inscriptions

and water channels. You can easily picture monks meditating in their cave retreats here.

Tours

Most places to stay can arrange for licensed guides if you'd like – useful if you want a deep understanding of Anuradhapura and its rich history. Rates start at about Rs 1500 for two hours with you providing the transport.

One of the best local guides is **Charitha Jithendra Jith** (☎077 303 7835; charithajithendra@gmail.com).

Festivals

Unduvap Poya RELIGIOUS
(☉Dec) Each December, thousands of pilgrims flock to Anuradhapura for Unduvap Poya, a festival that commemorates the arrival of the sacred bodhi tree from India.

Sleeping

Anuradhapura has some of the best-value budget accommodation in Sri Lanka, with dozens of excellent family-run guesthouses scattered around the pleasant leafy neighbourhoods southeast of Main St.

Prices given are for direct bookings. Rates for budget places on booking websites can be up to 50% higher; the opposite is true for top-end places. The oversupply of budget accommodation means there's room for bargaining here.

Note that commission-seeking hotel touts sometimes board trains a few stations outside of town and hassle visitors. Three-wheeler drivers can be equally pushy. Many places offer free pick-up from transport terminals.

Balcony Rest GUESTHOUSE $
(☎071 614 1590; balconyrestanuradhapura@gmail.com; 1160/B Nagasena Mawatha; s/d Rs 2000/2500; ❀☃) There are just two rooms at this stylish family home, so two couples could have the entire upper floor to themselves. Rooms are excellent value, with a spotless bathroom and a fine wooden balcony. The residential location is a bit out of the centre and hard to find, so call ahead. English teacher Nimali and her husband Jayantha are excellent hosts.

Melbourne Tourist Rest GUESTHOUSE $
(☎025-223 7843; www.melrest.com; 388/28 Rest House Rd, Stage 1; r Rs 2500-3000; ❀☃) This fresh and modern property run by Milano Tourist Rest has 10 tiled rooms, a large restaurant, garden seating and a quiet central location.

235

Milano is also building a modern new hotel nearby with 50 rooms, to open in 2018.

London Palace
GUESTHOUSE $

(☏ 025-223 5070; www.londonpalacesl.com; 119/29/1 Mailagas Junction; r Rs 3000-3500; ❄ @ ☎) Impressive two-storey place ('palace' is a little ambitious!) with 10 lovely, clean, bright and airy rooms with TV, fridge, neutral-colour schemes and balcony (except the single, which is worth avoiding). The six front rooms are best. The location is quite a way from the centre, but bikes are available (Rs 400). It's owned by the efficient people behind Milano Tourist Rest.

★ Milano Tourist Rest
HOTEL $$

(☏ 025-222 2364; www.milanotouristrest.com; 596/40 JR Jaya Mawatha; r Rs 3500; ❄ @ ☎) Hidden in a quiet residential street, Milano is a professionally run place in an elegant late-1950s house. The eight rooms are somewhat old-fashioned, but with a touch of class that belies the moderate prices. All rooms have thick mattresses, fridges and modern bathrooms. The restaurant is good (mains Rs 850) and there's a lovely garden for alfresco dining.

Gamodh Citadel Resort
HOTEL $$

(☏ 025-492 8906; www.gamodhcitadelresort.com; Lolugaswewa; r US$30-35, ste US$40-45; ❄ ☎ ☎) A terrific rural hotel, offering comfortable and excellent-value rooms in two new blocks, with slightly dated and smaller rooms in the old building. The landscaped grounds are relaxing, with tables dotted around a generously sized pool, and meals are very flavourful. It's 6km west of the commercial centre, but quite close to the western ruins.

Hotel Randiya
HOTEL $$

(☏ 025-222 2868; www.hotelrandiya.com; 394/19A Muditha Mawatha; r incl breakfast Rs 4500-8000; ❄ @ ☎ ☎) There are two distinct options at this hotel. The stylish, modern new building is all sleek lines and white walls, with a swimming pool and modern restaurant. The older, wood-lined villa boasts *walawwa* (minor palace) style architecture with cheaper and more characterful (but darker) rooms and an atmospheric old-school bar.

★ Ulagalla
BOUTIQUE HOTEL $$$

(☏ 025-205 0280, Colombo 011-232 8832; www.ugaescapes.com; Ulagalla Walawwa, Thirappane; s/d from US$395/460; ❄ ☎ ☎) Exclusive and stylish, the 20 villas in this remote rural retreat, 40km from Anuradhapura, are top of the line, with private plunge pools and relaxing decks, in addition to a lovely central pool. The century-old main building lends a classy colonial air, making it a superb place to unwind after touring the region's cultural sites.

The real highlight is the sense of privacy and space, but the luxury also comes with eco credentials; rain water is harvested and 50% of the electricity comes from solar power.

★ Lakeside at Nuwarawewa
HOTEL $$$

(☏ 025-222 1414; www.nuwarawewa.com; Dhamapala Mawatha; s/d/tr US$85/95/105; ❄ @ ☎ ☎) Renovated from top to tail, this modern hotel has a fine location near the lovely Nuwara Wewa tank. Rooms are stylish and fresh and come with a balcony or verandah; you can save a few dollars by ditching the pool view. It's good value, and the restaurant is excellent, with pleasant outdoor seating. Nonguests can use the pool for Rs 850.

THE ANCIENT CITIES ANURADHAPURA

ANURADHAPURA'S NEW STUPA

Two thousand years after the first of the great dagobas was constructed, a huge new stupa, the **Sandahiru Seya** (Moon-Sun Temple), is rising on the south side of Anuradhapura, commissioned by President Rajapaksa in 2010. Designed to reach 85m in height, with a circumference of 244m, it will eventually rise above the ancient dagobas of Jetavanarama and Abhayagiri (but will not surpass their original heights). Sandahiru Seya is being constructed from over 30 million bricks and will be plastered and then whitewashed when finished.

Controversially, this is just one of nine new stupas planned, on orders of the president 'in appreciation of the noble service rendered by the armed forces and police to defeat terrorism and bring lasting peace to the country'. However, some have objected to the principle of dedicating a Buddhist monument to the actions of the Sri Lankan military.

The pace of construction and flow of funds has slowed in recent years, so it could be many years before the huge dagoba is finished.

Sanctuary at Tissawewa HISTORIC HOTEL $$$
(☎ 025-222 2299; www.tissawewa.com; off Old Puttalam Rd; deluxe s/d incl breakfast US$130/140; ❄ ☎) For sheer colonial class this Raj-era relic (formerly a British governor's residence) can't be matched. It's been beautifully and respectfully restored – the stylish rooms boast all mod cons and the verandahs are a delightful place to enjoy a peaceful afternoon, overlooking the mature gardens dotted with mahogany and teak trees and home to peacocks and monkeys.

Palm Garden Village Hotel HOTEL $$$
(☎ 025-222 3961; www.palmgardenvillage.com; Old Puttalam Rd, Pandulagama; s/d from US$140/155; ❄ ☎ ☎) Set in 38 hectares of forest and gardens with a lovely pool area, this resort hotel has spacious rooms with fine terrace seating. Some bathrooms are better than others. Extras include an Ayurvedic spa and the occasional visiting wild elephant. Service is not the best, but the quiet location is very relaxing. It's 7km west of town.

Eating

Dining choices are surprisingly limited in Anuradhapura. Several hotels have good restaurants, including the Sanctuary at Tissawewa.

Lulu's Feeding Point SRI LANKAN $
(Hospital Rd; curries Rs 270-330) This self-service corner-shop joint is perfect for shoestringers staying at one of the many nearby budget guesthouses. The rice and curry, string hoppers, *kotthu* and some Chinese dishes are all good, plus there's airy roadside seating and the staff are friendly and helpful. Our go-to option for a cheap and cheerful meal.

Walkers SRI LANKAN $
(Rest House Rd; mains Rs 350; ⊙ 7am-9.30pm; ☎) Just east of the 'elephant' roundabout this modern cafe-restaurant-store is a popular spot for egg, curry and noodle dishes, including freshly squeezed orange juice. There's a side terrace for dining and staff are friendly. It can get hot here.

★**Hotel Shalini** SRI LANKAN $$
(☎ 025-222 2425, 071 807 3335; www.hotelshalini.lk; 41/388 Rest House Rd; set meals Rs 850; ⊙ noon-2pm & 6-11pm) With its airy, upper-storey pavilion and dripping eaves, this *haveli* (town house)-style building has a charming setting, but it's the food that really stands out. The menu changes daily, but the family recipes normally include the excellent lotus root salad, jackfruit curry and two delicious types of aubergine, along with unusual medicinal dishes such as the *kohilla* tuber. Bring mosquito repellent.

Mango Mango INDIAN $$
(☎ 025-222 7501; Jayanthi Mawatha; curries Rs 320-520; ⊙ 7-10am, noon-3.30pm & 6-10pm) The location in the southern outskirts of town is not the most convenient, but this bright and hip restaurant is worth the trip if you are in the mood for an Indian curry (dinner only). The tikka and tandoori dishes are good, as is the tasty chicken *kadahi masala* (cooked with onions, tomatoes and peppers). Set dinners are good value (Rs 290).

The counters of the attached fast-food-style cafe groan with desserts and cakes.

★**Sanctuary at Tissawewa** INTERNATIONAL $$$
(www.tissawewa.com; mains Rs 800-1600; ⊙ 7.30-9.30am, noon-3pm & 7.30-9.30pm; ☎) There is no more atmospheric place for a leisurely meal or drink than the verandah or dining room of this beautiful colonial hotel. Try the chilli-marinated grilled pork chops, a club sandwich or the four-course set dinner (Rs 1550), followed by coffee, served in white embossed china cups. No alcohol is served.

ℹ Information

Main St and Dhamapala Mawatha in the centre have banks and ATMs.

People's Bank (Main St; ⊙ 9am-5pm Mon-Fri)
Sampath Bank (Main St; ⊙ 8am-8pm) Long opening hours, no commission and fast service at this bank and ATM.

Seylan Bank (Main St; ⊙ 9am-5pm Mon-Fri)
Tourist Police (☎ 011-313 3686; Sri Maha Bodhi Mawatha; ⊙ 24hr) The place to come if you have an emergency.

ℹ Getting There & Away

BUS
Confusingly, Anuradhapura has no less than three bus stations. Unless noted otherwise, daytime service in all directions is frequent (every 30 minutes or so).

Colombo Bus Station
Private air-con and 'semi-comfortable' (larger seats, no air-con) buses leave from the small Colombo Bus Station near the Old Bus Station.

Buses to Colombo run via Dambulla and Kurunegala (bus No 15) or faster via Puttalam and Negombo (bus No 4). The fastest air-con intercity express buses to Colombo depart at 9.15am and 2.15pm.

Services include the following:

Colombo Rs 350 to 500, six hours

Dambulla Rs 190, 1½ hours; take a Kandy-bound minibus

Kandy Rs 340, 3½ hours; air-con minibuses are the fastest

New Bus Station

Buses heading to points east and north start from the New Bus Station. Services include the following:

Jaffna Rs 328, six hours, eight daily; en route from Colombo, so stops outside the bus station

Mihintale Rs 33, 30 minutes

Polonnaruwa Rs 150, three hours; bus is labelled 'Kaduruwela'; also for Habarana

Trinco Rs 180, 3½ hours, two daily; or change in Horowupotana

Old Bus Station

The Old Bus Station is mostly for local services, including to Kurunegala (Rs 140, three hours).

TRAIN

Anuradhapura's main train station is an art deco gem. Some services stop also at the new train station further south. Train services include the following:

Colombo 1st/2nd/3rd class Rs 900/450/280, five hours, five daily

Jaffna 1st/2nd/3rd class Rs 1000/500/130, 3½ hours, three daily

ⓘ Getting Around

The city's commercial district is quite compact, but the rest of the town is too spread out to investigate on foot. A three-hour taxi/three-wheeler tour costs about Rs 1500/1200. Bicycles are the best local means of transport and can be rented at most hotels and guesthouses (Rs 400 to 500 per day).

Mihintale

📋 025

This sleepy village and **temple complex** (Rs 500; ⊙24hr), 13km east of Anuradhapura, holds a special place in the annals of Sri Lankan lore. In 247 BC, King Devanampiya Tissa of Anuradhapura was hunting a stag on Mihintale Hill when he was approached by Mahinda, son of the great Indian Buddhist emperor, Ashoka. Mahinda tested the king's wisdom and, considering him to be a worthy disciple, promptly converted the king on the spot. Mihintale has since been associated with the earliest introduction of Buddhism to Sri Lanka.

As the climb takes 25 minutes, you may wish to visit early in the morning or late in the afternoon to avoid the midday heat. You can cut the walk in half by driving up the side Old Rd and starting near the Monks' Refectory. Wannabe guides charge about Rs 800 for a two-hour tour. If the guide follows you up the steps, you're committed, so make your decision clear before setting out.

⊙ Sights

Monks' Refectory & Relic House   RUINS

On the second landing is the monks' refectory with huge stone troughs that the lay followers kept filled with rice for the monks.

Nearby, on a raised platform identified as the monastery's relic house, are two inscribed stone slabs erected during the reign of King Mahinda IV (r 975–91). The inscriptions laid down the rules relating to the relic house and the conduct of those responsible for it.

One inscription clearly states that nothing belonging to the relic house shall be lent or sold. Another confirms the amount of land to be given in exchange for a reliable supply of oil and wicks for lamps and flowers for offerings. Also known as the Mihintale tablets, these inscribed stones define the duties of the monastery's many servants: which servants gather firewood and cook, which servants cook but only on firewood gathered by others, and so on.

There are also rules for monks: they should rise at dawn, clean their teeth, put on their robes, meditate and then go to have their breakfast (boiled rice) at the refectory, but only after reciting certain portions of the scriptures.

Assembly Hall   RUINS

On the same level as the relic house, this hall, also known as the convocation hall, is where monks met to discuss matters of common interest. The raised dais in the middle of the hall was where the most senior monk would have presided over the discussions. Sixty-four stone pillars once supported the roof. The main path to the Ambasthale Dagoba leads up from here.

★Sinha Pokuna   MONUMENT

Just below the monks' refectory on the second landing, and near the entrance if you are coming via Old Rd, is a small pool surmounted by a 2m-high rampant lion, reckoned to be one of the best pieces of animal

THE ANCIENT CITIES MIHINTALE

Mihintale

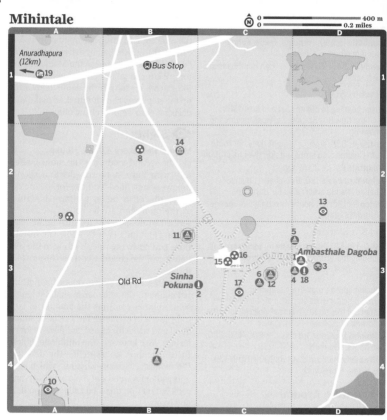

N
0 _____ 400 m
0 _____ 0.2 miles

Anuradhapura
(12km)
19

Bus Stop

14
8

9

13

11

5

15 16

Ambasthale Dagoba
1
3

Old Rd

Sinha
Pokuna
2

17

6
4 18

12

7

10

carving in the country. Anyone placing one hand on each paw would be right in line for the stream of water from the lion's mouth. There are some fine friezes around this pool.

★**Ambasthale Dagoba**   BUDDHIST STUPA
The main ceremonial stairway, lined with frangipani trees, leads to the Ambasthale Dagoba, built over the spot where Mahinda converted Devanampiya Tissa to Buddhism. A nearby **statue of the king** wearing traditional dress marks the spot where he met Mahinda. The name Ambasthale means 'Mango Tree' and refers to a riddle that Mahinda used to test the king's intelligence.

To the side, up a flight of rock-carved steps, is a large white **Buddha statue**.

The **bodhi tree** to the left of the steps leading to the Mahaseya Dagoba is said to be one of the oldest surviving trees in Sri Lanka. The tree is surrounded by a railing festooned with prayer flags left by pilgrims.

Mahaseya Dagoba   BUDDHIST STUPA
This dagoba (the largest at Mihintale) is thought to have been built to house relics of Mahinda. On the far side you'll find the original, smaller brick dagoba, one of the oldest in Sri Lanka and largely ignored by visitors. From here, there are views over the lakes and trees to Anuradhapura.

A small temple at the side of the dagoba has a reclining Buddha and Technicolor modern frescoes – donations are requested. A room at the side is a devale with statues of the gods Ganesh, Vishnu, Murugan (Skanda) and Saman.

Mahinda's Cave   CAVE
A path leads downhill from the back of the relic house courtyard, northeast of the Ambasthale Dagoba, for 10 minutes to a cave where there is a large flat stone where Mahinda lived. The track to the cave is hard on tender, bare feet.

Mihintale

Aradhana Gala VIEWPOINT
To the east of Ambasthale Dagoba is a steep path over sun-heated rock-carved steps leading up to a point with great views of the surrounding valley. A railing goes up all the way. Aradhana Gala means 'Meditation Rock'.

Naga Pokuna POND
Halfway back down the steep flight of steps from the Ambasthale Dagoba, a path leads to the left, around the base of the hill topped by the Mahaseya Dagoba. Here you'll find the Naga Pokuna (Snake Pool), so called because of a five-headed cobra carved in low relief on the rock face of the pool. Its tail is said to reach down to the bottom of the pool.

Continuing on from here, you eventually loop back down to the second landing. Alternatively, take the left trail up to the old stupa beside the Ambasthale Dagoba, or the right path up to Et Vihara.

Kantaka Chetiya BUDDHIST STUPA
At the first landing, a side flight of 100 steps branches right to this partly ruined dagoba, one of the oldest at Mihintale. It's 12m high (originally more than 30m) and 130m around its base. A Brahmi inscription decrees that funding for the dagoba came from taxes on a nearby water tank. Four stone flower altars stand at the cardinal points,

and surrounding these are sculptures of dwarfs, geese and other figures.

Et Vihara BUDDHIST STUPA
At an even higher elevation (309m) than the Mahaseya Dagoba is the little-visited and modest Et Vihara (literally, 'Elephant Monastery') stupa, which offers excellent views over the valley. It's a fine place to watch the sun set.

Mihintale Museum MUSEUM
(⏱8am-4.30pm) FREE This small museum on the road leading to the stairway base is worth a short visit for its modest collection of artefacts collected from Mihintale.

Hospital RUINS
The remains of a 9th-century hospital sit a stone's throw from the site museum. The hospital consisted of a number of cells. A *bat oruwa* (large stone trough) sits near the entrance. The interior of the trough is carved in the shape of a human form, and the patient would climb into this to be immersed in healing oils.

Inscriptions have revealed that the hospital had its specialists – there is reference to a *mandova*, a bone and muscle specialist, and to a *puhunda vedek*, a leech doctor. Surgical instruments were unearthed from the site.

Indikatu Seya Complex RUINS
On the road leading to Old Rd, west of the site proper, are the remains of a monastery enclosed in the ruins of a stone wall. Visible here are two dagobas, the larger known as Indikatu Seya (Dagoba of the Needle). Evidence suggests that this monastery was active in fostering Mahayana Buddhism. The main dagoba's structure differs from others in Mihintale in that it's built on a square platform.

Kaludiya Pokuna LAKE
(Dark Water Pond) On the southwest outskirts of Mihintale is the lovely Kaludiya Pokuna, an artificial pool that features a rock-carved bathhouse and the ruins of a small monastery. It's a charming spot for a quiet picnic.

 Festivals

Poson Poya RELIGIOUS
This large annual festival is held on the Poson full-moon night (usually in June) to commemorate the conversion of Devanampiya Tissa to Buddhism.

SCULPTURAL SYMBOLISM

The four *vahalkadas* (solid panels of sculpture) at the Kantaka Chetiya (p239) are among the oldest and best preserved in the country and are the only ones to be found at Mihintale.

Vahalkadas face each of the four cardinal directions and comprise a series of bands, each containing some sort of ornamentation. The upper part usually contained niches in which were placed sculptures of divine beings. At either end of each *vahalkada* is a pillar topped with the figure of an animal, such as an elephant or a lion. How or why these sculptural creations came into being is subject to speculation, but one theory is that they evolved from simple flower altars. Others suggest they were an adaptation from Hindu temple design.

The cardinal points in traditional sculptural work are represented by specific animals: an elephant on the east, a horse on the west, a lion on the north and a bull on the south. In addition to these beasts, sculptures also feature dwarfs (sometimes depicted with animal heads), geese (said to have the power to choose between good and evil), elephants (often shown as though supporting the full weight of the superstructure) and *naga* (serpents, said to possess magical powers). Floral designs, apart from the lotus, are said to be primarily ornamental.

🛏 Sleeping & Eating

Mihintale Rest House HOTEL $$
(☑ 025-226 6599; www.chcresthouses.com; Trincomalee Rd; s/r incl breakfast Rs 3740/4400; ❄ @ 🕷) As Mihintale is so close to Anuradhapura, few people overnight here, but this attractive hotel has a classy open-sided lobby lounge and spacious, if somewhat dated, rooms. Luxury rooms have nice views and better bathrooms for Rs 1000 more. The pavilion cafe serves a set lunch for Rs 700.

❶ Getting There & Away

Mihintale is 13km east of Anuradhapura. Buses run frequently (Rs 30, 30 minutes) from Anuradhapura's New Bus Station, with the last bus returning from a bus stop just north of the Mihintale site around 6.30pm.

A return taxi from Anuradhapura, with two hours to visit the site, costs about Rs 2500; a three-wheeler is about Rs 1500. It takes less than an hour to cycle here.

Yapahuwa Rock Fortress

Rising 100m from the surrounding plain like a mini Sigiriya, the impressive granite outcrop of Yapahuwa (Fire Rock; adult/child US$4/2; ⊘ 7am-6pm), pronounced yaa-pow-a, is off the beaten track, but it's a fascinating place with an important history.

There has been a Buddhist monastery at Yapahuwa since the 3rd century BC, but the site hit its zenith between 1272 and 1284, when King Bhuvanekabahu I used the rock fortress as his capital and housed Sri Lanka's sacred Buddha tooth relic here. Indians from the Pandavan dynasty captured Yapahuwa in 1284 and carried the tooth relic to South India, only for it to be recovered four years later by King Parakramabahu III. From this point onwards the capital shifted to Kurunegala.

The steep ornamental staircase of this dramatic rock fortress is perhaps its finest feature, and once led to the Temple of the Tooth. One of the lions near the top of the staircase appears on the Rs 10 note. The porches on the stairway had extraordinarily beautiful pierced-stone windows, one of which is in the National Museum in Colombo, while the other is in the on-site museum.

The small **museum** is off a parking area about 300m before the entrance to the steps. On display are stone sculptures of Vishnu and Kali, some illuminating displays in English, and coins showing trade connections as far away as China.

Past the museum you wander through the south gate and the inner and outer ramparts and moat protecting the **ancient fortress**. From here you climb past the ornamental staircase to the rock summit and its wonderfully breezy 360-degree views. There are faint traces of the stupa and bodhi tree shrine that once stood here.

Back on ground level, to the side of the main monastery buildings, a **cave temple** contains some lovely 13th-century frescoes and images of the Buddha made from wood and bronze. You may have to ask the monk to unlock the temple with its giant key.

ℹ Getting There & Away

Yapahuwa is 9km east of the Anuradhapura–Kurunegala highway, which is well served by buses. Three-wheelers charge Rs 1000 return (including waiting time) to the site from the highway junction at Daladagama.

Alternatively, bus No 57/7 runs from Kurunegala to Maho (Rs 75, two hours) every 15 minutes, from where it's a shorter 6km three-wheeler ride to the site.

Maho also has a railway station, where the Trincomalee line splits from the Colombo–Anuradhapura line.

Panduwasnuwara

Almost abandoned, the 12th-century ruins of the temporary capital of Parakramabahu I are spread across the countryside, about 36km northwest of Kurunegala. They are worth a stop if you have a particular interest in Buddhist ruins or are travelling between Negombo and the Ancient Cities.

Most people visit Panduwasnuwara as a day trip from Kurunegala or en route between Anuradhapura and Negombo.

The archaeological site is spread over a wide area. Near the entrance is a moat, a massive citadel wall and the remains of a royal palace. Further on are image houses, brick dagobas and monastic living quarters.

Follow the road as it branches left, and you'll eventually come to a restored tooth temple (Dalada Maligawa) with a bodhi tree, a colourfully painted sleeping Buddha temple and, behind that, the remains of a fascinating round palace (apparently once multistoreyed) enclosed in a circular moat.

ℹ Getting There & Away

Panduwasnuwara is about 20km southwest of Padeniya on the road between Wariyapola and Chilaw. The turn-off to the site is at Panduwasnuwara village, near the tiny museum.

Frequent buses (No 525) between Kurunegala and Chilaw pass Panduwasnuwara (Rs 60), from where you could hire a three-wheeler to take you around the ruins, the furthest of which are around 2km from the road.

Ridi Vihara

Literally the 'Silver Temple', **Ridi Vihara** (⊙7am-8pm) FREE was named for the silver ore that was discovered here in the 2nd century BC that financed the construction of the huge Ruvanvelisaya Dagoba in Anuradhapura.

The two Buddhist caves at the foot of the cliff face are off the beaten track, but the attached monastery is a welcoming place and is worth the trip to see its wonderful frescoes, unusual Dutch tiles and nearby giant Buddha carving.

The primary attraction at this Buddhist temple is the golden standing Buddha statue in the main cave called the **Pahala Vihara** (Lower Temple), which also houses a 9m recumbent Buddha resting on a platform decorated with a series of blue-and-white tiles. The tiles were a gift from the Dutch consul and depict scenes from the Bible, including animals entering Noah's ark two by two.

The next-door **Uda Vihara** (Upper Temple) was built by Kandyan King Kirti Sri Rajasinghe in the 18th century and features stunningly vibrant murals and carvings painted in yellows, reds and black. Some clever visual tricks were used by the fresco artists; in one case, above the exterior doorway to the right, what appears to be an elephant reveals itself on closer inspection to be a formation of nine maidens. Photos are not allowed inside either of the temples.

Outside the temple complex you can walk past an Indian-looking stone temple up the ceremonial pathway to a renovated dagoba. On the way up, to your right, is an ancient rock inscription.

Those with a special interest in Buddhism can overnight in the monastery guesthouse; otherwise, most people visit on a day trip from Kurunegala or en route between Dambulla and Kandy.

ℹ Getting There & Away

Ridi Vihara is situated east of the Kurunegala–Dambulla Rd, 2km southeast of Ridigama village.

From Kurunegala take the No 564 Keppitigala bus to Ridigama (Rs 40, one hour). Alternatively, take a No 556 Matale-bound bus, get off at the junction 2.5km north of Ridigama and take a three-wheeler from there.

> ### RIDIGAMA BUDDHA
>
> A 20m-tall sitting Buddha, **Monaragala Viharaya Buddha** (www.samadhibuddha statue.lk; Rambadagalla) is 4km southeast of Ridigama and was unveiled in 2015 as the largest (but not the loveliest) granite statue in the world. Set on a plinth of carved peacocks, elephants and lotus buds, the Buddha is in samadhi (meditation) pose. It's worth a quick visit if you have your own transport.

From Ridigama, a return three-wheeler to Ridi Vihara costs Rs 400.

Kurunegala

📱 037 / POP 34,500

Kurunegala is a bustling market town and transport hub between Colombo and Anuradhapura, and Kandy and Puttalam. The town is not a destination in itself, but there are a few diversions nearby.

◉ Sights

The large, smooth rocky outcrops that loom over the town are the most striking feature of this city. Named for the animals they appear to resemble (Tortoise Rock, Elephant Rock etc), the outcrops are, unsurprisingly, endowed with mythological status. It's said they were formed when animals that were endangering the free supply of water to the town were turned into stone.

Athagala   BUDDHIST SITE
(Elephant Rock) An atmospheric rock-cut staircase winds up Athagala, a large black rock outcrop on the eastern side of the city, to offer fine city views from a 22m-tall white Buddha statue. A road also winds up to the same spot. On the way up you pass a small monastery, the **Ibbagala Vihara**. A three-wheeler to the top costs Rs 700 return.

Padeniya Raja Mahavihara BUDDHIST TEMPLE
(donations appreciated; ⊘ dawn-dusk) About 85km south of Anuradhapura and 25km northwest of Kurunegala, where the Puttalam and Anuradhapura roads meet, is this Kandyan-style temple, which is worth popping into if you're passing by. It's a pretty, medieval temple with 28 carved pillars and a stunning elaborate door (said to be the largest in Sri Lanka) to the main shrine. There is also a clay-image house and a library, as well as a preaching hall with an unusual carved wooden pulpit.

🛏 Sleeping & Eating

Few travellers stay in Kurunegala, but there are a couple of accommodation options.

Hotel Viveka   HOTEL $$
(📱 037-222 2897; www.hotelviveka.com; 64 North Lake Rd; s/d Rs 3000/4000; 🅿 🛜) An elegant, if somewhat threadbare, colonial villa with a verandah overlooking the lake in a leafy part of town. Its four rooms have been renovated and have modern bathrooms. Take a sunset stroll around the lake. Viveka doubles as Kurunegala's most convivial bar and restaurant (mains Rs 500 to 700), so can be busy on weekends.

Littlemore Estate Bungalows   LODGE $$$
(📱 072 231 9443; reservations@ferncliff.lk; r incl breakfast US$115; 🅿 🛜 🍴) An intriguing accommodation option, Littlemore Estate is a 50-hectare coconut plantation bordered by paddy fields and woodland with a healthy local peacock population. There are three very tastefully presented modern rooms, and staff will show you around the estate and explain all about coconut harvesting. Meals are traditional Sri Lankan.

It's 9km northwest of Kurunegala; the turn-off is at the village of Pellandeniya on the A10 Hwy.

In & Out   SRI LANKAN $
(18 Puttalam Rd; mains Rs 200; ⊙ 6am-10pm) An unexpectedly modish bakery-restaurant, 30m from the bus station, with decent Sri Lankan and Western dishes. Omelettes are available as well as rice and curry (from 11.30am) and some good cakes.

ℹ Getting There & Away

Buses depart from a chaotic, fume-filled bus station in the very centre of town. Frequent services (every 20 minutes) include the following:

Anuradhapura express Rs 140, three hours
Colombo normal/express air-con Rs 120/240, 3½ hours
Dambulla Rs 100, two hours
Kandy normal/express air-con Rs 67/130, one hour
Negombo express Rs 195, three hours

Trains depart from a station 2km southwest of the town centre.

The East

Best Places to Eat

➡ Hideaway Restaurant (p250)

➡ Sana's (p267)

➡ Coconut Beach Lodge (p267)

➡ Sun Shine Cafe (p259)

Best Places to Sleep

➡ Stardust Beach Hotel (p249)

➡ Riviera Resort (p258)

➡ Laya Waves (p261)

➡ Hilltop Beach Cabanas (p252)

➡ Trinco Blu by Cinnamon (p266)

Why Go?

Maybe you're searching for somewhere in Sri Lanka a little less developed, a coastline that retains a more earthy, local feel. Or maybe you just want the best beach of your life. Well, the East might just offer that place and that beach.

Many people come here and start investigating how to delay their onward journey. Still a little rough around the edges, the East remains primarily a land of fishing villages, sandy lanes, chickens in the yard, and tradition. It's a culturally fascinating combination of ocean-orientated Muslim communities, astonishing Hindu temples, crumbling colonial forts, dazzling markets, and a coastline of killer surf, hidden bays and stretch-for-kilometres white-sand beaches.

The entire region is well linked to the rest of the country by road, bus and rail, so there's really no reason to skip the many allures of the East.

When to Go
Trincomalee

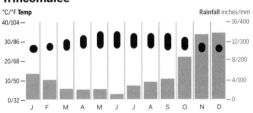

Mar–Apr The most reliable months for spotting blue whales in the seas off Trincomalee.

May–Jun This is shoulder season; nesting season in Kumana and good elephant-spotting.

Jun–Jul White-sand beaches (and surfing) from Nilaveli to Arugam Bay are at their prime.

The East Highlights

1 Uppuveli (p265)
Enjoying the chilled-out beach vibe at this strip of sand.

2 Kumana National Park (p254) Spotting a skittish leopard – or monitoring the road to avoid a rogue elephant – in this blissfully uncrowded park.

3 Pigeon Island National Park (p268) Snorkelling or diving with reef sharks around this gem of an island off Nilaveli.

4 Arugam Bay (p246) Hanging ten on the endless rights of this chilled-out surf mecca.

5 North of Nilaveli (p269) Venturing up the quiet B424 Hwy past empty idyllic beaches, lagoons and ancient cultural sites.

6 Pottuvil Lagoon (p251) Listening to the quiet ripple of the water and watching rainbow-coloured kingfishers flit around mangroves.

7 Batticaloa (p255) Losing yourself in the fort, before losing yourself in the old colonial town, before losing yourself in the beaches of Kallady.

8 Trincomalee (p261) Exploring the fortress, Hindu temples and sights in this historic port.

Monaragala

📞 055 / POP 10,400

If you're coming from the touristy Hill Country, then Monaragala will probably be your first stop in the East. A bustling place with a huge Sunday market, it's a good introduction to the region. The town nestles beneath Peacock Rock, a round-topped forest-covered mountain. Few travellers break their journey in Monaragala these days, but the town's unhurried ambience and leafy avenues have a certain appeal.

Sights & Activities

An easy but beautiful hike starts near the bus station. Walk five minutes past a colourful little Hindu **Ganesh Temple** to the ageing rubber factory, then veer left to a rock-paved footpath that climbs between attractive boulder fields through Monaragala's famous rubber plantations.

A much more demanding trek is the full-day round trip to the summit of the densely forested **Maragala Rock**. There is no set trail up the mountain and you'll need a guide, which can be organised through guesthouses for around Rs 1500 for the four-hour trek. From the summit, you can almost check the surf at Arugam Bay on a clear day.

Wijayawardana (VJ; 📞 077 649 1117) is a friendly English-speaking guide who charges Rs 4000 per day for organising and leading local hikes or trips in a three-wheeler.

Sleeping & Eating

There are a handful of places to stay, most right on the A4 Hwy.

Kanda Land Villa GUESTHOUSE $
📞 055-227 6925; raxawa@yahoo.com; Wellawaya Rd; r with fan/air-con Rs 2000/4000; ❄) This good guesthouse (in the old YMCA building) has four spacious rooms and a lounge, and is the best place to hook up with other travellers. Hikes to Maragala Rock and a rubber plantation are offered, the latter involving a night in a hilltop mountain lodge. There's decent food, too: rice and curry is Rs 350.

Victory Inn HOTEL $
📞 055-227 6100; www.victoryinnmonaragala.com; 5 Wellawaya Rd; r with fan/air-con Rs 3000/4000; ❄🛜) The Victory's smoked-glass facade looks dated. The 16 rooms here (some with balconies and most with wooden trim), are also old-fashioned, though comfortable enough. For a filling meal, the Rs 350 lunch buffet is

a great deal, and the restaurant serves both Western and local dishes. There's a full bar.

Pavilion SRI LANKAN $
(📞 055-227 6127; 1 Pottuvil Rd; mains Rs 250-700; ⊙9am-9pm) In the heart of town at the main circle, the Pavilion has a sit-down restaurant area where you can order the usual standards off a Sri Lankan menu or opt for the good lunch buffet (Rs 350). For more casual eats, the cafe area has rice and curry plus snacks – many good for the road.

🛈 Getting There & Away

Monaragala is a convenient junction town between the east, the south and the hills. Some handy bus routes include the following:

Ampara Rs 130, 2½ hours, hourly

Colombo regular/air-con Rs 345/630, seven hours, hourly

Ella Rs 125, two hours, six daily

Kandy Rs 215, five hours, five daily

Nuwara Eliya Rs 218, four hours, one daily

Pottuvil (for Arugam Bay) Rs 120, 2½ hours, seven daily

Wellawaya (via Buttala; for the Hill Country and south coast) Rs 74, one hour, every 20 minutes

Yudaganawa

In a forest clearing near the village of Buttala, the ancient, ruined dagoba (stupa) of Yudaganawa is an enigmatic and powerful site, well worth a detour.

⭐ **Yudaganawa Dagoba** RUINS
(off A4; Rs 100; ⊙6am-6pm) Only the bottom third remains of this ruined dagoba, but the setting is evocative and your imagination can run riot with thoughts of how amazing it must have looked back in its day. It's thought to have been an earthen stupa built some 2300 years ago, though various alterations over the years – including an ongoing renovation that began in the 1970s – have obscured its history.

The small building in front houses 300-year-old carved-wood Buddhas and some exquisite faded paintings; it probably dates to the 7th century. The entire site is impressively tidy.

Chulangani Vihara RUINS
The moss-encrusted ruins of the small 12th-century Chulangani Vihara have a pudding-shaped dagoba and fragments of a decapitated 7th-century Buddha. It is right before the main Yudaganawa dagoba.

SLEEPING IN THE TREES

The antidote to concrete resort hotels and national parks overrun with hundreds of jeeps, **Tree Tops Jungle Lodge** (☑ 077 703 6554; www.treetops junglelodge.com; Badeyaya; per person all-inclusive 1st night US$150, less each additional night) provides a true back-to-nature experience. Beautifully isolated at the base of the Weliara Ridge, 10km from Buttala, this wilderness lodge offers the chance to marvel at the dawn chorus, listen for wild elephants and be dazzled by the stars of the night sky.

Accommodation is in three spacious, canvas 'chalets' (tented huts on a raised, sand-filled platform with bathrooms). Food (mostly vegetarian), drinks and guided hikes with expert local trackers around the area, including to Arhat Kanda, the scenic 'Hills of Enlightenment', are included. Reserve ahead.

❶ Getting There & Away

Buses from Monaragala to Buttala (Rs 40, 25 minutes) run every 30 minutes, and a three-wheeler from Buttala to Yudaganawa costs Rs 400 return. A three-wheeler from Monaragala costs Rs 1300 return, or around Rs 3000 for both the Yudaganawa sites and Maligawila.

If driving, the turn for Yudaganawa is 1.5km west of Buttala on the A4. Turn north just west of the 232km marker. It's then 1.5km to the site.

Maligawila

Tucked away in the forest of Maligawila village are the extensive 7th-century remnants of Pathma Vihara and its two inscrutable Buddha statues. The surrounding village is so diffuse that it's virtually invisible. As part of your visit, you can also see the picturesque temple of Dematamal Vihara, 10km to the northwest.

Dematamal Vihara BUDDHIST TEMPLE
This gorgeous old temple is set amid a blanket of fertile green. It's roughly midway along the road between Buttala and Maligawila.

Pathma Vihara BUDDHIST SITE
(☉dawn-dusk) FREE Among the trees of verdant Maligawila lie the extensive remains of Pathma Vihara, including two graceful Buddha statues, carved by devotees in the 7th century. Once part of a grand monastic complex, the site is delightful, set in an appealingly shady forest glade.

❶ Getting There & Away

Maligawila is 17km east of Buttala along winding yet decent, roads.

A three-wheeler from Monaragala costs Rs 2000 return, or Rs 3000 for a Monaragala–Maligawila–Yudaganawa–Monaragala loop.

Frequent buses run to Maligawila from both Monaragala (Rs 60, 40 minutes) and Buttala (Rs 35). The journey to Maligawila from Monaragala, past jungles and paddy fields, is as much a highlight as the ruins themselves.

Arugam Bay
☑ 063
Lovely Arugam Bay, a moon-shaped curl of soft sand, is home to a famed point break that many regard as the best surf spot in the country. It's a tiny place, with a population of a few hundred, and everything is dotted along a single road which parallels the coast.

If you're not a surfer, there are plenty of other draws: beachfront guesthouses, oceanside restaurants and a mellow, swing-another-day-in-a-hammock kind of vibe that's totally removed from the brash west-coast beach resorts. The southern half is lined with fishing boats and you can watch the catch being brought in. Shacks for the hard-working crews are at the edge of the sand. At sunset locals gather to watch the reflected glow of the ocean.

Arugam Bay also makes a great base for several adventures in the surrounding hinterland. During the low season (November to April) things get extremely quiet and many places close altogether, but it can also be a serene time to visit, with few tourists and verdant landscapes.

🏃 Activities
Surfing
The famous, long right point break at the southern end of Arugam Bay offers consistent surf from April to September, with some good (and much quieter) days until November. (Some other points don't get going until May or June.)

Locals, as well as some travelling surfers, tend to overhype Arugam Bay as a world class spot, which is slightly fanciful to say the least. However, it consistently produces long and fairly fat slow-breaking waves that are ideal for intermediate surfers. Surf average

1m to 1.5m, with a few rare 2m days. On small days it can be very shallow and sectiony, while at any size there can be lots of boils and bumps to deal with. In season, it can get dangerously busy, and learners should stick to the gentle beach break further inside of the point, also known as **Baby Point**. A bit further south, **Surf Point** is good all-around.

There are many more breaks of similar quality, most of which need a decent-size swell. To the north, these include **Pottuvil Point**, which is a slow right-hander, ideal for learners (it tends to be better later in the season), and Whiskey Point (p252) and Lighthouse Point (p252), which are both also good for beginners. To the south are **Crocodile Rock**, **Elephant Rock** and **Peanut Farm** – the latter has two breaks (one of which is advanced). Further south, accessible via a dirt track, are **Panama**, which quite frankly no one likes, and Okanda (p253), which many consider the best of the lot.

Several surf shops rent out boards, give lessons and do camping trips to some of the further points. Surf camp tours allow you to start surfing first thing in the morning, and you don't have to worry about food or transport, but some surfers find it's just as easy, and cheaper, to make their own way.

Safa Surf School   SURFING
(☑ 077 955 2268; www.safaarugambay.com; Panama Rd; short & long board/body board rental per day Rs 1000/750, lessons from US$30) Well-organised surf shop run by local surfer Fawas Lafeer, offering lessons from native instructors, good-quality board hire and repairs.

Dylan's Surf Company   SURFING
(☑ 072 876 0737; www.dylanssurfcompany.com; Panama Rd; surfboard rental per day from Rs1000; lessons from Rs2500; ⊙ 9am-7pm) Slickly run surf shop with all types of gear. The rental boards are high-quality.

A-Bay Surf Shop   SURFING
(Panama Rd; bodyboard & surfboard rental per day from Rs 1000, lessons from Rs 2500; ⊙ 8am-8pm) A good selection of old boards suitable for learners, plus expert ding-repair service, wax and sunscreen.

Swimming

Seas are rough, but OK for swimming. It would be wise, however, to ask locals before plunging in at lesser-known beaches, where rips might be strong. There's safe swimming in shallow water at the southern end of Arugam Bay, where the beach bends around towards the point. However, this is essentially a fishing beach, so it is not ideal for lounging on.

Nature Watching

Mangrove Ecotours (p251) on Pottuvil Lagoon, just north of the bay, are superb and should not be missed. They are best organised directly via the boatmen. Tours to Kumana National Park (p254), home to leopards, elephants, wild buffalo, crocodiles and outstanding birdlife, can be set up by many guesthouses and hotels.

There's a good chance of seeing crocodiles and elephants around Crocodile Rock on Pasarichenai Beach, just south of Arugam Bay. For **birdwatching**, Pottuvil Lagoon and the ponds and lagoons between Arugam Bay and Panama are prime areas, attracting waterfowl and waders.

🛏 Sleeping

Most local hotels and guesthouses are on the beach or nearby. Many places have a kind-of homespun charm and remain family-owned. However, new glossy, commercial establishments are beginning to take over prime beachfront, often completely filling their small plots and imperilling the mellow vibe.

The term 'cabana' refers to anything from ultra basic plank or *cadjan* (coconut-frond matting) huts to luxurious full-facility bungalows. Low-season discounts of 20% to 50% are common.

★ Ranga's Beach Hut   HUT $
(☑ 077 160 6203; www.arugambaybeachhut.com; off Panama Rd; huts Rs 500-700, cabanas Rs 1000-1500; 🛜) A quirky, locally owned beachside place with loads of atmosphere and a loyal clientele of backpackers and surfers. There's a choice of 22 digs (all built from timber, bamboo and thatch), including tree-house-style cabanas and A-frame huts split across to neighbouring sites. Most are only steps from the ocean. The cheapest huts share bathrooms.

The restaurant to the rear has a large table for socialising, a shady terrace and good-value meals (Rs 400 to 700). Laundry and good local tours, including boat trips on the lagoon, are also offered.

Happy Panda   GUESTHOUSE $
(☑ 077 299 0779; www.happypandahotel.com; off Panama Rd; r Rs 2500-3000; 🛜) A tiny place 50m from the beach with three simple, clean, arty rooms and a very inviting porch-lounge

Arugam Bay

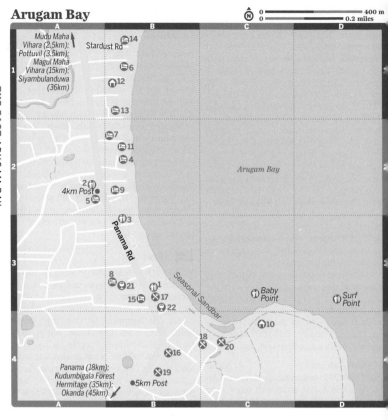

Arugam Bay

area, complete with hammocks. Happy Panda promotes its good breakfasts (Rs 400 to 500; French toast and tropical fruit salad with local curd) at its 'very small cafe'.

★ **Hotel Stay Golden**   INN $
(📞 075 064 4409; www.staygoldenarugam.com
Panama Rd; r US$20-65; ❄️ 🛜) This very larg
site spans the sandy ground from the road t

the beach. There are seven rooms, in wood and stucco cabana-style units. Some have 2nd-floor chill-out decks with hammocks and ocean views. The stretch of beach here is excellent.

⭐ **Sandy Beach Hotel**   HOTEL **$$**
(☑ 063-224 8403; www.arugambay-hotel.com; off Panama Rd; r Rs 4000-10,000; ❄ 🛜) This fine beachside two-storey hotel has 15 rooms – all beautifully presented and immaculately clean, and most boasting minibars, desks and attractive furniture – and one simpler A-frame cabana. The owner, Badur Khan, is totally charming, an educated and well-travelled host who goes the extra mile to ensure your stay is comfortable and loves chatting with his guests. Three rooms have ocean views.

⭐ **Galaxy Lounge**
Beachfront Cabanas   GUESTHOUSE **$$**
(☑ 063-224 8415; www.galaxysrilanka.com; off Panama Rd; cabanas Rs 5000-10,000; ❄ 🛜) A sociable place where many of the 11 spacious cabanas are raised on stilts and hammocks abound between the shore-side trees. Galaxy has charm and ambience: its posher cabanas are attractive. The beachfront location is superb, and the book exchange, board games and regular barbecues are bonuses.

Danish Villa   HOTEL **$$**
(☑ 077 695 7936; www.thedanishvilla.dk; Panama Rd; r Rs 2000-8000; ❄ 🛜) Set back from the west side of the main road, the Danish Villa has a lovely, peaceful garden (except when the odd troop of monkeys whoops by) and a classy, colonial-style ambience. There's a good choice of rooms, friendly staff, and fine Western and Asian food available. Service is pleasant and it gets a lot of repeat business.

Arugam Bay
Surfing Bay Resort   GUESTHOUSE **$$**
(☑ 071 640 9720; off Panama Rd; r Rs 2500-10,000; @ 🛜) Highly popular with travellers thanks to its gregarious vibe, guest kitchen and communal dining. The eight rooms here have bamboo frames topped with a thatch roof – though there are also cabanas and an Arabian-style tent. The restaurant offers good grub (meals Rs 400 to 900). Three of the units in the L-shaped site have fine surf views. Also offers board rental.

Nice Place   GUESTHOUSE **$$**
(☑ 077 341 2240; off Panama Rd; r Rs 3500-8000; ❄ 🛜) This guesthouse has 12 rooms with comfy touches, all about 100m back from

the beach. Recent expansions, however, have filled the site almost to bursting, so it generally feels cramped. Staff, though, are charmers. The cheapest rooms are fan-only.

⭐ **Stardust Beach Hotel**   HOTEL **$$$**
(☑ 063-224 8191; www.arugambay.com; Stardust Rd; cabanas s/d US$35/45, r US$70-80, apt US$95-110; 🛜) This Danish-run place sits at the north end of the bay. There's a magnificent open-sided restaurant-lounge-terrace facing the ocean, perfect for languid meals or a relaxed drink and chatting with friends. Rooms (in a two-storey block) and apartments are charming, with elegant furnishings (though they have cold-water bathrooms), while cabanas are simple, thatched and well-designed. The large grounds are shady. Yoga classes and massages are offered in season.

Hideaway   INN **$$$**
(☑ 063-224 8259; www.hideawayarugambay.com; Panama Rd; r US$40-120; ❄ 🛜 🍽) A fine place with atmospheric, boho accommodation scattered around a huge, shady garden plot. Stylistically, think hand-painted window shutters, tribal textiles and a nod to artful faux-distress. At the rear is a colonial-style villa draped in bougainvillea with four rooms and a restaurant. Some rooms have love porches, with lush views you can enjoy from cane loungers.

Surf N Sun   GUESTHOUSE **$$$**
(☑ 063-224 8600; Panama Rd; cottages incl breakfast US$40-100; ❄ 🛜) Deservedly popular place on the west side of the main road that definitely wins the 'garden of the year' award, with a lush, verdant Eden complete with pond and bursting with tropical greenery. The cottages, some with crazy trees growing out of the showers, are cosy, too. It's a well-designed place with lots of lounge space. Discounts are readily available at quiet times.

Mambo's   HUT **$$$**
(☑ 077 782 2524; www.mambos.lk; s/d from US$45/60, bungalows US$85-140; ❄ 🛜) Surfer favourite, right next to the main point, allowing you to tumble out of bed and land in the line-up. Offers isolated but attractive fan-only rooms in the guesthouse and excellent bungalows with window screens, earthy, simple decor and little porches in a delightful garden setting. The bar-restaurant has hammocks and Saturday-night parties. Prices vary a lot according to the season.

✖ Eating & Drinking

You'll find a great range of places to eat, with global flavours on menus, including lots of seafood. For inexpensive meals, many guesthouse owners will whip up a tasty rice and curry given a little notice.

In season, most places to eat in Arugam Bay serve beer and cocktails. In the low season, however, getting a cold beer can be a surprising challenge.

The rowdier restaurants all organise beach and full-moon parties in season. Many travellers also head north to the famous beach raves at Whiskey Point.

Siripala Place Surf Cafe   SEAFOOD $$

(off Panama Rd; mains Rs 400-1000; ⊙11am-11pm) This cafe is next to the spot where the fish are first hauled out of nets or off boats and loaded onto buffalo-drawn carts. But some stay right here, so the seafood is surf-fresh. The views and breezes from the terrace provide the perfect backdrop.

Meena   SRI LANKAN $$

(Panama Rd; meals Rs 200-550; ⊙8am-10pm) For a good local meal, this small place pumps out all the usual faves including string hoppers, rice and curry, *kotthu* (*rotti* chopped up and mixed with vegies) and fried rice. Sip on a tropical fruit juice while you savour the flavours.

Samanthi's Restaurant   SRI LANKAN $$

(☑077 175 9620; Freedom Beach Cabanas, off Panama Rd; mains Rs 250-700; ⊙8am-10pm; 🌿) Samanthi's, at Freedom Beach Cabanas, is run by a family of cheerful women. Order ahead for rice and curry (around Rs 350); other dishes are the standard A-Bay mix of Western and modified Sri Lankan (meaning toned down). Try the fresh fruit with honey and buffalo curd: the yoghurt is a regional speciality.

Perera Restaurant   SRI LANKAN $$

(Panama Rd; mains Rs 250-500; ⊙8am-10pm) Simple roadside joint that works well for a decent rice and curry and genuine Sri Lankan meals at affordable prices. Also serves some Western food, including breakfasts.

★ Seahorse Inn & Pizzeria   PIZZA $$$

(☑077 172 2356; www.seahorseinnabay.com; Panama Rd; mains Rs 700-1600; ⊙11am-late) The rooms at this inn are a little too close to the road, but the courtyard dining area is in back. It's all open air, with tables and lounging areas. The pizza is not just the best in Arugam Bay, but among the best in the country. It's

thin, crispy and topped with first-class ingredients. Fine drinks can be had from the bar.

★ Hideaway Restaurant   INTERNATIONAL $$$

(☑063-224 8259; www.hideawayarugambay.com; Panama Rd; mains Rs 900-1600; ⊙8am-10pm 🌐) This classy hotel restaurant features a menu that changes daily and lots of fresh locally sourced ingredients. Staff are professional and welcoming. Many dishes feature Mediterranean and East Asian influences There are also lots of vegetarian, vegan and gluten-free choices. The outside tables are in a lovely garden. The property also runs the Hideaway Blue cafe for coffee, paninis, juices and smoothies.

Stardust Restaurant   INTERNATIONAL $$$

(☑063-224 8191; www.arugambay.com; off Panama Rd; meals Rs 800-2000; ⊙11am-10pm; 🌐) For a memorable meal, this superb beachfront hotel restaurant is just the ticket, with expertly executed European and Asian dishes, wine by the bottle (and glass), and terrific juices lassis and espresso coffee. There's a lovely terrace and garden, as well as an open-sided dining area that catches the ocean breeze Excellent fresh seafood.

Surf N Sun   SEAFOOD $$$

(☑063-224 8600; www.thesurfnsun.com; Panama Rd; mains Rs 600-1500; ⊙11am-10pm; 🌐) Relax amid lush gardens on the broad outdoor deck lounge, with low-slung cushions, throw pillows, and candles and lanterns. Good food, too, including seafood, pizza and the occasional barbecue. There is a range of good drinks at the bar.

Hide & Chill Bar   LOUNGE

(☑063-224 8259; Hideaway Hotel, Panama Rd ⊙5pm-midnight) For divine cocktails under the stars, check out Hideaway Hotel's Hide & Chill Bar. There are all sorts of lounging areas where you can sprawl out after a long day and literally let the good times roll. This is Arugam Bay's classiest place for a drink.

Siam View Hotel   BAR

(www.arugam.com; Panama Rd; ⊙11am-late; 🌐 This ungainly-looking, rickety roadside party HQ creaks with action almost around the clock. It hosts a slew of party nights, with everything from tech-house DJs to local reggae bands rocking the dance floor. Expect to make new friends amid the rollicking atmosphere. Should you need it, there's a short menu of Thai-flavoured dishes. Look for the classic British phone box outside.

ℹ Information

Locals are used to seeing Western women in swimwear on the beach, but as this is a conservative Muslim community, consider wearing a T-shirt over your swimsuit, or even a T-shirt and shorts to avoid unwanted attention. It's considered respectful, for both men and women, to dress modestly; when off the beach, don't wander around in swimwear.

There have been cases of attempted sexual assault in secluded areas, particularly south behind the surf point.

If you have a matter for the police, make contact through your guesthouse or hotel.

There are a couple of ATMs on the main drag, Panama Rd. If they're misbehaving, you'll find many more just north in Pottuvil.

ℹ Getting There & Away

For bus transport, nearby Pottuvil is the gateway to Arugam Bay. You'll need to take a three-wheeler from Pottuvil to Arugam Bay (Rs 250). Note that you may need to change buses in Siyambulanduwa to reach Pottuvil.

Private air-con cars to/from Colombo cost about Rs 18,000 and take five to seven hours. They are easily arranged through any place to stay.

Virtually all guesthouses can arrange daily bicycle (about Rs 500) and motorbike (Rs 1000 to 1500) rental.

Direct buses to Pottuvil from other parts of the country are uncommon. However, you can get buses to Siyambulanduwa (a market town 37km to the west), where you can transfer to one of the frequent buses to Pottuvil (Rs 40).

Pottuvil & Around

📄 063

For most tourists, the small town of Pottuvil is simply the transport gateway for Arugam Bay, 3km further south. But Pottuvil has a spectacular lagoon to explore, a very good surf break and some intriguing ancient ruins.

◉ Sights & Activities

Mudu Maha Vihara   RUINS

Out near the ocean east of the centre are the ancient ruins of Mudu Maha Vihara. This moody little site, partly submerged in the encroaching sand dunes, features a fine 3m-high standing Buddha statue flanked by two bodhisattva figures. The **beach** just behind is wide, beautiful and undeveloped, but not safe for swimming. An excellent road leads here from the south.

Pottuvil Point   SURFING

At the end of a scenic peninsula-like stretch of sand, north of the centre and east of the lagoon, is beautiful Pottuvil Point, which is a slow right-hander ideal for learners. There are food vendors here and the luxurious Kottukal Beach House (p252) at the south end of the break. Pottuvil Point is Rs 1000 return by three-wheeler from Arugam Bay.

★ Mangrove Ecotours   TOURS

(📱 076 307 5516, 075 824 1432; 2hr tour per 2 people Rs 4000) These tours are one of the best reasons to visit Pottuvil. Outrigger canoes take visitors punting across the lagoon where you can potter about among the mangroves

THE EAST POTTUVIL & AROUND

WORTH A TRIP

MAGUL MAHA VIHARA

About 12km west of Pottuvil lies **Magul Maha Vihara**, an evocative 5th-century ruin, set in a peaceful forested spot. Probably built by King Dhatusena (r 459–77), the site was most likely part of a royal compound. At the foot of a former shrine is a beautiful and well-preserved moonstone; ringed with elephants, it's unusual for having little riders atop some of them. The site is 800m south of the A4 on a road just west of the 307km post.

There's also an elevated stupa, in good condition and guarded by stone lions, a *vat-adage* (circular relic house) on a cross-shaped platform that – in a stroke of ancient trompe l'oeil – is 'supported' by the stone pillars and crouched lions around its base, and a crudely patched up headless Buddha. Note the streamlined elephant-trunk railings along the site's staircases. Some sources contend that parts of the temple date to the 2nd century BC.

A little further east, between the 308km and 309km posts is **Kotawehera**, the ruined remains of an ancient brick stupa, which enjoys a magnificent situation upon a hilltop. On a clear day, there are spectacular vistas over forests to the wetlands around Pottuvil Lagoon.

Pottuvil

0 — 500 m
0 — 0.25 miles

Whiskey Point (8km);
Lighthouse Point (20km);
A4
Magul Maha Vihara (12km);
Siyambulanduwa (32km)
A4

Kottukal Beach
House (500m);
Pottuvil Point
(2km)
Pottuvil
Lagoon
Mangrove
Ecotours

Cargills

Market

Central Rd

Panama Rd

Mudu Maha
Vihara

1km Post

Arugam
Lagoon

Arugam Bay
(1km)

Arugam
Bay

searching for crocodiles, monkeys and myriad birds. It's best to go early in the morning or last thing in the evening. Ignore touts in Arugam Bay and arrange things here at the waterside office.

Sleeping & Eating

Pretty much everyone stays just south in Arugam Bay, although there is a beach retreat out near the surf break in Pottuvil, and there are a few options further north.

Pottuvil

Kottukal Beach House   BOUTIQUE HOTEL $$$
(📞 077 534 8807; www.jetwinghotels.com; r US$120-150; ❄ 🎤) This intimate, secluded beachfront villa hotel, 5km north of Arugam Bay, is managed by Jetwing, the well-regarded Sri Lankan hotel group. It's perfectly located for sybaritic surfers, as it's at the south end of the Pottuvil Point break. There are just four rooms (all large and with lashings of luxe), all in a two-storey, traditional-style beach villa. The common areas are commodious.

Cargills   SUPERMARKET $
(Panama Rd; ⊙8am-8pm) The reliable local chain has a good-sized outlet near the bus terminal. Stock up on Western foods and groceries.

Whiskey Point

Whiskey Point is a three-minute beach walk north from Pottuvil Point, but much further around by road. The point is good for beginners, and the waves are consistent from late April on. The beach has little shade; there are some unusual bulbous rocks at the southern end. Three-wheelers charge around Rs 1600 return, including three hours' waiting, from Arugam Bay (a 25-minute trip).

Paper Moon Kudils   INN $$$
(📞 071 997 9797; www.papermoonkudils.lk; r from US$60; ❄ 🎤 🏊) Upscale surfers' digs right on the beach. If the water seems too far, there's a big pool. Rooms are in bungalow-style units with thatched roofs. The restaurant and bar are good, with plenty of seafood and drinks specials.

SaBaBa Surf Café   CAFE $$
(📞 077 711 8132; mains Rs 350-1000; ⊙food 7am-10pm) This driftwood-vibe, boho joint is the centre of life in Whiskey Point. It has cushioned seating around its huge wooden deck, good food, beds on the beach and regular parties in surf season (usually Wednesdays and Fridays) with DJs playing full-on house and electronica till dawn (and beyond).

Lighthouse Point

Lighthouse Point, another beginner/medium right-hander, is 26km north of Arugam Bay. It's a lovely, isolated spot and its fine sandy beach is little visited. The surf season is May to October. **Green House**, another point further north, is a 15-minute walk along the beach.

If you can find something open in the low season and aren't worried about riding waves this would make an idyllic total beach escape. It's simply untouched and gorgeous here.

Three-wheelers charge Rs 3500 return from Arugam Bay. The roads on the 4km trek from the A4 are often impassable in the slow season (November to early April).

★ **Hilltop Beach Cabanas**   HUT $$
(📞 077 374 1466; www.hilltopcabanas.com; cabanas Rs US$30-50) This gorgeous place gets rave reviews thanks to the kindness and cooking (most meals Rs 300 to 600) of owner Dilani. Of the cabanas, the one on stilts is best, with million-dollar views shining through seashell garlands. Rooms have minimal solar-powered electricity (lights only), and bathrooms are outside under the trees.

Lighthouse Beach Hut HUT $$

(☑️077 317 9594; www.lighthousebeachhut.com; cabanas from Rs 3500) These eight rustic cabanas sit easy in their rural surrounds right by the break. Kanthan, the owner, worked in Arugam Bay for years, and is well versed in travellers' needs, preparing great local food (meals from Rs 300). It's solar powered, and there are often yoga classes during the main season. The tree-house huts are a climb, but have splendid views.

ℹ️ Getting There & Away

Pottuvil is the gateway to Arugam Bay, but you'll need to take a three-wheeler from Pottuvil to Arugam Bay (Rs 250). Note that you may need to change buses in Siyambulanduwa (p251) to reach Pottuvil.

Direct buses to Pottuvil are limited. Useful private and Central Transport Board (CTB) bus services from the **bus terminal** (Panama Rd):

Batticaloa Rs 160, three hours, 12 daily

Colombo regular/air-con Rs 425/750, eight hours, three daily

Wellawaya (for connections to the south coast) Rs 175, 2½ hours, two daily

Arugam Bay to Panama

Kilometres of untouched beaches stretch south of Arugam Bay. The region is a surfing heaven and a fine place for anyone who likes to stroll endless, perfectly empty sands.

The B374 from Arugam Bay to Panama stays somewhat inland, but intersects with lagoons where you can spot waterfowl, wading birds, water buffalo and even elephants. It's a beautiful, savanna-like landscape. In sleepy Panama, you can explore some of these areas on new eco-tours. It's all a good day trip from Arugam Bay.

🏃 Activities

Close-by surf points, reached via the coast road from Arugam Bay, include **Crocodile Rock** (Rs 800 return by three-wheeler), **Elephant Rock** (Rs 1000) and **Peanut Farm** (around Rs 1000).

At the northern end of Panama's beach, close to the jellyfish-processing plant (jellyfish are sent to East Asia for use in cooking), is a fairly lame right-point break that is good for novice surfers.

Panama Lagoon Eco Safari BOATING

(☑️071 175 6933, 076 719 1015; punchiralasomasiri@gmail.com; Panama Beach Rd; 3hr tours for 4 people from Rs 5000; ⊙tours at 6am & 3pm) Tour the local mangroves by slow boat and experience up close the great diversity of life below the water, on the marshes and in the sky. New floating boats (with ungainly seats) will take you on three-hour wildlife-watching journeys. The office and boats are 3km from town, where the dirt beach road ends at the sand and lagoon. Book in advance.

ℹ️ Getting There & Away

Panama is 13km south of Arugam Bay on the smooth B374. A three-wheeler costs Rs 2000 return. Only a handful of buses come here daily from Pottuvil (Rs 80, one hour).

Panama to Okanda

The road seems to end – literally – in Panama. Continuing south, the grandly designated B355 is really just a rough dirt track for the 16km to the Kumana National Park entrance and Okanda, a minute seasonal settlement for local fishers and an annual pilgrimage destination.

The drive to Okanda is sensational, albeit slow. The scenery is a mix of wetlands and savanna. There is oodles of wildlife and often elephants right in the road (you'll see their droppings everywhere). Watch for the huge and colourful painted storks. Add in a couple of interesting stops and this is a fine continuation of a day trip from Arugam Bay.

Once in Okanda, just a five-minute walk east from the Hindu temple lies a sweeping beige-white **beach** with an excellent right point break popular with surfers fleeing the crowds at Arugam Bay.

Kudumbigala Forest Hermitage RELIGIOUS SITE

(off B355) The superb 47-sq-km site of Kudumbigala Forest Hermitage is a marvellous jumble of forgotten Sigiriya-style outcrops set in dense jungle. Over 200 shrines and hermits' lodgings are set in caves or sealed rocky overhangs here. While none is individually especially interesting, the atmosphere is fantastic and the dagoba-topped summit of the highest rock offers vast panoramas across the eccentric landscape and expansive forest canopy. Kudumbigala is usually visited along with nearby Kumana and Okanda on tours. Drivers know where to stop and how to access it.

Okanda Sri Murugan Kovil HINDU TEMPLE

(off B355, Okanda) Though relatively small, the main temple here has a colourful *gopuram* (gateway tower) and is a major point on the

WORTH A TRIP

KUMANA NATIONAL PARK & KUMANA RESERVE

A lack of crowds, yet an abundance of beautiful scenery and wildlife, make **Kumana National Park** (☑ 063-363 5867; www.dwc.gov.lk; off B355; adult/child US$10/5, vehicle Rs 250, service charge per group US$8, plus overall tax 15%; ⊙ ticket office 6am-4pm) an excellent place to visit, particularly for bird enthusiasts.

This 357-sq-km park, once known as Yala East National Park, is much less frequently visited than its busy neighbour, Yala National Park. Consequently, it's a far less zoo-like experience and it never feels too crowded here, even during high season. Yes, the density of animals is lower, but it's not rare to spot a leopard, along with elephants, crocodiles, turtles, white cobras, wild buffalo and tonnes of birds. About a dozen bears live in the park, but they're rarely seen.

There are modest exhibits at the ticket office near the park entrance.

The park's best-known feature is the 200-hectare Kumana bird reserve, an ornithologically rich mangrove swamp 22km beyond Okanda. May to June is nesting season. There have been sightings of Sri Lanka's very rare black-necked stork, but more commonly spotted, even outside the bird reserve, are Malabar pied hornbills, green bee-eaters, blade-headed orioles and painted storks, among others. Watchtowers provide a terrific perspective for birdwatchers. Visitors regularly report seeing dozens of peacocks here.

Entry fees are myriad, and can really add up. A mandatory guide (who may not speak English) accompanies each vehicle. Guesthouses in Arugam Bay can arrange for a jeep and driver; the going rate is around Rs 8000 per day.

You can arrange camping trips within the park, which allow you to watch animals at dusk and dawn – the two best times.

Camping fees for the national park can seem convoluted. There's a US$15 per person camping fee, a US$20 per person park fee and a US$12 per person service fee, plus 15% tax. Normal park entrance fees are paid on top of all of this.

Overnight camping trips with gear can be arranged in Arugam Bay for about US$300 per two people; this includes morning and evening safaris.

From Arugam Bay, it takes up to 90 minutes to reach the park entrance and ticket office. There are not usually guides and drivers available to hire at the park, so you need to make arrangements in Arugam Bay (easily done, vendors are everywhere). If you just do the Rs 4000 day trip that includes Panama and Okanda, you won't see any of the park as there's nothing of great interest around the entrance.

Pada Yatra pilgrimage to Kataragama. Thousands of pilgrims gather here during the two weeks before the July *poya* (full moon) before attempting the last, and most dangerous, five-day leg of the 45-day trek from Jaffna. Some 25,000 make the trip each year.

ⓘ Getting There & Away

Expect the 16km drive on the rugged B355 from Panama to Okanda/Kumana National Park to take up to one hour each way. Day trips on three-wheelers from Arugam Bay can usually be arranged for about Rs 4000.

Ampara

☑ 063 / POP 44,300

Laid-back Ampara sits in the midst of countryside dappled with paddy fields, lakes and palm groves. Though the town itself won't hold you, the area has a couple of low-key sights.

◉ Sights

Deegawapi   RUINS
(Dighavapi Cetiya; off B92) According to legend, Deegawapi is the one place in southeastern Sri Lanka that the Buddha visited. The stupa was built during the reign of King Saddhatissa (137–119 BC) and patched up in the 2nd and 18th centuries AD before becoming lost in the jungle that was once here. The site is 19km east of Ampara via Eragama and the B439.

Rediscovered in 1916, it has for decades been at the centre of disputes; many Sinhalese say the area's predominantly Muslim population deliberately settled on ancient dagoba (read: Sinhalese) land, while many Muslims, who have lived in the region for centuries, see the claim as a bridgehead for Sinhalese colonisation.

The site might not be interesting enough to warrant the lengthy detour: the vast central red-brick dagoba stub is massive, but it acks a particularly scenic setting. An excavation is ongoing. The small, free **museum** (open 8am to 5pm) has a few archaeological exhibits.

Buddangala Rajamaha Viharaya
BUDDHIST SITE

(Buddhangala Rock Hermitage; off Buddangala Rd; donations accepted; ⊙ 6am-8pm) Rising above the forest north of Ampara, this 150m-high hill offers panoramic views from its rocky summit (including, occasionally, of wild elephants at dusk). Buddangala is said to be 1800 years old, and when the old temple, the remains of which are to the left of the main shrine, was excavated in 1964, a gold casket containing a tooth of the Buddha was discovered. It's now housed inside the dagoba and is on view every June for three days around poya day.

Within an ancient cave overhang, interesting museum-style treasures include a human skeleton, used in meditation. The site is beautiful, but without a guide or English signage, its spiritual relevance is somewhat lost; English-speaking monks may be around to chat. From Ampara, it's 6km northeast; three-wheelers cost Rs 1000 return, including waiting time.

Japanese Peace Pagoda
BUDDHIST SITE

(Sama Chaitya; off Inginiyagala Rd) This pagoda, 4km west of town, is a graceful stupa with a twist or two, including a vaguely Roman-looking colonnade ringing its lower level. Niches containing gilded Buddhas contrast superbly with the whitewashed body of the temple. To reach the site, follow DS Senanayake Rd from the clock tower, which heads towards Inginiyagala, passing scenic Ampara Tank. After 3km, a short right turn brings you to the pagoda.

The incense-smoked image room near the entrance, with its Buddha statues and colourful altar, is also fascinating, especially when the friendly resident monk and nun are drumming and chanting. Birdwatchers find the pagoda platform a handy perch for spotting hundreds of waterbirds that flit about the facing lake. Elephants that once passed here haven't been seen in years.

Sri Manika Pillaiyar
HINDU SITE

(Inginiyagala Rd) The Sri Manika Pillaiyar, which boasts an array of Hindu statuary illuminated by fairy lights, gives Ganesh a lovely view across Ampara Tank. It's about 4km west of the main traffic circle.

🛏 Sleeping & Eating

Ambhasewana Guest House
GUESTHOUSE $

(☏ 063-222 3865; cnr 1st & 4th Aves; r with fan/air-con from Rs 850/1800; ❄) Run by a welcoming family, this basic aqua-and-white guesthouse occupies a shady plot on a quiet side street, two blocks from the town centre. The nine airy rooms are simple and fine.

Terrel Residencies
GUESTHOUSE $$

(☏ 063-222 2215; terrelb@gmail.com; 153 Stores Rd; s/d with fan Rs 2000/2500, with air-con Rs 4750/5250; ⊙ restaurant 11am-10pm; ❄ 🛜) A bustling, attractive place set around a central garden, there are 11 large, clean and comfy rooms here in a two-storey block. The restaurant features lots of Chinese-style mains (Rs 300 to 600). The owner, the genial Terrel, can set up boat safaris (from Rs 4800) in the local lagoons and lakes.

Monty Guest House
HOTEL $$

(☏ 063-222 2169; 1st Ave; r Rs 3000-9000; ❄ 🛜 🏊) In a leafy neighbourhood 1km south of the centre, the likeable Monty is a well-run place. Design-wise, it's slightly quirky: some communal areas resemble a multistorey car park, while the contemporary lobby is tasteful. Fan rooms are functional and a tad dark, but air-con options boast modern furniture and clean lines. The restaurant (mains Rs 250 to 650) serves a range of local and Western dishes on its outdoor terrace or in the dining room.

Keells New City
SRI LANKAN $

(DS Senanayake Rd; meals Rs 150-300; ⊙ 7am-10pm) A good bet for a lunchtime rice and curry, *kotthu* in the evening or quick eats (deep-fried snacks and other small bites) for the times in between. There is an adjoining bakery and supermarket. It's just east of the 1980 clock tower in the heart of town.

❶ Getting There & Away

Ampara's new bus terminal is just south of the main clock tower and has CTB and private services. Services include the following:

Batticaloa Rs 98, three hours, four daily

Kandy Rs 381, 5½ hours, hourly

Pottuvil (for Arugam Bay) Rs 110, three hours, one daily

Batticaloa

☏ 065 / POP 93,600

Historic Batticaloa, Batti for short, enjoys a spectacular position surrounded by lagoons

Batticaloa

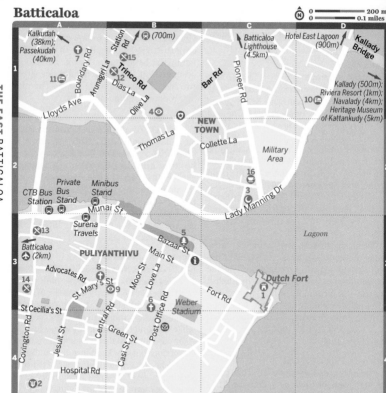

with palm-filtered sunlight glancing off the water. There's a mellow vibe to the town, and the compact centre and its huge fortress and many churches are well worth a half-day's exploration on foot.

To the east of Batti's centre, Kallady is a small town on a long, sandy isthmus. There are some great beaches out here and a growing number of places to stay. Exploring the entire region by bike is a delight.

◉ Sights

There are three distinct areas of interest in Batti, each divided by the waters of the Batticaloa lagoon.

◉ Puliyanthivu

The most atmospheric quarter, and the location of old Batti, is actually an island. It's home to the fort, several colonial-era churches and the bus stands. Wandering around

Old Batti is particularly atmospheric at night: cicadas call and water drips, but not a soul stirs on the eerily empty streets. As well as the landmarks of St Mary's Cathedral and St Anthony's Church, it's worth wandering past colonial survivors such as the **Methodist Church** (Post Office Rd; ⊘8am-5pm) and **St Michael's College** (Central Rd).

★ Dutch Fort   FORT
(Fort Rd, Puliyanthivu; ⊘8.30am-4.30pm) FREE
This once-mighty fort is now home to administrative offices, and though large sections of the structure are crumbling, it's still an evocative sight. It was built by the Portuguese in 1628, but the Dutch took over after just 10 years, followed by the British. Inside the courtyard are some dishevelled, yet colonnaded, old colonial buildings. Look for English cannons, surviving watchtowers and a ruined bell tower. Views across the lagoon are magnificent. There's a tiny **museum** with

Batticaloa

everal intriguing items labelled, alas, only in Tamil and you can glimpse the old jail (now a store).

Mahatma Gandhi Park   PARK
(Bazaar St, Puliyanthivu) This lovely modern park along Old Batti's waterfront is popular with strolling couples and includes features such as the Batticaloa Gate, which was a 19th-century welcoming arch to the harbour.

St Mary's Cathedral   CHURCH
(St Mary's St, Puliyanthivu) The grand, turquoise-coloured St Mary's Cathedral stands out among the many churches in Batti. St Mary's was rebuilt in 1994 following its partial destruction during fighting between local Tamils and Muslims.

Anipandi Sitivigniswara Alayar   HINDU SITE
(Hospital Rd, Puliyanthivu) Of the many Hindu temples, the expanding Anipandi Sitivigniswara Alayar is visually the finest, with a magnificent *gopuram* that's decorated with a riotous festival of intertwined god figures.

◉ New Town

Across the lagoon to the north of Puliyanthivu is the new town, the commercial hub with broad streets lined with shops and banks.

Batticaloa Lighthouse   LIGHTHOUSE
(off B46, Palameenmadu; boat trips Rs 400-3000; ⊙ boat trips 8am-7pm) At the end of a sandbar, surrounded by lagoons and mangroves, this 28m-tall lighthouse dates from 1913. The sheltered coastline around here is a popular family excursion (avoid weekends) and there's a play area for kids. Swimming in the calm water, surrounded by islands and inlets, is the main draw. Three-wheelers charge Rs 500 from Batticaloa. It's 5km northwest from New Town via the B46.

You can go on little boat trips in the surrounding waters, which can be especially scenic near sunset.

Imperial Saloon   SHRINE
(📞 077 248 7815; Trinco Rd; ⊙ 8.30am-8.30pm Mon-Sat, to 1pm Sun) Consider a haircut and head massage (Rs 400) at this utterly bizarre salon, a monument to kitsch. Every centimetre is covered in decorative painting, fake flowers, sequins, filigree, stained glass or tinsel garlands, and at the back of the salon, up towards the faux-sky ceiling, is an interfaith shrine, from where Durga, Mary and the Buddha keep an eye on things.

Our Lady of Sorrows   CHURCH
(Trinco Rd) Of the dozens of churches, the most eye-catching is the huge cerulean blue, eight-sided, unfinished Our Lady of Sorrows.

Auliya Mosque   MOSQUE
(Lady Manning Dr) The tiny Auliya Mosque has a curious green minaret. It's a great place to observe the Dutch Fort over the water.

◉ Kallady

On the east side of Batti is Kallady, which you reach on foot or by bike via the picturesque 1924 bridge (cars use a modern one). It has a busy commercial strip, leafy older quarters and large expanses of beach. You can see the effects of the 2004 tsunami in places, where the land still looks washed bare.

★ Heritage Museum of Kattankudy   MUSEUM
(📞 065-224 8311; A4; adult/child Rs 250/100; ⊙ 9am-6pm Sat-Thu) This fine new museum plunges deep into the history of Muslims and Arab traders locally. Spread over three floors, it tells a compelling story about centuries of culture through models, displays, recreations, artefacts and more. The English-speaking staff are very happy to show you around.

THE EAST BATTICALOA

Kallady & Navalady
Peninsula Beach   BEACH
This long beach follows the peninsula all the way north to the end. The swimming is usually good. With a bike, you can explore the beach, which has access at numerous places from Navalady Rd. Some areas have more shade than others.

Thiruchendur Murugan
Alayam Temple   HINDU SITE
(Navalady Rd) Built in 1984 as a stopping point on the Pada Yatra pilgrimage to Kataragama, the temple's Murugan image is said to have opened its own eyes before the painter could do the job. The structure was slammed by the tsunami, leaving its small *gopuram* leaning at an alarming angle. The colourful leaning tower sits near the beach between Third and Fourth Cross Sts in Kallady.

Activities & Tours

Exploring the area is one of the best activities in Batti, as is finding your perfect beach. You can usually hire a bike through your accommodation; the Kallady roads in particular are bike-friendly mellow.

Guests of the Riviera Resort can rent kayaks to explore the lagoon.

Sri Lanka Diving Tours   DIVING
(☎077 764 8459; www.srilanka-divingtours.com; Deep Sea Resort, off Navalady Rd, Kallady; 2-tank dive boat trip from US$70; ☺8am-6pm Mar-Sep) This professional dive school specialises in wrecks, and Batticaloa has a world-class one: the HMS *Hermes,* a British aircraft carrier that was sunk by Japanese bombers in 1942. This dive is for tech divers only (the five-day certification course, for very advanced divers, is also offered here), but there are several other dives in the area for those less advanced. There are also rooms you can stay in as part of packages.

★ East N' West On Board   CYCLING
(☎065-222 6079; www.eastnwestonboard.com; 65 Thiruchentoor Beach Rd, Kallady; bike rental per day Rs 500, tours for 2 people from Rs 7000; ☺8am-6pm Mon-Sat) A fantastic resource, this Sri Lankan–French initiative promotes tourism in the Batti region. Among the many services are bike rentals, free maps and plenty of advice. It also offers a range of local tours by bike and three-wheeler that visit villages and households where you can learn about local culture and food.

Sleeping

The Kallady area is pleasant, with the lagoon on one side and the beach on the other.

The cultural tour group East N' West On Board can arrange for stays at several cute and comfortable Kallady homestays. These are highly recommended and cost Rs 6000 for two people half-board.

★ Riviera Resort   HOTEL
(☎065-222 2165, 065-222 2164; www.riviera-online. com; New Dutch Bar Rd, Kallady; s/d with fan from Rs 2500/3000, with air-con from Rs 4500/5000; ❅@☎) Perched at the water's edge with serene views of Kallady Bridge and the lagoon, the Riviera is a peaceful, relaxing place to stay. The accommodation has some old-fashioned charm, especially the units with large patios. It's easy to overlook a slightly faded feel. There's a well-stocked bar and a restaurant (p259) offering good local cooking. Service is excellent.

Kayaks are available for hire (single/double Rs 500/800) for exploring the lagoon and there's also a good range of bikes.

Treatooo Lagoon View   GUESTHOUSE
(☎065-222 8929; www.treatooo.com; 103 Lady Manning Drive, New Town; s/d with fan from Rs 3000/3500, with air-con from Rs 5000/6000; ❅☎) This welcoming guesthouse has eight spacious rooms named after birds, some of which have balconies with lagoon views. The family owners look after travellers well, offering tasty local, Chinese and Western dishes (Rs 250 to 500), as well as good transport information and laundry. Its waterside location is restful.

YMCA   GUESTHOUSE
(☎065-222 2495; www.ymcabatticaloa.org; Boundary Rd, New Town; s/d with fan from Rs 1200/1500, with air-con from Rs 2000/2600; ❅☎) If you're really watching the rupees, well the Y is your place. The location is central, but quiet, and the staff are friendly, although, the large impersonal block offers near zero in terms of ambience; rooms are bare and the attached bathrooms are cold-water only.

Naval Beach Villa   GUESTHOUSE
(☎077 469 2121; School Rd, Kallady; s/d with fan from Rs 2000/2500, with air-con from Rs 4500/5000; ❅☎) A small, olive-green-walled compound some 100m from the beach. This is a convivial spot with some shared kitchen and grilling facilities. Rooms are basic, but large, and attract a fair number of budget-minded European

roup travellers. The family that runs it are helpful charmers. Enjoy the hammocks.

Hotel East Lagoon HOTEL **$$$**
(065-222 9222; www.hoteleastlagoon.lk; Munai Lane, Uppodai Lake Rd, New Town; r Rs 7200-12,000; ❄🛜☒) This modern four-storey colonial-style place enjoys a serene lagoon-side setting 1km northeast of the centre, with fine views over the water to Kallady from its spacious rooms. There's a good restaurant with an excellent lunch buffet (Rs 900) for great local food, including lots of vegetarian choices.

Naaval HOTEL **$$$**
(077 068 4905; 74/1 Mugathuwaram Rd, Kallady; r from US$50; ❄🛜) This new resort is near the northern tip of the peninsula. The land narrows here, so it has views of both the lagoon and the ocean. The 10 units have terraces and balconies plus mod cons. It's still a bit antiseptic, but there's no beating the pristine facilities.

🍴 Eating & Drinking

Only the higher-end hotels have bars; most restaurants do not serve alcohol.

⭐ Sun Shine Cafe SRI LANKAN **$**
(065-465 0650; 136 Trinco Rd, New Town; meals Rs 180-400; ⊙10am-10pm) Sun Shine has quite a reputation, and it's easy to see why. This modern, clean and welcoming place covers all bases with an amazing display of biryanis, curries (try the mutton) and pilau rice, as well as burgers, cakes and snacks (samosas for Rs 25), juices and lassis. The bakery sells good cupcakes.

Euro Veg Restaurant SRI LANKAN **$**
(Covington Rd, Puliyanthivu; meals Rs 180-450; ⊙8am-10pm) Eating here is a full sensory experience; the food has some spicy dash. There's excellent biryanis, noodles and *kotthu* served in bright surrounds.

Eat Me SRI LANKAN **$**
(Trinco Rd, New Town; mains Rs 150-400; ⊙9am-9pm) If only they sold T-shirts! This cute little shopfront sells various types of rice and curry in shiny surrounds. The motto: 'I'm healthy and tasty'. Indeed.

⭐ Riviera Resort SRI LANKAN **$$**
(065-222 2164; www.riviera-online.com; New Dutch Bar Rd, Kallady; meals Rs 350-1000; ⊙noon-3pm & 5-10pm; 🛜) Dining here evokes memories of colonial times, as waiters fix you up with a drink (ideally a gin and tonic) on the verandah, take your order and beckon you into the dining room (or onto the terrace), then set you up with all manner of dishes. The food is well worth the wait, including excellent crab curries and seafood.

RN Buffet & Take Away SRI LANKAN **$$**
(065-222 2684; 42 Covington Rd, Puliyanthivu; meals Rs 150-650; ⊙7.30am-6pm) A wonderful find, this hyper-busy little olive-coloured eatery, run by a delightful, industrious couple, has an excellent takeaway section (vegie/meat meals Rs 120/200) popular with office workers. Upstairs is a buffet restaurant; the lunchtime buffet (Rs 650) includes fish, chicken and lots of vegetarian dishes.

Tomato Restaurant INTERNATIONAL **$$**
(065-465 0650; 136 Trinco Rd, New Town; meals Rs 300-650; ⊙10am-10.30pm; 🛜) When the tropical heat becomes too much, the sanctity of air-conditioned Tomato is refreshingly welcome. This refined restaurant has Western food (pasta, sandwiches, salads, seafood and grilled lamb chops) as well as northern Indian specials from the tandoori oven (after 6pm), including naan bread and tikkas. No alcohol is served, but there's a good choice of juices. It's above Sun Shine Cafe.

Café Chill CAFE
(077 777 9598; 9 Pioneer Rd, New Town; ⊙9.30am-9pm Sun-Fri; 🛜) A meeting point for Batti's version of hipsters, this rustic little cafe serves fab coffee, tea (including herbal varieties), juices and lassis in a relaxed semi-alfresco setting close to the lagoon. Food, such as burgers, fries and samosas, is also available.

ℹ️ Information

There are numerous ATMs in all commercial areas.

Police station (Bar Rd; ⊙24hr)
Post office (Post Office Rd, Puliyanthivu; ⊙7am-8pm Mon-Fri, to 6pm Sat, to 5pm Sun) In a handy location.
Tourist information booth (Bazaar St, Puliyanthivu; ⊙hours vary) Has good maps, but keeps irregular hours.

ℹ️ Getting There & Away

AIR

The commuter carrier **Cinnamon Air** (Map p60; 011-247 5475; www.cinnamonair.com) links Colombo with Batticaloa once daily. Flights take one hour and fares start at Rs 40,000. Flights use Batticaloa Airport, which is 2km west of Puliyanthivu.

BUS

CTB buses, private buses and minibuses have adjacent bus stations on Munai St. Combined CTB and private departures include the following:

Ampara Rs 110, three hours, three daily

Badulla Rs 260, six hours, five daily

Colombo Rs 365, nine hours, three daily

Jaffna (via Vavuniya) Rs 515, seven hours, four daily

Polonnaruwa Rs 130, two hours, every 30 minutes

Pottuvil (for Arugam Bay) Rs 160, three hours, 12 daily

Trincomalee Rs 200, four hours, every 30 minutes

Valaichchenai (for Passekudah and Kalkudah) Rs 50, 50 minutes, every 20 minutes

Most people prefer taking a private bus to Colombo:

Surena Travels (☑ 065-222 6152; Munai St, Puliyanthivu; ⊙ 4.30-8.30pm) Ordinary/air-con Rs 600/1100, nine hours, two daily

TRAIN

Book ahead at the **railway station** (☑ 065-222 4471; Station Rd, New Town; ⊙ ticket office 8.30am-6pm) for trains to Colombo (1st/2nd/3rd class Rs 1250/630/480, nine hours, twice daily). Book the night train at least one week in advance.

Kalkudah & Passekudah

☑ 065

These spectacular back-to-back beaches, 34km north of Batticaloa, present as stark – and confusing – a juxtaposition as you could imagine. At the northern tip of the peninsula on a tightly enclosed bay, the breathtaking white sands of sickle-shaped **Passekudah beach** are being developed as a kind of mini-Cancun, a government-driven 'Special Economic Zone' with oodles of luxury hotels planned to ring the bay. With the resorts stretching into the distance, Passekudah's extremely shallow water heats up to bathtub temperatures on sunny days (you'll have to wade out some distance for a good swim). There's also lots of sharp coral mixed in with the sand, so take care if barefoot.

In contrast, **Kalkudah beach**, 2km east and south along the ocean, is mostly deserted – save for the odd fisherman and his boat. Good roads run inland from the sand and it may not be long before hotels again line the shore the way they did in places before the 2004 tsunami. In the meantime, while there's little shade, it's a delight to explore;

just wander along the shore until you find your own private patch of sand. Anchoring these two areas is the unappealing town of Valaichchenai, which is inland, has the bus stop and train station, and sits near the junction of the A11 and A15 highways.

◉ Sights

Coconut Cultural Park PARK
(☑ 065-365 9028; Coconut Board Rd, Passekudah; Rs 1300; ⊙ 7.30am-4.30pm Mon-Sat) Just behind the resorts, this attraction is dedicated to the coconut, surely the world's most remarkable plant, and inexorably linked with Sri Lanka (its cultivation is mentioned in the Mahavamsa). You can wander under coconut groves and learn about the coconut palm's many uses – timber for housing and shelter, coir rugs and rope, cooking oil and toddy. The coconut ice cream is a treat. And it's not just coconuts: other useful plants such as the papaya get their due, too.

🛏 Sleeping & Eating

Luxury resorts line the Passekudah shoreline. Budget and midrange places are concentrated inland along the Valaichchenai–Kalkudah Rd and in the nearby sandy lanes inland from Passekudah beach.

No matter where you stay, both beaches are very accessible. You'll never be more than 2km from a patch of sand.

Note that the Passekudah resort area – and its artful light poles lining Coconut Board Rd – is spread out. It's not really a place where you'll wander from resort to resort.

All the places to stay have restaurants where the prices tend to reflect the room rates. There is no strip of traveller-friendly cafes – at least for now.

Moni Guest House GUESTHOUSE
(☑ 077 392 6833, 065-365 4742; off Valaichchenai-Kalkudah Rd; s/d with fan from Rs 2000/2500, with air-con from Rs 3000/3500; ❄ 🛜) Moni is in the midst of things, but has a good family feel. The nine rooms are basic, but kept tidy, and the family owners prepare filling meals, including tasty fish curries and huge breakfasts. The garden is restful; watch the coconuts fall.

New Land Guesthouse GUESTHOUSE
(☑ 065-568 0440; 283 Valaichchenai-Kalkudah Rd, Passekudah; s/d with fan from Rs 2000/2500, with air-con from Rs 3000/3500; ❄ 🛜) A welcoming family-run place with a selection of very clean rooms with mosquito nets and wooden

urnishings; those in the new block are a bit maller. The seafood restaurant wins kudos; ook the spectacular lobster dinners one day n advance.

★ Roy's Inn
GUESTHOUSE **$$**

(☑ 077 503 6696, 065-205 0223; Mariyamman Ko-il Rd, Passekudah; s/d with fan from Rs 3000/3500, with air-con from Rs 4500/5000; ❄️🛜) The cottage-style rooms here are dotted around a pretty, peaceful garden. All the units boast high ceilings, terraces and good-quality beds and mattresses. It's signposted down a sandy lane, 300m inland from Passekudah Beach.

Nandawanam Guesthouse
GUESTHOUSE **$$**

(☑ 065-225 7258; www.nandawanam.blogspot.com; off Valaichchenai-Kalkudah Rd, Passekudah; r Rs 3300-7000; ❄️🛜) This green villa is set well back from the road in beautiful gardens. Rooms vary – those on the ground floor are more traditional, while upstairs they're modern – but all are very clean, tidy and boast good thick mattresses and cable TV. Meals are good; it also rents bikes.

★ Laya Waves
BOUTIQUE HOTEL **$$$**

(☑ 011-232 1122, 065-205 0500; www.layahotels.lk; Valaichchenai-Kalkudah Rd, Kalkudah; r from US$70; ❄️🛜🏊) Right at the northern end of Kalkudah Beach, this sprightly hotel is very well run. There are only eight rooms; all have terraces and views of the ocean (get a 2nd-floor unit for the very best view). For the moment, you have most of this endless beach to yourself.

Anilana Pasikuda
RESORT **$$$**

(☑ 065-203 0900; www.anilana.com/pasikuda; 14 Hotel Development Rd, Passekudah; r US$90-200; ❄️@🛜🏊) Around the bluff from the main trip, this tasteful beachfront resort offers modern styling tempered with thatched roofs and natural materials. All accommodation (in the main building or shore side) features hip lighting and modish bathrooms and is set around a lovely pool perfect for laps. There's a well-regarded spa.

Uga Bay
RESORT **$$$**

(☑ 065-567 1000; www.ugaescapes.com; Coconut Board Rd, Passekudah; r from US$140; ❄️🛜🏊) On a huge beachside plot in the middle of the resort strip, this luxury hotel offers beautifully finished rooms and suites (all with sea views) that combine dark wood, marble and contemporary detailing to achieve a pleasing vision of tropical chic. Kids will love the massive pool, and there's a spa and gym.

Anantaya Resort
RESORT **$$$**

(☑ 065-223 3200; www.anantaya.lk/passikudah; Coconut Cultivation Board Rd, Passekudah; r from US$140; ❄️@🛜🏊) Slightly smaller than its luxe brethren, the Anantaya is at the northern end of the strip and is fairly isolated from any crowds. The 55 rooms are scattered about the large site in a variety of soaring and dramatic two- and three-storey buildings. The free-form pool winding between the units is one of the area's largest.

❶ Getting There & Away

The town of Valaichchenai is the gateway to the beaches. Trains stop at the **Valaichchenai Railway Station** (Railway Rd, Valaichchenai; ⊙ ticket office 8am-6pm), which is just north of the A15. Services:

Batticaloa 1st/2nd/3rd class Rs 110/60/30, 45 minutes, twice daily

Colombo 1st/2nd/3rd class Rs 1230/630/380, eight hours, twice daily

There's no bus terminal, but buses do stop on the main road near the train station. Three-wheelers charge Rs 200 for the short hop between Valaichchenai and Passekudah or Kalkudah. Buses include the following:

Batticaloa Rs 50, one hour, every 30 minutes

Polonnaruwa Rs 97, 1½ hours, every 30 minutes

Trincomalee Rs 160, three hours, every 30 minutes

Trincomalee

☑ 026 / POP 101,100

Trincomalee (Trinco) sits on one the world's finest natural harbours. This historic city is old almost beyond reckoning: it's possibly the site of historic Gokana in the Mahavamsa (Great Chronicle), and its Shiva temple the site of Trikuta Hill in the Hindu text Vayu Purana. Most people just pass through the city on their way to the nearby beaches of Uppuveli and Nilaveli, but the town has some charm, plenty of history and an interesting melange of people.

Trincomalee's superb deep-water port has made it the target for all manner of attacks over the centuries: by the British takeover in 1795, the city had changed colonial hands seven times. It's easy to spend a day or more exploring the ins and outs of the myriad waterfronts and the fort and its famous temple.

◉ Sights & Activities

Trinco's most famous beaches are at nearby Uppuveli and Nilaveli, but picturesque Dutch

Trincomalee

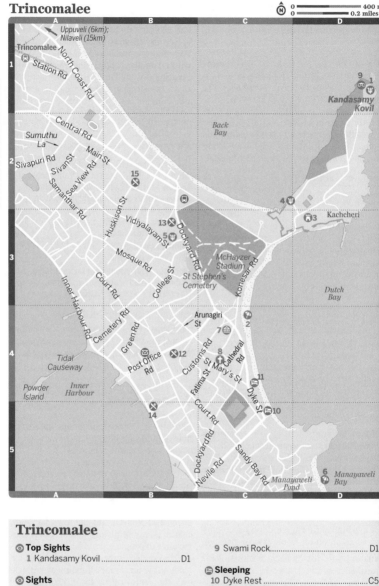

N

0 — 400 m
0 — 0.2 miles

Uppuveli (6km);
Nilaveli (15km)

Trincomalee
Station Rd
North Coast Rd
Central Rd
Sumuthu La
Sivapuri Rd
Sivan St
Samanthar Rd
Sea View Rd
Main St
Huskison St
Vidiyalayam St
Mosque Rd
Court Rd
College St
Inner Harbour Rd
Cemetery Rd
Green Rd
Post Office Rd
Customs Rd
Fatima St
St Mary's St
Court Rd
Dockyard Rd
Nevile Rd
Sandy Bay Rd
Dockyard Rd
Konesar Rd
Arunagiri St

Back Bay
Kandasamy Kovil
Kachcheri
Dutch Bay
McHayzer Stadium
St Stephen's Cemetery
Tidal Causeway
Powder Island
Inner Harbour
Manayaweli Pond
Manayaweli Bay

Trincomalee

Bay isn't bad, while Manayaweli Cove is quite good. Note that Inner Harbour and Back Bay are too polluted for swimming.

★ Kandasamy Kovil   HINDU SITE
(Koneswaram Kovil; Fort Frederick) This revered temple at the summit of a rocky outcrop is one of Sri Lanka's *pancha ishwaram,* five historical Hindu temples dedicated to Shiva and established to protect the island from natural disaster. It houses the *lingam* (Hindu phallic symbol) known as the Swayambhu Lingam. It's an ancient place of worship, but the current structure dates to 1952. Pilgrims from across the nation flock here; its *puja* (prayers) at 6.30am, 11.30am and 4.30pm are always well attended.

Fort Frederick   FORTRESS
(Konesar Rd) FREE Occupying the neck of a narrow peninsula, Fort Frederick has been a defensively important site for centuries. A fortress was initially constructed here by the Portuguese in 1623 and later rebuilt by the Dutch. The British took over in 1782 (look out for royal insignias crowning the tunnel-like gateway that pierces the fort's massively stout walls).

The fortress is used today by the Sri Lankan military, but you're able to explore most of the fort by foot or car. Assorted cannons and artillery are dotted around the enclave, which also contains a small number of spotted deer grazing under huge banyan trees.

Among the colonnaded colonial-era buildings, the impressive Georgian-style mansion (not open to visitors) is **Wellesley House**, named after a Duke of Wellington. It dates from the late 1700s. There's also a big standing **Buddha statue** at the **Gokana Temple**, from where there are fine views of Trinco and the coastline.

Maritime & Naval History Museum   MUSEUM
(Dockyard Rd; ⊙ 8.30am-4.30pm Wed-Mon) A grand 18th-century Dutch colonial building has been renovated and turned into a museum. Displays on the ground floor cover Sri Lankan naval history back to Marco Polo's time. Upstairs there's a lot of useful info on the flora and fauna of the east coast, especially that of Pigeon Island. Wide porches are fine places to pause and take in the views.

Manayaweli Cove   BEACH
(Sandy Bay Rd) Manayaweli Cove is an appealing curl of fishing beach with clean sand where you can also swim in the clear water; reach it by strolling past Manayaweli Pond, aka Dhoby Tank.

Dutch Bay Beach   BEACH
Right in the centre of Trinco is the attractive and picturesque Dutch Bay. Swimming is possible despite sometimes dangerous undertows. However, it's more a place for strolling with an ice cream from the many vendors.

St Mary's Cathedral   CHURCH
(St Mary's St; ⊙ 8am-5pm) Of the city's churches, the 1852 Catholic St Mary's Cathedral is particularly attractive, with a sky-blue neo-baroque frontage and a tiled, towered rear. Inside, portraits of saints gaze out between the columns.

Kali Kovil   HINDU TEMPLE
(Dockyard Rd) Kali Kovil has the most impressive, eye-catching *gopuram* of Trinco's many Hindu temples. It's always busy.

🛏 Sleeping

Most travellers (rightly) prefer the beachside accommodation in Uppuveli, just 6km north. But you can savour the charms of Trinco by staying right in town. There are some good guesthouses on Dutch Bay Beach.

★ Dyke Rest   INN $
(☑ 026-222 5313; www.facebook.com/DykeRest; 228 Dyke St; r with fan Rs 1500-2500, with air-con from Rs 4400; ❄ 🛜) Management couldn't be better at this two-storey gem with a great spot right on the beach. It doesn't look like much from the front, but head inside and check out the view. Two rooms upstairs have air-con, share a bathroom and have views. There's a lounging porch where you can gaze at the fort while you write your book.

DON'T MISS

WHALE WATCHTOWER

Jutting into the ocean on the east side of the city of Trincomalee, **Swami Rock (Fort Frederick)** has been declared by oceanographers the world's greatest vantage point for blue-whale spotting.

Blue whales are present in the seas off Trinco all year round, though sightings are most frequent between the months of February and November. Sperm whales also regularly cruise by.

So while you're exploring Kandasamy Kovil, spare some time to gaze at the big blue offshore for spouting cetaceans. And bring binoculars if you can.

THE EAST TRINCOMALEE

DRIVING SOUTH FROM TRINCO

Drive the 110km on the A15 Hwy nonstop between Trincomalee and Kalkudah and you can do the trip in two hours. But given the myriad attractions worth exploring tucked away in pockets off the road, you can also make an entire day of it.

Heading out of Trinco, the A15 loops around the fringes of giant bite-shaped Trincomalee Bay, passing the airport. After 17km there's a turn-off on the left for **Marble Beach** (📞026-302 1000; www.marblebeach.lk; off A15; per person Rs 20, parking Rs 50; ⊙dawn-dusk), signpost-ed just before the Kinniya bridge, a glorious cove bookended by wooded headlands. Run by the air force, there is a resort at the north end of the cove. But spend your time at the south end in the perfect water, enjoying the emerald and blue views and the sight of the odd passing freighter. Note that on weekdays, it can get overrun by school groups.

Continuing south over the Kinniya bridge, the A15 hugs the coastline until the Muslim town of **Mutur**, which has shops where you can buy refreshments.

Pushing on, turn off the A15 just south of the 101km post, then follow a partially paved road for 7.5km to **Seruwawila Rajamaha Viharaya**. (From the south, turn off just south of the 89km post and drive for 7km along mostly paved roads.) This is one of the holiest Buddhist monuments in Sri Lanka, founded in the 2nd century BC, but only redis-covered, and reconstructed, in the 1920s. The stupa pokes above the scrubby plains and was renovated in 2009. The tiny village here has snack vendors.

Continuing south, the A15 cuts through an ocean of rice paddies and then a very sparsely populated region of scrub bush and wetlands.

Just after the town of Vakarai and then the Panichchankeni bridge, at the 58km post, turn towards the ocean and drive 2.5km to the idyllic and untrammelled **beach**. Should you decide to stay here (and who wouldn't?), **Tranquility Coral Cottages** (📞011-262 5404, 077 735 4894; www.tccvakarai.com; Sallithievu Rd, Panichchankeni, Vakarai; cottages incl meals per person from Rs 8000) 🍃 offers an unplugged, off-the-grid beach experience. Here you can enjoy empty white sands, explore the Panichchankeni lagoon, snorkel the reefs around Sallithievu (an islet connected by a sandbar to the mainland) and taste home-style cooking. The wooden cottages are spacious, but perhaps a little pricey for true Robinson Crusoes.

Back on the A15, it's only 20km south to the twin beaches of Kalkudah and Passekudah.

Hotel Blue Ocean GUESTHOUSE $
(📞026-222 5578; 290 Dyke St; r from Rs 1500) Right on Dutch Bay Beach, this simple guest-house has a narrow front on the sand. The basic rooms, spread across three storeys, are clean.

✗ Eating

Ajmeer Hotel SRI LANKAN $
(Newraheemiya; 65 Post Office Rd; mains Rs 150-400; ⊙5.30am-10.30pm) Excellent rice and curry. The refills seem to never end, portions are enormous and the vibe is friendly.

Anna Pooram
Vegetarian Restaurant SOUTH INDIAN $
(415 Dockyard Rd; mains Rs 150-400; ⊙8am-10pm) Bustling vegie eatery excelling in Tamil dish-es, it's always packed at lunchtime (easy, given its small size). Famous for its *sambar* (soupy lentil dish with veg) and rice and cur-ry. It has a couple of tables, but it's mostly popular for its takeaway trade.

New Parrot Restaurant SRI LANKAN $
(📞026-326 7777; 96 Main St; mains Rs 150-500; ⊙8am-9pm Mon-Sat, to 4pm Sun) Head up the stairs to this tidy place that offers reliably good noodles, rice, *kotthu,* soup and 'devilled' dishes. Try the special fried rice with chicken or omelette. It's above a Nations Trust Bank.

Dutch Bank Cafe INTERNATIONAL $$$
(📞077 269 0600; 88 Inner Harbour Rd; meals Rs 600-1600; ⊙8am-10pm; 🛜) Central Trinco's most polished restaurant is in a historic build-ing that combines dramatic architectural fea-tures with contemporary design. Menu-wise there's everything from pizza, burgers and noodle dishes to Sri Lankan specials. Drinks-wise you'll find espresso and cappuccino, good juices and shakes. It faces the Inner Harbour and has air-con.

ⓘ Information

ATMs are common in Trinco. There is a **Post office** on Post Office Rd (⊙7am-7pm Mon-Sat, 8.30am-4.30pm Sun)

ℹ️ Getting There & Away

AIR

The commuter carrier **Cinnamon Air** (Map p60; ☏ 011-247 5475; www.cinnamonair.com) links Colombo with Trinco once daily. Flights take one hour and fares start at Rs 40,000. The airport is a 12km drive west of town.

BUS

CTB and private bus departures all use the same **bus terminal** (Dockyard Rd). Services include the following:

Anuradhapura Rs 200, four hours, six daily

Batticaloa Rs 200, four hours, every 30 minutes

Colombo regular Rs 450, seven hours, hourly

Colombo (air-con; book in advance) express/luxury Rs 600/950, six hours, six daily

Jaffna (via Vavuniya) Rs 320, seven hours, nine daily

Kandy Rs 250, 5½ hours, seven daily

TRAIN

There are two trains daily between Trincomalee and Colombo Fort, including a direct overnight sleeper service. Reserve at **Trincomalee station** (☏ 026-222 2271; Station Rd; ⊙ bookings 8am-4pm). You can also travel to Polonnaruwa and Batticaloa via a change in Gal Oya.

Colombo sleeper 1st-/2nd-/3rd-class sleeper Rs 1250/550/350, eight hours; reserve at least one week ahead

Colombo unreserved (transfer in Gal Oya) 2nd/3rd class Rs 480/305, eight hours

Uppuveli
☏ 026

Uppuveli, just 6km north from Trincomalee, is a fun little coastal enclave consisting of a fine beach of golden sand, a few hundred locals, a score of places to stay and eat, plus a seemingly unlimited supply of fresh seafood.

Although not exactly drop-dead gorgeous, it does have a distinctly local charm, an intimate feel and some good-value accommodation. It's many travellers' favourite hang-out in the East.

◉ Sights & Activities

Dive shops are mostly seasonal, generally opening during the local high season from April to October.

★ Uppuveli Beach   BEACH

Just an all-around great beach. The sand is honey-beige and the swimming generally good. There's always a pleasant vibe here as mellow locals wander about and travellers make new friends. Beach dogs try for a few laughs by snatching your T-shirt while you're swimming. A few simple cafes provide essentials.

Commonwealth War Cemetery   CEMETERY

(B424; ⊙dawn-dusk) For a break from the beach, stroll up to this beautifully kept cemetery. This is the last resting place for 364 Commonwealth servicemen who died at Trinco during WWII, most of them during a 1942 Japanese raid that sank over a dozen vessels.

You'll be shown around by the amiable caretaker, whose knowledge of the cemetery is encyclopedic – he'll lead you to specific graves, or those of the 13 nationalities buried here.

Salli Muthumariamunam Kovil   HINDU SITE

This beachfront temple is 4km by road from Uppuveli, but only a short wade (or hop by boat if the tide is high) from the north end of Uppuveli beach. It's across Fishermen's Creek, masked from view by green-topped rocks.

★ Angel Diving   DIVING

(☏ 071 275 8499; www.facebook.com/angeldiving srilanka; Uppuveli Beach; 2-tank boat dives from US$80; ⊙8am-6pm Apr-Sep) A very popular dive shop that is praised for its customer service. Located along the beach near the Golden Beach Cottage, it organises all manner of trips, including to Pigeon Island and the fabled HMS *Hermes*.

🛏️ Sleeping

There is a line of good-value places to stay right on the sand, with another line-up right behind.

Aqua Inn   HOTEL $

(☏ 071 251 9749; www.aquahotel-trincomalee.com; 12 Alles Garden; s/d with fan from Rs 2500/3000, with air-con from Rs 4500/5000; ✹ ☎ ☀) First the good points: it's cheap, sociable and the beachfront location is superb. Prepare yourself, however, for the fearsomely ugly concrete accommodation block and distinctly grim budget rooms (with a dim, bare light bulb for 'decor'); air-conditioned options are slightly better.

★ Coconut Beach Lodge   GUESTHOUSE $$

(☏ 026-222 4888; coconutbeachlodge@gmail.com; r Rs 5000-8000; ✹☎) Locally owned place with a blissful beachfront location. The garden compound is a delight; at its rear is an elegant villa-style structure for home-cooked meals and hanging out with other guests.

Uppuveli

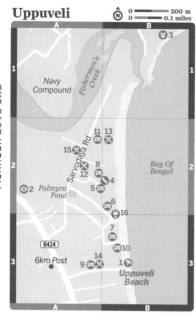

0 — 200 m
0 — 0.1 miles

Standard fan-only rooms are very popular, with nice touches such as artwork in the bathroom, while the air-con rooms have high ceilings and all mod cons.

Anantamaa HOTEL $$
(☎026-205 0250; www.anantamaa.com; 7/42 Alles Garden; r from US$50; ❄☎⊠) Back from the beach, but with its own private path to the sand, this professionally managed hotel has clean and comfortable rooms in two-storey blocks around a large pool.

Golden Beach Cottages GUESTHOUSE $$
(☎026-493 1210, 077 134 4620; www.goldenbeach cottages.com; r Rs 3500-7000; ❄☎) Offers good rates for its 10 remodelled rooms, which have little front porches for lounging. Various rooms here sleep from two to four people and are surprisingly spacious. The little cafe has tables on the sand.

Palm Beach Resort HOTEL $$
(☎026-222 1250; r from US$50; ❄☎) This well-run property has tasteful and no-surprises rooms all with dark-wood furniture and little porches, though bathrooms are cold-water and mattresses are foam slabs. The bird-call-filled shady gardens are a short stroll from the beach and there's excellent food. It's just back down a little lane from the beach.

Shiva's Beach Resort HOTEL $$
(☎026-222 8000; goldenbeachtrinco24@gmail. com; 178/32 Alles Garden; r Rs 3000-7000; ❄☎) Initial appearances are a little deceptive here as the slab-like concrete design looks rather soulless from the outside, but the 16 spacious, neat rooms are actually a good deal. Some budget rooms are fan-only. Down a little lane, it has some cabanas on the beach.

★ Trinco Blu by Cinnamon RESORT $$$
(☎026-222 2307; www.cinnamonhotels.com; off Sarvodaya Rd; s/d incl breakfast from US$90/110; ❄@☎⊠) Beautifully designed hotel that makes the most of its prime beachside plot, where all rooms face the ocean. Colour schemes – whitewashed walls and cobalt blues – are offset with punchy orange throw pillows, textiles and mosaic art. The expansive lawn is a great base for a day's lounging, with a lovely 30m pool. This place defines 'mellow retreat'.

✕ Eating & Drinking

Wander the beach at night to choose a place to drink and dine or pick a place from the high-quality choices on the little strip along Sarvodaya Rd away from the beach.

★ Coconut Beach Lodge SRI LANKAN $$

(📞 026-222 4888; meals Rs 350-700; 🖥) Coconut Beach is the best place in town for Sri Lankan–style home cooking. Rice and curry, grilled seer fish and giant prawns, plus vegie delights, are all prepared with love and served on a pretty candlelit patio. Reserve by 3.30pm.

Ceylon Seafood Cafe SEAFOOD $$

(📞 077 933 5858; Sarvodaya Rd; mains Rs 500-1200; ⏱ 7pm-midnight) You can't get more rustic than this totally open-air bamboo hut next to a lotus pond. Each night it displays a huge range of fresh fish, which you choose for staff to cook. Ask for extra pepper and garlic on your fish fillets. It's BYO beer, which you can buy from small shops nearby.

Tonic's SEAFOOD $$

(📞 026-493 1210; Golden Beach Cottage; meals Rs 500-1200; ⏱ 11am-10pm) The beachside restaurant of Golden Beach Cottage has just a touch of refinement to bring some style to its dinners. There's always fresh fish, which is served with salad and fries, and the battered calamari is excellent as well. Lots of fresh-off-the-boat specials.

★ Sana's SRI LANKAN $$$

(📞 077 700 4047; Sarvodaya Rd; mains Rs 500-2000; ⏱ 8am-10pm) An example of why the Sarvodaya Rd strip is becoming one of the most interesting eating neighbourhoods on the east coast. This restaurant is a two-level driftwood dream that's staffed by charmers. The main menu is mostly under Rs 800, but you can splurge on lobster and other interesting seafood creations.

Crab INTERNATIONAL $$$

(📞 026-222 2307; Trinco Blu by Cinnamon, off Sarvodaya Rd; meals Rs 1000-2800; ⏱ 5-11pm) A wonderful setting for a meal, this stylish hotel restaurant is perfect for a lazy dinner near the surf. You'll find a wide selection of dishes, with everything from Indonesian spicy rice with satay to succulent seafood (and a particularly fine crab curry). This is the most upscale option in Uppuveli. There's an open kitchen, full bar and good service.

Palm Beach ITALIAN $$$

(📞 026-222 1250; meals Rs 1300-2600; ⏱ 6.30-9pm Feb-Nov; 🖥) Authentic Italian food, including fine pasta and seafood; the menu changes daily, but always includes a special or two. Enjoying a good reputation, this restaurant is back from the beach, under some palms. Reserve ahead; dine inside or out.

Fernando's Beach Bar BAR

(📞 071 251 9749; Aqua Inn; ⏱ 7am-10pm) *The* beach bar in Uppuveli, many nights seem to start and end here. Sit on a pillow on the sand, at a table, or up on the driftwood-covered terrace. The beer is cold, the drinks potent and the vibe fun. Listen to the surf while you listen to stories from new-found friends. The food is simply OK.

ⓘ Getting There & Away

Irakkandy–Trincomalee buses run every 20 minutes along the B424; flag one down on the main road for Trincomalee (Rs 20, 20 minutes) or Nilaveli (Rs 20, 10 minutes). Three-wheelers cost Rs 500 to Trinco and Rs 600 to Nilaveli.

Nilaveli

📞 026

Nilaveli, the furthest north of the Trinco region's two beach resort areas, is more intimate than Uppuveli. Hotels are scattered up and down little lanes off the coast highway (B424) – it's around 6km from one end of the village to the other. If you're looking for some serious beach time, Nilaveli could be just the ticket, for the sands are golden and the ocean inviting.

Offshore, Pigeon Island offers fabled diving and snorkelling. Note that the recent surge in tourism has damaged the reef to a degree, so don't expect a pristine marine environment. Close to the shore, some day trippers stomp all over shallow coral.

◉ Sights & Activities

★ Nilaveli Beach BEACH

For years Nilaveli has been considered one of Sri Lanka's best beaches. It certainly has that feeling of paradise-island remoteness, with plenty of bending palms swaying over the golden sand. It's about 4km long, with modest resorts dotted along the shore. Looking east, you can see Pigeon Island beckoning you to snorkel.

★ Nilaveli Private Boat Service BOAT TRIP, SNORKELLING

(📞 071 593 6919, 077 886 9285; fishing trips 1-4 people Rs 6000, whale-watching trips per 2/4 people Rs 14,000/16,000) The local boat owners' association has set prices for the Pigeon Island trip – Rs 2000 per boat (not including park fees) while snorkelling gear costs Rs 600 per day to rent. Boat hire costs the same whether it's a full day (7am to 5.30pm) or a couple of hours because they shuttle back and forth all day and pick you up whenever you've specified. The captains (who don't speak much English) have a hut at the beach by the park office.

Fishing trips and whale-watching excursions are also offered. The latter are very popular as you often see blue whales. There are also various wildlife-watching tours of the local mangroves to choose from. During the peak season in July and August, you need to book your Pigeon Island trip at least a day ahead.

★ **Pigeon Island**

National Park   DIVING, SNORKELLING
(park fees 1/2 adults Rs 3150/4700, child Rs 950) Floating in the great blue 1km offshore, Pigeon Island, with its powdery white sands and glittering coral gardens, tantalises with possibilities. A nesting area for rock pigeons, the island is beautiful enough, with rock pools and paths running through thickets, but it's the underwater landscape that's the real star. The reef here is shallow, making snorkelling almost as satisfying as diving, and it's home to dozens of corals, hundreds of reef fish (including blacktip reef sharks) and turtles.

Poseidon Diving Station   DIVING
(☑ 091-720 1200; www.divingsrilanka.com; off B424, near 9km post; 2-tank boat dives from €80; ☉ Apr–Nov) This well-organised school offers

Nilaveli

lots of scuba action, including PADI Open Water certification courses (from €350), fun dives and snorkelling trips to Pigeon Island. Whale-watching boat trips, searching for blue whales and sperm whales, are also offered.

🛏️ Sleeping & Eating

Nilaveli has a growing number of places to stay and they are now scattered for about 6km, from roughly the 13km post through to the 19km post. Generally, the lodging is more expensive here than further south in Uppuveli. Note that in the low season things are very quiet. Virtually everywhere to stay serves food; indie restaurants have just started to appear.

That's Why   HUT $$
(☑ 077 175 6290; off B424; r Rs3500-5000) The convivial ringmaster Sameera has organised one big party at this beachfront collection of huts. You can't get any closer to the surf and not get wet. He has eight cone-shaped cabanas, which are really small huts. They're fan-cooled and comfortable in a '60s-throwback sort of way. The beach bar (11am to late) is *the* place to be for guests and the merry staff.

Seaway Hotel   HOTEL $$
(☑ 026-223 2212; www.seawayhotel.com; off B424; r Rs 3000-8000; ❄️ 🛜) Set just off the beach, the inviting Seaway offers a wide choice of accommodation in a huge grassy compound. There are three classes of rooms, from smallish, but clean, fan-cooled budget digs with cold-water bathrooms and front porches to attractive modern options with stylish furnishings, minibar, hot water and balconies.

Uga Jungle Beach Resort   RESORT $$$
(☑ 026-567 1000; www.ugaescapes.com/jungle beach; B424, 27km post, Kuchchaveli; cabins US$100-300; ❄️ 🛜 🏊) 🌿 This ecostyle resort built from natural materials (timber and thatch) enjoys a wonderful location just off a truly spectacular beach. All the rooms have been artfully constructed so there's lots of shade, greenery and resident birdlife. The pool area is gorgeous, ringed by foliage and bordering the restaurant. Guests can enjoy free yoga sessions and there's a spa. It's 9km north of Nilaveli.

Nilaveli Beach Hotel   RESORT $$$
(☑ 026-223 2296; www.nilaveli.tangerinehotels. com; off B424; r US$90-200; ❄️ 🛜 🏊) Nilaveli Beach Hotel definitely has the best grounds – sprawling, shady groves with hammocks and a gorgeous pool area – of any hotel in the

Nilaveli map

N   0 ——— 400 m
     0 ——— 0.2 miles

Pigeon Island Beach Resort
Pigeon Island National Park (1km)
Irakkandy (2km);
Kuchchaveli (16km);
Pulmoddai (36km)
Nilaveli Private Boat Service
18km Post   Anilana   Nilaveli
             Nilaveli Beach Hotel
Nilaveli Beach
Seaway Hotel
17km Post
NILAVELI VILLAGE
INDIAN OCEAN
Family Restaurant
16km Post
Irakkandy Lagoon
B424
15km Post   That's Why (1km)
14km Post
Uppuveli (6km); Trincomalee (12km)

NORTH OF NILAVELI

The beautiful B424 coastline road north of Nilaveli follows the shore, with the ocean on one side and lagoons inland. It's a great day out on a motorbike, in a car or, for those with some stamina, via bicycle (it is very flat). If you get lonely, there are wild donkeys, peacocks and monkeys all about.

Heading north, there's little of interest for the first 6km, but after you cross the river estuary at Kumpurupiddi the road runs very close to the beach, and then skirts a huge shallow lagoon on the west. A system of dykes and channels here enables sea water to be pumped into **salt pans** and salt to be harvested in the dry season.

Continuing north, you'll find the blockbuster (signposted) archaeological site of **Kuchchaveli** at the 34km post on the B424. Occupying a rocky point that juts into the Indian Ocean are the modest remains of a brick stupa. From the stupa's elevated position (50 steps up) there are spectacular views over a turquoise sea, across the white foam of the rollers, with stunning twin beaches to the north and south.

Around the 40km post the road traverses another lovely river estuary, the sandy shoreline dotted with colourful fishing boats. Then you pass through an area of dense mangrove forests, home to monitor lizards and prolific birdlife (including herons, storks and waders) before reaching an army checkpoint.

At the 45km post, tear your eyes away from the gorgeous beach view and turn west on a small road for 4km. At a shady parking area, stop and walk past an old pond with the remains of some complex carvings around the edges. Now climb up the hillside for some stunning views and the tattered remains of **Girihandu Seya**, which is thought to be the first Buddhist temple built in Sri Lanka, perhaps as far back as the 3rd century BC.

Back on the B424, it's a short trip to the isolated village of **Pulmoddai** at Km 54, which sits just inland from the **Kokkilai Lagoon**, an important bird sanctuary.

Buses (Rs 90, 1½ hours, hourly) connect Pulmoddai with Trincomalee, passing through Nilaveli and Uppuveli en route. Services (Rs 100, two hours, hourly) also head to Mullaitivu, offering a coastal route to northern Sri Lanka and Jaffna.

---

area, as well as a beautiful stretch of beach, with views across to Pigeon Island. The architecture is organic, with creative use of fountains and concrete and a harmonious balance of contemporary and earthy.

The restaurant is a temple of good seafood; spices come from the property's own garden. It's close to the Pigeon Island boats.

Anilana Nilaveli HOTEL $$$
(☏011-203 0900; www.anilana.com/nilaveli; off B424; r US$90-170; ✸@☎☀) This blinding-white-outside hip hotel ticks all the right contemporary boxes, with sleek accommodation finished in subtle shades of cream: all with gorgeous bathrooms and a balcony facing the beach or (less fun) one of the two huge pools. There's a wonderful deck for languid alfresco meals, and excellent Asian and Western food. There's also a spa.

Pigeon Island Beach Resort HOTEL $$$
(☏026-492 0633; www.pigeonislandresort.com; off B424; r incl breakfast from US$70; ✸☎☀)

This beachside hotel has attractive rooms in a long two-storey building, though only suites have sea views. It's worth a visit for lunch or dinner as a change of pace from your own hotel; the dining and lounge areas, with their antique furniture, wicker lamps and breezes, are charming. The beach is even quieter than usual here.

Family Restaurant SEAFOOD $$
(off B424; mains Rs 700-1000; ☺8am-9pm) Another fishing family makes good. All generations lend a hand at this bare-bones simple seafood restaurant that serves up whatever has been caught fresh. There are only eight tables, the floor is sandy and the welcome delightful.

❶ Getting There & Away

Flag down any passing bus along the B424 for Trincomalee (Rs 40, 30 minutes, every 20 minutes). A three-wheeler will cost around Rs 900, or Rs 600 to Uppuveli.

Jaffna & the North

Best Places to Eat

➡ Mangos (p278)

➡ Jaffna Heritage Hotel (p278)

➡ Hotel Rolex (p278)

➡ Green Grass (p278)

Best Places to Sleep

➡ Jetwing Jaffna Hotel (p278)

➡ Jaffna Heritage Hotel (p278)

➡ Sarras Guest House (p277)

➡ Shell Coast Resort (p292)

Why Go?

With towering, rainbow-coloured Hindu temples, sari-clad women on bicycles and a spectacular coastline fringed with palmyra and coconut palms, the North is a different world. Here the climate is arid for most of the year and the fields sun-baked. The light is stronger: surreal and white-hot on salt flats in the Vanni, bright and lucid on coral islands and northern beaches, and soft and speckled in Jaffna's leafy suburbs and busy centre. Look for the shimmer of colours from the wild peacocks that seem to be everywhere.

And, of course, there are the cultural differences. From the language to the cuisine to religion, Tamil culture has its own rhythms, and people here are proud of their heritage. Inevitably, given the region's recent history, there's still a noticeable military presence. But the ambience is relaxed as locals focus on building for the future and reviving the rich traditions of northern life.

When to Go
Jaffna

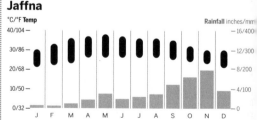

Feb The best month to view greater flamingos, present in their hundreds on Mannar Island.

Jun–Jul High season sees sunshine, moderate heat and delicious mangoes.

Jul–Aug Jaffna's extraordinary 25-day Nallur festival has parades, ice cream and ritual self-mutilation.

Jaffna & the North Highlights

1 Jaffna's Islands (p286)
Marvelling at the spectacular seascapes and surreal light while exploring offshore treasures such as Nainativu.

2 War Memorials (p287)
Understanding the war's destruction of communities at sites like the Sea Tiger Shipyard.

3 Mannar Island (p290)
Discovering ancient baobab trees, a historic fort, remote bays and a view almost to India.

4 Scenic Rides (p283)
Riding along spectacular coastal roads of the Jaffna.

5 Northeast Shore (p284) Finding your own

perfect palm-fringed ribbon of sand, such as isolated Manalkadu Beach.

6 Jaffna (p272)
Slipping into a trance during puja (prayers) at Nallur Kandaswamy Kovil, before appreciating the city's rebirth among the old walls of Jaffna Fort.

History

The North has always existed a bit apart from the rest of the island; even under colonial regimes the region remained highly autonomous. Jaffna, especially, has always been an important city, and one of the defining moments on the path to war came in 1981 when a group of Sinhalese burnt down Jaffna's library, seen as a violent affront to the Tamils' long and rich intellectual tradition.

The war began two years later, and Jaffna continued to be a hotspot for violence. For two decades the North was synonymous with death and destruction as the Liberation Tigers of Tamil Eelam (LTTE) and Sri Lankan military contested control. Since the war ended on the shores of Mullaittivu in 2009, a sense of calm and stability is at last returning to the North, though there is still much rebuilding to be done, both in terms of infrastructure and community relations.

Jaffna

📞 021 / POP 91,000

A bastion of Hindu tradition, art and creative culture, Jaffna welcomes visitors warmly. It's intriguing, unimposing, slightly off the beaten path and a thoroughly rewarding place to discover Sri Lankan Tamil culture. Inescapably, decades of war, emigration, embargoes and loss of life and property deeply affected this historic town, but the city is surprisingly green and leafy, with attractive palm-shaded colonial-era suburbs and beautiful temples and churches. Physically, new projects and upgraded transport connections show that Jaffna's days of isolation are long past.

Ancient sights both in the centre of town and on the outskirts make for compelling attractions. And while there is enough to do after dark to create a nascent buzz, it's still mellow enough that you won't get run over while walking. The city is an ideal base for forays to the idyllic islands just to the west and trips along the coastline and lagoons of the surrounding peninsula.

History

For centuries Jaffna has been Sri Lanka's Hindu-Tamil cultural and religious centre – especially during the Jaffna Kingdom, the powerful Tamil dynasty that ruled from Nallur for 400 years beginning in the 13th century. But the Portuguese tried hard to change that. In 1620 they captured Cankili II, the last king (his horseback statue stands on Point

Pedro Rd, near the Royal Palace ruins), then set about systematically demolishing the city's Hindu temples. A wave of mass Christian conversions followed.

Following a bitter three-month siege, the Portuguese surrendered their 'Jaffnapattao' to the more tolerant Dutch a few decades later, and Dutch Jaffna, which lasted for almost 140 years, became a major trade centre. Jaffna continued to prosper under the British, who took over in 1795 and sowed the seeds of future interethnic unrest by 'favouring' the Jaffna Tamils.

The city played a crucial role in the lead-up to the civil war and by the early 1980s escalating tensions overwhelmed Jaffna; for two decades the city was a no-go war zone. Variously besieged by Tamil guerrillas (the Liberation Tigers of Tamil Eelam, or LTTE), Sri Lanka Army (SLA) troops and a so-called peacekeeping force, the city lost almost half of its population to emigration. In 1990 the LTTE forced Jaffna's few remaining Sinhalese and all Muslim residents to leave. Jaffna suffered through endless bombings, a crippling blockade (goods, including fuel, once retailed here for 20 times the market price – one reason so many residents ride bicycles) and military rule after the SLA's 1995 recapture of the town.

Then in the peace created by the 2002 accords, the sense of occupation was relaxed and Jaffna sprang back to life: domestic flights began; refugees, internally displaced persons (IDPs) and long-absent émigrés returned; and new businesses opened and building projects commenced. Hostilities recommenced in 2006 and tension continued through to the end of the war in 2009.

Today a renewed focus on the future is palpable across Jaffna. New building projects are being launched and the last scars of the war have been erased – at least the physical ones.

◉ Sights

Jaffna is dotted with Hindu temples, easily identified by their red-and-white-striped walls. They range from tiny shrines to sprawling complexes featuring *mandapaya* (raised platforms with decorated pillars), ornate ponds and towering *gopuram* (gateway towers). The city also has its landmark fort and an abundance of churches, many located on shady streets east of the centre. Commercial activity is crammed into the colourful hurly-burly of Hospital, Kasturiya and Kankesanturai (KKS) Rds. To the northeast are some extraordinary ruins from the Jaffna Kingdom some four centuries ago.

⊙ Central Jaffna

You can walk between many of Jaffna's main sites. Bikes put everything in range.

★ Jaffna Fort   FORT

(Main St; ⊘ fort 8am-6pm, shop 8am-4.30pm Thu-Tue) **FREE** Sections of this vast complex overlooking the Jaffna lagoon have been recently restored, though much work continues. Once one of the greatest Dutch forts in Asia, it was built in 1680 over an earlier Portuguese original, and defensive triangles were added in 1792 to produce the classic Vaubanesque star form.

Jaffna's fort has been fought over for centuries. Today you're free to explore its walls, admire its gateways and moats, study some exhibits and view the city from its ramparts.

Long the gatehouse of the city, this citadel once housed thousands of troops and civilians. Many of its walls (constructed from coral, stone, brick and mortar) are still hidden beneath overgrown slopes.

During the war, government forces used it as an encampment, and in 1990 the LTTE – at the time in control of the rest of Jaffna – forced out government troops after a grisly 107-day siege. Today there is a room with exhibits about the archaeological history of the fort and other local sites inside the main portal. Across the way is a small **shop** with books about local heritage.

★ Nallur Kandaswamy Kovil   HINDU SITE

(Temple Rd; donations accepted; ⊘ 4am-7pm) This huge Hindu temple, crowned by a towering god-encrusted, golden-ochre *gopuram,* is one of the most significant Hindu religious complexes in Sri Lanka. Its sacred deity is Murugan (or Skanda), and during cacophonous *puja* – at 5am, 10am, noon, 4.15pm (small *puja*), 4.30pm ('special' *puja*), 5pm and 6.45pm – offerings are made to his brass-framed image and other Hindu deities like Ganesh in shrines surrounding the inner sanctum. It's about 1.5km northeast of the centre.

Jaffna Public Library   LIBRARY

(☑ 021-222 6028; http://english.jaffnalibrary.lk; Esplanade Rd; ⊘ 9am-7pm) Tellingly, one of the first major buildings to be rebuilt after the 2002 ceasefire was Jaffna's Public Library. It had been burnt down by pro-government mobs (some say forces) in July 1981, a destruction that many Tamils deemed a cultural attack – few acts were more significant in the build-up to civil war.

In its reconstruction, architects kept true to the elegant original neo-Mughal design from 1959. Today it's a bright spacious place that's very actively used by Jaffna's citizens.

Clock Tower   MONUMENT

(Vembadi St) An architectural curiosity, the spindly Clock Tower has a Moorish domed top, which makes it look like it belongs somewhere in North Africa. It was erected in 1875 to honour a visit by the Prince of Wales. In 2000 the current prince, Charles, donated the working clocks you see today to replace those damaged by fighting.

Old Park   PARK

(Kandy Rd) A grand expanse of grass with very old, huge shade trees, first laid out by the British in 1829. Besides a playground and the cute Dora Cafe (p278), it has the vaguely spooky ruins of the war-destroyed

JAFFNA & THE NORTH JAFFNA

THE MILITARY & TOURISM IN THE NORTH

Sri Lanka has a heavily militarised society, particularly in the north of the country, which was a war zone for decades and where many army divisions are still stationed.

Since the end of the war in 2009, the military has taken over large chunks of coastal land. The government considers this necessary to safeguard national security; protest groups deem many actions as profiteering land grabs. What's not in dispute is that villagers have been removed from their ancestral land and the military is increasingly involved in tourism in the north.

Some tourist facilities, such as Fort Hammenhiel (p288), are located on well-established military bases and are less contentious. Others, including the Thalsevana Resort at Kankesanturai on the Jaffna peninsula, have been built on land previously held by villagers. Meanwhile, the navy controls most ferry services around Jaffna's islands. It's expected that the military will play a role in developing the beautiful beaches in the former war zone along the coast north of Mullaittivu.

Jaffna

colonial-era Registry Office. They're like something from an Agatha Christie novel.

Jaffna Archaeological Museum MUSEUM
(Nawalar Rd; donations accepted; ⊙ 8am-4.45pm Wed-Mon) This small, unkempt but interesting museum is hidden away at the end of a messy garden behind a concrete events hall. At the door are a pair of rusty Dutch cannons from the fort and a set of whale bones. Inside, there are a few treasures, including some

15th-century Buddha torsos found at Kantarodai and a 14th-century 'seven-mouthed pot'.

St Mary's Cathedral CHURCH

(☎ 021-222 2457; Cathedral Rd; ⊗ 8am-5pm) Built by the Dutch along classical lines in the 1790s, St Mary's Cathedral is astonishingly large, but it's curious to see corrugated-iron roofing held up by such a masterpiece of wooden vaulting. It's the main church for Roman Catholics.

Jaffna

◉ **Top Sights**
1 Cankili Thoppu Archway H1
2 Jaffna Fort...A5
3 Nallur Kandaswamy Kovil.....................G1

◉ **Sights**
4 Clock Tower..C4
5 Jaffna Archaeological Museum.............E3
6 Jaffna Public Library B5
7 Mantiri Manai..H1
8 Old Park...G5
9 Our Lady of Refuge Church...................D4
10 Sangiliyan Statue...................................H2
11 St James' Church C6
12 St Mary's Cathedral..............................E6

🚴 **Activities, Courses & Tours**
13 Sri Lanka Click..D3

🛏 **Sleeping**
14 Green Grass Hotel E4
15 Jaffna Heritage Hotel F2
16 Jaffna Heritage Villa F2
17 Jetwing Jaffna Hotel...............................C4
18 Lux Etoiles...G3
19 Old Park Villa...F5
20 Sarras Guest House F5
21 Theresa Inn..G4

🍴 **Eating**
22 Cosy Restaurant D3

23 Dora Cafe...F5
Green Grass ....(see 14)
24 Hotel Rolex...B3
Jaffna Heritage Hotel....................(see 15)
25 Malayan Café B3
26 Mangos F1
27 Rio Ice Cream..F2
28 Rolex Bake Mart B2

🍸 **Drinking & Nightlife**
Jetwing Jaffna Rooftop Bar ....(see 17)

🎭 **Entertainment**
29 Alliance Française G4
30 British Council F4
31 Jaffna Cultural Centre B4

🛍 **Shopping**
32 Anna Coffee..B3
33 Art Gallery F4
34 Jaffna Market...B3
35 Rosarian Convent....................................H6
36 Zahra Tailors..B3

🚌 **Transport**
37 CTB Bus Stand B3
38 Minibus Stand..B3
39 Private Bus Stand....................................B3
40 Private Buses to Colombo B3

St James' Church CHURCH
(☎ 021-222 5189; Main St; ⊙ 8am-5pm) This is the grandest church in Jaffna, a classical Italianate edifice used by Anglicans that dates to 1827.

Our Lady of Refuge Church CHURCH
(☎ 075 064 9899; off Hospital Rd; ⊙ 6am-7pm) This unusual structure looks like a whitewashed version of a Gloucestershire village church.

◉ Jaffna Kingdom

Nallur was the capital of the Jaffna Kingdom for 400 years, beginning in the 13th century. A few weathered structures of the royal palace remain; they're well worth the short excursion to the northeast on Point Pedro Rd. Ride bikes out here or hop a three-wheeler for under Rs 250.

★**Cankili Thoppu Archway** HISTORIC BUILDING
(Sangili Thoppu; Point Pedro Rd) The provenance of this Jaffna Kingdom relic is fairly secure. This archway is thought to be one of the palace's original entrances. Among its weathered yet intricate carvings is an inscription to King Sangili from 1519.

Mantiri Manai HISTORIC BUILDING
(Mantri Manai; Point Pedro Rd) Set back from the road, it's easy to sense the beauty that was once part of this building's soul. Completely derelict now, and with walls covered in graffiti, the building keeps its secrets. There's much debate about its background. Some contend it dates back to the Jaffna Kingdom, when it would have been used as guest quarters for visiting ministers. Others place it in the Dutch or Portuguese colonial era, while some even claim it was built as recently as the 1890s.

Yamuna Eri HISTORIC SITE
(Chemmani Rd, off Point Pedro Rd) This U-shaped pool made of carved stones is neglected but still intact – it's thought to have been the women's bathing pool of the royal family. The tank is north of St James' Church, which is on Chemmani Rd (and not to be confused with the church of the same name on Main St). You reach it on narrow lane east of Point Pedro Rd. It's an evocative site; just tune out the nearby modern buildings.

Sangiliyan Statue
MONUMENT

(Point Pedro Rd) Glistening in the sun, this gold-hued statue was first erected in 1974. It portrays Cankili II, the last king of the Jaffna Kingdom (he died in 1623). During the war the statue was removed. It was restored in 2011 but not without the kind of controversy that is common in the north. Some Tamils contend that the current version lacks some of the heroic features of the original.

🏃 Activities

★ Sri Lanka Click
CYCLING

(☑077 848 8800; www.srilankaclick.com; 447 Stanley Rd; bike/motorbike rental per day from Rs 500/2000; ⊙8am-7pm) Great shop with a range or rental bikes, scooters and motor-bikes. Price includes helmet and lock. It can offer lots of good touring advice and also arrange a variety of tours by bike or vehicle of the region.

🎉 Festivals & Events

Nallur Festival
RELIGIOUS

Spread over a period of 25 days in July and/or August, this Hindu festival climaxes on day 24 with parades of juggernaut floats and gruesome displays of self-mutilation by entranced devotees.

🛏 Sleeping

Jaffna has a good selection of places to stay and the selection will only increase as investment and visitors pour in.

Sarras Guest House
GUESTHOUSE $

(☑021-567 4040, 021-222 3627; www.jaffnasarras.lk; 20 Somasutharam Rd; r Rs 2000-3500; ❄@🛜) Ageing colonial mansion with some (faded) character, including polished old floorboards and red-oxide flooring. The very spacious top-floor rooms are best; avoid the annex. The genial family running the place can pre-pare meals and advise on transport options. The cheapest rooms are fan-only; there are also family rooms. It has a communal fridge and microwave.

Senthil Complex
GUESTHOUSE $

(☑021-222 5226; www.senthilcomplex.com; 88 Sivapragasam Rd; r with fan/air-con from Rs 2500/3500; ❄🛜) Very basic accommodation at a small house just northwest of the centre. The two rooms are spotless and the family owners couldn't be nicer. There's a pleasant sitting area outside.

Theresa Inn
GUESTHOUSE $

(Do Drop Inn; ☑021-222 8615, 071 856 5375; calistusjoseph89@gmail.com; 72 Racca Rd; s/d from Rs 1700/1800, with air-con Rs 2800/3000; ❄🛜) A good choice, located on a leafy plot on a quiet street, with eight spartan, white rooms. The family owners are helpful, offer tasty meals and can organise bikes (Rs 350 per day), scooters (Rs 1500) or a car and driver (from Rs 6000).

Jaffna Heritage Villa
GUESTHOUSE $$

(☑021-222 2411, 021-222 2424; www.jaffnaheritage.com; 240 Temple Rd; r from US$40; ❄🛜) Run as an annex of the excellent Jaffna Heritage Hotel (p278), this fine guesthouse shows up separately in many booking sites. The rooms are large and have chic colonial-inspired style. The guesthouse is in an old villa, without a yard. This is an excellent bargain if you don't mind the main hotel services being across and down the road.

Margosa
HISTORIC HOTEL $$

(☑021-224 0242; www.bongostay.com; Puttur Rd/B380, Urelu North; s/d incl breakfast from US$45/50; ❄🛜) This stunning 19th-century colonial manor house in landscaped gardens has beautifully presented accommodation, most with open-air bathrooms. Perhaps a little overpriced, it's nonetheless worth a splurge; the restaurant has great local and Western food. It's 10km north of the city, in a quiet, leafy area. Listen to the birds.

Green Grass Hotel
HOTEL $$

(☑021-222 4385; www.jaffnagreengrass.com; 33 Aseervatham Lane, Hospital Rd; r from Rs 4000; ❄🛜☀) Architecturally it's a mess, but thanks to its attractive gardens and pool this place has some charm. Ask to see more than one room as renovations mean that standards vary (avoid the old, unfashionable ones obviously). Otherwise it's a good economical choice in a very central location, especially if you are using the train. The restaurant's outside tables are popular.

Lux Etoiles
HOTEL $$

(☑021-222 3966; www.facebook.com/HotelLux EtoilesJaffna; 34 Chetty St La; r from US$50; ❄🛜☀) Set on a quiet suburban street, Lux Etoiles creates a good initial impression – there's a vintage Austin automobile in the lobby that makes an art statement. The 24 rooms range in size from small to not so small after a recent expansion. The pool is large, although hemmed in by walls bearing vivid and unusual murals.

JAFFNA & THE NORTH JAFFNA

Old Park Villa
HOTEL $$

(☎ 021-222 3790; www.oldparkvillajaffna.com; 76 Kandy Rd; s/d incl breakfast from Rs 4000/5000; ❄ 🛜) A stylish converted heritage villa, with seven tastefully decorated rooms that feature handsome dark-wood furniture and ochre paintwork, and a lovely lounge with tribal artefacts. It's in a quiet setting back from the road. Excellent food is available, including Western breakfasts.

★ Jetwing Jaffna Hotel
HOTEL $$$

(☎ 021-221 5571; www.jetwinghotels.com; 37 Mahatma Gandhi Rd; r from US$100; ❄ 🛜) The big news in Jaffna is literally this high-rise hotel. The 55 rooms are compact but have intricate art, mod style and balconies. Those on higher floors have sweeping views of the region. Service is up to Jetwing's corporate standards. The rooftop bar (p279) is probably the best place in town for an evening cocktail.

★ Jaffna Heritage Hotel
BOUTIQUE HOTEL $$$

(☎ 021-222 2424; www.jaffnaheritage.com; 195 Temple Rd; r from US$75; ❄ 🛜 🏊) A superb modern hotel where the 10 rooms tick all the contemporary design boxes, with clean lines, high ceilings and stylish fittings; the expansive hotel grounds are fringed by coconut palms and there is a pleasant, upstairs terrace. Staff are very welcoming and the (all vegetarian) meals are excellent; it does a fine, upscale rice and curry. It also runs the nearby Jaffna Heritage Villa (p277).

🍴 Eating & Drinking

Jaffna is a good place to try South Indian–style cuisine. Red-hued *pittu* (rice flour and coconut, steamed in bamboo), *idiyappam* (string hoppers or steamed noodles) and *vadai* (deep-fried doughnut-shaped snacks made from lentil flour and spices) are local favourites. Look for typical snacks cooked up fresh from market vendors.

★ Mangos
SOUTH INDIAN $

(☎ 021-222 8294; off 359 Temple Rd; meals Rs 200-450; ⊙ 10.30am-10pm) With an open kitchen, lots of space and outdoor seating, Mangos is an atmospheric place to dine and is wildly popular with extended Tamil families and Westerners. The South Indian food is exceptional with around 20 dosas (try the ghee masala), great *parotta* (Keralan-style flat bread; the chilli version is sublime) and *idiyappam*. For lunch, the thali (Rs 200) can't be beaten. It's down a small lane and is close to Nallur Kandaswamy Kovil.

★ Rio Ice Cream
ICE CREAM $

(☎ 021-222 7224; 448A Point Pedro Rd; ice creams & sundaes Rs 60-250; ⊙ 9am-10pm) For a typical Jaffna treat, head to this popular ice-cream parlour near the landmark Nallur Kandaswamy Kovil. Rio is a local favourite; join the crowds enjoying sweets inside or pout on the nice covered terrace. It has a few savoury snacks and is the best of the small cluster of ice-cream places here.

Rolex Bake Mart
BAKERY $

(☎ 021-222 9402; 118 Kasthuriar Rd; snacks from Rs 100; ⊙ 7am-5pm) No you won't hear some knucklehead here bragging about his new US$4200 watch; rather, you can set your time to the excellent sweet and savoury treats that regularly emerge from the ovens. It's all takeaway.

Hotel Rolex
SRI LANKAN $

(☎ 021-222 2808; 340 Hospital Rd; meals Rs 100-300; ⊙ 8am-9pm) In the heart of the bustling centre, this local eatery is always busy and has friendly management, a good range of food options and 'nuts ice cream'.

Dora Cafe
CAFE $

(☎ 077 999 4045; Old Park Rd, Old Park; mains Rs150-300; ⊙ 9am-6pm) Smell the popcorn at this kid-friendly park cafe where you can get fresh juices, snacks and light meals.

Malayan Café
SRI LANKAN $

(☎ 021-222 2373; 36 Power House Rd; meals Rs 150-300; ⊙ 7am-9pm) Highly authentic and atmospheric old-school eatery in the market district with marble-topped tables, wooden cabinets, swirling fans and photos of holy men illuminated by bright fluorescent bulbs shining down on diners. The cheap, tasty vegetarian fare – dosas, rice and curry for lunch and light meals – is served on banana leaves and eaten by hand.

Jaffna Heritage Hotel
INDIAN, WESTERN $$

(☎ 021-222 2424; www.jaffnaheritage.com; 195 Temple Rd; meals Rs 600-1500; ⊙ 8am-10pm 🛜) For a refined ambience, the small open-air restaurant at the Jaffna Heritage Hotel (p278) is perfect. It offers excellent vegetarian Indian and Sri Lankan food, including wonderful coconut *rotti* and delicately spiced upscale curries. Also a good choice for a healthy, if pricey, Western breakfast. There's no alcohol.

Green Grass
SRI LANKAN $$

(☎ 021-222 4385; www.jaffnagreengrass.com; 3? Aseervatham Lane, Hospital Rd; mains Rs300-600

11am-11pm; 🛜) The restaurant at this hotel, with tables under a mango tree and around the pool, is a good spot for a meal, and also for an evening beer. Try the Tamil, Indian (crab curry, yum) and Chinese dishes. Avoid the stodgy indoor dining room.

Cosy Restaurant   NORTH INDIAN **$$**
(☑ 021-222 5899; 15 Sirampiyadi Lane, Stanley Rd; meals Rs 250-700; ⊙11am-11pm; 🛜) The lovely open courtyard seating is popular here as is the Jaffna-style crab curry. The big attraction is the tandoori oven, which fires up at 6pm daily and pumps out delicious naan bread, tikkas and tandoori chicken. It's BYOB.

★ **Jetwing Jaffna Rooftop Bar**   ROOFTOP BAR
(☑ 021-221 5571; www.jetwinghotels.com; 37 Ma-atma Gandhi Rd; ⊙6-11pm; 🛜) It gets no points for creative naming, but this place makes up for it with the sensational views. The rooftop bar at the hotel is breezy and has a variety of seating. It has a full range of cocktails and some light snacks. Make certain your beer is cold.

☆ **Entertainment**

Jaffna Cultural Centre   PERFORMING ARTS
(Esplanade Rd) Wow! India has gifted Jaffna a huge new cultural centre due for completion by 2019. It will include a large theatre, museum, art galleries and much more. The design takes cues from the neighbouring Jaffna Public Library. Once complete, it will truly be a very big deal and will revolutionise the cultural scene in the region.

British Council   CULTURAL CENTRE
(☑ 021-752 1521; www.britishcouncil.lk; 70 Racca Rd; ⊙9am-5pm Wed-Sun; 🛜) Has a library stocked with magazines, newspapers and English literature and hosts cultural events including art exhibitions.

Alliance Française   CULTURAL CENTRE
(☑ 021-2228093; http://lk.ambafrance.org/Alliance-Francaise-in-Jaffna; 61 Kachcheri-Nallur Rd; ⊙9am-5pm) Has a comfy lounge with English- and French-language newspapers and a library with books in French and English. Offers occasional film screenings.

🛍 **Shopping**

Jaffna Market   MARKET
(Grand Bazaar, Modern Market; Hospital Rd; ⊙7am-6pm Mon-Sat) Jaffna's colourful fruit and veg-etable market is west of the bus stand, but the greater market area encompasses several bustling blocks beyond that, including Power House Rd. You can easily spend a few hours wandering around.

Zahra Tailors   CLOTHING
(☑ 071 919 2908; 17 Jaffna Market, Power House Rd; ⊙9am-6pm Mon-Sat) Great little open-front tailor shop in the heart of the market. The talented guys here will mend clothing worn out by your touring while you wait. They can make you a bridal outfit too, should love strike.

Art Gallery   ARTS & CRAFTS
(☑ 021-222 7955; www.facebook.com/jaffnaartgallery; 15 Racca Rd; ⊙10am-3pm Wed-Mon) Jaff-na's first art gallery is in a striking white structure and showcases work by contemporary Sri Lankan artists.

Anna Coffee   COFFEE
(No 4, Jaffna Market; ⊙8.30am-6pm Mon-Sat) Sri Lankan coffee and tea from a venerable old shop in the market district. It also produces its own line of spices and even tooth powder.

Rosarian Convent   WINE
(Thoma Monastery; 48 Colombuthurai Rd; ⊙8.30am-1pm & 2-5.30pm Mon-Sat) The convent makes

ℹ **STAYING SAFE IN JAFFNA**

Foreigners visiting the north will typically see only a few vestiges of the high security that once dominated the area.

Checkpoints on the roads are a thing of the past, although some roads in the north around the Palali KKS Military Camp remain closed. You'll also notice numerous military bases dotting the countryside, with soldiers on guard duty doing their best to look alert.

However, politically active locals (and foreigners) still face state intimidation. Harassment, detentions and occasional disappearances continue. Most people are looking to the future and are relieved to put the war behind them, but old tensions remain under the surface.

Locals may not want to speak openly about politics or the war; use sensitivity and tact. International media coverage of the current situation in the North inevitably includes remarks about unsuccessful efforts to get locals to speak openly on the subject.

Rosetto 'wine' (from Rs 300 per bottle). Sweet and laced with cinnamon and cloves, it tastes like German *gluhwein*. There's also startlingly coloured grape 'juice' and 'nelli crush' (Rs 200), both nonalcoholic, flavourful fruit cordial concentrates.

ⓘ Information

You're never far from an ATM in central Jaffna.

Jaffna Teaching Hospital (☏ 021-222 3348; Hospital Rd; ⊙ 24hr) A large government hospital. The main facility in the North.

Post Office (Postal Complex, KKS Rd; ⊙ 7am-5pm Mon-Sat) Near the fort.

ⓘ Getting There & Away

BUS
Long-distance
From the **CTB bus stand** (☏ 021-222 2281; off Power House Rd) and neighbouring **private bus stand** (off Power House Rd) there are frequent long-distance services:

Anuradhapura Rs 400, four hours, three daily.
Kandy Rs 600, eight hours, nine daily.
Mannar Rs 185, three hours, 10 daily.
Trincomalee Rs 350, seven hours, five daily.
Vavuniya Rs 185, three hours, every 30 minutes.

Colombo
Numerous private bus companies offer overnight services to Colombo. Around a dozen offices are all grouped together on Hospital Rd near the **area** where you catch the buses. Most run overnight and take about eight to 10 hours.

Rates are Rs 700/900/1300 for an ordinary/semi-luxury/luxury air-con bus; the journey time is eight hours.

There are also CTB buses to Colombo (Rs 750, eight hours, eight daily).

Jaffna Peninsula
Destinations around the peninsula (including the islands) are served by both CTB buses from the CTB bus stand and private minibuses that use a **stop** (off Power House Rd) on Power House Rd. Be warned that local buses are slow and can be infrequent; check return times before you head out. Services include the following:

Kairanagar via Vaddukkoddai (782, 786) Rs 70, 1½ hours, every 30 minutes
Kayts (777) Rs 54, one hour, every 30 to 60 minutes (bus 780 also goes here but takes longer)
Keerimalai Spring (private minibuses 82, 87, 89) Rs 54, one hour, every 20 minutes
Kurikadduwan (KKD; 776) Rs 70, 1½ hours, hourly

Point Pedro via Nelliady (750) Rs 76, 1½ hours, every 30 minutes
Point Pedro via Valvettiturai (VVT; 751) Rs 80, 1½ hours, every 30 to 60 minutes
Tellippalai via Chunnakam (for Thurkkai Amman Kovil, Kantarodai, Keerimalai Spring 769) Rs 33, every 30 minutes

CAR & MOTORCYCLE
Many travellers prefer the freedom of renting a motorbike or car to explore the peninsula and islands. Traffic is light and roads are now in good condition. Scooters cost about Rs 1500 per day (excluding petrol), a car with driver around Rs 6500 per day. Most places to stay can arrange bike and car hire.

TRAIN
Trains on the Jaffna–Colombo line use the **Jaffna Railway Station** (Station Rd). This art-deco station has been beautifully restored. It has a small cafe offering drinks and food you can take on the train. There is an ATM.

Trains include a night train with sleeping berths and one InterCity train in each direction daily that goes significantly faster. Services include the following:

Anuradhapura 3rd/2nd/1st class Rs 190/340/600, three to four hours, four daily.
Colombo 3rd/2nd/1st class Rs 320/570/1100, six to eight hours, four daily.
Vavuniya 3rd/2nd/1st class Rs 150/280/520, two to three hours, four daily.

ⓘ Getting Around
Jaffna is not a large city and the central area is easily explored on foot or by bicycle.

Many guesthouses rent bikes (around Rs 350 to Rs 500 per day). An excellent rental source is **Sri Lanka Click** (p277).

Three-wheelers are very common and cost Rs 150 to Rs 300 for most trips. At night, locals recommend calling one (or having someone call one for you) for security reasons. Most places to stay can recommend local drivers.

Jaffna Peninsula
☏ 021

Once you get beyond Jaffna's already rustic outer boroughs, you're plunged into field of palmyra palms, technicolor temples, holy springs and miles of coastline. Few of the sights are individually outstanding, but together they make for interesting day trips especially if you have your own transport.

Many of the security concerns and road blocks that made travel here difficult have been removed, although a few remain and

Jaffna Peninsula

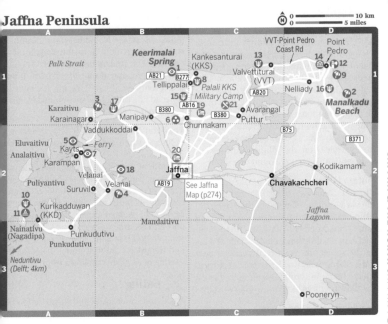

Jaffna Peninsula

prevent following the entire coastline. Make a few areas your focus: the sacred oceanside Keerimalai spring, the stunning coastal road between Valvettiturai and Point Pedro, and the northeast shore with its beautiful beaches.

Road conditions are good across the peninsula. There are some bus services (to Keerimalai spring and Point Pedro), but to really explore you'll want your own wheels. Riding bikes here is rewarding, especially along the lonely shore roads.

The North Coast & Keerimalai Spring

There are several important religious and ancient sites on the road to Kankesanturai (KKS). The town itself is right on the ocean in a pretty, tree-shaded setting. It is surrounded by military bases, but you can easily drive here for the fine water views (note a new army resort right on the water). However, blockades prevent you from driving west to stunning Keerimalai spring or east to Valvettiturai.

◉ Sights

★ Keerimalai Spring
HISTORIC SITE

(B277) This spring is a beautiful little spot: the men's side has a picturesque stepped pool of bright aquamarine water set against the ocean, while the women have a smaller pool nearby, surrounded by tall walls. The waters are supposed to be healing, and there are changing rooms on-site; women should bathe in something modest. Frequent Jaffna minibuses are Rs 54 to the spring, or get a three-wheeler from the Tellippalai bus stand for Rs 400/700 one way/round trip.

Kantarodai Ruins
RUINS

(off B380, Chunnakam; ⊘ 8.30am-5pm) Some 1km via a squiggle of lanes south of the B380 is the beautiful and mysterious Kantarodai Ruins – two dozen or so dagobas, 1m to 2m in height, in a palm-fringed field. Their origins are the subject of fierce controversy – part of the raging 'who was here first?' historical debate. It's an intriguing, albeit fenced, vista and the structures look quite otherworldly.

Naguleswaram Shiva Kovil
HINDU SITE

(B277, Keerimalai) Just before Keerimalai spring is the 6th-century-BC Naguleswaram Shiva Kovil, one of the *pancha ishwaram,* five temples dedicated to Lord Shiva in Sri Lanka. Before the civil war, this was a thriving Hindu pilgrimage site with several temples and six *madham* (rest homes for pilgrims) and *samadhi* shrines for holy men. Only traces of the original buildings survived after the temple was bombed by the army in 1990.

Maviddapuram
Kanthaswamy Kovil
HINDU SITE

(AB16, Tellippalai) Maviddapuram Kanthaswamy Kovil is now flourishing again after the war. The priests here are very friendly and will probably do a *puja* for you if you like (otherwise, it's at 11.30am). It's right by the road junction and is surrounded by fairly lush banana trees.

Thurkkai Amman Kovil
HINDU SITE

(AB16, Tellippalai; ⊘ 5.30am-7pm, closed 1-3pm some days) Beside the KKS road at the 13km marker, south of the village of Tellippalai, the vast Thurkkai Amman Kovil is set behind a fairly deep, stepped pool. The temple celebrates the goddess Durga and draws relatively large crowds, of women especially, on Tuesdays and Fridays, when devotees pray for a good spouse. *Puja* is at 8am, 11am, noon and 4pm, and the priests are welcoming. Look for the carving of elephants pulling a train.

✖ Eating

You'll find simple cafes and shops for food in the villages and at Keerimalai spring.

Sri Murugan Café
SRI LANKAN $

(off B380, Alaveddy Rd, Vakaiadi; mains from Rs 150; ⊘ 5am-9pm) The tasty old-fashioned Sri Murugan Café is 3km west of Puttur in a rural location. It serves rice and curry. There's not much English spoken here, but you just need to point. It's on the B380, which is the detour along the southern edge of the Palali KKS Military Camp.

TAMIL TIGER BURIAL GROUNDS

Although bodies of the deceased are generally cremated in Hindu tradition, the bodies of fighters for the Liberation Tigers of Tamil Eelam (LTTE) were buried instead, beneath neatly lined rows of identical stones. The fallen Tigers were called *maaveerar* – 'martyrs' or 'heroes' – and their cemeteries called Maaveerar Thuyilum Illam (Martyrs' Sleeping Houses). The tradition of burial began in the 1990s, not long after the 1989 initiation of Maveerar Naal, Heroes Day, held each year on 27 November. The cemeteries were controversial: many saw them as a natural way to honour those who died; for others, they were a propaganda tool.

When the Sri Lanka Army (SLA) took control of the Jaffna peninsula in 1995, it destroyed many of the cemeteries, only to have the LTTE build them up again after the 2002 ceasefire. But when the SLA conquered areas in the East in 2006 and 2007, and then again after the war's end in 2009, all cemeteries (and other LTTE monuments) across the North and East were bulldozed anew – to the distress of many Tamils, especially family members of the deceased.

Today, as the military builds monuments celebrating its victory in the war, many Tamils honour Maveerar Naal each year.

Getting There & Away

You have to detour around the huge Palali KKS Military Camp because roadblocks have closed the coast road. This means using the B380 to get between Chunnakam and Puttur. It's hoped that in the future restrictions will be lifted so that you can drive the coast all the way from Keerimalai spring east to VVT and on to Point Pedro.

Technically the rail line runs to KKS from Jaffna, but the trains are not frequent enough to make it a good option.

Valvettiturai

Valvettiturai (VVT) is a busy fishing village right on the Indian Ocean. To the west is Thondaimanaru and the useful new bridge over the tidal inlet. To the east is the beautiful coast road (p283) to Point Pedro.

Modest VVT was once a rich smuggling town. It's famous as the birthplace of LTTE leader Vellupillai Prabhakaran. Known for his extraordinary ruthlessness, charisma and single-minded strength of purpose, Prabhakaran's personality was considered by many to be the reason that the LTTE – of all the militant Tamil-rights groups that emerged in the 1970s – rose to prominence. Prabhakaran's death was reported during the final days of the war. Today there's nothing left of the Prabhakaran family home, which the army demolished in 2010, an action that many observers thought was to prevent it from becoming a tourist attraction, or even a kind of shrine.

Selvachannithy Murugan Kovil   HINDU SITE
(Thondaimanaru) The charming, waterfront Selvachannithy Murugan Kovil (also known as Sella Sannathy Kovil) is an important Murugan temple and a scenic stop, with a lively *puja*. It's 4km west of VVT.

Getting There & Away

Roads here are all sealed and in good shape. Visits here are usually part of a day trip by car or motorbike from Jaffna, which includes the beautiful coastal road to Point Pedro.

Point Pedro

Workaday Point Pedro is the Jaffna peninsula's second town. It has a few faint hints of a lingering colonial style and was hit hard by the 2004 tsunami: locals say fishing boats were found 1km inland. A busy commercial centre today, the town has some interesting places nearby and is connected to Valvettiturai (VVT) by a beautiful coastal drive.

COASTAL ROUTE

The coast road that runs 9km east from Valvettiturai (VVT) to the Point Pedro Lighthouse (p283) is easily one of the most beautiful drives in the north. It hugs the shore, with aquamarine waves breaking on rocks right alongside the road. At some points there are reefs right offshore. The views from the road are beautiful and panoramic.

You'll pass a succession of tiny fishing hamlets, with fish sun-drying in neat rows by the road.

The town is a small place with the usual market and a couple of commercial blocks. The namesake geographic landmark – with lighthouse and beaches – is 1.5km east.

Theru Moodi Madam   HISTORIC BUILDING
(Tollgate; Thumpalai Rd) These mysterious and elaborately carved ruins of a gate over the road are thought to date to Dutch colonial times. It's about 100m east of the heart of Point Pedro.

Munai Beach   BEACH
(off B370, Point Pedro) Simply a very fine beach, not far east of the Point Pedro Lighthouse. It's often good for swimming when the water is calm.

Point Pedro Lighthouse   LIGHTHOUSE
Occupies a prominent spot with sweeping views at the east end of the spectacular VVT–Point Pedro Coast Rd. Although the lighthouse is fenced off and photos are forbidden, there is a nice beach right beside it where you can have a dip or a picnic.

Vallipura Aalvar Kovil   HINDU SITE
The much-revered Vallipura Aalvar Kovil is 5km south from central Point Pedro. Its *gopuram* is painted in an unusually restrained colour palette and the temple interior has some very pretty Krishnas. It's famous for the boisterous, recently revived water-cutting festival in October, which attracts thousands of pilgrims. *Puja* is at 7am, 9.30am, noon, 4.15pm and, on Sunday, 6pm.

Getting There & Away

Point Pedro has regular buses from Jaffna (Rs 76, 90 minutes, every 30 minutes). Be prepared to walk to the beaches if you come this way.

Northeast Shore

Some of the region's best beaches are found on the northeast coast of the Jaffna peninsula. It's a very lonely region. Most of the abandoned houses visible along the shoreline to Point Pedro were destroyed by the 2004 tsunami.

A day trip here from Jaffna can be memorable. The B402 road turns east off the A9 some 9km north of the Elephant Pass Causeway. It heads north to the coast, 8km away. It's a gloriously isolated road, which traverses a couple of villages and a long slender lagoon before hitting the shore at Chempiyanpattu.

From Chempiyanpattu, you can follow the lonely B371 coastal road, which heads northwest up the narrow peninsula. It's a beautiful and stark 30km drive to Point Pedro. Along the way, expect to encounter monkeys, monitor lizards and lots of birdlife as well as beaches such as the idyllic one at Manalkadu.

★ Manalkadu Beach   BEACH
A small dirt road runs for 3.1km off the B371 to this lovely beach. There are a few fishing boats, some palm trees and not much else on the sand. The views extend up and down the sand as far as you can see. Back from the shore, the small **St Anthony's Church** sits in isolation and features a 6m-tall statue of Jesus. There are no vendors or services.

Chempiyanpattu Beach   BEACH
(off B402) There's a stunning beach here – a classic tropical picture of white sand, azure ocean and swaying coconut palms – though absolutely no facilities. Perfect if you want to get away from it all. Note the huge old baobab tree.

ⓘ Getting There & Away

The B371 and B402 roads are paved, albeit they're somewhat rough in parts. Some beach access roads are dirt, which is normally fine for cars in the dry season. This would be an ideal place for some bike touring.

Elephant Pass

Some 52km southeast of Jaffna via the A9 highway is Elephant Pass, a narrow causeway that connects Jaffna peninsula to the rest of Sri Lanka. There are vistas over the table-flat salt marshes here that extend for tens of kilometres. The actual pass gets its name from the hundreds of elephants that were herded through here en route to India between 300 BC and the 19th century.

For most Sri Lankans the name is inexorably linked with the civil war; for decades the government and Tamil Tigers contested control of this strategic spot – the gateway to Jaffna – with particularly bloody battles waged in 1991, 2000 and 2009.

Today it is the site of two major war memorials, which draw many tourists. The wetlands surrounding the causeway are beautiful, an aquamarine sea fringed by patches of white sand and mangroves, with lots of wading birds in evidence.

Buldozer Memorial   MEMORIAL
(A9) About 1km south of the causeway's southern end, there is a large memorial to Gamini Kularatne, a Sri Lanka Army soldier who single-handedly disabled an armoured LTTE bulldozer. The rusting vehicle – complete with a large hole from an explosion in its side – is mounted on a plinth. Nearby is a display about Kularatne's life, complete with letters to his mother, a pay stub and more.

ELEPHANT QUAY

Elephants were once indispensable to South Asian armies: they could transport troops through difficult terrain and waterways, carry heavy supplies, knock down the doors of forts and, when lined up with steel balls swinging from their trunks, scare the hell out of the enemy. Sri Lanka's elephants were known to be exceptionally strong, intelligent and large, and so the island became a major supplier to India – a practice that began around 300 BC and continued to the early 19th century.

Most elephants were caught in the Vanni, then marched through the Jaffna peninsula and shipped out from Elephant Quay in Kayts. (Elephant Pass, linking the Jaffna peninsula to the rest of Sri Lanka, really was an elephant pass.) They were shipped in custom-made wooden elephant boats constructed in Kayts, and the town was renowned as an elephant port.

As powerful as the elephants were, however, they were frightened and confused by loud noises, so the arrival of firearms put an end to their war prowess and the Kayts elephant trade.

THE PALMYRA PALM

Symbolising the North of the nation, the towering, fan-leafed palm tree known as the palmyra is abundant across the region, its graceful crown of leaves defining many a horizon at sunset. Of the estimated 11 million or so palmyra trees in Sri Lanka, 90% are found in the three provinces of Jaffna, Mannar and Kilinochchi.

An essential part of Tamil culture, palmyra has many uses: timber for construction; leaves for fencing, roofing and woven handicrafts; fibre for rope; and sap for drinking. If left to ferment for a few hours, the sap becomes a mildly alcoholic, fragrant toddy. Young palmyra roots are high in calcium and eaten as a snack and also ground to make flour for a porridge called *khool*. In markets across the North you'll find great blocks of jaggery (delicious golden-coloured unrefined palm sugar) made from unfermented palmyra toddy.

The Palmyrah Development Board (www.katpahachcholai.com) promotes a range of products, from shopping bags to shampoo, made from the palmyra.

Elephant Pass War Memorial MONUMENT
(A9) This grandiose, vaguely stupa-like monument glorifies the role of the Sri Lankan armed forces in defeating the LTTE and lauds the role of former President Rajapaksa. Huge bronze hands hold aloft a model of the country and are surrounded by bandoleer-wearing lions. It's at the north end of the causeway.

Getting There & Away
Your own wheels are the only practical way of visiting the monuments. Both memorials are right beside the A9, which is in excellent shape.

Jaffna's Islands

A highlight of the region, Jaffna's low-lying islands are a blissful vision of the tropics. The main pleasure is not any specific sight, but the hypnotic quality of the waterscapes and the escapist feeling of boat rides to end-of-the-earth villages. As the sea here is very shallow (only a metre or so deep in places) the light is very special indeed, with sunlight bouncing off the sandy seafloor. The islands are all dotted with spikey palmyra palms (p285); the salt flats often are dotted with pink flamingos.

Causeways and boat connections link the islands, making a number of idyllic day trips (p285) possible. The islands' beaches may not be quite as beautiful as those on the south coast, but they do offer pleasant swimming in balmy water. Women should swim in T-shirts and shorts.

You can assemble several adventuresome itineraries to explore Jaffna's islands. One option is to head from Jaffna city to Velanai and then to the island of Punkudutivu, ferry-hopping from here across to the temples of Nainativu and then returning by Kayts and Karaitivu island to the mainland. The second option is an excursion to the remote idyll of Neduntivu (Delft).

Getting Around
Bus connections to the islands from Jaffna are not that frequent. The ideal way to explore these islands is with your own wheels (ideally only two), giving you the freedom to pull over when and where you want. The terrain is very flat so it's perfect for covering while astride a bicycle or scooter; both can be loaded onto ferries between islands. Traffic is non-existent, so riding is relaxed. The navy operates most ferry services.

Velanai

Velanai island, connected by causeway to Jaffna, is sometimes referred to as Leiden, its Dutch name, or Kayts, after the village on its northeast coast. It's a beautiful but sparsely populated place.

Kayts VILLAGE
Kayts is a moody little village with a few scuttled fishing boats down by the ferry dock and some big old bayan trees. This was the port from which elephants were shipped to India, and you can still see traces of its colonial past. The waterfront has views of evocative Fort Hammenhiel (p288) across the shallow waters.

War Memorial MEMORIAL
(off AB19) About 2km north of the AB19 along a dirt track is a sombre memorial to Lieutenant General Denzil Lakshman Kobbekaduwa and others. In 1992, the LTTE set off a bomb that killed the general and much of the rest of the command staff of the Sri Lankan Army in the north. It was a major victory for the LTTE. Today this recently built site includes the remains of some of the vehicles of the motorcade. It's a lonely and solemn site.

St Anthony's Church   CHURCH
(AB19, Kayts) Built in 1820, this large colon-naded church is dishevelled, but the faithful have strung colourful garlands from the soaring rafters. Immediately west, ponder the ruins of **St Anthony's Villa**, which still has some beautiful and elaborate carvings set amid numerous grazing goats.

Chaatty Beach   BEACH
(Chaddy Beach; Velanai) Chaatty Beach is no white-sand wonder, but it's passable for swimming and has changing rooms, picnic gazebos and snack vendors. It's just 11km from Jaffna.

ℹ Getting There & Away
Bus 777 (Rs 54, one hour, every 30 to 60 minutes) runs to Kayts from Jaffna.

At Kayts, the free Velanai to Karaitivu ferry runs every 30 minutes from 6am to 6pm and takes 10 minutes to cross the narrow channel.

Karampan, 4km southwest of Kayts, is where navy-operated ferries depart daily (on a sporadic schedule) for the very quiet islands of Analaitivu and Eluvaitivu.

Note that many online maps and apps show a road across the water to the mainland from the little isthmus north of Velanai village. This does not exist. The AB19 is the only road link to the island.

Punkudutivu
A very long causeway links Velanai to the island of Punkudutivu. Notice the lagoon fishermen who use wade-out traps and sail in little wind-powered canoes. The village of Punkudutivu has an eye-poppingly colourful Hindu temple. Many old houses lie in various stages of decay. Smaller causeways link Punkudutivu to the ferry dock at Kurikadduwan (KKD), from which navy-run boats depart to Neduntivu and Nainativu.

Bus 776 links to the ferry dock at Kurikadduwan (KKD; Rs 70, 1½ hours, hourly) from Jaffna. If driving, it takes about 40 minutes.

Nainativu (Nagadipa)
Known as Nainativu in Tamil and Nagadipa in Sinhalese, this 6km-long lozenge of palmyra groves is holy to both Buddhist and Hindu pilgrims. It's a quiet place, with barely 2500 inhabitants. *Poya* (full-moon) days are observed by both Hindus and Buddhists on the island; expect crowds.

Nagadipa Temple   BUDDHIST SITE
(Nainativu) This is the North's only major Buddhist pilgrimage site. According to legend,

the Buddha came to the island to prevent war between a *naga* king and his nephew over ownership of a gem-studded throne. The solution: give it to the temple instead. The precious chair and original temple disappeared long ago, but today there is an attractive silver-painted dagoba. Just behind, three happy-looking Buddhas sit in a domed temple. It's a 10-minute walk south from Naga Pooshani Amman Kovil along the coast road.

Naga Pooshani Amman Kovil   HINDU SITE
(Nainativu) This lovely complex is an airy Hindu temple set amid mature neem trees. The main temple deity is the *naga* goddess Meenakshi, a consort of Shiva. (The term *naga* refers variously to serpent deity figures and to the ancient inhabitants of the island.) Women wishing to conceive come here seeking blessings, delivered during the trance-inducing midday *puja*. An impressive festival is held in June/July every year and attracts over 100,000 people. It's directly in front of the ferry jetty.

ℹ Getting There & Away
Navy-run ferries (Rs 30, 20 minutes) depart Kurikadduwan (KKD) on Punkudutivu island for Nainativu every 30 minutes or so from 7.30am to 4.30pm. The ride takes 20 minutes; on some trips you can bring a motorbike for Rs 100. During festival times, the wait for ferry passage can last hours.

Neduntivu (Delft)
The intriguing, windswept island of Neduntivu (Delft) is 10km southwest of KKD or Punkudutivu island. Around 6000 people live here, but it feels deserted. Dirt roads run through coconut-palm groves, and aquamarine water and white sand fringe the shore. Diverse flora populates the island, including neem, vines that you can swing from, and a rare, ancient baobab tree.

Of the various islands in the Jaffna region this is the one if you simply want to leave the world behind. Unlike Nainativu, it has no important religious shrines.

In 2011 Basil Rajapaksa (the ex-president's brother) announced plans for new resorts and roads. However, the clan's fall from favour ended this threat to the island's quietude. Don't be surprised, however, if new development schemes do emerge.

Hundreds of field-dividing walls are hewn from chunks of brain and fan corals. Delft ponies descended from Dutch mounts roam barren fields edged by rocky coral shores

MULLAITTIVU DRIVING TOUR

The region in the northeast around Mullaittivu today looks broadly pastoral and green. But in 2009 it was anything but. This is where the decades-long civil war came to an end as the Sri Lankan military waged an all-out assault on the LTTE.

This is the centre of allegations of human-rights abuses by the shelling of civilians, atrocities that have yet to be investigated, despite urging from the UN and the international community.

For now, it is a region in transition, with white beaches in stark contrast to towns such as Puthukkudiyiruppu that are still filled with shell-marked buildings. Elsewhere, however, there is new development and construction. Some of the latter is in the form of memorials being built by the military. It's well worth taking the detour here via the A34 and A35 on your journey to and from Jaffna.

The beach at Mullaittivu is long, white and beautiful. It's undeveloped, although there is some construction in the town as stores are being built. There is a simple cafe run by a military officer back behind the sand. The surf ranges from mild to treacherous.

About 3km north on the A35 is the **Vaddu Vakal Bridge** (A35). This single-lane concrete veteran still bears war scars. When the fish are running, the sides are lined with people casting nets; it's one of the few times you'll see a crowd in the region. The lagoon is normally placid and a bird haven.

Continue on the road north for about 6km and look for a dirt road turning east. There may be a sign that says 'museum' or some such. Follow the road for about 500m and you'll encounter a scene that might have you holding your jaw in place. The **Sea Tiger Shipyard** (off A35; ☉dawn-dusk) FREE was a base for the LTTE navy, a guerrilla force that operated for decades, often launching suicide attacks on government ships and ports. This site is where experimental submarines and fast boats were built to carry out missions. Really just a clearing in the dunes, there are more than a dozen craft here in bizarre shapes and stages of construction. There's even the remains of a rudimentary canal used to bring the vessels to and from the ocean.

The subs in particular are fascinating to look at. Utterly Rube Goldberg, they were constructed with simple tools and scrap metal for deadly missions. There are a couple of snack stands and usually some soldiers lounging around.

A small dirt road near the shipyard runs northwest and is back from the beach. Go about 1km from the A35 and stop near a military-base entrance. The grass-covered ground here is pocketed and uneven. It's odd until you realise that this is a **shelling zone** (off A35), one of the places where Tamil civilians were shelled in the war's final days in February, 2009. These events remain very controversial, with much blame cast in all directions, but the evidence that thousands were killed is overwhelming, as detailed in UN reports among others. No marker or memorial exists here.

Back on the A35, driving west about 4km from the shipyard road, is the army's **Monument of Victory** (A35). Set amid a marsh, a huge gold-coloured torso of a soldier juts up from the ground. It's bombastic to say the least; nearby a small building houses map displays that attempt to show the final months of the military campaign, but they are basically incomprehensible.

As you drive the A34 and A35 to and from Mullaittivu, you'll often see signs of a return to normalcy. Farmers take over huge swaths of the lightly travelled road to dry rice. New roadside shrines to the Virgin Mary are proliferating.

The major roads on the 100km loop out to Mullaitivu from the A9 are the A35 from Paranthan and the A34 from Mankulam, both in excellent condition. There is no easy way to do this area by bus.

There is a **giant rock** that is said to be growing and is therefore worshipped, and a small, very ruined **Dutch fort**, close to the ferry dock.

A rusty Sri Lanka Navy–operated ferry (free or Rs 85 depending on the sailing, one hour) departs KKD about four times a day between 8am and 4.30pm. The vessels get crowded, so arrive early and prepare to jam aboard for the uncomfortable, if memorable, trip.

If you're travelling by bus from Jaffna, you'll need to catch the 6.40am departure to KKD to make a ferry connection.

It's impossible to explore Neduntivu without transport. Three-wheelers/pick-ups (Rs 1500/4500 for two hours) can be rented for island tours from the dock.

Karaitivu

Karaitivu has several appeals: ferry access to Kayts; the crossing from the mainland across a long, water-skimming causeway, with views of wading fishermen and shrimp traps; a good public beach; and an atmospheric old fort.

⊙ Sights

Casuarina Beach BEACH
(New Rd; per person Rs 20, plus motorbike Rs 20, car Rs 50; ⊙ ticket office 7am-6pm) An attractive stretch of sand with good swimming and, as the name indicates, a shoreline backed by mature casuarina trees. It's popular with folks from Jaffna on weekends and has a couple of food vendors for a bite to eat and a drink. Buses from Jaffna to Karainagar pass within 2km of the beach. There are three-wheelers available for onward transport.

Fort Hammenhiel HISTORIC SITE
(☏ 021-381 8216; ☎) A tiny islet in the bay is home to the pocket-sized Fort Hammenhiel, a small Portuguese-built bastion that passed on to the Dutch in the 1650s. The thick coral walls are over 4m high. Access to the fort is very difficult. The navy has built a tiny officers-only resort inside the walls. If you have lunch at the resort's landside restaurant (p288), you might be able to beg a visit on one of the boats that makes the five-minute trip.

Varatharaja Perumal Kovil HINDU SITE
(off AB21) This temple is 1.1km north of the start of the Karaitivu causeway on the mainland. It's visible on the right as you start your crossing. There's a towering *gopuram* done up in polychromatic glory.

✕ Eating

Fort Hammenhiel Resort MULTICUISINE **$$**
(☏ 021-381 8216; Karaitivu; meals Rs 400-800; ⊙ 8.30am-10pm; ☎) The historic fort is part of a navy-run resort. There's a restaurant right on the waterfront with great views of the fort. It's a big place with a big menu and is a good stop for lunch. It's open to the public and is 1km

west of the Kayts ferry jetty. Because it's inside the naval base you need to present a copy of your passport for access. There are hotel rooms out on the fort, but they are restricted to people who have made reservations 'through an admiral', as the management explained.

ⓘ Getting There & Away

Buses from Jaffna run to Kairanagar via Vaddukkoddai (782, 786; Rs 70, 1½ hours, every 30 minutes). On the south end of the island, the free Karaitivu to Velanai ferry runs every 30 minutes from 6am to 6pm and takes 10 minutes to cross the narrow channel.

Kilinochchi & Around

The town of Kilinochchi radiates the kind of economic energy that is spreading through the North. It's unremarkable except for one sight that is a lasting image of the war, when this was a centre of LTTE power. Right near the centre of town, an enormous concrete **water tower** (A9, Kilinochchi; ⊙ site 24hr, shop 9am-5pm) lies on its side where it was toppled in the final days of the war in 2008. Its sheer size and the obvious violence needed to destroy it are sobering. A gift shop on site has a big sign that reads 'Souvenir Galore'. Items for sale include T-shirts with the slogan 'Re-awakening K-town!'

North of town, you'll travel through a stark savanna-like area with a minimalist beauty until you reach Elephant Pass. Frequent buses pass through town between Jaffna and points south. You can easily stop off and catch a later bus. There is also a train stop.

Vavuniya

☏ 024 / POP 79,000
A transport hub, the bustling town of Vavuniya (*vow*-nya) has few sights, but an afternoon pause here isn't unpleasant. Now that road and rail links to Jaffna are in good shape, few travellers stop in Vavuniya these days, but there are a few adequate hotels and places to eat.

⊙ Sights

The town arcs around an attractive tank that's best observed from **Kudiyiruppu Pillaiyar Kovil** (Pandaravanniyan Rd), a sprawling and ramshackle Ganesh temple. The market area surrounding the **Grand Jummah Mosque** (Horowapatana Rd) is easily the most interesting part of town for a wander.

Vavuniya

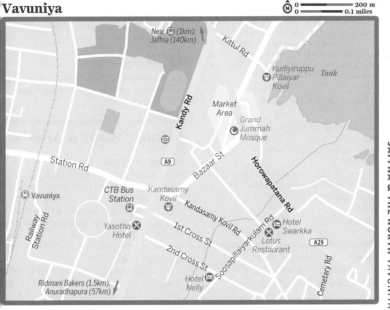

Madukanda Vihara BUDDHIST SITE
(Horowapatana Rd/A29) The quietly charming Madukanda Vihara is a Rs 250 three-wheeler ride from central Vavuniya, beyond the 3km post southeast on the A29. It was reputedly the fourth resting point in the journey of the sacred Buddha tooth relic from Mullaittivu to Anuradhapura during the 4th-century reign of King Mahsen.

Kandasamy Kovil HINDU SITE
(Kandasamy Kovil Rd) This photogenic Murugan (Skanda) temple has a very ornate, if faded, *gopuram* (gateway tower) and a gold-clad image in its sanctum. Walk back through the surrounding buildings to appreciate it, as it's somewhat obscured.

🏨 Sleeping & Eating

Hotel Nelly HOTEL **$**
(☑ 024-222 4477; www.nellystarhotel.com; 84 2nd Cross St; r with fan/air con from Rs 2200/3000; ❄ 🞿 ☒) The Nelly has an ungainly appearance. You enter through a banquet hall. But its wide choice of large rooms offer decent value and are the best choice in the area (the choice is limited). There is a small restaurant in a claustrophobic room walled off with heavy curtains (mains Rs 300 to Rs 600) and a bar with beer. It does a big business in takeaway pizza.

Hotel Swarkka GUESTHOUSE **$**
(☑ 024-222 1090; Soosapillaiyarkulam Rd; s/d with fan Rs 1500/2000, with air-con Rs 1750/3000; ❄) If you're really on an economy drive, this dated hotel might suffice for a night. Rooms, with TV and mossie nets, are spacious but ageing.

Yasotha Hotel SRI LANKAN **$**
(138 Kandy Rd; mains Rs130-250; ⊘ 8am-10pm) The cook is making *kotthu* (*rotti* chopped up and mixed with veggies etc) right in the front window at this clean and spiffy snack spot by the bus terminal. Choose from cheese, chicken or beef. The Yasotha Hotel has been proudly serving food since 1994.

Ridmani Bakers BAKERY **$**
(Kandy Rd/A9; snacks from Rs 50; ⊘ 7am-9pm) This roadside bakery 1km south of the centre is small, but it has a big selection that is fresh all day. Choose from savoury items such as rolls filled with veggies, chicken and fish, or just grab a few cookies.

Lotus Restaurant SRI LANKAN **$**
(Soosapillaiyarkulam Rd; mains Rs150-300; ⊘ 8am-10pm) This little cafe could not be cleaner. There's no printed menu, but you can choose between string hoppers and curries to enjoy in the large, covered open-air dining area. It is in front of the Hotel Swarkka (p289).

ℹ️ Information

Vavuniya is full of transient characters, and the streets are quiet after dark. Solo women should exercise caution when going out at night. There are numerous ATMs in the centre of town. The **post office** (Kandy Rd; ⊙ 8am-8pm Mon-Sat) is centrally located off Kandy Rd.

ℹ️ Getting There & Away

BUS
Vavuniya's Central Tourist Board (CTB) **bus station** (Kandy Rd) is by the clock tower. Less organised private buses, with similar fares, line 2nd Cross St.

A new bus station serving all buses is set to open 1km north of town on the Kandy Rd.

Anuradhapura Rs 100, one hour, every 20 minutes

Colombo CTB/private 'semi-luxury' Rs 330/440, 6½ hours, every 30 minutes

Jaffna Rs 185, three hours, every 30 minutes

Kandy Rs 220, five hours, 12 daily

Mannar Rs 111, 2½ hours, hourly

Trincomalee Rs 130, 3½ hours, hourly

TRAIN
Vavuniya's **railway station** (☑ 024-222 2271; Railway Station Rd; ⊙ booking office 7-10am & 4-5pm) has pleasant, shady platforms. Lines have been rebuilt and service restored north to Jaffna.

Anuradhapura 3rd/2nd/1st class Rs 50/90/160, one hour, six daily

Colombo 3rd/2nd/1st class Rs 185/330/600, five to seven hours, six daily

Jaffna 3rd/2nd/1st class Rs 150/280/520, two to three hours, four daily

ℹ️ Getting Around

Many of Vavuniya's three-wheelers are equipped with meters, so prices for short hops around town are reasonable.

Mannar Island & Around
☑ 023

Sun-blasted Mannar Island is a dry near-peninsula with lots of white sand and palm trees, gulls and terns, wild donkeys and fishing boats. Culturally, it's an intriguing place: it's dotted with ancient baobab trees (native to Africa and said to have been planted by Arab merchants many centuries ago) and crumbling colonial edifices built by the Portuguese, Dutch and Brits.

Once a prosperous pearling centre, today Mannar is one of the poorest corners of Sri Lanka. The island was once a major exit and entry point to India, just 30km away, but those services are now a distant memory. Thousands of Muslims were driven out by the LTTE in 1990.

Way out here, the island still feels like a world apart, with dusty streets, a slightly forlorn appearance and more than its share of trash and mosquitoes. That said, the people are welcoming and there's a hint of adventure.

◉ Sights

◉ Mannar Town

Reached via a 3km-long causeway from the mainland, Mannar town is a somewhat scruffy transport hub. Excepting the fort there's not that much for tourists, but as most accommodation is based here, this is where most travellers pause.

★**Dutch Fort**   FORT
(Mannar Town) An imposing Portuguese-Dutch construction, this fortress is situated right by the causeway to the island and is ringed by a moat. It's a bit shambolic, but the walls are atmospheric and contain the roofless remains of a chapel, dungeon and Dutch bell tower. Climb the ramparts for an impressive perspective of the town and the Gulf of Mannar. Don't miss the carved details on the entrance to the central courtyard (where you can park).

TEMPLE OF PROTECTION

On the mainland, 10km east of Mannar Town, **Thirukketeeswaram Kovil** (off A32) is one of the *pancha ishwaram,* the five historical Sri Lankan Shiva temples established to protect the island from natural disaster. It's an imposing site, with a towering, colourful *gopuram*. Ranged around the temple are pavilions containing five gigantic floats, called juggernauts, which are wheeled out each February for the impressive Maha Sivarathiri festival. The entire complex is in the midst of a vast reconstruction and expansion.

Thirukketeeswaram Kovil is 1km north off the A32, about 3km east of the Mannar causeway. Buses from Mannar are regular; three-wheelers charge Rs 1000 for the round trip. There are a few stands offering drinks and snacks; peacocks strut their stuff.

PEARL ISLAND

The shallow seas around Mannar have been associated with pearls since antiquity. Ancient Greek and Roman texts mention pearling here, and the Chinese monk Fa-hsien (Faxian) documented Mannar's exceptional pearls in 411, as did Marco Polo. Arab sailor Ibn Batuta (who passed by in 1344) reported seeing precious collections of pearls in the Mannar royal treasury. The British also benefited substantially from pearl profits. Between 1796 and 1809, £517,481 (a vast sum in those days) was credited as revenue into the Ceylon treasury from pearls. Over 200 pearling boats would set sail each day to comb the shallow waters of the Gulf of Mannar, each boat containing a government-employed 'shark charmer' who would perform ceremonies to safeguard divers against underwater attack.

Profits from pearling declined steeply in the late 19th century, possibly due to dredging, over-exploitation and the emergence of cultured pearls. The last pearling season in Sri Lanka, 1906, was a commercial failure.

Baobab Tree Pallimunai LANDMARK

(Palimunai Rd, Mannar Town) An offbeat attraction, this ancient baobab tree was allegedly planted by Arab traders. It has a circumference of 20m and is believed to be over 700 years old. In Africa the baobab is sometimes called the upside-down tree (because its branches look like roots); locals in Mannar refer to it as the *ali gaha* (elephant tree) since its tough, gnarled bark resembles the skin of an elephant. It's 1.2km northeast of the town centre.

Around the Island

The island is not endowed with beautiful stretches of sand, but **Keeri Beach** has good swimming, though no shade. Expect some trash. It's fringed by a small palmyra palm forest that's home to monkeys; it's located 5km west of Mannar Town.

Heading northwest from Mannar Town you pass a cluster of **baobab trees** after about 3km. Around the 8km marker is **Our Lady of the Martyrs**, a church and huge meditation hall where many hundreds gather to pray and meditate (Thursdays, 4pm to 7pm).

Continuing west you pass a vast lagoon (look out for flamingos in February, white and blue herons most times) and the small town of Pesalai before approaching the port of Talaimannar, 38km from Mannar Town.

Talaimannar

This was once the passage to India. Until 1990 ferries departed to Rameswaram in India from this tiny port on the island's western extreme. But those days are long gone – the last ferry departed in 1994, with a load of refugees fleeing the violence. Today you feel at the end of the world here. A lonely **lighthouse** (off A14, Talaimannar) stands near the old rusty ferry pier. There are some sunken fishing boats among the working ones. There are few people about and no services, but signs describe the local history, and the views over the turquoise water are alluring.

Offshore is **Adam's Bridge** – a chain of reefs, sandbanks and islets that nearly connects Sri Lanka to the Indian subcontinent. In the Ramayana these were the stepping stones that the monkey king Hanuman used in his bid to help rescue Rama's wife Sita from Rawana, the demon king of Lanka.

The narrow beach around the old pier is OK for swimming. It's better at the village of **Urumale**, 1km east of the lighthouse, where fishermen specialise in catching stingrays – you'll see (and smell) chunks drying in the sun here. Boats line the beach in front of the village, but there are empty sands a short walk away to the east.

Sleeping & Eating

Mannar Town has the most organised places to stay. There are some very basic roadside guesthouses in Pesalai midway along the island. There is no place to stay in Talaimannar.

Mannar Guest House GUESTHOUSE $

(077 316 8202, 023-222 2006; www.mannarguesthouse.com; 55/12 Uppukulam, Mannar Town; s/d with fan Rs 1500/2000, with air-con Rs 2000/2500; ❄☏) In a mixed Hindu/Muslim residential neighbourhood, this well-run, architecturally eclectic guesthouse has 21 rooms all with private bathrooms. The English-speaking owner's family live at the rear of the compound and can provide meals if organised in advance.

Baobab Guest House GUESTHOUSE $

(023-222 3155; 70 Field St, Mannar Town; s/d with fan Rs 1750/2000, with air-con Rs 2750/3000; ❄☏) A cheerful, welcoming place run by

WORTH A TRIP

CHURCH OF MIRACLES

This mainland church, **Our Lady of Madhu Church** (Madhu; ⊙ church 5.30am-7.30pm, information office 7.30am-5.30pm), is Sri Lanka's most hallowed Christian monument (though it's thought to be have been constructed over an ancient Hindu shrine). Its walls shelter Our Lady of Madhu, a diminutive but revered Madonna-and-child statue brought here in 1670 by Catholics fleeing Protestant Dutch persecution in Mannar. Our Lady is 12km along Madhu Rd, which branches off the A14 at Madhu Junction on the 47km marker.

The statue rapidly developed a reputation for miracles – it was particularly revered as offering protection from snake bites – and Madhu has been a place of pilgrimage ever since. The vast Madhu compound also served as a refuge for those fleeing the civil war when refugee camps ringed the complex.

The present church dates from 1872 and is quite austere but has soaring central columns. Outside, the most striking feature is the elongated portico painted cream and duck-egg blue. The church attracts huge crowds of pilgrims to its 10 annual festivals, especially the one on 15 August. The grounds now boast huge golden statues representing the stations of the cross.

Vavuniya–Mannar buses stop at Madhu Junction. From here three-wheelers cost Rs 900 return, including waiting time. A partially paved road runs east from the church and eventually joins the A30, giving a shortcut to Vavuniya.

Jerome (who will do train-station pick-ups), Baobab has a quiet location, an attractive living/dining room, a porch for relaxing, and good meals (order ahead). The traditional red-oxide floors and window screens add a touch of the tropics. It's a 10-minute walk from the centre of town. As there are only four rooms, book ahead.

Four Tees Rest Inn   LODGE **$**
(☎ 023-323 0008; Station Rd, Thoddaveli; ⊙ s/d with fan & shared bathroom Rs 1500/2000; ✳) This likeable albeit isolated lodge, 9km northwest of Mannar Town, offers a quiet, rural base and is shaded by mature trees. It's particularly popular with birders. Manager Mr Lawrence is a great source of information and can organise birdwatching excursions. Good meals (around Rs 500) are available. It's close to the Thoddaveli train stop.

Shell Coast Resort   HOTEL **$$$**
(☎ 077 144 9062; www.shellcoastresort.com; s/d incl breakfast from US$75/80; ✳ 🛜 🌊) Offering beachside accommodation on Mannar, this resort, 6km south of Pesalai, offers comfy octagonal wooden cabanas with terraces and attractive rooms with shared verandahs. The rustic setting will suit those searching for a back-to-nature vibe. You can arrange for meals (a good idea as you're quite isolated here).

Palmyrah House   HOTEL **$$$**
(☎ 011-259 4467; www.palmyrahhouse.com; off A14, Karisal; s/d inc breakfast from US$85/110; ✳ 🛜 🌊) 🌿 Offers five tasteful, colonial-style rooms in a custom-built two-storey building with wide, shady porches. It's in a tranquil location around 12km northwest of Mannar Town; the ambience and service are refined. You can also arrange for half- and full-board. Borrow a bike for the five-minute ride to a decent beach.

❶ Getting There & Away

The A14 to Mannar Town is in excellent condition. From here west to Talaimannar, it's sealed but rough. There is no sign that ferries to Rameswaram (India) will ever resume.

BUS

Buses from Mannar's **bus station** (A14, Mannar Town) include the following:

Colombo Rs 550, eight hours, seven daily.

Jaffna Rs 180, three hours, 10 daily.

Tallaimannar Rs 65, 30 minutes, hourly.

Thirukketeeswaram Kovil Rs 25, 20 minutes, nine daily.

Vavuniya Rs 120, 2½ hours, hourly.

TRAIN

Trains run from Colombo via the junction at Medawachchiya to Mannar, where the **railway station** (S Bar Rd, Mannar Town) is 2.3km west of town. Trains continue on to Talaimannar and a quiet station near the lighthouse, making numerous whistle stops across the island.

Trains from Mannar include the following:

Colombo 3rd/2nd/1st class Rs 620/350/205, eight hours, two daily.

Talaimannar 3rd/2nd/1st class Rs 50/90/160 45 minutes, two daily.

Understand
Sri Lanka

Sri Lanka Today

As the physical and economic consequences of the country's long civil war recede, tourists continue to pour into Sri Lanka in ever greater numbers. The country had a surprising election result in 2015 that saw a new coalition come to power. Much of the current government's attention continues to be focused on unravelling the legacy of the former president Mahinda Rajapaksa.

Best on Film

Dheepan (2015) Refugees try to escape human rights abuses in Sri Lanka by fleeing to France, but it's not that easy. It won the Palme d'Or at Cannes.

Flying Fish (2011) Set in his hometown of Trincomalee, director Sanjeewa Pushpakumara creates an anthology about people trying to live through the war.

Karma (2013) An award-winning mature drama by director Prasanna Jayakody. It depicts adults trying to make sense of their lives and desires in Colombo.

Best in Print

On Sal Mal Lane (Ru Freeman; 2013) Weaves together the many strands of Sri Lankan society in a beautiful novel set down a Colombo lane.

Anil's Ghost (Michael Ondaatje; 2000) The Booker Prize–winning author's haunting novel about human rights amid the turmoil of late-20th-century Sri Lanka. The book has received international commendation and some local condemnation.

Monkfish Moon (Romesh Gunesekera; 1992) Nine short stories, by the Booker Prize–nominated writer, provide a diverse glimpse of Sri Lanka's ethnic conflict. His *Reef* is also widely praised.

Human Rights Concerns

Over eight years after the war ended, Sri Lanka continues to struggle with its aftermath. While some infrastructure across the north and east has been rebuilt (some of the country's best roads and mobile-phone reception are now in these regions), it will take much longer for other scars to heal.

One major sore point is land. Beginning in the 1990s huge numbers of people were forcibly removed from their land by the military. Many of these families were Muslims, who ended up living as refugees in India or in local 'resettlement camps'. Now these displaced people (estimated at over 250,000) are demanding the return of their lands and, starting in 2016, there have been public protests. While the military has never released figures showing how much land it seized, the areas are massive, especially around Mannar and the regions north and east of Jaffna.

The Sri Lankan military claims it has released over 28,000 hectares to its owners (usually small-scale farmers), but it refuses to say how much remains under its control. Meanwhile, returning families are demanding that money spent on the roads and mobile-phone towers extend to electricity and clean water for their reclaimed lands. Many are expressing growing discontent with President Maithripala Sirisena, whom they helped elect in 2015 with the hope they'd get a new start in life.

Investigations over human rights abuses during the last years of the war continue to dog Sri Lanka. Although the current government has been somewhat supportive of the concept, no official or independent investigation has begun and international groups and governments are becoming increasingly impatient. While Sirisena won praise for establishing an Office of Missing Persons, he has been criticised for not pushing a real investigation forward. The EU has said there will need to be human rights improvements before it will extend trade and tariff benefits to Sri Lanka.

The UN Committee Against Torture released a report in 2016 that decried the continued 'brutal' torture of Tamils with even the vaguest suggestion of past Liberation Tigers of Tamil Eelam (LTTE) links, and it said that 'white van' abductions and disappearances continue. The Sri Lankan government has denied the allegations.

Other obstacles blocking true peace are a spate of new military-built monuments celebrating victory, which locals have protested as insensitive, and new military-owned resorts planned for prime pieces of land in the North and East.

Foreign Relations

Sri Lanka is dealing with many international challenges beyond those related to the legacies of the war. The previous Rajapaksa government's massive Chinese-financed construction schemes have run up a huge debt. China has made no secret of its expectation that it will receive something in return, beyond debt repayment. However, locals are pushing back. An agreement to give the Chinese government permanent freehold of a large area of the new Hambantota port was scaled back to a 99-year lease by the Sirisena government after violent protests broke out.

Closer yet, the Indian government, seeing China establish a foothold close to its coast, is also vying for Sri Lanka's attention, with various schemes such as massive investments in the Tamil north. Even here, though, the relationship is complicated. An offer by Sri Lanka to give India control of the Trincomalee port to offset the Chinese control of the Hambantota port was rejected, as developing it will require enormous investment.

Tourists Everywhere

Visitor numbers to Sri Lanka continue to boom. Consider: in 2005 there were barely 550,000 foreign visitors to the country. In 2010, the year after the war ended, there were 655,000. From there, the numbers have simply shot up, averaging a 22% increase a year. In 2016, a whopping 2.1 million tourists arrived. (To put that into perspective, however, that same year the island of Bali received 4 million visitors, and Thailand 32.6 million.)

This influx of visitors has driven a huge amount of investment in businesses geared to tourism, from Jaffna to Galle. Huge hotels are in the works backed by multinational corporations, but so too are family-run guesthouses. Tourism now accounts for 11% of the economy and with so much of the nation's gorgeous coast undeveloped, it seems there is no reason to expect that the numbers won't keep growing.

In the meantime, infrastructure is struggling to keep up. For many involved in tourism, the new terminal at Bandaranaike International Airport – slated for completion in 2020 – can't come soon enough.

POPULATION: **22.3 MILLION**

AREA: **65,610 SQ KM**

GDP: **US$80.6 BILLION**

ANNUAL INFLATION: **6.9%**

UNEMPLOYMENT: **4.6%**

if Sri Lanka were 100 people

75 would be Sinhalese
11 would be Sri Lankan Tamils
9 would be Sri Lankan Moors
4 would be Indian Tamils
1 would be other

belief systems
(% of population)

70 Buddhist

13 Hindu

10 Muslim

7 Christian

population per sq km

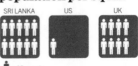

SRI LANKA   US   UK

≈ 35 people

History

Sri Lanka's location – near India and along hundreds of ancient trade routes – has for ages made it attractive to immigrants, invaders, missionaries, traders and travellers from India, East Asia and the Middle East. Many stayed on, and over generations they assimilated and intermarried, converted and converted back. Although debates still rage over who was here first and who can claim Sri Lanka as their homeland, the island's history, like that of its ethnicities, is one of shifting dominance and constant flux.

Prehistory & Early Arrivals

Sri Lanka's history is a source of great pride to both Sinhalese and Tamils, the country's two largest ethnic groups. The only problem is, they have two completely different versions. Every historical site, religious structure, even village name seems to have conflicting stories about its origin, and those stories are, in turn, blended over time with contrasting religious myths and local legends. The end results are often used as evidence that the island is one group's exclusive homeland; each claims first dibs.

Did the Buddha leave his footprint on Adam's Peak (Sri Pada) while visiting the island that lay halfway to paradise? Or was it Adam who left his footprint embedded in the rock while taking a last look at Eden? Was the chain of islands linking Sri Lanka to India the same chain that Rama crossed to rescue his wife Sita from the clutches of Rawana, demon king of Lanka, in the epic Ramayana?

Possible Early Iron Age Sites

....

Sigiriya

....

Kantarodai

....

Tissamaharama

Whatever the legends, the reality is that Sri Lanka's original inhabitants, the Veddahs (or, as they refer to themselves, Wanniyala-aetto: 'forest dwellers'), were hunter-gatherers who subsisted on the island's natural bounty. Much about their origins is unclear, but anthropologists generally believe they are descended from people who migrated from India, and possibly Southeast Asia, and existed on the island as far back as 32,000 BC. It's also likely that rising waters submerged a land bridge between India and Sri Lanka in around 5000 BC.

Historians and archaeologists have differing interpretations of its origins, but a megalithic culture emerged in the centuries around 900 BC

TIMELINE	Pre-6th century BC	6th century BC	3rd century BC
	The island is inhabited by Veddahs (Wanniyala-aetto), a group of hunter-gatherers who anthropologists believe were descendants of a society that existed on Sri Lanka since 32,000 BC.	Vijaya, a shamed North Indian prince, is cast adrift, but makes landfall on Sri Lanka's west coast. He settles around Anuradhapura and establishes the island's first recorded kingdom.	Indian emperor Ashoka sends his son and daughter to spread the Buddha's teachings. Anuradhapuran King Devanampiya Tissa accepts them, beginning Sri Lanka's ties between government and religion

with striking similarities to the South Indian cultures of that time. Also during this early Iron Age, Anuradhapura grew as a population centre.

Objects inscribed with Brahmi (an ancient 'parent' script to most South Asian scripts) have been found from the 3rd century BC; parallels to both North Indian and South Indian Brahmi styles have been made, though Tamil words are used in many of those found in the north and east of the island. Sri Lankan historians debate these details fiercely, as do many Sri Lankans, but rather than there being two distinct ethnic histories, it is more likely that migrations from West, East and South India all happened during this time and that those new arrivals all mixed with the indigenous people.

Anuradhapura

The 5th-century-AD Pali epic, the Mahavamsa, is the country's primary historical source. Although it's a somewhat faithful record of kingdoms and Sinhalese political power from around the 3rd century BC, its historical accuracy is shakier – and indeed full of beautiful myths – before this time. Nonetheless, many Sinhalese claim they're descended from Vijaya, an immoral 6th-century-BC North Indian prince who, according to the epic, had a lion for a grandfather and a father with lion paws who married his own sister. Vijaya was banished for bad behaviour, with a contingent of 700 men, on dilapidated ships from the subcontinent.

Landing near present-day Mannar, supposedly on the day that the Buddha attained enlightenment, Vijaya and his crew settled around Anuradhapura, and soon encountered Kuveni, a Yaksha (probably Veddah) who is alternately described as a vicious queen and a seductress who assumed the form of a 16-year-old maiden to snag Vijaya. She handed Vijaya the crown, joined him in slaying her own people and had two children with him before he kicked her out and ordered a princess – and wives for his men – from South India's Tamil Pandya kingdom. (That, by this account, the forefathers of the Sinhalese race all married Tamils is overlooked by most Sri Lankans.) His rule formed the basis of the Anuradhapura kingdom, which developed there in the 4th century BC.

The Anuradhapura kingdom covered the island in the 2nd century BC, but it frequently fought, and coexisted with, other dynasties on the island over the centuries, especially the Tamil Cholas. The boundaries between Anuradhapura and various South Indian kingdoms were frequently shifting, and Anuradhapura was also involved in conflicts in South India. A number of Sinhalese warriors arose to repel South Indian kingdoms, including Vijayabahu I (11th century AD), who finally abandoned Anuradhapura and made Polonnaruwa, further southeast, his capital.

For centuries, the kingdom was able to rebuild after its battles through *rajakariya,* the system of free labour for the king. This free labour provided the resources to restore buildings, tanks and irrigation systems and to

The indigenous Veddahs were called Yakshas, or nature spirits, by the island's early arrivals. No one knows if this is because the Veddahs were so at home in nature or because they prayed to their departed ancestors – spirits known as *nae yaku.*

Veddah Place Names

....

Gal Oya National Park

....

Nanu Oya

....

Kelaniya Ganga

205–161 BC	103–89 BC	1st century BC	4th century AD
Reign of Chola King Elara, described in the Mahavamsa as a just leader. Although Tamil and Hindu, he offers alms to Buddhist monks and employs both Sinhalese and Tamils.	Five Tamil kings from India invade Anuradhapura and rule for 14 years. King Valagamba is forced to flee and shelters in the caves around Dambulla.	The Fourth Buddhist council is held in Aluvihara. The Buddha's teachings, previously preserved by oral tradition, are written down for the first time.	Buddhism is further popularised with the arrival in Anuradhapura of the sacred tooth relic of the Buddha. It becomes a symbol of both religion and sovereignty over the island.

develop agriculture. The system was not banished from the island until 1832, when the British passed laws banning slavery.

The Buddha's Teaching Arrives

Buddhism arrived from India in the 3rd century BC, transforming Anuradhapura and possibly creating what is now known as Sinhalese culture. The mountain at Mihintale marks the spot where King Devanampiya Tissa is said to have first received the Buddha's teaching. The earliest Buddhist emissaries also brought to Sri Lanka a cutting of the bodhi tree under which the Buddha attained enlightenment. It survives in Anuradhapura, now garlanded with prayer flags and lights. Strong ties gradually evolved between Sri Lankan royalty and Buddhist religious orders. Kings, grateful for monastic support, provided living quarters, tanks (reservoirs) and produce to the monasteries, and a symbiotic political economy between religion and state was established – a powerful contract that is still vital in modern times.

Buddhism underwent a further major development on the island when the original oral teachings were documented in writing in the 1st century BC. The early Sri Lankan monks went on to write a vast body of commentaries on the teachings, textbooks, Pali grammars and other instructive articles, developing a classical literature for the Theravada (doctrine of the elders) school of Buddhism that continues to be referenced by Theravada Buddhists around the world. The arrival of the Buddha's tooth relic at Anuradhapura in AD 371 reinforced the position of Buddhism in Sinhalese society, giving a sense of national purpose and identity and inspiring the development of Sinhalese culture and literature.

The bodhi tree in Anuradhapura has a 2000-year history of human care and custody, making it the world's oldest tree of this kind.

TANK-BUILDING

The science of building tanks, studying gradients and constructing channels is the key to early Sri Lankan civilisation. The tanks, which dot the plains of the ancient dominions of Rajarata (in the north-central part of the country) and Ruhuna (in the southeast), probably started as modest structures. But by the 5th century BC they reached such dimensions that local legends say they were built with supernatural help. It is claimed that Giant's Tank near Mannar Island was built by giants, while other tanks were said to have been constructed by a mixed workforce of humans and demons.

The irrigation system, developed on ever-greater scales during the millennium before the Common Era, ranks with the ancient *qanats* (underground channels) of Iran and the canals of Pharaonic Egypt in sophistication. These dry-zone reservoirs sustained and shaped Sri Lanka's civilisation for more than 2500 years, until war and discord overtook the island in the 12th to 14th centuries AD.

5th century	5th century	7th–15th century	11th century
After engineering his father's death and expelling his older brother Mugalan, King Kasyapa constructs the rock fortress at Sigiriya. With the assistance of Indian mercenaries, Mugalan finally retakes the throne.	Indian scholar-monk Buddhaghosa arrives in Sri Lanka and writes the Visuddhimagga, a manual for the Buddha's teachings. His explications become part of the Theravada canon and are still studied today.	Arab traders settle in Sri Lanka, marrying locally and establishing Islam on the island. They maintain trade with the Middle East and coexist peacefully with both Tamils and Sinhalese.	Weary of continued conflict with Tamil neighbours, King Vijayabahu I defeats the Cholas and moves the Sinhalese capital southeast to Polonnaruwa; a brief golden age follows.

Polonnaruwa

The next capital, at Polonnaruwa, survived for over two centuries and produced two more notable rulers. Parakramabahu I (r 1153–86), nephew of Vijayabahu I, expelled the South Indian Tamil Chola empire from Sri Lanka, and carried the fight to South India, even making a raid on Myanmar. He also constructed many new tanks and lavished public money to make Polonnaruwa a great Asian capital.

His benevolent successor, Nissanka Malla (r 1187–96), was the last king of Polonnaruwa to care for the well-being of his people. He was followed by a series of weak rulers, and with the decay of the irrigation system, disease spread and Polonnaruwa was abandoned. The lush jungle reclaimed the second Sinhalese capital in just a few decades.

After Polonnaruwa, Sinhalese power shifted to the southwest of the island, and between 1253 and 1400 there were another five different capitals, none of them as powerful as Anuradhapura or Polonnaruwa. Meanwhile, the powerful kingdom of Jaffna expanded to cover a huge part of the island; when Arab traveller Ibn Batuta visited Ceylon in 1344, he reported that it extended south as far as Puttalam.

With the decline of the Sinhalese northern capitals and ensuing Sinhalese migration south, a wide jungle buffer separated the northern, mostly coastal Tamil settlements and the southern, interior Sinhalese settlements. For centuries, this jungle barrier kept Sinhalese and Tamils largely apart, sowing the seeds for Sri Lanka's ethnic dichotomy.

Trade & Conquest
Enter the Portuguese

At the heart of the Indian Ocean, Sri Lanka had been a trading hub even before Arab traders arrived in the 7th century AD with their new Islamic faith. Gems, cinnamon, ivory and elephants were the valued items of commerce. Early Muslim settlements took hold in Jaffna and Galle, but the arrival of a European power, focused as much on domination as trade, forced many Muslims inland to flee persecution.

When the Portuguese arrived in 1505, Sri Lanka had three main kingdoms: the Tamil kingdom of Jaffna and Sinhalese kingdoms in Kandy and Kotte (near Colombo). Lourenço de Almeida, the son of the Portuguese Viceroy of India, established friendly relations with the Kotte kingdom and gained a monopoly on the valuable spice trade. The Portuguese eventually gained control of the Kotte kingdom.

Tamil–Portuguese relations were less cordial, and Jaffna successfully resisted two Portuguese expeditions before falling in 1619, at which point the Portuguese destroyed Jaffna's many beautiful Hindu temples and its royal library. Portugal eventually took over the entire west coast, then the east, but the Kandyan kingdom in the central highlands resisted domination.

Descendants of Mozambican slaves brought to Sri Lanka by the Portuguese are almost totally assimilated. Their most obvious contributions to Sri Lankan culture are *bailas*, love songs with Latin melodies and African rhythms.

1216	1505	1658	1796
As Polonnaruwa declines, the Tamil kingdom of Jaffna is established and briefly becomes a feudatory of South India's Pandya kingdom before gaining independence. It survives for four centuries.	Following Polonnaruwa's decline, Sinhalese power is with the Kotte in the southwest and Kandy. The Portuguese arrive and conquer the entire west coast, but Kandy defeats their advances.	Following a treaty with the Kandyan kingdom, the Dutch, who arrived in 1602, establish a monopoly on the spice market and wrest control of coastal Sri Lanka from the Portuguese.	The Netherlands, under French control, surrenders Ceylon to the British. The shift is initially thought to be temporary, and the British administer the island from Madras, India.

European-Era Forts

Batticaloa

Jaffna

Matara

Trincomalee

Galle

Mannar

Sunil S Amrith's *Crossing the Bay of Bengal: The Furies of Nature and the Fortunes of Migrants* tells the human, economic and environmental history of the bay whose 'western gateway' was once Ceylon.

The Portuguese brought religious orders, including the Dominicans and Jesuits. Many coastal communities converted, but resistance to Christianity was met with massacres and the destruction of temples. Buddhists fled to Kandy and the city assumed its role as protector of the Buddhist faith, a sacred function solidified by another three centuries of unsuccessful attempts at domination by European powers.

The Dutch

In 1602 the Dutch arrived, just as keen as the Portuguese on dominating the lucrative traffic in Indian Ocean spices. In exchange for Sri Lankan autonomy, the Kandyan king, Rajasinha II, gave the Dutch a monopoly on the spice trade. Despite the deal, the Dutch made repeated unsuccessful attempts to subjugate Kandy during their 140-year rule.

The Dutch were more industrious than the Portuguese, and canals were built along the west coast to transport cinnamon and other crops. Some can be seen around Negombo today. The legal system of the Dutch era still forms part of Sri Lanka's legal canon.

The British

The British initially viewed Sri Lanka in strategic terms, and considered the eastern harbour of Trincomalee as a counter to French influence in India. After the French took over the Netherlands in 1794, the pragmatic Dutch ceded Sri Lanka to the British for 'protection' in 1796. The British moved quickly, making the island a colony in 1802 and finally taking over Kandy in 1815. Three years later, the first unified administration of the island by a European power was established.

The British conquest unsettled many Sinhalese, who believed that only the custodians of the tooth relic had the right to rule the land. Their apprehension was somewhat relieved when a senior monk removed the tooth relic from the Temple of the Sacred Tooth Relic, thereby securing it (and the island's symbolic sovereignty) for the Sinhalese people. Sinhalese angst grew when British settlers began arriving in the 1830s. Coffee and rubber were largely replaced by tea from the 1870s, and the island's demographic mix was profoundly altered with an influx of Tamil labourers from South India. (These 'Plantation Tamils' were – and still are – separated by geography, history and caste from the Jaffna Tamils.) Tamil settlers from the North made their way south to Colombo, while Sinhalese headed to Jaffna. British colonisation set the island in a demographic flux.

The Road to Independence
Growing Nationalism

The dawning of the 20th century was an important time for the grass-roots Sri Lankan nationalist movement. Towards the end of the 19th

1802	1815	1832	1843–59
After the decline of the Dutch, Sri Lanka becomes a British colony. The island is viewed as a strategic bulwark against French expansion, but its commercial potential is soon recognised.	Determined to rule the entire island, the British finally conquer the Kandyan kingdom. It's the first (and only) time all of Sri Lanka is ruled by a European power.	Sweeping changes in property laws open the door to British settlers. English becomes the official language, state monopolies are abolished and capital flows in, funding the establishment of coffee plantations.	Unable to persuade the Sinhalese to labour on plantations, the British bring in almost one million Tamil labourers from South India. Today 'Plantation Tamils' are 4% of the population

century, Buddhist and Hindu campaigns were established with the dual aim of making the faiths more contemporary in the wake of European colonialism, and defending traditional Sri Lankan culture against the impact of Christian missionaries. The logical progression was for these groups to demand greater Sri Lankan participation in government, and by 1910 they had secured the minor concession of allowing Sri Lankans to elect one lonely member to the Legislative Council.

By 1919 the nationalist mission was formalised as the Ceylon National Congress. The Sinhalese-nationalist activist Anagarika Dharmapala was forced to leave the country, and the mantle for further change was taken up by a variety of youth leagues, some Sinhalese and some Tamil. In 1927 Mahatma Gandhi visited Tamil youth activists in Jaffna, providing further momentum to the cause.

Further reform came in 1924, when a revision to the constitution allowed for representative government, and again in 1931, when a new constitution finally included the island's leaders in the parliamentary decision-making process and granted universal suffrage. Under the constitution no one ethnic community could dominate the political process, and a series of checks and balances ensured all areas of the government were overseen by a committee drawn from all ethnic groups. However, both Sinhalese and Tamil political leaders failed to thoroughly support the country's pre-independence constitution, foreshadowing the problems that were to characterise the next eight decades.

From Ceylon to Sri Lanka

Following India's independence in 1947, Ceylon (as Sri Lanka was then called) became fully independent on 4 February 1948. Despite featuring members from all of the island's ethnic groups, the ruling United National Party (UNP) really only represented the interests of an English-speaking elite. The UNP's decision to try to deny the 'Plantation Tamils' citizenship and repatriate them to India was indicative of a rising tide of Sinhalese nationalism.

In 1956 this divide increased when the Sri Lankan Freedom Party (SLFP) came to power with an agenda based on socialism, Sinhalese nationalism and government support for Buddhism. One of the first tasks of SLFP leader SWRD Bandaranaike was to fulfil a campaign promise to make Sinhala the country's sole official language. Under the British, Tamils had become capable English speakers and were overrepresented in universities and public-service jobs, which created Sinhalese resentment, especially during the slow economy of the 1950s. The main political parties played on Sinhalese fear that their religion, language and culture could be swamped by Indians, perceived to be natural allies of Sri Lankan Tamils. The Tamils, whose Hindu identity had become more pronounced in the lead-up to independence, began to find themselves in the position of threatened minority.

Sir James Emerson Tennent's affable nature shines through in his honest and descriptive writing about 19th-century Sri Lanka, now in the public domain online at www. gutenberg.org.

HISTORY THE ROAD TO INDEPENDENCE

Not an easy read but an important one, *When Memory Dies*, by A Sivanandan, is a tale of the ethnic crisis and its impact on one family over three generations.

1870s	late 19th century	1919	1931
The coffee industry drives the development of roads, ports and railways, but leaf blight decimates the industry and plantations are converted to growing tea or rubber.	The Arwi language, a combination of Tamil and Arabic that evolved among Sri Lankan Moors, is at its peak, with the publication of several important religious works.	Following the British arrest in 1915 of Sinhalese leaders for minor offences, the Ceylon National Congress unifies Sinhalese and Tamil groups to further nationalist and pro-independence goals.	A new constitution introduces power sharing with a Sinhalese-run government. Universal suffrage is introduced as the country is the first Asian colony to give women the right to vote.

WHAT'S IN A NAME?

Changing the country's name from Ceylon to Sri Lanka in 1972 caused considerable confusion for foreigners. However, for the Sinhalese the country had always been known as Lanka and for the Tamils as Ilankai; the Ramayana, too, describes the abduction of Sita by the king of Lanka. The Romans knew the island as Taprobane and Muslim traders talked of Serendib, meaning 'Island of Jewels' in Arabic. The word Serendib became the root of the word 'serendipity' – the art of making happy and unexpected discoveries. The Portuguese somehow twisted Sinhala-dvipa (Island of the Sinhalese) into Ceilão. In turn, the Dutch altered this to Ceylan and the British to Ceylon. In 1972 'Lanka' was restored, with the addition of 'Sri', a title of respect.

The Sinhala-only bill disenfranchised Sri Lanka's Hindu and Muslim Tamil-speaking population: almost 30% of the country suddenly lost access to government jobs and services. Although tensions had been simmering since the end of colonial rule, this decision marked the beginning of Sri Lanka's ethnic conflict.

A similar scenario played out in 1970, when a law was passed favouring Sinhalese for admission to universities, reducing numbers of Tamil students. Then, following an armed insurrection against the government by the hardline anti-Tamil, student-led People's Liberation Front (Janatha Vimukthi Peramuna or JVP), a new constitution, which changed Ceylon's name to Sri Lanka, gave Buddhism 'foremost place' in Sri Lanka and made it the state's duty to 'protect and foster' Buddhism.

Unrest grew among northern Tamils, and a state of emergency was imposed on their home regions for several years from 1971. The police and army that enforced the state of emergency included few Tamils (partly because of the 'Sinhala only' law), creating further division and, for Tamils, an acute sense of oppression.

Enemy Lines: Warfare, Childhood, and Play in Batticaloa, by Margaret Trawick, describes living and working in eastern Sri Lanka and witnessing the recruitment of teenagers to the LTTE cause.

Birth of the Tigers

In the mid-1970s several groups of young Tamils, some of them militant, began advocating for an independent Tamil state called Eelam (Precious Land). They included Vellupillai Prabhakaran, a founder of the Liberation Tigers of Tamil Eelam (LTTE), often referred to as the Tamil Tigers.

Tamil had been elevated to the status of 'national language' for official work, but only in Tamil-majority areas. Clashes between Tamils and security forces developed into a cycle of reprisals, all too often with civilians in the crossfire. Passions on both sides rose, and a pivotal moment came in 1981, when a group of Sinhalese rioters (some say government forces) burnt down

1948	1956	1958	1959
Ceylon becomes an independent member of the Commonwealth six months after neighbouring India. The United National Party (UNP) consolidates power by depriving Plantation Tamils of citizenship.	The Sri Lankan Freedom party (SLFP) defeats the UNP on a socialist and nationalist platform. Protests, ethnic riots and conflict break out after a 'Sinhala only' language law is passed.	The country sees its first island-wide anti-Tamil riot. It lasts for days, leaves more than 200 people dead in violent attacks (and some revenge attacks) and displaces thousands of Tamils.	Despite coming to power in 1956 with a Sinhalese-nationalist manifesto, SWRD Bandaranaike begins negotiating with Tamil leaders for a federation, resulting in his assassination by a Buddhist monk.

Jaffna's library, which contained, among other things, various histories of the Tamil people, some of which were ancient palm-leaf manuscripts.

Small-scale reprisals followed, but the world only took notice two years later, in 1983, when full-scale anti-Tamil massacres erupted in Colombo in response to the Tigers' ambushing and killing of 13 soldiers in the Jaffna region. In a riot now known as Black July, up to 3000 Tamils were clubbed, beaten, burned or shot to death, and Tamil property was looted and burned. Several Tamil-majority areas, including Colombo's Pettah district, were levelled, and violence spread to other parts of the country.

The government, the police and the army were either unable or unwilling to stop the violence; some of them assisted. Hundreds of thousands of Tamils left the country or fled to Tamil-majority areas in the North or East – and many joined the resistance. (Many Sinhalese, meanwhile, moved south from the North and East.) The horror of Black July prompted a groundswell of international sympathy for Tamil armed resistance groups, and brought funding from fellow Tamils in southern India, as well as from the government of Indira Gandhi.

Revenge and counter-revenge attacks continued, and grew into atrocities and massacres – on both sides. The government was widely condemned for acts of torture and disappearances, but it pointed to the intimidation and violence against civilians, including Tamils and Muslims, by the Tamil fighters. Implementation of a 1987 accord – offering limited Tamil autonomy and formalising Tamil as a national language – never happened, and the conflict escalated into a 25-year civil war that eventually claimed upwards of 100,000 lives.

Attempts at Peace
Indian Peacekeeping

In 1987 government forces pushed the LTTE back into Jaffna as part of a major offensive. India pressed the Sri Lankan government to withdraw, and the two heads of state, JR Jayawardene and Rajiv Gandhi, negotiated an accord: the Sri Lankan government would call off the offensive, Tamil rebels would disarm and an Indian Peace Keeping Force (IPKF) would protect the truce. Tamil regions would also have substantial autonomy, as Colombo devolved power to the provinces.

It soon became clear the deal suited no one. The LTTE complied initially but ended up in battle with the IPKF when it refused to disarm. Opposition to the Indians also came from the Sinhalese, a revived JVP and sections of the *sangha* (community of Buddhist monks and nuns), leading to violent demonstrations.

In 1987 the JVP launched a second revolution with political murders and strikes, and by late 1988 the country was terrorised, the economy crippled and the government paralysed. The army struck back with a

William Mc-Gowan's *Only Man Is Vile* is an incisive, unrelenting account of ethnic violence in Sri Lanka, penetrating deeply into its complexities.

1959	1970s	1972	1979
Widow Sirimavo Bandaranaike assumes her late husband's SLFP post, becoming the world's first female prime minister. She is appointed prime minister several more times before her death in 2000.	Young Tamils begin fighting for an independent Tamil state called Eelam (Precious Land) in Sri Lanka's north. The Liberation Tigers of Tamil Eelam (LTTE) emerge as the strongest group.	A new constitution is created. It changes Ceylon's name to Sri Lanka, declares, once again, Sinhalese to be the official language and gives Buddhism 'foremost place' among the island's religions.	Sri Lanka enacts the Prevention of Terrorism Act. Police may detain for up to 18 months anyone thought to be connected with unlawful activities. The Act is still in effect.

ruthless counter-insurgency campaign. The insurrection was put down, but not before tens of thousands died.

By the time the Indian peacekeepers withdrew, in March 1990, they had lost more than 1000 lives in just three years. But no sooner had they left than the war between the LTTE and the Sri Lankan government escalated again. By the end of 1990 the LTTE held Jaffna and much of the North, although the East was largely back under government control. In May 1991 Rajiv Gandhi was assassinated by a suicide bomber; it was blamed on the LTTE, presumably in retaliation for consenting to the IPKF arrangement.

The 2002 Ceasefire

Although most Tamils and Sinhalese longed for peace, extremists on both sides pressed on with war. President Premadasa was assassinated at a May Day rally in 1993. The LTTE was suspected but never claimed responsibility. The following year, the People's Alliance (PA) won the parliamentary elections; its leader, Chandrika Bandaranaike Kumaratunga, the daughter of former leader Sirimavo Bandaranaike, won the presidential election. The PA had promised to end the civil war, but the conflict continued in earnest.

In 2000 a Norwegian peace mission brought the LTTE and the government to the negotiating table, but a ceasefire had to wait until after the December 2001 elections, which handed power to the UNP. Ranil Wickremasinghe became prime minister, and economic growth was strong while peace talks appeared to progress. Wickremasinghe and President Chandrika Bandaranaike Kumaratunga, however, were from different parties, and circled each other warily until 2003, when Kumaratunga dissolved parliament and essentially ousted Wickremasinghe and his UNP.

In 2002, following the Norway-brokered ceasefire agreement, a careful optimism reigned. In the North, refugees, internally displaced persons and long-absent émigrés began to return, bringing an economic boost to devastated Jaffna. Nongovernmental organisations started tackling, among other things, an estimated two million land mines.

But peace talks stumbled, and the situation was ever more fraught. Accusations of bias and injustice were hurled from all sides. In October 2003 the US listed the LTTE as a Foreign Terrorist Organisation. Some believed this to be a positive move; others saw it as an action that would isolate the LTTE, causing further strain and conflict. In early 2004 a split in LTTE ranks added a new dynamic, and with killings, insecurity, accusations and ambiguities, the Norwegians left. At that stage, almost all of Sri Lanka, including most of the Jaffna peninsula, was controlled by the Sri Lankan government. The LTTE controlled a small area south of the Jaffna peninsula and pockets in the East, but it still had claims on land in the Jaffna peninsula and in the island's northwest and northeast.

At least one million land mines were laid during the civil war in the 1990s. Efforts to clear the mines meant that thousands of displaced people were moved and resettled.

In *Crucible of Conflict: Tamil and Muslim Society on the East Coast of Sri Lanka,* Dennis McGilvray argues that peace in Sri Lanka requires recognising the country's cultural diversity.

1981	1983	July 1987	1987–89
Jaffna's Public Library, home to many ancient Tamil works and a symbol of Tamil culture and learning, is burnt down by Sinhalese mobs, galvanising the Tamil separatist movement.	The ambush of an army patrol near Jaffna ignites widespread ethnic violence. Up to 3000 Tamils are estimated killed by Sinhalese rioters in what is now known as Black July.	An accord is signed, with India's involvement, granting Tamils an autonomous province in the country's north, but disagreements over its implementation prevent it from going into effect.	The JVP launches a second Marxist insurrection, and attempts a Khmer Rouge–style peasant rebellion in the countryside. When the uprising is finally crushed, up to 60,000 people have died.

After the Tsunami

An event beyond all predictions struck on 26 December 2004, affecting not only the peace process but also the entire social fabric of Sri Lanka. As people celebrated the monthly *poya* (full moon) festivities, the waves of a tsunami pummelled the country, killing 30,000 people and leaving many more injured, homeless and orphaned. Initial optimism that the nation would come together in the face of catastrophe soon faded into arguments over aid distribution, reconstruction, and land tenure and ownership.

Meanwhile, Kumaratunga, seeking to extend her presidential term, sought to alter the constitution. Thwarted by a Supreme Court ruling, presidential elections were set for 2005. Among the contenders, two candidates were the most likely victors – the then prime minister, Mahinda Rajapaksa, and opposition leader, Ranil Wickremasinghe. With an LTTE voting boycott, Rajapaksa narrowly won. The LTTE's motives for the boycott were unclear, but their actions cost Wickremasinghe an expected 180,000 votes and the presidency and, perhaps, a better chance at peace.

President Rajapaksa pledged to replace Norwegian peace negotiators with those from the UN and India, renegotiate a ceasefire with the LTTE, reject Tamil autonomy and refuse to share tsunami aid with the LTTE. Such policies didn't auger well for future peace. Meanwhile, LTTE leader Prabhakaran insisted on a political settlement during 2006, and threatened to 'intensify' action if this didn't occur. Tensions were high, and again Sri Lanka was perched on a precipice. Killings, assaults, kidnappings and disappearances occurred on both sides, and commentators predicted the worst.

The 2004 Indian Ocean tsunami killed more than 225,000 people in 14 countries. The waves, which were in some places more than 30m tall, travelled as far as the East African coast.

The End of the War

An Elusive Ceasefire

The path to peace was marked by some of the worst violence of the entire civil war. Another ceasefire was signed in early 2006, but cracks soon appeared and by mid-year the agreement was in tatters. Major military operations by both sides resumed in the North and East, and a wave of disappearances and killings in 2006 and 2007 prompted human rights groups and the international community to strongly criticise all belligerents. By August the fighting in the northeast was the most intense since the 2002 ceasefire, and peace talks in Geneva failed again. The optimistic days of negotiation and ceasefire seemed more distant than ever.

In January 2008 the Sri Lankan government officially pulled out of the ceasefire agreement, signalling its dedication to ending the 25-year-old civil conflict by military means. Later in the year, the LTTE offered a unilateral 10-day ceasefire in support of the South Asian Association for Regional Cooperation (SAARC) summit being held in August in Colombo.

1991	1994	1995–2001	2002
A Black Tiger (an LTTE fighter trained in suicide missions) kills former Indian Prime Minister Rajiv Gandhi, presumably to protest the IPKF, in the world's first female suicide bombing.	President Chandrika Kumaratunga comes to power pledging to end the war with the LTTE. Peace talks are opened, but hostilities continue. In 1999 she survives a suicide-bomb attack.	Hostilities between the Sri Lanka military and the LTTE intensify; following more failed attempts at negotiation, the LTTE bombs Kandy's Temple of the Sacred Tooth Relic in 1998.	After two years of negotiation, a Norwegian peace mission secures a ceasefire. Sri Lankans, especially in the North and East, return to a new normal; many émigrés return.

The government, suspicious that the LTTE planned to use the ceasefire a a time to shore up its strength, responded with an emphatic no.

Cornering the LTTE

A change in military strategy saw the Sri Lankan security forces fight fir with fire with an increase in guerrilla-style attacks, and by August the Sr Lankan Army (SLA) had entered the LTTE's final stronghold, the jungl area of the Vanni. The Sri Lankan government stated that the army wa on track to capture the LTTE capital Kilinochchi by the end of 2008. Face with a series of battleground defeats, the LTTE struck back with anothe suicide bomb in Anuradhapura, killing 27 people.

In September 2008 the Sri Lankan government ordered UN agencie and NGOs to leave the Vanni region, saying it could no longer guarante their safety. This may have been true, but their withdrawal denied a be leaguered population of Tamils access to humanitarian support and th security of a human rights watchdog. The departure of the NGOs an the barring of independent journalists from the site of the conflict mad (and continues to make) it impossible to verify claims made by either sid about the final battles of the war.

Government and LTTE forces remained dug in around Kilinochchi the de facto capital of the unofficial Tamil Eelam state since 1990 – unt the SLA declared victory there in January 2009. This was followed rapidl by claims of control throughout the Vanni, and by February, the LTTE ha lost 99% of the territory it had controlled just 12 months earlier.

Government advances pushed remaining LTTE forces and the 300,00 Tamil civilians they brought with them to an increasingly tiny area in th northeast near Mullaittivu. Amid growing claims of civilian casualties an humanitarian concerns for the noncombatants hemmed in by the fighting foreign governments and the UN called for an immediate ceasefire in Feb ruary 2009. Military operations continued, but escape routes were opene for those fleeing the fighting to move to no-fire zones, where there was t

A FLAG FOR COMPASSION

Sri Lanka's flag was created in 1948 and took on many changes over the years. The core element was the lion on a crimson background, which had been used on flags throughout Sri Lankan history, beginning with Prince Vijaya, who is believed to have brought a lion flag with him from India. The lion, then, represented the Sinhalese people, and the gold is said to signify Buddhism. The flag was adopted in 1950, and as Sri Lanka settled into independ- ence, it evolved: in 1951 green and orange stripes were added to signify Sri Lanka's Muslims and Hindus, respectively, and in 1972 four bodhi-tree leaves were added to represent *metta* (loving-kindness), *karuna* (compassion), *upekkha* (equanimity) and *muditha* (happiness).

2004	2005	2008	2008–2009
A tsunami devastates coastal Sri Lanka, leaving 30,000 people dead. It's thought the disaster will bring unity, but the government and LTTE are soon wrangling over aid distribution and recon- struction.	Sinhalese nationalist Mahinda Rajapaksa wins presidential elec- tions. Before the elec- tion Rajapaksa signs a deal with the Marxist JVP party, rejects Tamil autonomy outright and denies tsunami aid to the LTTE.	The government pulls out of the 2002 cease- fire agreement, signal- ling a single-minded focus on a military solution. From 1983 to 2008, an estimated 70,000 people have died in the conflict.	In the war's fina months, up to 40,00 civilians are killed according to a late report by a UN specia panel. The Sri Lanka government denies any civilian deaths

further transport to welfare centres. The military, claiming that attacks were being launched from within the safe zones, then shelled them for days.

With claims that the SLA was bombing civilians in 'safe areas', and counter-claims that the LTTE was using Tamil civilians as human shields and stopping them from leaving the conflict zone, the UN High Commissioner for Human Rights Navi Pillay accused both sides of war crimes. But the international community remained largely quiet.

The Bitter End

By April, tens of thousands of Tamil civilians along with LTTE fighters were confined to a single stretch of beach, where they were bombarded from all sides. The LTTE offered the Sri Lankan government a unilateral ceasefire, but given that the Sri Lankan military's objectives were so close to being fulfilled, it was dismissed as 'a joke' by the Sri Lankan Defence Secretary. Other efforts by Swedish, French and British diplomats to inspire a truce were also dismissed by a Sri Lankan government with ultimate battleground success in its sights after three decades.

The government forces finally penetrated the LTTE and implored trapped war refugees to move to safe areas. According to UN investigations, the Tigers allegedly blocked many from leaving and killed others; refugees reported that government forces raped and executed many who surrendered.

The end finally came in May 2009 when the Sri Lankan military captured the last sliver of coast and surrounded the few hundred remaining LTTE fighters. The LTTE responded by announcing they had 'silenced their weapons' and that the 'battle had reached its bitter end'. Several senior LTTE figures were killed, including leader Vellupillai Prabhakaran, and the war that terrorised the country for 26 years was finally over.

Fast Change

The end of war was quickly followed by an inrush of money and tourists to Sri Lanka. Foreign investment from China and India quickly manifested itself in development schemes in Colombo that included expanded ports and commercial areas. Meanwhile in the south, President Rajapaksa embarked on enormous schemes involving his family around his home town of Hambantota. A new port, airport and numerous public facilities were built at a cost of billions of dollars, often with loans from China.

Around the country a building program produced new toll roads and repaired infrastructure in the East and North that had been damaged during the war. And tourists poured in, with visitor totals increasing by 20% each year. This enlivened investment across the nation, as new hotels, guesthouses, cafes, tour companies and more materialised to serve the new demand. Visitors returning for the first time since the 2005 tsunami were awestruck by the changes.

Although its authorship and veracity have been disputed, *Tamil Tigress*, by Niromi de Soyza, tells the engrossing story of a child who left school at 17 to join the Tamil Tigers.

May 2009	2013	2015	2016
After almost 30 years, Asia's longest-running war ends in May when the LTTE concedes defeat after a bloody last battle at Mullaitivu. Tamil aspirations and grievances remain.	The Commonwealth Heads of Government Meeting is meant to showcase the nation under the rule of President Mahinda Rajapaksa. However, it galvanises protests over human rights abuses and three nations refuse to attend.	In a shock, political strongman Mahinda Rajapaksa loses his bid for reelection after his own party abandons him to protest his autocratic rule. His former lieutenant Maithripala Sirisena is elected president.	The UN releases a report detailing continued human rights abuses of the Tamil population. It cites murky quasi-military groups that continue to settle scores dating back to the war.

Environmental Issues

At first glance, Sri Lanka looks like a Garden of Eden. The country positively glows i
greens and is filled with the noise of endlessly chirping, cheeping, buzzing, growling an
trumpeting animals. Add to that the sheer diversity of landscapes and climatic zone
and you get a natural wonderland. But it's a wonderland under serious threat thanks to
combination of deforestation, rapid development, pollution and human—wildlife conflic

Pear-Shaped Treasure

Looking a lot like a plump pear, the island country of Sri Lanka dangle
into the Indian Ocean off the southern tip of India. At roughly 66,00
sq km, it's slightly smaller than Ireland, but sustains 4.5 times as man
people. That's 22 million in a space stretching 433km from north to sout
and only 244km at its widest point – like the entire population of Austra
ia taking up residence in Tasmania.

Thrust up out of the encircling coastal plains, the southern centr
of the island – the core of the pear – is dominated by mountains an
tea-plantation-covered hills. The highest point is broad-backed Mt P
durutalagala (Mt Pedro; 2524m), rising above the former colonial se
tlement of Nuwara Eliya. However, the pyramid profile of 2243m-hig
Adam's Peak (Sri Pada) is better known and far more spectacular.

Hundreds of waterways channel abundant rain from the south-centra
wet-zone uplands – haven of the country's surviving rainforests – dow
through terraced farms, orchards and gardens to the paddy-rich plain
below. The Mahaweli Ganga, Sri Lanka's longest river, has its source clos
to Adam's Peak and runs 335km to Koddiyar Bay, the deep-sea harbou
of Trincomalee.

North-central Sri Lanka is home to high, rolling hills, including som
fantastically dramatic landscapes like the area around the Knuckle
Range. These hills give way to plains that extend to the northern tip o
the island. This region, portions of the southeast and most of the eas
comprise the so-called dry zone.

Sri Lanka's coastline consists of hundreds of mangrove-fringed lagoon
and marshes – some now protected wetlands – interspersed with fin
white-sand beaches, the most picturesque of which are on the south
west, south and east coasts. A group of low, flat islands lies off the Jaffn
peninsula in the north, off-limits during the civil war, but now openin
up again to tourism.

Largest
Surviving
Tracts of
Rainforest
....
Sri Pada Peak
Wilderness Reserve
(224 sq km)
....
Knuckles Range
(175 sq km)
....
Sinharaja Forest
Reserve (189 sq
km)

Flora

The southwestern wet zone is home to the country's surviving tropica
rainforest, characterised by dense undergrowth and a tall canopy of hard
wood trees, including ebony, teak and silkwood. The central hill zone ha
cloud forests and some rare highland areas populated by hardy grass
lands and elfin (stunted) forests.

Other common trees are the banyan, bodhi (also known as *bo* or *peepu*
of religious significance to Hindus and Buddhists), flame, rain, Ceylo
ironwood and neem – an assortment of names as colourful as their barks

eaves and especially flowers. There are traditional medicinal uses for almost all of them. In the Hill Country, towering eucalyptuses provide shade in tea estates.

Native fruit trees such as mangoes, tamarinds, wood apples and bananas grow in many private gardens, supplemented by introduced species like papayas and guavas. The jackfruit and its smaller relative, the *del* (breadfruit), will certainly catch your eye. The jackfruit tree produces the world's largest fruit; these sacklike, green and knobbly skinned fruit can weigh up to 30kg and hang close to the trunk rather than dangling from the branches.

Fauna

When it comes to animals, it's not just elephants in Sri Lanka; the island has a huge range of animals for such a small area. And where Africa has its famous 'Big Five' (lion, leopard, elephant, rhino and Cape buffalo), Sri Lanka has a 'Big Four' plus one (leopard, elephant, sloth bear and wild Asiatic water buffalo, plus the ginormous blue whale found offshore).

Sri Lanka's Elephants

Elephants occupy a special place in Sri Lankan culture. In ancient times they were Crown property and killing one was a terrible offence. Legend has it that elephants stamped down the foundations of the dagobas (stupas) at Anuradhapura, and elephant iconography is common in Sri Lankan art. Even today elephants are held in great affection. Of those in captivity, the Maligawa tusker, which carries the sacred tooth relic for the Kandy Esala Perahera (p159), is perhaps the most venerated of all. In the wild, one of Sri Lanka's most incredible wildlife events is 'the Gathering' in Minneriya National Park.

Despite being held in high regard, Sri Lanka's elephant population has declined significantly. Their plight has become a powerful flashpoint in the ongoing debate about human–animal conflict.

In recent years, attitudes have begun to change regarding the use of elephants in religious rituals such as the Kandy Esala Perahera and as temple guardians. Conservation groups have questioned the ethics of chaining elephants inside temple compounds for traditional (but now increasingly controversial) religious purposes. Sri Lanka's strong conservation lobby has also firmly opposed the export of elephants as gifts to other nations. Nandi, a young elephant from Pinnewala (p151), was donated as a gift to Auckland zoo by President Maithripala Sirisena, but protestors stopped her export in April 2017.

Dwindling Numbers

At the end of the 18th century an estimated 10,000 to 20,000 elephants lived unfettered across Sri Lanka. By the mid-20th century small herds of the decimated population (perhaps as few as 1000) were clustered in the low-country dry zone. Natural selection had little to do with that cull: under the British, big-game hunting delivered a mighty blow to elephant life expectancy. Today experts disagree about whether numbers

What Tree Is That? by Sriyanie Miththapala and PA Miththapala contains handy sketches of common trees and shrubs in Sri Lanka, and includes English, Sinhala and botanical names.

ENVIRONMENTAL ISSUES SRI LANKA'S ELEPHANTS

Save the Elephants

Don't feed elephants in the wild.

Don't patronise places where they're in chains.

Do visit them in national parks to support conservation.

BIOLOGICAL HOT SPOT

Sri Lanka's superlatives extend to its natural world. Conservation International has identified Sri Lanka as one of the planet's 25 biodiversity hot spots, which means the island is characterised by a very high level of 'endemism' (species unique to the area). Sure enough, Sri Lanka tops the charts, with endemism in 23% of the flowering plants and 16% of the mammals. On the other hand, hot spots are targeted as habitats seriously at risk and that's very much the case with Sri Lanka.

are increasing or diminishing, but the population is believed to be around 4000 in the wild, half of which live on protected land, plus about 300 domesticated animals.

Human–Elephant Conflict

Farmers in elephant country face an ever-present threat from animals that may eat or trample their crops, destroy their buildings and even take their lives. During the cultivation season, farmers maintain round-the-clock vigils for up to three months to scare off unwelcome raiders. For farmers on the breadline, close encounters with wild elephants are a luxury they can't afford.

Meanwhile, elephants, which need about 5 sq km of land each to support their 200kg-per-day appetites, no longer seem to have sufficient stock of food staples in the small wildlife safety zones where they are protected. Hunger (and perhaps curiosity) is driving them to seek fodder in other areas – such as arable land abutting their 'secure' habitats. The resulting conflict pits elephants against farmers – both just trying to secure their own survival.

Contributing to the vicious circle is unfortunate behaviour on both sides, much of it caused by fencing. Electric fences installed around national parks to contain elephants prevent the animals seeking out neighbouring grasslands (their preferred diet) for grazing. Migration patterns are also disturbed. This leads to elephants going hungry, and possibly starving, according to the Born Free Foundation.

Some elephants leave parks through damaged fences and rampage through farmers' land. Also, as can be seen at Uda Walawe National Park,

RESPONSIBLE TRAVEL IN SRI LANKA

The best way to responsibly visit Sri Lanka is by trying to be as minimally invasive as possible. This is, of course, easier than it sounds, but consider the following tips:

Demand green Sri Lanka's hotel and guesthouse owners are especially accommodating and, as visitor numbers soar, most are keen to give customers what they want. Share your environmental concerns and tell your hosts that their green practices – or lack thereof – are very important to you.

Watch your use of water Travel in the Hill Country of Sri Lanka and you'll think the island is coursing with water, but demand outstrips supply. Take up your hotel on its offer to save itself big money, er, no, to save lots of water, by not having your sheets and towels changed every day.

Don't hit the bottle Those bottles of water are convenient but they add up and are a major blight. Still, you're wise not to refill from the tap, so what to do? Ask your hotel if you can refill from their huge containers of drinking water.

Conserve power Sure you want to save your own energy on a sweltering afternoon, but using air-con strains an already overloaded system. Electricity demand in Sri Lanka is soaring. Try to save as much energy as possible and act as if you are paying your own electricity bill.

Don't drive yourself crazy Can you take a bus or, even better, a train, instead of a hired car? Even Colombo is more walkable than you may think. And encourage the recent trend of hotels and guesthouses providing bikes for guests. Large swaths of Sri Lanka are best toured during the day on two wheels.

Bag the bags Say no to plastic bags (and plastic straws, too) – a ban on single-use plastic bags came into effect on 1 September 2017.

Elephant tourism Sri Lanka has several elephant camps of dubious conservational merit. Avoid anywhere that offers elephants walks using howdah. These magnificent mammals are definitely best seen in a national park.

ENDANGERED SPECIES

The International Union for Conservation of Nature's Red List of Threatened Species counts over 60 species in Sri Lanka as endangered or critically endangered. They include the Asian elephant, purple-faced langur, red slender loris and toque macaque. All five of Sri Lanka's marine turtle species are threatened, as are the estuarine crocodile and the mild-mannered dugong, all of which are killed for their meat. Also under threat are several species of birds, fish and insects.

endors have set up fruit stands where the park borders the highway, so tourists can feed elephants. An increasing number of elephants now hang out all day by the roadside waiting for their tasty handouts. The idea of actually foraging for their normal diet is soon forgotten.

Possible Solutions

Some people are looking for long-term solutions to the conflict. One involves fencing *humans in;* or, rather, elephants out of human areas. This approach has been proven effective by the **Sri Lanka Wildlife Conservation Society** (SLWCS; ☑072 999 9520; www.slwcs.org; Udahamulla, Nugegoda), an award-winning wildlife conservation group. Another is to give farmers alternative livelihood solutions and land practices that incorporate elephants. The collection and commercial use of elephant dung is one such enterprise. Spreading around the economic benefits that come from scores of visitors coming to see elephants is another solution.

Finally, encouraging the cultivation of crops which elephants find unpalatable like chillies, citrus fruits and *thibbatu* (baby aubergines) has proved a successful way to counter human–elephant conflict.

Deforestation & Overdevelopment

Sri Lanka's biggest environmental threat is arguably deforestation and overdevelopment leading to serious habitat loss. At the beginning of the 20th century about 70% of the island was covered by natural forest. By 2005 this had shrunk to about 20%. Worse, in recent years Sri Lanka has had one of the highest recorded rates of primary-forest destruction in the world: an 18% reduction in forest cover and 35% loss of old-growth tracts.

Chena (shifting cultivation) is blamed for a good part of this deforestation, but irrigation schemes, clearance for cultivation and land 'development', armed conflict and, obviously, illegal logging have all been contributing factors.

The boom in Sri Lanka's economy brought about by peace is bound to put even more pressure on the environment. With tourism increasing rapidly, new construction projects are proliferating. And the track record is not good: after the 2004 tsunami, laws were put in place that banned construction of hotels and restaurants within 100m of the high-tide line, but in many southern and western coastal areas new buildings have been built virtually at the water's edge.

The Nature of Sri Lanka, with stunning photographs by L Nadaraja, is a collection of essays about Sri Lanka by eminent writers and conservationists.

The People of Sri Lanka

Every day in Sri Lanka, families bring flowers to white-domed dagobas (stupas), women in bright saris walk to rainbow-coloured Hindu temples with offerings for their gods, and whitewashed mosques call the faithful to prayer in the cool dawn. Of course, the country has seen decades of war and violence, and tensions remain. But the traditions continue and Sri Lankans somehow manage to find moments of peace, all the while greeting visitors with warmth and hospitality as they've done for millenniums.

Tradition & Ethnicity

Traditional Sri Lankan life was centred on the *gamma* (village), a highly organised hub of activity, where everyone fulfilled specific roles. Agriculture was the mainstay, and some villages focused on particular products – even today you might pass through a 'cane-furniture *gamma*'. Every village had a protector deity (or several), usually associated with aspects of nature.

To learn more about historical and contemporary Veddah life and customs, see www.vedda.org.

Veddahs

The Veddahs (Hunters) or, as they refer to themselves, Wanniyala-aetto (People of the Forest), are Sri Lanka's original inhabitants. Each wave of migration to Sri Lanka left the Veddahs with less forest on which to subsist. Today they are so few in number that they don't even make the census, and only a tiny percentage of those retain a semblance of their old culture, which comprises a hunter-gatherer lifestyle and close relationships to nature and their ancestors. The Kele Weddo (jungle-dwelling Veddahs) and Can Weddo (village-dwelling Veddahs) live mainly in the area between Badulla, Batticaloa and Polonnaruwa.

Sinhalese

The predominantly Buddhist Sinhalese sometimes divide themselves into 'low country' and 'high country' (ie Kandyan). The Kandyan Sinhalese are proud of the time when the Hill Country was a bastion of Sinhalese rule, and still consider Kandy to be the island's spiritual hub. Although the Buddha taught universalism, the Sinhalese have a caste system, with everyone falling somewhere along the spectrum between aristocrat and itinerant entertainer.

In Hindu mythology elephants are seen as symbols of water, life and fortune. They also signify nobility and gentleness, the qualities achieved when one lives a good life. In Sri Lanka, only the elephant parades with sacred Buddhist relics and Hindu statues.

Tamils

Most Tamils are Hindu and have cultural and religious connections with South Indian Tamils across the water, though they generally see themselves as a distinct group. Broadly, there are two Tamil groups in Sri Lanka. 'Jaffna Tamils' live mostly in the North and East and have been settled in Sri Lanka for many centuries. 'Plantation Tamils' on the other hand were brought by the British from India in the 19th century to work on tea farms.

The vast majority of Tamils are Hindu, and caste is an important cultural factor. Jaffna Tamils are mainly of the Vellala caste (landlords and blue bloods), while Plantation Tamils mainly come from lower castes. Times are changing, however, and traditional caste distinctions are grad ally eroding. That said, intermarriage between castes can be controversial and is often opposed in rural areas.

Moors

The island's Muslims – called Sri Lankan Moors – are descendants of Arab or Indian traders who arrived around 1000 years ago. To escape Portuguese persecution, many moved into the Hill Country and the east coast, and you'll still see predominantly Muslim towns like Hakgala near Nuwara Eliya. Most Moors speak Tamil.

Burghers

The Burghers are mixed-race descendants of the Portuguese, Dutch and British. Even after independence, Burghers had a disproportionate influence over political and business life. When growing Sinhalese nationalism reduced their role, many Burghers emigrated. Look out for surnames like Fernando, de Silva and Perera.

Religion

Religion has been the cause of much division in Sri Lanka, but the often-overlooked reality is that Sri Lanka's many religions mix openly. Buddhists, Hindus, Muslims and Christians visit many of the same pilgrimage sites, a Catholic may pay respect to a Hindu god, and Sri Lankan Buddhism has Hindu influences and vice versa.

Buddhism

Buddhism is the belief system of the Sinhalese and plays a significant role in the country, spiritually, culturally and politically. Sri Lanka's literature, art and architecture are all strongly influenced by it. Strictly speaking, Buddhism is not a religion but a practice and a moral code espoused by the Buddha. Although 'Buddhist' now is a deeply entrenched cultural and ethnic identifier, the Buddha taught meditation to people of various religions, and emphasised that no conversion was necessary (or even recommended) to benefit from his teachings, also known as the Dhamma.

Born Prince Siddhartha Gautama in modern-day Nepal around 563 BC, the Buddha abandoned his throne to seek a way out of suffering. After years of rigorous training, the Buddha discovered the Four Noble Truths: existence itself is suffering; suffering is caused by craving for sensual and material pleasures as well as existence itself; the way out of suffering is through eliminating craving; and craving can be eliminated by following a path of morality and the cultivation of wisdom through meditation. After many states of spiritual development – and, probably, many lifetimes – nirvana (enlightenment, or *nibbana* in Pali) is achieved, bringing freedom from the cycle of birth and death.

Historical Buddhism

King Devanampiya Tissa's acceptance of the Buddha's teaching – brought to the island in the 3rd century BC by the son of the Indian emperor Ashoka – firmly implanted Buddhism in Sri Lanka, and a strong relationship developed between Sri Lanka's kings and the Buddhist clergy.

Worldwide there are two major schools of Buddhism: Theravada and Mahayana. Theravada (way of the elders) scriptures are in Pali, one of the languages spoken in North India in the Buddha's time, while Mahayana (greater vehicle) scriptures are in Sanskrit. Theravada is regarded as more orthodox, and Mahayana more inclusive of later traditions.

Mahayana Buddhism is practised in Sri Lanka, but the Theravada tradition is more widely adopted. Several factors have consolidated Buddhism, especially the Theravada stream, in Sri Lanka. Sinhalese Buddhists attach vital meaning to the words of the Mahavamsa (Great Chronicle; one of

In *Buddhism: Beliefs and Practices in Sri Lanka,* Lynn de Silva combines lucid writing, fascinating information and a scholarly (but accessible) approach to shed light on the island's Buddhist tradition.

Multifaith Pilgrimages

Adam's Peak

Kataragama

Nainativu

POYA DAYS

Poya (or *uposatha*) days fall on each full moon and have been observed by monks and laypeople since the time of the Buddha as times to strengthen one's practice. Devout Buddhists visit a temple, fast after noon and abstain from entertainment and luxury. At their temple they may make offerings, attend teachings and meditate. *Poya* days are public holidays in Sri Lanka and each is associated with a particular ritual.

Duruthu (January) Marks the Buddha's first supposed visit to the island.

Vesak (May) Celebrates the Buddha's birth, enlightenment and *parinibbana* (final passing away).

Poson (June) Commemorates Buddhism's arrival in Sri Lanka.

Esala (July/August) Sees the huge Kandy festival, which observes, among other things, the Buddha's first sermon.

Unduvap (December) Celebrates the visit of Sangamitta, who brought the bodhi tree sapling to Anuradhapura.

their sacred texts), in which the Buddha designates them protectors of the Buddhist teachings. This commitment was fuelled by centuries of conflict between the Sinhalese (mainly Buddhist) and Tamils (mainly Hindu).

For some Sinhalese, Mahayana Buddhism resembled Hinduism – and indeed was followed by many Tamils in early times – and therefore defence of the Theravada stream was considered crucial. Many Buddhist sites in India were destroyed in the 10th century AD, around the time of a Hindu resurgence (and a popular Hindu text that described the Buddha as a wayward incarnation of Vishnu), further reinforcing the Sinhalese commitment to protecting the tradition.

Buddhist Nationalism

Since the late 19th century an influential strand of 'militant' Buddhism has developed in Sri Lanka, centred on the belief that the Buddha charged the Sinhalese people with making the island a citadel of Buddhism in its purest form. It sees threats to Sinhalese Buddhist culture in Christianity, Hinduism and, more recently, Islam. Sri Lankan Buddhism is historically intertwined with politics, and it was a Buddhist monk, dissatisfied with Prime Minister SWRD Bandaranaike's 'drift' from a Sinhala-Buddhist focus, who assassinated him in 1959, in contradiction of the very first Buddhist precept against killing. Many Buddhist monks have also strongly opposed compromise with the Tamils.

In 2007, hard-line Sinhalese-nationalist monks achieved leverage in the Sri Lankan government through the Jathika Hela Urumaya (JHU; National Heritage Party). In 2012 a group of monks who felt the JHU was not aggressive enough in protecting Buddhism founded the Bodu Bala Sena (BBS; Buddhist Power Force), which has, along with other radical groups, been implicated in several protests and attacks against Muslim and Christian communities in recent years. At a 2013 opening for a BBS training school, Defence Secretary (and brother of the president) Gotabhaya Rajapaksa said in a speech that 'it is the monks who protect our country, religion and race'.

In 2014 the BBS was widely blamed for inciting anti-Muslim riots in Dharga Town which resulted in four deaths and the burning and looting of Muslim shops, and forced 10,000 people to flee their homes.

Hinduism

Tamil kings and their followers from South India brought Hinduism to northern Sri Lanka, although the religion may have existed on the island well before the arrival of Buddhism, as a result of the island's proximity to India and the natural cultural exchange that would have taken place. Today, Hindu communities are most concentrated in the north, the east and tea plantation areas.

Hinduism is a complex mix of beliefs and gods. All Hindus believe in Brahman: the myriad deities are manifestations of this formless being, through which believers can understand all facets of life. Key tenets include belief in ahimsa (nonviolence), samsara (the cycle of births and deaths that recur until one reaches a pure state), karma (the law of cause and effect) and dharma (moral code of behaviour or social duty).

Hindus believe that living life according to dharma improves the chance of being born into better circumstances. Rebirth can also take animal form, but it's only as a human that one may gain sufficient self-knowledge to escape the cycle of reincarnation and achieve moksha (liberation).

For ordinary Hindus, fulfilling one's ritual and social duties is the main aim of worldly life. According to the Hindu text Bhagavad Gita, doing your duty is more important than asserting your individuality.

The Hindu pantheon is prolific: some estimates put the number of deities at 330 million. The main figures are Brahma, who created the universe, and his consort Saraswati, the goddess of wisdom and music; Vishnu, who sustains the universe and is lawful and devout, and his consort Lakshmi, the goddess of beauty and fortune; and Shiva, the destroyer of ignorance and evil, and his consort Parvati, who can be the universal mother or the ferocious and destructive Kali. Shiva has 1008 names and takes many forms: as Nataraja, lord of the *tandava* (dance), his graceful movements begin the creation of the cosmos.

In the modern age Shiva, Vishnu and their associated consorts are the most revered deities, while Brahma – once the most important deity in Hinduism – has been demoted to a minor figure.

> For more information on Hinduism, see www.bbc.co.uk/religion/religions/hinduism.

Islam

Sri Lanka is home to almost two million Muslims – many of whom are descendants of Arab traders who settled on the island from the 7th century, not long after Islam was founded in present-day Saudi Arabia by the Prophet Mohammed. Islam is monotheistic, and avows that everything has been created by Allah.

After Mohammed's death the movement split into two main branches, the Sunnis and the Shiites. Sunnis emphasise following and imitating the words and acts of the Prophet. They look to tradition and the majority views of the community. Shiites believe that only imams (exemplary leaders) can reveal the meaning of the Quran. Most of Sri Lanka's Muslims are Sunnis, although small communities of Shiites have migrated from India.

All Muslims believe in the five pillars of Islam: the shahada (declaration of faith: 'there is no God but Allah; Mohammed is his prophet'); prayer (ideally five times a day); the zakat (tax, usually a donation to charity); fasting during the month of Ramadan; and the hajj (pilgrimage) to Mecca.

Religious Hubs

....

Nallur Kandaswamy Kovil, Jaffna

....

Temple of the Sacred Tooth Relic, Kandy

....

Our Lady of Madhu Church, Madhu

....

City of Anuradhapura

Christianity

Christianity in Sri Lanka potentially goes back to the Apostle Thomas in the 1st century AD, and it's certain that in the early centuries AD small numbers of Christians established settlements along the coast.

With the Portuguese in the 16th century, Christianity, specifically Roman Catholicism, arrived in force, and many fishing families converted. Today, Catholicism remains strong among western coastal communities, such as Negombo. The Dutch brought Protestantism and the Dutch Reformed Church, mainly present in Colombo, while evidence of the British Christian denominations includes the stone churches that dot the Hill Country landscape.

Sri Lankan Tea

The Dutch may have come to the island in search of spices, but the country is now more associated with an imported plant – tea, introduced by the British. Today, Sri Lanka is among the world's top tea-producing nations and Ceylon tea is perhaps the nation's most powerful, internationally recognised brand.

Shaping the Nation

Tea came to Sri Lanka when extensive coffee plantations were decimated by disease in the 19th century. The first Sri Lankan tea was grown in 1867 at the Loolecondera Estate, southeast of Kandy. Plantation owners discovered that the Hill Country combines a warm climate, altitude and sloping terrain: a winning trifecta that's perfect for growing tea.

Shipments of Ceylon tea began filling London warehouses in the 1870s. The public's thirst for a cuppa proved nearly unquenchable. Fortunes were made by the early growers, which included a name still famous worldwide today: Thomas Lipton. By the 1890s, Lipton's tea plantations were exporting around 30,000 tonnes of tea annually back to London.

Tea production continued to spiral upwards in the 20th century. Forests were cleared and plantations greatly expanded. A running war was fought with various pests and diseases that afflicted the crops, and all manner of chemicals were created to keep the tea plants healthy.

Today Sri Lanka is the world's fourth-biggest tea-producing nation with 288 million kg yielded in 2016. Sri Lankan tea (branded internationally as 'Ceylon' tea) enjoys a premium positioning and its sale prices are well above those of rival nations. Income from tea exports topped US$1.2 billion in 2016.

Despite the British roots of the industry, Ceylon tea today is exported across the globe. Russia is the largest importer of Sri Lankan tea, followed by Iran, Iraq and Turkey.

Besides the various forms of ubiquitous black tea, Sri Lanka produced 2.37 million kg of green tea in 2016, which is known for its more pungent flavour, and white tea, which is among the most premium of teas and is often called 'silver tips'.

Quality

The many varieties of tea are graded by size (from cheap 'dust' through fannings and broken grades to 'leaf' tea) and by quality (with names such as flowery, pekoe or souchong). Obviously, tea sized as dust is rather inferior. Anything graded in the leaf category is considered the minimum designation for respectable tea. In terms of quality designations, whole leaves are best and the tips (the youngest and most delicate tea leaves) are the very top tier.

The familiar name pekoe is a superior grade of black tea. Interestingly, there is no definitive record of where the 'orange' in the popular orange pekoe moniker comes from. It definitely has nothing to do with flavour but rather is either an artefact of a designation used by early Dutch tea

Tea plantations cover about 1900 sq km. This is primarily in the Hill Country and adjoining regions, especially in the south.

aders or a reference to the colour of the leaves when dried. Either way, range pekoe is a very superior grade of Ceylon black tea.

Altitude is another vital indication of tea quality. Udawatte (high-rown tea) is considered the finest; it grows slowly, but has a delicate, sub-e flavour that makes it greatly sought after – Dimbula, Nuwara Eliya and va are three prime growing districts. Udawatte is grown above 1200m.

Medawatte (mid-grown tea) has floral and malty notes and a fullness f body, but is less refined; Kandy is the main centre of production. It's icked at altitudes of 600m to 1200m, and occupies the middle ground price and quality.

Yatawatte (low-grown tea) is stronger, higher in caffeine and more ro-ust, but it's not considered as complex; it's found below 600m. The foot-ills inland of the coast are centres of low-grown production: Ratnapura nd Galle are two important districts.

Cultivation

ea bushes are typically planted a metre or so apart on contoured terraces help irrigation and to prevent erosion. A tea bush is around 1m in eight, and is regularly pruned to encourage new shoots, prevent flower-ng and fruit formation and maximise leaf production. Adequate rainfall essential, as is fertilisation.

Tea leaves are plucked by hand every seven to 14 days, a task tradition-lly carried out by Tamil women in Sri Lanka. The pluckers have a daily arget of between 20kg and 30kg. After plucking, the tea leaves are taken) a factory where they are left to wither (demoisturised by blowing air t a fixed temperature through them). You'll spot the huge factory build-ngs throughout tea-growing country. Many are more than 100 years old.

The partly dried leaves are then crushed, starting a fermentation pro-ess. The green leaves quickly turn a coppery brown as additional heat applied. The art in tea production comes in knowing when to stop the ermentation, by 'firing' the tea at an even higher heat to produce the nal, brown-black leaf that will be stable for a reasonable length of time. inally the tea is separated and graded according to leaf size.

The workers who regulate the myriad variables to take a day's pickings nd produce proper tea, which will demand the premium prices Sri Lan-an tea producers count on, are high up the ladder on the plantations. here is a definite art to the process, which has been refined over decades.

DRINKING TEA

Although black tea is fairly forgiving, there are still right and wrong ways to prepare a cup. For maximum enjoyment, keep the following points in mind.

➡ Store tea in an airtight container, whether it is loose or in tea bags. It's prone to absorbing odours, which are especially harmful to some of the delicate blends or flavoured teas.

➡ Use fresh water and boil it (water that's been boiling for a while or which was previously boiled gives you a flat-tasting cup of tea).

➡ Too accustomed to tea bags? With loose tea, it's one teaspoon per average-sized cup plus one extra if you're making a pot.

➡ Let the tea brew. It takes three to five minutes for tea to fully release its flavour.

➡ Conversely, once the tea is brewed, toss the tea leaves, whether they were loose or in a tea bag. Tea leaves quickly become bitter once brewed.

➡ For milk tea, pour the milk into the cup and then add the tea: the flavours mix better.

BEST TEA PLANTATIONS & FACTORIES

Some of our favourite places to get up close and smell the tea include:

Ceylon Tea Museum (p166) Near Kandy. An informative early stop in your tea tour.

Hundungoda Tea Estate (p124) Near Koggala. Produces over 25 varieties of tea, including many rare varieties.

Pedro Tea Estate (p176) Near Nuwara Eliya. Has tours of the factory, which was originally built in 1885.

Dambatenne Tea Factory (p184) Near Haputale. Built by Sir Thomas Lipton in 1890 and offers good tours.

Mackwoods Labookellie Tea Factory (p173) A factory well positioned by the Nuwara Eliya road; handy if you're in a hurry.

It takes only 24 hours from the time tea is picked to process it and load it into bags for shipment.

Tea Workers

Sri Lanka's tea industry is responsible for more than one million jobs about 5% of the entire population. Wages are very low: in October 201 the minimum daily rate for tea pluckers was raised to Rs 730 (less tha US$5). Compulsory pension and funeral payments further erode salarie

Most families live in seriously substandard housing, barracks-lik buildings (known as 'lines') on the fringes of plantations. Few have run ning water or electricity, and wood and coal stoves used for cooking an heating cause respiratory diseases.

The vast majority of tea workers are Tamils. Originally, the British te barons intended to hire Sinhalese workers, but the labour was unappea ing to locals, so plantation owners looked to India. Huge numbers c Tamils were brought over. Today they remain one of the most margina ised groups in the nation. Most are landless, classified as 'Indian Tamil and disadvantaged by linguistic and cultural differences.

All the island's teas are branded with a 'Lion Logo', which denotes that the tea was produced in Sri Lanka.

Visiting a Tea Plantation

A great introduction to the endless rolling green fields of the Hill Cour try's tea plantations is riding the train from Ella to Haputale. In just few hours you'll see dozens of plantations and their emerald-green car pets of tea bushes. Amid it all you'll see sari-clad pluckers toiling unde the sun, busily meeting their quotas for the day.

Tea factories and plantations throughout the Hill Country provid tours to explain the process, usually using machinery and technolog that are largely unchanged since the 19th century.

Buying Tea

Tea is inexpensive, easy to pack and much loved by almost everyone, so makes an excellent gift for others at home – or yourself. The tea factorie and plantations in the Hill Country have a bewildering array of option on offer. There are also many good shops in Colombo, Kandy and Galle

Ceylon black tea is the best known and is famous for its citrusy tast Green Ceylon is characteristically pungent, with a slightly nutty flavou Ceylon silver tips tea is produced from very young buds that are silver white, have a delicate flavour and command premium prices.

Survival Guide

Directory A–Z

Accommodation

Sri Lanka has all types of accommodation ranging from rooms in family homes to five-star resorts. With tourism booming, prices have increased rapidly. Accommodation is rarely great value (compared to other Asian countries), so expect to fork out more for your bed here compared to, say, India or Southeast Asia. Wherever you stay, try to bargain over the price, as negotiation is common.

Rates are very seasonal, particularly at beach resorts; look for good discounts in the low season. The high season is December to April on the west and south coasts, and April to September on the east coast.

Note that there are reports of a few hotels refusing to honor prepaid reservations made on sites like www.agoda.com. They'll tell you that if you want to stay you'll need to pay rack rate (always inflated) and that you will then need to get your money back from the booking website. This is usually a scam.

Bring printed confirmations and have the local contact number for the booking website. One call should sort things out, as the hotel won't want to be banned from the booking website.

Some midrange and top-end hotels quote room prices in US dollars or euros, but accept the current rupee equivalent. Note that a service charge of 10% will usually be added to the rate you're quoted. At many hotels an additional value added tax (VAT) and other local taxes can add up to 15% to your bill, which can make for a large surprise at check-out.

Note that many hotels are not licensed to sell alcohol (but are usually fine about you bringing your own). Most places are nonsmoking.

Types of Accommodation

Guesthouses and hotels provide the majority of places to sleep in Sri Lanka. In rural areas, almost every place is a guesthouse. The difference is that hotels will usually be larger and offer more services beyond a person minding the

desk. Often guesthouses are family run.

Almost every place to stay will serve meals. Note that it's easy to stumble upon places that are quite inferior whether it's a guesthouse renting rooms by the hour or top-end hotels that have ossified. There are almost always better choices nearb so look around.

BUDGET

There are budget guesthouses, hostels and a few budget hotels across Sri Lanka; they vary widely in standards and price.

Expect the following amenities:

➡ fans in most rooms, air-co in only one or two (fans are fine in the Hill Country and right on the beach)

➡ maybe hot water

➡ private bathroom (except in hostel dorms where

shared facilities are more common) with shower and sit-down flush toilet

➡ wi-fi

➡ simple breakfast.

MIDRANGE

Midrange guesthouses and hotels are the most common choices throughout Sri Lanka. Most provide a decent level of comfort, although some can be quite nice with a range of services and views. Choices include well-run colonial-era lodges and stylish places on or near a beach.

Expect the following amenities:

➡ maybe a balcony/porch/patio

➡ satellite TV

➡ small fridge

➡ air-con in most if not all rooms

➡ wi-fi

➡ maybe a pool.

TOP END

Top-end hotels range from small, stylish, boutique affairs in colonial mansions to lavish five-star resorts.

Expect the following amenities:

➡ good service

➡ usually enticing views – ocean, lush valleys and rice fields or private gardens

➡ usually a pool

WHERE TO STAY

No matter what kind of travel experience you're looking for, Sri Lanka delivers.

Those exploring the Ancient Cities and the great cultural monuments will find Anuradhapura, Giritale and Habarana ideal bases.

Beach seekers should head to established southern resorts like Mirissa and Tangalla or less-developed coves like Talalla or Hiriketiya. On the west coast, Bentota and Hikkaduwa are very popular, while over on the east coast try either Arugam Bay or the beaches north of Trincomalee.

Up in the Hill Country there are myriad choices, but Nuwara Eliya can't be topped for colonial ambience, while historic Kandy is a cultural mecca.

➡ spa

➡ restaurant (licensed to sell alcohol).

Villa rentals are taking off in beachy areas, especially along the south coast. Speciality accommodation includes the former homes of British tea-estate managers in the Hill Country, which have been converted into guesthouses or hotels, often with beautiful gardens and antique-stuffed living rooms.

Customs Regulations

Sri Lanka has the usual list of prohibited imports, including drugs, weapons, fresh fruit and anything remotely pornographic.

Items allowed:

➡ 0.25L of perfume

➡ 1.5L of alcohol.

There are duty-free shops in the arrivals area before you reach baggage claim at the airport. Besides booze, they include appliances like blenders and refrigerators.

Sri Lanka Customs has full details on its website (www.customs.gov.lk).

Discount Cards

An International Student ID Card is not widely recognised in Sri Lanka.

Electricity

The electric current is 230V, 50 cycles. Plugs come in a bewildering range of variations. Besides the primary plug type, which is similar to Indian plugs, you may well find US-, EU- and British-style plugs in your room.

Adaptors are readily available at markets, supermarkets and tourist shops for under Rs 500.

Type D
220V/50Hz

Embassies & Consulates

It's important to realise the limits of what your embassy can do if you're in trouble. Generally speaking, their hands are tied if you've broken Sri Lankan law. In real emergencies you might get some assistance, but only if all other channels have been exhausted. Embassies can recommend hospitals, doctors and dentists.

Unless otherwise indicated, the following embassies are in Colombo:

Australian High Commission (Map p64; ☎011-246 3200; www.srilanka.embassy.gov.au; 21 RG Senanayake Mawatha (Gregory's Rd), Col 7; 8.30am-5pm Mon-Fri)

Canadian High Commission (Map p64; 011-532 6232; www.srilanka.gc.ca; 33A 5th Lane, Col 3; 8am-4.30pm Mon-Thu, to 1.30pm Fri)

French Embassy (Map p64; 011-263 9400; www.lk.ambafrance.org; 89 Rosmead Pl, Col 7; 8.30am-1pm & 2.30-4pm Mon-Thu, to 1pm Fri)

German Embassy (Map p64; 011-258 0431; www.colombo.diplo.de; 40 Alfred House Ave, Col 3; 7.30am-4pm Mon-Thu, to 1pm Fri)

India Visa Office (Map p64; 011-255 9435; www.ivsvisalanka.com; 129 Phillip Gunawardena Mawatha, Col 4; submissions 8.30am-2pm Mon-Fri)

Indian High Commission (Map p64; 011-232 7587; www.hcicolombo.org; 36-38 Galle Rd, Col 3; 9am-5.30pm Mon-Fri)

Maldivian High Commission (Map p72; 011-551 6302; www.maldiveshighcom.lk; 25 Melbourne Ave, Col 4)

Netherlands Embassy (Map p64; 011-251 0200; www.nederlandwereldwijd.nl/landen/sri-lanka; 25 Torrington Ave, Col 7; 8.30am-5pm Mon-Thu, to 2pm Fri)

UK High Commission (Map p64; 011-539 0639; www.gov.uk/government/world/organisations/british-high-commission-colombo; 389 Bauddhaloka Mawatha; 8.30am-12.30pm & 1.30-4.30pm Mon-Thu, 8.30am-1pm Fri)

US Embassy (Map p64; 011-249 8500; https://lk.usembassy.gov; 210 Galle Rd, Col 3; 8.30am-4.30pm Mon-Thu, to noon Fri)

Food & Drink

Sri Lanka has a fine range of eating options (p34). The most popular high-end restaurants in Colombo and at the main resorts should be booked in advance; elsewhere, it's very rarely necessary to book.

Restaurants Found in the capital, Galle, Kandy, beach resorts and upmarket hotels throughout the country. Tend to be expensive and quite formal; usually offer alcohol.

Hotels Not 'hotels' in the usual sense, these basic local eateries serve no-nonsense local grub at affordable prices.

Cafes Found in cities and beach resorts; serve sandwiches and snacks.

Bakeries Offer 'short eats': bread rolls, pastries, patties, *vadai* (deep-fried doughnut-shaped snacks).

Gay & Lesbian Travellers

Same-sex sexual activity is illegal in Sri Lanka and the subject is little discussed publicly. No one has been convicted for over 60 years, but it pays to be discreet. There is no legislation to protect LGBT people from harassment, but the situation is changing slowly, and Colombo has a low-key scene. You can be more open in cosmopolitan areas like Col 1, Col 3 and Col 7.

Equal Ground (011-567 9766; www.equal-ground.org) is a Colombo-based organisation that supports gay and lesbian rights, sponsors pride events, offers counselling services and has useful online resources.

Insurance

Unless you are definitely sure that your health coverage at home will cover you in Sri Lanka, you should take out travel insurance – bring a copy of the policy as evidence that you're covered.

Worldwide travel insurance is available at www.lonelyplanet.com/travel-insurance. You can buy, extend and claim online anytime – even if you're already on the road.

EATING PRICE RANGES

The following price ranges refer to a standard main course.

$ less than Rs 250

$$ Rs 250–800

$$$ more than Rs 800

Internet Access

Wi-fi in guesthouses and hotels is the norm. Mobile data is reasonably quick (at least 3G speeds) in larger towns and all cities. You may get no signal in rural areas.

Legal Matters

Sri Lanka's legal system is a complex, almost arcane mix of British, Roman-Dutch and national law. The legal system tends to move slowly, and even a visit to a police station to report a small theft can involve much time-consuming filling out of forms. The tourist police in major towns and tourist hot spots should be your first point of contact in the case of minor matters such as theft.

Drug use, mainly locally grown marijuana, but also imported heroin and methamphetamine, occurs in tourist centres such as Hikkaduwa, Negombo and Unawatuna. Dabbling is perilous; you can expect to end up in jail if you're caught using anything illegal and your home government may be unable to help beyond putting you in touch with a local lawyer.

Maps

Digital maps – online and in apps by Apple, Bing and Google – are mostly up-to-date but beware of errors, especially in the North where on-the-ground conditions may not have made it to the the digital world.

Money

ATMs

ATMs are easily found in towns and cities of any size. ATMs often issue Rs 5000 notes. Try to break a few as soon as possible as small vendors may not accept large notes: you can usually do this inside the bank that operates the ATM.

Cash

Any bank or exchange bureau will change major currencies in cash, including US dollars, euros and British pounds. Change rupees back into hard currency at the airport (before security, there are no exchange counters after) prior to leaving, as even nearby countries may not exchange Sri Lankan currency.

Credit & Debit Cards

MasterCard and Visa are the most commonly accepted credit cards. Cards are generally accepted at most mid-range and all top-end hotels and restaurants.

Currency

The Sri Lankan currency is the rupee (Rs), which is divided into 100 cents; pricing in cents is rare. Rupee coins come in denominations of one, two, five and 10 rupees. Notes come in denominations of 10, 20, 50, 100, 200, 500, 1000, 2000 and 5000 rupees.

Money Changers

Money changers can be found in Colombo and major tourist centres. Their rates are competitive, but choose carefully, as money-exchange scams abound. Stick to banks or reputable offices, such as those at the airport. ATMs are safer and more reliable.

Taxes & Refunds

The VAT (value added tax) in Sri Lanka is 15%. It may or may not be already included in the prices of goods and services. Make certain you don't pay it twice. There is no tourist refund scheme for VAT.

Opening Hours

Apart from tourist areas, much is closed on Sunday.

Bars Usually close by midnight, last call is often a sobering 11pm.

Restaurants and cafes 7am to 9pm daily, later in areas popular with travellers

Shops 10am to 7pm Monday to Friday, 10am to 3pm Saturday

Shops and services catering to visitors 9am to 8pm

Photography

➡ Most Sri Lankans love getting their picture taken, but it's common courtesy to ask permission. A few business-oriented folk, such as the stilt fishermen at Koggala, will ask for payment.

➡ It's forbidden to film or photograph dams, airports, road blocks or anything associated with the military.

➡ Never pose beside or in front of a statue of the Buddha (ie with your back to it), as this is considered extremely disrespectful.

➡ Flash photography can damage age-old frescoes and murals, so respect the restrictions at places like Dambulla and Sigiriya.

Post

Sri Lanka Post (www.slpost. gov.lk) has offices in most towns and cities. Service to the outside world is slow.

Public Holidays

With four major religions, Sri Lanka has a lot of public holidays; also, all *poya* (full moon) days are public holidays and much is closed.

New Year's Day 1 January

Tamil Thai Pongal Day 14 January, Hindu harvest festival

Independence Day 4 February

Good Friday March/April

Sinhala and Tamil New Year 14 April

Labour Day 1 May

Id ul-Fitr Marks the end of Ramadan. Date varies with the lunar calendar: falls 14 June 2018, 4 June 2019

Christmas Day 25 December

Safe Travel

With the end of the civil war, Sri Lanka does not present any extraordinary concerns about safe travel.

➡ Travellers with Buddha tattoos or images of the deity on clothing have been denied entry into the country or arrested and deported.

➡ Also show respect to any statue or other representation of Buddha.

Telephone

Mobile Phone Companies

Mobile coverage across Sri Lanka is good in built-up areas and cheap. You can get a SIM card that has data and voice credit for as low as Rs 700 with a domestic call cost of Rs 2 per minute.

The main mobile companies have booths in the arrivals area of Bandaranaike International Airport; compare prices as there are wide variations in rates. Major providers include the following:

Dialog (www.dialog.lk)

Hutch (www.hutch.lk)

Mobitel (www.mobitel.lk)

Time

Sri Lanka Standard Time (GMT/UTC + 5½ hours) is the same as India Standard Time. There is no summer/daylight savings time.

Sri Lankan time, being 30 minutes off the top of the hour used in much of the world, bedevils many a traveller. Sri Lanka is 4½ hours behind Australian EST and 10½ hours ahead of American EST.

Toilets

➡ All top-end and midrange accommodation has sit-down flush toilets.

➡ Only budget places that don't get a lot of tourists have squat toilets and lack toilet paper.

➡ Public toilets are scarce (and are usually grim when they exist, although some have attendants).

➡ Use restaurants, hotels and attractions like tea-plantation visitor centres.

Tourist Information

Sri Lanka Tourist Board (SLTB; Map p64; ☎011-243 7059; www.srilanka.travel; 80 Galle Rd, Col 3, Colombo;

⊙7am-9pm) The Colombo main office has useful glossy brochures and maps.

Elsewhere, tourist offices are uncommon.

Travellers with Disabilities

Sri Lanka is a challenge for travellers with disabilities, but the ever-obliging Sri Lankans are always ready to assist. If you have restricted mobility, you may find it difficult, if not impossible, to get around on public transport, as buses and trains don't have facilities for wheelchairs. Moving around towns and cities can also be difficult for those in a wheelchair and for the visually impaired because of the continual roadworks and frequently poor roads; don't expect many smooth footpaths. The chaotic nature of Sri Lankan traffic is also a potentially dangerous challenge. A car and driver is your best transport option. If possible, travel with a strong, able-bodied person.

Apart from some top-end hotels, accommodation is not geared for wheelchairs. However, many places can provide disabled travellers with rooms and bathrooms that are accessible without stairs.

Download Lonely Planet's free Accessible Travel guide from http://lptravel.to/AccessibleTravel.

Visas

Transit visas good for 48 hours are free. Thirty-day visitor visas cost US$25 to US$100, depending on your nationality. Apply in advance online (www.eta.gov.lk).

Obtaining a Visa

Before visiting Sri Lanka, do the following to get a 30-day visa:

➡ Visit the Sri Lanka electronic visa website

GOVERNMENT TRAVEL ADVICE

The following sites have useful safety tips:

Australia: www.smartraveller.gov.au

Canada: http://travel.gc.ca

Germany: www.auswaertiges-amt.de/DE/Laender informationen/01-Reisewarnungen-Liste_node.html

Japan: www.mofa.go.jp/region/index

Netherlands: www.government.nl/topics/travelling -abroad

New Zealand: www.safetravel.govt.nz

UK: www.gov.uk/foreign-travel-advice

US: https://travel.state.gov

www.eta.gov.lk) several days before arriving.

Follow the online application process and pay with a credit or debit card.

Once approved, print out the visa confirmation.

You can also obtain visas at Sri Lankan embassies abroad and there is a counter at Bandaranaike International Airport for people who arrive without a visa, although you'll have to wait with the other visa-less masses (which can take several hours) and pay a higher fee: US$40.

Visa Extensions

You can renew a 30-day tourist visa twice, for 30 days each time. Contact the **Department of Immigration and Emigration** (☑011-532 5000; www.immigration.gov.lk; Sri Subuthipura Dr, Battaramulla; ☺8:30am-4:15pm). Extensions are not hard to get but require jumping through some bureaucratic hoops and downloading some forms. To complete the process in one day, arrive to the office by 10am and expect it to take at least four hours.

Volunteering

There are fewer volunteer opportunities available now than there were in the years after the 2004 tsunami. Still, or people with time – and especially expertise – there re some ways you can be actively involved in helping others.

Lonely Planet cannot vouch for organisations that we do not work with directly, so you should always carry out your own research to make sure that any volunteer placements are ethical and beneficial to local people. Organisations offering placements include the following:

International Volunteer HQ (IVHQ; ☑+64 6758 7949; www.volunteerhq.org; Kandy) Organises a wide range of volunteer experiences, including teaching, medical care and temple renovation. Based in New Zealand, it runs programs in and around Kandy.

Sri Lanka Wildlife Conservation Society (SLWCS; ☑072 999 9520; www.slwcs.org; Udahamulla, Nugegoda) Offers paid volunteer roles for people interested in wildlife data collection and teaching opportunities.

Volunteer Sri Lanka (☑077 791 0747; www.volunteersri lanka.net; Galle) Can arrange short-term volunteer positions, especially for teachers but also for unskilled positions.

Women Travellers

Women travelling alone may experience uncomfortable levels of male attention. Outside Colombo, it is a good idea to cover your legs and shoulders, though you'll be stared at no matter what you wear. Tight tops are a bad idea. And away from the popular tourist beaches of the South, East and West, consider swimming in a T-shirt and shorts.

In Colombo and popular tourist areas you can relax the dress code. 'Are you married?' could be the snappy conversation starter you hear most often, so if you are single consider wearing a fake wedding ring and carrying a few pics of your imaginary partner back home.

Women travelling alone may be hassled while walking around day and night, or while exploring isolated places. Physical harassment (grabbing and groping) can occur anywhere. Single women may be followed, so try to be connected with larger groups of people. There have also been cases of solo women being attacked by guides at heritage sites; again, don't go alone.

However, travelling in Sri Lanka is not one long hassle. Unpleasant incidents are the exception, not the rule. But remember there are many social environments that are almost exclusively male in character – local bars, for example.

Stock up on tampons as they can be very hard to find.

Work

Sri Lanka is not a place to seek work, even in tourist places such as beach cafes or dive shops. The only foreigners who normally work in the country are hired for specific roles by companies ready to deal with a significant bureaucratic process.

Transport

GETTING THERE & AWAY

Air links to Sri Lanka become more extensive each year, but there are currently no sea routes to the island.

Flights, cars and tours can be booked online at lonely planet.com/bookings.

Entering the Country

Immigration at Bandaranaike International Airport is straightforward.

You must have your passport with you at all times in Sri Lanka. Before leaving home, check that it will be valid for at least six months after you plan to leave Sri Lanka.

Air

Airports

On paper, Sri Lanka has two international airports, but in practice, almost all airlines fly into **Bandaranaike International Airport** (CMB; ☎011-226 4444; www.airport.lk), located at Katunayake, 30km north of Colombo. There are 24-hour money-changing facilities in the arrivals and departures halls as well as ATMs, mobile-phone dealers, taxi services and more.

Arriving is fairly hassle-free as touts are mostly kept away. Transit passengers and those checking in early should note, however, that the terminals remain very spartan in terms of amenities.

The airport is the hub for the national carrier, **SriLankan Airlines** (☎011-777 1979; www.srilankan.aero), which operates an extensive network to Asia and the Middle East. It has a safety record on par with other international carriers. Local connections are provided by **Cinnamon Air** (Map p60; ☎011-247 5475; www.cinnamonair.com).

Mattala Rajapaksa International Airport (www.airport.lk/mria) is 15km north of Hambantota near the south coast. A notorious white elephant, it normally has one scheduled flight a day, on a budget carrier to Dubai. Media reports note that these flights often carry no passengers. The large terminal is shiny, but normally there are no services. If you are flying in, be sure to have transportation arranged in advance.

Airlines Flying to & from Sri Lanka
ASIA

Sri Lanka is well served by major Asian carriers, including budget favourite Air Asia. Service from India is competitive between several carriers.

Many visitors combine a visit to Sri Lanka with the Maldives. SriLankan Airlines and Emirates fly between Colombo and Malé.

CLIMATE CHANGE & TRAVEL

Every form of transport that relies on carbon-based fuel generates CO_2, the main cause of human-induced climate change. Modern travel is dependent on aeroplanes, which might use less fuel per kilometre per person than most cars but travel much greater distances. The altitude at which aircraft emit gases (including CO_2) and particles also contributes to their climate change impact. Many websites offer 'carbon calculators' that allow people to estimate the carbon emissions generated by their journey and, for those who wish to do so, to offset the impact of the greenhouse gases emitted with contributions to portfolios of climate-friendly initiatives throughout the world. Lonely Planet offsets the carbon footprint of all staff and author travel.

USTRALIA & EW ZEALAND

onnections are on Asian arriers such as Singapore irlines and Thai Airways. Us-g Emirates requires major acktracking.

UROPE

riLankan Airlines links Co-mbo nonstop with London. onnecting through on a arrier such as Austrian, Brit-h Airways, Emirates, Etihad irways, Qatar Airways and urkish Airlines is common.

ORTH AMERICA

ou're literally going halfway round the world from Can-da and the USA; from the est coast connect through sia, from the east coast onnect through the Middle ast or India.

Sea

is not currently possible to avel to Sri Lanka by sea. A ervice linking Colombo and uticorin (Tamil Nadu) in In-ia lasted only a few months 2011. Prior to the civil war, ferry service linked Mannar northwest Sri Lanka to ameshwaram in India; there as been talk of reviving this oute for several years, but here are few signs that this ight actually materialise.

GETTING AROUND

ome useful points to con-ider when getting around ri Lanka:

Domestic flights in Sri anka are quite limited, istances are not vast nd new expressways are hrinking travel times.

Travelling on public ransport is a choice etween buses and trains: oth are cheap. Trains can e crowded, but it's nothing ompared with the huge umber of passengers that quash into ordinary buses. tanding on a train is better han standing on a bus.

➜ On the main roads from Colombo to Kandy, Negombo and Galle, buses cover around 40km to 50km per hour. On highways across the plains and to the North, it can be 60km or 70km an hour. In the Hill Country, it can slow to just 20km an hour.

➜ All public transport gets crowded around *poya* (full moon) holidays and their nearest weekends, so try to avoid travelling then.

Air

Options for flying within Sri Lanka are very limited.

Bandaranaike International Airport (p326) Has connecting domestic flights provided by **Cinnamon Air** (p326). It offers a limited schedule of expensive flights to destinations that include Batticaloa, Dikwella, Sigiriya and Trincomalee. Service is on small planes, some using airforce bases, others with floats that land on lakes and lagoons. It also offers charter flights to points around the country at fares which start at US$3000.

Colombo Airport, Ratmalanae (www.airport.lk/rma) 15km south of Colombo, this is an airforce base with a terminal that handles some domestic air charters.

Bicycle

Cycling around historic areas such as Anuradhapura and Sigiriya is the best and most enjoyable ways to see these important sites. Bikes are also an ideal way to explore the North and East via the lightly travelled roads typical of these regions. More and more hotels and guesthous-es have bicycles that guests can hire.

Hire

Simple, cheap mountain bikes make up many of the rentals you'll find in guesthouses and hotels. Rates average about Rs 500 per day.

➜ If your accommodation doesn't hire bikes, it can usually hook you up with someone who does. Many places rent bikes to nonguests.

➜ Bikes available for day use typically are not suitable for long-distance riding. Bike-rental shops offering quality long-distance machines are rare. Consider bringing your bike from home if you plan on serious cycle touring.

Bike Tours

Tour and outfitting companies organise cycling tours of Sri Lanka and may also help you get organised for independent travel. Some operators are:

Eco Team (Map p64; 011-583 0833; www.srilankaecotourism. com; 20/63 Fairfield Gardens, Colombo)

SpiceRoads Cycle Tours (in Thailand 02 381 7490; www. spiceroads.com)

Srilanka Bicycle Trips (011-622 3378; www.srilankabicycle trips.com; tours from Rs 10,500)

Long-Distance

➜ Keen long-distance cyclists will enjoy Sri Lanka, apart from the steeper areas of the Hill Country and the busy roads exiting Colombo. When heading out of Colombo in any direction, take a train to the edge of the city before you start cycling.

➜ Start early in the day to avoid the heat, and pack water and sunscreen. Your daily distances will be limited by the roads; be prepared for lots of prudent 'eyes down' cycling as you negotiate a flurry of obstacles from potholes to chickens. Remember, too, that speeding buses, trucks and cars use all parts of the roadway and shoulder, so be cautious and wear visible clothing.

➜ If you bring your own bicycle, also pack a supply of spare tyres and tubes. These suffer from the poor road surfaces, and replacement parts can be hard to obtain. The normal bicycle tyre size in Sri Lanka is 28in by 1.5in. Some imported 27in tyres for 10-speed bikes are available, but only in Colombo.

➡ Keep an eye on your bicycle at all times and use a good lock.

➡ When taking a bicycle on a train, forms must be filled out, so deliver the bicycle at least half an hour before departure. At Colombo Fort train station you may want to allow up to two hours. It costs about twice the 2nd-class fare to take a bicycle on a train.

Boat

With the exception of ferries used to reach the islands southwest of Jaffna, there are no ferry services of note in Sri Lanka.

Bus

Bus routes cover about 80% of the nation's 90,000km of roads. There are two kinds of bus in Sri Lanka:

Central Transport Board (CTB) buses These are the default buses and usually lack air-con; they ply most long-distance and local routes. You'll also see buses with a Sri Lanka Transport Board (SLTB) logo.

Private buses Independent bus companies have vehicles ranging from late-model coaches used on intercity-express runs to ancient minibuses on short runs between towns and villages. Private air-con intercity buses cover some major routes. For long-distance travel they are more comfortable and faster than other bus services. Note that completion of the Southern Expressway has sparked the introduction of express services in fully modern air-con coaches between Colombo and Galle.

General Tips

Bus travel in Sri Lanka can be interesting and entertaining. Many locals speak some English, so you may have some enjoyable interactions. Vendors board to sell snacks and gifts on long-distance routes.

Important considerations for bus travel:

➡ Major routes will have service several times an hour during daylight hours.

➡ Finding the right bus at the chaotic bus stations of major cities and towns can be challenging, although almost all buses now have part of their destination sign in English.

➡ Many buses operate on fixed routes with a route number, which makes it easier to locate the correct bus.

➡ There is usually no central ticket office; you must locate the right parking area and buy your bus ticket either from a small booth or on board the bus.

➡ You may be able to reserve a seat on a bus in advance; check at the station.

➡ 'Semi-comfortable' (or 'semi-luxe') buses are run by private companies and have larger seats and window curtains compared to CTB buses, but lack the air-con of the best intercity buses.

➡ Most people at bus stations and on buses will help you with your questions.

➡ Luggage space is limited or nonexistent; you may have to buy a ticket for your bag.

➡ The first two seats on CTB buses are reserved for clergy (Buddhist monks).

➡ To guarantee a seat, board the bus at the beginning of its journey.

➡ When you arrive at your destination, confirm the departure details for the next stage of your journey.

Costs

In most cases, private bus companies run services parallel to CTB services. Intercity expresses charge about twice as much as CTB buses, but are more than twice as comfortable and usually faster. Fares for CTB buses and ordinary private buses are very cheap.

Car & Motorcycle

➡ Self-drive car hire is possible in Sri Lanka, though it is far more common to hire a car and driver. If you're on a relatively short visit to Sri Lanka on a midrange budget, the costs of hiring a car and driver can be quite reasonable.

➡ When planning your itinerary, you can count on covering about 35km/h in the Hill Country and 55km/h in most of the rest of the country.

➡ Motorcycling is an alternative for intrepid travellers. Distances are relatively short and some of the roads are a motorcyclist delight; the trick is to stay off the main highways. The quieter Hill Country roads offer some glorious views, and secondary roads along the coast and the plains are reasonably quick. But you will have to make inquiries, a motorcycle rental is nowhere near as commonplace as it is in much of the rest of Asia.

➡ Throughout Sri Lanka, Mw is an abbreviation for Mawatha, meaning 'Avenue'.

Hiring a Car & Driver

A car and a driver guarantee maximum flexibility in your travels, and while the driver deals with the chaotic roads, you can look out the window and – try to – relax.

You can find taxi drivers who will happily become your chauffeur for a day or more in all the main tourist centres. Guesthouses and hotels can connect you with a driver, which may be the best method. Travel agencies also offer various car and driver schemes, although these car cost considerably more.

COSTS

Various formulas exist for setting costs, such as rates per kilometre plus a lunch and dinner allowance and separate fuel payments. The simplest way is to agree on a flat fee with no extras. Expect to pay Rs 8000 to 11,000 per day (US$60 is a good average), excluding fuel, or more for a newer air-con vehicle. Other considerations:

➡ Most drivers will expect a tip of about 10%.

➡ Meet the driver first as you may sense bad chemistry.

➡ Consider hiring a driver for only two or three days at first to see if you fit.

➡ You are the boss. It's great to get recommendations from a driver, but don't be bullied. Drivers are known to dissuade travellers from visiting temples and other sights where there are no commissions.

➡ Unless the driver speaks absolutely no English, a guide in addition to the driver is unnecessary.

Drivers make a fair part of their income from commissions. Most hotels and guesthouses pay drivers a flat fee or a percentage, although others refuse to. This can lead to disputes between you and the driver over where you're staying the night, as the driver will literally wish to steer you to where the money is. Some hotels have appalling accommodation for drivers; the smarter hotels and guesthouses know that keeping drivers happy is good for their business, and provide decent food and lodgings.

Recommended companies with drivers include the following (there are many more; the Lonely Planet Thorn Tree Forum is a good source of driver recommendations):

Ancient Lanka (☑077 727 7780; www.ancientlanka.com)

Let's Go Lanka (☑077 630 0070; www.letsgolanka.com)

Self-Drive Hire

Colombo-based company **Shineway Rent a Car** (☑071 378 9323; http://rentalcarsrilanka.com; 45/15 Nawala Rd, Narahenpita, Col 5) offers self-drive car hire. You'll find other local firms as well as very small operations in tourist towns. You can usually hire a car for about US$30 per day with 100km of included kilometres. But it is still uncommon to see visitors driving themselves in Sri Lanka.

Motorbike rentals run about Rs 1500 per day across the country.

DRIVING LICENCE
An International Driving Permit (IDP) can be used for driving in Sri Lanka; it's pricey, valid for three months to one year and is sold by auto clubs in your home country. Note that many travellers never purchase an IDP and have no problems.

Road Conditions
Driving in Sri Lanka requires constant attention to the road. Country roads are often narrow and potholed, with constant pedestrian, bicycle and animal traffic to navigate. Note, however, that Sri Lanka's massive road-building program is improving roads across the nation, especially in the North and East.

Punctures are a part of life here, so every village has a repair expert.

It's dangerously acceptable for a bus, car or truck to overtake in the face of oncoming smaller road users. Three-wheelers, cyclists, and smaller cars and vans simply have to move over or risk getting hit. To announce they are overtaking, or want to overtake, drivers sound a shrill melody on their horns. If you're walking or cycling along any kind of busy main road, be very alert.

Road Rules
➡ Speed limit 50km/h in towns, 70km/h in rural areas and 100km/h on the new expressways.

➡ Driving is on the left-hand side of the road, as in the UK and Australia.

Hitching
Hitching is never entirely safe, and Sri Lanka's cheap fares make it an unnecessary option. We don't recommend it,

---

SRI LANKA'S NEW HIGHWAYS

Various new expressways are opening over the next few years. Most will be toll roads, with relatively cheap tolls.

Colombo–Katunayake Expressway Greatly reducing travel time between Bandaranaike International Airport and the city. From its start 4km northeast of Fort at Kelani Bridge, you can reach the airport in 30 minutes. Unfortunately, during the day the city streets remain as congested as ever between Fort and the entrance.

Outer Circular Expressway Completed in 2017, this belt road runs through the far eastern suburbs of Colombo. It links the Southern Expressway to the Katunayake Expressway, which means you can drive from the airport to Galle in well under three hours, a huge time saving.

Southern Expressway The first new expressway completed. It is 161km long and runs from Colombo's southern suburb of Kottawa, near Maharagama, to Matara via an exit near Galle. Until linking roads are complete, it can take as long to get from Fort to the expressway entrance as it does from there to Galle – or even longer. Plans call for the road to eventually be extended to reach Hambantota.

Colombo–Kandy Expressway Approved in 2012, this road is expected to reduce travel time to close to an hour, but as yet there is no confirmed opening date.

and travellers who do choose to hitch should understand that they are taking a small but potentially serious risk.

Local Transport

Many Sri Lankan towns are small enough to walk around. In larger towns, you can get around by bus, taxi or three-wheeler.

Bus

Local buses go to most places, including villages outside main towns, for fares from Rs 10 to 50.

Taxi

Sri Lankan taxis are common in all sizable towns, and even some villages. Only some are metered (mostly in Colombo), but over longer distances their prices are comparable to those of three-wheelers, and they provide more comfort and security. You can count on most taxi rides costing around Rs 60 to 100 per kilometre.

Hotels and restaurants can usually get you a ride for a modest cost. In Colombo you can count on taxis dispatched via apps such as Uber.

Three-Wheeler

Three-wheelers, known in other parts of Asia as tuk-tuks, *bajajs* or autorickshaws, are waiting on nearly every corner. Use your best bargaining skills and agree on the fare before you get in. Some keen drivers will offer very extensive tours; use your discretion.

As a rule of thumb, a three-wheeler should cost no more than Rs 200 per kilometre, but this can prove elusive depending on your negotiating skills. Note that three-wheelers with meters are somewhat prevalent in Colombo.

Three-wheelers and taxis waiting outside hotels and tourist sights expect higher-than-usual fares. Walk a few hundred metres to get a better deal.

Train

Sri Lanka Railways (☎011-243 2908; www.railway.gov.lk; Colombo Fort Train Station, Col 11) runs the nation's railways, and trains are a great way to cross the country. Although they are slow, there are few overnight or all-day ordeals to contend with. A train ride is almost always more relaxed than a bus ride. Costs are in line with buses: even 1st class doesn't exceed Rs 1000. Most stations have helpful information windows where English is spoken.

In addition, a couple of companies run private air-con train cars, which are attached onto regular trains. Although more expensive and less atmospheric than the 1st-class observation cars on Sri Lanka Railways, these private cars offer air-con and snacks and may have seats available when regular classes are already fully booked. **Rajadhani Express** (☎071 453 6840; www.rajadhani.lk) runs to Kandy, Badulla, Galle and Matara, while **Expo Rail** (☎011-522 5050; www.exporail. lk/ExpoRail.php) serves Kandy and the Hill Country.

There are three main rail lines in Sri Lanka.

South from Colombo A scenic delight. Recently renovated, runs past Aluthgama and Hikkaduwa to Galle and Matara.

East from Colombo To the Hill Country, through Kandy, Nanu Oya (for Nuwara Eliya) and Ella to Badulla. A beautiful route, the portion from Haputale to Ella is one of the world's most scenic train rides.

North from Colombo Through Anuradhapura to Mannar and also to Jaffna. One branch reaches Trincomalee on the east coast, while another serves Polonnaruwa and Batticaloa.

Other Lines The Puttalam line runs along the coast north from Colombo, although rail buses run between Chilaw and Puttalam. The Kelani Valley line winds 60km from Colombo to Avissawella.

Trains are often late. As traffic surges and efforts at upgrading the system struggle, long delays of an hour or more are not uncommon.

Two good independent references for Sri Lanka trains:

www.seat61.com/SriLanka A good overview.

http://slr.malindaprasad.com Schedules and some fares.

Classes

There are three classes on Sri Lankan trains (although many have no 1st class):

1st class Comes in three varieties: coaches, sleeping berths and observation saloons (with large windows). The latter are used on some trains east and north from Colombo and are the preferred means of travelling these scenic lines. Some have large rear-facing windows and vintage interiors.

2nd class Seats have padding and there are fans. On some trains (but not to Galle) these seats can be reserved in advance.

3rd class Seats have little padding and there are no reservations. The cars accommodate as many as can squeeze in and conditions can be grim.

The air-con train cars run by private companies are slightly more expensive than regular 1st class; fares average around US$12.

Reservations

➜ You can reserve places in 1st class and 2nd class on many intercity expresses.

➜ Always make a booking for the 1st-class observation saloons, which are very popular. Sleeping cars also book far in advance.

➜ Reservations can be made at train stations up to 30 days before departure.

➜ If travelling more than 80km, you can break your journey at any intermediate station for 24 hours without penalty. You'll need to make fresh reservations for seats on the next leg.

Health

Before You Go

Insurance

Even if you're fit and healthy, don't travel without health insurance: accidents do happen. A travel or health insurance policy is essential. You may require extra cover for adventure activities, such as scuba diving. If your normal health insurance doesn't cover you for medical expenses abroad, get extra insurance. If you're uninsured, emergency evacuation is expensive, and bills of more than US$100,000 are not uncommon.

Recommended Vaccinations

The only vaccine required by international regulations is yellow fever. Proof of vaccination will only be required if, in the six days before entering Sri Lanka, you have visited a country in the yellow-fever zone.

The US Centers for Disease Control (CDC) recommends that travellers to Sri Lanka consider the following vaccinations (as well as being up to date with measles, mumps and rubella vaccinations):

Adult diphtheria and tetanus Single booster recommended if none in the previous 10 years.

Hepatitis A Provides almost 100% protection for up to a year.

Hepatitis B Now considered routine for most travellers.

Japanese encephalitis Recommended for rural travel, people who will be doing outdoor activities or for anyone staying longer than 30 days.

Polio Incidence has been unreported in Sri Lanka for several years but must be assumed to be present.

Rabies Three injections in all. A booster after one year will then provide 10 years' protection.

Typhoid Recommended for all travellers to Sri Lanka, even if you only visit urban areas.

Varicella If you haven't had chickenpox, discuss this vaccination with your doctor.

In Sri Lanka

Availability & Cost of Health Care

Medical care, and its cost, is hugely variable in Sri Lanka. Colombo has some good clinics aimed at expats; they're worth using over options aimed at locals because a superior standard of care is offered. **Nawaloka Hospital** (Map p64; ☑011-557 7111; www.nawaloka.com; 23 Deshamanya HK Dharmadasa Mawatha, Col 2) in Colombo also has a good reputation and English-speaking doctors. Embassies and consulates often have lists of recommended medical providers. Elsewhere in Sri Lanka, hotels and guesthouses can usually steer you to a local doctor for at least initial treatment.

Self-treatment may be appropriate if your problem is minor (eg traveller's diarrhoea). If you think you may have a serious disease, especially malaria, do not waste time: travel to the nearest quality facility to receive attention. It is always better to be assessed by a doctor than to rely on self-treatment.

Before buying medication over the counter, always check the use-by date and ensure the packet is sealed. Colombo and larger towns all have good pharmacies;

FOOD SAFETY

Dining out brings with it the possibility of contracting diarrhoea. Ways to help avoid food-related illness:

➡ eat only freshly cooked food

➡ avoid shellfish and buffets

➡ peel fruit

➡ cook vegetables

➡ soak salads in iodine water for at least 20 minutes

➡ eat in busy restaurants with a high customer turnover.

most medications can be purchased without a prescription.

Infectious Diseases

Dengue fever This mosquito-borne disease is becomingly increasingly problematic across Asia. As there is no vaccine available, it can only be prevented by avoiding mosquito bites at all times. Symptoms include high fever, severe headache and body ache and sometimes a rash and diarrhoea. Treatment is rest and paracetamol – do not take aspirin or ibuprofen as it increases the likelihood of haemorrhaging. Make sure you see a doctor to be diagnosed and monitored.

Hepatitis A This food- and water-borne virus infects the liver, causing jaundice (yellow skin and eyes), nausea and lethargy. There is no specific treatment for hepatitis A, you just need to allow time for the liver to heal. All travellers to Sri Lanka should be vaccinated against hepatitis A.

Hepatitis B This sexually transmitted disease is spread by body fluids and can be prevented by vaccination. The long-term consequences can include liver cancer and cirrhosis.

Hepatitis E Transmitted through contaminated food and water, hepatitis E has similar symptoms to hepatitis A, but is far less common. It is a severe problem in pregnant women and can result in the death of both mother and baby. There is no commercially available vaccine, and prevention is by following safe eating and drinking guidelines.

HIV Spread via contaminated body fluids and present in Sri Lanka. Avoid unsafe sex, unsterilised needles (including in medical facilities) and procedures such as tattoos.

Influenza Present year-round in the tropics, influenza (flu) symptoms include fever, muscle aches, a runny nose, cough and sore throat. It can be severe in people over the age of 65 or in those with medical conditions such as heart disease or diabetes – vaccination is recommended for these individuals.

There is no specific treatment, just rest and paracetamol.

Japanese B encephalitis This viral disease is transmitted by mosquitoes and is rare in travellers. Most cases occur in rural areas and vaccination is recommended for travellers spending more than one month outside cities. There is no treatment, and it may result in permanent brain damage or death. Ask your doctor for further details.

Malaria Malaria was formerly a serious problem, but the World Health Organization declared Sri Lanka malaria-free in 2016. Doctors presently advise that anti-malarial drugs are not necessary.

Rabies This fatal disease is spread by the bite or possibly even the lick of an infected animal – most commonly a dog or monkey. You should seek medical advice immediately after any animal bite and commence postexposure treatment. Having pretravel vaccination means the postbite treatment is greatly simplified. If an animal bites you, gently wash the wound with soap and water, and apply iodine-based antiseptic. If you are not prevaccinated you will need to receive rabies immunoglobulin as soon as possible, and this can be expensive and tricky to find in some areas.

Tuberculosis While TB is rare in travellers, those who have significant contact with the local population (such as medical and aid workers and long-term travellers) should take precautions. Vaccination is usually only given to children under the age of five, but adults at risk are recommended to have pre- and post-travel TB testing. The main symptoms are fever, cough, weight loss, night sweats and fatigue.

Typhoid This serious bacterial infection is also spread via food and water. It gives a high and slowly progressive fever and headache, and may be accompanied by a dry cough and stomach pain. It is diagnosed by blood tests and treated with antibiotics. Vaccination is recommended for all travellers who are spending more than a week in Sri Lanka. Be aware that vaccination is not 100% effective, so you must still be careful with what you eat and drink.

Traveller's Diarrhoea

This is by far the most common problem affecting travellers in Sri Lanka. It's usually caused by a bacteria, and thus responds promptly to treatment with antibiotics.

Traveller's diarrhoea is defined as the passage of more than three watery bowel actions within 24 hours, plus at least one other symptom, such as fever, cramps, nausea, vomiting or feeling generally unwell.

Treatment consists of staying well hydrated; rehydration solutions like Gastrolyte are the best for this. Antibiotics such as ciprofloxacin or azithromycin should kill the bacteria quickly. Seek medical attention quickly if you do not respond to an appropriate antibiotic.

Loperamide is just a 'stopper' and doesn't get to the cause of the problem. It can be helpful, though (eg if you have to go on a long bus ride). Don't take loperamide if you have a fever or blood in your stools.

Amoebic dysentery Amoebic dysentery is very rare in travellers but is quite often misdiagnosed by poor-quality labs. Symptoms are similar to bacterial diarrhoea: fever, bloody diarrhoea and generally feeling unwell. You should always seek reliable medical care if you have blood in your diarrhoea. Treatment involves two drugs: tinidazole or metronidazole to kill the parasite in your gut and then a second drug to kill the cysts. If left untreated, complications such as liver or gut abscesses can occur.

Giardiasis Giardia is a parasite that is relatively common in travellers. Symptoms include nausea, bloating, excess gas, fatigue and intermittent diarrhoea. The parasite will eventually go away if left untreated, but this can take months; the best advice is to seek medical treatment. The treatment of choice is tinidazole, with metronidazole being a second-line option.

Women's Health

For gynaecological health issues, seek out a female doctor.

Birth control Bring adequate supplies of your own form of contraception.

Sanitary products Pads, but rarely tampons, are readily available.

Thrush Heat, humidity and antibiotics can all contribute to thrush. Treatment is with antifungal creams and pessaries such as clotrimazole. A practical alternative is a single tablet of fluconazole (Diflucan).

Urinary-tract infections These can be precipitated by dehydration or long bus journeys without toilet stops; bring suitable antibiotics.

Environmental Hazards
AIR POLLUTION

Air pollution, particularly vehicle pollution, is an increasing problem in most urban hubs. If you have severe respiratory problems, speak with your doctor before travelling. It's worth taking a disposable face mask if you are affected by air quality.

HEAT

Lowland areas of Sri Lanka can be hot and humid throughout the year. For most visitors, it takes around two weeks to comfortably adapt to the hot climate. Swelling of the feet and ankles is common, as are muscle cramps caused by excessive sweating. Prevent these by avoiding dehydration and excessive activity in the heat. Don't eat salt tablets (they aggravate the gut); drinking rehydration solution or eating salty food helps. Treat

AYURVEDA

Ayurveda (eye-your-veda) is an ancient system of medicine using herbs, oils, metals and animal products to heal and rejuvenate. Influenced by the system of the same name in India, Ayurveda is widely used in Sri Lanka for a range of ailments.

Ayurveda postulates that the five elements (earth, air, ether, water and light) are linked to the five senses, which in turn shape the nature of an individual's constitution – his or her *dosha* (life force). Disease and illness occurs when the *dosha* is out of balance. The purpose of Ayurvedic treatment is to restore the balance.

For full-on therapeutic treatments, patients must be prepared to make a commitment of weeks or months. It's a gruelling regimen featuring frequent enemas and a bare minimum diet of simple vegetable-derived calories.

Much more commonly, tourists treat themselves at Ayurvedic massage centres attached to major hotels and in popular tourist centres. Full treatments take up to three hours and include the following relaxing regimens:

➡ Herbal saunas (Sweda Karma) are based on a 2500-year-old design. The plaster walls are infused with herbal ingredients, including honey and sandalwood powder. The floor of the sauna is covered with herbs. Like a European sauna, a steady mist of medicinal steam is maintained with water sprinkled onto hot coals.

➡ The steam bath (Vashpa Swedanam) looks like a cross between a coffin and a torture chamber. Patients lie stretched out on a wooden platform, and a giant hinged door covers the body with only the head exposed. From the base of the wooden steam bath, up to 50 different herbs and spices infuse the body.

➡ The so-called Third Eye of the Lord Shiva treatment (Shiro Dhara) is the highlight for many patients. For up to 45 minutes, a delicate flow of warm oil is poured slowly onto the forehead and then smoothed gently into the temples by the masseuse.

While there are numerous spas with good international reputations, the standards at some Ayurvedic centres are low. The massage oils may be simple coconut oil and the practitioners may be unqualified, and in some instances may even be sex workers. As poisoning cases have resulted from herbal treatments being misadministered, it pays to enquire precisely what the medicine contains and then consult with a conventional physician.

For massage, enquire whether there are both male and female therapists available; we've received complaints from female readers about sexual advances from some male Ayurvedic practitioners. In general, it's not acceptable Ayurvedic practice for males to massage females and vice versa.

cramps by resting, rehydrating with double-strength rehydration solution and gently stretching.

Dehydration is the main contributor to heat exhaustion. Recovery is usually rapid, and it is common to feel weak for some days afterwards. Symptoms include the following:

➡ feeling weak

➡ headache

➡ irritability

➡ nausea or vomiting

➡ sweaty skin

➡ a fast, weak pulse

➡ normal or slightly elevated body temperature.

Treatment for dehydration:

➡ get out of the heat

➡ fan the sufferer

➡ apply cool, wet cloths to the skin

➡ lay the sufferer flat with their legs raised

➡ rehydrate with water containing one-quarter teaspoon of salt per litre.

Heatstroke is a serious medical emergency. Symptoms include the following:

➡ weakness

➡ nausea

➡ a hot, dry body

➡ temperature of over 41°C

➡ dizziness

➡ confusion

➡ loss of coordination

➡ seizures

➡ eventual collapse.

Treatment for heatstroke:

➡ get out of the heat

➡ fan the sufferer

DIVING & SURFING

Divers and surfers should seek specialised advice before they travel to ensure their medical kit contains treatment for coral cuts and tropical ear infections. Divers should ensure their insurance covers them for decompression illness – get specialised dive insurance through an organisation such as Divers Alert Network (www.danasiapacific.org). Certain medical conditions are incompatible with diving; check with your doctor.

➡ apply cool, wet cloths to the skin or ice to the body, especially to the groin and armpits.

Prickly heat is a common skin rash in the tropics, caused by sweat trapped under the skin. Treat it by moving out of the heat for a few hours and having cool showers. Creams and ointments clog the skin so they should be avoided. Locally bought prickly-heat powder can be helpful.

INSECT BITES & STINGS

Bedbugs Don't carry disease, but their bites can be itchy. You can treat the itch with an antihistamine.

Lice Most commonly appear on the head and pubic areas. You may need numerous applications of an antilice shampoo such as pyrethrin.

Ticks Contracted while walking in rural areas. Ticks are commonly found behind the ears, on the belly and in armpits. If you have had a tick bite and have a rash at the site of the bite or elsewhere, fever or muscle aches, see a doctor. Doxycycline prevents tick-borne diseases.

Leeches Found in humid rainforest areas. They do not transmit any disease, but their bites are often itchy for weeks and can easily become infected. Apply an iodine-based antiseptic to

any leech bite to help prevent infection.

Bee and wasp stings Anyone with a serious bee or wasp allergy should carry an injection of adrenalin (eg an Epipen).

SKIN PROBLEMS

Fungal rashes There are two common fungal rashes that affect travellers. The first occurs in moist areas, such as the groin, armpits and between the toes. It starts as a red patch that slowly spreads and is usually itchy. Treatment involves keeping the skin dry, avoiding chafing and using an antifungal cream such as clotrimazole or Lamisil. The second, Tinea versicolor, causes light-coloured patches, most commonly on the back, chest and shoulders. Consult a doctor.

Cuts and scratches These become easily infected in humid climates. Immediately wash all wounds in clean water and apply antiseptic. If you develop signs of infection (increasing pain and redness), see a doctor.

SUNBURN

Even on a cloudy day sunburn can occur rapidly.

➡ Use a strong sunscreen (factor 30) and reapply after a swim.

➡ Wear a wide-brimmed hat and sunglasses.

➡ Avoid lying in the sun during the hottest part of the day (10am to 2pm).

If you become sunburnt, stay out of the sun until you have recovered, apply cool compresses and, if necessary, take painkillers for the discomfort. One percent hydrocortisone cream applied twice daily is also helpful.

WATER

Tap water is not safe to drink. Use bottled or filtered water; for the former, look for the small round 'SLSI' logo, which shows the water has been tested by the government's Sri Lanka Standards Institution (the majority of local brands).

Language

Sinhala and Tamil are national languages in Sri Lanka, with English commonly described as a lingua franca. It's easy to get by with English, and the Sri Lankan variety has its own unique characteristics – 'You are having a problem, isn't it, no?' is one example. However, while English may be widely spoken in the main centres, off the beaten track its spread thins. In any case, even a few words of Sinhala or Tamil will go a long way.

SINHALA

Sinhala is officially written using a cursive script. If you read our coloured pronunciation guides as if they were English, you shouldn't have problems being understood. When consonants are doubled they are pronounced very distinctly, almost as separate sounds. The symbols t and d are pronounced less forcefully than in English, th as in 'thin', dh as the 'th' in 'that', g as in 'go', and r is more like a flap of the tongue against the roof of the mouth – it's not pronounced as an American 'r'. As for the vowels, a is pronounced as the 'u' in 'cup', aa as the 'a' in 'father', ai as in 'aisle', au as the 'ow' in 'how', e as in 'met', i as in 'bit', o as in 'hot', and u as in 'put'.

Basics

| Hello. | aayu-bowan |
| Goodbye. | aayu-bowan |

> **WANT MORE?**
>
> For in-depth language information and handy phrases, check out Lonely Planet's *Sinhala Phrasebook*. You'll find it at **shop.lonelyplanet.com**, or you can buy Lonely Planet's iPhone phrasebooks at the Apple App Store.

Yes.	owu
No.	naha
Please.	karuna kara
Thank you.	istuh-tee
Excuse me.	samah venna
Sorry.	kana gaatui
Do you speak English?	oyaa in-ghirisih kata karenawa da?
What's your name?	oyaaghe nama mokka'da?
My name is ...	maaghe nama ...

Accommodation

Do you have any rooms available?	kaamara thiyanawada?
How much is it per night?	ek ra-yakata kiyada
How much is it per person?	ek kenek-kuta kiyada
Is breakfast included?	udeh keh-emath ekkada?
for one night	ek rayak pamanai
for two nights	raya dekak pamanai
for one person	ek-kenek pamanai
for two people	den-nek pamanai
campsite	kamping ground eka
guesthouse	gesthaus eka
hotel	hotel eka
youth hostel	yut-hostel eka

Eating & Drinking

Can we see the menu?	menoo eka balanna puluvandha?
What's the local speciality?	mehe visheshayen hadhana dhe monavaadha?

I'd like rice and curry, please.	bahth denna
I'm a vegetarian.	mama elavalu vitharai kanne
I'm allergic to (peanuts).	mata (ratakaju) apathyayi
No ice in my drink, please.	karunaakarala maghe beema ekata ais dhamanna epaa
That was delicious!	eka harima rasai!

Please bring a/the...	... karunaakarala gennah
bill	bila
fork	gaarappuvak
glass of water	vathura veedhuruvak
knife	pihiyak
plate	pingaanak

bowl	vendhuwa
coffee	koh-pi
fruit	palathuru
glass	co-ppuwa
milk	kiri
salt	lunu
spoon	han-duh
sugar	seeni
tea	thay
water	vathura

NUMBERS – SINHALA

0	binduwa
1	eka
2	deka
3	thuna
4	hathara
5	paha
6	haya
7	hatha
8	atta
9	navaya
10	dahaya
100	seeya
200	deh seeya
1000	daaha
2000	deh daaha
100,000	lakshaya
1,000,000	daseh lakshaya
10,000,000	kotiya

Emergencies

Help!	aaney!/aaeeyoh!/ammoh!
Call a doctor!	dostara gen-nanna!
Call the police!	polisiyata kiyanna!
Go away!	methanin yanna!
I'm lost.	maa-meh nativelaa

Shopping & Services

What time does it open/close?	ehika kiyatada arinneh/vahanneh?
How much is it?	ehekka keeyada?
big	loku
medicine	behe-yat
small	podi/punchi
bank	bankuwa
chemist/pharmacy	faahmisiya
... embassy	... embasiya
market	maakat eka
my hotel	mang inna hotalaya
newsagency	pattara ejensiya
post office	tepal kantohruwa
public telephone	podu dura katanayak
tourist office	sanchaaraka toraturu karyaalayak

Time & Dates

What time is it?	velaave keeyada?
morning	udai
afternoon	havasa
day	davasa
night	raah
week	sumaanayak
month	maasayak
year	avuurudeh
yesterday	ee-yeh
today	ada (uther)
tomorrow	heta
Monday	sandu-da
Tuesday	angaharuwaa-da
Wednesday	badaa-da
Thursday	braha-spetin-da
Friday	sikuraa-da
Saturday	senasuraa-da
Sunday	iri-da

SIGNS – SINHALA

ඇතුල්වීම	Entrance
පිටවීම	Exit
විවෘතව ඇත.	Open
වසා ඇත.	Closed
තොරතුරු දැන්වුම	Information
තහනම් වේ.	Prohibited
පොලිස් ස්ථානය	Police Station
කාමර ඇත.	Rooms Available
කාමර නැත.	No Vacancy
වැසිකිළි	Toilets
පුරුෂ	Men
ස්ත්‍රී	Women

Transport & Directions

When does the next ... leave/arrive?	meelanga ... pitaht venne/paminenne?
boat	bohtuwa
bus (city)	bus eka
bus (intercity)	bus eka nagaraantara
train	koh-chiya
I want to get off.	mama methana bahinawa
I'd like a one-way ticket.	mata tani gaman tikat ekak ganna ohna
I'd like a return ticket.	mata yaam-eem tikat ekak ganna ohna
1st class	palamu veni paantiya
2nd class	deveni paantiya
3rd class	tunveni paantiya
bus stop	bus nevathuma
ferry terminal	totu pala
timetable	kaala satahana
train station	dumriya pala
I'd like to hire a ...	mata ... ekak bad-dhata ganna ohna
bicycle	baisikeleya
car	kar (eka)
Where is a/the ...?	... koheda?
Go straight ahead.	kelinma issarahata yaanna
Turn left.	wamata harenna
Turn right.	dakunata harenna
near	lan-ghai
far	durai

TAMIL

The vocabulary of Sri Lankan Tamil is much the same as that of South India – the written form is identical, using the traditional cursive script – but there are marked differences in pronunciation between speakers from the two regions. In this section we've used the same pronunciation guides as for Sinhala.

Basics

Hello.	vanakkam
Goodbye.	poytu varukirehn
Yes.	aam
No.	il-lay
Please.	tayavu saydhu
Thank you.	nandri
Excuse me.	mannikavum
Sorry.	mannikavum
Do you speak English?	nin-gal aangilam paysu-virhalaa?
What's your name?	ungal peyr en-na?
My name is ...	en peyr ...

Accommodation

Do you have any rooms available?	ingu room kideikkumaa?
How much is it per night/person?	oru iravukku/aalukku evvalavur?
Is breakfast included?	kaalei unavum sehrtha?
for one/two nights	oru/irandu iravukku
for one/two people	oruvarukku/iruvarukku

SIGNS – TAMIL

வழி உள்ளே	Entrance
வழி வெளியே	Exit
திறந்துள்ளது	Open
அடைக்கப்பட்டுள்ளது	Closed
தகவல்	Information
அனுமதி இல்லை	Prohibited
காவல் நிலையம்	Police Station
அறைகள் உண்டு	Rooms Available
காலி இல்லை	No Vacancy
மலசலகூடம்	Toilets
ஆண்	Men
பெண	Women

LANGUAGE TRANSPORT & DIRECTIONS

NUMBERS – TAMIL

0	saifer
1	ondru
2	iranduh
3	muundruh
4	naan-guh
5	ainduh
6	aaruh
7	ealluh
8	ettu
9	onbaduh
10	pat-tuh
100	nooruh
1000	aayirem
2000	irandaayirem
100,000	oru latcham
1,000,000	pattuh lat-chem
10,000,000	kohdee

campsite	mukhaamidum idahm
guesthouse	virun-dhinar vidhudheh
hotel	hotehl
youth hostel	ilainar vidhudheh

Eating & Drinking

Can we see the menu?	unavu pattiyalai paarppomaa?
What's the local speciality?	ingu kidaikkak koodiya visheida unavu enna?
I'd like rice and curry, please.	sorum kariyum tharungal
I'm a vegetarian.	naan shaiva unavu shaappidupavan
I'm allergic to (peanuts).	(nilak kadalai) enakku alejee
No ice in my drink, please.	enadu paanaththil ais poda vendaam
That was delicious!	adhu nalla rushi!

Please bring a/the...	... konda varungal
bill	bill
fork	mul karandi
glass of water	thanni oru glass
knife	kaththi
plate	oru plate

bowl	kooppai
coffee	kahpee

fruit	paadham
glass	glass
milk	paal
salt	uppu
spoon	karandi
sugar	seeree
tea	te-neer/plan-tea
water	than-neer

Emergencies

Help!	udavi!
Call a doctor!	daktarai kuppidunga!
Call the police!	polisai kuppidunga!
Go away!	pohn-goh!/poi-vidu!
I'm lost.	naan vali tavari-vittehn

Shopping & Services

What time does it open/close?	et-thana manikka tirakhum/mudhum?
How much is it?	adhu evvalavu?
big	periyeh
medicine	marunduh
small	siriyeh
bank	vanghee
chemist/pharmacy	marunduh kadhai
... embassy	... tudharalayem
market	maarket
my hotel	enadu hotehl
newsagency	niyuz paper vitku-midam
post office	tafaal nilayem
public telephone	podhu tolai-pessee
tourist office	toorist nilayem

Time & Dates

What time is it?	mani eth-tanai?
morning	kaalai
afternoon	pit-pahel
day	pahel
night	iravu
week	vaarem
month	maadhem
year	varudem
yesterday	neh-truh
today	indru
tomorrow	naalay

Monday	tin-gal
Tuesday	sevvaay
Wednesday	budahn
Thursday	viyaalin
Friday	vellee
Saturday	san-nee
Sunday	naayiru

Transport & Directions

When does the next ... leave/arrive?	eththanai manikku aduththa ... sellum/varum?
boat	padakhu
bus (city)	baas naharam/ul-loor
bus (intercity)	baas veliyoor
train	rayill
I want to get off.	naan iranga vendum
I'd like a one-way ticket.	enakku oru vahly tikket veynum
I'd like a return ticket.	enakku iru vahlay tikket veynum

1st class	mudalahaam vahuppu
2nd class	irandaam vahuppu
bus/trolley stop	baas nilayem
luggage lockers	porul vaikku-midam
timetable	haala attavanay
train station	rayill nilayem
I'd like to hire a ...	enakku ... vaadakhaikku vaynum
bicycle	sai-kul
car	car
Where is it?	adhu en-ghe irukkaradhu?
Where is a/the ...?	... en-ghe?
Go straight ahead.	neraha sellavum
Turn left.	valadhur pakkam tirumbavum
Turn right.	itadhu pakkam thirumbavum
near	aruhil
far	tu-rahm

SRI LANKAN ENGLISH

Greetings & Conversation
Go and come. – farewell greeting, similar to 'See you later' (not taken literally)
How? – How are you?
Nothing to do. – Can't do anything.
What to do? – What can be done about it? (more of a rhetorical question)
What country? – Where are you from?
paining – hurting
to gift – to give a gift

People
baby/bubba – term used for any child up to about adolescence
batchmate – university classmate
peon – office helper
uncle/auntie – term of respect for elder

Getting Around
backside – part of the building away from the street
bajaj – three-wheeler
bus halt – bus stop
coloured lights – traffic lights
down south – the areas south of Colombo, especially coastal areas
dropping – being dropped off at a place by a car
get down – to alight (from bus/train/three-wheeler)

normal bus – not a private bus
outstation – place beyond a person's home area
petrol shed – petrol/gas station
pick-up – 4WD utility vehicle
seaside/landside – indicates locations, usually in relation to Galle Rd
two-wheeler – motorcycle
up and down – return trip
up country/Hill Country – Kandy and beyond, tea plantation areas
vehicle – car

Food
bite – snack, usually with alcoholic drinks
boutique – a little, hole-in-the-wall shop, usually selling small, inexpensive items
cool spot – traditional, small shop that sells cool drinks and snacks
hotel – a small, cheap restaurant that doesn't offer accommodation
lunch packet/rice packet – rice/curry meal wrapped in plastic and newspaper and taken to office or school for lunch
short eats – snack food

Money
buck – rupee
last price – final price when bargaining
purse – wallet

GLOSSARY

ambalama – wayside shelter for pilgrims

Aurudu – Sinhalese and Tamil New Year, celebrated on 14 April

Avalokitesvara – the *bodhisattva* of compassion

Ayurveda – traditional system of medicine that uses herbs and oils to heal and rejuvenate

bailas – folk tunes based on Portuguese, African and local music styles

baobab – water-storing tree *(Adansonia digitata)*, probably introduced to Mannar Island and the Vanni in northern Sri Lanka by Arab traders

bodhi tree – large spreading tree *(Ficus religiosa)*; the tree under which the Buddha sat when he attained enlightenment, and the many descendants grown from cuttings of this tree

bodhisattva – divine being who, although capable of attaining *nirvana*, chooses to reside on the human plane to help ordinary people attain salvation

Brahmi – early Indian script used from the 5th century BC

bund – built-up bank or dyke surrounding a *tank*

Burgher – Sri Lankan Eurasian, generally descended from Portuguese-Sinhalese or Dutch-Sinhalese intermarriage

cadjan – coconut fronds woven into mats and used as building material

Ceylon – British-colonial name for Sri Lanka

chetiya – Buddhist shrine

Chola – powerful ancient South Indian kingdom that invaded Sri Lanka on several occasions

CTB – Central Transport Board, the state bus network

dagoba – Buddhist monument composed of a solid hemisphere containing relics of the Buddha or a Buddhist saint; a *stupa*

devale – complex designed for worshipping a Hindu or Sri Lankan deity

dharma – the word used by both Hindus and Buddhists to refer to their respective moral codes of behaviour

eelam – Tamil word for precious land

gala – rock

ganga – river

gedige – hollow temple with thick walls and a corbelled roof

gopuram – gateway tower

guardstones – carved stones that flank doorways or entrances to temples

Hanuman – the monkey king from the *Ramayana*

Jataka tales – stories of the previous lives of the Buddha

juggernaut – decorated temple cart dragged through the streets during Hindu festivals (sometimes called a 'car')

kachcheri – administrative office

kadé – Sinhalese name for a streetside hut (also called boutiques); called *unavakam* by Tamils

Karava – fisherfolk of Indian descent

karma – Hindu-Buddhist principle of retributive justice for past deeds

Kataragama – see *Murugan*

kiri bath – dessert of rice cooked in coconut milk

kolam – meaning costume or guise, it refers to masked dance-drama; also the rice-flour designs that adorn buildings in Tamil areas

kovil – Hindu temple dedicated to the worship of Shiva

kulam – Tamil word for water tank

lakh – 100,000; unit of measurement in Sri Lanka and India

lingam – phallic symbol; symbol of Shiva

LTTE – Liberation Tigers of Tamil Eelam, also known as the Tamil Tigers; separatist group fighting for an independent Tamil Eelam in the North and the East

Maha – northeast monsoon season

Mahaweli Ganga – Sri Lanka's longest river, starting near Adam's Peak and reaching the sea near Trincomalee

Mahayana – later form of Buddhism prevalent in Korea, Japan and China; literally means 'greater vehicle'

Mahinda – son of the Indian Buddhist emperor Ashoka, credited with introducing Buddhism to Sri Lanka

mahout – elephant master

Maitreya – future Buddha

makara – mythical beast combining a lion, a pig and an elephant, often carved into temple staircases

makara torana – ornamental archway

mandapaya – a raised platform with decorative pillars

masala – mix (often spices)

moonstone – semiprecious stone; also a carved 'doorstep' at temple entrances

mudra – symbolic hand position of a Buddha image

Murugan – Hindu god of war; also known as *Skanda* and *Kataragama*

naga – snake; also applies to snake deities and spirits

nirvana – ultimate aim of Buddhists, final release from the cycle of existence

nuwara – city

ola – leaves of the talipot palm; used in manuscripts and traditional books

oruva – outrigger canoe

oya – stream or small river

Pali – the language in which the Buddhist scriptures were originally recorded

palmyra – tall palm tree found in the dry northern region

perahera – procession, usually with dancers, drummers and elephants

pirivena – centre of learning attached to monastery

poya – full-moon day; always a holiday

puja – 'respect', offering or prayers

rajakariya – 'workers for the king', the tradition of feudal service

Ramayana – ancient story of Rama and Sita and their conflict with *Rawana*

Rawana – 'demon king of Lanka' who abducts Rama's beautiful wife Sita in the Hindu epic the *Ramayana*

relic chamber – chamber in a *dagoba* housing a relic of the Buddha or a saint and representing the Buddhist concept of the cosmos

Ruhunu – ancient southern centre of Sinhalese power near Tissamaharama that survived even when Anuradhapura and Polonnaruwa fell to Indian invaders

samudra – large *tank* or inland sea

Sangamitta – sister of *Mahinda;* she brought the sacred *bodhi tree* sapling from Bodhgaya in India

sangha – the community of Buddhist monks and nuns; in Sri Lanka, an influential group divided into several nikayas (orders)

Sanskrit – ancient Indian language, the oldest known member of the family of Indo-European languages

sari – traditional garment worn by women

Sinhala – language of the Sinhalese people

Sinhalese – majority population of Sri Lanka; principally Sinhala-speaking Buddhists

Skanda – see *Murugan*

stupa – see *dagoba*

Tamils – a people of South Indian origin, comprising the largest minority population in Sri Lanka; principally Tamil-speaking Hindus

tank – artificial water-storage lake or reservoir; many of the tanks in Sri Lanka are very large and ancient

Theravada – orthodox form of Buddhism practised in Sri Lanka and Southeast Asia, which is characterised by its adherence to the *Pali* canon

unavakam – Tamil name for a streetside hut; called kadé or boutiques by the Sinhalese

vahalkada – solid panel of sculpture

vatadage – circular relic house consisting of a small central *dagoba* flanked by Buddha images and encircled by columns

Veddahs – original inhabitants of Sri Lanka prior to the arrival of the Sinhalese from India; also called the *Wanniyala-aetto*

vel – trident; the god *Murugan* is often depicted carrying a *vel*

vihara, **viharaya** – Buddhist complex, including a shrine containing a statue of the Buddha, a congregational hall and a monks' house

Wanniyala-aetto – see *Veddahs*

wewa – see *tank*

Yala – southwest monsoon season

Behind the Scenes

SEND US YOUR FEEDBACK

We love to hear from travellers – your comments keep us on our toes and help make our books better. Our well-travelled team reads every word on what you loved or loathed about this book. Although we cannot reply individually to your submissions, we always guarantee that your feedback goes straight to the appropriate authors, in time for the next edition. Each person who sends us information is thanked in the next edition – the most useful submissions are rewarded with a selection of digital PDF chapters.

Visit **lonelyplanet.com/contact** to submit your updates and suggestions or to ask for help. Our award-winning website also features inspirational travel stories, news and discussions.

Note: We may edit, reproduce and incorporate your comments in Lonely Planet products such as guidebooks, websites and digital products, so let us know if you don't want your comments reproduced or your name acknowledged. For a copy of our privacy policy visit lonelyplanet.com/privacy.

OUR READERS

Many thanks to the travellers who used the last edition and wrote to us with helpful hints, useful advice and interesting anecdotes: Adam Grubb, Adam Krigel, Adrie Pouwer, Aishling Middelburg, Alex Smith, Alex Wharton, Alexandra Forest, Aline Pabst, Andreas Rohner, Anja Biedermann, Anja Stumpf, Annalisa Cavallini, Anne Klier, Anthony Redden, Astrid Lenz, Becca Lumley, Bernhard Bouzek, Brian Jones, Caroline Schouten, Chen Xiaoqin, Chloë Eelen, Chris Bachmann, Chris Rowland, Chris Sutton, Chris Tuck, Christopher Rowland, Clare Foxon, Colin Stevenson, Darius Bazazi, Dennis Walker, Donald Ross, Elaine Cadzow, Elicia Murdoch, Elizabeth Miller, Femke Koek, Filip Tanay, Francis Lu, Frank Höppener, George Barrow, Gerrie Bakker, Greg Kiriakou, Gregory Rose, Heather O'Callaghan, Herman Fuglestvedt, Hollis Burbank-Hammarlund, Jack Clancy, Jamie Witton, Jane Havell, Jan-Willem Overbeek, Jaymini Shah, Jean-Philippe Castellani, Jeremy Dodd, Jessi Johnson, Jhone Guken, Jim Robertson, Joanne Antonetti, Joe Lim, Joyman Lee, Julia Lawrence, Julie Woods, Kaye Kent, Keith Liker, Lars Sander-Green, Louis de Moor, Luuk & Marion Sommers, Maarten van Krimpen, Malcolm Skinner, Mandy Kellagher, Mark Thamel, Marta Cardoso, Martin Abrahams, Martin Wyss, Mary Pelton, Matt Garner, Meaghan Philpott, Mehves Evin, Melanie Luangsay, Michael Gurney, Michal Rudziecki, Milena Artner, Mogens Frandsen, Mollie Jones, Neil Passmore, Nils Klahr, Noah Impekoven, Noelia Rivas, Ole Nielsen, Paul Reynolds, Peter Phillips, Peter Svensson, Petra O'Neill, Petra Sigrist, Piotr Suffczynski, Rachael Glazier, Robin Daus, Ruben Baumgarten, Rutger van den Groenendaal, Sam Fenning, Sarah Meixell, Sarah Phillips, Sheila Miller, Silvia Durrsperger, Stefan Schmidt, Stephen Drewe, Tahira Sheriff, Tamar Drori, Tatjana & Teodora Gazibara, Verena Pietsch, Willemijn Brouwer, Willem-Jan Altena, William Hall, Zubair Khawar

WRITER THANKS
Ryan Ver Berkmoes

Thanks to all those who won't let the appalling events of 2009 be forgotten. And thanks to all those who have made the last 20 years at Lonely Planet an incredible run, with life-changing travel, remarkable creativity and more than 100 fabulous books. But most important are the life-long friendships with some magnificent people. And then there's love: without LP, no Alexis Ver Berkmoes! Finally, because he's been there from the start, Samuel L Bronkowitz has been an inspiring muse.

Bradley Mayhew

Many Sri Lankans helped out with the logistics of research, especially Dimuthu Priyadarshana in Giritale, and also A Malik in Kandy, and Mali and Niksan Peiris in Alankuda. Thanks to Roy in Sigirya for letting me drive the tuk-tuk and to Martin Fullerton for his generous help.

Iain Stewart

It was a utter pleasure to revisit Sri Lanka, such a very special country. Thanks to Somey, my friend, driver and guide in the South and Hill Country, Nisha for the motorbike loan and company in Kandy, Juliet Coombe for her help and tips in Galle, Herman, the Bedspace boys around Mirissa, the Chill team in Ella and Joe Bindloss and all the Lonely Planet crew.

ACKNOWLEDGEMENTS

Climate map data adapted from Peel MC, Finlayson BL & McMahon TA (2007) 'Updated World Map of the Köppen-Geiger Climate Classification', *Hydrology and Earth System Sciences*, 11, 163-344.

Cover photograph: Buddhist monk on Weligama beach, Tuul & Bruno Morandi/4Corners ©

BEHIND THE SCENES

THIS BOOK

This 14th edition of Lonely Planet's *Sri Lanka* guidebook was curated by Anirban Mahapatra and researched and written by Ryan Ver Berkmoes, Bradley Mayhew and Iain Stewart. The previous two editions were written by Stuart Butler, Ryan Ver Berkmoes, Amy Karafin and Iain Stewart .

This guidebook was produced by the following:
Destination Editor Joe Bindloss
Product Editor Grace Dobell
Senior Cartographer David Kemp
Book Designer Virginia Moreno
Assisting Editors Imogen Bannister, Michelle Bennet, Janice Bird, Anne Mulvaney, Saralinda Turner, Simon Williamson, Maja Vatrić
Assisting Cartographer Diana Von Holdt
Cover Researcher Naomi Parker
Thanks to Katherine Marsh, Claire Naylor, Karyn Noble, Lauren O'Connell, Kirsten Rawlings, Amanda Williamson

Index

Map Legend

Sights

- Beach
- Bird Sanctuary
- Buddhist
- Castle/Palace
- Christian
- Confucian
- Hindu
- Islamic
- Jain
- Jewish
- Monument
- Museum/Gallery/Historic Building
- Ruin
- Shinto
- Sikh
- Taoist
- Winery/Vineyard
- Zoo/Wildlife Sanctuary
- Other Sight

Activities, Courses & Tours

- Bodysurfing
- Diving
- Canoeing/Kayaking
- Course/Tour
- Sento Hot Baths/Onsen
- Skiing
- Snorkelling
- Surfing
- Swimming/Pool
- Walking
- Windsurfing
- Other Activity

Sleeping

- Sleeping
- Camping
- Hut/Shelter

Eating

- Eating

Drinking & Nightlife

- Drinking & Nightlife
- Cafe

Entertainment

- Entertainment

Shopping

- Shopping

Information

- Bank
- Embassy/Consulate
- Hospital/Medical
- Internet
- Police
- Post Office
- Telephone
- Toilet
- Tourist Information
- Other Information

Geographic

- Beach
- Gate
- Hut/Shelter
- Lighthouse
- Lookout
- Mountain/Volcano
- Oasis
- Park
- Pass
- Picnic Area
- Waterfall

Population

- Capital (National)
- Capital (State/Province)
- City/Large Town
- Town/Village

Transport

- Airport
- Border crossing
- Bus
- Cable car/Funicular
- Cycling
- Ferry
- Metro station
- Monorail
- Parking
- Petrol station
- Subway station
- Taxi
- Train station/Railway
- Tram
- Underground station
- Other Transport

Routes

- Tollway
- Freeway
- Primary
- Secondary
- Tertiary
- Lane
- Unsealed road
- Road under construction
- Plaza/Mall
- Steps
- Tunnel
- Pedestrian overpass
- Walking Tour
- Walking Tour detour
- Path/Walking Trail

Boundaries

- International
- State/Province
- Disputed
- Regional/Suburb
- Marine Park
- Cliff
- Wall

Hydrography

- River, Creek
- Intermittent River
- Canal
- Water
- Dry/Salt/Intermittent Lake
- Reef

Areas

- Airport/Runway
- Beach/Desert
- Cemetery (Christian)
- Cemetery (Other)
- Glacier
- Mudflat
- Park/Forest
- Sight (Building)
- Sportsground
- Swamp/Mangrove

Note: Not all symbols displayed above appear on the maps in this book

Iain Stewart

The South, Hill Country, Wildlife & Environmental Issues, People of Sri Lanka, Sri Lankan Tea Iain first hit the road during his university years, hitch-hiking around Europe followed by short forays into Turkey, Israel and Egypt. He then spent more than two years travelling the world – from India to Honduras – in the early 1990s, a trip that included a stint in Tokyo teaching English. Skint and without a career on his return to the UK, he trained as journalist and then worked as a news reporter and a restaurant critic in London. Iain started writing guidebooks in 1997 and has worked for six publishers (including Lonely Planet, Rough Guides and DK Eyewitness) and penning over 30 books for destinations as diverse as Ibiza and Cambodia. Iain's worked on titles including *Mexico, Indonesia, Croatia, Vietnam, Bali & Lombok* and *Southeast Asia on a Shoestring* for Lonely Planet. He also writes regularly for the *Independent, Observer, Daily Telegraph* and *Wanderlust*. He'll consider working anywhere there's a palm tree or two, a beach of a generally sandy persuasion, a night club and a cocktail list. After 18 years in South London, Iain moved to Brighton in 2003 and lives close to sea, within firing range of the city's wonderful south-facing horizon.

OUR STORY

A beat-up old car, a few dollars in the pocket and a sense of adventure. In 1972 that's all Tony and Maureen Wheeler needed for the trip of a lifetime – across Europe and Asia overland to Australia. It took several months, and at the end – broke but inspired – they sat at their kitchen table writing and stapling together their first travel guide, *Across Asia on the Cheap*. Within a week they'd sold 1500 copies. Lonely Planet was born.

Today, Lonely Planet has offices in Franklin, London, Melbourne, Oakland, Dublin, Beijing and Delhi, with more than 600 staff and writers. We share Tony's belief that 'a great guidebook should do three things: inform, educate and amuse'.

OUR WRITERS

Anirban Mahapatra

Curator Anirban Mahapatra multitasks as a multimedia travel journalist, iPhone photographer and independent filmmaker. Since 2007, his role as a Lonely Planet writer has seen him research, write, edit and curate multiple editions of Lonely Planet's bestselling *India* travel guidebook, several region-specific India handbooks, as well as country guidebooks *Bangladesh, Sri Lanka* and *Bhutan*. Apart from authorial roles, he has also designed content models and held training workshops for new authors for Lonely Planet's India operations. Among his video pursuits, he has produced travel and cultural documentary films under the aegis of the Ministry of Culture and the Ministry of Information & Broadcasting (Govt of India), and is currently working on an experimental documentary on the ancient Himalayan kingdom of Mustang. When not roaming the world on work or personal explorations, he reads up on Buddhism, hosts barbecues and listens to the blues in his homes in Kolkata and Dhaka.

Ryan Ver Berkmoes

Colombo, The East Coast, Jaffna & the North, Plan chapters Ryan Ver Berkmoes has written more than 110 guidebooks for Lonely Planet. He grew up in Santa Cruz, California, which he left at age 17 for college in the Midwest, where he first discovered snow. All joy of this novelty soon wore off. Since then he has been travelling the world, both for pleasure and for work—which are often indistinguishable. He has covered everything from wars to bars. He definitely prefers the latter. Ryan calls New York City home. Read more at ryanverberkmoes.com and at @ryanvb.

Bradley Mayhew

The West Coast, The Ancient Cities Bradley has been writing guidebooks for 20 years now. He started travelling while studying Chinese at Oxford University, and has since focused his expertise on China, Tibet, the Himalaya and Central Asia. He is the co-author of Lonely Planet guides to *Tibet, Nepal, Trekking in the Nepal Himalaya, Bhutan, Central Asia* and many others. Bradley has also fronted two TV series for Arte and SWR, one retracing the route of Marco Polo via Turkey, Iran, Afghanistan, Central Asia and China, and the other trekking Europe's 10 most scenic long-distance trails. His first gigs with Lonely Planet were guides to Pakistan and the Karakorum Highway and he progressed from there to write for first editions of *Southwest China* and *Shanghai*.

OVER PAGE MORE WRITERS

Published by Lonely Planet Global Limited
CRN 554153
14th edition – Jan 2018
ISBN 978 1 78657 257 8
© Lonely Planet 2018   Photographs © as indicated 2018
10 9 8 7 6 5 4 3 2 1
Printed in Singapore